Remaking Management

Debates about the consequences for work practices posed by the rapidly growing transnationalisation of business have become increasingly central to management studies, sociology, political science, geography and other disciplines. *Remaking Management* brings together a range of international contributors from different sub-disciplines in management to examine current theories of change or continuity in relation to work practices, in the context of fashionable claims about unstoppable globalisation or immovable national business systems. It provides theoretical and empirical challenges to both of these explanations, rejecting an overemphasis on inevitable convergence and enduring divergence. The book reveals a mix of international, national and organisational influences on workplace practice, providing a rich and wide-ranging resource for graduate students and academics concerned with how organisations are responding to an increasingly complex commercial environment.

CHRIS SMITH is Professor of Organisational Studies at Royal Holloway, University of London.

BRENDAN MCSWEENEY is Professor of Management at Royal Holloway, University of London.

ROBERT FITZGERALD is Reader in Business History and International Management at Royal Holloway, University of London.

REMAKING MANAGEMENT

Between Global and Local

Edited by

Chris Smith

Brendan McSweeney

Robert Fitzgerald

CAMBRIDGE UNIVERSITY PRESS
Cambridge, New York, Melbourne, Madrid, Cape Town, Singapore, São Paulo, Delhi

Cambridge University Press
The Edinburgh Building, Cambridge CB2 8RU, UK

Published in the United States of America by Cambridge University Press, New York

www.cambridge.org
Information on this title: www.cambridge.org/9780521861519

First published 2008

Printed in the United Kingdom at the University Press, Cambridge

A catalogue record for this publication is available from the British Library

ISBN 978-0-521-86151-9 hardback

Contents

Tables

Notes on contributors

Editors

Chris Smith (Ph.D. Bristol) is Professor of Organisational Studies at the School of Management, Royal Holloway, University of London. He was previously at the University of Aston, and has held visiting positions at the Universities of Hong Kong, Sydney, Wollongong and Griffith. His main research interests are the sociology of professions, labour process theory and the comparative analysis of work. Some of his books are: *Technical Workers* (1987); *Reshaping Work: The Cadbury Experience* (1990) (with John Child and Michael Rowlinson); *Global Japanization?* (1994) (with Tony Elger); *Engineering Labour* (1996) (with Peter Meiksins); and *Assembling Work: Remaking Factory Regimes in Japanese Multinationals in Britain* (2005) (with Tony Elger). He has conducted fieldwork-based research in Australia, China, Mexico and the United Kingdom.

Brendan McSweeney (Ph.D. LSE) is Professor of Management at Royal Holloway, University of London. He has published papers on a variety of issues in journals such as: *Accounting, Organizations and Society; Human Relations; Journal of International Business Studies; Journal of Organizational Change Management*; and *The Political Quarterly*. He has undertaken field studies in Belgium, Ireland, Italy, the United Kingdom and the United States.

Robert Fitzgerald (Ph.D. Royal Holloway London) is Reader in Business History and International Management at Royal Holloway, University of London. He has published on international and comparative business and on business history. In addition to numerous articles in academic journals, he has been responsible for a wide range of monographs and edited books, including *Rowntree and the Marketing Revolution* (1995), *Origins of Japanese Industrial Power* (1995) and *Development of Corporate Governance in Japan and Britain* (2003), and he is currently writing *Corporation: Rise of the Global Company*. He has conducted research in the United Kingdom, the United States, Canada, Australia, South Africa, Ireland, Japan and South Korea.

Contributors

Rajeswary Ampalavanar Brown (Ph.D. SOAS) is Reader in Business History at the School of Management, Royal Holloway, University of London. She has published the following single-author monographs: *The Indian Minority and Political Change in Malaya, 1945–1957* (1981); *Capital and Enterpreneurship in South East Asia* (1994); *Chinese Big Business and the Wealth of Asian Nations* (2000); and *The Rise of the Corporate Economy in South East Asia* (2006). She is currently working on Islamic banks and Islamic philanthropy in South-East Asia and their global connections. She has carried out research in South-East Asia, East Asia and the Middle East.

Ed Clark (Ph.D. Glasgow) is Reader in Organisation Studies at the School of Management, Royal Holloway, University of London. He has been conducting research into the trasformation of management and organisation in post-socialist Europe since 1991, using intensive fieldwork methods to examine the different processes of change undertaken within former state-owned enterprises. He has published widely in international journals such as *Organization Studies, Human Relations, Journal of Management Studies, Work, Employment and Society* and the *International Journal of Human Resource Management*. He has conducted fieldwork in the Czech Republic and Slovenia.

Jos Gamble (Ph.D. SOAS) is Reader in Asia Pacific Business at the School of Management, Royal Holloway, University of London. In addition to a research monograph *Shanghai in Transition* (2003) he has published in journals such as: *Journal of Management Studies; International Journal of Human Resource Management; Work, Employment and Society; Journal of World Business; Asia Pacific Business Review; Asian Business and Management*; and *Modern China*. He has undertaken field research in China, Japan, South Korea, Malaysia and Thailand.

Michael Gold (Ph.D. Edinburgh) is Senior Lecturer in European Business and Employee Relations at the School of Management, Royal Holloway, University of London, and publishes principally in the field of European employment policy. His articles have appeared in numerous academic journals, and he is currently editing a second edition of his book *The Social Dimension: Employment Policy in the European Community*, to be published in 2008. He has carried out research extensively for the European Foundation for the Improvement of Living and Working Conditions, based in Dublin. He has undertaken field work in Austria, Belgium, Denmark, France, Greece, Ireland, Italy, Malta, the Netherlands, Spain and the United Kingdom, and within the European Commission.

Chris Hackley (Ph.D. Strathclyde) is Professor of Marketing at the School of Management, Royal Holloway, University of London. His work has appeared in various journals, including the *British Journal of Management, the International Journal of Advertising,* the *Journal of Advertising Research, Consumption, Markets and Culture,* the *Journal of Management Studies* and the *Journal of Business Ethics.* His books include *Marketing and Social Construction* (2001), *Doing Research Projects in Marketing, Management and Consumer Research* (2003) and *Advertising and Promotion: Communicating Brands* (2005). He has conducted fieldwork in advertising agencies in the United Kingdom, the United States and Thailand.

Axel Haunschild (Dr. rer. pol. Hamburg) is Senior Lecturer in Human Resource Management (HRM) at the School of Management, Royal Holloway, University of London, and a Guest Professor of HRM at University of Innsbruck. His work has been published in journals such as *Human Relations, International Journal of Human Resource Management, British Journal of Industrial Relations, Creativity and Innovation Management* and *Journal of Organizational Behavior.* He has undertaken field studies in Germany, the United Kingdom and Austria.

Alice Lam (Ph.D. LSE) is Professor of Organisation Studies at the School of Management, Royal Holloway, University of London. Her research focuses on the relationship between organisational forms, knowledge creation and societal institutions. Her current work is exploring the innovative employment dynamics of network organisations in knowledge-intensive sectors. She has published widely in a range of academic journals, including *Organization Studies, Journal of Management Studies* and *Industrial Relations.* She has undertaken fieldwork in Japan and the United Kingdom.

Dirk Matten (Dr. rer. pol., Dr. habil., Heinrich-Heine-Universität Düsseldorf) holds the Hewlett-Packard Chair in Corporate Social Responsibility at the Schulich School of Business, York University, Toronto. From 2004 to 2006 he was a Professor of Business Ethics at the School of Management, Royal Holloway, University of London, and he remains a Visiting Professor at the School. His work has appeared in a number of journals, including *Academy of Management Review, Journal of Management Studies, Organization Studies, Human Relations, Business Ethics Quarterly* and *Journal of Business Ethics.* He has taught and carried out research at universities in Australia, Belgium, Canada, the Czech Republic, France, Germany, Italy, the United Kingdom and the United States.

Fiona Moore (Ph.D. Oxford) is currently Lecturer in International Human Resource Management at the School of Management, Royal Holloway, University of London. She has conducted research with German businesspeople in the City of London and Frankfurt, the managers and workers of a German automobile manufacturer's British and Bavarian plants, and Korean expatriates in Surrey. Her publications include the monograph *Transnational Business Cultures: Life and Work in a Multinational Corporation* (2005) and papers in the *Journal of International Human Resource Management, Management International Review* and *Global Networks.*

Gül Berna Özcan (Ph.D. LSE) is Senior Lecturer in Corporate Governance and European Business at the School of Management, Royal Holloway, University of London. She has published papers on a variety of issues in journals such as: *World Development; Comparative Economic Studies; Environment and Planning C: Government and Policy*; and *Entrepreneurship and Regional Development.* Her book *Building States and Markets: Enterprise Development in Central Asia* was published in 2007. She has carried out research in Italy, Turkey and three Central Asian states: Kazakhstan, Kyrgyzstan and Uzbekistan.

Alan Pilkington (Ph.D. Aston University) is Senior Lecturer in Operations and Technology Management at the School of Management, Royal Holloway, University of London. His current research includes developing patent analysis techniques to explore inventor and technology networks, analysing bibliometric data to define emerging research streams, and the adoption of process improvement methodologies for strategic advantage. He has published in many journals, including: *California Management Review, Technovation* and *International Journal of Operations and Production Management.* He has conducted field research in Europe, North America, the Far East and Australia.

Andrew Popp (Ph.D. Sheffield Hallam) is Senior Lecturer in Business History, Royal Holloway, University of London. He has published widely on subjects in British business history in journals such as: *Business History, Economic History Review, Enterprise and Society, Organization Studies* and *Management and Organizational History.* To date his archival research has been conducted in the United Kingdom.

Lutz Preuss (Ph.D. King's College London) is Lecturer in European Business Policy at the School of Management, Royal Holloway, University of London, where he is also Programme Director of the M.Sc. Sustainability and Management. His research has been published in journals, such as *Journal of Business Ethics, Business Strategy and the Environment* and *Journal of Public Affairs.* He is also the author of *The Green Multiplier* (2005). He has undertaken fieldwork in a number of European countries, including the United Kingdom and Germany.

Amy Rungpaka Tiwsakul (M.Sc. Birmingham) is Tutor in Marketing at the School of Management, University of Surrey. Her Ph.D., which is in progress at Royal Holloway, University of London, is based on fieldwork with advertising and media practitioners and young consumers in the United Kingdom and Thailand. Her research into consumer, ethical and regulatory issues in product placement on television has been published in the *International Journal of Advertising*, the *Journal of Marketing Communications* and *Advances in Consumer Research (Asia Pacific)*. She has conducted research in the United Kingdom and Thailand.

1 Remaking management: neither global nor national

Brendan McSweeney, Chris Smith and Robert Fitzgerald

Introduction

The chapters in this volume were written as a collective contribution to the current debate in management and sociology on the forces shaping work practices at the local level. In contrast to the fashionable predilection for single determinant explanations, the empirical case studies in the book reveal a mix of international, national and company-level influences on action in organisations. These influences are complex and not always coherent. Furthermore, actors at the case study sites of action are shown not to be mere passive relays and responders to these influences but formative exercisers of agency. As a result, although there is change, it is not always uniform or predictable.

During the past decade or so two frameworks have dominated the debate on change within countries: globalisation and comparative (or varieties of) capitalism. In one there is a persistence of differences through the local embedding of each 'capitalist' experience, while in the other there is a tendency for that experience to become a common one. This book recognises variation, rivalry and conflict, both beyond and within national territories. At the same time, it judges capitalism as never quite settling into any one national costume, but as possessing 'natural' or systemic features that constantly undermine such territorial constraints, while nevertheless not operating completely outside such constraints. In other words, there is fluidity and contradiction within a political economy that has inherent global reach, but in the practical experience of actors is always located or uneasily resident within a particular set of local rules and practices.

Accounts founded on the perspectives either of globalisation or of comparative capitalism each possess some explanatory power, but too often one or the other is treated as a sufficient explanation. Furthermore, the processes through which each is perceived to preserve or change work practices is underspecified. Pressure for change frequently comes from outside. Unless change is coercively imposed, however, what happens inevitably involves endogenous influences, and an extensive literature points to distinct and long-standing differences (institutional and other) *within* regional, national and local territories. In this volume we envisage a more complex world for management and workers (especially within the internationalising firm) than that suggested by the discourses of convergence or divergence. In this world, national and local routines, international competition and universal 'best practice' concepts elide and interact, and outcomes never favour one force over another straightforwardly. The variety and unpredictability of developments in actual workplaces are, in key respects, at odds with that predicted by either of the two established models.

If globalisation were a sufficient explanation, the case studies in this volume would observe clone-like transformations of different host-country organisations. Local values, desires and institutions, and everything else running counter to the externally sought changes, would have been ineffectual in resisting globalising standards (however problematic to define). On the other hand, if a national variety of capitalism were an adequate constraint, the case studies would record the rejection or neutralisation of externally derived changes. Neither unequivocal convergence-colonisation nor divergence-indigenicity is identified, however. Both the exogenous and the endogenous are influential. Furthermore, neither set of factors is always internally coherent. Because of the dynamics between the exogenous and the endogenous, what occurred at the sites of action was much more complex than the effect of a singularity (global *or* national) or a conflict between singularities (global *and* national).

We chart, as it were, a third way between, on the one hand, convergence through unstoppable globalisation and, on the other, enduring national divergence. Against the absoluteness of two irreconcilable frameworks we seek, in this volume, to move towards a framework that better fits the empirics of actual change rather than conforming to ideal or normative types. We do so largely through in-depth empirical case studies of sites of change and through discussion of the methodological problems of the dominant explanation types. Moreover, the various chapters in the book stress the significance of 'actors' shaped by past action that influences but does not determine their actions. Actors are makers and remakers of their social world, not passive victims of its incontrovertible effects.

The book is more unified, however, than a simple set of case study chapters that ground management practice in local contexts; it offers theoretical coherence (without obscuring complexities). The empirical chapters are related to a comparative framework that seeks to move beyond the convergence–divergence discourse discussed so far, and to different degrees individual contributions use this framework to anchor arguments against determinant globalising or diversifying forces. The 'system, society and dominance' (SSD) framework (see chapter 2 for a full account) suggests that a 'natural' or systemic political economy exists as both a heuristic and realistic force – a way of thinking about capitalism as not quite a 'variety', since there are by definition common characteristics, such as the market mechanism or waged employment relationships, evident wherever capitalism is present. In this sense, uncovering these underlying structural forces provides a guide to action choices. The societal element within the analysis, however, says that such action choices have local colour and difference of a non-trivial character. The third part of the triplet implies that the localisation of capitalist relations is inherently conflictual and unsettled, because systemic competition creates uncertainty. Moreover, capitalist societies do not face each other as equals, and thus there is an observed tendency for one strong player to evolve patterns of management or work organisation deemed 'modern' or 'dominant', whether this is 'scientific management' from the United States or 'lean production' from Japan. Fads and fashions for managing the workplace flow from cyclical patterns of dominance. In practice, the triple determination of action implied by the SSD framework gives a more nuanced account of life in the internationalised workplace for managers and workers, because structural forces impacting on workplaces are not simply local norms or rules or global standards but a contradictory mixture of elements from the local, the common and the temporarily dominant. Managers and workers within actual work sites have to work with and through these different tendencies.

Globalisation

Globalisation is a periodisation theory: an older epoch or age is said to have been, or to be in the process of being, inevitably superseded by a new one. Broadly, the term is used in two related senses. First, it is the contemporary causal force. The motor of this dynamic is usually seen as economic but there are also benign or predatory political hegemony or 'society in dominance' versions (usually identified as the United States). Secondly, it refers to the supposed uniform consequences of globalisation.

Almost everywhere we see a lowering of barriers to the international transfer of capital, goods, services, culture and information. The prevailing trend in advanced economies at least is towards 'liberalisation'. The Cold War had abated by the 1970s, and its end in the 1980s marked the closure of a distinct era in geopolitics and international relations. The ideal – or fear – of an alternative to capitalism has gone. Arguably, capitalism has begun to reshape the institutions and organisations that had been built to 'civilise' it (Kristensen, 2005). Increasingly we see changes in the structure of income distribution and the comparative rights of capital and labour (Traxler, Blaschke and Kittel, 2001). Does that actually and necessarily mean an increasing homogenization of work practices, however? This remains a contested question.

By the late 1980s most commentators preferred the term 'globalisation', albeit often in a compressed and underspecified manner, to the more restricted sense of 'internationalisation'. The term 'globalisation' highlights how the re-internationalisation of the world economy after the hiatus during and between World Wars I and II is not just about trade and capital flows between nations but is characterised by much wider and deeper economic and other transnational engagements (Drucker, 1989). Whilst there are still deviations from these developments (North Korea, for instance), economies that previously were largely isolated – such as the People's Republic of China – or highly protected – such as India – are now energetically engaged.

Employment of the expression 'globalisation' also indicates the growing scale and greater geographical dispersion of transnational corporations (TNCs) – also known as multinational corporations (MNCs) – than heretofore and the organisational integration of their supply, production and demand chains. The linkings of national economic development and foreign direct investment (FDI) and the economic and social policy changes made to attract and retain TNCs are significant. There is also considerable evidence of the growing transnationalisation of capital flows and equity ownership. Large pension funds and other institutional investors such as private equity funds, most obviously in the United States and United Kingdom, own substantial stakes in 'overseas' corporations. The California Public Retirement System (CalPERS), as the largest US public retirement fund holds nearly $20 billion in foreign equities, representing almost 20 per cent of its total equity investment. On average, 35 per cent of the shares in the forty largest companies in the Paris Stock Exchange and more than 40 per cent of equivalent Dutch companies are held by American and British institutional investors and pension funds

(Gilson, 2001). There have also been flows in the opposite direction. By the end of 2004 non-US investors held about one-quarter of all bonds of US corporations. Significant as these developments are, they do not constitute either a single unidirectional force, nor are their consequences always inevitable or predictable (Hirst and Thompson, 1999).

'Globalisation' implies that the world is shrinking, and – more controversially – converging, as opposed to remaining different or becoming increasingly divergent, at the levels of technology, production, consumption and political economy (Wolf, 2005; Friedman, 2005). New international norms, institutions and regimes operating in the areas of human rights and the environment, among others, have curtailed the formerly prevailing notion of non-interference in the 'internal' affairs of nation states. Capitalism – seen as a singularity – has triumphed on the world stage; consumption habits and leisure pursuits are being homogenised through the standardisation of retailing and instant communication systems. Within this shrinking world framework, economic actors, such as companies, are transforming themselves into international or transnational institutions, establishing extensive production chains, marketing to the globe and searching out labour, technology and other resources from everywhere. At the same time, manufactured goods, such as electronic products, are designed as mass or global artefacts, sometimes modified only superficially for national markets. Further, it is arguable that radical developments in and reduced usage costs of information and communication technologies, including the internet, and mass air travel have removed or diminished many barriers to knowledge transfers. Insofar as companies face globally similar problems they will apply similar solutions to issues of standardisation in production and markets. Work practices are thus seen as becoming inevitably uniform. This is seen functionally as the spread of 'best standard' practice, rationally welcomed or coercively imposed.

Until the early 1980s the setting of formal standards was seen primarily as a national matter. There were exceptions, of course, including agreement to drive on the right in most countries; QWERTY keypads; the dimensions of freight carriers; the thread thickness of screws; the thickness of credit cards (0.76 mm); or the number of survival suits held on ships sailing in cold waters. Overwhelmingly, however, national processes and decisions dominated. In contrast, over the past twenty years or so there has been a remarkable growth in the number of international and regional standards, and the production of national standards has dramatically declined. The International Organization for Standardization (ISO) and its sister organisation the International Electrotechnical Commission (IEC) once stood in the shadow of powerful national organizations, such as DIN (the German Institute for Standardisation) or BSI (the British Standards Institution). Today, however, they jointly account for approximately 85 per cent of known international technical standards, and their annual output of agreed standards has doubled since the early 1980s (Mattli and Büthe, 2003). Other international organisations, such as the World Trade Organization (WTO) and the European Commission, clearly have transnational influence (Chorev, 2005).

Nonetheless, the vision of an inevitably homogenising world is contestable. It supposes that barriers (institutional, cultural or otherwise) are absent or ineffective, and, relatedly, that the prior sources of diversity have been vanquished or will readily be vanquished. It assumes that globalisation is itself a homogeneous force with uniform outcomes.

Far from originating from a single 'global' source, the diverse forces and processes collectively labelled as 'globalisation' emanate from and are historically embedded within particular sociocultural conditions. Even the most ardent supporter of the notion of globalisation as a deterministic force would acknowledge that international diversity continues to exist – although it is assumed that differences will ultimately disappear. Work practices brought to a host country will not therefore be globally universal ones but will be those preferred by, and that characterise, each investing company. Even if the notion of common national practices is supposed (something that is questioned below and elsewhere in this volume) and if global forces are seen as wishing to and being capable of replacing the local, those local practices would be replaced in diverse ways and not by uniform global practices (Doremus *et al.*, 1998). Transnational corporations do not all seek to impose common operational practices: some try to do so with varying degrees of success; others seek to fit or modify them more to circumstances such as local labour and product markets.

Not all goods can be consumed globally. Not all services have international reach, and they can be tied to territory. Live performances, real estate, holiday destinations, or even attendance at Harvard Business School, have capacity restraints. The perceived authenticity of the good or service is often linked to location, and, as such, global access is not possible without the transformation of a particular good's or service's unique character. Companies, as human organisations, have exclusive narratives, not just universal ones.

Convergence (either as domination or fusion) is incomplete. Empirical descriptions of convergence are sustainable only at very high levels of aggregation. To the extent that its advocates provide illustrative examples, they usually do so by selecting cases of convergence but ignore, pass over lightly or deem to be temporary instances of continuing difference or divergent trends (Ruigrok and van Tulder, 1995; Hirst and Thompson, 1999). Examples of recent differences include: the US/EU trade disputes over Airbus–Boeing, bananas, beef, cement, genetically modified foods and steel; anti-'dumping' measures against China by both the United States and the European Union in relation to shoes, textiles and automobile parts; severe criticisms from many countries, including Japan, regarding China's lax record on the protection of intellectual property rights (IPR); Chinese, Indian, Russian and US doubts about the necessity and effectiveness of the Kyoto protocol; and even the refusal of the US government to participate in the International Criminal Court.

The research presented in this book indicates that the scale and implications of the globalisation of work practices have been exaggerated. As a result, the diversity of management and the complexity of work organisation and company change have been underestimated. On the other hand, though, the conservative bias in the varieties of capitalism and similar literature is unwarranted.

Varieties of capitalism

Notwithstanding the volumes published on globalisation, for more than two decades or so the dominant trend in social science analysis has been towards privileging the particular. An approach to understanding the organisation of economic relations that emphasises national patterns emerged within organisational sociology during the 1970s, and produced ideas spreading across industrial sociology, international relations, industrial relations, labour process analysis and accounting. National 'systems' (institutional, cultural or other), it is argued, are characterised by persistence or path dependency. The initial conditions may be determined by an accident of history or the design of politics, or some determining embedded values can set a 'country' (or, rather, features of it) down a particular 'path'. The approach emphasises the persistence of uniformity within and between the institutions and/or cultures of countries or regions. Counter to generalisations about globalisation, such writers insist on the power of the past to continue to deliver significant, non-trivial nationally or regionally distinct uniformities. As we shall see elsewhere in this volume, there are other interpretations of history – that do not depend on overgeneralised, uniform and linear pathways; do not have a preoccupation with the nation or culture as the singular motor of internal conformity and external difference; and do not suffer from a lack of evidence at the sites of action at workplaces.

Theories of this type are territorial: distinct ideas, institutions and/or cultures are said to characterise particular territories. In the main, these spaces specified in these geo-institutional or geo-cultural theories are said to be countries or nations. Early contributions include Andrew Shonfield's 1965 *Modern Capitalism*; Jacques Horovitz's 1980 *Top Management Control in Europe*; Geert Hofstede's 1980 *Culture's Consequences*; and Michael Porter's 1990 *The Competitive Advantage of Nations*. There is also a considerable body of work focusing on clusters of countries that are contrasted with each other. A major influence on that approach is Michel Albert's 1993 *Capitalism vs. Capitalism*, which distinguishes between two broad types of capitalism, namely one 'Rhineland' and another 'Anglo-Saxon' type (see also Whitley, 1992; Nelson, 1993). The currently popular 'varieties of capitalism' model (Hall and Soskice, 2001) has drawn on Albert's work (Crouch, 2005).

The notion of a country, state or nation as a perfectly woven and all-enmeshing 'fabric' echoes down the centuries: German Romanticism; Ruth Benedict's 'cultural patterns'; Mary Douglas's notion of 'one single, symbolically consistent universe'; Pitirim Sorokin's insistence on the internal logic of culture; and Talcott Parsons' 'central-value system'. Anthony Giddens's account of 'de-routinization' sidesteps the possibility of variations within national configurations as the genesis of change, supposes institutional/cultural coherence and relies on exogenous events to explain change. Even today, there remains a stubborn resistance to acknowledging cultural and institutional diversity within the same society and the openness of societies to ideas and influences from outside the national territory (McSweeney, 2002).

Whether conceived as differences between individual countries or between families of countries, the identified characteristics are seen as significant, enduring and uniform (or coherent) across the specified territory. The literature adopting a varieties of capitalism or similar approach (such as national business systems) provides a valuable service in pointing to the importance of diversity, but two methodological aspects lead to an over-emphasis on the homogeneity of institutions or culture. As a result, heterogeneity within and across nations is largely unrecognised – indeed, it is unrecognisable. The first methodological approach is that comparisons at the level of the chosen territory (country or cluster of countries) emphasise, or even predetermine, the 'discovery' of national unity and cross-national differences. The second is that there is a disregard of deviant data not fitting the overall characterisations of a given national or 'super-national' system or an inclination to treat dissonant traits as untheorised, empirical 'noise' to be ignored 'in the interests of an elegant and sharply profiled account' (Crouch and Farrell, 2004: 33).

Comparative analysis undertaken between what is already supposed to be nationally representative inevitably relies on the supposition of national uniformities, because, without that supposition, international comparisons cannot be undertaken. Uniformity is constructed either through comparisons of averages or by unwarrantedly taking a single or a few examples as nationally typical. The problem with the former is the requirement for smoothing out internal differences in order to arrive at the idea of the national average essential for comparative or clustering purposes. For the latter, the invalid assumption that the singular or few examples are nationally typical has to be made. As Peer Hull Kristensen (2005: 387) observes, '[D]istinct modelling of particular national systems circumscribes both their internal complexity, their complementarity and coherence, and also their internal incoherence and conflicts.' Even with the recent attempts to recognise 'diversity within' and 'diversity between' nation states (Jacoby, 2005) there is still a requirement for constructing what is nationally typical and atypical, and many of the procedural difficulties in framing comparative differences, as criticised above, remain. Harry Katz and Owen Darbishire's (2000) concept of 'converging divergences', greater industry- or sector-level commonalities *across* countries producing more variation *within* countries, has the advantage of specifying structures of global standardisation (sectors), but overcomes neither the puzzle of describing the national nor the need to account for firm-level differences.

The practices *in* a company in a country are not necessarily the practices *of* that country. 'Societal effects' (Maurice, Sellier and Silvestre, 1982, quoted in Sorge, 1991) include, but are not reducible to, national effects. As Chris Smith (2005: 605–6) observes, '[C]omposite, large-scale societies contain variety, not uniform societal effects and sectors are diverse within national territories, responding to global or international pressures in different ways, depending upon their exposure to world markets, global competition, and international technological forces' (see also Hollingsworth, Schmitter and Streeck, 1994; Dörrenbächer, 2002). National organisations, the production or other activities of which are exclusively or primarily located in just one territory, and their employees are not isolated from ideas, values, pressures, examples, images and norms, from multiple and even non-national sources. A physical limit is not an ideational boundary; and those that originate from within a national territory can be diverse as well as plural.

Recently, the notion that national institutions and values are always harmonious, coherent and enduring has been challenged from within the neo-institutionalist camp. There is a growing acknowledgement that there is within nations 'a higher level of diversity than has previously been supposed' (Morgan, 2005: 3). Wolfgang Streeck and Kathleen Thelen's (2005) volume of case studies, for instance, is a very valuable addition to the study of institutional continuity *and* change. As the primary object of their analysis is national institutions, however, those case studies are undertaken at the level of the nation state. The object of our analysis is work practices, and so the case studies in this volume are not examinations at country level but primarily of *organisation within nations*. We do not presuppose that what is examined is typical of the country in which the case is located. Generalising nationally or regionally from single or a few cases is unwarranted – and therefore we do not do so. The varieties of capitalism literature rarely engages with local sites of action – organisations – but these are, for our purposes, where analysis can be fruitfully focused. Where seen to be significant, the national is acknowledged but it is not supposed that *all* relevant influences on work practices come from and can be understood at the level of the nation state. Even if it is supposed that there is continuity in a national institution or values, one cannot validly conclude that this will lead to uniformity of practice at a site of action: institutions or value sets may have no influence because they are unrelated to the action; formal continuity may mask internal change and/or diversity; and, particularly pertinent for the purposes of this volume, at the organisational level the institution (or set of institutions) can be used or filtered in different ways even by the same actors (Jackson and Deeg, 2006). The conclusion is that the deterministic notion of coherent, and continuous, national institutions or values should not be a research presupposition.

We do not have a preformed ideal model into which data fit, or are forced to fit, or as a result of which data are discarded. In their discussion of innovation Peter Hall and David Soskice (2001) unambiguously describe the US system as 'liberal market'; and yet an account of significant aspects of innovation within the United States, including that 'by' private corporations, would need to factor in the considerable financial and others roles of government defence spending (O'Sullivan, 2000). The performance of some industries in both the United Kingdom and United States are not explicable solely in terms of a singular system. For example, the aeronautical industry in the United States and the pharmaceutical industry in the United Kingdom have clearly been dependent on public expenditures and specifications. The rise of Silicon Valley – and its specific location – is not explicable without factoring in defence-related procurement. Soskice (1999: 125) depicts Ireland as a liberal market economy from which 'labor has been progressively excluded'. In some sections of the economy – especially in many multi-national subsidiaries – this is true, but not in others, to the extent that 'labor', through a powerful trade union movement, has for many years had a key role in national tripartite policy-making fora. Too often the national or regionally uniform descriptions of the varieties of capitalism suffer from conceptual overreach: the allocation of countries to their categories is not consistent with the empirical facts.

The comparative capitalism or varieties of capitalism literature highlights the importance of diversity but, locked within a state framework, it inadequately restricts those differences to the international. It is incapable of acknowledging plurality *within* nations, and, therefore, is equally incapable of credibly theorising change. As Colin Crouch and Henry Farrell (2004: 33) critically observe, 'change is [conceived of as] likely to occur only when whole systems change,' and transformations can be theorised as exogenous only because internally the system is supposed to be coherent. Exogenous shocks, furthermore, have local modifying or hybrid consequences. They can be conceived of only as being rejected or very occasionally creating a 'big bang' change (Lane, 2005; Vogel, 2005). Sometimes historic convulsive ruptures occur, but they are not typical.

Conclusions

The research presented in this book indicates that the scale of homogenisation through globalisation has been exaggerated. As a result, the diversity of management and the complexity of work organisation and company change have been underestimated. On the other hand, the research also shows that the continuity asserted by the comparative capitalism or varieties of capitalism literature ignores the extent and variations of change not only across but also within nations. By overemphasising the level of uniformity and embeddedness of differences in national competitive advantages, institutions or culture, it is an approach that ignores the impact of internationalisation on indigenous systems and attitudes. As the contributors to this volume lay bare, it offers intransigent assumptions about the nature of economies and societies, and their transformation.

The globalisation model overstates the scale and uniformity of change and disregards endogenous forces. The varieties of capitalism model understates the extent of change and reifies endogenous constraints. The case studies in this volume and the discussion chapters explore the significance of both the exogenous and the endogenous, and consider their complex and unpredictable interplay at sites of real action–crossroads at which multiple potential influences from diverse sources and levels elide. Pure endogenicity and pure exogenicity are end points of a continuum, not absolutes. There are uniformities within and between nation states, but there is also considerable transnational and intranational heterogeneity. Some, but by no means all, come from the national; some, but by no means all, come from common international sources.

We suggest, therefore, that both the globalisation and the varieties of capitalism models ignore the iterative and complex nature of change in favour of a few 'fixed' causes. Such 'templates' are ahistorical and at variance with what is currently happening on the ground. It is the roles of actors, their motives and the effects generated in a variety of circumstances that are relevant. The process and outcomes are neither predeterminable nor linear. They produce complexity.

An analysis that takes adequate account of the international, national and company-level issues evident in the current making and remaking of work practices requires a number of characteristics. These we have sought to achieve in this volume.

First, it needs a complex view of the factors involved. Openness to multiple levels, a variety of points of influence and diverse characteristics is required. Societal effects will often include national effects but are not limited to them. Studies that are restricted to one type may provide valuable insights, but not if power attributed exclusively to that level creates impoverished deterministic claims.

Second, the uniformity or coherence of institutions or values should not be presupposed. The notion excludes the possibility of change, unless, bizarrely, change is generated only exogenously, or, paradoxically, is uniform and predictable.

Third, actors should not be theorised as mere relays but as having agency. Actors may be embedded but they are reflexive and not necessarily trapped by their context (which, in any case, may be transforming and incoherent, and as a result likely to engender uncertainties). Nor is the embeddedness of actors the same – a salient point in workplaces with greater national, gender and age diversity, as well as the widening biographical diversity of individuals.

Fourth, analysis should balance case material and exceptions with theoretical understanding and generalisations. Data should not be forced into pre-established ideal types. Contrary data should not be dismissed. There should be no prior commitment to 'confirming' the coherence or uniformity of national or other sets of institutions or values.

Fifth, we need an historical perspective of work practice formation and change that understands them to be iterative as well as complex processes. If change (or stasis) is attributed to a single, unchanging determinant force then what occurs will be theorised as enduring, and there is a risk of over-privileging some 'formative' critical period. Actual change is generated through the inter-playing of heterogeneous and mutable factors, however. Reinforcing processes ('feedback loops') may occur at the site of action, and can be detected only by longitudinal analysis, but their understanding does not rest on some over-theorised uniformity. Nor should we assume that they produce optimum outcomes in terms of social embeddedness (due to differential value) or com-petitive advantage (due to variations in factor and demand conditions). They may also create vested interests or longer-term institutional sclerosis, all in turn capable of stimulating conflict and new sources of action.

Finally, we need to differentiate between institutions/values and conse-quences/'functions'. There is no linear cause and effect relationship. Norms and practices do not necessarily cohere within or between the various levels of scale under study. Diversity within a single setting (national or other) is all too possible and potentially significant

After this introductory chapter, the volume opens with three discussion chapters in Part I, each written by one of the volume's editors. Chapter 2, by Chris Smith, distinguishes three distinct approaches to the analysis of con-temporary capitalism and considers the role that they allocate to business organisation. It identifies merits in all three positions but argues that none recognises the complexity of real economies or is able to explain the overlaid reality of change and continuity. An alternative argument is developed in favour of the system, society and dominance model (Smith and Meiksins, 1995).

Chapter 3 is by Brendan McSweeney. Through a rereading of the key literature claiming that national culture is both *the* bedrock of unique national practices (including those within organisations) and the master key to identifying, explaining and predicting them, he argues for the existence of dynamic diversity *within* countries. The implications of that heterogeneity for cross-national comparative analysis and for the possibilities of work practice continuity or change are considered.

Chapter 4, by Robert Fitzgerald, argues that historical analysis can be a valuable corrective to totalising and determining theories about societies, since it can reveal how traditions and cultures are often less historically rooted and more contingent than originally assumed. In particular, national institutions and culture can be revealed as less solid and less determinative of the pathways through which business systems have evolved. The value of a historical perspective to comparative analysis is also addressed.

The remainder of the volume contains the empirical case studies. These chapters are divided into three Parts, corresponding to the 'system', 'society' and 'dominance' categories developed by Chris Smith and Peter Meiksins (1995). Each of these sections also begins with a brief overview of the case studies.

The contributions represent a diverse set of evidence and perspectives, but none is reliant on attenuated notions of convergence through unstoppable globalisations or enduring divergence due to uniform national differences. By looking first at the reality of the workplace and at sites of action, they can then consider the impact of and response to complex and sometimes contradictory forces. Their insights can accommodate rather than simplify away the global and national dimensions of making and remaking management.

References

Albert, M. (1993) *Capitalism vs. Capitalism: How America's Obsession with Individual Achievement and Short-term Profit Has Led It to the Brink of Collapse*, New York: Four Walls Eight Windows.

Chorev, N. (2005) The institutional project of neo-liberalism: the case of the WTO, *Theory and Society*, 34, 317–55.

Crouch, C. (2005) *Capitalist Diversity and Change: Recombinant Governance and Institutional Entrepreneurs*, Oxford: Oxford University Press.

Crouch, C., and H. Farrell (2004) Breaking the path of institutional development? Alternatives to the new determinism, *Rationality and Society*, 16, 1, 5–43.

Doremus, P. N., W. W. Keller, L. W. Pauly and S. Reich (1998) *The Myth of the Global Corporation*, Princeton, NJ: Princeton University Press.

Dörrenbächer, C. (2002) *National Business Systems and the International Transfer of Industrial Models in Multinational Corporations: Some Remarks on Heterogeneity*, discussion paper, Wissenschaftszentrum Berlin für Sozialforschung.

Drucker, P. F. (1989) *New Realities*, London: Butterworth.

Friedman, T. L. (2005) *The World is Flat*, New York: Farrar, Straus and Girroux.

Gilson, R. J. (2001) Globalizing corporate governance: convergence of form or function, *The American Journal of Comparative Law*, 49, 2, 329–57.

Hall, P. A., and D. Soskice (eds.) (2001) *Varieties of Capitalism: The Institutional Foundations of Comparative Advantage*, Oxford: Oxford University Press.

Hirst, P., and G. Thompson (1999) *Globalization in Question* (2nd edn.), Cambridge: Polity Press.

Hofstede, G. (1980). *Culture's Consequences: International Differences In Work-related Values*, Beverly Hills, CA: Sage.

Hollingsworth, J. R., P. C. Schmitter and W. Streeck (eds.) (1994) *Governing Capitalist Economies: Performance and Control of Economic Sectors* Oxford: Oxford University Press.

Horovitz, J. H. (1980) *Top Management Control in Europe*, London: Palgrave Macmillan.

Jackson, G., and R. Deeg (2006) *How Many Varieties of Capitalism? Comparing the Comparative Institutional Analyses of Capitalist Diversity*, Discussion Paper 06–02, Cologne: Max Planck Institute for the Study of Societies.

Jacoby, S. M. (2005) *The Embedded Corporation*, Princeton, NJ: Princeton University Press.

Katz, H. C., and O. Darbishire (2000) *Converging Divergences: Worldwide Changes in Employment Systems*, Ithaca, NY: ILR/Cornell University Press.

Kristensen, P. H. (2005) Modelling national business systems and the civilizing process, in G. Morgan, R. Whitley and E. Moen (eds.) *Changing Capitalisms? Internationalization, Institutional Change, and Systems of Economic Organization*, Oxford: Oxford University Press, 383–414.

Lane, C. (2005) Institutional transformations and system change: changes in corporate governance of German corporations, in G. Morgan, R. Whitley and E. Moen (eds.) *Changing Capitalisms? Internationalization, Institutional Change, and Systems of Economic Organization*, Oxford: Oxford University Press, 78–109.

McSweeney, B. (2002) Hofstede's model of national cultural differences and their consequences: a triumph of faith – a failure of analysis, *Human Relations*, 55, 89–117.

Mattli, W., and T. Büthe (2003) Setting international standards: technological rationality or primacy of power?, *World Politics*, 56, 1–42.

Maurice, M., F. Sellier and J.-J. Silvestre (1982) *Politique d' éducation et organisation industrielle en France et en Allemagne: essai d' analyse sociétale*, Paris: Presses Universitaires de France.

Morgan, G. (2005) Introduction, in G. Morgan, R. Whitley and E. Moen (eds.) *Changing Capitalisms? Internationalization, Institutional Change, and Systems of Economic Organization*, Oxford: Oxford University Press, 1–18.

Nelson, R. R. (1993) *National Innovation Systems: A Comparative Analysis*, Oxford: Oxford University Press.

O'Sullivan, M. (2000) *Contests for Corporate Control*, Oxford: Oxford University Press.

Porter, M. E. (1990) *The Competitive Advantage of Nations*, New York: Free Press.

Ruigrok, W., and R. van Tulder (1995) *The Logic of International Restructuring*, New York: Routledge.

Shonfield, A. (1965) *Modern Capitalism: The Changing Balance of Public and Private Power*, Oxford: Oxford University Press.

Smith, C. (2005) Beyond convergence and divergence: explaining variations in organizational practices and forms, in S. Ackroyd, R. Batt, P. Thompson and P. S. Tolbert (eds.) *The Oxford Handbook of Work and Organization*, Oxford: Oxford University Press, 602–25.

Smith, C., and P. Meiksins (1995) System, society and dominance effects in cross-national organizational analysis, *Work, Employment and Society*, 9, 2, 241–67.

Sorge, A. (1991) Strategic fit and the societal effect: interpreting cross-national comparisons of technology, organization and human resources, *Organization Studies*, 12, 2, 161–90.

Soskice, D. (1999) Divergent production regimes: coordinated and uncoordinated market economies in the 1980s and 1990s, in H. Kitschelt, P. Lange, G. Marks and J. D. Stephens (eds.) *Continuity and Change in Contemporary Capitalism*, Cambridge: Cambridge University Press, 101–34.

Streeck, W., and K. Thelen (eds.) (2005) *Beyond Continuity: Institutional Change in Advanced Political Economies*, Oxford: Oxford University Press.

Traxler, F., S. Blaschke and B. Kittel (2001) *National Labour Relations in Internationalized Markets*, Oxford: Oxford University Press.

Vogel, S. K. (2005) Routine adjustment and bounded innovation: the changing political economy of Japan, in W. Streeck and K. Thelen (eds.), *Beyond Continuity: Institutional Change in Advanced Political Economies*, Oxford: Oxford University Press, 145–68.

Whitley, R. (1992) *Business Systems in East Asia: Firms, Markets and Societies*, London: Sage.

Wolf, M. (2005) *Why Globalization Works*, New Haven, CT: Yale University Press.

Part I

Conceptualising International and Comparative Management

Preface: Dominance, diversity and the historical process in management practice

Chris Smith, Brendan McSweeney and Robert Fitzgerald

The three chapters in this section offer a commentary on and an alternative account to theories of internationalisation that stress either unrelenting globalisation, or the resilience of national management patterns and actions or a division of the world into fixed varieties of capitalism, effectively constructed with more or less market and state. All three offer a critique of claims for an enduring and nationally uniform business practice. In anticipation of empirical chapters that reveal a within-country change and diversity at odds with notions of unchanging national homogeneity, the three demonstrate the significance of endogenous (and not just exogenous) sources of change – a possibility inconceivable within variety of capitalism and national business system perspectives. They stress the remaking of management as a more dynamic, recurrent and variable practice, reflecting the fact that the integration of firms and national territories is more fluid and diverse than suggested by national business system approaches.

Chapter 2 outlines different approaches to the internationalisation of business and implications for management action within the firm, and suggests an alternative framework for thinking about and researching these processes. Three theories are reviewed: globalisation, national business systems and varieties of capitalism. This is followed by an exposition of the system, society and dominance framework that the book is informed by.

Globalisation implies a convergence of action around one set of best or standard efficiency practices, which are diffused through the market, technology and multinational agencies and which place all national or local models of action under intense competitive pressure. This approach is problematic, not just in defining what practices constitute globalised standards (typically a neoliberal model of capitalism) but, more importantly, in its implications of an inevitable linear movement towards such standards by all countries. In direct contradiction to globalisation is the idea that national boundaries pattern firm and management action into distinct country codes and cultures.

This is also problematic as an absolute, because national economies are open-ing up to international influences, such as transnational firms. Management education and training is not simply local but permissive, embracing a variety of local, sectoral, national and international influences. Moreover, as other chapters in this section show, the integrity of a homogeneous national cultural or institutional practice is dubious, given within-country diversity and across-country influences, as well as uneven temporal change to something as dynamic as management practices. Finally, the grouping of capitalist societies together into determinate 'varieties' breaks away from the notions of numerous national stories and a single global one, but remains problematic in suggesting that 'capitalism' is somehow multiple, rather than essentially systemic, as a political economy. Following these criticisms, chapter 2 supports a way of framing management action within the firm through the SSD perspective, on the grounds that this appears more sensitive to competing and conflicting influences and choices of action in the modern business environment.

The SSD framework suggests that political economies, such as capitalism or state socialism, are systemic rather than contingent in influence. French or Chinese capital owners are positioned by common sets of interests, structures and processes as capitalists, in the same way that Chinese or French workers are positioned by determinant features of waged labour. System effects ensure that countries are pulled into common or interdependent social relations when firms in these different countries participate in market transactions and production for the purpose of profit. Reducing management activity in particular countries, sectors or times to a functional reflex of capitalist social relations, however, can only ever be a partial account of real histories and experiences. This is because any particular capitalist firm has a home, a history and a context, and is not a structural abstraction, and such firms compete with other companies that have their own, divergent, homes and histories, adding layers of difference and nuance to their competitive rela-tions. Moreover, while markets, the price mechanism, technologies and competition favour dominant survival pathways and rationalise action along efficiency lines, strong historical traditions, national institutional rules and customs, and distinct but equally effective ways of combining capital and wage labour create robust boundaries around agents and inter-ests, especially national or societal boundaries. In this sense, societal effects filter and infuse systemic social relations, making national prefixes to man-agement and worker actions meaningful if only partial filters of action.

The final element in the framework is the idea of dominance, which builds on the observation that capitalist societies do not compete as equals but in hierarchical ensembles, in which 'leadership' circulates on the basis of economic performance, but also through subsystem innovations and fads that animate management agents to move with the spirit of the age, and particular management concepts to move in and out of fashion. Dominance effects were evident in the 1980s, when American and European manufacturing employers were compelled to imitate all things Japanese in order to maintain competitive position. Dominance effects are equally observable in concepts such as 'flexible labour markets', 'privatisation', 'lean production' or 'business process re-engineering', which are advocated and proselytised as essential solutions to common management problems irrespective of the context, history and market position of particular firms.

Dominant management concepts find an audience through symbolic as much as actual efficacy, and management as an agency is prone to whims and fashions, on account of the stress on the novel within management discourse and increased competitive pressures to keep up with what seems to be 'flavour of the month'. It is also the case, however, that 'leading firms' (Microsoft, McDonald's, Toyota, Tesco and Wal-Mart today, or Ford and GM in the past) evolve methods of working and managing that others seek to emulate, both within and beyond the particular business niche. In this way dominance can be about firms, countries or management concepts, and, while linked to economic performance at a macroeconomic level, need not always be so. Dominance effects are useful in avoiding the treatment of capitalism as homogeneous and societies as uniformly institutionally bounded.

Chapter 2 sets up a point of reference, which is used by many chapters within the book in their consideration of transitions between political economies, or diversity between societal forms of management or the rise of new management concepts, such as corporate social responsibility (CSR).

Chapter 3 contributes to critiques of the model of unchanging national uniformity and of the model of unstoppable global homogenisation. Through that process, it provides part of a conceptual framework for understanding heterogeneous change within countries inconceivable within either of those two models.

Explanations of supposedly enduring national uniformity rely on notions either of determinant national institutions or, alternatively, of determinant national culture. Although there is little intellectual crossover between the institutional and the cultural literatures, they have much in common. Both depict countries as characterised by patterns of persistently reproduced actions and practices. Essentially, they differ only in what is deemed to be the enduring source of those patterns: unchanging national institutions or culture. Insofar as the institutional literature engages with cultures or values, these are usually said also to be institutions. Whenever the national culture literature refers to institutions, these are treated as dependent variables, as consequences of national culture. Both culture and institutions are intermediary concepts between 'society', 'organisations' and 'individuals'. Attempting to define them differently in terms of content results in problems and perplexities, because the terms contain so many overlapping elements. The criticisms of national culture in chapter 3 therefore also apply to the notion of nationally uniform and enduring institutions. As both models suppose institutional or cultural coherence within countries, neither can conceive of change other than as a consequence of rare and profound external shock. Further, as the resulting change is imaginable only as nationally uniform, no old or new local change or variation can be acknowledged. Thus, the two models are fundamentally ill-equipped to explain the smaller-scale, variable and unpredictable remakings described in the case and field studies in this book.

Chapter 3 advances the development of a framework that can both acknowledge variety of practices within countries and explain change in that variety on grounds that are not entirely exogenous. It does so by countering the notion of national uniformity with that of 'dynamic diversity' within countries. This view is explored and argued for, first, by a rereading of a number of seminal national cultural works that have based their claims on data from sources as wide-ranging as questionnaires and novels. Unpacking them reveals a range of ways in which that literature either ignores evidence of intranational diversity or inappropriately homogenises it. Key categories and concepts, when opened up, reveal change and diversity, not singular continuity. Within each country, variety and variation are, it is argued, the appropriate reading of the national culturalists' own foundation material. Secondly, the legitimacy claimed by some from anthropology for their bedrock notion of uniform and enduring patterns of action is shown, at best, to rely on views long peripheralised, indeed discredited, in that discipline. Both oversocialised and overintegrated conceptions of humans are critiqued. That diversity is seen as the product of two related sources: (i) the existence of a variety of values (and/or institutions) within countries; and (ii), without jettisoning the influence of historical legacies, individuals are theorised as capable of agency.

The arguments for 'dynamic diversity', for variety and variation within countries, also have implications for the inexorable global homogenisation model. In its most uniform sense, 'globalisation' in that model is presented as a monolithic and always standardising process. More sophisticated versions acknowledge national varieties – but still presuppose the national uniformity of the originating country. Companies, or whatever other 'globalising' force, from a particular country may indeed be the product in part of nationally uniform influences, but they may also be shaped by variety within countries. What comes into a country, even from the same originating country, will not necessarily be identical, and thus there is the potential for dissimilar outcomes. Furthermore, what is 'met' within a 'host' country will also have some variety. The combination of both types of differences multiplies the possibility of variations in practices. A relentless uniformity from abroad does not therefore meet an effete national uniformity: variety engages with variety. The consequence may be repulsion or replacement, but, equally, may not be. Frequently the outcome is remixing in zones of interaction. That is not to discount what might be nationally uniform either from the home country or in the host country, but to reject a reductionism that ignores all else and, specifically, the reality and influence of national 'dynamic diversity' in home and host countries.

Chapter 4 argues that influential propositions on the origin and nature of business systems fail adequately to accommodate the roles of firms and individuals, and the complex and contradictory processes by which developments occur over time. These models lack nuance and empirical justification, reverting instead to explanations based on simple functionalism, or linear ideas about a fundamental cause at a key point in time having widespread and uniform effects. They cannot, therefore, fully explain how business systems are made, and, since circumstances and responses continue to evolve, they cannot explain how they are subsequently remade. Nor can they explain instances of diversity within as well as between societies. Institutionalist perspectives in the management literature and the 'varieties of capitalism' model fail to account for the history of business systems in particular countries, and so make unjustifiable claims in their comparisons between nations.

The chapter argues that the comparative method should (a) have a better appreciation of the historical method and (b) abandon the idea of national homogeneity (in culture, institutions or business systems) in favour of an approach that accepts intranational differences as forces of change (including discussion of general economic trends, and business systems). It points out that historians generally reject single explanatory factors (whether 'nation' and culture, or 'global' forces), and would more readily accept a more complex standpoint incorporating and comparing developments at many levels and intersections.

Chapter 4 provides a detailed analysis of institutionalism and the varieties of capitalism perspective by challenging their simplistic historical method and unfamiliarity with historical research. The point is important, because these perspectives rest upon the idea of formative (but questionable) influences that shape the nature of national business systems at key turning points in history. The chapter considers the major arguments of the institutionalist theories ('national business systems', 'varieties of capitalism' and so forth), which presuppose and focus on national institutional homogeneity and outcomes. It identifies a common fault in their approach, rooted largely in dubious historical and comparative methods and assumptions. In addition, the failure of 'institutionalism' to incorporate ideas on the influence of economic development processes (and their varied outcomes) is analysed.

In common with chapter 3, the chapter further challenges ideas of nationally homogeneous systems because of their reliance on notions of influential and identifiable national cultures, which are often ahistorical, and at best unconvincing historically as a strong determinant factor. These cultural (or 'civilisational') notions, familiar to an earlier generation of historians, have long been abandoned in historiography. Chapter 4 also reviews the historical importance of the international economic system, undermining the argument that 'globalisation' is new, but, more particularly, indicating how this adversely affects institutionalism and the varieties of capitalism perspective (which deny the importance of international forces). It follows that recent attempts belatedly to incorporate 'globalisation' alongside so-called business systems rooted in a 'national' past are misplaced.

The chapter emphasises the flawed nature of the national culture concept and ideas of homogeneous national business systems (as both are models of stasis they ignore the contingencies of history); the need to investigate a range of influences on the continuous remaking of management, and at several levels; and the use of empirical evidence to illustrate the capacity of business systems to vary. As a result, chapter 4 (which provides a fuller historical analysis of management systems) is a useful accompaniment to chapter 2 (which considers the continuous interplay of the varied forces remaking management) and to chapter 3 (which deals with the conceptual and empirical inadequacy of ideas based on national homogeneity and determinant national cultures).

2 Work organisation within a dynamic globalising context: a critique of national institutional analysis of the international firm and an alternative perspective

Chris Smith

Introduction

In the modern world globalising forces are helping to challenge structures of national difference. The outcome of this process is not some set of 'worldly' or 'global' best practices, however, but instead more hybridity and blending of practices drawn from different histories and environments. Rather than universalism or nationalism within economic action at the level of the firm, we have a much more nuanced, layered and dynamic set of competing actions, which draw from a discourse of global practices but are not global; and a discourse of institutional specificity, but one that is not functionally bounded. This chapter examines these tensions and, at the same time, proposes a framework to theorise the sources of diversity and convergence that operate within organisations exposed to internationalising processes

Three distinct positions will be distinguished. First, there are those attached to the idea of distinctive 'national business systems', who retain a belief in the distinctive organisation of work, management and employment relations characterised by a *national* system of institutions and cultural legacies. Such writers argue the case for the persistence of national differences and the continuation of diversity based on the 'embedding' of the organisation within these institutional rules. Moreover, any external international forces, such as multinational firms, that come into these national environments become local players, not destroyers of local action.

Second, there are those who argue for the importance of globalising trends and the convergence between organisational forms and policies and, by extension, a more homogeneous character to economic organisations. Convergence forces for these writers are carried forward by worldwide agencies, in particular transnational corporations and their global institutional supporters, such as the World Trade Organization. This is an argument that tends in the opposite direction to that of national business systems, and suggests the gradual removal of diversity and increased homogenisation of management practice.

Third, between the extremes, there are arguments that there are a small number of distinctive patterns to 'varieties of capitalism' that can be distinguished, based on forms of market and state coordination of economic activity, and that these 'varieties of capitalism' are reasonably robust and self-perpetuating.

It is argued here that there is some merit in all these positions, but none of them quite recognises the complexity of real economies, and therefore they are unable to explain the extent of change and continuity that actually exists. The nature of work within the modern international organisation is more complex than global/local, universal/national and convergence/divergence dichotomies. By way of an alternative, an argument will be developed in favour of what is called the system, society and dominance model. In the central sections of the chapter it is argued that capitalism, as a political economy (based on distinctive property rights, accumulation through competition and incessant innovation of the means and forces of production), possesses a generic form, but one that presents distinctive characteristics according to the organisation of institutional actors, especially firms, labour and the state. It is argued, however, that these forms are not fixed, as there are globalising forces operating on all businesses, particularly those exposed to internationalising markets (Traxler, Blaschke and Kittel, 2001).

Moreover such forces are filtered through nationally distinctive institutional settlements, which have 'societal effects' (Maurice, Sellier and Silvestre, 1986) on the way work is organised, authority constructed and patterns of industrial relations enacted. Within the international firm, therefore, we have, on the one hand, permanent tensions between generic features of capitalism and particular forms of management and labour derived from the nationally embedded contexts in which the firm originated and the subsidiaries are currently located, and, on the other, standardising forces derived from dominant or global actors as they represent the 'modern' to the firm. We have a context of complexity, and it is hoped that the chapter will advance a model of cross-national organisational analysis that will contribute to an understanding of this growing complexity.

Alternative accounts of continuity and change

National business systems

An approach to understanding the organisation of economic relations that emphasises *national* patterns emerged within organisational sociology in the 1970s, and produced ideas that have spread across economic sociology, industrial relations and labour process analysis. Arguments of this kind make conditional or context-dependent statements about the world and work organisations. The approach emphasises the persistence of the variations within capitalism carried by cultural or ideational uniqueness located within national and subnational institutions that are inimitable to societies as they emerge from unique, path-dependent developments during transitions into capitalist economic organisation. This stress on national institutional analysis can be found in: 'national innovation systems' (Nelson, 1993); 'business systems' (Whitley, 1992a, 1992b; Whitley and Kristensen, 1997); 'training systems' (Crouch, Finegold and Sako, 1999); 'education systems' (Lorenz, 2000; Dosi and Kogut, 1993); 'trade unions' (Streeck, 1992; Ferner and Hyman, 1992; Traxler, Blaschke and Kittel, 2001; Hyman, 2001); and 'management styles and philosophy' (Redding, 1990; Hampden-Turner and Trompenaars, 1993). Reacting against generalisations about globalisation, convergence or the dominance of neoliberal practices (such as shareholder value, open capital markets and flexible labour markets), such writers stress the power of the past to continue to deliver significant, non-trivial national differences between capitalist societies. They continue to invest value in path dependencies to 'reproduce national specificities' (Sorge, 1991) irrespective of the increasing economic and institutional integration of economies as a consequence of global economic and political activities.

Most prominent within this 'systems' approach to economic action has been Richard Whitley (1992a). Through a critique of universalist neoclassical views of economic action, he has highlighted the way that institutions fit together to embed and integrate the capitalist firm in complementary and integrating ways that introduce differentiation and not standardisation to economic action. Writing against neoclassical economics, classical management and Marxist views of the capitalist firm as exhibiting one form or evolving towards one efficient outcome, Whitley suggests that there are different ways of producing the firm depending on how it is formed (by families, banks, states or other combinations) and how it relates to secondary institutions, such as the political system, finance system, educational system and labour system. Drawing from the functional sociology of Talcott Parsons, Whitley sees the organisation as formed within the divergent processes of industrialisation, which create distinct path-dependent processes, and formed within different financial, educational, training and industrial relations subsystems, which have the effect of producing different 'national' business systems.

While initially acknowledging that there can be 'a *variety* of distinct business systems *within* different nation states' (Whitley, 1992a: 15; emphasis added), the powerful role allocated to the state in forming subsystem institutions means that his institutional account of economic action has attracted the prefix 'national' and plural combinations have become singular national systems. Indeed, in his classic statement *Business Systems in East Asia* he slips between terms such as 'major' business systems or 'different' business systems to 'national business systems' (1992a: 28) or the 'Japanese business system' (28) or 'Japanese employment system' (34), implying a single national business system per nation rather than multiple competing business systems based on different ethnic, cultural and institutional patterns of formation and reproduction. Nevertheless, a tension remains, and Whitley differentiates between strong states with 'cohesive configurations of institutions', such as Japan or South Korea, and those that are more 'differentiated with a plural configuration', such as the United Kingdom. In nations with a weak central state, such as Italy, there are 'regional' variations to business systems within the same country.

The question remains as to what underlies these differences. Here, Whitley returns to cultures that animate institutional formation, and, like Parsons, he holds that it is 'values' that hold systems together. So 'nation states with relatively homogeneous cultures and institutions generate more distinctive business systems than those characterised by greater heterogeneity' (1992a: 14). The problem with this homogeneous/heterogeneous differentiation is that it begs the question of what exactly produces these features. Moreover, the logic of a more globalising and integrating business world is towards more standardisation. More recently, Whitley (2005) has returned to the tension between the national and non-national business systems, but he remains remarkably close to the integrative and differentiated role of institutions and the place of the state in society in upholding 'rules of the game' discussed in *Business Systems in East Asia*. He concludes that 'the national specificity and distinctiveness of business systems depends on the extent to which characteristics of states and related institutions are complementary in their implications for firms and markets, as well as the active structuring and coordination of interest groups and their interrelationships by state agencies' (2005: 224). He acknowledges the impact of growing FDI on national economies and the emergence of international institutions and agencies, while remaining convinced that it is institutions within the national arena – especially the state – that act to mediate these internationalising forces, and as such reinforce rather than undermine the national.

In favour of this approach is the fact that the condensation of business systems – distinctive ways of doing things – within particular territories is observable across time. In other words, sunk fixed costs and psychological attachment amongst national actors to particular rules of the game exist and persist, and societies clearly exhibit certain path-dependent qualities. Societal effects thinkers would suggest that there is 'fit' between national institutions and the competitive advantages offered by different societies. Ronald Dore (2000) describes the links between the national economy and society in terms of an 'institutional interlock', and Rogers Hollingsworth and Robert Boyer (1997) invoke 'social systems of production' (see Hyman, 2006: 242–3) in order to stress the role of self-reinforcing linkages and supports. Invoking *fit* reinforces the functional theoretical heritage of the approach, however, with a stress on complementarities and not contradictions between actors in the economy and society. Arndt Sorge and Marc Maurice (1993) support this functionality between society and economy, to the point of suggesting (76) that there are *competitive advantages* at the level of the nation, whereby each society retains unique and non-imitative sectoral characteristics:

[o]rganisational structures and processes are interdependent with the firm's business strategy and market segment ... Firms will survive and grow when there is a relatively good fit between societal and sectoral or market segment characteristics. Hence, there is, for instance, a large and successful population of medium size investment goods engineering firms in Germany. In Britain and France, large batch producers or defence, electronics, and specialised high tech manufacturers are more competitive.

In the United Kingdom, for example, if the technical education of workers is of a lower magnitude compared to Germany or Japan this is functional, because these societies have more need for higher volumes of technical labour as the nature of their competitive advantage requires more technical labour. Alternatively, if the hierarchical ordering of management specialisms is also different and persistently so between countries, with accounting and finance in a dominant position in the United Kingdom relative to the power of engineers in, say, Germany and Japan, then this is because of the underlying functional needs of the national system. The role of the City of London as a major global finance centre might explain the functional need for more accountants in the United Kingdom compared with Germany or France. Raising capital has also been consistently different, with the United Kingdom having greater reliance on stock markets and less on industrial banks (which do not really exist in the United Kingdom). Inter-firm investments and investment through retained profits are more common in Japan and Germany (Lane, 1997). We can continue to elaborate the 'facts' of comparative difference, but they speak only to one constituent of practices within firms: namely that given by a particular national set of institutional arrangements. To explain these 'facts' with reference to 'functional fit', however, is to view institutions as *knowing strategic agents*, and national business systems as unchanging, when, in practice, institutions arise, decay and change – through the force of outside events, the rise of new interest groups or class struggle between collective actors (such as that between the Thatcher government and the miners), which can lead to the recasting of national settlements in novel ways (Morgan, 2005: 427).

Firms are embedded and marked by their national origins in profound and lasting ways. Firms, especially large ones, are also key actors in shaping their environments, however, because they have desirable or scarce products, locational choice or power, and under neoliberal world rules they can 'regime shop' or use their bargaining power to create conditions within states that favour their interests. As Glenn Morgan (2005) and Colin Crouch (2005) note, boundary-spanning actors such as TNCs can change themselves, and not simply exhibit patterns of isomorphism. Because firms exist within the terrain of *competing* practices, with senior management cadres drawn from different 'business systems', different sectors, different national educational backgrounds and training, this means that the firm is far less likely to be *nationally* homogeneous. In other words, firms and states can be in a *contradictory*, not corresponding, relationship. Recent research into work and authority relations within organisations that cross different national environments have shifted from stressing the formal hierarchical features of TNCs, with headquarters enforcing rules on subsidiaries in the interests of efficiency, control, coordination and knowledge transfer, to a view of work relations within TNCs as political relations in sets of social networks through which transnational 'practices' are evolved and enacted, but not imposed in a linear, rational manner (see readings in Ferner, Quintanilla and Sánchez-Runde, 2006, and Geppert and Mayer, 2006). In other words, the structure of the international firm has changed in response to globalising economic forces, and this is changing the character of national/international differentiation.

The national business systems approach underestimates the way in which firms borrow and adopt practices, say by employing managers from firms from other territories, or by learning through partnerships or transplant operations. Moreover, societal effects theory operates with an oversocialised view of action: action is determined by inputs or the supply side, with different ingredients producing different national cakes. This ignores cross-national learning through the transnational firm, and internal variation within states based on region, ethnicity and the embeddedness of particular industrial complexes and sectors (Smith and Elger, 2000). Put another way, composite, complex societies contain variety, not uniform 'societal effects'. Invoking history to explain the routes of diversity is misleading, for, as Anna Pollert (1999: 57) has noted, the 'concept of "path dependence" begs the question of which path, out of a multiplicity of historical processes, is being followed'. In other words, writers in constructing a past to explain the present functional arrangement of institutions that make up a business system are necessarily *selective* – choosing certain institutions, such as long-term employment in large-scale Japanese firms, but ignoring other histories, such as the persistence of insecure employment in small-scale companies (see Chalmers, 1989). As Fitzgerald (chapter 4) notes, the role of interest groups, accidents and power, rather than path dependence, is important for seeing the way that institutions are remade at different times and that they are not simply self-reproducing once initiated (see also Wailes, Ramia and Lansbury, 2003, on the critical relationship between interest groups and institutions). As Hyoong-ki Kwon (2004) has noted, the reform of Japanese employment relations has not followed a path-dependent route; rather, reform has revealed other aspects of the Japanese system that were always present, but that had been lost in the story of 'alliance capitalism' projected in the 1980s when the Japanese economy was in a more symbolically dominant position.

Convergence through globalisation

It is evident today that there are convergence forces that are carried by world-wide agencies. In particular, there is the transnational corporation, the policies of which are producing an emergent process of globalisation. As Leslie Sklair (2001: 48) has noted: '[G]lobalizing corporations are those consciously denationalizing from their domestic origins in the course of developing genuinely global strategies of operation.' Here 'globalising' is a verb, a process and practice, rather than something that already exists. Thus, 'transnational corporations are said to be globalizing, not global, to the extent that they operate in a world made up of nation states, though not necessarily dominated by them economically, politically or in terms of culture-ideology' (48). Because this is an argument for a long-term tendency, this is not similar to the technological determinism of Clark Kerr, John Dunlop, Frederick Harbison and Charles Myers (1960), or the production determinism suggested by Harry Braverman (1974) or the naïve views of 'one best way' principles of business organisation of Frederick Taylor, Elton Mayo and Henri Fayol.

Alongside these wide policy and structural forces of convergence, we also have, *within* the firm, management being subject to globalising management concepts as the fashions, practices and professional projects of competing management cadres. For example, in the 1980s and 1990s it was 'lean production' and an associated 'Japanisation' that spread through the business schools and into practising management. Later, it was 'business process re-engineering' that emerged as an American reaction to non-American rationalisation recipes. Nonetheless, such *recipes* or *new management concepts* are carried within TNCs, and the strategies they are pursuing on a global basis. Further, the internationalisation of consumer *markets* means that global brands and TNCs are challenging local producers with bigger marketing budgets and more purchasing power. TNCs are forcing the globalising of brands and the internationalising of production. They create pressures on price, which reinforce cost reduction through an international division of labour (Froebel, Heinrichs and Kreye, 1980), forcing manufacturers and, increasingly, services to flee from embedded, high-cost institutional environments to source parts and assembly or commercial servicing processing in low-cost areas, such as India, China and the Association of South East Asian Nations (ASEAN) countries, Mexico and South America or central and eastern Europe (Taylor and Bain, 2005). Exporting assembly jobs creates longer production chains, integrates new states into the global market and undermines national institutional settlements, which are predicated on national manufacturing and corporate bargaining.

Discussions around the idea of the 'globalisation' of the labour process suggest ever more limited space for local and national patterns of workplace relations, as factories and offices disintegrate vertically and spatially, and are recombined through international supply chains, strategic alliances, transnational companies, and producer and consumer commodity chains

(Gereffi, 1994). Globalisation suggests a shrinking or 'runaway' world (Giddens, 2001), but such concepts, as discussed by Fitzgerald (chapter 4) and McSweeney, Smith and Fitzgerald (chapter 1), overstate the amount of economic activity taking place across borders, which is limited and concentrated in certain industrial sectors; present a zero-sum relationship between the national and the global, whereas states both aid and inhibit internationalisation; and, moreover, stress one-way trends towards the global market, even though there are countervailing political and economic pressures at national and regional levels that constrain such unidirectional change (see Tilly, 1995, and the replies by Wallerstein, Zolberg, Hobsbawm and Beneria in the special issue of *International Labor and Working Class History* entitled 'Scholarly controversy: global flows of labor and capital', for debate on the impact of 'globalisation' on work and workers' rights; the reply by Beneria, 1995, is particularly useful).

While Sklair conceives TNCs as 'globalising' agents, others judge them as national firms with international operations often engaged in transferring their home-country advantages to other foreign spaces, or having to negotiate the weight of host-country practice within their subsidiary operations (see Edwards and Rees, 2006, for a review). In other words, TNCs retain *national* identities and engage national institutional practices as they internationalise, rather than simply exhibiting a 'transnational' identity. While Morgan's (2001: 12–20) concept of the TNC as inhabiting 'transnational social space' with regard to corporate governance, internal management systems and work organisation opens up useful conversation on the limitation of a purely national or context-dependent rationality for the international firm, it is hard for the analysts of actually existing TNCs to interrogate the firm without introducing context-dependent rationality – that is, without bringing into play the role of national institutions and agents. Simply being boundary-spanning, transnational agents of an 'in-between' national space does not make TNCs non-national or worldly actors operating across anonymous space. Japanese firms in the United Kingdom retain important elements of their Japanese*ness* while also interacting within distinctively British rules of the game, especially with regard to the management of workers (Elger and Smith, 2005).

It is important not to exaggerate or misunderstand what is being claimed here. In its most effective form the convergence case is largely a structural argument. It is to be distinguished from arguments for globalisation based on the diffusion of consumption patterns. The 'McDonaldisation' thesis of George Ritzer (1993), for example, suggests that national boundaries are being dissolved. Talk of global consumption standards, of world factories and of shared management education through such programmes as the Master of Business Administration (MBA), however, is as sterile and unbalanced as the national partisanship of the business systems approach. Clearly, there is also a need to avoid polarised general theory: convergence versus divergence, national versus global, particular societies versus international practices. Rather, we should seek to capture the contradictions between the different structures and actors – states, markets, regional blocs, globalising firms, employers and worker's organisations – at the same time as being careful with both the level and the unit of analysis, and being clear what is it is we are trying to demonstrate: difference or similarity.

Varieties of capitalism

The divergence and convergence arguments considered so far might be thought to be resolved by the 'varieties of capitalism' approach to comparative analysis (Albert, 1993; Esping-Anderson, 1990; Crouch and Streeck, 1997; Hall and Soskice, 2001; Boyer *et al.*, 1998; Coates, 2000) or rival capitalist business models (Lazonick, 1991; Chandler, 1990). Such approaches argue that there are some distinctive patterns of institutions that allow societies displaying similar institutional configurations to be identified. Such arguments typically focus on the role of state policy and practice, welfare or societal institutions (such as industrial relations or the organisation of business and management) in furnishing distinctiveness and diversity. These approaches mainly offer an assessment of 'national political economies' as both self-contained and stable spaces for the reproduction of difference. The constancy of state welfare and differing institutional practices has been called into question, however, by the challenges to the nation state posed by internationalising product and service markets, globalising or transnational companies, and the general increased mobility and deterritorialisation of capital (Sklair, 2001).

Varieties of capitalism frequently divide between coordinated and market forms, with one promoting more corporate and integrated states and the other championing flexibility and market responsiveness. So-called 'cooperative' capitalism can be produced either through powerful legislative frameworks, cartel-like inter-firm links and powerful trade unions, typical of German-inspired 'cooperative capitalism' (Chandler, 1990), or from the dominance of giant enterprises, extensive inter-firm, long-term, relational subcontracting networks and the integration of labour into secure employment, typical of Japanese-inspired 'alliance' (Gerlach, 1992) or 'collective capitalism' (Lazonick, 1991: 24). In theories of 'varieties of capitalism', however, there remains an unresolved tension between *national-institutional* or embedded conceptions of capitalism, tied to a particular society, and *national-systemic* conceptions, which posit looser relations between society and system, and raise the idea of decoupling 'national competitive advantages' from national context, and their packaging and diffusion as techniques, models and principles learnable in other societies. For example, Mark Fruin (1992: 318) berates managerialist efforts to learn from Japan by abstracting practices such as just-in-time, quality circles and the like and bolting these onto the Western firm as fundamentally misunderstanding the institutionally embedded nature of the 'Japanese enterprise system'. Managerialists (Vogel, 1979; Pascale and Athos, 1982; Ouchi, 1981; Womack, Jones and Roos, 1990) have a tendency to abstract the paradigmatic case from the national, whereas business and economic historians (Chandler, 1990; Fruin, 1992; Lazonick, 1991) either remain at the level of national historical specificity or build more cautious 'national systemic' models that lack generalisability.

One of the criticisms of the 'varieties of capitalism' approach is that variety is constructed around bipolar contrasts between the role of the state and of the market in the economy. Richard Hyman (2006: 239–55), in reviewing the impact of neoliberalism in the European Union, contrasts the force of markets against social regulation, and notes that 'all markets are institutionally embedded, but some are more embedded than others' (228). In other words, in some societies the market has more autonomy and in others it is more constrained or embedded by social regulation. Embedding is thus conceived as a quantitative not a qualitative process – a 'more or less' question, not a 'different forms and processes' question. It seems sensible to stress that the market or international capital is never fully constrained by social regulation at national or regional level. International markets always possess an external or independent influence. Nevertheless, the quantification of differences between capitalist societies by contrasting more or less market, more open or constraining regulation, misses the deeper patterns of cultural and ideological differentiation, which are not simply about the abstracted operation of state or market rationalities. Sanford Jacoby (2005: 158–9), in an excellent comparison of the changing nature of HRM practices in Japan and the United States, also operates with bipolar concepts: market and organisation; make or buy decisions; internal or external labour markets; commodity or resource views of labour; and shareholder or stakeholder conceptions of the firm. Thus, movement along these bipolar lines leads to societies ebbing towards or away from each other. As Japan relies on more market and less organisation, more buying in of resources (including human resources) and less making, and an increasing commodification of labour (moving workers out from the protection of the organisation), then one can say that *Japan is moving closer to the US model*. The problem with bipolar readings, and, again, a quantitative analysis (*more or less* market or organisation), is that comparisons of different types of market contracts (long-term versus short-term, for example) and different forms of organisation are missed.

Varieties of capitalism have their roots within particular national contexts and have always existed in writing about business organisations, employment relations and the labour process. Karl Marx wrote through the British experience to speak of capitalism in general, when the United Kingdom was far from archetypal. Braverman (1974) used the United States as typical of 'monopoly capital' in general. Given that 'pure' capitalism cannot exist, then historical accounts of capitalist organisations are always *particular* stories. Caution is therefore required when attempting to abstract from history 'common' or 'typical' features of a 'system', or to create the idea of permanent 'varieties' to capitalism. Varieties of capitalism are in tension, however, with neoliberal variants more dominant of late, and hence the question of 'dominance' or rivalry is important. Secondly, there are systemic or 'natural' features to capitalism, as discussed below, and these get submerged within a national or contextual characterisation of this political economy by the 'varieties' school (see also Block, 2002: 222).

We have to disentangle the various levels of influence offered by the international trends and forces of international capital, the distinct institutional patterning of work within a given country, the borrowing and diffusion of new 'best practices' and the specificities of workplace-level historical and local contingencies. In some instances, the national speaks to the experience of labour process organisation across industrial sectors and geographical exigencies; in others, the autonomy of the workplace and local labour market conditions and patterns override any national or international typicality of standards. Theoretically, we cannot a priori rank such influences; we can only suggest methodologies and research strategies that will capture the nuances of analysing the labour process in today's more complex workplace.

The stability of the nation state during the post-war boom was supported by welfarism, Keynesism, financial or exchange controls on the movement of capital, and nationally centred pacts between states, employers and workers' organisations. The resurgence of the market, international capital and the greater mobility of financial and physical capital through TNCs have challenged these policies and institutional arrangements since the late 1970s. Therefore, the perspective of competing capitalism has been threatened by a resurgence of neoliberalism and international market forces (Traxler, Blaschke and Kittel, 2001).

States, rather than reinforcing national institutional settlements and differences on the basis of competition with other states, begin to come under pressure from internationalising firms to deregulate (or homogenise) their national territories, open up state activities to market forces and transform state practices into a common agenda of a 'competition' state (Cerny, 1990). Such states have standard policy incentives to pull in FDI, flexibilise their workforces, deregulate their labour markets and weaken trade unions and local institutional actors. Beginning in more marketised economies – Australia, the United States and United Kingdom – this liberal market philosophy has been spreading to corporatist, regulated and 'more embedded' institutionalised states, such as Germany (Jürgens, Naumann and Rupp, 2000) and Japan (Dore, 2002; Morgan and Takahashi, 2002).

States, firms and change

It is sensible to concede that national, state and institutional arrangements within states create practices that are relatively *stable*. States (and the social institutions within them) do not encounter profound *ownership* change to the national in the same way as private firms, but they do make structural adjustments, such as the shift from Keynesianism to neoliberalism from the late 1970s. International 'competitiveness' between states is unlike that between firms, however, because states do not go bankrupt or get taken over, and therefore they behave differently from firms (Krugman, 1994). As Ricardo Petrella (1996: 73) has noted, '"[G]oing global" has been far easier for firms than for governments, parliaments, trade unions or universities, which are not sufficiently flexible institutions ready to adapt easily or quickly to changing conditions.' We therefore need to separate states and firms in comparative analysis and to note the patterns of interaction between them.

When they move, firms carry the traits of the national environment in which they originated, and typically they retain most production capability, market, senior staff and research and development (R&D) capability. Furthermore, although states and firms both change, states do so more slowly than firms, so they can be seen plausibly as the context within which firms operate. They are not constrained by these, however, as capital is mobile, labour is mobile through and between the firm, and increasingly state policy is 'transferred' through what Sklair (2001) calls 'transnational' practices and institutions, such as the European Union (see chapter 13). States and national institutions change more slowly because they are not as institutionally subject to the rationalising forces of international markets, competition and the technological forces of capitalism. Firms are more dynamic – changing ownership, and integrating activities cross-nationally, operating with a global reach that few states (or national institutions) can possess as they are tied to *territory* in a way that capital, and to a lesser extent labour, are not.

Firms are more receptive to change than states. Moreover, production systems may be more heterogeneous, combining elements of 'old' (Fordist) and new (innovative/experimental) practices. Further, firms, unlike states, can experiment within national systems, and across national territories, because capital, unlike national institutions, is mobile (and increasingly so under neoliberal economic management practices). The recent Japanese *transplant* debate (Oliver and Wilkinson, 1992; Womack, Jones and Roos, 1990; Milkman, 1991; Kenney and Florida, 1993; Abo, 1994; Elger and Smith, 1994, 2005; Liker, Fruin and Adler, 1999; and others), discussion on the diffusion of management ideas (Kogut, 1993), the role of international business consultants (Kipping and Engwall, 2002) and of international firms in diffusing transnational or 'world best practice' (Sklair, 2001; Morgan, Kristensen and Whitley, 2001) make firms more, not less, likely to exhibit tensions within their practices, rather than the homogeneous national traits implied by societal effects theory (Maurice and Sorge, 2000).

In a recent book on reform of 'the Japanese model' (Inagami and Whittaker, 2005), global dimensions are kept at arm's length and reform is seen as a largely national process, ignoring the internationalisation of Japanese capital and capitalism as a system. Part of the reason for the challenge to the Japanese model is due to the internationalisation of Japanese firms, however, through FDI and access to labour markets in which employment conditions are different and the rationalisation of labour much easier. Consolidated overseas production in Hitachi, for example, grew from 6.5 per cent to 13.4 per cent in six years (Inagami and Whittaker, 2005). This doubling of overseas production for Hitachi is significant in itself, for the Japanese model and for the experimentation with different ways of putting the employment relationship together – dimensions not really covered by the authors. Thus, while the Japanese 'model' has structure, institutions and ideology in which 'corporate communities' are constructed and bounded, capitalism is not nationally constrained within such Durkheimian constructs, and all societal models have to interact with other models and global capitalism. So, although Takeshi Inagami and Hugh Whittaker acknowledge the role of class struggle in the construction of the Japanese model, they seem not to continue with this analysis when discussing the challenges to the system (see Elger and Smith, 2005: 26–9, for a discussion).

'Americanisation' as a prescription has been talked about throughout the period of economic recession since the early 1990s, but it is only recently that the impact of foreign firms operating in Japan has been researched. George Olcott (2008) has studied the effects of foreign entrants in Japan to see if they have opened up the Japanese model in more direct ways than that prescribed by consultants, advisers and academics, concluding:

The introduction of a controlling foreign shareholder was indeed found to cause extensive organisational change at Japanese firms. There was a greater emphasis on what the new management called 'performance culture' which led to the introduction of a wide range of market-oriented HR practices. These practices emphasised, for example, individual contribution and accountability over the traditional principles of equality and consensus that characterise Japanese organisations. Important conventions such as lifetime employment and generalist career paths were also affected. There was a dispersal of power away from the traditionally highly centralised HR Department to the operating divisions, with a corresponding increase in the significance of the finance function.

An alternative framework: distinguishing system, society and dominance effects

In a recent review of theories of the employment relationship, Peter Ackers (2005) criticises the incompleteness of the account offered by materialist analysis based on irreconcilable structural conflict between labour and capital within the capitalist labour process. Such an approach, he suggests (540), does not explain differences in work and employment relations *between* branches of industry or *between* countries:

[M]aterialism is flawed because it is a base–superstructure model. The effect is to overextend the explanatory power of the employment relationship and draw too much from what can only be tensions and tendencies. Once we start asking important questions, such as why are there more strikes in manufacturing than in retail, or more in France than in the UK, the employment relationship per se can tell us little, the labour process not so much more. Instead, we turn to institutions (in their broadest sense) for explanation. And were these institutions grown from the seed of an employment relationship? Well, yes, in a certain very generic sense, as with trade unions and employer associations, but they grew on very different soil, in traditional societies that existed before capitalism, and shaped its local development. The employment relationship is a useful ideal type to build IR [industrial relations] around, but institutions are the historical forces that pour life into it (see Jacoby 1990: 319).

Ackers is rightly acknowledging the power culture and pathways taken by different societies into capitalism and the persistence of different traditions, institutions and ideas of what constitutes work, workers, authority transactions and employment relations. Equally, however, one can say that to begin with society and institutions, and ignore the systemic commonalities and forces of a global, deterritorialising and permissive capitalism, is to end up telling half the story. Indeed, it is to end up with the mess of grubby empiricism. Instead of structural materialism, caricatured above, *historical materialism* takes underlying forces, such as ownership and control differences between workers and managers, and suggests that these need to be contextualised through their specific manifestations or appearances within particular societies, periods and contexts. As Tony Elger and Chris Smith (2005: 7) put it, 'Work organization is always context-dependent. Management policies and organizational or technological repertoires cannot determine the social relations of work independently of the wider contextual features that surround the enterprise and workplace.'

Within comparative organisational analysis, the international firm is a site for the social interaction of distinct forces, and not simply a universal set of economically 'efficient' organisational practices versus a local set of institutional rules, customs, laws and relations. To explain this better, a model of system, society and dominance effects, described below, grew out of comparative research on the engineering profession (Smith, 1990, 2005; Smith and Meiksins, 1995), and was extended through research on Japanese transplants in the United Kingdom (Smith and Elger, 1997, 2000; Elger and Smith, 2005). The model is an attempt to create a dynamic, synthetic and integrated approach to cross-national organisation analysis, and was built upon and reacted to the work of John Child (1981) and Christel Lane (1989).

The utility of the analysis is demonstrated by the fact that international organisations indicate a three-way interaction of contextual and interest group effects from different structural sources. Actors operate within and outside the organisation, and ensure that any common structural pressures are mediated and negotiated in divergent ways that reflect actor interests and not straightforwardly local institutional rules (Edwards *et al.*, 2006; Wailes,

Ramia and Lansbury, 2003). The structural forces can be conceived of as a triple determination: first, there is the political economy or mode of production ('system effects'); second, there is the effect of unique national institutions, cultures and histories ('societal effects'); and, third, there is the diffusion of best practices or modernisation strategies by the 'society in dominance' at any particular period of global competition. In recent decades it has been the United States or Japan that has exercised these 'dominance effects'.

The value of the approach has been highlighted in a number of ways. It has been considered in reviews of British economic sociology (e.g. Dodd, 2000), and diffused through influential critical British organisation studies textbooks (especially Thompson and McHugh, 2002). The latter elaborates the 'model by Smith and Meiksins', with political economy (system effects), national institutions (societal effects) and global forces (dominance effects) mutually interacting together and upon work organisation (82–3). More recently, Jill Rubery and Damian Grimshaw (2003: 47) have built a model of the international pressures on societal employment systems that 'has close parallels to that proposed in the various writing of Elger, Meiksins and Smith'. They in particular accept the idea of dominance, and see it as being an advance on the ideas of societal effects institutionalists. They use the SSD model to identify the competing pressures of divergence *and* convergence within the firm as introduced by different forces.

Other writers have used the model to critique cultural and institutional approaches, and stress the importance of 'system' features of generic conflict in employment relations in the globalisation of the service sector (Sturdy, 2001) or in debate on new production concepts diffused by Japanese firms (Delbridge, 1998; Sharpe, 2001). Those closer to the societal effects model have tried to 'test' and 'weigh' the relative importance of societal effects *against* dominant country effects, concluding that societal institutions carry *more effect* on, in this case, supply relations than current global 'best practice', such as vogue solutions from Japan (Lane, 1997). Nonetheless, it is not the aim of the SSD model to elevate one effect above another but, rather, to locate analytically the sources of change and continuity within the international firm. It is an inappropriate use of the model to attempt to rank the relative importance of different effects, as is attempted by Lane (1997). The assumption is that system, society and dominance effects may all be present and may work in inconsistent or consistent directions. Discussion of the intervention of a dominant player with global work organisation practices in the United Kingdom, in the form of Japanese TNCs, highlights their selective application of their own business systems, selective disregard of national practices and innovation and varying degrees of resistance from employees. Rather less than complete subordination of British workers to Japanese employment relations and work organisation practices is found in the work of Elger and Smith (2005). Lane's case study in a sector not exposed to international competition might explain why she found societal arrangements 'in tact' rather than complicated by dominance effects.

The dominance idea has been picked up by writers on TNCs (Edwards, 2004; Ferner, Quintanilla and Sánchez-Runde, 2006) and extended to describe the actions of dominant firms, such as Tony Royle's (2005) work on McDonald's in Europe, as much as the idea of dominance as a country model:

'[D]ominance' could also be associated with the influence of a small number of firms or even one highly influential firm in a particular sector. In other words, that where the appropriate sectoral characteristics apply, competing firms could be driven by the 'one best way' logic of the sector to emulate a dominant firm's employment practices across national borders and regardless of considerable differences in the national industrial relations systems. (Royle, 2005)

Maurice and Sorge (2000: 391–2), in defending the 'societal effects' approach against criticism from the SSD model, argue that 'societal effects may be amplified' by globalisation forces, reinforcing existing structures rather than changing them. This may indeed occur. On the other hand, the opposite may be true. Work on Japanese transplants in the United Kingdom, discussed below, highlights the subnational variations in practice applied by TNCs, and the innovative practices developed by dominant players within particular societal conditions, rather than simply the further reproduction of the same institutional practices and effects. One of the locational preferences for international firms, especially mass manufacturing companies, appears to be for clustered concentrations in 'special zones', 'new towns' or growth regions, which frequently lie 'outside' national 'rules of the game' or permit 'experimentation' within 'national rules', often influenced by alliances between local states and international capital. In these contexts, general societal values and rules may not apply in the same way to international firms (Smith and Elger, 2000; Elger and Smith, 2005).

The SSD model is not unidirectional and overly structural in emphasis. It allows that the firm does select policies and options and often does make its own environment. Research into Japanese TNCs in the United Kingdom based on the SSD model highlights the agency of the firm in managing its environment (Elger and Smith, 2005). This research is supported by the work of others (Clark and Mueller, 1996), who have tried to interrogate the action of the large firm within the context of societal constraints, developing what Michael Mayer and Richard Whittington (1999: 936) call a 'reflexive recombination of local and international practices', or what Morgan (2005: 424) sees as the *strength* of firms and *weakness* of institutions: 'Firms are "strong" not in the sense that they are immortal but in the sense that even within institutional constraints, they are centralized decision-making actors which have to make choices if they are to grow and develop. Institutions are "weak" in the sense that they do not have a centre of decision-making.' While one might argue that political institutions are also centralised decision-makers, in general Morgan is right to emphasise the greater capacity of firms to act and act more quickly across institutional spaces.

System effects: universalism

To begin to explore the three effects in more detail, 'system' is understood in a broad sense of a pure model or typology, which is not contextualised within any particular society but, rather, operates both within and against institutional boundaries. So, for example, capitalism is a 'political economy', a system with definite characteristics and common social relations that create recurrent problems, regardless of the country context within which capitalist social relations operate. System effects come through common social relations or purposes – for example, the motivation to work for private gain, rather than enhanced community status or common bonds of group or collective interest. 'System' refers to the sharing of fundamental factors, regardless of how they may have been introduced or arrived at. State socialism had generic features, typically an accentuated role for the state in economic affairs, the planning and management of the firm, control of labour allocation and constraints on managers' freedom to hire and fire workers. In addition, 'system' can refer to common elements of industrial society such as global technology or techniques, and ways of working that are diffused as common standards through such channels as management textbooks and common programmes such as the MBA. Capitalist competition, technological dynamism and capital–labour conflict underpin and exert common pressures on all specific manifestations of capitalist social relations, whether within enterprises, sectors or national economies. It is these underlying dynamics, with their associated conflicts and uncertainties, that go under the heading of *system imperatives*. Moreover, market relations, while embedded within societal institutions in different degrees, as noted earlier, are also autonomous, and international product and service markets impact on different societies and challenge locally derived societal rules (Traxler, Blaschke and Kittel, 2001; Hyman, 2006).

Systemic features of capitalism begin with property rights, owners and non-owners and the capitalist employment relationship. Paid work in a capitalist society requires waged labour dependent on employers for work and is structured by the drive for capital accumulation and profitable production. This motivates firms, which are activated by actors, managers and workers drawn into definite social relations for this purpose. Workers are motivated (compelled and facilitated) to sell their labour power to survive. Managers have to take this human 'raw material' and combine it with social forces of production (tools, equipment and technology and material objects for work) and a purpose (profitable production), which animate the rules of capitalist economic action. Within relations between waged workers and employers (or their 'representatives') there is an exchange, an employment relationship in which wages are exchanged for labour services. The precise amount of work or labour effort to be expended for economic return is left open-ended, however, as is the precise nature of the tasks to be performed, their sequencing, the particular standard of work, the performance criteria and the quality of the authority and human relations between those who employ and those who are employed. The capitalist employment relationship within different societies has different structures and rules, but institutional pluralism does not mean that systemic features of capitalism are overcome or transformed, although differences between capitalist societies can persist in a structural way for long periods.

Universal or 'systemic' theorising assumes a standardised or standardising workplace in which technology, science and managerial discourse aims at creating common methodologies regardless of the sector or country in which the firm is operating. System thinking is common to all deductive reasoning, which builds on abstract concepts, in which context-dependent rationality is suspended for the purposes of building ideal or pure typologies. Following a realist method, 'system' represents an underlying dynamic, which nevertheless receives varied manifestations. It is critically important to retain a separation between, say, 'pure' capitalism and actual capitalist societies, as to do otherwise is to assume that societies can overcome capitalist social relations independently, when, at most, individual societies can deviate from the law of value or the international marketplace only for a certain period or under certain conditions.

Societal effects: national divergence

The societal effects school frequently suggests an *irreducible* diversity to work organisation, regardless of common factor inputs or modes of systemic rationalising (Maurice and Sorge, 2000). This is because the 'rules of the game' under which managers and workers interact are formed by nationally specific cultural and institutional codes, not common or systemic rules of political economy. As these particular codes or rules emerge through the historical process within each country, they are unique. Any systemic thinking on work organisation according to this logic will be filtered through distinctive, inimitable agencies, and therefore be set to reproduce diversity perpetually. A country's history cannot be wiped clean, or only in exceptional circumstances of wars or colonisation, and even then cultural differences persist at subnational levels. Culture is important for embedding or framing action, which is always socially constructed, and hence derived from local values.

Societal effects or national business systems assume that there is no single 'best way' to organise work but, rather, that efficiency can be produced in 'functionally equivalent' ways. Therefore, there is no imperative to adopt one standard or 'best way', because such a notion is simply a reflection of current fashion or what could be called the practices of a society in dominance at any given moment. Societies are different because of historical legacies that act in 'self-perpetuating' ways, and as such ensure that material forces, such as organisations, are context-dependent and not subject to standardising or universal rationality. There is within this school of thought a differentiation between culture defined as abstract and ahistorical values (as promoted by Hofstede – see chapter 3) and claims that embed values and beliefs within social institutions, such as those of education, training, finance, etc., which may be strongly or weakly embedded at the national level and therefore more or less easy to change. In general, societal rules of the game, because they evolve from past actions and set up powerful 'routines and cultures', are hard to change and become habit-forming.

In extreme form, a focus on societal differences discounts the idea of the capitalist labour process; all that exists are national variants of 'ways of working', a menu of social relations prepared by national histories and not economic or functional structures of a supranational capitalist system. British writers using this approach (such as Lane, 1989) have critiqued the universalism of Braverman's deskilling thesis, for example, by bringing into focus different patterns of training and skill formation between capitalist societies, suggesting that social 'institutions' mould capitalist social relations in distinctly 'national' ways, so that there in no generalised tendency for capitalism to deskill or for the labour process to express the same antagonistic relationships between labour and capital as seen in the United Kingdom or United States. Workers' and managers' expectations and perceptions of each other are partially cultural – that is, they are informed by historical experience, and are partially the products of institutional genesis.

According to this view, national rules exist as external facts pressing down on individuals and ensuring, like language rules, that they obey the rules so as to enable social action. This Durkheimian view is clearly present in the quote below, which looks at the institutional rules at the national-sectoral level, and how these limit choices for social actors:

National-sectoral regimes of economic governance *evolve over time* and constitute *historically grown social facts* for each generation of traders. At any given point, economic actors are confronted with a legacy of local social institutions that are not of their making; not subject to their choosing; not in principle amenable to contractual reordering; and whose functional and evolutionary logic is different from that of a market or a formal-organizational hierarchy. At the centre of this logic is the ability of governance regimes to impose *socially constructed collective obligations* on individuals, if necessary against their resistance ... In the real world, the 'givenness' of an industrial order is visible in its ability to *socialize* its subjects into distinctive identities. While individuals 'belonging to' a particular order may undertake to remake it – for example, in line with the perceived imperatives of efficiency and 'economizing' – in doing so they are forced to observe its present modus operandi and the constraints it imposes upon them (in other words, to accept its 'path dependency'). (Hollingsworth, Schmitter and Streeck, 1994: 278–9; emphasis in original)

'Country' boundaries around work (through social institutions, laws, values and attitudes) remain one of the key features by which organisations are distinguished in this model.

We might observe, though, that supranational forces – technology, science, management best practices, international firms – operate to challenge national 'rules of the game' and create economic complexity, and are not simply internal, national institutional rules of the game. Moreover, it is clear that international organisations move between societies and are not 'nationally bounded', but draw from an internationally diverse range of practices and operate within Morgan's (2001) 'transnational social space'. Therefore, it becomes an open research question whether host or home practices, or a hybrid or combination of the two, shape work organisation and employment relations in transnational firms. The range of practices brought into action means that the TNC is able to draw upon divergent policies, practices and individuals with differing orientations to work from those simply present within the host society. This diversity produces varied organisation 'learning' and the leverage of coercive comparison.

Dominance effects

The third element in the framework concerns the uneven nature of economic power, and the tendency for one society to take the lead in evolving work organisation or business practices considered more efficient than those operating within other countries. These lead societies create 'dominance effects' that circulate as 'best practices' or temporary global standards that are emulated by other societies. In this way, societies do not face each other as equals but with uneven capabilities, which encourages the process of learning and borrowing or diffusion and dominance. Added to which, the globalisation of capital means that international companies operate in several regions and societies, and home practices might be retained only if they are judged to yield competitive advantage to the firm.

Within the contemporary debate, there are those who emphasise a plurality of equally effective national solutions to common economic problems, and those who search for a 'best' solution, and hence an arrangement of social institutions that delivers superior economic performance. As Crouch (2001: 132) has noted, the search for the 'best' model – Sweden, Germany, Japan or the United States in recent years – has short-term currency, as the economies of these countries begin to underperform, and today's model of emulation is tomorrow's model of aversion. Echoing the SSD framework, Jacoby (2005: 16) says that the 'dominant-model' form of convergence suffers from the problem of selection, namely the question of whether the parts of a country's institutional practice that others are being urged to copy are the actual parts that produced the associated economic success in the first place. This is not a straightforward question of identifying successful factors, such as quality circles, performance-related pay, team working, flexible labour markets or whatever. The same practice can, under different macroeconomic conditions, be seen as positive or negative. Hence, the same practices can be lauded and lamented at different times – such as Japan's corporate governance model being praised for its cooperation at one moment and damned for its cronyism at another. Similarly, the shareholder value model of US corporate governance that produced apparent financial transparency also produced Enron. Furthermore, when dominance is tied to a particular society, internal divisions are ignored as they do not fit the frame of the dominant model. As noted earlier, Japan has two economies, big business and small, and most complex societies have diverse rather than uniform business systems – and within-country differences are suppressed when a country is elevated as projecting one dominant form.

The search for 'dominance' is not really explained by Crouch (2001). Jacoby (2005: 16) suggests that this is ingrained in economists' thinking as they look for 'single peak optimality' when 'the historical evidence suggests that a wide variety of economic systems foster growth – that there are multiple equilibria – and what appears as the best model is shaped as much by fad and fashion as by evidence'. There is a lot in this, but I would suggest that the urge to emulate follows the systemic competition between states and capital, but also that the unevenness between societies produces a sort or rotating dominance and an associated fashionable urge to follow whichever leading country or firm is judged to be ahead.

Dominance may also be 'symbolic', tied to the cyclical patterns of economic success of one nation or region. Because 'efficiency' is *institutionalised* in the form of a strong 'society' or 'country case', rather than simply abstracted concepts of growth, output and productivity, it is inevitable that comparative modelling and diffusion take on a cognitive and symbolic dimension. Following institutional theory, one would expect that the urge to emulate these perceived (and real) dominant economies is stimulated as much by conformity, fashion and the need to overcome the uncertainties of capitalist competition (DiMaggio and Powell, 1983). For example, Japan and the so-called Asian 'tiger' economies, founded as they were on export processing and not import substitution strategies, were successful, dominant and therefore worthy of both emulation, promoted through management and firms, or coercive isomorphism, fostered through state direction. When the cycle moves, however, the stars of yesterday become the dogs of today, and the 'learning from' literatures move on to new talents. In this way, 'dominance' rotates and has a cognitive or perceived/symbolic element, as well as representing real efficiency differences between societies.

Applying the SSD model

Using the SSD framework, one can see that ideas or practices associated with economic success have national, systemic and dominant elements. Within the debate on the Japanese model, we have seen a clear relationship between the economic success of Japan and the intense interest by firms and governments in wishing to 'learn' from and 'borrow' Japanese ideas when the Japanese economy was strong in the 1980s. Dominance effects signal the idea that one society originates ideas, and may seek to diffuse these, as new standards, but through the process of diffusion there occurs a distillation of the ideas into 'societal' and 'systemic' elements. In order to make emulation more acceptable or to neutralise societal origins, systemic and non-societal technical terms are invented, such as 'lean production' or 'total quality management' (TQM) or 'continuous improvement'. Although they originated in Japan, the circulation of these practices creates a different discourse, and association with the Japanese context may be broken; this was especially important as the 'dominance' of the Japanese economy faded in the 1990s. This is clear in the Japan debate, and was also evident in earlier debates on Taylorism:

> Taylorism . . . was initially bounded by the constraints of American capitalism; but its diffusion transformed it into a 'best practice' which was seen as a system requirement in some economies . . . The identification of Taylorism with American economic success made it difficult to resist. Disentangling the three influences of society, system and dominance has always been part of the critique of Taylorism as it became a dominant ideology and began to diffuse to Europe and Japan; but we could say that it was only with the emergence of other dominant capitalist states, in Europe and Japan, that such a critique has been able to separate these levels, and identify what in Taylorism is specific to America, what is part of capitalism, and what held sway only through American economic hegemony and not intrinsic qualities of Taylorism itself. (Smith and Meiksins, 1995: 263–4)

While there are undoubtedly some important 'societal effects', the most significant problem for this approach is in explaining, theoretically, why there are continued convergence pressures within supposedly nationally bounded economies. The imperative of efficiency (i.e. abstract economic or market principles) applies to all capitalist societies as *system* imperatives. Establishing the efficiency even of non-complex and bounded systems is notoriously difficult, however. On the other hand, it is clear that dominant countries provide models of 'best practice' that involve the packaging of national operations into apparently neutral requirements, which actually involve the selective borrowing of 'best practices' from national agendas; this is because of the economic inequality between societies and the nature of capitalist competition.

Thus, whilst the theorists of societal effects have begun to develop valuable accounts of the sources of diversity in national trajectories of capitalist development and class relations, these accounts have concentrated upon the internal logics of institutional development, which are held to explain persistent distinctiveness, while giving little attention to the ways in which evolving relations among states alter the terrain upon which national 'systems' operate.

Dominance and diffusion

The SSD model suggests that capitalist production rationalisation has 'national' traits, such as the link between Taylor, Taylorism and the United States, or Toyota, 'Toyotaism' and Japan. It also suggests, however, that the diffusion of new production and employment ideas through international firms, consultancy channels, academic discourse and universal management educational processes (such as the global commodity of the MBA) aims to delink the sources of ideas (Taylorism and Fordism in the United States, Toyotaism in Japan) from national contexts through the process of diffusion (Kogut and Parkinson, 1993; Smith and Meiksins, 1995). Delinking stresses the universal efficiency gains that all organisations will receive from the adoption of new 'best practices'. Nevertheless, the application and adaptation of novel practices within the workplace, especially for TNC subsidiaries, will raise themes of 'ownership', until techniques become 'global best practices' (Sklair, 2001), denationalised, and diluted or altered, through the diffusion process.

The system, society and dominance model aims to capture the complexity of 'transfer' within the modern, internationalised workplace. It locates the sources of differences, which come into the firm through home or local practices (societal contexts), standard or system forces, given by the definite relations of production of a particular political economy. Finally, it stresses the importance of a 'society in dominance' or standard-setter for modern employment and work relations, which continually fuels competition between companies and nations by holding up the latest business, production or employment practice originating in an apparently *more* efficient/dominant society or company within a market, sector or region, diffused through various agencies that gain from packaging and trading 'best practice' knowledge and information.

As research into the activities of Japanese transplants reveals, while there is not a simple diffusion of something called 'the Japanese model', or a generic process of Japanization, there are certainly real traces of borrowing, learning, transfer and transformation through the interaction of internationally dominant TNCs in national economies (Smith and Elger, 2000; Elger and Smith,

2005). Throughout the 1980s and 1990s there was an active debate on the transfer of Japanese management techniques from Japan to the West through the agency of the Japanese transnational company. At different moments and in different societal contexts, 'applying' Japanese practices to new locations was considered straightforward, due to their inherent and irresistible efficiency superiority, and thus normatively essential for the competitive survival of the Western firm (Womack, Jones and Roos, 1990; Florida and Kenney, 1991). At other times it was regarded as a more interactive and problematical process of application and adaptation, involving considerable compromise for the Japanese firm (Abo, 1994, 1998; Itagaki, 1997), or as very creative and dynamic, whereby relocation produced new work forms, different both from those in Japan and from within the host society, and therefore unanticipated and unimagined prior to the process of Japanese subsidiary formation (Jürgens, Malsch and Dohse, 1993; Kenney and Florida, 1993; Smith, 1996; Boyer *et al.*, 1998; Liker, Fruin and Adler, 1999; Freyssenet *et al.*, 1999). In other words, diffusion has systemic (universal), societal (adaptation) and dominant (best practices) elements, rather than being something simple, as in technology transfers or capital relocation.

TNCs affect global, regional and trans-state forms of interdependence and integration, however, often based on cost-driven and market-driven business strategies, or the construction of different 'global commodity chains' (Gereffi and Korzeniewicz, 1994). These, while not suppressing institutional and value differences between societies, tend to create common policy responses and instruments within states desperate to attract foreign direct Investment – such as low/no tax incentives and special labour codes, as found in new towns and 'special' development regions and zones (Dicken, 1998; Sklair, 2002). The 'competition state' (Cerny, 1990; Elger and Burnham, 2001) and globalisation reinforce each other, and the national is not a source of simple diversity but convergence to standards that fit the process of the internationalisation of capital. It is the adoption of these common policy instruments designed to pull in FDI, and the consequent clustering of manufacturing capital, that create distinctive management and labour responses – especially high turnover and management retention/adaptation strategies such as process deskilling, inter-firm collusion, contract segmentation, neo-paternalism and worker substitution (Smith and Elger, 2002).

Capitalist firms in different societies are not all equivalent in terms of efficiencies and productivity, and when economic goods are tradable through TNCs such differences inform location choices, and also national policy-makers, who place comparative economic advantage on the agenda, and press towards the adoption of modern technologies, techniques and practices to 'compete with the best'. Such emulation – again, present in the Japanisation debate – creates homogenisation or globalisation pressures, which tend to test and erode local or national institutional rules and practices. The comparative evaluation of the economic performance between countries raises borrowing as a possibility, even though, in practical terms, taking practices and policies from one country and 'transferring' them to another is far from straightforward – as discussed above (Jacoby, 2005; Elger and Smith, 2005). Nevertheless, the fact that the idea of transfer occurs repeatedly needs explaining, and is not self-evident from a purely 'societal effects' perspective in which countries compete with each other through divergent, but *functionally equivalent*, organisational means and methods. This leads to a discussion of differences between societies, and the 'dominance effects' these create through the competitive pressure of the global marketplace.

Despite evident system properties, every consideration of the social relations in organisational change must take into account actor consciousness, the actions and reaction of groups of actors. This was either not considered by societal effect theorists or, if it was, it was treated as marginal to the theme of 'transfer' and 'transplantation', which was a largely mechanical or technical process, and not one mediated through human agency and so not requiring interpretation. Modern management practices and production systems were judged like bits of technology, and thought capable of isolation and transfer (Ferner, 1997). Ethnographic accounts of workers' 'life on the line' in Japanese subsidiaries or emulator plants highlighted a much more mundane, routine and pressured picture of work and authority relations, however (Graham, 1995; Delbridge, 1998; Palmer, 1996; Sharpe, 1997, 1998). Nonetheless, this research also highlighted 'movable' and 'immovable' practices. Rick Delbridge (1998: 203–4), for example, notes that certain 'technical' aspects of the Japanese production system were present in his two case companies: quality regime, inventory control and the grouping of activities; none of the 'social' side of the Japanese model was present, however (security of employment, team working and seniority pay), echoing earlier work by Ruth Milkman (1991) in the United States and Vagelis Dedoussis (1995) in Australia.

Conclusions: transnational firms and the SSD model

Transnational companies are globalising, not globalised, as Sklair suggests, and therefore their organisations will be marked by both their origins and the strength of the local practices embedded within any particular subsidiary, as well as the prevailing forces within the world market and production system. States or national business systems are always penetrated by the international division of labour, the world market and competition between rival capitalist societies, and are never 'islands' of self-sustaining diversity. They are also increasingly divergent, as different sectors of industry and services integrate into the global economy at different rates. Hence, there may be 'two-speed' sectors, and international differentiation within national economies and between national economies (Katz and Darbishire, 2000; Katz, 2005).

The idea that globalisation, best practices or the latest, 'one best way' modernisation recipe will sweep away diversity is misleading, however. What flows from the arguments presented here is that interplay between different processes, often pulling in contradictory directions, is a more feasible scenario. As such, the new international division of labour within global capitalism may confirm some countries within already dependent, peripheral or subordinate positions within the order of global capitalism. New entrants may also create different ways of organising the firm, employ-ment relations, work organisation and supplier relations, however, and redefine themselves and influence others in the system. Japan played this role in the 1980s, exercising a profound influence on work organisation outside the country. Finally, whatever value there is in particularising the nature of organisation, work, and employment relations by reference to country or production metaphors (Fordism or Toyotaism, for example), the universal or systemic social relations given by the political economy will always be present within all these diverse representations or appearances. In other words, capital–labour contestation is structurally endemic to capital-ism, but is expressed in manifold ways, and mediated through a great variety of institutional forms.

The transferred or internationalised workplace condenses the effects of globalising capitalist forces, national institutional rules and 'world best prac-tice' work and employment standards within local and unique work situations. Nevertheless, it is only through social interaction that groups and individuals negotiate which of these different (and perhaps competing) ways of working, standards of quality, authority relations and methods of employment will actually shape particular work situations. It is therefore important to retain a research focus on the workplace, as it is here that the working out of workplace *rules* and *practices* emerges. The *unpredictability* of workplace relations comes from the system effects within employment relations, but so does the impos-sibility of knowing, from the outside, how the contingent combinations of particular workers and managers, in particular locations, sectors and contexts, will actually interact to produce definite work and employment relations. It is both the systemic and contingent contradictions that necessitate empirical enquiry, as social agents are reflexive, and have choices over how they interact within the constraints they find themselves in.

Note

This chapter is an expanded version of Smith (2005).

References

Abo, T. (ed.) (1994) *Hybrid Factory: The Japanese Production System in the United States*, Oxford: Oxford University Press.

  (1998) Hybridization of the Japanese production system in North America, newly industrializing economies, South-east Asia and Europe: contrasted configurations, in R. Boyer, E. Charron, U. Jürgens and S. Tolliday (eds.) *Between Imitation and Innovation: The Transfer and Hybridization of Productive Models in the International Automobile Industry*, Oxford: Oxford University Press, 216–30.

Ackers, P. (2005) Theorizing the employment relationship: materialists and institutionalists, *British Journal of Industrial Relations*, 43, 3, 537–60.

Albert, M. (1993) *Capitalism vs. Capitalism: How America's Obsession with Individual Achievement and Short-term Profit Has Led it to the Brink of Collapse*, New York: Four Walls Eight Windows.

Beneria, L. (1995) Response: the dynamics of globalization, *International Labor and Working Class History*, 47, 45–52.

Block, F. (2002) Rethinking capitalism, in N. W. Biggart (ed.) *Readings in Economic Sociology*, Oxford: Blackwell, 219–30.

Boyer, R. E. Charron, U. Jürgens and S. Tolliday (eds.) (1998) *Between Imitation and Innovation: The Transfer and Hybridization of Productive Models in the International Automobile Industry*, Oxford: Oxford University Press.

Braverman, H. (1974) *Labor and Monopoly Capital: The Degradation of Work in the Twentieth Century*, New York: Monthly Review Press.

Cerny, P. G. (1990) *The Changing Architecture of Politics: Structure, Agency and the Future of the State*, London: Sage.

Chalmers, N. J. (1989). *Industrial Relations in Japan: The Peripheral Workforce*, London: Routledge.

Chandler, A. D. (1990) *Scale and Scope: The Dynamics of Industrial Capitalism*, Cambridge, MA: Harvard University Press.

Child, J. (1981) Culture, contingency and capitalism in the cross-national study of organisations, in B. M. Staw and L. L. Cummings (eds.) *Research in Organizational Behavior*, vol. III, Greenwich, CT: JAI Press, 303–56.

Clark, P., and F. Mueller (1996) Organisations and nations: from universalism to institutionalism, *British Journal of Management*, 7, 2, 125–40.

Coates, D. (2000) *Models of Capitalism: Growth and Stagnation in the Modern Era*, Cambridge: Polity Press.

Crouch, C. (2001) Heterogeneities of practice and interest, *New Political Economy*, 6, 1, 131–5.

  (2005) Complementarity and fit in the study of comparative capitalisms, in G. Morgan, R. Whitley and E. Moen (eds.) *Changing Capitalisms? Internationalization, Institutional Change, and Systems of Economic Organization*, Oxford: Oxford University Press, 167–9.

Crouch, C., and W. Streeck (eds.) (1997) *Political Economy of Modern Capitalism: Mapping Convergence and Diversity*, London: Sage.

Crouch, C., D. Finegold and M. Sako (1999) *Are Skills the Answer? The Political Economy of Skill Creation in Advanced Industrial Societies*, Oxford: Oxford University Press.

Dedoussis, V. (1995) Simply a question of cultural barriers? The search for new perspectives in the transfer of Japanese management practices, *Journal of Management Studies*, 32, 6, 731–46.

Delbridge, R. (1998) *Life on the Line in Contemporary Manufacturing: The Workplace Experience of Lean Production and the 'Japanese' Model*, Oxford: Oxford University Press.

Dicken, P. (1998) *Global Shift: Transforming the World Economy* (3rd edn.), London: Paul Chapman.

DiMaggio, P. J., and W. W. Powell (1983) The iron cage revisited: institutional isomorphism and collective rationality in organizational fields, *American Sociological Review*, 48, 147–60.

Dodd, N. (2000) Economic sociology in Britain, *Economic Sociology European Electronic Newsletter*, 2, 1, 3–12.

Dore, R. (2000) *Stock Market Capitalism: Welfare Capitalism: Japan and Germany versus the Anglo-Saxons*, Oxford: Oxford University Press.

  (2002) Stock market capitalism and its diffusion, *New Political Economy*, 7, 1, 115–21.

Dosi, G., and B. Kogut (1993) National specificities and the context of change: the coevolution of organization and technology, in B. Kogut (ed.) (1993) *Country Competitiveness: Technology and the Organizing of Work*, Oxford: Oxford University Press, 249–62.

Edwards, T. (2004) International human resource management and industrial relations: a framework for analysis, in A.-W. Harzing and J. Van Ruysseveldt (eds.) *International Human Resource Management*, London: Sage, 389–410.

Edwards, T., X. Coller, L. Ortiz, C. Rees and M. Wortmann (2006) National industrial relations systems and cross-border restructuring: evidence from a merger in the pharmaceuticals sector, *European Journal of Industrial Relations*, 12, 1, 69–88.

Edwards, T., and C. Rees (2006) *International Human Resource Management: Globalization, National Systems and Multinational Companies*, Harlow: Pearson Education.

Elger, T., and P. Burnham (2001) Labour, globalization and the 'Competition state', *Competition and Change*, 5, 3, 245–68.

Elger, T., and C. Smith (1994) Introduction, and Global Japanization? Convergence and competition in the organization of the labour process, in T. Elger and C. Smith (eds.) *Global Japanization? The Transnational Transformation of the Labour Process*, London: Routledge, 1–24, 31–59.

  (2005) *Assembling Work: Remaking Factory Regimes in Japanese Multinationals in Britain*, Oxford: Oxford University Press.

Esping-Anderson, G. (1990) *Three Worlds of Welfare Capitalism*, Princeton, NJ: Princeton University Press.

Ferner, A. (1997) Country of origin effects and HRM in multinational companies, *Human Resource Management Journal*, 7, 1, 19–37.

Ferner, A., and R. Hyman (1992), *Industrial Relations in the New Europe*, London: Blackwell.

Ferner, A., J. Quintanilla and C. Sánchez-Runde (eds.) (2006) *Multinationals, Institutions and the Construction of Transnational Practices*, Basingstoke: Palgrave Macmillan.

Florida, R., and M. Kenney (1991) Organisation versus culture: Japanese automotive transplants in the United States, *Industrial Relations Journal*, 22, 3, 181–96.

Freyssenet, M., A. Mair, K. Shimizu and G. Volpato (eds.) (1999) *One Best Way? Trajectories and Industrial Models of the World's Automobile Producers*, Oxford: Oxford University Press.

Froebel, F., J. Heinrichs and O. Kreye (1980). *The New International Division of Labour*, Cambridge: Cambridge University Press.

Fruin, W. M. (1992) *The Japanese Enterprise System: Competitive Strategies and Cooperative Structures*, Oxford: Clarendon Press.

Geppert. M., and M. Mayer (eds.) (2006) *Global, National and Local Practices in Multinational Companies*, Basingstoke: Palgrave Macmillan.

Gereffi, G. (1994) Capitalism, development and global commodity chains, in L. Sklair (ed.) *Capitalism and Development*, London: Routledge, 211–31.

Gereffi, G., and M. Korzeniewicz (eds.) (1994) *Commodity Chains and Global Capitalism*, Westport, CT: Praeger.

Gerlach, M. (1992) *Alliance Capitalism: The Social Organization of Japanese Business*, Berkeley, CA: University of California Press.

Giddens, A. (2001) *Runaway World: How Globalization is Reshaping Our Lives*, London: Routledge.

Graham, L. (1995) *On the Line at Subaru-Isuzu: The Japanese Model and the American Worker*, Ithaca NY: ILR/Cornell University Press.

Hall, P. A., and D. Soskice (2001) An introduction to varieties of capitalism, in P. A. Hall and D. Soskice (eds.) *Varieties of Capitalism: The Institutional Foundations of Comparative Advantage*, Oxford: Oxford University Press, 1–69.

Hampden-Turner, C., and F. Trompenaars (1993) *The Seven Cultures of Capitalism*, London: Piatkus.

Hollingsworth, J. R., and R. Boyer (1997) *Contemporary Capitalism: The Embeddedness of Institutions*, Cambridge: Cambridge University Press.

Hollingsworth, J. R., P. C. Schmitter and W. Streeck (eds.) (1994) *Governing Capitalist Economies: Performance and Control of Economic Sectors*, Oxford: Oxford University Press.

Hyman, R. (2001) *Understanding European Industrial Relations: Between Market, Class and Society*, London: Sage.

  (2006) Structuring the transnational space: can Europe resist multinational capital?, in A. Ferner, J. Quintanilla and C. Sánchez-Runde (eds.) *Multinationals, Institutions and the Construction of Transnational Practices*, Basingstoke: Palgrave Macmillan, 239–55.

Inagami, T., and D. H. Whittaker (2005) *The New Community Firm: Employment, Governance and Management Reform in Japan*, Cambridge: Cambridge University Press.

Itagaki, H. (ed.) (1997) *The Japanese Production System: Hybrid Factories in East Asia*, London: Macmillan.

Jacoby, S. M. (1990). The new institutionalism: what can it learn from the old?, *Industrial Relations*, 29, 316–59.

(2005) *The Embedded Corporation*, Princeton, NJ: Princeton University Press.

Jürgens, U., K. Naumann and J. Rupp (2000) Shareholders in an adverse environment: the German case, *Economy and Society*, 29, 1, 54–79.

Jürgens, U., T. Malsch and K. Dohse (1993) *Breaking from Taylorism: Changing Forms of Work in the Automobile Industry*, Cambridge: Cambridge University Press.

Katz, H. C. (2005) The causes and consequences of increased within-country variance in employment practices, *British Journal of Industrial Relations*, 43, 4, 577–83.

Katz, H. C., and O. Darbishire (2000) *Converging Divergences: Worldwide Changes in Employment Systems*, Ithaca, NY: ILR/Cornell University Press.

Kenney, M., and R. Florida (1993) *Beyond Mass Production: The Japanese System and its Transfer to the US*, Oxford: Oxford University Press.

Kerr, C., J. T. Dunlop, F. Arbison and C. A. Myers (1960) *Industrialism and Industrial Man: The Problems of Labor and Management in Economic Growth*, Cambridge, MA: Harvard University Press.

Kipping, M., and L. Engwall (eds.) (2002) *Management Consulting: Emergence and Dynamism of a Knowledge Industry*, Oxford: Oxford University Press.

Kogut, B. (ed.) (1993) *Country Competitiveness: Technology and the Organizing of Work*, Oxford: Oxford University Press.

Kogut, B., and D. Parkinson (1993) The diffusion of American organizing principles to Europe, in B. Kogut (ed.) *Country Competitiveness: Technology and the Organizing of Work*, Oxford: Oxford University Press, 179–202.

Krugman, P. (1994) Competitiveness: a dangerous obsession, *Foreign Affairs*, 73, 2, 28–44.

Kwon, H.-k. (2004) Japanese employment relations in transition, *Economic and Industrial Democracy*, 25, 3, 325–45.

Lane, C. (1989) *Management and Labour in Europe: The Industrial Enterprise in Germany, Britain and France*, Aldershot: Edward Elgar.

(1997) 'The governance of inter-firm relations in Britain and Germany: societal or dominance effects?, in R. Whitley and P. H. Kristensen (eds.) *Governance at Work: The Social Regulation of Economic Relations*, Oxford: Oxford University Press, 62–85.

Lazonick, W. (1991) *Business Organisation and the Myth of the Market Economy*, Cambridge: Cambridge University Press.

Liker, J. K., W. M. Fruin and P. S. Adler (1999) Bringing Japanese management to the United States: transplantation or transformation?, in J. K. Liker, W. M. Fruin and P. S. Adler (eds.) *Remade in America: Transplanting and Transforming Japanese Management Systems*, Oxford: Oxford University Press, 3–35.

Lorenz, E. (2000) Societal effects and the transfer of business practices to Britain and France, in M. Maurice and A. Sorge (eds.) *Embedding Organizations: Societal Analysis of Actors, Organizations and Socio-Economic Context*, Amsterdam: John Benjamin's, 241–56.

Maurice, M., F. Sellier and J. J. Silvestre (1986) *The Social Foundations of Industrial Power: A Comparison of France and Germany*, Cambridge, MA: MIT Press.

Maurice, M., and A. Sorge (2000) Conclusions, in M. Maurice and A. Sorge (eds.) *Embedding Organizations: Societal Analysis of Actors, Organizations and Socio-economic Context*, Amsterdam: John Benjamin's, 389–99.

Mayer, M., and R. Whittington (1999) Strategy, structure and 'systemness': national institutions and corporate change in France, Germany and the UK, 1950–1993, *Organization Studies*, 20, 6, 933–59.

Milkman, R. (1991) *Japan's California Factories: Labor Relations and Economic Globalisation*, Ithaca, NY: ILR/Cornell University Press.

Morgan, G. (2001) The multinational firm, in G. Morgan, P. H. Kristensen and R. Whitley (eds.) *The Multinational Firm: Organizing across Institutional and National Divides*, Oxford: Oxford University Press, 1–24.

  (2005) Multinationals and work, in S. Ackroyd, R. Batt, P. Thompson and P. S. Tolbert (eds.) *The Oxford Handbook of Work and Organization*, Oxford: Oxford University Press, 555–76.

Morgan, G., P. H. Kristensen and R. Whitley (eds.) (2001) *The Multinational Firm: Organizing across Institutional and National Divides*, Oxford: Oxford University Press.

Morgan, G. and Y. Takahashi (2002) Shareholder value in the Japanese context, *Competition and Change*, 6, 2, 169–91.

Nelson, R. R. (ed.) (1993) *National Innovation Systems: A Comparative Analysis*, Oxford: Oxford University Press.

Olcott, G. (2008) *Take-over and Non-take-over Firms in Japan*, Cambridge: Cambridge University Press.

Oliver, N., and B. Wilkinson (1992) *The Japanisation of British Industry: New Developments in the 1990s* (2nd edn.), Oxford: Basil Blackwell.

Ouchi, W. G. (1981) *Theory Z: How American Business can Meet the Japanese Challenge*, New York: Avon Books.

Palmer, G. (1996) Reviving resistance: the Japanese factory floor in Britain, *Industrial Relations Journal*, 27, 2, 129–43.

Pascale, R. T., and A. G. Athos (1982) *The Art of Japanese Management*, London: Allen Lane.

Petrella, R. (1996) Globalization and internationalization: the dynamics of the emerging world order, in R. Boyer and D. Drache (eds.) *States Against Markets: The Limits of Globalization*, London: Routledge, 62–83.

Pollert, A. (1999) *Transformation at Work in the New Market Economies of Central Eastern Europe*, London: Sage.

Redding, S. G. (1990) *The Spirit of Chinese Capitalism*, Berlin: de Gruyter.

Ritzer, G. (1993) *The McDonaldization of Society*, London: Sage.

Royle, T. (2005) The dominance effect and the five lane low road: multinational corporations in the Italian quick food service sector, mimeo, Department of Management, St Anthony's College, National University of Ireland, Galway.

Rubery, J., and D. Grimshaw (2003) *The Organization of Employment: An International Perspective*, Basingstoke: Palgrave.

Sharpe, D. R. (1997) Managerial control strategies and sub-cultural processes: on the shopfloor in a Japanese manufacturing organisation in the UK, in S. A. Sackmann (ed.) *Cultural Complexity in Organisations: Inherent Contrasts and Contradictions*, London: Sage, 228–51.

(1998) Shop floor practices under changing forms of management control: a comparative ethnographic study, Ph.D. thesis, University of Manchester.

(2001) Globalization and change: organizational continuity and change within a Japanese multinational in the UK, in G. Morgan, P. H. Kristensen and R. Whitley (eds.) *The Multinational Firm: Organizing across Institutional and National Divides*, Oxford: Oxford University Press, 196–224.

Sklair, L. (2001) *The Transnational Capitalist Class*, Oxford: Basil Blackwell.

(2002) *Globalization: Capitalism and Its Alternatives*, Oxford: Oxford University Press.

Smith, C. (1990) How are engineers formed? Professionals, nation and class politics, *Work, Employment and Society*, 3, 4, 451–70.

(1996) Japan, the hybrid factory and cross-national organisational theory, *Österreichische Zeitschrift für Soziologie*, 3, Special Issue (Vernetzung und Vereinnahmung-Arbeit zwischen Internationalisierung und neuen Managementkonzepten), 105–30.

(2005) Beyond convergence and divergence: explaining variations in organizational practices and forms, in S. Ackroyd, R. Batt, P. Thompson and P. S. Tolbert (eds.) *The Oxford Handbook of Work and Organization*, Oxford: Oxford University Press, 602–25.

Smith, C., and T. Elger (1997) International competition, inward investment and the restructuring of European work and industrial relations, *European Journal of Industrial Relations*, 3, 3, 279–304.

(2000) The societal effects school and transnational transfer: the case of Japanese investment in Britain, in M. Maurice and A. Sorge (eds.) *Embedding Organizations: Societal Analysis of Actors, Organizations and Socio-Economic Context*, Amsterdam: John Benjamin's, 225–39.

(2002) The transferred workplace: towards a theory of work in the transnational firm, paper presented at the 18th European Group for Organization Studies colloquium, Barcelona, 4–6 July.

Smith, C., and P. Meiksins (1995) System, society and dominance effects in cross-national organisational analysis, *Work, Employment and Society*, 9, 2, 241–67.

Sorge, A. (1991) Strategic fit and the societal effect: interpreting cross-national comparisons of technology, organization and human resources, *Organization Studies*, 12, 2, 161–90.

Sorge, A., and M. Maurice (1993) The societal effect in the strategies of French and West German machine tool manufacturers, in B. Kogut (ed.) *Country Competitiveness: Technology and the Organizing of Work*, Oxford: Oxford University Press, 75–95.

Streeck, W. (1992) National diversity, regime competition and institutional deadlock: problems in forming a European industrial relations system, *Journal of Public Policy*, 12, 4, 301–30.

Sturdy, A. (2001) The global diffusion of customer service: a critique of cultural and institutional perspectives, *Asia Pacific Business Review*, 7, 3, 75–89.

Taylor, P., and P. Bain (2005) 'India calling from far away towns': the call centre labour process and globalization, *Work, Employment and Society*, 19, 2, 261–82.

Thompson, P., and D. McHugh (2002) *Work Organisations* (3rd edn.), Basingstoke: Palgrave.

Tilly, C. (1995) Globalization threatens labor's rights, *International Labor and Working Class History*, 47, 1–23.

Traxler, F., S. Blaschke and B. Kittel (2001) *National Labour Relations in Internationalized Markets*, Oxford: Oxford University Press.

Vogel, E. (1979) *Japan as No. 1: Lessons for America*, Cambridge, MA: Harvard University Press.

Wailes, N., G. Ramia and R. Lansbury (2003) Interests, institutions and industrial relations, *British Journal of Industrial Relations*, 41, 4, 617–37.

Whitley, R. (1992a) *Business Systems in East Asia: Firms, Markets and Societies*, London: Sage.
  (ed.) (1992b) *European Business Systems: Firms and Markets in Their National Contexts*, London: Sage.

Whitley, R., and P. K. Kristensen (eds.) (1997) *Governance at Work: The Social Regulation of Economic Relations*, Oxford: Oxford University Press.
  (2005) How national are business systems? The role of states and complementary institutions in standardizing systems of economic coordination and control at the national level, in G. Morgan, R. Whitley and E. Moen (eds.) *Changing Capitalisms? Internationalization, Institutional Change, and Systems of Economic Organization*, Oxford: Oxford University Press, 190–231.

Womack, J. D., P. T. Jones and D. Roos (1990) *The Machine that Changed the World: The Triumph of Lean Production*, New York: Rawson Associates.

3   Cultural diversity within nations

Brendan McSweeney

> The appeal to national character is generally a mere confession of ignorance.
>
> Max Weber (1992 [1904–5]: 88)

Introduction

Are workplace practices shaped by national context? Are those practices embedded, inflexible, path-dependent? Is there a national path? Is there a single 'best fit' between practices and specific national contexts? Norbert Elias observes that '[s]ocial norms are often discussed in a manner which suggests that the norms of one and the same society are all of a piece' (1996: 158). Belief in such uniformity is the bedrock of the notion of enduring and determining national culture popular in the management literature (Oyserman, Coon and Kemmelmeier, 2002; Søndergaard, 1994). In contrast to national homogeneity claims, however, Elias argues that '[i]n societies above a specific level of differentiation, inherently contradictory codes of norms can co-exist in varying degrees of amalgamation and separation. Each may be activated in different situations and at different times.'

    In line with Elias's view, and against the image of static mono-national cultures, the existence of *dynamic cultural diversity* within countries is argued for in this chapter. It does so through a rereading of the national cultural literature itself against a backdrop of contrary data. An analysis of the key categories and claims in the national culture literature and of its reliance on discarded concepts from other disciplines shows that it inappropriately represents national heterogeneity as homogeneity. It spreads, as Maurice Farber says, a 'homogeneous semantic veneer over the cracks in the social structure of nations' (1950: 311).

Compressed categories and unwarranted claims: the culture of what, who, how and when?

Four categories that are conflated within the notion of *national* culture are first examined: nation; nationally common; cultural causality; and enduring.

Nation (whose culture?)

What does the 'national' in 'national culture' refer to? National culture one might reasonably suppose to be the culture of a 'nation'. A striking feature of the national culture literature, however, is the conflation of the word 'nation' with that of 'country' or 'state' (in the sense of a territorial juridical unit) (see Hofstede and Hofstede, 2005, or Lewin and Kim, 2004, for instance). A state is easily conceptualised at a particular point in time in quantitative terms. 'Peru, for illustration, can be defined … as the territorial-political unity consisting of sixteen million inhabitants of 514,060 square miles located on the west coast of South America between 69° and 80° West, and 2° and 18° South' (Connor, 1994: 36). Defining a nation is much more difficult and is, as a result, the object of extensive and long-standing scholarly debates between the primordialsts, perennialists, symbolists, modernists and others (e.g. Gorski, 2000; Smith, 1998; Singer, 1996; Hutchinson and Smith, 1994; Eller and Coughlan, 1993; Stokes, 1986; Robinson, 1979).

Were all states nation states – in the sense of each nation having a state – the distinction between 'nation' and 'state' would not be important, but many states include multiple nations (and therefore should more accurately be called plural national states, or state nations). Ernest Gellner, for instance, estimated in 1983 that there were about 8,000 nations, yet only 159 states. Equally, there are nations without states.

A nation may comprise part of a state (e. g. the Basques) or extend beyond the borders of a single state (e.g. the Kurds). State boundaries may be unstable. Poland, for instance, as a nation state ceased to exist in the late eighteenth century, and was not reconstituted, with quite different borders, until the Treaty of Versailles in 1919, when the borders of many other European countries were radically altered. After World War II Poland's (and many other countries') borders were changed again. Land and people formerly in one state may be redesignated as being part of another state. For example, Alsace-Lorraine was returned to France most recently in 1945 (having yo-yoed back and forth between France and Germany over the previous century). Whole states or parts of states may be annexed, as the north of Cyprus was by Turkey. New states may be formed by seceding from other states (e.g. Bangladesh). Some multinational states are very stable (e.g. Switzerland), some are very volatile (e.g. Iraq). States may be formed by the voluntary or involuntary combination of multiple states (for instance, Germany in the late nineteenth century, and again in the late twentieth century). States may fragment into multiple states, violently (for example, the break-up of Pakistan into [West] Pakistan and Bangladesh) or peacefully (for example, the separation of Czechoslovakia into the Czech Republic and Slovakia).

Despite the use of the term 'national culture', its champions' descriptions, measurements and comparisons are of states or countries, not nations. If the existence of unique national cultures is supposed, the state data analysed will almost invariably be from territories with multiple nationalities, and therefore each state must logically have multinational cultures, not a common national culture. A state is a political unit. It is inappropriate to use citizenship as a proxy for sampling an unwarrantedly supposed cultural unity (Fiske, 2002). A *data unit* – that is, the category used in the data collection and analysis – should not be confused with an *explanatory unit* – that is, the unit that can account for patterns of results (observed practices or whatever) (Ragin, 1987; Stannard, 1971).

Causality (how is it supposed to influence?)

We can take meaning or values very seriously without accepting the static singularity of the national cultural literature (Leung *et al.*, 2005; Collins, 1998). It is possible to suppose the existence of national cultures without attributing deterministic powers to them. If national cultures exist they might be non-causal, or be causal outcomes rather than causal forces, or have limited causality, or be just one component in a fixed or varying cocktail of influences (Caudill, 1973). These other influences may be seen as cultural and/or non-cultural, and to have originated from within or from outside a country (Pries, 2001).

Even *within* a wholly culturalist explanation of social action, attributing causality to just one type of culture, 'national' or whatever, is far too simple. The assumption of coherence of national culture and the exclusion of any other cultural influence (subnational and/or from outside the nation) necessarily excludes the possibility of any divergent cultural interpretations, and thus of the variety of social actions within the same national space. If culture is defined as influential, however, then it is illogical to exclude the possibility of the influences of other cultures within a nation. These cultures are by definition not national, and so they are *not* represented even by national culturalists as being uniformly present across a nation. Thus, if causal influence is attributed to culture, then logically it must be concluded that the acknowledged cultural diversity must create national heterogeneity, not homogeneity of practices. Even if a common national culture is supposed to be somehow present at every site of practice, in action it will also be a varying cocktail of other cultures with differential embeddedness and characteristics, and thus – even within a wholly culturalist view of the world – uniform national practices cannot logically be deduced (Scheuch, 1967).

A move beyond the exclusiveness of culturalist explanations problematises further the characterisation of national practices as 'culture's consequences' (Hofstede, 2001). Common social action may result from common values, but common action does not require such unity, nor does such action necessarily result from common values (Archer, 1989; Schudson, 1994; Campbell, 1998). An extensive post-Parsonian literature argues on both theoretical and empirical grounds against both the conflation of values and social action and also, alternatively, against the treatment of one or other as merely a dependent variable (see Schmid, 1992, for instance). To draw a distinction between national culture, or culture much more widely, and social action is not necessarily to deny the effects of culture on action, but it does exclude a restricted focus on culture as the independent variable or determining force. The champions of national culture obfuscate the notion of uniform culture and uniform action. Nonetheless, these *are* theoretically and empirically distinct; hence they can vary independently of one another (Allaire and Firsirotu, 1984; Archer, 1989).

One of a number of non-cultural explanations for uniform practice is *coercion*. A glaring case is that of fascism in Germany, where considerable behavioural uniformity coexisted with both substantial doctrinal inconsistencies within Hitler's entourage and significant reservations amongst the population of the country. Although German detainees (Jewish and non-Jewish) constituted a comparatively small minority of the concentration camp prison population, in absolute terms their number was significant. In addition, repression against non-Jewish German citizens in Germany became increasingly severe during World War II. About 50,000 *non*-Jewish German citizens were condemned to death by German courts. Approximately 15,000 Wehrmacht soldiers were executed after court martials, whereas in the course of World War I only 48 German soldiers were condemned to death and executed (Burrin, 2005). Hitler's *New Order* was a coercive order (Gellner, 1987). Why should national cultural – or cultural in general – causality be privileged over administrative, coercive or other means of social integration/control? Their exclusion is reckless and unwarranted. As Adam Kuper states:

No worthwhile theory of change can exclude social relations that constrain choices, the organization of power, and the capacity of people with guns to impose new ways of thinking and acting on those without them. It is equally the case that no history can afford to ignore ideas that motivate and inform actions ... Culture does not provide scripts for everything ... (1999: 199)

Nationally common I

National culture is represented as nationally common in two ways in the devotee literature (sometimes in the same work). First, as individually carried by, everyone in a nation. 'Mexicans remain Mexicans, Turks remain Turkish, Finns remain Finnish' (Hickson and Pugh, 1995: 25). Second, as a national average, as an 'average tendency' (Hofstede, 1991: 253). The former is discussed first and then the latter.

Cultural pluralism or oscillation is denied, as are ideational or value ambiguities and contradictions within, or between, sets of ideas/values. The individual is not conceived of as a potential innovator but as a cultural carrier who has passively and indelibly received and internalised national values. To 'illustrate' this view, Geert Hofstede and Gert Jan Hofstede (2005) give the example of the juror who remains polite despite being confronted by other angry jurors in the play/film *Twelve Angry Men*. The juror retains his composure because he is an Austrian who 'still behaves the way he was raised. He carries within himself an indelible pattern of behaviour' (2005: 2). The very impolite Austrian Adolf Hitler seems somehow not to have been programmed by Austrian 'national culture'. Hofstede sometimes argues that country-level analysis does not explain individual behaviour, and yet at other times he claims that it does have the ability to do so (Roberts and Boyacigiller, 1984). 'Weber, we are told [in Hofstede, 2001], could only have come from Germany, Freud's theory is essentially Austrian, Fayol was French to his fingertips, Taylor had to be American' (Smith, 2002: 122). Nevertheless, contrary and different views from those of these writers from *within* the same country of origin can readily be identified (McSweeney, 2002b).

Theorising national culture as common to all national individuals makes 'identification' easy. On the grounds that what is true of one is true of all, depictions of national cultures or of the supposed consequential national organisational practices have all been based on studies of minuscule numbers of individuals or firms. Claims about entire national populations are based on very small-scale studies (for example, the attendees at single undergraduate, postgraduate or management development courses categorised on the basis of their nationality), or practices *in* a single organisation become the window through which an entire national culture is identified (for an overview of such such studies, see Oyserman, Coon and Kemmelmeier, 2002).

What evidence supports the assumption that 'national' culture is common to individuals within a nation? Beneath its scientific veneer, research that relies on this concept of national culture necessarily employs stereotyping, a notion that has a long, but dishonourable, history (Lippmann, 1997 [1922]). In effect, this sense of 'national culture' is a politically correct euphemism for race (Kuper, 1999). As Weber said, 'The appeal to national character is generally a mere confession of ignorance ... To ascribe a unified national character ... would be simply to falsify history' (1992 [1904–5]: 88). Any national stereotype can always be countered by actual counter-examples from the same country. Although Myra Hindley was English and a child-killer, not all English people are child-killers. There is counter-evidence even within the national culture literature itself. For example, '[US] IBM respondents tended to score much more individualist than Japanese [IBM] respondents. However, some Japanese respondents gave quite individualist answers. Some Americans scored quite collectivist, more collectivist than the average for Japanese IBMers' (Hofstede, 1991: 253; see also Takano and Osaka, 1999). As Daphna Oyserman, Heather Coon and Markus Kemmelmeier observe, based on a meta-analysis of studies of individualism and collectivism, 'Our ability to make generalizations on the basis of the current body of empirical research is limited by significant within-group heterogeneity in regional, country, and ethnic group comparisons' (2002: 30; see also Fiske, 2002, and Lenartowicz, Johnson and White, 2003).

If national culture were commonly shared and identifiable, what would be found for one would be true for all. It is not. This has long been recognised within anthropology – and, indeed, within management. As Michael Bond states, '[A]s has been shown by *many authors*, the patterns of correlations at the national (or organizational, or group) level is not replicated at the individual level ... [n]ation-level constructs are not logically or empirically constituted the same way as individual-level constructs, convenient as it would be' (2002: 75; emphasis added).

Nationally common II

Another move within the national cultural literature is to change the level of abstraction at which national culture is supposed to exist and be identified. It is not theorised as something borne by all, some or even any individuals within a nation but by the nation or state. It is a national 'mode' (Inkeles and

Levinson, 1969), 'national norm' (Hofstede, 1980b: 45) or national 'average' (Trompenaars, 1993: 25).

A measure of an average value or central tendency (mean, median, mode or whatever) can always be extracted from any set of data, but it is representative of the entire population only if all the data are available or the sample can confidently be deemed to be representative. Neither condition is satisfied in the calculations of national culture as a national average. Note that the national average or whatever it is called is not said to be the dominant culture or the culture of a political elite – but an average. Asymmetries of power are ignored (cf. Sagiv and Schwartz, 2000; Licht, Goldschmidt and Schwartz, 2005) – the 'rich man is in his castle and the poor man at his gate' – but somehow each contributes to and is shaped by the same national norm that determines 'everything' (Hickson and Pugh, 1995: 90). As William Starbuck observes, however: 'Since social phenomena often give overlapping frequency distributions, comparisons between averages may say nothing about specific instances' (2004: 1245; see also Lenartowicz and Roth, 2001; Lenartowicz, Johnson and White, 2003).

Treating *statistical* averages as a social force is an early nineteenth-century notion, a phenomenon that Ian Hacking calls 'statistical fatalism' (1990). What came to be called *Quetelismus* (after the Belgian astronomer Adolphe Quetelet, who on the basis of statistical averages sought to identify social forces or 'penchants', which he believed acted like physical forces such as gravity) was widely satirised – as early as 1859 by the novelist Charles Dickens (Kern, 2004).

In summary: individual-based notions of national culture unsatisfactorily rely on stereotyping, which unwarrantedly generalises; 'central tendency' notions confuse statistical averages with actual causal forces.

Enduring

The general concept of culture is not necessarily static and can be employed to explain both change and stability (Schmid, 1992; Chabal and Daloz, 2006). National culturalists' absolute notion supposes continuity over lengthy periods of time, however: 'National values,' Hofstede and Hofstede (2005) state, are 'as hard as a country's geographic position' (13), and, 'while change sweeps the surface, the deeper layers remain stable, and the [national] culture rises from its ashes like the phoenix' (36). The 'national culture' of the United States, for instance, has – according to Hofstede (2001: 34) – been the same since 1782 (cf. Bateson, 1973: 67–8) despite continuous waves of immigration from multiple countries. Manfred Kets de Vries states that there is a 'stability to the essential nature' of national character that retains its 'significance regardless of place, time or regime' (2001: 597; see also Newman and Nollen, 1996). National culture is a theory of stasis based methodologically on a bracketing of history and suppression of the agency of people in creating history. As Ludwig Wittgenstein emphasised, however – the possibility of creative interpretations exists:

A rule stands like a sign-post ... Does the sign-post leave no doubt open about the way I have to go? Does it shew me which direction I am to take when I have passed it ... ? And if there were, not a single sign-post, but a chain of adjacent ones or of chalk marks on the ground ... is there only *one* way of interpreting them? (1953: sect. 85; emphasis in original)

National culturalists' supposition of enduring national culture allows them to assert prolonged influence – but it disables them from engaging with change (Burke, 1962, Volkman, 1984; Swidler, 1986; Archer, 1989; Morawska, 1994). In the short and medium term, at least, the supposed stability (and coherence) of cultures within a nation excludes the possibility of national cultural change – through conflicts, mutations, contradictions or whatever.

The possibility of other culture 'arriving' somehow from another nation is not excluded, but, locked into its theoretical lacuna, national culture has no leverage to engage with the meetings of, the interrelationships between, an immigrant culture, or culturally created practices, and those in the host country. Even if we accept that the new arrival 'meets' national culture there is nothing in the national cultural literature that provides insights into the outcomes – other than generalised and largely content-free notions such as 'resistance', 'repulsion' or 'disregard'. Even such blandness exceeds what most national culturalists can legitimately claim, however. They cannot even go so far as to say that every attempted change – for example, attempts via foreign direct investment to impose different management practices – will even encounter national culture. Why? Because the sites of such new cultural 'immigration' is not the nation as a whole, the level at which national culture as the 'central tendency' or 'norm' or 'average' is supposed to exist, but at micro-sites – for example, a factory plant, the readers of a particular book, the viewers of a specific film, and so forth. If 'national culture' is theorised as a national average or central tendency – and not something that is present everywhere – then it cannot logically be said that the immigrant culture or cultural practice will meet anything national, as 'national' culture is not necessarily present where the immigrant culture 'arrives'.

When the possibility of change is acknowledged (and it rarely is), it is conceived of as uniformly and simultaneously happening – i.e. across a country, and not just in some organisations within a country. There must be a 'big bang', a national discontinuity and transformation (Lane, 2005). Intra-state differentiation as a consequence is inconceivable for national culturalists, as that would mean acknowledgement of the end of *national* culture. What is deemed to be true of one location in a country must, it is supposed, be true of all in that country; as the cause of action is national, any change must also be nationally pervasive. Bizarrely, Hofstede even goes further in claiming that, on the rare occasions when there is a change in a national culture, the change occurs not only across that country but also within all countries throughout the world, so that the 'relative positions of national cultures are almost as solid as the countries' geographical positions' (2005: 40). National cultures very rarely change, he states, but when they do 'they change in formation' across the globe (2001: 36).

So, what can the notion of national culture tell us about the meeting of the exogenous with the endogenous, the alien and the national? Frankly, nothing, because only two implausible answers are possible without under-mining the notion of national culture itself. First, it may be supposed that no change occurs: national cultures are robust enough to withstand any attempt to change them. This characterisation of enduring isolation, of the unfailing capacity of the local to repel anything new, is inconsistent with many local studies (see Gamble, 2000, for instance). Secondly, and alter-natively, it may be supposed that if a change occurs at a site of action it must also somehow happen simultaneously at every other national loca-tion. Such rapid national transformation is contradicted by just about every historical study of national change. An acknowledgement of the possibility of change that would *not* also occur everywhere else in the same country would be inconsistent with the master assumption of *nationally uniform* culture.

Empirical evidence

A riposte from national culturalists might be that its the descriptions of national cultures or national cultural differences are based on extensive and carefully analysed empirical evidence. Bond states that 'Hofstede's (1980 [a]) Herculean achievement was to provide the social sciences with an *empirical* mapping of 40 countries ... [s]ocial scientists were galvanized [and] cross-cultural psychologists . . . felt . . . unleashed because we now enjoyed an empirical justification . . .' (2002: 73; emphasis added).

The fuzziness of the notion of 'national culture', and its inconsistent use (discussed above), make the empirical identification of national cultures' characteristics and outcomes problematic, however. So too does the disregard for non-cultural influences. There are many other methodological doubts and weaknesses, moreover (see Ragin, 1987, Smelser, 1992, and McSweeney, 2002a, 2002b, for instance). For example, cross-national comparisons will inevitably – like most other comparisons – show differences. Unless the population of each comparator is homogeneous and the data compared are robustly representative, however, general claims about the characteristics of each of the populations on the basis of the comparative data are not valid. What is true of some or many may not be true for all. Even if somehow a valid national cultural average could be identified, what is true as an average is not necessarily true in particular. On average men are taller than women, but is Edward taller than Eve?

Furthermore, depictions of differences derived from comparisons based on attitudinal responses to surveys, or however else derived, do not constitute adequate grounds for identifying the cause(s) of the difference(s) nor for supposing that the degree of agreement shown indicates a similar level of uniformity at the levels of practices. A cross-*national* survey is not necessarily a cross-*cultural* study (Sparrow and Wu, 1998). For instance, the World Value Surveys indicate that a far higher proportion of the population of Pakistan than in the United Kingdom say that 'God is extremely important in their lives' (Inglehart and Baker, 2000: 25), but that does not mean that there are not different views on that issue within both of the countries; nor that those who hold the majority view do so because of 'national culture'; nor that there is more uniformity of practices within Pakistan than in the United Kingdom (Pandey, 1999; Hechter, 1975). Analysis that is based only on macrosocial differences and similarities, even if correctly identified/ measured, is not truly comparative (Przeworski and Teune, 1970).

Identifying national culture

To a large extent two 'data' sources have been employed to identify the characteristics of 'national cultures': (1) answers to attitudinal questions obtained usually by questionnaires, sometimes by interviews, from individuals (overwhelmingly these have been undergraduates) (Oyserman, Coon and Kemmelmeier, 2002); and (2) analysis of artefacts (such as organisational literature, novels, films, and so forth). Both data sources – answers and artefacts – are treated as expressions of national cultures and 'windows' into those cultures.

Answers to attitudinal questions

Problems with treating culture as declarative knowledge – that is, regarding answers to attitudinal questions as a means of identifying, as 'windows' into, national culture – have been discussed in a range of literature (see Oyserman, Coon and Kemmelmeier, 2002, Kitayama, 2002, and McSweeney, 2002a, for reviews). Here just one of a number of crucial assumptions that have to be made when individuals' answers are used to yield up 'national cultures' is considered, namely that the groups of people whose answers are analysed are nationally representative.

Respondents are deemed to be nationally representative in one of two ways. Either each individual is treated as the carrier of a common national culture, or an averaging of the respondents' views supposedly identifies the national average or 'central tendency'. Confusingly, many national culturalists treat these two quite different views of national culture as one and the same.

Taking individuals as being representative, first, in this approach, regardless of diversity within national populations (of age, region, gender, class, education, and so forth) and individuals' reflexivity, each individual is treated as a 'perfect [national] sample' (Mead, 1953: 648). It is 'as if all members of a nation were envisaged as having been immersed in the homogeneous fluid of national culture' (Farber, 1950: 307). Thus, for example, at an executive course in a business school in France, the answers given by an affluent, agnostic, forty-year-old, female, multilingual Pakistani senior manager of a large multinational corporation who completed her postgraduate studies in the United Kingdom, whose office is located in New York and who holidays in the West Indies and Italy with her Colombian husband are – based on the assumption of representativeness – treated as typical of all Pakistanis, such as a nineteen-year-old, ill-educated, impoverished, Hindko-speaking, religiously devout man who works fifteen hours a day, for a pittance, sewing clothes.

In response to such a critique, some national culturalists argue that they are not identifying or comparing the national cultures of the individuals in a nation but comparing the culture of one nation with another (Søndergaard, 2002). As discussed above, 'national culture' is instead, or additionally, defined as a national norm or central tendency. How is this done? The views of a group, or groups, composed of individuals of the same nationality are treated as nationally representative. Intra-group diversity is sometimes acknowledged amongst the individuals in the chosen group, but nonetheless it is asserted that the national norm is identifiable in the group.

Generalisation to the national level by statistically averaging highly varied responses might seem more sophisticated than treating one respondent as representative of all. In practice there is little difference, however. The numbers studied are always minuscule proportions of their national populations. Instead of each individual being defined as carrying a national culture, the national culture is held to be present and identifiable within the group being studied; it could be any group sharing the same nationality.

Benedict Anderson has famously described a nation as 'an imagined community' the individual members of which 'will never know most of their fellow members, meet them or hear of them, yet in the mind of each lives the image of their communion' (1983: 15). National culturalists who suppose that, on the basis of a few answers, they have identified that nation's culture similarly make the assumption of communion. Fons Trompenaars, for example, relies on samples that were as low as '100 people [white-collar employees]' for each country (1993: 1). These were drawn from one or, at most, a few organisations in each country. Daniel Bollinger (1994) 'identifies' the 'mentality' of Russia (with a population in excess of 150 million) from a study of fifty-five managers on a management course in Moscow (see also Kets de Vries, 2001). William Bigoness and Gerald Blakely (1996) rely on average 'sample' sizes of forty-seven senior, mainly male, English-speaking managers who had attended courses at a business school in Switzerland to describe the national cultures of twelve 'nations'. They acknowledge limitations as a result of their partial 'samples'. Hofstede's depictions of national cultures are statistical averages of answers provided by quantitatively and qualitatively nationally unrepresentative groups of sales and service staff to an IBM survey (not Hofstede's) that was designed primarily to obtain data to boost staff morale. The unrepresentativeness of his 'samples' can be gauged, for instance, by the fact that the first survey he relied on in Pakistan was of only thirty-seven urban dwellers, the second of seventy urban dwellers (1980a: 73). At the time of the surveys the population of Pakistan was about 65 million, of whom over three-quarters lived in rural areas. In the Philippines, the answers of 158 respondents in the first survey and 161 in the second are deemed to be sufficient to identify the 'national culture' of a country with at least 65 million people on over 7,000 islands with more than 100 different dialects.

Even if somehow these tiny numbers of respondents whose answers are relied on by national culturalists were nationally representative, there is a further problem. The answers provided to questionnaires or in interviews always show diversity. The national culturalist response in order to escape from this heterogeneity is to average the diverse individual responses and depict the result as 'national culture'. Labelling that arithmetical mean as 'national culture' or 'national cultural difference' is a conclusion too far, however.

A mean can always be produced from any data set – but what are the data representative of? Does an average even report the 'culture' of the organisation or class of students from which it was extracted? Even if, heroically, it is assumed to do so, there are no reasonable grounds for supposing that the norm would be the same in every other organisation in the same country. Is it reasonable to suppose that the norms of the editorial staff of the Ku Klux Klan's 'White Pride Internet TV' would be the same as amongst the attendees at the 'Friends of Lesbian, Gay, Bisexual, Transgender, and Queer Concerns' gathering at the US Quakers' annual general conference? Is it reasonable to suppose that, whilst French 'national culture' as a norm would *not* be shared by an enclosed order of nuns in France with those in a similar convent in Spain, it would be shared by the French nuns with all French nationals in a French brothel and with every other grouping of persons in France? It is possible that there is not even cultural homogeneity *within* each of those groups. Only by *presupposing* the national representativeness of the chosen organisation can the averaging of the views of a minuscule proportion of the population (those in the studied organisation or classroom) be described as a *national* culture.

There are many other methodological problems with the claims to have derived national culture or national cultural differences from responses to questions (see, for example, Sivakumar and Nakata, 2001, and McSweeney, 2002a, for additional critique). The critique above is sufficient, however, to demonstrate that only through prior supposition of the existence of such cultures can the empirical identification claims be made.

Artefacts

The second national culture empirical identification approach is now considered, and shown to disregard diversity inappropriately. As national culture is said to 'underlie everything' (Hickson and Pugh, 1995: 90) then, in principle, a national culture can be identified through everything and anything; and, indeed, a wide variety of artefacts – 'explicit products' (Trompenaars, 1993: 22) – have been used to 'demonstrate' or confirm the existence of specific features of national cultures and identify some of the consequences. The artefacts analysed have included newspapers, popular magazines, institutional structures, regulations, novels, children's stories, folklore, plays, films, television programmes, websites, art, folk tales *and* organisational practices. The core assumptions are (a) that the chosen arte-fact(s) is/are national cultural products and (b) that the characteristics and consequences of that causal culture can be discerned from an analysis of the artefact(s). Kets de Vries (2001), for instance, draws on the works of nineteenth-century Russian novelists Ivan Goncharov and Maxim Gorky as evidence that 'anarchy' is central to the Russian 'culture', 'character', 'mind-set' or 'psyche' (terms he uses without distinction).

An obvious concern is the representativeness of the examined artefacts. Treating Leni Riefenstahl's movies, for example, as products of a German national culture is to ignore the extensive suppression and destruction by the Nazis of movies with different messages, the death in extermination camps of many film industry personnel and the large number of distinguished German movie directors who fled to the United States and elsewhere (Rentschler, 1996; Jackson, 2001). Hofstede (2001) and Kets de Vries (2001), for instance, go even further in claiming to be able to discern national character from just one character in one novel.

Goncharov's novel *Oblomov* (2005 [1859]), from which Kets de Vries largely draws on in generalising about the character of all Russians, is a satirical portrait of what Goncharov regarded as an idle and decaying nineteenth-century Russian aristocracy, *not* of all Russians. The aristocrat Oblomov avoids work and postpones change, but that attitude is not true even of all characters in that novel. In real life, moreover and in literature even of limited sophistica-tion, individual characters will be complex. As Mikhail Bakhtin (1984 [1929]: 228), commenting on the work of Fyodor Dostoevsky, states: 'A single con-sciousness is *contradictio in adjecto*. Consciousness is in essence multiple.'

The hugely reductionist idea that Russian (or any other) national character/ psyche/culture can be discerned by selecting any one character (or an aspect of one character) from just one novel from the immensely varied creations of Bunin, Chekhov, Dostoevsky, Goncharov, Gorky, Lermontov, Nabokov, Pasternak, Pushkin, Sholokhov, Tolstoy or Turgenev, as well as a multitude of hack socialist realists apologists for Stalin's regime, for instance, or from the poetry of Akhmatova, Baratynsky, Blok, Dementyev, Fet, Gippius, Ivnev, Kapnist, Mandelshtam, Myakovsky or Tsvetaeva, for example, is an absurdly shallow view, but it is consistent with – indeed, a logical consequence of – national culturalism's determinism. Which character in which novel of Balzac, Camus, de Laclos, Flaubert, Sartre, Stendhal, the Marquis de Sade, Proust, Voltaire, Zola, and so forth, represents French national culture? Which in the novels of Alcott, Carleton, Collins, Faulkner, Fitzgerald, Ford, Hawthorne, Hurston, James, Keillor, Lee, Smiley, Spillane, Stowe or Wharton, for example, represents the culture of the United States of America? A national culturalist can take his/her pick and select any character he/she wishes from the novel/play/movie or whatever he/she has picked. Unaware of or indifferent to the enormous diversity and complexity in literature, the confirmatory bias of national culturalism allows unwarranted generalisation.

That is not to deny that the analysis of certain artefacts *can* be valuable in understanding the internal dynamics of particular nations. For instance, Siegfried Kracauer's (1947) analysis of filmic images in his book *From Caligari to Hitler* provides a rich depiction of the events and conditions that made possible the rise of Nazism. It did not claim to have unearthed a nationally shared and socially determining national culture, however. Which movie character, if any, represents *the* US 'national culture': *Dirty Harry*, in which the cop is tougher than the villains, or *Colombo*, in which the cop is smarter than the villains? Insofar as the notion of national culture makes any sense, should we not consider each in their differences to be part of a complex and heterogeneous US culture? The diversity of films being produced even from quite centrally controlled countries such as Iran is indicative of heterogeneity within countries. Timothy Mitchell's studies on Spain, including bullfighting (1991), flamenco song and dance (1994) and the sexual abuse of women and children by Spanish clergy (1998), do not propose a uniform Spanish national culture but richly explore intranational diversity. David Riesman's *The Lonely Crowd* (1950) is often cited as a description of 'the' American national character or culture (see Hofstede, 2001, and Potter, 1954, for instance), but, as Riesman himself states (1967), his book does not 'attempt to deal with national character as such, but to suggest a hypothesis about changes in upper middle-class social character in the twentieth century'. As Kuper says, '[U]nless we separate out the various processes that are lumped together under the heading of culture, and then look beyond the field of culture to other processes, we will not get very far in understanding any of it' (1999: 247; see also Smelser, 1992: 24).

A problem additional to the questionable representativeness of the selected artefacts is the assumption of national purity. Even a modest familiarity with management textbooks, novels or films would show how much multi-/inter-/transnational influence and borrowing routinely occurs. To take an Irish example, the classic memoirs of Tómas Ó Crohán (*An tOileannach/ The Islander*) and Muirís Ó Súilleabháin (*Fiche Blian ag Fás/Twenty Years a'Growing*) have often been taken as narratives embodying the pure experience of life in a western Irish island life, and that for national culturalists it therefore reflects (as does every artefact), and is a means of access to, what is quintessentially national (Kiberd, 1995). It turns out, however, that Ó Crohán's and Ó Súilleabháin's books were in fact directly shaped by reading Gorky's *My Childhood*, lent by a visiting intellectual (Foster: 1998: 39). Ó Crohán was aware how atypical his, and his fellow islanders', life was – and that it would not endure. As he said, he sought 'to set down the character of the people about me so that some record of us might live after us, for the like of us will never be seen again' (my translation from the original Munster Gaelic).

Again, as in questionnaire- or interview-based claims to have identified national cultures, we have the unwarranted leap by the national culturalists from the micronational to the macronational on the basis of a founding *a priori* of national uniformity: what was to be investigated had already been assumed to exist. Heterogeneous data are ignored or processed into an artificial homogeneity.

Fables: so yesterday

Within the academy, management was not the first discipline to develop or employ the notion of uniform, causal and enduring national culture. It drew on what was already well 'known'. Those other disciplines in which that idea was once dominant have long abandoned or peripheralised it, however.

Of course, in the popular media, and elsewhere, the idea of a common national culture (or 'character' or 'psyche') is still often taken as self-evident – as common sense. One manifestation is the periodic calls for a recognition of, and commitment to, what are said to be unique 'core' national values by some politicians. The United Kingdom's previous Chancellor of the Exchequer, for instance, has stated: 'We can find common qualities and common values that have made Britain the country it is. Our belief in tolerance and liberty which shines through British history.' Yet he also (inconsistently) argues that 'the days of Britain having to apologise for our history [of intolerance] are over' (Brown, 2005). Tolerance is indeed a very desirable value, but to the extent that it exists in contemporary Britain it is not unique to that country, and as such is not a distinctive national value.

Historiography and anthropology were the pioneering employers of the notion of national culture within the academy. Sir Ernest Barker, for example, in his lectures on 'National character and the factors in its formation', delivered in 1922–6, asserted that national culture was 'a mental organization connecting the minds of all members of a national community by ties as fine as silk and as firm as steel' (quoted in Cubitt, 1998b: 16).

Key national culturalists have both explicitly and crudely drawn on those disciplines. Whilst the idea of national culture or national character was once a standard orthodoxy in anthropology and historiography, however, it is now at most a peripheral, indeed discredited, notion (Bock, 1999, 2000; Kuper, 1999; Stannard, 1971). Within the academy, it is within parts of the discipline of management alone that it retains a significant following.

Anthropology

In early anthropology, culture was regarded as undifferentiated along class or other principles of social division: it was a concept that applied to the whole of society. For instance, after the United States had entered World War II, a number of prominent anthropologists moved to Washington to take part in research and planning (Bock, 1999; Shannon, 1995). Cultural anthropology promised practical pay-offs. During that war, profiling the supposed national character of Germans and Japanese was the main focus of the co-opted anthropologists' analysis – even writers such as Eric Fromm and Theodor Adorno travelled on the national stereotyping 'bandwagon'. In the early Cold War period the Russian national character became the focus of research. Those were heady days, when the leading anthropologists of the day, Alfred Kroeber and Clyde Kluckhohn, could pronounce in 1952 that culture 'in explanatory importance and in generality of application . . . is comparable to such categories as gravity in physics, disease in medicine, evolution in biology' (quoted in Kuper, 1999: x).

Even before World War II there were critics of the then dominant anthropological views. Karl Renner accused the then new 'social science' of anthropology of making an academic discipline out of ancient cultural hatred. Weber inveighed against what he dubbed the 'racial mythology'. As early as the 1930s Ruth Benedict, often regarded as a key exponent of national cultural uniformity, acknowledged that she had found extreme incoherence in some cultures; in particular, she described 'our society [the United States, United Kingdom, etc.]' as 'an extreme example of lack of integration' (quoted in Smelser, 1992: 6). Her two symbols of the chrysanthemum and the sword in her 1946 book *The Chrysanthemum and the Sword: Patterns of Japanese Culture* embody the contradictions *within* Japan.

Increasingly, the cultural characterisations – of common values – in classical anthropology – even within 'cultural anthropology' – were challenged through their reinterpretation, the deperipheralisation of counter-stories, and by new studies (Yengoyan, 1986). Gellner (1979: 36) describes the coherence 'findings' in early anthropology as 'unwittingly quite *a priori* ... the principle employed has ensured in advance of any inquiry that nothing may count as ... inconsistent or categorically absurd though it may be'. Referring to Sir Edward Evans-Pritchard's pioneering and highly influential study of 'Zande culture', he states that it was 'ironical that this culture [that of Zande – described by Evans-Pritchard in a seminal anthropological study in 1937] of shreds and patches, incorporating at least 20 culturally alien groups and speaking at least 8 diverse languages in what is but part of its total territory, should have come to have been systematically invoked by philosophers making facile and superficial use of anthropology as an illustration of the quite erroneous view that cultures are islands unto themselves' (Gellner, 1974: 143–4).

By the 1960s the national cultural (or national character) assumption was 'pretty well discredited' in anthropology (Bock, 1999: 104). As anthropologist Adam Kuper states, 'Things look very different today' (1999: x), and as Philip Bock, formerly president of the Society for Psychological Anthropology, has emphatically stated, '[T]he uniformity assumption is false' (1999: 111; see also Yengoyan, 1986: 368). Today, however, the leading figures amongst the national culturalists continue to cite this now jettisoned anthropological work as if it were the contemporary view in anthropology, so as to provide scholarly legitimacy for their view of culture (see Hofstede and Hofstede, 2005, Hofstede, 2002, 2001, 1980a, Kets de Vries, 2001, and Trompenaars, 1993, for example). They fail to realise, or acknowledge, that, as Michael Schudson states, citing anthropologists Akil Gupta and James Ferguson (1992), '[I]t is now recognised that "the territorially distinct cultures" anthropologists claimed they were studying were never as autonomous as they imagined' (1994: 37).

Classical anthropology studied (apparently) simple societies, providing some rationale for the formerly dominant supposition that each society has a common, coherent culture. The national culturalists in management, however, have taken that idea – long after it was abandoned in anthropology – and applied it to widely differentiated and diversified modern societies and organisations. It is desirable that the disciplines of management draw from and contribute to other disciplines. It behoves scholars of management to keep up to date with developments and debates in relevant non-management disciplines. Over the past few decades, however, whilst the field of organisation theory has engaged with a wider cultural literature and revealed complex cultural processes and characteristics in organisational contexts, the national cultural literature has theoretically atrophied. It remains fixated with a view of culture that was once dominant but is now at best peripheralised.

Even its employment of earlier anthropological research in the national cultural literature has been partial. For example, Kluckhohn's analysis is often cited by leading management national culturalists, but the subtleties, nuances and qualifications in his work are ignored (see Kets de Vries, 2001: 597, and Hofstede, 2001: 10, for instance). Kluckhohn distinguishes between situational and absolute culture: the former is incompatible with the notion of national culture. He gives the example of Japanese prisoners of war who 'in situation A [prior to capture] publicly observed the rules of the game with a fervor that impressed Americans as "fanaticism". Yet the minute [they were] in situation *B*, the rules for situation *A* no longer applied' (1957: 137). The idea that the rules we follow, the way we behave, the practices we accept or reject are situationally influenced, other than by the national, is irreconcilable with the notion of determinate national culture, however. As Sorge states, 'A large power distance in the enterprise, for instance, does not necessarily imply a correspondingly large power distance in the family, such as between father and children' (1983: 628). Moreover, behaviour 'in the enterprise' may be influenced by multiple sub-enterprise situations (see Lane, 1989, Kondo, 1990, Triandis, 1994, and McSweeney, 1995, for instance).

Historiography

The assumption of a common national character or culture in earlier anthropology had already been well established in historiography. With the rise of nationalism across nineteenth-century Europe there was an increasing essentialising of alleged national characteristics, or culture. Numerous historians in the nineteenth century, and well into the twentieth century, employed race as a synonym for nation, references to a 'German race' or to an 'English race', for instance, being quite common. As Nicholas Stargardt (1998: 22) points out, '[T]he establishment of modern history as a full academic discipline in the nineteenth century was intimately connected with writing political and even social history within a national framework ... Assumptions about the inherently national character of modern history ... remained safely ensconced in their dominance well into the post-1945 era.'

By the 1960s, however, as in anthropology, conceptions of the nation as an imagined, invented or hybrid category had become the standard orthodoxy in historiography. The 'evidence' in historical studies of long-standing cultural distinctiveness had come to be seen as largely fictive, and indeed often invented or counterfeited (Hobsbawm and Ranger, 1983; Schudson, 1994; Cubitt, 1998; Oergel, 1998). The past preoccupation with the degree of coherence of national culture has now virtually disappeared in historiography as motifs of domination, strategy, usage, politics and practice have emerged. The fictive bases of the narratives of the purveyors of the notion of a unitary nation were increasingly exposed as based on acts of faith, not evidence. The field remains riven by disagreements and is divided by rival approaches, but compared with the previously dominant national essentialist models they demonstrate a much greater level of sophistication and understanding of the complexity of nations. Nations are not revealed realities; their existence is always ontologically unstable: '[N]ations remain elusive and indeterminate, perpetually open to contest, to elaboration and to imaginative reconstruction' (Cubitt, 1998b: 3).

The national culturalist literature has ignored these debates and developments, however. Indeed, compared even with the earlier models, its singular primordialism seems crude and simplistic. The idea of a national culture or character as a product of a common national history relies on *volkisch* fantasies, not on scholarly historiography.

Belief in national cultural uniqueness and of individuals as passive recipients has long ceased to have a following in disciplines in which it once was the dominant view. Nevertheless, the devotees of national culture in management unquestioningly suppose it. That dogged commitment is not based on engagement with and rejection of the pertinent debates and conclusions in the disciplines that have jettisoned national culture. Thirty years and more of developments are simply ignored; they are not even acknowledged. Instead of standing on the shoulders of giants, the devotees of uniform, ensuring and determinant national culture are standing on graves.

National identity and fictive kinship

It is important to distinguish between national identity (a belief in, and commitment to, a sense of a shared identity or indeed identities: Sen, 2006) and national culture as empirical fact (a belief that everyone with the same nationality shares the same culture, or that each nation has a unique culture: Gellner, 1983; Zimmer, 1998). As Wolfgang Welsch states, the idea that 'an individual's cultural formation must be determined by his or her nationality or national status . . . belongs among the mustiest assumptions' (1999: 199). A rejection of national culture as empirical fact does not debar one from 'feeling patriotic'.

It is possible to have an acute sense of commitment to a community or communities (national or other) and yet at the same time repudiate the cult of shared values. Nonetheless, the notion of the uniqueness of nations or states – what Annette Ching calls the 'social construction of primordiality' (quoted in Yelvington, 1991: 165) – is continuously perpetuated in multiple explicit and symbolic ways, including country-specific ones: passports, stamps, flags, capital, anthems, civil services, police forces, taxes, maps, heroes (and villains), elections, state funerals, nationally regulated examinations, aggregate statistics, routines of international comparisons, from exports to sporting achievements, and notions such as national competitiveness (Tooze, 1998; Firth, 1973). These features of 'banal nationalism' (Billig, 1995) contribute to the construction and maintenance of the illusion of national homogeneity. Attempts to define something unique – even in behaviour – about the population of states *or* nations – always fail, however, ineptly relying on empirically groundless stereotypes ([all] English people are emotionally repressed), features that are not unique (like an English breakfast), historical myths (the English have always been distinguished by their tolerance) or generalisations based on the preferences or dislikes of one subgroup or another ('they' prefer sweet sherry). Attempts to capture that elusive quality of 'Englishness', or Frenchness', or 'Germanness' or whateverness always flounder in essentialist impressionism (Cubitt, 1998a). A constitutive idea does not have to be empirically true, however.

Discussion and conclusions

Albeit through an engagement with a largely different literature, with greater emphasis on micro-level sites of action and a focus on culture rather than institutions, the findings and conclusions in this chapter are broadly in line with those of a new wave of neo-institutionalism, which is not analytically a 'prisoner of the nation state' as it does not treat the nation as *the* unit of analysis nor as a discrete unit of analysis (see Djelic and Quack, 2005, Crouch, 2005, and Streeck and Thelen, 2005, for instance). That is not a rejection of 'societal effects' but of reducing and restricting 'society' merely to that of nationally uniform and determinant context.

National culturalism's organising concepts are fuzzy and often applied illogically and inconsistently; its assumption of the internal coherence of subjective culture debars engagement with diversity, with counterfactual data and with contemporary developments in anthropology, historiography and organisation theory, and elsewhere, that predominantly conceive of cultures as multiple, fragmented, internally contested and porous. Its determinism – the supposition and claim that autonomous national culture shapes just about everything – unrealistically, indeed foolishly, excludes the influence of other cultural and non-cultural factors. Its conflation of the unit of data (the 'nation') with the unit of explanation (the sources of action *within* a 'nation'), its erasure of intranational differences and its commitment to an unchanging and nationally uniform culture debar it from engaging with change and differences within and between local sites of action. Its claims to have empirically measured national cultures or national cultural differences relies on reckless methodological errors, central to which is the circularity of presupposing the existence of what it purports to identify.

At best national culture is 'much ado about nothing', but at worst it leads to sterile theoretical entrapment and misleading advice. In claiming to have found the key to understanding 'everything' (Hickson and Pugh, 1995), the 'rules by which people in different cultures think, feel, and act in business, family, schools, and political organizations' (Hofstede and Hofstede, 2005), it explains nothing. Practices rarely have a single cause; causes rarely work in isolation; multiple causes act in varying combinations, not merely additively – thus a change in one will not necessarily produce a different outcome or a predictable outcome; and causes may have contradictory effects depending on context (Ragin, 1987; McSweeney, 1995). The study of culture, its intertwining (conceivable in multiple ways) with the non-cultural, and its possible consequences have considerable potential for understanding continuity and change in organisational and wider social practices, but only if culture is treated not as wholly autonomous and coherent but as containing diverse and conflicting elements and as a result is contestable, elastic and situated.

Cross-*national* studies that have not overlooked within-country differences often provide much richer insights than those that treat average or aggregate country data as the sole unit of analysis (O'Sullivan, 2000; Agnew, 1989; Kohn, 1987; Scheuch, 1967).

Take the example of homicide. Rates vary not only between countries and over time but also within them. They vary immensely across different locations, socio-economic, gender and ethnic groups. Within the United States, for example, the annual homicide rate per 100,000 of the population in 2003 in the states of Louisiana and Maryland was 13.0 and 9.5, but at the other end the rates were 1.2 and 1.3 in Maine and South Dakota respectively. Nisbett and Cohen (1996) find that, among white men, homicide in response to insults occurs at rates several times higher in the southern US states than in the northern states (Fiske, 2002; Akerlof and Kranton, 2005). Sub-state analysis of homicide (and multiple other practices) would demonstrate further spatial heterogeneity at sub-county or sub-city level, and so forth (see Law *et al.*, 2004, for instance).

Subnational analysis based on *social* rather than *geographical* heterogeneity also demonstrates the information poverty of national averages. For example, in the United States in 2002 blacks were seven times more likely to commit homicide and were six times more likely to be victims of homicide than whites. In the same year, and in the same country, it was men and not women who committed 93 per cent of felony murders, 91 per cent of gun homicides, 80 per cent of arson homicides and 63 per cent of poison homicides. Oyserman, Coon and Kemmelmeier (2002) find that very few of the international comparisons they analysed included any information on the ethnic composition of their samples. That is not to define countries as composed of plural monocultures, as the term 'multiculturalism' is often employed; internally each such sub-national group ('ethnic', ' class', 'gender', 'class-gender', and so forth) has a homogeneous or coherent culture. There is cultural diversity also within those groupings (Higham, 1993; Fiske, 2002; Sen, 2006).

Progress towards understanding intranational continuity and change requires a jettisoning of the presupposition of static uniform national culture. Culture, circumstances and agency should not be treated as variables to be considered separately but studied in their complex interactions. The antique notion of *national* culture as stable, domineering, acontextual and depictable by bipolar 'dimensions' leads into a sterile conceptual cul-de-sac (Fiske, 2002). Attempts to explain macro and micro social behaviour through these dimensions is alchemic, its equivalent to reducing physics to meter reading (Chomsky, 1968). As Weber has observed, '[A]n exhaustive causal investigation … is not only practically impossible – it is simply nonsense' (quoted in Shils and Finch, 1949 [1904]: 78).

References

Agnew, J. A. (1989) The devaluation of place in social science, in J. A. Agnew and J. S. Duncan (eds.) *The Power of Place*, Boston: Unwin Hyman, 9–29.

Akerlof, G. A., and R. E. Kranton (2005) Economics and identity, in G. A. Akerlof (ed.) *Explorations in Pragmatic Economics: Selected Papers of George A. Akerlof (and Co-authors)*, Oxford: Oxford University Press, 67–99.

Allaire, Y., and M. E. Firsirotu (1984) Theories of organizational culture, *Organization Studies*, 5, 3, 193–226.

Anderson, B. (1983) *Imagined Communities: Reflections on the Origin and Spread of Nationalism*, London: Verso.

Archer, M. S. (1989) *Culture and Agency: The Place of Culture in Social Theory*, Cambridge: Cambridge University Press.

Bakhtin, M. (1984 [1929]) *Problems of Dostoevsky's Poetics* (ed. and trans. C. Emerson), Manchester: Manchester University Press.

Bateson, G. (1973) *Steps to an Ecology of Mind*, St Albans: Paladin.

Bigoness, W. J., and G. L. Blakely (1996) A cross-national study of managerial values, *Journal of International Business Studies*, 27, 4, 739–52.

Billig, M. (1995) *Banal Nationalism*, London: Sage.

Bock, P. K. (1999) *Rethinking Psychological Anthropology* (2nd edn.), Prospects Heights, IL: Waveland.

    (2000) Culture and personality revisited, *American Behavioral Scientist*, 44, 1, 32–40.

Bollinger, D. (1994) The four cornerstones and the three pillars in the 'House of Russia' management system, *Journal of Management Development*, 13, 2, 49–54.

Bond, M. H. (2002) Reclaiming the individual from Hofstede's ecological analysis – a 20-year odyssey: comment on Oyserman *et al.* (2002), *Psychological Bulletin*, 128, 1, 73–7.

Brown, G. (2005) Speech by the Rt. Hon. Gordon Brown, Chancellor of the Exchequer, at the CBI Annual Conference, London, 28 November, available from http://www.hm-treasury. gov.uk/newsroom_and_speeches/press/2005/press_99_05.cfm [accessed 29 November 2006].

Burke, K. (1962) *A Grammar of Motives and a Rhetoric of Motives*, Cleveland, OH: World Publishing.

Burrin, P. (2005) *From Prejudice to the Holocaust: Nazi Anti-Semitism* (trans. J. Lloyd), New York: New Press.

Campbell, C. (1998) *The Myth of Social Action*, Cambridge: Cambridge University Press.

Caudill, W. (1973) The influence of social structure and culture on human behaviour in modern Japan, *Ethos*, 1, 3, 343–82.

Chabal, P., and J.-P. Daloz (2006) *Culture Troubles: Politics and the Interpretation of Meaning*, London: Hurst and Company.

Chomsky, N. (1968) *Language and Mind*, New York: Harcourt Brace Jovanovich.

Collins, D. (1998) *Organizational Change: Sociological Perspectives*, London: Routledge.

Connor, W. (1994 [1978]) A nation is a nation, is an ethnic group is a . . ., in J. Hutchinson and A. D. Smith (eds.) *Nationalism*, Oxford: Oxford University Press, 36–46.

Crouch, C. (2005) *Capitalist Diversity and Change*, Oxford: Oxford University Press.

Cubitt, G. (ed.) (1998a) *Imagining Nations*, Manchester: Manchester University Press.

    (1998b) Introduction, in G. Cubitt (ed.) *Imagining Nations*, Manchester: Manchester University Press, 1–21.

Djelic, M. -L., and S. Quack (2005) Rethinking path dependency: the crooked path of institutional change in post-war Germany, in G. Morgan, R. Whitley and E. Moen (eds.) *Changing Capitalisms? Internationalization, Institutional Change, and Systems of Economic* Organization, Oxford: Oxford University Press, 137–66.

Elias, N. (1996) *The Germans*, Cambridge: Polity Press.

Eller, J., and R. Coughlan (1993) The poverty of primordialism: the demystification of ethnic attachments, *Ethnic and Racial Studies* 16, 2, 183–202.

Farber, M. L. (1950) The problem of national character: a methodological analysis, *Journal of Psychology*, 30, 307–16.

Firth, R. (1973) *Symbols: Public and Private*, London: George Allen and Unwin.

Fiske, A. P. (2002) Using individualism and collectivism to compare cultures – a critique of the validity and measurement of the constructs: comments on Oyserman *et al.* (2002), *Psychological Bulletin*, 128, 1, 78–88.

Foster, R. (1998) Storylines: narratives and nationality in nineteenth-century Ireland, in G. Cubitt (ed.) *Imagining Nations*, Manchester: Manchester University Press, 38–56.

Gamble, J. (2000) Localizing management in foreign-invested enterprises in China: practical, cultural, and strategic perspectives, *International Journal of Human Resource Management*, 11, 5, 883–903.

Gellner, E. (1974) *Legitimation of Belief*, Cambridge: Cambridge University Press.

(1979) Concepts and society, in B. R. Wilson (ed.) *Rationality: Key Concepts in the Social Sciences*, Oxford: Basil Blackwell, 18–49.

(1983) *Nations and Nationalism*, Ithaca, NY: Cornell University Press.

(1987) *Culture, Identity, and Politics*, Cambridge: Cambridge University Press.

Goncharov, I. (2005 [1859]) *Oblomov* (trans. D. Magarshack), London: Penguin Books.

Gorski, P. S. (2000) The mosaic moment: an early modernist critique of modernist theories of nationalism, *American Journal of Sociology*, 105, 5, 1428–68.

Gupta, A., and J. Ferguson (1992) Beyond 'Culture': space, identity, and the politics of difference, *Cultural Anthropology*, 7, 2, 6–23.

Hacking. I. (1990) *The Taming of Chance*, Cambridge: Cambridge University Press.

Hechter, M. (1975) *Internal Colonialism: The Celtic Fringe in British Development, 1536–1966*, Berkeley, CA: University of California Press.

Hickson, D. J., and D. S. Pugh (1995) *Management Worldwide: The Impact of Societal Culture on Organizations around the Globe*, London: Penguin Books.

Higham, J. (1993) Multiculturalism and universalism: a history and a critique, *American Quarterly*, 45, 204–5.

Hobsbawm, E., and T. Ranger (eds.) (1983) *The Invention of Tradition*, Cambridge: Cambridge University Press.

Hofstede, G. (1980a) *Culture's Consequences: International Differences in Work-related Values*, Beverly Hills, CA: Sage.

(1980b) Motivation, leadership and organization: do American theories apply abroad?, *Organizational Dynamics*, 9, 1, 42–63.

(1991) *Cultures and Organizations: Software of the Mind*, London: McGraw-Hill.

(2001) *Culture's Consequences: Comparing Values, Behaviours, Institutions and Organizations across Nations* (2nd edn.), Thousand Oaks, CA: Sage.

(2002) Dimensions do not exist: a reply to Brendan McSweeney, *Human Relations*, 55, 11, 1355–61.

(2005) Constant culture: interview with Janet Cooper, *hrmonthly*, August, 36–41.

Hofstede, G., and G. J. Hofstede (2005) *Cultures and Organizations: Software of the Mind* (2nd edn.), New York: McGraw-Hill.

Hutchinson, J., and A. D. Smith (eds.) (1994) *Nationalism*, Oxford: Oxford University Press.

Inglehart, R., and W. E. Baker (2000) Modernization, cultural change, and persistence of traditional values, *American Sociological Review*, 65, 19–51.

Inkeles, A., and D. J. Levinson (1969) National character: the study of modal personality and sociocultural systems, in G. Lindzey and E. Aronson (eds.) *The Handbook of Social Psychology*, vol. IV, Reading, MA: Addison-Wesley, 418–506.

Jackson, J. (2001) *France: The Dark Years – 1940–1944*, Oxford: Oxford University Press.

Kern, S. (2004) *A Cultural History of Causality*, Princeton, NJ: Princeton University Press.

Kets de Vries, M. F. R. (2001) The anarchist within: clinical reflections on Russian character and leadership style, *Human Relations*, 54, 5, 585–627.

Kiberd, D. (1995) *Inventing Ireland*, Cambridge, MA: Harvard University Press.

Kitayama, S. (2002) Cultural psychology of the self: a renewed look at independence and interdependence, in C. von Hofsten and L. Bäckman (eds.) *Psychology at the Turn of the Millennium, vol. II, Social Developments and Clinical Perspectives*, New York: Taylor and Francis, Chap. 15.

Kluckhohn, C. (1957) *Mirror for Man*, New York: Premier.

Kohn, M. L. (1987) Cross-national research as an analytic strategy, *American Sociological Review*, 52, 713–31.

Kondo, D. K. (1990) *Crafting Selves: Power, Gender, and Discourses of Identity in a Japanese Workplace*, Chicago: University of Chicago Press.

Kracauer, S. (1947) *From Caligari To Hitler: A Psychological History of German Film*, Princeton, NJ: Princeton University Press.

Kuper, A. (1999) *Culture: The Anthropologists' Account*, Cambridge, MA: Harvard University Press.

Lane, C. (1989) *Management and Labour in Europe: The Industrial Enterprise in Germany, Britain and France*, Aldershot: Edward Elgar.

  (2005) Institutional transformations and system change: changes in corporate governance of German Corporations, in G. Morgan, R. Whitley and E. Moen (eds.) *Changing Capitalisms? Internationalization, Institutional Change, and Systems of Economic Organization*, Oxford: Oxford University Press, 78–109.

Law, D. C. G., M. L. Serre, G. Christakos, P. A. Leone and W. C. Miller (2004) Spatial analysis and mapping of sexually transmitted diseases to optimize intervention and prevention strategies, *Sexually Transmitted Infections*, 80, 294–9.

Lenartowicz, T., J. P. Johnson and C. T. White (2003) The neglect of intracountry cultural variation in international management research, *Journal of Business Research*, 56, 12, 999–1008.

Lenartowicz, T., and K. Roth (2001) Does subculture within a country matter? A cross-cultural study of motivational domains and business performance in Brazil, *Journal of International Business Studies*, 32, 2, 305–25.

Leung, K., R. S. Bhagat, N. R. Buchan, M. Erez and C. B. Gibson (2005) Culture and international business: recent advances and their implications for future research, *Journal of International Business Studies*, 36, 357–78.

Lewin, A. Y., and J. Kim (2004) The nation-state and culture as influences or organizational change and innovation, in M. S. Poole and A. H. Van de Ven (eds.) *The Oxford Handbook of Organizational Change and Innovation*, Oxford: Oxford University Press, 324–53.

Licht, A. N., C. Goldschmidt and S. H. Schwartz (2005) Culture, law, and corporate governance, *International Review of Law and Economics*, 25, 2, 229–55.

Lippmann, W. (1997 [1922]) *Public Opinion*, New York: Free Press.

McSweeney, B. (1995) Accounting in organizational action: a subsuming explanation or
situated explanations?, *Accounting, Management and Information Technologies*, 5, 3/4,
245–82.

(2002a) Hofstede's model of national cultural differences and their consequences: a triumph
of faith – a failure of analysis, *Human Relations*, 55, 1, 189–117.

(2002b) The essentials of scholarship: a reply to Hofstede, *Human Relations*, 55, 11,
1363–72.

Mead, M. (1953) National character, in A. L. Kroeber (ed.) *Anthropology Today: An
Encyclopedic Inventory*, Chicago: University of Chicago Press, 642–67.

Mitchell, T. (1991) *Blood Sport: A Social History of Spanish Bullfighting*, Philadelphia:
University of Pennsylvania Press.

(1994) *Flamenco Deep Song*, New Haven, CT: Yale University Press.

(1998) *Betrayal of the Innocents: Desire, Power, and the Catholic Church in Spain*,
Philadelphia: University of Pennsylvania Press.

Morawska, E. (1994) *Insecure Prosperity: Small-town Jews in Industrial America, 1880–1940*,
Princeton, NJ: Princeton University Press.

Newman, K. L., and S. D. Nollen (1996) Culture and congruence: the fit between management
practices and national culture, *Journal of International Business Studies*, 27, 4, 753–79.

Nisbett, D., and R. E. Cohen (1996) *Culture of Honor: The Psychology of Violence in the South*,
Oxford: Westview Press.

Oergel, M. (1998) *The Return of King Arthur and the Nibelungen: National Myths in
Nineteenth-Century English and German Literature*, New York: de Gruyter.

O'Sullivan, M. (2000) *Contests for Corporate Control*, Oxford: Oxford University Press.

Oyserman, D., H. M. Coon and M. Kemmelmeier (2002) Rethinking individualism and
collectivism: evaluation of theoretical assumptions and meta-analyses, *Psychological
Bulletin*, 128, 1, 3–72.

Pandey, G. (1999) Can a Muslim be an Indian?, *Comparative Studies in Society and History*, 41,
4, 608–29.

Potter, D. M. (1954) *People of Plenty: Economic Abundance and the American Character*,
Chicago: Chicago University Press.

Pries, L. (ed.) (2001) *New Transnational Social Spaces*, London: Routledge.

Przeworski, A., and H. Teune (1970) *The Logic of Comparative Social Inquiry*, New York: Wiley
Interscience.

Ragin, C. C. (1987) *The Comparative Method: Moving beyond Qualitative and Quantitative
Strategies*, Berkeley, CA: University of California Press.

Rentschler, E. (1996) *The Ministry of Illusion: Nazi Cinema and Its Afterlife*, Cambridge, MA:
Harvard University Press.

Riesman, D. (1967) Some questions about the study of American character in the twentieth
century, *Annals of the American Academy of Political and Social Sciences*, 370, 1, 36–47.

Roberts, K., and N. Boyaciciller (1984) Cross-national organizational research: the grasp of the
blind man, in B. M. Staw and L. L. Cummings (eds.) *Research in Organizational Behavior*,
vol. VI, Stanford, CT: JAI Press, 423–75.

Robinson, F. (1979) Islam and Muslim separatism, in D. Taylor and M. Yapp (eds.) *Political Identity in South Asia*, London: Curzon Press, 78–112.

Sagiv, L., and S. H. Schwartz (2000) A new look at national culture: illustrative applications to role stress and managerial behavior, in N. Ashkenasy, C. Wilderom and M. Peterson (eds.) *Handbook of Organizational Culture and Climate*, London: Sage, 417–37.

Scheuch, E. K. (1967) Society as context in cross-cultural comparisons, *Social Science Information*, 6, 5, 7–23.

Schmid, M. (1992) The concept of culture and its place within a theory of social action: a critique of Talcott Parson's theory of culture, in R. Münch and N. J. Smelser (eds.) *Theory of Culture*, Berkeley, CA: University of California Press, 88–120.

Schudson, M. (1994) Culture and the integration of national societies, in D. Crane (ed.) *The Sociology of Culture*, Oxford: Basil Blackwell, 21–43.

Sen, A. (2006) *Identity and Violence: The Illusion of Destiny*, New York: Norton.

Shannon, C. (1995) A world made safe for differences: Ruth Benedict's 'The Chrysanthemum and the Sword', *American Quarterly*, 47, 4, 659–80.

Shils, E. A., and H. A. Finch (trans. and eds.) (1949 [1904]) Objectivity in social science and social policy, in *Max Weber: The Methodology of the Social Sciences*, Glencoe, IL: Free Press, 49–112.

Singer, B. C. J. (1996) Cultural versus contractual nations: rethinking their opposition, *History and Theory*, 35, 3, 309–37.

Sivakumar, K., and C. Nakata (2001) The stampede towards Hofstede's framework: avoiding the sample design pit in cross-cultural research, *Journal of International Business Studies*, 32, 3, 555–74.

Smelser, N. J. (1992) Culture: coherent or incoherent, in R. Münch and N. J. Smelser (eds.) *Theory of Culture*, Berkeley, CA: University of California Press, 3–28.

Smith, A. D. (1998) *Nationalism and Modernism*, London: Routledge.

Smith, P. B. (2002) Culture's consequences: something old and something new, *Human Relations*, 55, 1, 119–35.

Søndergaard, M. (1994) Hofstede's consequences: a study of reviews, citations and replications, *Organization Studies*, 15, 3, 447–56.

(2002) In my opinion, *European Business Forum*, 9, 40–1.

Sorge, A. (1983) Review of 'Culture's Consequences: International Differences in Work-related Values', *Administrative Science Quarterly*, December, 625–9.

Sparrow, P., and P.-C. Wu (1998) Does national culture really matter? Predicting HRM preferences of Taiwanese employees, *Employee Relations*, 20, 1, 26–56.

Stannard, D. E. (1971) American historians and the idea of national character: some problems and prospects, *American Quarterly*, 23, 2, 202–20.

Starbuck, W. H. (2004) Why I stopped trying to understand the *real* world, *Organization Studies*, 25, 7, 1233–54.

Stargardt, N. (1998) Beyond the liberal idea of a nation, in G. Cubitt (ed.) *Imaging Nations*, Manchester: Manchester University Press, 22–37.

Stokes, G. (1986) How is nationalism related to capitalism? A review article, *Comparative Studies in Society and History*, 28, 3, 591–8.

Streeck, W., and K. Thelen (eds.) (2005) *Beyond Continuity: Institutional Change in Advanced Political Economies*, Oxford: Oxford University Press.

Swidler, A. (1986) Culture in action: symbols and strategies, *American Sociological Review*, 51, 273–86.

Takano, Y. and E. Osaka (1999) An unsupported common view: comparing Japan and the US on individualism/collectivism, *Asian Journal of Social Psychology*, 2, 311–41.

Tooze, J. A. (1998) Imagining national economies: national and international economic statistics, 1900–1950, in G. Cubitt, *Imagining Nations*, Manchester: Manchester University Press, 212–28.

Triandis, H. C. (1994) Theoretical and methodological approaches to the study of collectivism and individualism, in U. Kim, H. C. Triandis, Ç. Kâgitçibasi, S. Choi and G. Yoon (eds.) *Individualism and Collectivism*, Thousand Oaks, CA: Sage, 41–65.

Trompenaars, F. (1993) *Riding the Waves of Culture: Understanding Cultural Diversity in Business*, London: Nicholas Brealey.

Volkman, T. A. (1984) 'Great performances': Toraja cultural identity in the 1970s, *American Ethnologist*, 11, 1, 152–3.

Weber, M. (1992 [1904–5]). *The Protestant Ethic and the Spirit of Capitalism* (trans. T. Parsons 1930), London: Routledge.

Welsch, W. (1999) Transculturality: the puzzling form of cultures today, in M. Featherstone and S. Lash (eds.) *Spaces of Culture*, London: Sage, 194–213.

Wittgenstein, L. (1953) *Philosophical Investigations* (trans. G. E. M. Anscombe), Oxford: Basil Blackwell.

Yelvington, K. A. (1991) Ethnicity as practice? A comment on Bentley, *Comparative Studies in Society and History*, 33, 1, 158–168.

Yengoyan, A. A. (1986) Theory in anthropology: on the demise of the concept of culture, *Comparative Studies of Culture*, 28, 2, 368–74.

Zimmer, O. (1998) In search of natural identity: Alpine landscape and the reconstruction of the Swiss nation, *Comparative Studies in Society and History*, 40, 4, 637–65.

4 Business systems, institutions and economic development: the value of comparison and history

Robert Fitzgerald

Introduction: making and remaking management

Most people think, at some level, that history matters. Personal genealogy is, for many, an issue of significance. Some have a natural interest in the values and circumstances of the past, since they can highlight contrasts with their own lives; others look for insight into the concerns and controversies of the present, and hold them up to the test of former achievements and follies. There is, moreover, a human tendency to regard the policies of specific interest groups or social change as more acceptable once associated with established traditions or an 'unstoppable' course of events (Hobsbawm and Ranger, 1983). Conversely, historical research should be a powerful corrective to 'invented traditions', the assumption of 'inevitable' outcomes or the idea of 'natural' solutions for a given society. Detailed evidence frequently disinters the complexity of the past. It throws boulders in the path of simple, linear explanations; it reveals the limits of generalisations when applied too easily to whole societies; it questions attempts to identify and date significant periods of change, when based on a single event or trend; it prefers instead the numerous and frequently contradictory factors that influence the process of change; and it raises the problem of distinguishing 'long-term' or more consequential developments from those that are 'short-term'. Close analysis discloses the uncertainty of the past, in which decisions and institutional settlements are the result of contest, subject to later challenges and, in actuality, 'conflicted' rather than general or 'natural'. Furthermore, deeper insights into society and the economy and the causes of change require comparative methods, and comparative analysis, in turn, can be strengthened through the test of history. Since the comparative approach frequently focuses on differences between nation states, it carries with it the danger of simplifying or even exaggerating those differences, failing adequately to demonstrate the complex and continuous processes of change. Those engaged in the matching and contrasting of nations often fail, too, to acknowledge the importance of external influences. The rising interest in 'global history', however, seeks to reveal the long-term implications of the 'interactions' that have occurred between nations.

Those who study business systems usually acknowledge the durable influence of past choices, yet the practice of history and the social science of management studies are rarely cooperating partners. This statement may, on first reading, appear strange. There is a well-known interest in historically embedded national institutions that determine the basic structure of business systems and, as a result, differences between the business systems of nations. Nonetheless, this management literature carries assumptions about the nature of historical change, specifically concerning the formation of nations and national institutions. It demonstrates limited knowledge of alternative interpretations, which may have equal or greater power to explain, and even less concern for the richness of historical case evidence. In other words, the analysis is 'over-structured', and downplays the role of 'events' and their ambiguous consequences. More fundamentally, the institutionalist perspective is associated with challengeable ideas about the reality and significance of national cultures. Indeed, nation states themselves can be seen, historically, as in flux not only geographically but in terms of popular identity. The redrawing of borders is a notable characteristic of history. An explicit association between ideas of statehood, ethnicity or language is historically recent (200 years or so), and too often illusory in reality. A strong sense of the nation or nationalism has an even shorter heritage (from the late nineteenth century onwards), and was fostered and given form by actors and events. In 1918 the leader of the soon to be newly independent Poland, Marshal Józef Pilsudski, gave the succinct practitioner's viewpoint: 'It is the state which makes the nation and not the nation the state.' In order to forget the role of chance accident, internal conflict or the exercise of political and social power by formative interest groups, it has frequently been necessary to 'reinvent' tradition and culture as part of the process of state formation and as a means of encouraging unity and conformity. New ways are adopted as 'old' and 'natural'. Change (especially economic growth, industrialisation and urbanisation) may in fact bring or even require the replacement of national traits by others. It follows that nations, tradition and culture appear, on examination, less historically rooted and more contingent than originally assumed, and not an expression of an innate and inevitable force that drives the rest of history. Similarly, national institutions may seem less solid and less determinant of the pathways by which business systems have evolved.

Another uncertainty in the complex journey called historical pathways is the extent to which national economies have interacted and cross-fertilised each other. Inevitably, the degree to which any nation is open to international influences will vary; similarly, industries or firms in a single country may vary in their openness to international trends in management and markets. International interaction has in the past been closely connected with the very process of economic development, however. It is hard to argue for the purity of national institutions when, historically, the world has been subject to international forces of change. For every occasion on which we are told that the world and its economy are currently undergoing a profound and even unprecedented transformation, we might equally be reminded of the need for greater historical perspective. John Maynard Keynes, in the aftermath of the World War I, looked back nostalgically to a world being lost: 'What an extraordinary episode in the economic progress of man that age which came to an end in 1914! The inhabitant of London could order by telephone . . . the various products of the whole earth . . . he could at the same moment and by the same means adventure his wealth in the natural resources and new enterprises of any quarter of the world . . .' (Keynes, 1919). The initial advance of 'globalisation' (before 1914), its retreat (from 1914–45) and then ensuing return (since 1945) reveal cautionary lessons. Keynes believed that the victorious states that signed the Versailles Treaty had the power to undermine the welfare of an economically interdependent globe. The current wave of internationalisation began as a policy formulated, or more grudgingly accepted, by key nations in the post-war decades, and, just as their choice was not an inevitable one, so arrangements and outcomes within the 'global' economy have been complex and varied.

This is a plea for a more detailed and more explicitly historical understanding of how business systems, national institutions and international markets relate to each other. While employing comparative approaches to the deeper understanding of national economies and their individual evolution, we need an equally long-term appreciation of external international influences and two-way interactions between countries.

The end result of all these considerations may not lead to a tidy or embracing theory. The making of management is a continuous process of change, adaptation and events that includes both compatible and conflicting elements. The actions of business leaders, management systems and national and international product markets are not passive but continuously interact and influence national institutions and popular attitudes. Similarly, the international economy, or globalisation, is neither a magic formula nor an untainted benefit, but a consequence of choices by nations and businesses. Decisions are made and events occur that have important and widespread results, and the outcomes of such decisions and events are complex and possibly uncertain.

On one side is the 'end of history' advocate, looking forward to the global victory of a single system of political economy (essentially, Georg Hegel's triumph of an idea or the spirit of the age). To make his case, Francis Fukuyama (1992) had to overlook the complexities of markets and international business, and ignore a chief characteristic: their formidable ability to generate change. On the other side is the concept of determinant national institutions, which argues instead for global diversity. It emphasises a set of national institutional characteristics or a culture. These institutions and culture are formed at a particular time, and become to a large extent fixed. They then shape a national business system formed at a subsequent point in time. For Fukuyama, it is the Anglo-American form of political economy (already fully formed and fixed for eternity) that has subsequently begun to shape the world. Either separate national institutions determine at a turning point in history the long-term characteristics of very individual business systems or, alternatively, a single system of political economy determines at a turning point in history the long-term characteristics of the other business systems. Both are appeals to the court of historical understanding, but the cases are flawed. Management might instead be seen as being made and continuously remade by a diverse range of factors, in response to both internal and external pressures, through a more complex and less obviously linear process (Thompson, 1963).

Comparative history: economic development

Comparison when mixed with history has an authoritative pedigree. In attempting to describe the origins of wealth, Adam Smith (1776) decided upon an historical account of nations and their trading relationships. He pointed to the productive efficiencies that flowed from the division of labour and the specialisation of skills, which were associated in turn with operational scale and the size of the market. Trade expanded the size of the market, and an international division of labour enabled countries to specialise in certain products in mutually beneficial exchange for others. A nation would export whenever it possessed an absolute advantage, or, in Smith's terms, lower production costs. His linking of developments in business systems, national economies and international trade places a powerful analytical tool at the centre of his thesis, in which a comparative and historical approach links the organisational and the contextual. Alongside his labour theory of value, David Ricardo (1817) is famous for introducing the notion of comparative advantage: a country might still import a good for which it enjoyed an absolute lead in productivity, so long as it utilised its pool of resources to export goods for which it had even greater relative advantage. Interestingly, Smith and Ricardo were both dismal about the long-term impact of higher consumption and population growth on the 'fixed' supply of land, a theory more famously linked to the name of Thomas Malthus (1798): unsustainable demands on natural resources would lead to shortages and famine.

The pessimism of classical economists reflected the uncertain beginnings of industrialisation and occurrences of widespread economic hardship. John Stuart Mill (1848) was not quite so dismal a practitioner of the new 'science'. Since another generation had passed by the time he wrote, he could be more confident that improvements in business organisation and technology might offer more far-reaching possibilities and achieve a permanent economic and social transformation. 'One of the changes which most infallibly attend the progress of modern society,' he asserted, 'is an improvement in the business capacities of the general mass of mankind.' Previous writers had perceived wealth and trade flows as being shaped and constrained principally by a nation's natural resources, and, despite their interest in work organisation, they were unable to envisage the potential of human-created endowments. Like the classical economists, Marx (1909 [1867]) analysed economics within the framework of politics, society and international markets. He also considered the importance of technology, business systems and human skills as sources of economic and social change. He recognised the possibilities of future growth, but focused on capitalism's exploitative characteristics and internal contradictions, since his view was that they would ultimately bring about its collapse and transformation. His analysis was, like that of predecessors, rooted in the use of comparison and history. Nonetheless, Marx viewed history as a series of stages to be followed by all societies, in accordance with the European experience, and he evinced a low understanding of non-European societies. Historical evidence exposes important differences between capitalist societies (rather than a single model) and in the pathways by which they develop.

The framers of neoclassical economics offered a logically coherent and abstract theory, with two significant outcomes. First, by the end of the nineteenth century, industrialisation and trade were firmly rooted within many leading nations, and, indeed, defined them. The new economists were, as a consequence, drawn to the optimal workings of a given market, and they were less concerned with the sources of economic growth and change. Neoclassicists concentrated primarily on the laws of supply and demand, not the means of expanding these factors. They focused their interest on movements in prices, suggesting that they would in the longer term influence the allocation of productive resources. Market analysis prevailed over the finer understanding of firms, technological innovation, production organisation and human relations. Second, abstract modelling inevitably discouraged detailed, contextual and comparative understanding of business systems, and static market analysis left little room for historical perspective. It is worth adding that Alfred Marshall showed through many of his writings that economics needed history, but he did not, seemingly, know how to fit history into his economics (Jevons, 1871; Marshall, 1895, 1919). We can, then, fully appreciate Joseph Schumpeter's achievement: for him, profit was the result of innovation in new methods and products, or part of the economics of growth. Rivalry and competition, integral to change and progress, force prices and markets towards a continuous state of flux over time, contrary to the static model of efficiency conceived by the neoclassicists. He saw population growth not as preparation for a natural disaster but as part of the growth process. By concentrating on technology, entrepreneurship, innovation and organisation as the roots of development and productivity, he broadened the argument beyond prices, costs and profit maximisation. Schumpeter instilled a sense of dynamism and change into his theories, and he is, therefore, more accommodating to historical explanations (Schumpeter, 1934 [1912], 1942). Nevertheless, the events of the inter-war period turned attention towards the evils of the business cycle, for which Keynes (1936) offered his path-breaking solution. A preoccupation with economic growth and its origins returned only with the formation of the post-1945 world, correcting decades of neglect.

The tradition of comparative history was continued in the field of sociology. Both Max Weber and Emile Durkheim had an interest in industrial society, and both advocated the application of comparison and history as the basis for deep analysis. Such a combination helped to disentangle, over the long term, the determinant characteristic from the accidental. Weber, as is well known, distinguished between the natural and social sciences by arguing

that the former is theoretically driven and more conducive to general conclusions. As a result, the social scientist could propose individuals, beliefs,
organisations or actions that were typical of a society or period, or types
towards which a society or period would tend. The existence of these types
would not depend on or predict, within a given society, total conformity. On
the contrary, by investigating aspirations to ideal rather than actual patterns of
behaviour, it would be possible to detect the sources of change within a society.
Facts and detailed evidence, placed under these frames of reference, could
validate generalisations. Through comparison of one society with another,
the factors that are consistent or significant causes of change may reveal
themselves. Though drawn to the interpretation of motives, Weber recognised
the need to explore situational elements and structural conditions, including
politics, law and the economy, as well as culture. The bulk of his historical
analysis is much more wide-ranging than his best-known work, *The Protestant
Ethic and the Spirit of Capitalism*, which was one part of a collection of lecture
notes published after his death. He proposed frameworks for interpreting
historical change and demonstrating the transition from traditional societies
to rational, capitalist economies. Weber was intrigued by differences between
Europe and Asia, but, like Marx, his examination of historical change is
Eurocentric and Europe-driven (Weber, 1978 [1914], 2003 [1923], 1992
[1904–5]). Durkheim's confidence in the value of comparison and history
was highly explicit. Natural sciences could reach conclusions through experiments in 'artificial' laboratory conditions, but students of society, who could
never have this advantage, had to employ 'indirect experimentation' or 'the
comparative method'. There was only one way to demonstrate if one phenomenon was the cause of another, and that was to compare cases where they were
both simultaneously either present or absent. The differing contexts and
circumstances of any two cases inevitably produce some variations in cause
and effect, however, and so deeper understanding relies on tracing patterns of
cause and effect over significant periods of time (Durkheim, 1895). As
Durkheim states: 'In reality, so far as I know there is no sociology worthy of
the name which does not possess a historical character' (1908).

When political and academic interest in economic growth revived, in the
quest for post-war reconstruction and international economic interdependence, prominent amongst contributors was Simon Kuznets (1966). Having
become an architect of national income accounting, he then established
himself as a leading figure in both comparative economics and history, and
demonstrated concern for both quantification and institutional and organisational development. His *Modern Economic Growth* offers a comprehensive

insight into the pace of economic growth in numerous countries, and presents an analysis of its key elements and major effects. Kuznets poses a question that motivates all growth economists: why have some nations succeeded and others not? Kuznets sees world economic development in terms of epochs that are differentiated from preceding periods by 'epochal innovations'. These sources of change include the technological and the economic, but, in additional, the cultural, political, organisational and institutional, and the relationship between all these factors. Economic growth can be detected throughout human history, but dramatic transformations have occurred only in recent centuries. For Kuznets, the epoch of 'modern' economic growth is marked by 'the extended application of science to the problems of economic production', and concomitant modifications in workplace organisation, management, government, finance systems, infrastructure, international trade, consumption and other aspects of society. It superseded the earlier epochal innovation of world trade, and has associations with Weber's belief in capitalist societies being founded on 'rational', scientific methods and organisation. The economic growth of nations is defined, by Kuznets, as a sustained increase in per capita or per worker product, most often accompanied by sweeping structural changes. He is attempting to capture, like Schumpeter, the dynamic qualities of economic growth. Sweeping changes in economic structure – the movement of labour and other resources from one set of industries to another, more productive set of industries – are required. Structural adjustments reflect the processes of innovation, industrialisation, technology application and product development.

Kuznets's conclusion is, inappropriately, modest, however: he states that his historical and comparative analysis measured the scale and the impact of growth, but merely revealed the cultural, political, organisational and institutional foundations of the growth phenomenon that had altered human history (see also Gould, 1972). The concept of epochal innovation is valid, but too generalised to supply deep insight. The study of economic growth has different objectives and more eclectic concerns than the neoclassical approach, and Kuznets then called for more detailed investigation of its foundations. Angus Maddison (1995) has continued Kuznets's work on the comparative measurement of economic change. He specifies the 'proximate' sources of growth, such as increased capital investment or human skills, and the 'ultimate' sources, such as culture, politics, organisation and institutions, that drive the 'proximate' (see also Maddison, 2003). Jeffrey Sachs (2005), in his examination of global poverty, employs the agenda and framework of modern economic growth.

Walt Rostow (1960) argues that there are a number of key characteristics common to all cases of modern economic growth. He contends that the process of industrialisation can be divided into distinct phases. In the 'pre-conditions stage', nations undergo an industrial apprenticeship, in which agriculture and food production advance, rates of investment improve, technological experiments occur, institutions begin to modernise and real incomes and population expand to a degree. Then, the 'take-off stage' follows, in which levels of investment rise, growth rates accelerate and living standards improve dramatically. When a critical mass is reached, industria-lisation and economic growth become a self-sustaining process, labelled the 'mature stage'. By associating macroeconomic change with the institutional, organisational, technological and cultural, Rostow finds accord with the classical economists and Kuznets. Later works of history, however, have questioned Rostow's belief in the critical role of leading industries or in specific levels of capital accumulation. It is impossible, in practice, to date or clearly define the sequential stages of growth. Detailed research, almost inevitably, has raised awareness of complexity and diversity within societies at any juncture. Others have wondered if his model is especially suited to instances of industrialisation in the United Kingdom and United States, based largely on the lengthy emergence of market-driven systems. They doubt if nations nowadays could adopt the same institutional, organisational and technological means of development (see also Rostow, 1990). Whatever the many, acknowledged advances found in Rostow's work, it suggests a 'one best way' to economic development, and its comparative analysis relies on an inflexible model of stages that becomes suspect under detailed probing.

Alexander Gershenkron's (1965) name is not so well known outside the field of economic history, yet it is well regarded within it. Students of contemporary business systems have, nonetheless, been able to apply his thesis of 'late industrialisation' or 'late development' (Amsden, 1989, 2001; Hikino and Amsden, 1994; Nolan, 2001; Sutherland, 2003). In the first instance, it is a flexible model of development that allows for strategic and organisational diversity in response to differences in circumstance and events. Secondly, not only are variations in the pathway of development allowed for within the concept, they are explicable. Thirdly, the original concept of late development relied on the measuring of differential growth rates, but concentrated on a detailed analysis and explanation of technologies, organisations and institutions. The basic premise is that the degree of back-wardness within an economy on the eve of industrialisation fundamentally determines the rate and pattern of its subsequent economic growth. As ever, the delineation of national periods of industrialisation remains a difficulty, but faster rates of economic growth have, historically, been easier to achieve at an early stage, in part because of the initially low starting base. With respect to patterns of development, 'backward' economies do not have to await the 'preconditions' apprenticeship detected by Rostow, but can find alternative institutional and organisational means to speed up the lengthy establishment of markets, capital accumulation or social capital. One key reason is that 'follower' nations do not engage in the slow process of inventing core technologies, but can instead copy the breakthroughs of 'leaders', or simply purchase them internationally.

When home markets are inchoate, institutions and organisations can act as 'market substitutes', an historical fact or pattern that does not accord with the neoclassical tradition. A frequent driver of industrialisation, and the most important institution, is the state: it actively assists in the transfer of technologies; controls exchange and capital in pursuit of long-term objectives; and, for a crucial period, it might protect nascent industries against foreign competition. The state will channel scarce resources towards a narrow range of strategic heavy industries, usually with the cooperation of several big companies or business groups. These advanced enterprises will differ from the rest of the economy in their technological demands, capital requirements and size of operations. So, the whole economy does not progress through distinct, characteristic 'stages' (homogeneity) but by reason of its unevenness (internal contrasts). As these leading companies cannot rely on a readily available pool of engineering, work or managerial experience, they may demonstrate a particular interest in production management, skills training or business organisation. State activity, bank–industry relationships and horizontally and vertically integrated business groups all act as market substitutes, in order to accelerate the pace of economic growth, to share the risks of financing and poor demand conditions, and to encourage long-termism in managerial objectives and national strategic goals (see also Lewis, 1955). They are the foundations of national systems that differ from those associated with so-called 'early development' or more market-orientated mechanisms, as in the United Kingdom or United States.

It is the processes of change in differing national contexts and varying strategic considerations – and not some universal economic theory, or a fixed and static notion of national characteristics and 'best' management practice – that potentially explain the nature of business systems and corporate organisation. There is an obvious link between the late industrialisation perspective and pathway analysis, in which the sequence of choices and events within firms, nations and even the international economy is connected to the development of differing capabilities. Specific competencies are locked within unique organisations, institutions and contexts, and determine the range of future effective choices (Nelson and Winter, 1982; Teece, 1998). The phrase 'late development' can be seen as confusing when it is applied to both nineteenth-century Germany and modern-day China, but it is the choice between development strategies that is critical and not the historical timing. Nevertheless, the thesis has nothing to say about the appropriateness of late development institutions and business systems once an economy becomes classified as developed or internationally competitive, at which point, arguably, more advanced technologies or alternative forms of corporate governance are required. In other words, business systems are not fixed during a specific period of industrialisation (which itself presents common problems of definition and dating); they are made and subsequently remade. After the initial period of economic development, for which they might claim responsibility, certain interest groups may become unwilling to undertake further economic and social reforms. Nor has the late development thesis adapted to several decades of globalisation, the declining economic sovereignty of the nation state or the fact of international pressure against trade barriers.

Contrary to popular conviction, history is not an effective guide to predicting a future course of events, yet it may help to locate or clarify those issues affecting current society. For most historians, the past is 'of its own kind', and their desire to test generality with realism challenges universal theories and models. Investigators of contemporary business systems, often with a background in sociology or economics, tend to perceive history as a form of structural analysis, which focuses on broad categories or patterns of change. They are less aware of detailed work in general and economic history, and, more especially, in the field of business history. The focus on individuals, groups, firms and events is, by its nature, more empirical, sceptical and contextual. The perceived contrast between historical and 'actor-centred' approaches is, therefore, a false one. Kuznets is admired, quite rightly, for his intellectual and methodological grasp of macro factors, but even he urges the type of detailed analysis that enables fuller interpretation of the data. The role of entrepreneurs, the ability to utilise technology, legal systems and the building of managerial hierarchies are only the beginning of a potentially long topic list. The late development thesis, originating with Gershenkron, suggests the possibility of variation in patterns of historical change, as exposed by research into the actual events of transforming economies. Nonetheless, it too discovers insightful points of comparison in the similar and dissimilar institutional, organisational, political and cultural characteristics of economic growth. Although historians do not reject generalisations, they are wary of models that seek to be representative of realities rather than acting as tools of analysis. They hold that detail, complexity and variety, as revealed over time, offer a fuller understanding of the human condition. As the historian J. B. Bury (quoted in Temperley, 1930) outlined, we can give reasons why a British prime minister might walk down a street, and we can explain the physics that would loosen a roof tile; we are more challenged to develop a theory of why roof tiles kill prime ministers, yet it is the unpredictable conjuncture of two events that becomes important.

A number of themes or approaches do emerge from the work of major historians who have sought to evaluate the economic growth of nations however. First, we have to link general trends with knowledge of their foundations amongst individuals, firms, industries, regions and institutions. We must appreciate, in addition, the impact of events and a cumulative sequence of events on choices, outcomes, and organisational and institutional settlements. Second, interpretations of national economic development distinguish between the exploitation of 'limited' natural resources and the 'limitless' possibilities of human-created endowments and innovation in products, systems and skills. Since, as industrialising countries mature, they may depend more on the latter advantages, the need to evaluate the human and organisational foundations of growth are re-emphasised. Analysis needs to be awake to the causes of further change in business systems and core capabilities. Third, although the study of economic development may take the nation as its unit of analysis, no nation can be studied in isolation. The international aspects of economic development have been historically important, as well as currently far-reaching. Fourth, our understanding of the impact on institutions and businesses at a national, local or firm level must depend on an appreciation of complexity, variety and unpredictable outcomes.

National systems: national management

Why have certain developing and developed nations, all seemingly accepting competitive markets and private capital, achieved higher growth rates than others? One response has been to argue that modern capitalist economies in fact came in different varieties, and that fundamental differences in business systems, management and work methods have shaped economic performance. Amongst those who emphasise national rather than international sources of economic success, Porter (1990) is most prominent. When companies acquire basic types of organisational capabilities through the exploitation of natural resources, that is international comparative advantage, but higher rates of wealth and innovation rest on human skills and systems that are turned into an international competitive advantage. Porter reformulates the question of why nations prosper into why certain countries become the home base for internationally successful industries. National competitiveness depends on the productivity of industries, and competitive advantage flows from individual firms that offer the lowest prices or the most differentiated products. A firm does not exist in isolation, however. Efficient suppliers and distributors, supporting industries, access to technology and knowledge, labour pools and good government all add to the productivity of the value chain through locational advantages and clustering effects. Industries may have, consequently, a regional as well as a national dimension. Firms are motivated by competitive rivalry, and successful firms stimulate the growth of clusters in a virtuous circle of accumulating advantages. More complex business systems, innovation and high-value output are related to levels of clustering. Industries utilise the competitive strengths honed in home markets to reap further gains from global operations. In essence, a successful national economy is composed of successful industrial clusters.

Although the evolution of industrial regions contains an obvious temporal dimension, Porter's approach cannot capture the complex origins of clusters and business networks (Sabel and Zeitlin, 1997; Scranton, 1997). The absence of historical perspective is general. Firstly, Porter does provide a framework of how firms and industrial sectors may progressively derive competitive advantage, but he states that their interaction with national factor and demand conditions is an essential ingredient. He is seeking to show how internationally competitive firms and industries emerge in particular nations. Why is the German economy so successful at businesses that are science-intensive, or why has the powerhouse of the Japanese economy so far been located in machinery and transport manufacturing? Individual national environments provide the factor and demand advantages that shape the evolution of firms and industries, which, in turn, then enhance national strengths. Checklists of factor and demand conditions suggest the range of advantages that may or may not exist, but, since no reason why they actually exist in any one nation is provided, they do not add up to a theory or full explanation. A strong R&D base will encourage the growth of knowledge-driven businesses, so generating high-value-added output and good living standards. There is a strong element of tautology in this explanation, however, unless we can explain the origins of national science institutions. Historical perspective would have offered the resources and analytical tools with which to describe the economic development of specific countries. As in Porter's portrayal of clustering, the analysis of national competitive advantage and its causes tends to be a static template within the neoclassical tradition.

Secondly, therefore, Porter does not add to his description of how nation, firm and cluster interact to create competitive advantage. He offers, to be exact, a sketch of the movement from factor to innovation stages of 'national competitive development', which does have a possible temporal dimension. Interestingly, this proposal is reminiscent of Rostow's belief that all nations undergo the same process of economic development in clearly definable 'stages'. To meet the facts and varied cases of real history, a more flexible framework is needed. Both Rostow and Porter, furthermore, stress the importance of markets and competition to an extent that overlooks 'market substitutes' at the initial phase of growth, because inchoate markets have yet to be fully formed, and because markets offer disproportionate advantages to 'leader' nations. Porter cannot accommodate his sidelining of the state, which has had a major role in the development of most economies. Nor does he admit that business groups and networks, when acting as market substitutes, have furthered the emergence of national clusters. We require a comparative approach that takes better account of how industrialisation is achieved historically, since the framework of national competitive advantage seems more appropriate to mature economies that have already industrialised. Thirdly, Porter stands accused of not giving enough weight to the international origins of competitive advantage. He argues, with some force, that trade and FDI are determined by the existence of locational advantages, which are contained within clusters of production. Large multinationals will invest in areas that best meet their production requirements, and clusters, being examples of specialisation and comparative advantage, will determine the structure of exports and trade. Historical perspective reveals that the international economy is not a new phenomenon, however, and that international trade and investment have affected, as well as been shaped by, the emergence of national economies.

Alfred Chandler (1990) is the author of a famous book on comparative business, and one of few historians to influence the wider field of management studies (for example, Whittington and Mayer, 2000). Like Porter, he looks for the economic success of nations amongst their business systems; unlike Porter, he has a definitive theory and management model. His concept of the managerial enterprise has challenged assumptions about the relevance of perfectly competitive markets, since it is large and oligopolistic corporations that dominate modern economies. It is the 'visible hand' of management within these enterprises that deliver goods and services rather than Smith's 'invisible hand'. Mass technologies and mass consumption bring returns to scale and scope that are best captured within the organisational capabilities of large firms, accounting for new growth industries, structural change and productivity gains. Neither could have been implemented effectively, however, without the more critical organisational innovation of managerial hierarchy and the profession of management itself. It is no accident that the United States is portrayed as the joint home of mass manufacturing, mass consumption and modern management. The 'strategy and structure' concept is a genuine theory, in which technological and market frontiers determine strategic options, and the effective implementation of strategy depends on the nature of business organisation. Chandler's work moves from an analysis of four leaders in management to an evaluation of corporate America generally. Then, his *Scale and Scope* poses the core question of why certain economies have succeeded or sunk into decline. It argues that Germany followed the US investment in managerial hierarchies, and that an inability to change family ownership and non-professionalised systems explains the United Kingdom's 'personal capitalism' and relative failure. The influence of Weber is noteworthy. The large corporation, supported by systems of professionalised managerial hierarchy, represents a universal system of rational bureaucracy. Chandler's comparative historical analysis, like that of his predecessors, is concerned with the macroeconomic implications of organisational capabilities at the level of firms. In addition, though, he contends that the performance of national economies is influenced principally by internal management characteristics. He attempts to demonstrate that the United States, Germany and the United Kingdom evolved across their leading firms distinct national patterns of management.

Chandler's work displays the case-centred and data-rich strengths of the historian. All the same, while the interest in corporate management is legitimate, the lack of weight given to national context and complexities is problematic, and the application of comparative method has weaknesses. Challenging the repercussions of 'personal capitalism', other historians quote the United States, Europe and Asia as examples where family ownership can exist in combination with professionalised management. The information as presented too easily suits a pattern of US/German success and British failure, when individual cases are capable of different interpretations, and it ignores important variations between firms in the same country. By concentrating so emphatically on internal firm structures, Chandler does not account for other important factors. He believes that the British style of personal management inhibited the growth of large-scale firms, managerial teams and national growth rates. Alternatively, in comparison with the United States, the smaller home markets in the United Kingdom and Germany limited the potential magnitude of firms, reduced capital demands, maintained family owner involvement and determined the size of managerial teams. In different national contexts, organisational choices were similarly different but not necessarily inferior. Furthermore, Chandler overlooks the role of the state, finance systems and the labour force. He ignores the external dimensions of firms, such as business groups and networks, which serve as alternatives to markets, internal scale and managerial organisation (Fruin, 1992; Cassis, 1997). The list contains neglected topics of immediate interest to the late development thesis, notably the state, bank–industry relationships and business groups, and the circumstances of industrialisation directly shape the choices that firms make on strategy, size and organisation. By applying a single model of management to all nations, when it is perhaps best suited historically to US conditions, Chandler is advocating a 'one best way' approach in managerial practice. He does not, moreover, sufficiently address the role of smaller-scale enterprise and clusters, vital if we are fully to evaluate the characteristics of national economies (Scranton, 1997).

There remains a further question of why, according to Chandler, US and German business owners and managers were inclined or able to transform the size and structures of their enterprises, and why their British counterparts failed. He does not fully address this point. He is uninterested in the role of the state or varying market opportunities, preferring to emphasise the determinant influence of internal management capabilities on national economic advantage. Why, though, would US managers transform their methods, and why would their British counterparts fail to follow? Chandler suggests that the answer is a difference in the business cultures of the large firms to be found in each nation. Those that advocate the key importance of national institutions, such as the state, finance, education systems or labour movements, do so in the alternative belief that they determine the nature of management and business organisation: just as national business cultures shape differences in institutions, varying national institutions shape business systems. They argue, with effectiveness, that business systems are socially constructed. Business systems within firms are particular arrangements of hierarchy–market relations, which become institutionalised and relatively successful in specific contexts. Markets are more complex phenomena than neoclassical models would allow, and so the internal control and organisation of firms *do* matter. Since markets are imperfect, and knowledge is bounded, efficient structures are dependent upon beliefs, priorities and value judgements. The national institutional context, especially the state, reinforces and rewards certain types of 'successful' behaviour. At the time of industrialisation, it leaves a determinant, initial imprint on the characteristics of business systems, which may begin to exercise degrees of autonomy at a later stage (Whitley, 1992a, 1992b; Maurice and Sorge, 2000; Morgan, Whitley and Moen, 2005; Sorge and Warner, 1986; Sorge, 2005).

The analysis raises a number of issues. First, it is argued that institutions reflect pre-industrial patterns of social organisation. The approach rests on the paradoxical idea that historical processes matter and that the chief cause of change is a 'fixed' or static culture. It assumes that national institutions and national cultures have permanent characteristics that serve as a 'natural' reference point for the creation of national business systems. Presumably, these characteristics can be located as exerting their long-term influence at some notional but critical date in the past. Cultures and institutions may emerge as much from conflict as consensus, however, and they remain fluid, malleable and subject to change. Cultures and institutions were and are 'contested terrains', representing the motivation and influence of various actors, and, in seeking to characterise a society, we cannot ignore the tensions and differences within them (Edwards, 1979). 'Institutionalism' tends to a certain interpretation of historical change, or, arguably, towards an ahistorical analysis. It acknowledges that the strength of a culture and levels of conformity vary, but this concession begins to raise issues about other factors that might be brought into the equation. The thesis fails to look at how national culture, assuming this exists, or observable forms of behaviour are themselves altered by the requirements of industralisation. The causal relationship between attitudes, national institutions and business systems is not linear, since all these factors constantly interact and change in a complex manner.

Second, one proponent of the institutional approach, Whitley, states that his analysis does not consider the evolution of any particular institution in detail – the very example that would intrigue an historian. Nor does he believe 'general processes of economic development' to be significant for long-term outcomes. As we have seen, economic and business historians are fundamentally interested in these processes, because the evidence suggests that they had a direct bearing on the nature of national business systems.

What is missing from 'institutionalism' is a convincing explanation of why industrialisation takes place, and a description of the necessary changes in management and business systems that underpin industrialisation itself. This is partly because the economic, technological, organisational and market demands of industrialisation do have implications for business systems, even if they are not the sum total. 'Institutionalism' argues that pre-industrial patterns of social organisation and the relationships of village communities were able to leave a large legacy on East Asia because of the speed of industrialisation, yet, on the contrary, active state involvement and choices in business systems were used to transform perceived culture or former practices, when they are seen as a barrier to economic development. The demands of technology, business organisation, events and contested social and political settlements during the achievement of industrialisation may have had a greater impact on culture than culture has had on the path of economic development. Historical evidence suggests, for example, that events and choices made in the 1940s and 1950s were much more critical to the creation of the 'Japanese enterprise system' than the Tokugawa period of the 1860s. Structures were more mixed and fluid in the decades before World War II. The characteristics of the 'classic' Japanese model, frequently associated with a particular cultural and feudal inheritance, were formed and agreed in response to specific events and choices on technology, human relations and managerial organisation that would facilitate rapid economic development. Entrepreneurs and firms were 'actors' rather than passive responders to institutional and cultural frameworks, influential in the formation of state policy, and at times capable of resisting the wishes of government. The overemphasis on culture as cause and the lack of history are especially notable in the case of Hofstede's work (Hofstede, 1980, 1991).

Third, theorists of 'institutionalism' possess marginal interest in levels of competitiveness, which may be connected to the variations within business systems. They evince little knowledge of the far-reaching consequences of economic growth and economic development historically in terms of work organisation, finance systems, living standards, urbanisation or international engagement. Institutions and business systems change, progressively or suddenly, after the beginnings of industrialisation, and cultural assumptions and national identity are subject to the same processes of transformation. Arguably, economic change requires institutional and organisational transformations and not institutional continuities. The works of Weber on Protestantism and Gordon Redding (1990) on the Chinese family business have, undoubtedly, influenced the institutionalist theory and its central notion that markets and business success are socially constructed. It is surprising that Fukuyama, having in effect predicted the triumph of one style of capitalism, wrote another book on the cultural origins of business systems (1995). We have noted that Weber's ideas on Protestantism represent only part of his general output on economic development, although it is perhaps his most famous theory. Historians have, since his death, challenged his interpretation on the grounds that, even if Calvinist beliefs influenced the behaviour of many leading businessmen, capitalism would have arisen in northern Europe whether or not Calvinism had existed (Tawney, 1938 [1926]). Weber's view (1951 [1916]) that Confucianism was, in antithesis to Protestantism, the explanation for Chinese relative decline fits uneasily with contemporary views of the East Asian 'miracle'. Since Confucianism has been both the explanation for Asian economic failure and Asian economic success, we might make two conclusions: either culture is so flexible a concept that it can explain any social, political or economic phenomena; or political and economic changes in Asian societies have had an impact on popular interpretations of Confucianism.

World systems: global management

One further criticism might be added to the idea of national institutions determining the nature of business systems. Over recent decades, undeniable trends towards further globalisation have demonstrated clearly that international forces do shape business systems. From an historical perspective, this factor is even more problematic for 'institutionalist' analysis, since these international forces have been significant for centuries and, undeniably, critical over the whole post-war period. It is fair to state that 'globalisation' may appear an inflexible and simplified concept. It ignores the relevance and the importance of differences between nations, regions and companies as the long-term origin of core competencies, and, indeed, these differences are a main cause of international interaction itself. The internationalisation of the world economy is not an automatic, inevitable or mystical process but the result of historical choices. Nations, like companies, do not instinctively favour the transfer of knowledge and competence. They utilise institutional barriers in order to slow their imitation, and so maintain a competitive advantage. They nonetheless accept some level of international economic interaction when it offers net as well as mutual benefit (even if the pressure is actually political or diplomatic). Nation states and companies were two active elements in the growth of the international economy during the post-war period. Governments created the General Agreement on Tariffs and Trade (GATT) and, subsequently, the World Trade Organization, although the last has been given greater independence and authority as a body regulating and promoting free trade. They oversee the International Monetary Fund (IMF), the World Bank and a vast range of institutional, regulatory and exchange relations. The post-war commitment of nation states, especially the United States, to free trade, foreign direct investment and internationalisation has had significant implications. The scale and scope of multinationals have, almost inevitably, increased alongside the rise of the international economy. According to multinational business theory, firms engage in overseas expansion because they have particular organisational capabilities, which are or have been rooted in their home economy; locational advantages in production or marketing, moreover, flow from operating overseas; and the scale and scope returns emerge from the coordinating of international transactions, which would be paramount in a truly globalised world (Dunning, 1993). When, in the 1960s, the term 'multinational' was coined, it was an acknowledgement of the increasing importance of world trade and investment, and the greater organisational complexity of a business phenomenon.

The term 'globalisation' has a twofold objective. In the first place, it highlights the continued internationalisation of the world economy; the exaggerated notion and benefits of a single global marketplace; the scale of so-called 'global' businesses; and the possibility of 'footloose' international capital with little loyalty to any nation state (Ohmae, 1990, 1995, 2005; Reich, 1991). Nevertheless, global production, trade and FDI flows remain remarkably concentrated between the 'triad' of North America, western Europe and the Asia-Pacific region. Home-country origins remain the main marketplace for most of the world's largest companies, and they continue to stamp and assert a major influence on the nature of their management and core capabilities. The global market remains far from homogeneous, and multinational companies differ markedly in their operations and capabilities. The degree of international integration – that is, the value of FDI stocks in relation to world value added – reached a high point in 1914, when World War I ended a period of extending free trade, or, if preferred, the 'first era of globalisation'. The inter-war decades show that events and nation states can reverse the process of internationalisation in pursuit of greater self-sufficiency and protectionism. Interestingly, tariff barriers and market access, not free trade, then became the main rationale for multinational investment. From 1945 onwards the growth of the international economy surpassed in most decades the rise in world output, as did the increase in TNC activity. It was not until 2004, however, that the FDI stock relative to the size of the world economy overtook the former peak of 1914. For Fukuyama (1992), globalisation symbolised the cessation of the Cold War and disputes over systems of political economy. A new era without precedent had begun. He was inspired by Hegel's belief in looking beneath the real events of history into its mystical 'controlling' undercurrents. The world had been moving in one direction, and finally produced a single, dominant and imitable form of market capitalism and political democracy, based, as in previous decades, on the US model. Nonetheless, Kuznets's writings were not alone, or the first, in noting the economic, social and political impact of trade over many centuries.

In the second place, the term 'globalisation' highlights the application of so-called 'best standard' practice, applicable in all cases, or internationally applicable in the long term. It is a simplified version of the international economy and of the economic 'interactions' between nation states. During the 1990s there were notable changes in the strategy, scale and organisational complexity of TNCs, and an increase in the levels of international integration. Although output and trade remained geographically concentrated, giant firms could acquire greater advantage from their transnationality. For the proponents of globalisation, they would ultimately impose converging management and operations systems throughout their operations and influence the future direction of host economies. The benefits of international scale and scope would bring similarities in business ownership, administrative procedures, work and cultural attitudes, most apparently in line with the Anglo-American variant of capitalism. Conceptually underwriting this trend is the notion of 'best practice' management, systems and institutions, in which follower nations raise competitiveness merely by replicating the activities of leaders. On the other hand, previous examples of 'best practice' – scientific management, Fordism, lean production or the McKinsey model of business organisation – were varied in application at the national, industrial or corporate level.

By its nature, successive and detailed research discovers the complexity and diversity of the past, and asks different questions to those tracing 'overall' trends. It re-emphasises the influence of context on variety, but looks, also, at contest, interaction and the motivations of interest groups. There is a danger that reminders of precedents and continuity go too far, and in effect deny the importance of change. International influences in the form of technology, systems and capital have historically been a feature of industrialisation and economic growth, but the international economy of the last few decades does have new characteristics, just as it did in the immediate post-war years. If we agree that history is no predictor of future events, we could grant that it uncovers the contemporary issues at stake: greater degrees and differing mechanisms of internationalisation, certainly, but, at the same time, the complexities of economic activity occurring at the local, national, regional and global levels simultaneously, and the unpredictable consequences of human motivation and agency. Unless we assume, as Fukuyama might, that the world's economic system can now be perfected, future sources of change and growth depend on variety, contrast, contest and the disruption of established technologies, business systems and product markets.

One major agent of globalisation is the transnational corporation, due to its ability directly and rapidly to transfer technology and systems (Chandler and Mazlich, 2005). If TNCs become more powerful than governments, and if international competitive advantages become greater than national sources, they emerge as the major forces of economic change. It has been easy to exaggerate the size and power of multinationals in relation to many states, merely by comparing, incorrectly, corporate revenues with national value added (gross domestic product – GDP). Their means to export 'best practice' is an extension of Chandler's integrating managerial hierarchy, and, therefore, Weber's bureaucratic, rational organisation, as models to be imitated by all. The emphasis is on the growth effects of internal management structures rather than on factors external to the firm. Historians have been slow to incorporate the role of the TNC into well-known historical concepts such as 'world systems'. They have not in the main connected debates on globalisation with the tradition of world history, which is concerned with understanding the forces that have most profoundly shaped human existence (Hopkins, 2002, 2006). World, or global, history shifts the focus away from the study of individual nation states towards the international 'interactions' between them. Alternatively, it seeks to understand the development of any one country through a framework of comparative analysis and understanding. These two objectives are not mutually exclusive.

In commentaries on world history, the first to be quoted is often Oswald Spengler (1932). He contends that politics can be understood only in relation to artistic and philosophical developments, and that leading civilisations capable of international influence emerge independently of external influences because they are directed by their 'soul' or core culture. For modern readers, the idea of a 'soul' or core culture seems mystical, and yet there is a link with current arguments for a determinant national culture that will configure national institutions and business systems. Arnold Toynbee

(1934–61) conceives of civilisations that, larger than individual states, are (very vaguely) defined by shared cultural characteristics. A 'creative minority' formulates responses to internal and external challenges, and civilisations undergo inevitable cycles of growth and disintegration. Although the analysis of historical change is elitist and narrow, Toynbee does identify interest groups as the drivers of change. Nonetheless, cultural characteristics that are shared by collections of nations or regions still determine world history, and detailed research is capable of challenging an overgeneralised concept. William McNeill (1963), in his highly regarded book, challenges the Spengler–Toynbee view that separate civilisations have been largely autonomous in their evolution, and argues that human cultures have interacted throughout history. Writing at the high point of US world power, he outlines too how the West has had a dramatic impact on the rest of the world. McNeill's account remains predominantly 'civilisational' in approach, and it emphasizes the one-directional influence of the West on the rest of the world. Interestingly, Samuel Huntington (1996) seeks to challenge Fukuyama's assertion that ideological debates between nations has ended. He suggests instead that the clash between the West and Islam in particular has replaced the tensions of the Cold War. The thesis is more ideological than the former writings of historians, and rests on highly challengeable assumptions about the role of culture and civilisations in world history. He, similarly, imposes uniformity on the national groupings he terms 'civilisations', and ignores their complexity and plurality.

The preoccupation of world historians with defining civilisations has sometimes led them to depend on debatable notions of innate culture. Moreover, it has downplayed the role or economics and business. It is this lacuna that Fernand Braudel (1972–3 [1949]) has attempted to bridge. He formulated the idea of a 'world system' by examining the regional economy and trade around the Mediterranean in the sixteenth century. Braudel argues that it comprised 'a' world economy, even if 'the' world economy had not yet formed. The preoccupation with autonomous civilisations (McNeill apart) sidelined the historical interaction of nations and world regions with each other, hiding those occasions and areas of collision. Immanuel Wallerstein (1974, 1980, 1989), the author most famously associated with world history, attempts to address this issue too. He asserts that the period after 1500 is a discontinuity because Europe produced a world system, namely capitalism, that could exist for the first time separately from political power or imperial exploitation. The age of exploration and trade was suited to its influence and dispersal. Capitalism was a 'best practice' business system that restructured the world into either industrialised states or the rest – that is, the core and a periphery.

Wallerstein sees the system as exploitative of workers and the peripheral states, and tends to suggest that the inequalities are embedded and permanent. Numerous criticisms, with similarities to those surrounding contemporary globalisation, have been levelled at the thesis. Wallerstein's definition of capitalism is simplistic, and his description of its influence remains Eurocentric and linear. The system arises in a particular country or region, and forms the 'best practice' that must be imitated by the rest. Although the historical impact of western Europe and, more latterly, the United States is difficult to deny, detailed research can reveal examples of international interaction in technology, systems and products prior to industrialisation itself and during the process of modern economic growth. The giants of India and China had a noteworthy influence on Europe. Moreover, 'capitalism' is not formed, fixed, at a specific and identifiable historical juncture, but undergoes continuous adaptations over time and between countries. Within his 'world system', Wallerstein underestimates the complexities of economic development and the existence of national varieties within capitalism. He ignores the differing pathways in industrialisation, as suggested by the late development thesis, and fails to account for the ways that nations can overcome the assumed 'permanence' of economic backwardness. Wallerstein focuses on the topics of property rights, individual enterprise, freedom, wealth creation, markets, limited government and democracy, as definitions of the capitalist system originating in Europe and shaping the rest of the world. As historical evidence demonstrates, and contemporary examples illustrate, there have been cases of successful industrialisation that did not rely on all these elements. Market substitutes and developmental states have been prominent in many, if not all, cases. China has returned as an economic giant despite a lack of democratic credentials, pushing as a result through the delicate envelope that is Fukuyama's 'end of history' thesis.

Although inspired by Marx, Wallerstein's description of capitalism and its global influence has one parallel with the institutionalist analysis of leading economic historians. This group asks why it is that certain countries have achieved modern economic growth. They answer that political accountability and just legal systems secure property rights, and, when those responsible for entrepreneurship and innovation receive the rewards of profit, economic growth and dynamism follow. The correct political and legal systems enable the correct working of market mechanisms. Unlike those institutionalists who hold markets to be socially constructed, markets are seen as essentially economically driven. Rather than differing national institutions generating varieties of capitalism, sound national governance produces market systems that are in principle similar (North, 1990). This interpretation of institutionalism is effectively integrated with long-term historical and macroeconomic trends, and certainly adds subtlety to the neoclassical perspective by seeking the origin of growth-inducing markets. It also simplifies the comparative historical experience of many industrialised countries, however, and overlooks the significance of national variations within capitalism.

Sales of world history books have proved popular in recent times. These publications have been critical of former interpretations that identified civilisation with Europe and progress with 'Western' supremacy (if only because of the unfortunate occurrence of two world wars, which Fukuyama dismisses as an insignificant diversion from the historical evolution of a dominant US political economy). They consider the development of individual states, empires and civilisations, but also seek a detailed understanding of how ideas, technologies and systems are transferred between human communities. They offer a wealth of detail, and outline the sequence of events. Their existence is a challenge to general models of historical change (Fernandez-Armesto, 1995; Davies, 1996; Ponting, 2000; Hobsbawm, 1994). In trying to understand the increasingly 'globalised' world, we are not presented with a smooth 'scientific process' but have, instead, a 'contested terrain' (to borrow the phrase of one well-known book). While not denying the impact of contingent events, it can be argued that language, culture, power, authority, government and systems are rarely just historical accidents. Someone or some interest group shapes their evolution in pursuit of specific goals. Resistance, differences in self-interest and misunderstanding can be as relevant as cooperation and conformity. The point is not the wholesale adoption of one management system, even less its final evolution and triumph, but the nature of its making and subsequent remaking (to borrow another famous title). The emphasis is on the intricacies of the historical process and its almost inevitable complexity. Analysis needs perspectives that are local, national, regional and international. While looking for general trends, and dominant forces, it should seek out the comparative patterns or contrasts that are thrown up by interactions between the numerous parties involved. Dominant nations and systems are indications of change and international interaction, but variety and complexity are the potential forces of future change.

References

Amsden, A. H. (1989) *Asia's Next Giant: South Korea and Late Industrialization*, Oxford: Oxford University Press.

  (2001) *The Rise of the Rest: Challenges to the West from Late Industrialising Economies*, Oxford: Oxford University Press.

Braudel, F. (1972–3 [1949]) *The Mediterranean and the Mediterranean World in the Age of Philip II* (trans. S. Reynolds) (2 vols.), New York: Harper and Row.

Cassis, Y. (1997) *Big Business: The European Experience in the Twentieth Century*, Oxford: Oxford University Press.

Chandler, A. D. (1990) *Scale and Scope: The Dynamics of Industrial Capitalism*, Cambridge, MA: Harvard University Press.

Chandler, A. D., and B. Mazlich (2005) *Leviathans: Multinational Corporations in Global History*, Cambridge: Cambridge University Press.

Davies, N. (1996) *Europe: A History*, Oxford: Oxford University Press.

Dunning, J. H. (1993) *Multinational Enterprises and the Global Economy*, Wokingham: Addison-Wesley.

Durkheim, E. (1895) *The Rules of Sociological Method*, Paris: Machette.

  (1908) Pacifisme et patriotisme, *Bulletin de la Société Française de Philosophie*, 8, 44–67.

Edwards, R. (1979) *Contested Terrain: The Transformation of the Workplace in the Twentieth Century*, New York: Basic Books.

Fernandez-Armesto, F. (1995) *Millennium: A History of the Last Thousand Years*, New York: Scribner.

Fruin, W. M. (1992) *The Japanese Enterprise System: Competitive Strategies and Cooperative Structures*, Oxford: Clarendon Press.

Fukuyama, F. (1992) *The End of History and the Last Man*, New York: Free Press.

  (1995) *Trust: The Social Virtues and the Creation of Prosperity*, New York: Free Press.

Gershenkron, A. (1965) *Economic Backwardness in Historical Perspective*, Cambridge, MA: Harvard University Press.

Gould, J. D. (1972) *Economic Growth in History: Survey and Analysis*, London: Methuen.

Hikino, T., and A. H. Amsden (1994) Staying behind, stumbling back, sneaking up, soaring ahead: late industrialization in historical perspective, in W. J. Baumol, R. R. Nelson and E. N. Wolff (eds.) *Convergence of Productivity: Cross-national Studies and Historical Evidence*, Oxford: Oxford University Press, 285–315.

Hobsbawm, E. (1994) *The Age of Extremes: The Short Twentieth Century, 1914–1991*, London: Michael Joseph.

Hobsbawm, E., and T. Ranger (1983) *The Invention of Tradition*, Cambridge: Cambridge University Press.

Hofstede, G. (1980) *Culture's Consequences: International Differences in Work-related Values*, Beverley Hills: Sage.

  (1991) *Cultures and Organizations: Software of the Mind*, London: McGraw-Hill.

Hopkins, A. G. (2002) *Globalization in World History*, New York: Norton.

(2006) *Global History: Interactions between the Universal and the Local*, Basingstoke: Palgrave Macmillan.

Huntington, S. P. (1996) *The Clash of Civilizations and the Remaking of World Order*, New York: Simon and Schuster.

Jevons, W. S. (1871) *The Theory of Political Economy*, London: Macmillan.

Keynes, J. M. (1919) *The Economic Consequences of the Peace*, London: Macmillan.

(1936) *The General Theory of Employment, Interest and Money*, Cambridge: Cambridge University Press.

Kuznets, S. (1966) *Modern Economic Growth: Rate, Structure and Spread*, New Haven, CT: Yale University Press.

Lewis, W. A. (1955) *Theory of Economic Growth*, London: George Allen and Unwin.

McNeill, W. H. (1963) *The Rise of the West: A History of the Human Community*, Chicago: University of Chicago Press.

Maddison, A. (1995) *Explaining the Economic Performance of Nations: Essays in Time and Space*, Aldershot: Edward Elgar.

(2003) *The World Economy: Historical Statistics*, Paris: Organisation for Economic Co-operation and Development.

Malthus, T. (1798) *An Essay on the Principle of Population*, London: J. Johnson.

Marshall, A. (1895) *Principles of Economics* (3rd edn.), London: Macmillan.

(1919) *Industry and Trade: A Study of Industrial Technique and Business Organization*, London: Macmillan.

Marx, K. (1909 [1867]) *Capital: A Critique of Political Economy* (ed. F. Engels, trans. E. Untermann), Chicago: Cherles Kerr.

Maurice, M., and A. Sorge (eds.) (2000) *Embedding Organizations: Societal Analysis of Actors, Organisations and Socio-economic Context*, Amsterdam: John Benjamin's.

Mill, J. S. (1848) *Principles of Political Economy*, London: John W. Parker and Son.

Morgan, G., R. Whitley and E. Moen (eds.) (2005) *Changing Capitalisms? Internationalization, Institutional Change, and Systems of Economic Organization*, Oxford: Oxford University Press.

Nelson, R. R., and S. G. Winter (1982) *An Evolutionary Theory of Economic Change*, Cambridge, MA: Harvard University Press.

Nolan, P. (2001) *China and the Global Economy*, Basingstoke: Palgrave Macmillan.

North, D. C. (1990) *Institutions, Institutional Change and Economic Performance*, Cambridge: Cambridge University Press.

Ohmae, K. (1990) *The Borderless World: Power and Strategy in the Interlinked Economy*, London: HarperCollins.

(1995) *The End of the Nation State: The Rise of the Regional Economies*, New York: Free Press.

(2005) *Next Global Stage: Challenges and Opportunities in Our Borderless World*, Upper Saddle River, NJ: Wharton.

Ponting, C. (2000) *World History: A New Perspective*, London: Chatto and Windus.

Porter, M. E. (1990) *The Competitive Advantage of Nations*, New York: Free Press.

Redding, S. G. (1990) *The Spirit of Chinese Capitalism*, Berlin: de Gruyter.

Reich, R. B. (1991) *The Work of Nations: Preparing Ourselves for 21st-Century Capitalism*, New York: Vintage Books.

Ricardo, D. (1817) *On the Principles of Political Economy and Taxation*, London.

Rostow, W. W. (1960) *Stages of Economic Growth: A Non-Communist Manifesto*, Cambridge: Cambridge University Press.

(1990) *History, Policy, and Economic Theory: Essays in Interaction*, Boulder, CO: Westview Press.

Sabel, C. F. and J. Zeitlin (1997) *World of Possibilities: Flexibility and Mass Production in Western Industrialization*, Cambridge: Cambridge University Press.

Sachs, J. (2005) *The End of Poverty: How We Can Make It Happen in Our Lifetime*, London: Penguin Books.

Schumpeter, J. A. (1934 [1912]) *The Theory of Economic Development: An Inquiry into Profits, Capital, Credit, Interest and the Business Cycle* (trans. R. Opie), Cambridge, MA: Harvard University Press.

(1942) *Capitalism, Socialism and Democracy*, New York: Harper and Row.

Scranton, P. (1997) *Endless Novelty: Speciality Production and American Industrialization, 1865–1925*, Princeton, NJ: Princeton University Press.

Smith, A. (1776) *An Inquiry into the Nature and Causes of the Wealth of Nations*, London: Cadell and Davies.

Sorge, A. (2005) *The Global and the Local: Understanding the Dialectics of Business Systems*, Oxford: Oxford University Press.

Sorge, A., and M. Warner (1986) *Comparative Factory Organization: An Anglo-German Comparison of Manufacturing, Management and Manpower*, Aldershot: Gower.

Spengler, O. (1932) *The Decline of the West*, Oxford: Oxford University Press.

Sutherland, D. (2003) *China's Large Enterprises and the Challenge of Late Industrialisation*, London Oxford: Routledge Curzon.

Tawney, R. H. (1938 [1926]) *Religion and the Rise of Capitalism*, London: Pelican Books.

Teece, D. J. (1998) *Economic Performance and the Theory of the Firm*, Cheltenham: Edward Elgar.

Temperley, H. (1930) *Selected Essays of J. B. Bury*, Cambridge: Cambridge University Press.

Thompson, E. P. (1963) *The Making of the English Working Class*, London: Penguin Books.

Toynbee, A. J. (1934–61) *A Study of History* (12 vols.), Oxford: Oxford University Press.

Wallerstein, I. (1974) *The Modern World System: Capitalist Agriculture and the Origins of the European World-Economy in the Sixteenth Century*, New York: Academic Press.

(1980) *The Modern World System II: Mercantilism and he Consolidation of the European World-Economy, 1600–1750*, New York: Academic Press.

(1989) *The Modern World System III: The Second Era of Great Expansion of the Capitalist World-Economy, 1730–1840s*, San Diego: Academic Press.

Weber, M. (1951 [1916]) *The Religion of China: Confucianism and Taoism* (trans. M. H. Gerth), New York: Free Press.

Weber, M. (1978 [1914]) *Economy and Society* (trans. G. Roth and C. Wittich), Berkeley, CA: University of California Press.

Weber, M. (1992 [1904–5]) *The Protestant Ethic and the Spirit of Capitalism* (trans. T. Parsons, 1930), London: Routledge.

Weber, M. (2003 [1923]) *General Economic History* (trans. F. H. Knight), New York: Dover Publications.

Whitley, R. (1992a) *Business Systems in East Asia: Firms, Markets and Societies*, London: Sage.

(ed.) (1992b) *European Business Systems: Firms and Markets in Their National Contexts*, London: Sage.

Whittington, R., and M. Mayer (2000) *The European Corporation: Strategy, Structure and Social Science*, Oxford: Oxford University Press.

Part II

Systems in Transition

Preface: System as same and different

Brendan McSweeney

These chapters are structured around a notion of 'system' as developed in the system, society and dominance framework (see chapter 2). This notion of 'system' does not follow Niklas Luhmann's definition of system as 'a single mode of operation' (2006: 37), nor is it tautological in the sense that 'a system is difference – the difference between system and environment' (38). Rather, it is used here to mean specifically a system of political economy – capitalism – that is 'a complicated network of similarities overlapping and criss-crossing: sometimes overall similarities, sometimes similarities of detail' (Wittgenstein, 1953: 66).

Each of the three countries in which the chapter's studies are located – the Czech Republic, China and Turkey – have recognisably moved towards, or have extended their commitment to, the 'system' of capitalism, but there remain differences both within and between these countries. Moreover, what they are becoming differs – though not completely – from what they were. There is historical dependency, but not as the causal determinism of prior conditions. Change is mixed and uneven. For instance, even when the Czech Republic was a 'socialist' economy, there were capitalist activities, albeit on a much smaller scale. Now that it is a capitalist economy the power of capital is not unregulated. Anthony Giddens's advocacy of 'the third way' supposes that the two alternatives are pure forms. They never were.

One pure form, a system in the Luhmannian sense of singularity, is the normative ideal of neoliberal economists and politicians. For them, globalisation is an immutable, equilibrating market force that eliminates differences and creates perfect competition. Existing differences are regarded as flaws that should and can be eradicated to reach an idealised global uniformity. Local differences are not seen as sustaining but hampering efficiency and effectiveness. For neoliberal politicians and (some) corporate leaders, this ideal allows them to present their (sectional) interests as a rational and natural analysis and the only feasible response to economic imperatives (Peck, 2003).

A variation of this totalising rhetoric – a supposition of geographical unity – is the speculative epochal assertion that the old Fordist system has now been replaced globally by another, but different, monolith, namely post-Fordism. Its stylised depiction rests on a very narrow empirical foundation (McSweeney, 2006; Peck, 2000). Although in geography the fashionable bubble of post-Fordism seems to have been burst – in management it retains a following.

What comes to a country from outside – even from the same country – is not always the same. Thus, although transformations – national and transnational – are readily conceivable within a notion of a system as potentially pluralist, the idea of global convergence to a single model is incoherent because the endogenous is heterogeneous not homogeneous. So, too, the endogenous contains diversity as well as uniformity. From a pluralist systems perspective, a meeting of the exogenous and the endogenous is therefore not a meeting of the global and the national but of a variety of the foreign with a variety of the local at specific sites of action. That which is locally encountered may indeed be an instance of what is uniformly and robustly national, but not necessarily. Either the local may be nationally atypical or the grip of the national may be weak.

The reviews and empirically grounded case studies in this section point to pluralism – similarities but also differences: not 'a single mode of operation' – in their descriptions of what came into each country, what was encountered and what changed. Each demonstrates the value of a 'bottom-up' approach that seeks to identify the real patterns of actions, institutions and so forth, rather than deploying empirics to illustrate a supposed national uniformity of continuity or change. A unitary supposition leads to a denial or disregard of the non-nationally uniform, whereas from a pluralist perspective divergence is unsurprising but the specificities of the mosaic of heterogeneity and the process of its construction are features requiring explanation. They also need to be taken into theory.

Ed Clark, in chapter 5, observes that our understanding of 'processes and tendencies of globalisation' have been, and can be, greatly enriched by studying the transformations in the post-socialist countries – Russia and the former Soviet republics. In these countries there was widespread and intensive disillusionment with state socialism and financial weakness, and they were, and remain, the objects of extensive and explicit efforts from multiple and powerful sources, including the IMF, the World Bank and the European Bank for Reconstruction and Development (EBRD), which through a variety of processes and incentives have sought the adoption or imposition of a robust version of 'free' market capitalism. Pressure for change was therefore especially strong, and the desire and ability to resist, it might seem, comparatively weak.

Whilst substantial and wide-ranging transformations have occurred in these countries, convergence in the sense of unaltered and unvaried adoption of a neoliberal model has not occurred. Clark identifies a number of reasons for this diversity. First, the fact that 'post-socialist managers have informed their new practices by drawing on a variety of resources'. Although at national policy-making levels there was probably a broad consensus from advisers and advocates, such as the IMF, ideas – and, indeed, actions – from other sources such as some foreign direct investors, whilst quite different from those of the former state socialism, were not all of one kind. Second, there was diversity and the potential for the exercise of agency within the countries. Clark's findings are based both on an extensive literature review and his own fieldwork (with Anna Soulsby) in engineering enterprises in the Czech Republic. Drawing on his own joint case studies, and the findings of most of the others who have also studied changes in post-socialist organisations, he observes that 'the reality of the restructuring process is far more varied than would be expected from theoretical predictions' – that is, from predictions based on theories that presupposed unstoppable global homogenisation. 'Detailed studies of the transformational potential and internationalising consequences of FDI injections into post-socialist organisations demonstrate that these processes are more complex and less predictable than have been projected by researchers' working within 'hyperglobalisation' models.

Clark's chapter ranges across macro- and micro-level processes in a number of countries. The author's own empirically grounded fieldwork was in Czech manufacturing companies. Jos Gamble's chapter focuses on the transfer of one organisational function (human resource management) by one retail company (StoreCo) to a subsidiary (UK-Store) in one country (China). In contrast with the countries studied by Clark, where state socialism had collapsed and the economies were debilitated, at least at the time of the study, overall the economy of China is strengthening and the Chinese Communist Party maintains substantial control. Pressure on UK-Store to conform to local practices might also be seen to be especially strong, because as a retail store it was (a) not part of an integrated international production network and (b) 'it' dealt directly with local Chinese customers. Did the HRM practices of the UK subsidiary in China become a replication of those in the United Kingdom, were 'Chinese' practices adopted or did something else happen?

Gamble queries the pure notion of 'country of origin' with regard to practices. Just because a company is 'from' – located in – a specific country, it does not mean that its practices will be the same as those of every other company also located in that country. To say that a company is British could mean that it is located in, or incorporated in, the United Kingdom, or that its headquarters are in the United Kingdom or that the majority of its share-holders are British, but it does not necessarily imply that its practices are uniformly or uniquely British. Gamble points out that researchers have reported major sectoral differences in UK management practices: 'Even amongst firms in the retail sector [in which StoreCo is located] there appear to be substantial divergences.' StoreCo is noted for its relatively flat and porous hierarchy, whereas internal labour markets have 'bifurcated into a primary "managerial" segment and a secondary "shopfloor" segment'; an 'absence of mobility between segments' has also been found in the UK retail sector. In contrast with the finding by some researchers in 1995 of 'very strong resistance' in China to linking reward more closely with performance and to the introduction of pay differentials, UK-Store's employees complained to Gamble that the firm had not yet introduced a performance-related bonus system, even though their preference was for department-wide bonuses based on performance rather than individual-performance-based bonuses. StoreCo succeeded in transferring its relatively flat hierarchal struc-ture to China. Gamble contrasts this with the much more rigid hierarchy in state-owned companies in China. He observes that, whilst commitment to hierarchy has been defined as a characteristic of a supposedly uniform Chinese national culture (derived, it has been argued, from 'Confucian values'), there was an emphasis amongst employees at UK-Store on com-munality and the value of egalitarianism. He surmises that, though there may be a focus on hierarchy at the top of Chinese society, there is not at the bottom. He warns against overessentializing 'culture', as 'cultural values are not monoliths but a fluid and shifting repertoire with diverse strands'. Gamble also questions the existence of elements of 'a specifically Chinese HRM system', pointing out, for instance, that there are substantial differences in China between the HRM practices in private firms and in state-owned firms.

What emerged in UK-Store was neither purely that of the United Kingdom (or, rather, of Store-Co, since UK retailing does not have uniform practices) nor purely that of China, as in that country there is also intra-sector diversity in retailing. Amongst the non-national (UK or Chinese) practices by UK-Store observed by Gamble was the volume and type of information provided to its employees. Although the scale and range is less than that given to employees in the United Kingdom, it is far greater than in Chinese state-owned enterprises (SOEs), which are characterised by secrecy and limited cross-department sharing. Commenting on possible isomorphic pressures on UK-Store, he observes that they are only partly derived from domestic institutions, as employees' backgrounds were not only in Chinese (public and/or private) organisations but also in various types of foreign enterprises, including Japanese, German, French, Thai, Malaysian and American firms.

Chapter 7, by Gül Berna Özcan, also examines the transplantation of a retail organisation from one country to another. In this case the move was from Switzerland to Turkey, which, like China, has undergone considerable social and economic change, albeit of quite a different type. The originating company in Gamble's case study was a for-profit organisation; in Özcan's study the initial mover was a cooperative. Özcan's chapter provides a longitudinal study from 1954 to 2005 of 'many temporal and spatial discontinuities from its origins in Switzerland to its domestication as part of the Koç conglomerate of Turkey'. Domestication cannot be conflated with a notion of Turkishisation, however. The local context – or, rather, contexts – were a vital part of the transformations, but the various paths chosen were not inevitable. The ultimate outcome differs both from Migros-Türk's originating Swiss company's business model and from its domestic rivals.

The description of the early years of the company in Turkey vividly describe many differences between Switzerland and Turkey, including price controls on food products and poor roads, and contrast sharply with current conditions in Turkey. Trucks were uncommon in Turkey in the 1950s. The arrival of the company's first twenty trucks (imported from the United Kingdom) into Istanbul turned into a state celebration: the trucks were paraded through Istanbul, accompanied by motorcycle policemen and greeted by excited crowds. The company now operates 853 stores, has expanded out of Turkey, employs more than 10,000 people and has an annual turnover of about €1.2 billion. The chapter traces the uneven development of the company, weaving descriptions of challenges and choices into accounts of the political, social and economic changes occurring in Turkey. The process of hybridisation, it is argued, took 'decades of organisational deployment, periodic hibernation and a determined and patient source of capital [from both domestic and non-national sources]' against a background of political and social volatility, increasing market liberalisation but also state intervention.

References

Luhmann, N. (2006) System as difference, *Organization*, 13, 1, 37–57.

McSweeney, B, (2006) Are we living in a post-bureaucratic epoch?, *Journal of Organizational Change Management*, 19, 1, 22–37.

Peck, J. (2000) Doing regulation, in G. L. Clark, M. P. Feldman and M. S. Gertler (eds.) *The Oxford Handbook of Economic Geography*, Oxford: Oxford University Press, 61–80.

Wittgenstein, L. (1953) *Philosophical Investigations* (trans. G. E. M. Anscombe), Oxford: Basil Blackwell.

5 The post-socialist transformation and global process: knowledge and institution building in organisational settings

Ed Clark

Introduction

The theoretical debates about the processes and tendencies of globalisation have been profoundly enriched by the research undertaken over the last seventeen years on the post-socialist transformation. Following the collapse of state socialism, there were many questions about how – and how far – these societies of central and eastern Europe (CEE)[1] would become integrated into the wider context of international capitalism, from which they were more or less isolated from the late 1940s to 1990. There was intense discussion within social science about whether it would be possible to design a path towards a form of market capitalism that would be acceptable to those who saw the events of the late 1980s as an ideological and political victory for the 'West'. As an example of large-scale societal transformation, the institutional starting point of post-socialism was so distinctive that the CEE region was presented as an 'immense social laboratory' (Whitley and Czaban, 1998: 260) for the study of change at all levels of social, economic and political organisation.

The organisational repercussions of the institutional upheaval wrought by the end of state socialism could be conceptualised and explored in terms of internal processes of socio-economic change. External, international and particularly 'Western'[2] influences were so strong and deliberate during the 1990s, however, that issues of internal societal transformation could not be credibly separated from those of global power, dominant world ideologies and international institutional fashions. In this vein, I examine the theoretical arguments and empirical findings that have emerged from research into the socio-economic transformation of the former communist countries as they throw light on the processes and consequences of globalisation. This chapter focuses in particular on the ways in which post-socialist organisation and management have been transformed over the last seventeen years, in the face of international pressures to become more like Western business.

The theoretical framework through which I explore the relationship between post-socialism and globalisation is founded on the following concepts and logic. The transformation of management and organisation is conceptualised as a process of institution building. Institutions as cultural rules and cultural accounts (Meyer, Boli and Thomas, 1994; Scott, 1994) find their expression in society through social constructions, such as events, structures, organisations, regulatory systems, procedures, artefacts and patterns of behaviour. While they are most visibly embodied in *formal* structures, systems and laws, they most directly influence social behaviour through their shaping of *informal* (institutionalised) practices (Clark and Soulsby, 1999; North, 1990). In the process of transformation, formal structures and informal practices that were deeply embedded in historical institutional systems give way to new patterns of organising and managing that are more attuned to changing circumstances. Institution-building processes are necessarily informed by flows of new ideas, values and knowledge, which over time become accepted, internalised and reproduced in action. In this conception, therefore, knowledge and knowledge processes are central to and formative of new institutional patterns of organising, which, in turn, may in varying degrees reflect the institutionalised order that prevails in the wider world.

In principle, these knowledge processes can give rise to three types of institutional outcome. 'Convergence' results when new post-socialist patterns of organisation and management are similar to globally available practices; 'diversity' occurs when they retain their local distinctiveness; and we can speak of 'hybrid' patterns of organisation when they represent some combination of global and local institutional norms. The discussion below examines the theoretical rationales underpinning each of these post-socialist patterns and considers the empirical evidence for them.

Much of the debate about the post-socialist transition has been conducted within influential economic and institutionalist frameworks, the theoretical efforts of which are directed towards constructing structural generalisations and attributing – by inference rather than observation – *generic* motives to key social actors, such as owners and managers. It is my view that these structuralist approaches do not *in themselves* adequately appreciate or explain the intricate, complex and ambiguous patterns of transformation as a globally influenced process. Indeed, I argue that it is only by examining the values, motives and actions of locally situated actors that we can truly understand the microeconomic transformation. This focus places at the centre of discussion those processes whereby new ideas, knowledge and practices are drawn into post-socialist management from different sources, including external and domestic theory and ideology.

The arguments unfold in the following way. The first section outlines the nature of the post-socialist context, identifying the major institutional and knowledge gaps that existed in 1990 at the level of organisation and management. The chapter then examines three main types of transformation argument and their theoretical origins. The second section considers how these arguments have influenced our understanding of post-socialist organisational institution building through knowledge flows and evaluates their implications for the globalisation debate. The third section matches these arguments against empirical findings from different organisational settings, looking at how different patterns of ownership relate to different transformation and globalisation outcomes. This brings the chapter to some general conclusions about the importance of seeing both transformation and globalisation from a 'bottom-up' perspective that appreciates the diversity of real patterns of institution building.

The post-socialist transformation

The decades of communist rule in the Soviet Union and CEE had led to the institutionalisation of a distinctive form of social, political and economic organisation – state socialism – though how it worked in practice was surprisingly diverse across the region. Some countries, such as Hungary from the late 1960s and Poland during the 1980s, took on more liberalised and marketised patterns, while others, notably East Germany, Bulgaria and post-1968 Czechoslovakia, developed more rigid, hard-line neo-Stalinist practices that persisted until the collapse of the regimes in 1989. Yet others developed structural idiosyncrasies that reflected the power and interests of their influential leaders – e.g. Tito's Yugoslavia, Ceauşescu's Romania and Hoxha's Albania. Despite this diversity, the state socialism of CEE was *significantly* different in terms of institutional principles and practices from the market-economic forms of capitalism that prevailed in western Europe, Japan and North America. The ideological divide between communism and capitalism had served to minimise contact between the two blocs, and to isolate the CEE region from the globalisation processes that had emerged through the international expansion of capitalism.

In the aftermath of the fall of the Berlin Wall, the ideological and institutional differences between the two blocs that had dominated global geopolitics since the Russian Revolution were transmuted into problems of societal change. That is, these differences became institutional 'gaps' that needed to be closed if the socialist countries were to 'modernise' and 'catch up' with Western societies (Habermas, 1990). The failure of the command economy was interpreted by most social scientists and business commentators as proof of the inadequacy of socialist management and organisational practices. Existing knowledge was deemed 'worthless' (Geppert and Merkens, 1999), experiences 'invalid', confidence 'lacking' (Czeglédy, 1996) and capabilities irrelevant and insufficient to bridge the institutional gaps.

Much has been written about the problems of operating within the economic constraints presented by the central planning system (Arnot, 1988; Dyker, 1981; Kornai, 1980; Lane, 1987; Wolchik, 1991). The main unit of production in the command economy was the state-owned enterprise, and its internal organisation was an institutional reflection of the centralised planning environment in which it had to operate (Clark and Soulsby, 1995; Tsoukas, 1994). It had a simple functional structure with no strategic 'brain', since the task of the SOE was to receive instructions handed down from central organs and to organise and administer production processes to meet given targets. At the start of the economic transformation in 1990 the SOE was seriously maladapted to the modern business environment, and post-socialist managers had enormous knowledge deficiencies (see table 5.1).

The typically hierarchical, bureaucratic structures and associated managerial incentive structures encouraged inertial and compliant rather than flexible and innovative behaviour (Clark and Soulsby, 1995; Kozminski, 1995). Enterprise managers did not have experience of markets and marketing, up-to-date technical know-how such as quality assurance, or sufficient understanding of proactive strategic management to deal with competitive demand conditions and dynamic task environments (Myant, 1993; Newman, 2000; Soulsby and Clark, 1996a; Wolchik, 1991). Moreover, the function of human resource management was tainted by the political monitoring activities that it had performed for the Communist Party (Koubek and Brewster, 1995; Soulsby and Clark, 1998). SOE managers developed ways of coping with the operating idiosyncrasies of a command-economic environment, constructing and utilising the networks founded on the Party, the industrial ministries, partner suppliers and partner clients; but the

Table 5.1 The institutional gap

Characteristics	State-owned enterprise	Market-economic private enterprise
Organisation		
Ownership	State property	Private property
Control	Political-administrative	Shareholder control
Goals	Externally and politically defined	Profits, market-oriented
Formal structures	Simple, functional bureaucracy	Decentralised, divisionalised
Financial control	Weak, soft budgets	Strong, hard budgets
Key functions	Production, technical	Marketing, accounting
Management		
Education	Technological, engineering	Business management
Selection	Communist Party affiliation	Competitive appointment
Key 'market' problem	Shortage of supplies	Demand constraints
Primary strategy	External bargaining with centre	Seek competitive advantage
Top management focus and style	External networking, autocratic style	Strategic, devolved style
Middle management role	Routine administration, compliance with norms	Devolved, responsible decision-makers
Key values	Social, ideological	Economic, pragmatic
Attitude to employees	Hoard as valuable resource	Intensification, cost to be controlled
Attitude to work	Low motivation, avoidance of risk and responsibility	Involved, intrapreneurial, learning

Source: Based on Clark and Soulsby (1999: 106), Child (1993) and Kozminski (1995).

management skills and practices engendered by these experiences were mostly out of kilter with the emergent market-economic conditions. The transformation of post-socialist business required managers with 'outdated' education and experience to adopt more market-oriented ideas and practices. Only when these new practices were repeated across the organisation and habitualised over time would they become part of the institutionalised stock of management knowledge – i.e. the development of cognitive, normative and regulative foundations (Scott, 1995).

The more authoritarian the communist regime was the larger the institutional gap with the market-economic system, based on the principles of decentralised structures, differentiated tasks and information-diffusing practices (Child, 1993). Closing this gap demanded that post-socialist organisations restructure to take on these institutional principles and therefore conform to the business norms of international capitalism. Since these new organising templates were not present in the societies undergoing institutional upheaval (Newman, 2000), enterprises and their managers needed to look to other sources for the relevant knowledge.

Of particular importance were the ideas and policies of neoclassical economists, who saw the 'transition' as an ideal opportunity to disseminate their ideas by proposing ways of redesigning the CEE region's macroeconomic and microeconomic systems to reflect market-capitalist rules. Their concrete influence on the CEE region was promoted through the Washington Consensus doctrines of transition (Stiglitz, 1999) and operationalised through the lending policies of transnational institutions such as the IMF, the World Bank and the EBRD (Amsden, Kochanowicz and, Taylor 1994; Pollert, 1999; Radice, 1995). The political weakness and financial straits of interim or newly elected post-socialist governments made them especially receptive to the economic medicine prescribed by the influx of Western economic advisers (Clague, 1992; Lavigne, 1995; Parker, 1993). The central microeconomic tenet of the transition doctrines was the privatisation of the huge SOEs. Many scholars and practitioners saw this as a prerequisite for reinstitutionalising business, organisation and management (Fischer, 1992), especially when accompanied by appropriate incentive schemes and forms of corporate governance (Frydman, Rapaczynski and Earle, 1993; Frydman, Gray and Rapaczynski, 1996; Frydman and Rapaczynski, 1994).

The economic transformation concerns how local organisational settings such as former SOEs have through restructuring became integrated into the wider process of globalisation. It is also about how former management practices, forged within a centrally planned environment, have been reinstitutionalised to reflect new market-economic contexts. In short, at this microeconomic level, post-socialism is the story of how organisation and management have taken on the institutional characteristics that are associated with 'normal' Western business.

Nonetheless, this dominant economic account of the post-socialist transition, strongly contested by researchers from a variety of theoretical traditions, is not the whole story. Findings from transformation research suggest that the transfer of Western management knowledge and models is by no means a simple issue. In practice, post-socialist managers have informed their new practices by drawing on a variety of knowledge resources, which result not only from the simple transfer and implementation of imported ideas. What sources they turned to, what they adopted and the degree to which new knowledge affected actual management practice have been subjects of debate and disputation. Overall, post-socialist management and organisation seem to have taken on forms that, despite the isomorphic power of global business and the ideological power of neoclassical economics, refract Western knowledge through the prism of local values and customs, developing idiosyncrasy and sustaining diversity through the emergence of hybrid forms.

The central argument of this chapter therefore addresses the processes by which managers in post-socialist organisational settings have been able to acquire, assimilate and enact knowledge that allows them to operate in the transformed circumstances of an emergent open market economy. To develop this argument, I draw on the standard distinction between 'explicit knowledge' and 'tacit knowledge' (e.g. Nonaka, 1994). Explicit knowledge refers to ideas and practices that are codified or codifiable, such that they can more or less easily be 'packaged' into 'objects' and moved between social actors in different locations, without the source and the recipient having to know each other (Czarniawska and Joerges, 1996). On the other hand, tacit knowledge is located within individuals and requires deep levels of interpersonal understanding in order for it to pass from one person or context to another. It is very difficult to formalise tacit knowledge as rules and procedures, and challenging to assemble it into a 'culture-free' portable package that could be received and interpreted elsewhere without ambiguity.

We now turn to an examination of the range of arguments that social scientists have developed in their studies of the post-socialist transformation. Each form of argument makes different assumptions about the dominant knowledge process and how this impacts on the emergence of new institutionalised practices. As a result, they have quite different implications for the transformation and global incorporation of post-socialist management and enterprise.

Theorising the transformation of organisation and management

The dominant ways of examining the transformation and internationalisation of post-socialist economies have tended to adopt a structural mode of theorising, developing generalised arguments that attribute a deterministic role to institutional and technical-economic factors. The arguments fall within three broad categories, according to how they theorise relationships between knowledge processes as a source of new management practices, the nature of the change brought about within the post-socialist organisation and the implications of these changes for more general processes of globalisation (see table 5.2). The first type of argument highlights the tendencies towards a convergence of post-socialist organisation around

Table 5.2 Post-socialist organisational change, knowledge processes and globalising implications

	Conception of post-socialist change	Dominant knowledge process	Implications for globalisation	Relevant contexts	Typical approaches
Structural convergence arguments	Teleological transition from command to market-economic structures and practices	Inward, top-down transfer of (formal) management knowledge from Western sources	Convergence around globalised Western templates of corporate and management practices	MNCs as major instrument; neo-Fordist global industries (e.g. automotive); FDI-dominated countries (e.g. Hungary); ethnocentric MNC orientation; later transition	Low context: transition economics, structural institutionalism
Structural diversity arguments	Path-dependent transformation of management and organisation with unknown destination	Recombination of historically legitimate internal (tacit) knowledge	Continuity and reinforcement of local practices sustains diversity	SOEs and privatised enterprises; traditional domestic industries (e.g. heavy engineering); economies privatised through voucher schemes; polycentric MNC orientation; early transition	High context: historical institutionalism, national-cultural theory
Hybrid structural arguments	Emergent, phased transformation as 'negotiation' between institutional actors	Accommodation (mediation, translation) of external and internal knowledge	Hybrid forms of local practices, indicating both continuing diversity and global integration	MNCs as transnational social spaces; new private business; internationalised industries with strong local features; geocentric MNC orientations; later transition	Comparative institutionalist studies of internationalisation; symbolic and discourse approaches
Hybrid actor-centred arguments	Transformation as contested and negotiated between powerful social actors in specific settings	Local and Western knowledge as politically engaged management resources	Hybrid forms of local practices, indicating both continuing diversity and global integration	All contexts	Social institutionalism and other actor-centred approaches

global Western norms; the second identifies factors that reinforce existing patterns of diversity; and the third suggests that transformation results in hybridised forms of post-socialist management and organisation. In contrast to these structural explanations, actor-centred views consider the economic transformation and its globalisation implications to be socially constructed in many micro-organisational settings. In that they examine knowledge processes and institution building across a variety of settings, their conclusions tend to support the hybridisation thesis.

Institutional transfer, economic transition and global convergence

Early studies of changes in the post-socialist economy were strongly influenced by neoclassical economics, which in turn shaped the dominant policy advice offered to the new governments (Sachs, 1989, 1992). For these economists, the economic transition was a major experiment in 'designer capitalism' (Stark, 1992), in which the failed socialist economies could be brought into the international fold by copying Western market-economic laws and institutions into the local social system. This view finds theoretical support from structural versions of neo-institutionalist theory, in which non-conforming (post-socialist) organisations are subject to isomorphic pressures to become more like those (Western) models of business that constitute the internationally legitimate template for market-economic conduct (DiMaggio and Powell, 1983; Meyer and Rowan, 1977).

In the immediate post-1989 period the superiority of Western management and the inadequacy of CEE management served as working assumptions for microeconomic policy advisers and business consultants (Child and Czeglédy, 1996; Soulsby and Clark, 1996a). Institutions were directly imported from Western business systems to provide the legal framework for private business operations and for the regularisation of the transfer of state assets to private hands. The standard approach to privatisation was modelled on methods tried and tested – albeit on a relatively minuscule scale – in the 1980s in the United Kingdom (Fischer, 1992). The implementation of the formal institutions was expected to have an almost immediate and similar impact on key actors at the level of the enterprise. For example, in line with the logic of principal–agent and transaction cost theories, the introduction of private ownership and rules of corporate governance would change the incentives for owners and managers to run enterprises so as to increase shareholder value and enforce disincentives to be 'malfeasant' or self-serving (Frydman and Rapaczynski, 1994).

Multinational corporations were naturally hailed as major and direct conduits for the transfer of market-economic knowledge and the subsequent restructuring of local organisational settings. They would introduce Western capabilities to address the weaknesses in post-socialist organisation, filling crucial knowledge gaps in subsidiaries and other ventures in which they participated (Child and Czeglédy, 1996; Lyles and Salk, 1996; Meyer and Lieb-Dóczy, 2003; Uhlenbruck and de Castro, 2000). In line with international management research, scholars expected MNCs to spread new practices in order to improve control (Gupta and Govindarajan, 1991), technology (Kedia and Bhagat, 1988; Kogut and Zander, 1993), human resource management (Beechler and Yang, 1994; Ferner and Quintanilla, 1998; Hetrick, 2002; Rosenzweig and Nohria, 1994; Sparrow, Schuler and Jackson, 1994), quality management (Dobosz and Jankowicz, 2002; Kostova and Roth, 2002), strategic management (Birkinshaw and Hood, 1998; Kostova, 1999) and innovation (Ghoshal and Bartlett, 1988; Nobel and Birkinshaw, 1998). In accepting investment from a Western corporation, formerly socialist enterprises would be restructured through the acquisition of such new practices. Moreover, with capital starvation and market-economic inexperience, technologically backward local enterprises could enter the global economic environment under the wing of experienced and well-connected MNCs.

Whether the rationale for knowledge transfer is based on making organisational practices more 'normal', 'modern', 'professional' or relevant for growth (Lang and Steger, 2002), Western economic values and business norms are portrayed as the universal aim of the transition process (Stark, 1996; Whitley, 1995). Supported by these infusions of Western knowledge, the economic transition – at macro, meso and micro levels of society – is taken to represent an inexorable movement from a command to a market-based economy.

In whatever form, this argument theorises the same set of relationships between knowledge process, institution building and globalisation outcomes. The generalised and 'inevitable' nature of the propositions, however, leaves it unclear why and how the relationships are socially realised at the level of the enterprise. By implicitly assuming the superiority of the Western knowledge, adopting a Western perspective on transformation and applying structural logic, these arguments give little or no attention to the social and economic actors who populate the transforming enterprises. Child (2000) refers to such knowledge transfer views as 'low context', because they downplay the relevance of local business practices and imply some form of universalism. Post-socialist managers are assumed to be enthusiastic to learn from, or at least uncritical imitators of, the Western 'master logics' that are presented from the outside and implemented from the top (Child and Czeglédy, 1996; Geppert and Clark, 2003; Pollert, 1999). In order for Western knowledge to be accepted, integrated into local repertoires and enacted without question, it must take an essentially explicit – and therefore fully decodable – form (Djelic and Quack, 2002; Griffith, Zeybek and O'Brien, 2001). The 'underlying teleology' of the economic transition, driven by these processes of institutional mimicry, moves the nature of business and management towards an end state defined by convergence around global market-economic norms (Stark, 1996).

Knowledge recombination, path-dependent transformation and continuing diversity

Alternative ways of theorising the role of knowledge processes in the post-socialist transformation emerged from the critical evaluation of convergent theories of economic transition. Representing a largely neo-institutionalist research tradition, scholars have emphasised the idiosyncrasies of CEE institutional systems and identified indigenous tendencies to resist the simple importation of foreign knowledge while reproducing historically accepted ways of managing and organising. In contrast to convergence theorists' predilection to evaluate post-socialism from a Western perspective, neo-institutionalists have focused on CEE management and organisation as a set of historically located practices. With its legitimacy firmly rooted in state socialist experience and operation, CEE business cannot be understood – or changed – without examining how knowledge processes are affected by their contexts of use (Soulsby and Clark, 1998). It is argued that, when faced with the high levels of uncertainty and ambiguity that characterise 'institutional upheaval' (Newman, 2000) and render modern business rationality problematic, post-socialist management has naturally fallen back on its well-understood 'taken for granted' knowledge repertoires, as inscribed in the national institutional setting (Whitley, 2001).

From a Western economic perspective, these legacies may seem to be an irrational and outdated brake on changes imposed rationally from the outside. From an internal CEE perspective, however, they serve as cultural resources on which management can draw to make sense of the complex and shifting realities (Weik, 2001). David Stark's (1992, 1996) analysis of Hungarian enterprises demonstrates the rationality of recombining familiar practices and contextualised knowledge in the transient circumstances of the early transition period, with its complex blending of institutional (market-economic) discontinuities and (command-economic) continuities.

The 'rubble of 45 years of communist rule', of which Sachs (1992: 3) writes so negatively, thus provides for Stark (1996: 994) the raw materials of reconstruction. Evidence from research in other post-socialist economies – for example, Gerald McDermott (1997) in the Czech Republic and Christian von Hirschhausen (1995) in eastern Germany – echoes the conclusion that organisational possibilities in transforming societies are *necessarily* given shape by decisions and structures that have been institutionalised in inherited practices. Richard Whitley and Laszlo Czaban (1998) show that it is not only the restructuring of Hungarian former SOEs that is constrained by inherited custom and practices but also the conduct of foreign-owned and -controlled firms.

In contrast to convergence arguments, these findings suggest that the process and outcomes of economic transformation do not result from the unproblematic acquisition and enactment of Western knowledge, defining a linear route towards a Western-style market economy. Rather, indigenously legitimate ideas and values can be recombined innovatively and former practices and structures revisited in ways that make the transformation historically path-dependent and nationally distinctive. In that there are many useful recombinations of local knowledge, the transformation unfolds without a known destination, though its direction is affected by its provenance.

This high-context argument (Child, 2000) recognises the importance of national, regional and local features in explaining the movement and acquisition of ideas. The nature of the economic transformation is affected by the inertial effects of historical legacies and existing management practices, the application of which, in times of institutional upheaval, lead to more rational responses than their pure market-economic counterparts (Clark and Soulsby, 1999; Peng, 2003; Soulsby and Clark, 1996b). Since all knowledge is intrinsic to the context in which it is socially embedded, moving it between business systems is difficult in principle (Czarniawska and Joerges, 1996). This problem is exacerbated because of the hostility or resistance shown to the acquisition and integration of ideas originating from alien institutional and cultural contexts (see below). It is not enough for Western management ideas to be defined in formal and explicit packages, because the essence of management is tacit and highly contextualised.

The danger in this type of argument is that, in challenging ideological notions of global convergence, it becomes drawn towards a similar, if historically, deterministic polarised position. By highlighting the power of internal institutional forces to ward off external globalising influence, the insistence on diversity can leave little space for the social construction of future processes (Pollert, 1999).

Translation, accommodative transformation and hybridisation

Arguments about the early post-socialist transformation broadly passed through two phases. The early dominance of the transition-economic view, represented in the Washington Consensus, with its 'optimistic' assumptions about institutional change, gradually gave way to theoretical critiques emphasising the importance of path-dependent factors. If the power of the transition-economic viewpoint reflected the confidence of Western capitalist values following the fall of the Berlin Wall, the success of the institutionalist critique was based partly on convincing and consistent findings from organisation- and industry-level research. The latter showed that, in the early 1990s, managers and owners were not responding as predicted to formal institutional changes by altering their behaviour and their enterprises into Western-type patterns (Clark and Soulsby, 1995; McDermott, 1997; Stark, 1996; Whitley and Czaban, 1998). There was a simultaneous recognition, even among those responsible for administering the transition-economic medicine, that the Western prescriptions were based on 'excessively simplistic textbook models of the market economy', which presented 'misunderstandings' of how 'modern capitalism' actually worked in advanced economies (Stiglitz, 1999: 4).

In this theoretical context, there emerged a further set of arguments about the integration of post-socialism into the global economy. These can broadly be understood as a reconciliation of the 'hyperglobalist' view of homogenisation and convergence and 'global sceptic' arguments about contextualisation and diversity (Morgan, 2001b). This 'third way' seems, on the one hand, to be a pragmatic response to the impossibility of sustaining the level of generalisation about global trends while, on the other hand, reflecting empirical findings, which rarely supported 'pure' conformity to either global or local norms. Indeed, case study research has tended to discover complex and diverse patterns of management and organisational change, indicating, for example, that even individual organisations in the same industrial and national contexts may take very different routes to transformation. The outcome, in terms of the globalisation debate, has been to highlight the emergence of empirical transformation patterns that in different ways combine features of both Western and local practices.

This hybridisation argument has been reinforced in three theorising themes that have become influential in transformation research. First, there is increasing support for the view that economic transitions pass through multiple phases. There is some level of agreement that inertial historical forces prevail in the early phase because they play a crucial role in coping with the ambiguities of institutional transience (Clark and Soulsby, 1999; Newman, 2000; see above). Thus, the continued power of *nomenklatura*[3] managers in all spheres of economic activity reflected both the poverty of relevant experience outside this fading management class and their ability to use influence and connections to acquire capital, start small businesses and pull off commercial sales (Clark, 2000; Clark and Soulsby, 1996). Former communist directors of state exporting agencies, for example, walked into important marketing directorships within privatised enterprises because they were virtually the only people in the command economy to have had direct experience of working with Western customers in developed market economies. Later on, however, as the newly installed formal institutions began to take root in the economic system and as market exchange became the normal way of transacting, organisations and management systems increasingly responded to the isomorphic pressures to become more Western (Peng, 2003). By this stage, though, important historical practices had become socially re-embedded, and, to the extent that they were perceived to be legitimate and/or useful, they blended with market-economic norms to create hybrid management patterns.

The hybridisation argument finds further theoretical support from discourse or narrative theories, which present organisational change as 'a story of ideas turning into actions in ever new localities' (Czarniawska and Joerges, 1996: 13). This approach recognises the knowledge and institutional gap between post-socialist enterprises and their Western counterparts, and examines how ideas such as marketing, human resource and quality management are unpacked from their original cultural context and transported to their destination (Dobosz and Jankowicz, 2002; Hetrick, 2002). MNCs are seen most often as the vehicles for the 'travel of ideas', but they can equally move via third parties, such as management consultants, policy advisers and management educators. Central to this analysis is the view that management knowledge is deeply impregnated with tacit and context-specific aspects that lose their precise meaning once 'disembedded' or uprooted from their origins in Western practice, and therefore, instead of being mechanistically transferred or diffused, are 'translated'. As a consequence, the 'content' of an idea drifts as it travels across borders, since its original meaning is subtly affected through processes of acquisition, re-embedding and regularisation in the new location.

Third, recent developments in the national business systems approach to comparative institutional research have offered novel ways of conceptualising the complexities of internationalisation processes (Morgan, Kristensen and Whitley, 2001). In 'transnational social spaces' constituted by MNCs, in which actors of different nationalities meet and in which divergent logics of action coexist, there are crucial empirical questions about how cultural and ideological differences are resolved within the framework of management power and politics (Morgan, 2001a; Kristensen and Zeitlin, 2001). Despite the hegemonic tendencies and structural asymmetries immanent in post-socialist settings involving foreign MNCs, the need to act 'collaboratively' creates organisational practices as much through conflict and contestation as consensus and mimicry (Geppert and Clark, 2003). From this perspective, the political process of reconciling the priorities and values of Western MNCs and CEE post-socialist logic leads inevitably to the construction of new hybrid forms of local institution, thereby enriching the diversity of internationalisation outcomes.

These arguments describe hybridisation as an inevitable structural process with structural causes, and many case studies of post-socialist organisation have been interpreted as support for this thesis. There has been another micro-sociological tradition, however, which theorises the transformation as a process of institution building, resulting from the political and sense-making activities of social actors striving to resolve their everyday organisational dilemmas. This 'bottom-up' argument has been present in versions of institutionalism that are sensitive to the transformation as social construction (Clark and Soulsby, 1999; Geppert and Clark, 2003). It has the potential to increase our understanding of how internationalisation is shaped by political processes of conflict, contestation and negotiation, the conception at the heart of MNCs as transnational social spaces (Morgan, Kristensen and Whitley, 2001).

A bottom-up approach to institution building places motivated social actors at the centre of processual explanations of post-socialist transformation, providing an alternative to structuralist generalisation about causation. Post-socialism and its globalising consequences are therefore the product of social actors seeking to make sense of organisational settings characterised by institutional ambiguity and business uncertainty, and thereby making decisions about how to restructure and change. To manage their organisations through transforming circumstances, enterprise managers draw on whatever means are available, including power, knowledge (from whatever source) and other cultural, social and material resources. Since managers vary in their backgrounds and social capital and since organisational settings differ in their objective and perceived features, organisational transformation is likely to be a highly variable process, rather than some generalised or predetermined pattern of institutional mimicry or habit.

This argument holds so long as there is sufficient strategic space for managers to be able to express their values and objectives in making their decisions (Child, 1997; Clark, 2004). From this bottom-up perspective, the research problem is to study patterns of institution building within their complex organisational settings and to develop explanations that expose the internal situational logic of how and why social actors have taken particular decisions about change. Instead of generalising from macro-organisational data to the transformation in micro-organisational situations, explanation is constructed in the opposite way. From the range of institutionalising processes observed within specific post-socialist organisational settings, it is possible to construct an aggregate, if messy, picture of what is happening. Case study research into processes of transformation in organisational settings reveals a variety of pathways, most of which suggest that hybridisation is the norm and that convergence around global business norms is an unlikely outcome of post-socialism.

The remainder of the chapter examines in greater detail the logic and relevance of the hybridisation argument that results from this micro-sociological attention to social process and human agency. In the conclusion, I return to the central relationships between knowledge processes, transformation as institution building and the globalisation debate.

Institution building in different organisational settings

The three generic arguments present different expectations about the shape and direction of the transformation that results from knowledge and institution-building processes within post-socialist organisations. A priori, each of these arguments may logically be expected to hold in different organisational, industrial and country contexts (see table 5.2).

We might expect structural convergence through knowledge transfer and institutional imitation to occur more often in those enterprises (e.g. acquisitions), industrial sectors (e.g. those characterised by rationalised neo-Fordist operations) and countries (e.g. Hungary) that have been associated with foreign direct investment. Convergence will be increased to the extent that an MNC is 'ethnocentric' in its orientation (Perlmutter, 1969) and 'globalised' in its control structure (Bartlett and Ghoshal, 1989). Structural diversity arguments that emphasise path-dependent institution building and knowledge recombination might have more empirical likelihood in enterprises with a socialist history (e.g. state-owned and domestically privatised), traditional and staple domestic industries (e.g. heavy engineering) and those countries that have tackled their transformation largely using indigenous means (e.g. many former Soviet states). Structural hybridisation arguments, finally, are characterised by 'negotiated' institutions and forms of knowledge sharing. These might be empirically linked to newly founded businesses with entrepreneurial values, industries in which foreign owners are dependent on local managers for tacit management knowledge (e.g. localised customer tastes or specialised local networks) and countries with acclaimed research and innovation capabilities. They may also be typically expected when MNCs have 'geocentric' mentalities, operate through 'transnational' structures and diffuse 'diversified quality production' technologies (Bartlett and Ghoshal, 1989; Ferner and Quintanilla, 1998; Geppert, 2003; Perlmutter, 1969).

Cutting through the complexity of explaining the patterns of post-socialist transformation, scholars have tended to alight on the organisation's ownership pattern as the most important contingent factor affecting institution building – reflecting the central role attributed to the privatisation process. Mike Peng (2003) argues that foreign-owned firms, domestic firms and entrepreneurial start-ups are likely to make different strategic responses to the same transforming business environment because they experience its pressures differently. Similarly, Whitley and Czaban (1998) expect ownership patterns to have an important influence on the ways in which enterprises change (i.e. become more market-oriented and efficient) and the degree to which deep restructuring programmes are implemented. Most case study research that has examined how organisational transformation has taken place, however, has found that the reality of restructuring processes is far more varied than would be expected from theoretical predictions.

Foreign-influenced firms

Transformation scholars had high expectations of the influence of MNCs on microeconomic change and the internationalisation processes. Whether investing in the acquisition of SOEs as subsidiaries, building greenfield facilities or establishing joint ventures or strategic alliances, MNCs were proposed as a prerequisite for the effective and rapid transformation – 'deep restructuring' – of post-socialist organisation and the development of local management expertise and practices (Carlin and Aghion, 1996; Thomas,

1992). FDI-influenced enterprises were expected to be more likely to break from the past, take on Western knowledge and practices, restructure in line with Western business norms and adopt an identity that was recognisably convergent with globally institutionalised templates (Newman, 2000).

Intensive research into knowledge flows and organisational learning within MNC-influenced organisational settings underlines their potentially political and contested nature, however. Post-socialist managers have sometimes claimed that 'rational' Western values and practices, such as tight financial control and downsizing, clash with local traditions, such as the value of labour and the duty of employee care (Brouthers and Bamossy, 1997; Clark and Soulsby, 1998). Their introduction has been judged to be assertions of Western power or unwelcome forms of colonialism (Simon and Davies, 1996) or paternalism (Markóczy, 1993; Villinger, 1996). When Western ideas are seen as intrusive (Child and Czeglédy, 1996) and culturally coercive (Czeglédy, 1996), post-socialist managers may attempt to assert their autonomy as an expression of national pride in the face of the 'arrogance' of Western knowledge (Markóczy, 1993; Simon and Davies, 1996). They may distort or withhold information, or be generally hostile to knowledge that originates from foreign sources (Michailova and Husted, 2003). In these circumstances, managers may rely on their former practices and recombine them to suit changing circumstances (Jankowicz, 2001). Post-socialist responses might take more subtle or unintentional forms, such as 'unwilling implementation' (Child and Markóczy, 1993) or linguistic misinterpretation (Simon and Davies, 1996; Spicer, 1997; Villinger, 1996).

Once we concede that transnational settings are politicised social spaces in which institutions are constructed through the interaction of actors subscribing to different value systems, structural predictions become less robust (Geppert and Clark, 2003). In practice, MNCs do not always effect Westernised changes in management conduct and enterprise structures (Pollert, 1999), and may even bow in significant ways to local practices (Whitley and Czaban, 1998). Detailed studies of the transformational potential and the internationalising consequences of FDI injections into post-socialist organisations demonstrate that these processes are more complex and less predictable than have been projected by researchers working within structuralist traditions.

State-owned and privatised enterprises

There are strong and consistent expectations that state-owned and privatised firms are particularly prone to institutional inertia (Peng, 2003). Their historical and social embeddedness is likely to create path dependence tendencies, a preference for recombinant knowledge, a sense of national and organisational identity and resultant resistance or hostility to transfers of Western ideas. These characteristics, it is argued, lead to a greater likelihood of inadequate adaptation to emergent market conditions (cf. Newman, 2000).

Nevertheless, when Anna Soulsby and I examined the restructuring of a number of privatised Czech enterprises without FDI and subject to the same kinds of institutional pressures, we found varied management responses and internal change processes with different trajectories. From many examples that I could offer, consider the decentralisation of organisational structures, a classic symbol of the Westernisation of post-socialist enterprises. Using real-time and retrospective data from a longitudinal study, among the mechanical engineering enterprises there were clearly very different management practices at work, leading to diverse transformation processes. The managers in each of three enterprises were aware of, even rehearsed, the Westernised rhetoric of profit centres, divisionalisation and holding companies, yet their professional values and personal motives led to divergent strategic decisions. One management team decided on a path of radical Westernisation, leading to mass lay-offs and a rapid decentralisation of structures, while another consciously advocated protection of its work force and incremental change (Clark and Soulsby, 1998, 1999).

It appears that, so long as the business environment allows sufficient space for the exercise of managerial discretion (Hambrick and Finkelstein, 1987; Child, 1997), post-socialist managers of former SOEs were able to exercise strategic choice in restructuring of their enterprises (Clark, 2004). As with foreign-influenced organisations, research seeking explanation from *within* the organisational process indicates that the transformation of domestic enterprises can be both complex and diverse.

New private business

Among economic and institutional scholars, it was conventional wisdom to argue that path-dependent effects would limit the role of SOEs and privatised enterprises in advancing the transformation. As a result, special significance has been attributed to the founding of totally new private firms, the management of which would be untainted by the past and more likely to be influenced by standards associated with the Western ideal of entrepreneurial risk-taking and profit-driven motives (Benáček, 1997; Kornai, 1990; Ners, 1994).

Social scientists envisaged small firms being founded either by former black economy 'operators' able to legitimise their pre-1990 activities (Łos, 1994) or through the entrepreneurial spirit unleashed by the rise of new market opportunities (McDermott and Mejstřik, 1992). While most post-socialist economies did experience a huge increase in individuals registering new firms (Frydman, Rapaczynski and Earle, 1993; Bohatá, 1996), the vast majority of these remained on paper only. In my research within a Czech industrial town that had been dominated by four large SOEs, local respondents identified five small businesses as being especially successful in 1996–7. Field research revealed that they were all run by a third type of business founder – the *nomenklatura* entrepreneur (Clark, 2000; see also Róna-Tas, 1994, and Sik, 1994). When interviewed, with only one exception, each founder sought to conceal his (they were all men) Communist Party background, which was, in fact, critical in understanding how the firm was financed, founded and expanded. The scope of their pre-1990 social networks and of their social capital allowed these founders to gain access to material, financial and information resources, as well as connecting them to senior managers (former Communist Party colleagues) in the local privatised enterprises.

These findings might at first appear incidental, but they are important for two reasons. First, secondary sources and self-reporting questionnaire methods, which are the empirical foundation of structuralist theorising, would be very unlikely to pick up the true extent of this pattern of ownership and founding. Second, these fieldwork studies demonstrate clearly that there are multiple patterns of business foundation in transforming economies and that these may have very different implications for emerging management practices within this sector. Since *nomenklatura* founders have different values and motives and are integrated in distinctive social structures, they depart in significant ways from the Western entrepreneurial ideal or the converted black economy operator (see Łos, 1994).

No one was in a better position than former state socialist managers to exploit the institutional ambiguities of early post-socialism and work on its ill-defined and poorly understood margins of legality and illegality. The rise of the powerful oil and gas tycoons in Russia is the well-publicised face of this phenomenon, but, on a smaller and more discreet scale, many well-connected former *nomenklatura* managers have recycled themselves into important ownership positions in the business community. We might draw two important inferences. First, patterns of management in this organisational setting are likely to be more diverse that initially predicted. Second, they are more likely than initially expected to be embedded in the local context and less likely to echo the Western institutions of private business.

Conclusions

In this chapter I have examined the transformation of post-socialist management and organisation and considered its implications for debates about globalisation. In contextualising the post-socialist transformation, I outlined the state socialist heritage and identified the institutional gaps that had to be filled with flows of knowledge before the former communist countries could be integrated into the wider community of capitalist nations. Theoretically, the argument has focused on the ways in which the microeconomic transformation has been influenced by knowledge processes and their impact on institution building within different kinds of organisational setting. In particular, the chapter has identified three basic forms of argument that connect knowledge flows and institution building within organisations to transformation as a process of integration into the global economy.

First, I have referred to convergence arguments based around notions of Western knowledge transfer and institutional mimicry, leading to generalised expectations that post-socialist management and organisation would be transformed around global business norms. Second, I have outlined diversity arguments that emphasise internal recombinant knowledge processes and path-dependent institution building, which presage continuing differences in the ways that organisations are managed in CEE countries. The third type of argument acts as a compromise between the first two, pointing to the hybridisation of post-socialist management and organisation. In this case, mediation or translation processes lead to knowledge accommodation and negotiated institutions, sustaining degrees of diversity of management patterns, but indicating also some reconciliation with global norms.

The dominant structural arguments about transformation have tended to underplay the degree of diversity that exists within the post-socialism transformation. Micro-sociological approaches such as social institutionalism, however, offer alternative ways of exploring knowledge processes, institution building and the process of transformation *from below*. In examining how this approach has helped to flesh out our knowledge of management patterns within foreign-influenced, domestic and small business organisational settings, I have demonstrated the importance of knowing the values and motives of key players such as the managers themselves. Bottom-up studies suggest that Western knowledge imported directly into post-socialist transnational sites is unlikely to be accepted passively and without some contestation, mediation or translation. Further, it is difficult to generalise about path dependence in state-owned and privatised enterprises, because their managers' political agendas can promote both inherited priorities and Western institutional practices. New private firms in post-socialist contexts are also a conundrum that can be figured out only with close-up knowledge of ownership and management. They may well support institution building in ways that are unknown in stable market economies.

My arguments from transformation research into post-socialist organisation and management highlight the weaknesses in both the simple convergence and the simple diversity positions. The limits to global convergence are empirically defined, lying in the sheer range of management practices unearthed by post-socialist organisation studies. The institutions built within organisations vary from country to country, industry to industry, ownership type to ownership type, within ownership types and between organisations that are in the same country, in the same industry and owned in the same way. If our theories of organisational transformation can be improved by conceptualising it as a social construction, research requires some real attention to the values and motives of the key decision-makers and how they seek to realise them within the institutional and economic conditions of the business environment.

The limits to the diversity argument are defined by the severity of the constraints imposed by the business environment. Economic and institutional constraints can make it difficult for senior managers to exercise discretion and express their values and priorities in their decisions over the long haul. When the product or capital markets are financially tight, for instance, managers can pursue their own ambitions only so far. The managers of a privatised enterprise may have to contain the expression of their values (e.g. protecting employment) within the boundaries set by the institutionalised demands of just-in-time (JIT) practices from Japanese clients. Nonetheless, it should also be recognised – and of this I have first-hand research experience – that strategic managers can often insist on making the 'wrong' choices over many years, so that the limits to diversity may be postponed for some time (cf. Clark, 2004).

To conclude, the post-socialist microeconomic transformation comprises social processes that are constructed through the motivated interactions of key social actors with the power to realise their preferences within an institutional context characterised by inertia, ambiguity and change. How the transformation unfolds and the degree of globalisation that ensues depend on how these social actors enact this business environment, and this in part reflects how they use local and Western knowledge to inform their management practices. Given the reality of institutional diversity and the limits to management discretion, the transformation process is most likely to result in further socio-economic variations on the theme of market capitalism. Organisation and management norms will continue to evolve into increasingly stable yet hybrid forms that reference both their historical legacies and the dominant business systems of the era.

Notes

Many people over many years have influenced the arguments in this chapter. My fieldwork would not have been possible without the support and assistance of lots of colleagues – too many to mention – at the Technical University (VUT) of Brno in the Czech Republic. My ideas have been routinely aired and critically reviewed over the last ten years at dedicated sessions of the European Group for Organization Studies (EGOS) colloquia, and I am grateful to fellow transformation researchers from Europe and beyond. Some key arguments in this chapter about political and knowledge processes within transnational settings reflect my ongoing discussions with Mike Geppert (University of Surrey), to whom I am indebted. Most of all, however, the themes and thesis of this chapter are the product of an enduring research partnership with Anna Soulsby from Nottingham University Business School; although unnamed up-front, her imperceptible contributions make her a virtual co-author.

1. By CEE, I mean those communist countries of Europe that were outside the Soviet Union. In developing the arguments that follow, I refer mostly to these CEE countries, drawing occasionally on research in Russia and the former Soviet republics where relevant.

2. Given the limitations of space, I follow, with apologies for resultant imprecision, the rather loose convention of using the term 'Western' to describe countries with advanced market economies, thereby failing to discriminate between the institutional varieties of 'capitalism' (Hall and Soskice, 2001; Maurice and Sorge, 2000; Whitley, 1999). The debate about the direction of the post-socialist transition has often concerned the specific role of Anglo-American economic ideology and institutions (see sections 1 and 2) in relation to those of neighbouring European countries, such as Germany. In making general theoretical remarks, however, I would not want to exclude the substantial influence of, for example, Japanese ideas and practices.

3. The *nomenklatura* (or cadre) system identified those positions of authority that, according to the central Communist Party, required incumbents who were 'trustworthy'. Many senior managers appointed before 1990 had therefore been screened, and most had shown themselves to be reliable members of the Party.

References

Amsden, A. H., J. Kochanowicz and L. Taylor (1994) *The Market Meets Its Match: Restructuring the Economies of Eastern Europe*, Cambridge, MA: Harvard University Press.

Arnot, B. (1988) *Controlling Soviet Labour: Experimental Change from Brezhnev to Gorbachev*, London: Macmillan.

Bartlett, C. A., and S. Ghoshal (1989) *Managing across Borders: The Transnational Solution*, Boston: Harvard Business School Press.

Beechler, S., and J. Z. Yang (1994) The transfer of Japanese-style management to American subsidiaries: contingencies, constraints, and competencies, *Journal of International Business Studies*, 25, 3, 467–91.

Benáček, V. (1997) Private entrepreneurship and small businesses in the transformation of the Czech Republic, in G. Grabher and D. Stark (eds.) *Restructuring Networks in Post-socialism: Legacies, Linkages and Localities*, Oxford: Oxford University Press, 209–42.

Birkinshaw, J. M., and N. Hood (1998) Multinational subsidiary evolution: capability and charter change in foreign-owned subsidiary companies, *Academy of Management Review*, 23, 4, 773–95.

Bohatá, M. (1996) *Small and Medium-sized Enterprises in the Czech Manufacturing Industry*, Working Paper no. 94, Prague, CERGE-EI.

Brouthers, K. D., and G. J. Bamossy (1997) The role of key stakeholders in international joint venture negotiations: case studies from eastern Europe, *Journal of International Business Studies*, 28, 285–308.

Carlin, W., and P. Aghion (1996) Restructuring outcomes and the evolution of ownership patterns in central and eastern Europe, *Economics of Transition*, 4, 2, 371–88.

Child, J. (1993) Society and enterprise between hierarchy and market, in J. Child, M. Crozier and R. Mayntz (eds.) *Societal Change between Market and Organization*, Aldershot: Avebury, 203–26.

  (1997) Strategic choice in the analysis of action, structure, organizations and environment: retrospect and prospect, *Organization Studies*, 18, 1, 43–76.

  (2000) Theorizing about organizations cross-nationally, in J. L. C. Cheng and R. B. Peterson (eds.) *Advances in International Comparative Management*, vol. XIII, Stamford, CT: JAI Press, 27–75.

Child, J., and A. Czeglédy (1996) Managerial learning in the transformation of Eastern Europe: some key issues, *Organization Studies*, 17, 2, 167–80.

Child, J., and L. Markóczy (1993) Host-country managerial behaviour and learning in Chinese and Hungarian joint ventures, *Journal of Management Studies*, 30, 4, 611–31.

Clague, C. (1992) Introduction: the journey to the market economy, in C. Clague and G. C. Rausser (eds.) *The Emergence of Market Economies in Eastern Europe*, Oxford: Basil Blackwell, 1–22.

Clark, E. (2000) The role of social capital in developing Czech private business, *Work, Employment and Society*, 14, 3, 439–58.

  (2004) Power, action and constraint in strategic management: explaining enterprise restructuring in the Czech Republic, *Organization Studies*, 24, 4, 607–27.

Clark, E., and A. Soulsby (1995) Transforming former state enterprises in the Czech Republic, *Organization Studies*, 16, 2, 215–42.

  (1996) The re-formation of the managerial elite in the Czech Republic, *Europe–Asia Studies*, 48, 2, 285–303.

  (1998) Organization–community embeddedness: the social impact of enterprise restructuring in the post-communist Czech Republic, *Human Relations*, 51, 1, 25–50.

(1999) *Organizational Change in Post-communist Europe: Management and Transformation in the Czech Republic*, London: Routledge.

Czarniawska, B., and B. Joerges (1996) Travel of ideas, in B. Czarniawska and G. Sevón (eds.) *Translating Organizational Change*, Berlin: de Gruyter, 13–50.

Czeglédy, A. (1996) New directions for organizational learning in Eastern Europe, *Organization Studies*, 17, 2, 327–41.

DiMaggio, P. J., and W. W. Powell (1983) The iron cage revisited: institutional isomorphism and collective rationality in organizational fields, *American Sociological Review*, 48, 147–60.

Djelic, M.-L., and S. Quack (2002) From national configuration to transnational recombination, paper presented at the 18th European Group for Organization Studies colloquium, Barcelona, 4–6 July.

Dobosz, D., and A. D. Jankowicz (2002) Knowledge transfer of the Western concept of quality, *Human Resource Development International*, 5, 3, 353–67.

Dyker, D. (1981) Planning and the worker, in L. Shapiro and J. Godson (eds.) *The Soviet Worker: Illusions and Realities*, London: Macmillan, 39–75.

Ferner, A., and J. Quintanilla (1998) Multinationals, national business systems and HRM: the enduring influence of national identity or a process of 'Anglo-Saxonization', *International Journal of Human Resource Management*, 9, 4, 710–30.

Fischer, S. (1992) Privatization in East European transformation, in C. Clague and G. C. Rausser (eds.) *The Emergence of Market Economies in Eastern Europe*, Oxford: Basil Blackwell, 227–43.

Frydman, R., C. W. Gray and A. Rapaczynski (1996) *Corporate Governance in Central Europe and Russia*, Budapest: Central European Press.

Frydman, R., and A. Rapaczynski (1994) *Privatization in Eastern Europe: Is the State Withering Away?*, London: Central European University Press.

Frydman, R., A. Rapaczynski and J. Earle (1993) *The Privatization Process in Central Europe*, Budapest: Central European Press.

Geppert, M. (2003) Sensemaking and politics in MNCs: a comparative analysis of vocabularies within the global manufacturing discourse in one industrial sector, *Journal of Management Inquiry*, 12, 4, 312–29.

Geppert, M., and E. Clark (2003) Knowledge and learning in transnational ventures: an actor-centred approach, *Management Decision*, 41, 5, 433–42.

Geppert, M., and H. Merkens (1999) Learning from one's own experience: continuation and organizational change in two East German firms, *Human Resource Development International*, 2, 1, 25–40.

Ghoshal, S., and C. A. Bartlett (1988) Creation, adoption, and diffusion of innovations by subsidiaries of multinational corporations, *Journal of International Business Studies*, 19, 365–88.

Griffith, D., A. Y. Zeybek and M. O'Brien (2001) Knowledge transfer as a means for relationship development: a Kazakhstan–foreign international joint venture illustration, *Journal of International Marketing*, 9, 1, 1–18.

Gupta, A. K., and V. Govindarajan (1991) Knowledge flows and the structure of control within multinational corporations, *Academy of Management Review*, 16, 4, 768–92.

Habermas, J. (1990) *Die nachholende Revolution*, Frankfurt: Suhrkamp.

Hall, P. A., and D. Soskice (eds.) (2001) *Varieties of Capitalism: The Institutional Foundations of Comparative Advantage*, Oxford: Oxford University Press.

Hambrick, D. C., and S. Finkelstein (1987) Managerial discretion: a bridge between polar views of organizational outcomes, in L. L. Cummings and B. M. Staw (eds.) *Research in Organizational Behavior*, vol. IX, Greenwich, CT: JAI Press, 369–406.

Hetrick, S. (2002) Transferring HR ideas and practices: globalization and convergence in Poland, *Human Resource Development International*, 5, 3, 333–51.

Jankowicz, A. D. (2001) Limits to knowledge transfer: what they already know in the post-command economies, *Journal of East–West Business*, 7, 37–59.

Kedia, B. L., and R. S. Bhagat (1988) Cultural constraints on transfer of technology across nations: implications for research in international and comparative management, *Academy of Management Review*, 13, 4, 559–71.

Kogut, B., and U. Zander (1993) Knowledge of the firm and the evolutionary theory of the multinational corporation, *Journal of International Business Studies*, 24, 625–45.

Kornai, J. (1980) *Economics of Shortage* (2 vols.), Amsterdam: North Holland.

   (1990) *The Road to a Free Economy: Shifting from a Socialist System, the Example of Hungary*, New York: Norton.

Kostova, T. (1999) Transnational transfer of strategic organizational practices: a contextual perspective, *Academy of Management Review*, 24, 2, 308–24.

Kostova, T., and K. Roth (2002) Adoption of an organizational practice by subsidiaries of multinational corporations: institutional and relational effects, *Academy of Management Journal*, 45, 1, 215–33.

Koubek, J., and C. Brewster (1995) Human resource management in turbulent times: HRM in the Czech Republic, *International Journal of Human Resource Management*, 6, 2, 223–47.

Kozminski, A. K. (1995) From communist nomenklatura to transformational leadership: the role of management in the post-communist enterprises, in B. Grancelli (ed.) *Social Change and Modernization*, Berlin: de Gruyter, 83–105.

Kristensen, P. H. and J. Zeitlin (2001) The making of a global firm: local pathways to multi-national enterprise, in G. Morgan, P. M. Kristensen and R. Whitley (eds.) *The Multinational Firm: Organizing across Institutional and National Divides*, Oxford: Oxford University Press, 172–95.

Lane, D. (1987) *Soviet Labour and the Ethic of Communism: Full Employment and the Labour Process in the USSR*, Brighton: Wheatsheaf Books.

Lang, R., and T. Steger (2002) The odyssey of management knowledge to transforming societies: a critical review of a theoretical alternative, *Human Resource Development International*, 5, 3, 279–94.

Lavigne, M. (1995) *The Economics of Transition: From Socialist Economy to Market Economy*, Basingstoke: Macmillan.

Łos, M. (1994) From underground to legitimacy: the normative dilemmas of post-communist marketization, in B. Dallago, G. Ajani and B. Grancelli (eds.) *Privatization and Entrepreneurship in Post-socialist Countries: Economy, Law and Society*, Basingstoke: Macmillan, 111–42.

Lyles, M. A., and J. E. Salk (1996) Knowledge acquisition from foreign parents in international joint ventures: an empirical examination in the Hungarian context, *Journal of International Business Studies*, 27, 877–903.

McDermott, G. A. (1997) Renegotiating the ties that bind: the limits of privatization in the Czech Republic, in G. Grabher and D. Stark (eds.) *Restructuring Networks in Post-socialism: Legacies, Linkages and Localities*, Oxford: Oxford University Press, 70–106.

McDermott. G. A., and M. Mejstřik (1992) The role of small firms in the industrial development and transformation of Czechoslovakia, *Small Business Economics*, 4, 179–200.

Markóczy, L. (1993) Managerial and organizational learning in Hungarian–Western mixed management organizations, *International Journal of Human Resource Management*, 4, 2, 277–304.

Maurice, M., and A. Sorge (2000) *Embedding Organizations: Societal Analysis of Actors, Organizations and Socio-economic Context*, Amsterdam: John Benjamin's.

Meyer, J. W., J. Boli and J. Thomas (1994) Ontology and rationalization in the Western cultural account, in W. R. Scott and J. W. Meyer (eds.) *Institutional Environments and Organizations: Structural Complexity and Individualism*, London: Sage, 9–27.

Meyer, J. W., and B. Rowan (1977) Institutionalized organizations: formal structures as myth and ceremony, *American Journal of Sociology*, 83, 340–63.

Meyer, K. E., and E. Lieb-Dóczy (2003) Post-acquisition restructuring as evolutionary process, *Journal of Management Studies*, 40, 2, 459–82.

Michailova, S., and K. Husted (2003) Knowledge sharing hostility in Russian firms, *California Management Review*, 45, 59–77.

Morgan, G. (2001a) The multinational firm, in G. Morgan, P. M. Kristensen and R. Whitley (eds.) *The Multinational Firm: Organizing across Institutional and National Divides*, Oxford: Oxford University Press, 1–24.

(2001b) Transnational communities and business systems, *Global Networks*, 1, 2, 113–30.

Morgan, G., P. H. Kristensen and R. Whitley (eds.) (2001) *The Multinational Firm: Organizing across Institutional and National Divides* Oxford: Oxford University Press.

Myant, M. (1993) *Transforming Socialist Economies: The Case of Poland and Czechoslovakia*, Aldershot: Edward Elgar.

Ners, K. (1994) Privatisation (from above, below, or mass privatisation) versus generic private enterprise building, *Communist Economies and Economic Transformation*, 7, 1, 105–16.

Newman, K. (2000) Organizational transformation during institutional upheaval, *Academy of Management Review*, 25, 3, 602–19.

Nobel, R., and J. M. Birkinshaw (1998) Innovation in multinational corporations: control and communication patterns in international R&D operations, *Strategic Management Journal*, 19, 479–96.

Nonaka, I. (1994) A dynamic theory of organizational knowledge creation, *Organization Science*, 5, 1, 14–37.

North, D. C. (1990) *Institutions, Institutional Change and Economic Performance*, Cambridge: Cambridge University Press.

Parker, D. (1993) Unravelling the planned economy: privatization in Czechoslovakia, *Communist Economies and Economic Transformation*, 5, 3, 391–404.

Peng, M. W. (2003) Institutional transitions and strategic choices, *Academy of Management Review*, 28, 2, 275–96.

Perlmutter, H. (1969) The tortuous evolution of the MNC, *Columbia Journal of World Business*, 4, 9–18.

Pollert, A. (1999) *Transformation at Work in the New Market Economies of Central Eastern Europe*, London: Sage.

Radice, H. (1995) The role of foreign direct investment, in H.-J. Change and P. Nolan (eds.) *The Transformation of Communist Economies*, London: Macmillan, 282–310.

Róna-Tas, Á. (1994) The first shall be last? Entrepreneurship and communist cadres in the transition from communism, *American Journal of Sociology* 100, 1, 40–69.

Rosenzweig, P. M., and N. Nohria (1994) Influences on human resource management practices in multinational corporations, *Journal of International Business Studies*, 25, 2, 229–51.

Sachs, J. (1989) My plan for Poland, *International Economy*, 3, 24–29.

   (1992) The economic transformation of eastern Europe: the case of Poland, *American Economist*, 36, 2, 3–11.

Scott, W. R. (1994) Institutions and organizations: toward a theoretical synthesis, in W. R. Scott and J. W. Meyer (eds.) *Institutional Environments and Organizations: Structural Complexity and Individualism*, London: Sage, 55–80.

   (1995) *Institutions and Organizations*, Thousand Oaks, CA: Sage.

Sik, E. (1994) Network capital in capitalist, communist and post-communist societies, *International Contributions to Labour Studies*, 4, 73–93.

Simon, L., and G. Davies (1996) A contextual approach to management learning: the Hungarian case, *Organization Studies*, 17, 2, 269–89.

Soulsby, A., and E. Clark (1996a) The emergence of post-communist management in the Czech Republic, *Organization Studies*, 17, 2, 227–47.

   (1996b) Economic restructuring and institutional change: post-communist management in the Czech Republic, *Journal of Socio-Economics*, 25, 4, 473–96.

   (1998) Controlling personnel: management and motive in the transformation of the Czech enterprise, *International Journal of Human Resource Management*, 9, 1, 79–98.

Sparrow, P., R. S. Schuler and S. E. Jackson (1994) Convergence or divergence: human resource practices and policies for competitive advantage worldwide, *International Journal of Human Resource Management*, 5, 2, 267–99.

Spicer, A. (1997) Culture and knowledge transfer: conflict in Russian multinational settings, Briareliff Manor, NY: *Academy of Management Annual Meeting Best Paper Proceedings*, 194–8.

Stark, D. (1992) Path dependence and privatization strategies in east central Europe, *East European Politics and Societies*, 6, 1, 17–51.

   (1996) Recombinant property in east European capitalism, *American Journal of Sociology*, 101, 4, 993–1027.

Stiglitz, J. (1999) Whither reform? Ten years of the transition, keynote address presented at the World Bank's Annual Conference on Development Economics, Washington, DC, 28–30 April.

Thomas, S. (1992) The political economy of privatization: Poland, Hungary and Czechoslovakia, in C. Clague and G. C. Rausser (eds.) *The Emergence of Market Economies in Eastern Europe*, Oxford: Basil Blackwell, 279–95.

Tsoukas, H. (1994) Socio-economic systems and organizational management: an institutional perspective on the socialist firm, *Organization Studies*, 15, 1, 21–45.

Uhlenbruck, K., and J. O. de Castro (2000) Foreign acquisitions in central and eastern Europe: outcomes of privatization in transitional economies, *Academy of Management Journal*, 43, 3, 381–402.

Villinger, R. (1996) Post-acquisition managerial learning in central east Europe, *Organization Studies*, 17, 2, 181–206.

von Hirschhausen, C. (1995) From privatization to capitalization: industrial restructuring in post-socialist central and eastern Europe, in E. J. Dittrich, G. Schmidt and R. Whitley (eds.) *Industrial Transformation in Europe: Process and Contexts*, London: Sage, 54–78.

Weik, E. (2001) Myths in transformation processes, *International Studies of Management and Organization*, 31, 2, 9–27.

Whitley, R. (1995) Transformation and change in Europe: critical themes, in E. J. Dittrich, G. Schmidt and R. Whitley (eds.) *Industrial Transformation in Europe: Process and Contexts*, London: Sage, 11–29.

(1999) *Divergent Capitalisms: The Social Structuring and Change of Business Systems*, Oxford: Oxford University Press.

(2001) How and why are international firms different? The consequences of cross-border managerial coordination for firm characteristics and behaviour, in G. Morgan, P. M. Kristersen and R. Whitley (eds.) *The Multinational Firm: Organizing across Institutional and National Divides*, Oxford: Oxford University Press, 27–68.

Whitley, R., and L. Czaban (1998) Institutional transformation and enterprise change in Hungary, *Organization Studies*, 19, 2, 259–80.

Wolchik, S. (1991) *Czechoslovakia in Transition: Politics, Economics and Society*, London: Pinter.

6 The diffusion of HRM practices from the United Kingdom to China

Jos Gamble

Introduction

Substantial effort has been devoted to exploring the extent to which human resource management practices can be transferred from one national context to another. Particular attention has been paid to the manufacturing sector, to countries with 'strong' HRM traditions and to transfers between economically developed countries. This chapter addresses the transfer of a retail sector firm's HRM practices from the United Kingdom to China. Despite its significance both in economic terms and as a source of employment, the transfer of HRM in the service sector, and retailing in particular, has been rather neglected. Similarly, despite the global orientation of many UK firms, few studies have explored the extent to which they have transferred their HRM approach overseas. By contrast, numerous studies have explored the transfer of HRM practices from countries such as Japan, where these are seen to be a source of competitive advantage (e.g. Gill and Wong, 1998; Purcell *et al.*, 1999). When research has focused on UK firms, the exploration tends to remain within the realm of economically developed countries (e.g. Edwards, Ferner and Sissons, 1996; Edwards, Rees and Coller, 1999).

It is thus a timely point to focus on the transfer of HRM practices from a UK multinational retailer (hereafter StoreCo) to its subsidiary (UK-Store) in China. Since the early 1990s China has been the recipient of vast amounts of foreign direct investment, including substantial investment from the United Kingdom. Recent years have also witnessed the increased internationalisation of service sector firms. UK retailers have joined this trend with increasing investments in the Asia-Pacific region. Foreign companies have been allowed to participate in China's retail sector since 1992. By the end of 2005 there were 4,502 foreign operated stores in China (Ernst and Young, 2006).

From a variety of perspectives the expectation might be that the transfer of parent-country practices in this instance would be limited: HRM has not been considered a particular strength of UK firms; retail firms operate in a multi-domestic context serving local customers directly rather than as part of an integrated international production network; and there is a large cultural distance between the United Kingdom and China. Several aspects of HRM transfer are explored briefly: communication with the workforce, work patterns, the age composition of the workforce, reward systems, training and employee representation. Attention then focuses on the transfer of the firm's relatively flat organisational structure to a country that is perceived to place a high value on hierarchy and in which hierarchies tend to be quite rigid and clearly demarcated. The chapter seeks to provide fresh insights into the phenomenon of transfer by adopting a qualitative case study approach. This study also focuses on shopfloor employees' perspectives rather than purely the view of managerial staff, as has tended to be the case.

Factors affecting the transfer of HRM practices to overseas subsidiaries

A range of factors can promote or inhibit the transfer of HRM practices from TNCs' parent-country operations to their overseas subsidiaries. These can be categorised broadly as aspects that are either external or intrinsic to the firm. External factors include structural characteristics such as the country of origin, the degree of international production integration and the nature of product markets. Another set of external factors inheres in the particular legislative, institutional and cultural framework of the host country. At the firm level, key aspects include the structure of the company, its commitment to the dissemination of HRM practices and the resources it devotes to this end.

Country of origin

A starting point for many analysts who seek to understand the nature of transfer to overseas subsidiaries has often been the national business system (Whitley, 1992) and 'varieties of capitalism' approach (Hall and Soskice, 2001). In these approaches, businesses are considered to derive enduring and distinctive features from their embeddedness in national institutional structures The expectation is that nationally specific characteristics are likely to influence the way in which TNCs manage HRM in their overseas subsidiaries

(Ferner, 1997). Researchers have found evidence of distinctive national paths to internationalisation (Sally, 1994; Ferner and Quintanilla, 1998; Lane, 1998).

UK and Chinese national business systems

The national business systems approach provides a useful starting point, but it has limitations in terms of identifying and analysing practices in individual firms (Smith and Thompson, 1998). Movements of capital, people and ideas, for instance, are differentially constrained by national boundaries. The national business systems approach also tends to cryogenise national 'models' and ignore continued development. In addition, firm action is overdetermined and the potential for human agency neglected.

The national business systems approach has particular limitations in the context of this chapter. There are difficulties in assessing what constitutes either a UK or a Chinese national business system and distinctively 'British' and 'Chinese' approaches to HRM. Researchers report major sectoral differences in UK management practices (Child, Faulkner and Pitkethly, 2000). Even amongst firms in the retail sector there appear to be substantial divergences. A distinctive feature of StoreCo is its relatively flat hierarchy. Nonetheless, Peter Turnbull and Victoria Wass (1998) describe a UK retail store with an internal labour market bifurcated into a primary 'managerial' segment and a secondary 'shopfloor' segment, with an absence of mobility between segments. Turnbull and Wass report employees' comments on being 'treated as if you're nothing' (108) and 'it's very "Them and Us" ' (106). The contrast between these comments and the findings from UK-Store could not be more marked. Both are UK retail firms, but the managerial style and approach appear to be quite different.

It is also increasingly difficult to isolate key elements of a specifically Chinese HRM system. During the Maoist period it was relatively straightforward to delineate a range of features that applied, at least, to the larger state-owned enterprises. Chief aspects included centrally planned job allocation, guaranteed lifetime employment, egalitarian pay systems and extensive cradle-to-grave welfare benefits. With the increasing internationalisation and commercialisation and enhanced enterprise autonomy of the post-Mao era, and especially since the early 1990s, it has become more problematic to isolate a 'Chinese' approach to HRM. Researchers characterise China's labour management system as being in a state of transition (Warner, 1999; Ding, Goodall and Warner, 2000). Labour markets have become more fluid, reward systems reformed and the provision of benefits such as housing and medical care disentangled from enterprises. There are also substantial differences between HRM practices in private and state-owned Chinese firms (Zhu, 2005).

In some instances, SOEs begin to look more like joint ventures in their management approach, while earlier joint ventures retain older SOE-related characteristics (Warner, 1997). The interweaving of 'Western' HRM and 'iron rice-bowl' practices is such that Keith Goodall and Malcolm Warner (1998: 18) comment: 'We were able to identify in our sample very few practices or procedures that we could with confidence characterize as "local".' Faced with rapid change and growing complexity in the way multi-national and local elements of HRM practice combine, researchers argue for the necessity to describe and analyse each HRM practice separately rather than generalising about across-the-board approaches to HRM (Lu and Björkman, 1997).

A further limitation of the national business systems approach that became apparent in the analysis of StoreCo and its China subsidiary is that inputs to the firm's organisational milieu are diverse and cannot be captured by the notion of a national business system; it is difficult to state categorically what is 'British' about StoreCo. Since its establishment in the late 1960s the company has copied elements, such as aspects of store layout and the company uniform, from the US retailer Home Depot. StoreCo's chief executive in China was a Chinese national with experience of SOEs who had also lived and worked in North America. After encountering Home Depot in the United States, his intention had been to replicate this business in China. Whilst in the process of establishing China's first 'do-it-yourself' (DIY) company, however, he had been recruited by StoreCo, which provided him with additional training in the United Kingdom.

These global borrowings and interconnections are further complicated by the firm's prior experience in Taiwan, where it has had stores since the early 1990s. This experience is now both structured within the firm and embodied within the individuals who have worked there. The employee handbook used in the mainland, for instance, was originally translated from English to Chinese for use in Taiwan, and it was this version that was adapted for use in China. UK-Store's mainland China HRM consultancy firm, an American TNC, also had an input into the final version of the handbook. The consultants' advice was based upon their global experience and that of other firms in China. When they helped adapt the firm's pay and benefits scheme, for instance, this was done on the basis of benchmarking against other foreign retailers already operating in Shanghai. These instances indicate how business practices and ideas can ricochet back and forth across the globe, undermining the 'national', and highlight the need to incorporate other elements into our understanding of the transfer of business practices.

Degree of production integration and nature of product markets

It is argued that TNCs are more likely to diffuse their parent-country HRM practices when there is a high degree of production integration across countries (Edwards, Rees and Coller, 1999: 287). By contrast, in industries that are more 'polycentric' in structure, with subsidiaries geared to serving local markets rather than part of an international division of labour, the expectation is that there will be less imperative to transfer parent-country practices (Ferner, 1997). Transferring parent practices may be more problematic in service sector multinationals than in manufacturing firms, to the extent that the former deal not only with local employees but also the differing expectations and cultural values of customers. Since the stores studied in this chapter are not part of an integrated international production network and their express purpose is to serve local customers, the expectation might be that the firm would be inclined to adopt local HRM practices.

Host-country factors preventing diffusion and promoting local isomorphism

Host-country regulatory conditions, labour market conditions, local employees' institutionalised views about management practices, and cultural factors may all constrain TNCs from transferring their parent-country HRM policies and practices to overseas subsidiaries. In China, for instance, local employees' expectations have been shaped by their experience in the dependency conditions fostered by the state socialist system, and this may inhibit diffusion. Corinna-Barbara Francis (1996), for instance, finds evidence of 'institutional continuities' with the state-owned enterprise system among Chinese high-tech firms, with the reproduction in them of SOE-style benefits, including the provision of housing and social security benefits.

Host-country employees have various sources of power that they can use to block diffusion and promote local isomorphism, including those derived from their greater familiarity with the language and culture of the host country. This potential may be enhanced when the host-country's culture and language are conspicuously different from those of the TNC's parent country. In China, few expatriates can speak *putonghua*, the national Chinese language, never mind regional dialects such as that spoken in Shanghai, and even fewer can read it;

they cannot talk directly to their staff, let alone read legislation in Chinese. There may be considerable scope for local employees to resist company practices.

Cultural differences

Much attention has focused on the extent to which cultural differences influence management behaviour. It has been suggested that the greater the 'cultural distance' between the parent country and the host country the less subsidiaries will conform to local practices (Beechler and Yang, 1994). A contrasting view is that, faced with significant 'cultural distance', TNCs may seek to 'fit in' by imitating local practices (Rosenzweig and Nohria, 1994).

As a country perceived to have a culture markedly different from that of the United Kingdom, China provides a useful testing ground for such hypotheses. Many commentators argue that Chinese culture is a strong determinant of the way Chinese organisations are managed (Lockett, 1988; Easterby-Smith, Malina and Lu, 1995). Key aspects of Chinese culture are taken to be: respect for age and hierarchical position; group orientation; the concept of *face*; and the importance of relationships (Lockett, 1988). In the Chinese context, cultural differences are seen to inhibit transfer and enhance the need for local isomorphism. Previous studies have indeed found considerable disparity of HRM practices between China and Western countries (Child, 1994; Easterby-Smith, Malina and Lu, 1995). On the basis of comparative research conducted at UK and Chinese firms, Mark Easterby-Smith, Danusia Malina and Yuan Lu (56) conclude that, 'despite a few areas of similarity between the UK and China, there are strong cultural factors which limit the adoption of many features of HRM in China'. Martin Lockett (1988) reaches a similar conclusion, and suggests that Western management methods need to be adapted to fit better with Chinese conditions and culture.

Firm-level decisions and responses

Razeen Sally (1994: 165) is critical of international business analysts' tendency 'to abstract the firm from its national and international political economy context.' At the same time, it would be a mistake to underestimate the agency located within individual firms. Firms are important actors in their own right: each has its own 'institutionalised stock of knowledge' (Beechler and Yang, 1994: 5), and many seek to develop a distinctive approach to work organisation.

Nitin Nohria and Sumantra Ghoshal (1994) distinguish between firms that make a strategic decision to develop 'differentiated fit' with distinctive local conditions and those that promote global 'shared values' across the company. Sully Taylor, Schon Beechler and Nancy Napier (1996) identify three generic strategic international HRM orientations that firms may pursue when setting up an overseas subsidiary: adaptive, exportive and integrative. These approaches delineate firms that, respectively, adapt HRM systems for subsidiaries to reflect the environment of the host country; export wholesale the parent firm's HRM system to overseas subsidiaries; and attempt to integrate the 'best' practices from both local and parent country and use them throughout the organisation. Anthony Ferner (1997) indicates that other variants are also possible: multinationals may, for example, create a hybrid, in which host-country norms mediate the influence of the parent-country blueprint.

The extent to which firms actively encourage diffusion and coordinate it from the centre differs considerably (Ferner and Varul, 2000). Moreover, not all firms act strategically in this regard. Although firms may repackage their approach retrospectively as 'strategic', even in large TNCs much decision-making is reactive and opportunistic. Organisational inertia probably accounts for much that TNCs do with regard to the management of HRM in their overseas subsidiaries. Expatriate managers and headquarters have their own set of institutionalised views on what constitute efficient HRM practices, and will tend to introduce in the subsidiary features of the parent-country culture. In UK-Store's case, the transfer of its parent-country HRM practices appeared to stem largely from 'taken-for-granted assumptions, rather than consciously strategic choices' (DiMaggio and Powell, 1983: 149). Proponents of differentiated fit also overlook the fact that headquarters and expatriate managers with responsibility for policy-making might have limited understanding of host-country institutional and cultural environments.

Finally, the nature of the subsidiary plays a part in the extent of diffusion. Subsidiaries established on greenfield sites are better able to adhere to their foreign parents' operations than those acquired through acquisitions. Such operations do not face existing highly institutionalised practices and have greater scope to establish the employment 'ground rules' and recruit employees who 'fit' with their corporate culture.

Means of transfer

HRM practices can be diffused from the parent country to overseas subsidiaries through various routes. In the manufacturing sector, benchmarking is a common instrument of 'coercive comparison' between plants and a powerful means to enhance the transfer of practices (Mueller and Purcell, 1992).

At UK-Store's first China store, in the north-east suburbs of Shanghai, benchmarking was largely implicit: it resided in the UK experiences of the two expatriate managers and the more limited experience that selected Chinese employees had gained in training visits to the United Kingdom. When the second store was set up, however, in the west of Shanghai, the first store became a direct benchmark for the new store, with monthly competitions between them to see which had the higher turnover. This intra-store competition constituted a subtle form of pressure on the new store's managers to adopt the practices employed at the first store, which were seen as the source of its success.

The presence of expatriates is anticipated to facilitate the dissemination of standardised multinational practices. The expectation is that subsidiaries with a high expatriate presence will adhere more closely to the management practices of the parent firm (Rosenzweig and Nohria, 1994). Expatriate managers typically serve a key 'control function' in areas such as finance management and setting overall strategy (Gamble, 2000). They also fulfil a crucial role in the transfer of firms' 'administrative heritage' (Bartlett and Ghoshal, 1998). Expatriates spread explicit knowledge through such means as the introduction and dissemination of employee handbooks, training manuals and standard operating procedures. They also bring substantial intangible resources, chief amongst these being tacit knowledge of ways of managing the business (Taylor, Beechler and Napier, 1996).

Inevitably, the transmission of explicit and tacit knowledge overlaps. Thus, at UK-Store, expatriate managers not only introduced and activated training, selection and recruitment and promotion procedures, they also participated in and oversaw their operation. In selection procedures, for instance, they introduced and established the recruitment criteria and actively selected recruits who possessed the 'motivational characteristics and skills mix appropriate to the imported form of organisational practice' (Ferner, 1997: 26). In addition, in their daily behaviour and example they indicated to local employees the kind of work style and approach that was sought and sanctioned and would be rewarded by the firm. Their presence enabled an ongoing dialectic with local employees in which cultural values and expectations were negotiated on both sides. Despite the assumption that greater numbers of expatriates facilitates diffusion, UK-Store's example demonstrates that even small numbers can have a great impact. For the first year of its operation, UK-Store had just two expatriates. Despite this, at the apex of the management structure, they fulfilled a pivotal and critical role in diffusing the company's parent-country practices.

Research methodology

Most studies on the transfer of HRM practices are based on large-scale surveys conducted using questionnaires or by interviews with managers and professionals. Detailed, qualitative case studies provide the opportunity to investigate hypotheses developed in larger survey-type studies and an ideal means to explore the intricacies involved in the reception of transferred practices. The fact that a subsidiary has introduced, say, performance appraisal or quality circles tells us little about the actual operation of these practices, and even less about the experiences and perceptions of those who participate in them. Studies on the transfer of HRM practices run the risk of becoming like butterfly collecting, with elements apparently transferred simply being ticked off a list. This overlooks the likelihood that transferred elements may be interpreted very differently in novel contexts (Ferner and Varul, 2000).

The research for this chapter included interviews by the author with employees from all levels of the hierarchy. Even in economically developed countries, research on HRM practices often neglects the 'voice of those at the receiving end' (Clark, Mabey and Skinner, 1998: 10). In cross-national research, given language difficulties and access constraints, these voices are even more muted. Research based solely on managerial responses airbrushes out workers' perspectives. Even within the United Kingdom, the gulf between managerial rhetoric and employees' experiences can be dramatic, as demonstrated in Turnbull and Wass's (1998) study. The potential for overlooking such divergences is greater still in cross-national contexts.

Research was conducted at a UK-owned multinational retailer in both China and the United Kingdom. In June 1999 StoreCo became the first major UK retailer to enter mainland China when it opened a decorative materials warehouse store, UK-Store, in Shanghai. Although UK-Store is a minority holder (30 per cent) in a joint venture with two Chinese firms, the UK side had full operational control over the store. A second store, also in Shanghai, opened in May 2000, and the company planned further rapid expansion. The first store had 190 employees and the second store 185; 68 per cent of the employees were male and 32 per cent were female.

In China, research was undertaken during two visits, each of three weeks' duration, in 1999 and 2000. In 1999 research focused on the first store; in 2000 research was undertaken at both stores. The twelve-month interval provided a diachronic perspective. Semi-structured interviews were conducted with a cross-section of seventy employees. Some employees were interviewed on more than one occasion. The author was given a free hand to select interviewees, and they were chosen from a range of departments and every level in the firm's hierarchy. Several factors fostered a good relationship between the author and interviewees. In particular, the author's facility in Chinese permitted interviews with local employees to be conducted on a one-to-one basis and for them to be transcribed directly by the author during the interview; tape-recording interviews would have increased interviewees' reluctance to speak openly. The six-week research period ensured that the author became a familiar figure to employees. In addition, the author has extensive experience of conducting research in China (e.g. Gamble, 2003, 2006a, 2006b, 2007) and is alert to Chinese discourse patterns and body language that indicate evasiveness or reluctance to speak frankly.

Research in the United Kingdom provided a basis upon which comparisons could be made. Interviews were conducted in 2000 and 2001 with eighteen employees and managers at one of StoreCo's London stores, with the firm's director of human resources and its international development director. The direct comparison of actual workplaces means that the variables of business sector and company are held constant, allowing these aspects to be largely discounted in the analysis.

Several studies have explored the extent of divergence and convergence between 'traditional' Chinese HRM and Western-style HRM practices. Typically, the comparison is between ideal-type models of Western HRM and state-owned enterprise practices. The interview-based case study approach employed in this chapter enabled the author to elicit employees' reports of their own experiences of differing HRM regimes. Chinese employees were asked to contrast their experiences at UK-Store with those in their previous employers. This provided comparisons of HRM practices in a foreign-invested enterprise against actual practices in other workplaces in China.

Findings from UK-Store

StoreCo enjoys considerable success in its home market, and its basic approach in China has been to replicate as closely as possible its UK operation. With respect to HRM, UK-Store's senior expatriate manager emphasised: 'StoreCo has a strong culture, we want to bring this to China.' This approach was facilitated by operating on greenfield sites with no established workforce and by the UK side of the joint venture having full operational control. Overall business strategy was set by the corporate head-quarters in the United Kingdom, which had ultimate authority over all the overseas operations, including that in Taiwan, but with substantial input from senior managers in China. In terms of HRM, UK-Store's training manager explained that 'we get an outline' (*kuangzi* – literally 'a frame') from the United Kingdom and Taiwan, but that 'we should develop it in our own way'.

The extent to which the firm's parent-country HRM practices had been transferred to UK-Store is indicated in table 6.1. The final column,

Table 6.1 HRM practices transferred from the United Kingdom to China

HRM dimension	UK-Store (Shanghai)	StoreCo (London)	State-owned enterprises
Communication with workforce	Less disclosure than in United Kingdom	Extensive briefing on sales targets and company strategy, etc.	Secretive, information retained by higher levels and within departments
Hierarchy	Flat hierarchy	Flat hierarchy	Multi-layered
	Casual, informal:	Casual, informal:	Formal, hierarchical:
	first-name terms; accessible managers; open-plan offices; same uniform for all employees	first-name terms; accessible managers; open-plan offices; same uniform for all employees	job titles; remote managers; offices enclosed; previously single-status uniform for all employees
Reward system	Mainly fixed for lower levels; company profit bonus	Mainly fixed for lower levels; company profit bonus	Fixed rates; few performance-related rewards
Differentials	Mostly graduated differentials but some exceptions	Graduated differentials within and between categories	Limited differentials within and between categories
Non-wage benefits	Meals benefits provided after much debate	No meals benefits	Canteens
Work pattern	Full-time	Full-time and part-time	Full-time
Age composition of workforce	Mainly young employees, but older than many joint ventures (average age 27–8)	Older employees (average age 35)	Older employees (e.g. average age over 40 in an adjacent Shanghai store)
Training	At least as much as in United Kingdom, increasing provision of off-the-job training	Increasingly systematic provision and more off-the-job training	Minimal and mainly enterprise-based
Employee representation	Trade union; 'Grass Roots'	No trade union; 'Grass Roots'	Trade union

summarising practices in SOEs, is based primarily upon comments made by UK-Store's employees during interviews. As indicated, the firm had transferred many of its UK practices. Moreover, many local employees appeared, at least, to have internalised many of the company's values.

Communication with the workforce

In the United Kingdom, StoreCo provides its workforce with information on details ranging from sales targets and daily turnover to company strategy. This information is communicated through means, such as daily morning briefings, that are attended by all staff, the company magazine and workplace 'huddles'. By contrast, Chinese SOEs have tended to be secretive, with information retained both by higher levels and within departments (Child and Markóczy, 1993). UK-Store appeared to be midway between the practices of SOEs and those of its parent company, with less disclosure to employees than in the United Kingdom but more than in state firms. Arguments for less disclosure tended to come from the firm's Chinese director, who cited the need for security in a highly competitive marketplace – an aspect that could be attributed to the institutional legacy of state-owned enterprises.

Work pattern

StoreCo has a large proportion of part-time employees. This parallels a general trend in the UK labour market; the proportion of part-time workers in the retailing workforce rose from 35 percent in 1971 to 49 percent in 1993 (Townsend, Sadler and Hudson, 1996: 211). By contrast, UK-Store only had full-time employees. This divergence can be related not to cultural factors but to the different labour markets; for instance, China's lower labour costs permitted greater use of full-time employees.

Age composition of workforce

In the United Kingdom, StoreCo actively recruits older workers; each store had a target for 18 percent of employees to be over fifty years old. The average age of employees in London was thirty-five. In China, UK-Store employed mainly younger employees, with a notional upper age limit of forty-five. The average age of employees was twenty-seven to twenty-eight, although more older employees were recruited than in many joint ventures. This divergence from the United Kingdom can be accounted for by a variety of institutional and cultural factors. In UK home improvement stores, older employees are often able to provide product-related information because they have personal experience of the difficulties faced by customers when carrying out DIY tasks (Harris, Baron and Davies, 1999). In Shanghai there is no tradition of DIY, so both younger and older recruits lack such experience. As in other foreign-invested enterprises (Gamble, 2000), UK-Store's expatriate staff expressed concern that poor working habits in state enterprises had become ingrained in older workers. By contrast, younger recruits were considered easier to train. Indigenous Chinese stereotypes also supported this view; interviewees suggested that older employees would be physically incapable of the work involved as well as less adaptable.

Reward system

A national wage system was introduced in China during the 1950s. This model was characterised by an egalitarian ethos, with minimal reward differentials both within categories of worker and between management and shopfloor staff. Companies also provided extensive benefits in kind, including accommodation and free medical care. In a comparative study of UK and Chinese companies, Easterby-Smith, Malina and Lu (1995) found sharp differences with regard to pay and reward systems. In particular, differentials between top managers and average wages were much greater in the UK firms than the Chinese firms. In the latter, there was 'very strong resistance' to linking rewards more closely with performance and to the introduction of pay differentials. Easterby-Smith, Malina and Lu attribute such resistance to cultural factors and anticipate that 'there may be deep-seated differences between the two countries with regard to attitudes towards rewards which will limit the transferability of HRM ideas in this area' (30). In recent years, though, reward systems in China have begun to change. Material rewards have become more predominant, with a shift away from egalitarian pay and perks towards a greater emphasis on individual performance-related rewards with greater differentials.

In StoreCo and UK-Store, payment levels for employees in lower grades are relatively fixed and bonuses are based upon company-level performance. Unlike StoreCo, UK-Store's employees can reimburse a percentage of medical care costs and, from 2000, have received a meals subsidy. These two aspects can both be considered as examples of local isomorphism, but the drivers were rather different in each instance. The provision of medical cover was necessitated by the absence of society-wide health care. The meals subsidy, which was introduced only after a year of heated debate, appeared to be driven partly by institutional and cultural factors. In part, employees had grown accustomed to meals provided while on duty in other workplaces, and additionally Chinese generally eat a cooked meal at lunchtime. Staff also complained about the cost of buying meals out and the lack of suitable restaurants in the vicinity. During interviews in 1999 this issue was employees' main source of dissatisfaction with UK-Store.

In 2000 employees expressed more general dissatisfaction over the reward system. Chief aspects of concern were pay levels, the bonus system and, especially among older employees, the low level of medical benefits and lack of a pension system. Ironically, given Easterby-Smith, Malina and Yuan's findings, UK-Store's employees complained that the firm had yet to introduce a performance-related bonus system, the preference being for department-wide bonuses based on performance rather than individual performance-based bonuses.

Employees' aspirations and expectations, voiced through mechanisms such as 'Grass Roots' (see below), constituted a force for local isomorphism. Their expectations were derived partly from UK-Store's own self-presentation but also from comparisons with other firms. Employees brought with them a range of prior work environment experiences, not least because a minimum of one year's work experience was a requirement for new recruits, with preference given to candidates who had worked in foreign-invested stores. Employees had previously worked in state enterprises, collective firms, private firms and various types of foreign enterprise, including Japanese, German, French, Thai, Malaysian and American firms. These experiences provided the basis for a range of 'persuasive comparisons'.

From the interviews it was apparent that UK-Store's employees engaged in continual comparison of their salary levels, bonuses, welfare benefits and working conditions with those in employees' former workplaces and reported from firms of family members and friends. The main point of reference or benchmark against which UK-Store was judged was not so much provision by 'traditional' SOEs but that offered by other foreign enterprises. Moreover, by consistently describing itself as 'the number one' European firm in its line of business, UK-Store had made a rod for its own back, since it enabled employees to benchmark their own pay and conditions against those of competitor firms. Employees reasoned that, if UK-Store was 'number one', then, logically, their pay and benefits should match this status. Thus, isomorphic pressures were only partly derived from domestic institutions. Pressures to resemble state enterprises were at best second-hand – that is, to the extent that other foreign firms had succumbed to pressures to resemble state enterprises.

Employees' comparisons, while not coercive, could be persuasive and were not easily ignored. Workers' power to push for improvements rested on two main factors. First, UK-Store needed employees' active and enthusiastic involvement to provide the kind of customer service seen as vital for the business. Second, employment in a foreign enterprise enhanced employees' employability and the 'quit option' was a potent threat, especially given that UK-Store's plans for rapid expansion were predicated on the promotion of employees trained in-house.

An unexpected aspect of divergence was the level of differentials. Within and between categories of store-level employees, differentials were similar to those in the United Kingdom. Although precise details were difficult to obtain, however, it was apparent that differentials between shopfloor workers and head office professional staff were greater in nominally socialist China than in the United Kingdom. While store employees' compensation amounted to around one-eighth the level of their UK counterparts, professional staff were paid similar amounts to their UK equivalents. If expatriate managers' compensation packages were factored into this equation then differentials were greater still. The marked disparity in differentials can be attributed to the shortage of and pressure to retain appropriately skilled managers.

Training

Training in state-owned enterprises has traditionally been quite limited and mainly enterprise-based (Cooke, 2005). In the United Kingdom, training at StoreCo has tended to be piecemeal, ad hoc and on-the-job, especially for shopfloor staff. Recently, though, there has been a trend for more systematic provision and increased use of off-the-job training. In China, training provision at UK-Store was often more systematic and extensive than in the parent-country stores, including ongoing product knowledge training and a locally developed system of product knowledge certificates for customer assistants (Gamble, 2006a). In part, this divergence relates to the labour market. DIY skills and product knowledge are widely dispersed in the United Kingdom and many employees already possess such capabilities before they join the company. In China, these capabilities are less available: DIY is a new phenomenon, it is difficult for UK-Store to 'buy in' employees with appropriate skills and greater attention has to be devoted to training.

A lower-cost labour market in Shanghai compared to the United Kingdom also allowed for more training. Although the Chinese stores had more staff than comparably sized UK stores, total staff costs were roughly a half those of a UK store. The expatriate operations manager commented that, while the company considers training and skills development as equally important in the United Kingdom, tight manning often precluded staff taking time off for training. In the United Kingdom, StoreCo did not provide ongoing product knowledge training. This manager remarked that 'you may get product knowledge training on new products, otherwise you just get thrown in the pool'. What he described as 'the luxury of 4 percent staff costs' in China allowed for more concentration on training.

Even though both business sector and firm are held constant in this study there are still implicit differences. In China, for instance, simply being a large multinational is a source of competitive advantage, at least in the recruitment of employees. In popular perceptions, foreign enterprises are desirable employers (Gamble, 2000). The expectation is that a foreign firm, and especially a Western TNC, would provide better pay, conditions, training and promotion prospects than local firms. This enabled UK-Store to select from a larger pool of applicants and to recruit people of a higher educational standard than would be usual in the United Kingdom. What might be perceived as rather routine, dead-end jobs in Britain are more desirable in China. In early 2000, for instance, 1,000 applicants responded to a recruitment advert; fewer than twenty were offered jobs. Arguably, recruits in China are generally more trainable and enthusiastic to receive training than their counterparts in the United Kingdom (Gamble, 2006a).

Employees remarked upon the substantial degree of training offered by the firm. A decoration department deputy supervisor, previously employed at a state retail store, observed that, in comparison, 'at UK-Store there's an emphasis on the long term. There's a strong company culture because we have a training department. I've learnt a lot here. People make progress every day. We're taught about new products and can tell the customers.'

Multinationals' subsidiaries sometimes pursue more sophisticated human resource management practices than the parent. In some instances there is 'reverse diffusion', with these practices transferred to the firm's headquarters or to other plants within the corporation (Monks, 1996). StoreCo's director of human resources suggested that UK-Store's programme of product knowledge training with certificates for shopfloor staff might provide a model for the UK operation.

Employee representation

SOEs invariably have trade unions, and foreign enterprises are legally committed to establish a union if requested by employees. In the United Kingdom, StoreCo does not recognise a trade union, although individual employees are not constrained from joining one. The firm does operate an in-house representative consultation system called 'Grass Roots', however, in which employees are encouraged to voice their grievances. Once issues raised in this forum have been addressed, details of action taken and decisions reached are fed back to employees. UK-Store has a union, although its only role appeared to be organising leisure activities for employees. UK-Store has, however, introduced 'Grass Roots'. Local employees considered this a brave action on the part of the firm, one that few other foreign enterprises would dare to implement, since they would be wary of permitting employees the opportunity to voice discontent over company practices. In the Chinese context, the transfer of this mechanism constituted a progressive development (cf. Ferner, 1997: 32).

Transferring a flat hierarchy

The company culture at UK-Store is very different to that at my previous company [a Hong-Kong-owned store]. There's no sense of distance with higher staff. We feel that we're friends. There's no feeling that 'I'm the one in charge (*dangguan de*), I'm the boss (*tou*), you're the common people (*laobaixing*)'. This is from [H – first name of senior executive] down; everybody is very polite and treated equally. In my last job, it was a case of 'I'm the boss, you're the workers; so I look down on you'. (customer assistant)

Respect for hierarchy is one of the Chinese cultural values that Lockett (1988) anticipates will inhibit technical and organisational innovation. He adds that a high degree of differentiation of activities is a basic feature of Chinese organisations. The pattern of organisational structure in state-owned enterprises that emerged from interviews was, indeed, of multi-layered hierarchies, with diverse job titles and managers who were remote from the shopfloor staff. Typically, this remoteness is symbolised in managers' offices, which tend to be large, plushly decorated and well enclosed. Given the cultural and institutional differences between China and the United Kingdom, the prospects for StoreCo to transfer its relatively flat organisational hierarchy did not look promising. In fact, this transfer appeared to have been successful, although, as will be shown, cultural and institutional differences coloured local employees' reception of the transferred practices.

The situation at StoreCo in the United Kingdom is markedly different from that depicted in SOEs. The hierarchy is quite flat and interactions between staff at all levels are casual and informal, a situation symbolised in and encouraged by the use of first-name terms throughout the company and single-status uniforms. Managerial offices are open-plan, cramped and quite spartan. Moreover, managers are often not in their offices but visibly on the shopfloor.

Employees described UK-Store's management style as 'modern', 'scientific', 'systematic', 'civilised' and 'egalitarian' and as having 'human feeling' (*renqing-wei*). The two expatriate managers were described as 'polite' and 'friendly' and as having respect for employees and their opinions. A warehouse worker who had previously worked in a state-owned store described UK-Store's management style in these terms:

Very tolerant and warm-hearted, the managers show concern for you. In the state store, even though I was there for one year, the managers didn't even know my name. Here we're very familiar with both [I and B – first names of the two expatriate managers]. Workers have a spirit of unity [*tuanjie jingshen*]; at the old company it always felt that 'workers were workers and managers were managers', but here we feel that workers and managers are together, it's harmonious.

Many shopfloor staff expressed the view that workplace relations were 'fraternal' (*xiongdi guanxi*) and that the firm had an 'extended family atmosphere' (*da jiating fengwei*) or a 'family-like feel' (*qinqi ganjue*). In the loss prevention section, one of the store's oldest employees commented, 'I joke that UK-Store's way of having no distance between people is like China in the 1950s. Then everybody tightened their belts and worked together.'

A valuable team spirit had been built up during UK-Store's start-up phase. There was great enthusiasm for the project and many out-of-work activities, such as meals, karaoke, dancing and bowling, in which both local and expatriate staff participated. StoreCo also transferred the key aspects of its relatively flat organisational structure (see table 6.2).

For the first year of operations grades six and seven were filled by two expatriate managers, one of whom had previous experience in Taiwan, but neither of whom knew any Chinese language. In 2000 both expatriates remained in China but were promoted to executive roles. Three new expatriates arrived in 2000, each assigned to roles requiring particular technical skills. Although StoreCo had careful screening to select expatriates, cultural awareness training was minimal. In 2000 a newly arrived expatriate at

Table 6.2 Grading structure in UK-Store

Grade 2	Customer assistants, receiving desk staff, warehouse staff, clerical workers
Grade 3	Customer advisers, deputy supervisors
Grade 4	Supervisors
Grade 5	Deputy managers/team leaders
Grade 6	Assistant store manager
Grade 7	Store general manager

UK-Store commented, 'I just came in, it's typical StoreCo. The approach is "just get in and stop whinging".' Responsibility for the day-to-day management of the two stores had been transferred to locally recruited managers. Three team leaders were each responsible for three or four departments. Each of the trading departments had one supervisor, one deputy supervisor, one or two customer advisers and between four and eight customer assistants.

Messages about the company's culture and management style were delivered during the three-day induction training. During this period employees learnt that both the expatriate managers and the company's international development director had all been promoted from the lowest levels of the company. Two new recruits, interviewed immediately after their induction training, had both been left with the strong impression that the atmosphere was 'very egalitarian' and that there was 'no gap between the foreign managers and employees'. These messages were reinforced by the use of first-name terms and the single-status uniform. In the context of contemporary Shanghai, where managers now generally wear suits and ties to differentiate themselves from shopfloor staff, UK-Store's use of a common uniform constituted a reversion to the practice common during the Maoist era. The daily morning briefings also provided a means to help ameliorate vertical divisions that could develop between departments.

The positive acceptance of the relative lack of hierarchy cannot, however, be divorced from the daily example and self-presentation of the two expatriate managers. Both these managers operated as they had done in the United Kingdom, spending much time on the shopfloor and making every effort to be approachable. Initially, the operations manager had found that, in contrast to the UK stores, 'everyone here is very conscious of their level, they don't question those above them'. He added, however, that 'this is changing gradually as we get the message across'. Similarly, his senior expatriate colleague had found on his arrival that Chinese employees 'all expected me to be unapproachable'.

Local employees contrasted UK-Store's expatriate managers favourably both with other foreign managers and Chinese managers they had encountered. A deputy supervisor made this observation:

The UK managers are very polite, we like working with them; they're easy-going and treat us as equals (*pingyi jinren*). Chinese managers in other companies are separated from the masses (*tuoli qunzhong*) and not willing to interact with workers.

Another deputy supervisor, in the timber section, remarked:

It's very difficult to find this kind of boss; they talk openly (*tanxin* – literally 'speak from the heart') with us and don't just talk about salary. It's difficult to find a good job; it's even harder to find a good boss – finding both is really hard!

These comments indicate the successful transfer of a non-hierarchical workplace. Sometimes, though, cultural differences did emerge. For instance, employees often expressed what could be construed as a sense of loyalty to the company. This was invariably articulated in terms of an 'emotional' (*ganqing*) attachment to the particular expatriate managers, however. It could be that the emphasis upon personal relationships in China facilitated the adoption of a non-hierarchical structure.

All the staff were given English first names, which appeared alongside their Chinese names on their uniforms. In part, this practice was considered helpful for foreign customers, and it was also intended to create an atmosphere of informality. In Chinese companies, lower-ranking staff generally address staff senior to them in a quite formal manner, typically using both surname and job title; one customer assistant described it is a 'military-style' approach. Thus, the introduction of first-name terms across the company was a radical innovation. A trade desk deputy supervisor remarked that the main difference between UK-Store and his previous employer, a state-owned enterprise, was that

[t]he differences between the higher and lower levels are not sharply demarcated, the gap between them isn't great. Everyone uses first names. We feel that we're all in the same company, we're all co-workers and all have the same objective. Here the management don't just issue orders, it's very harmonious. It's like an extended family. This is due to UK-Store's culture; it has entered the employees.

The transfer and use of first-name terms could be taken to indicate the transfer of a non-hierarchical approach. During interviews, however, it became apparent that, while this was broadly the case, there were nuances that could be overlooked; whilst the form had been transferred the content meant something rather different in the Chinese context. In practice, the use of the English names was confined to particular circumstances; notably, while customer assistants sometimes addressed deputy supervisors and supervisors by their English names, they invariably used these names for managerial staff. This could be construed as a minimising of hierarchies, and customer assistants did, indeed, describe this usage as being 'harmonious' and remarked that using their Chinese names would increase the sense of distance. A deputy supervisor added, however, that she called staff in positions above her by their English names, since 'to call them by their Chinese first names would not be best because they're managers'. It appears that employees used the English names to rearticulate hierarchy in a new style.

Conclusions

This chapter has suggested that firm-specific practices and institutional features of the host-country environment, rather than country of origin, level of international production integration or product market, are the most relevant factors to analyse the transfer of HRM practices. The competitive assets of the multinational researched for this chapter appear largely firm- rather than nation-specific. Expectations that service sector firms are more likely to embrace local HRM practices rather than transfer those from the parent country are not supported. UK-Store's HRM practices largely followed those of the parent company, although there were also hybrid elements with particular features influenced by local (or localised) institutional norms and expectations. The firm's transfer of its parent-country HRM practices could be characterised as 'organisational inertia' as much as being derived from a deliberate decision to promote 'globally shared values'. Moreover, any strategic decision to seek 'differentiated fit' would, in any event, have been problematic, to the extent that the firm's head office and expatriate staff, initially at least, had little idea what cultural and institutionally derived expectations they would need to fit with.

This chapter has indicated that 'cultural distance' does not present an insurmountable barrier to the transfer of HRM practices (see also Gamble, 2006b). We should avoid overessentialising 'culture': cultural values are not a monolith but a fluid and shifting repertoire with diverse strands. In transferring its relatively flat hierarchical structure, for instance, UK-Store tapped into an egalitarian ideal that was out of kilter with contemporary trends but reminiscent of China in the early 1950s. It could be added that, although hierarchy is typically perceived as a major aspect of Confucian values, it might be that those at the top of society place most value on hierarchy, while those at the bottom tend to stress commonality and the value of egalitarianism.

The critical role played by key expatriate managers was evident, both in the communication and transfer of the explicit knowledge as well as the tacit knowledge of company practices and management approach. UK-Store's apparent business success in China can be attributed in part to the transfer of the firm's 'administrative heritage', particularly its organisational structure and management style. Nevertheless, the human agency of the particular expatriate managers involved was vital to this transfer. When expatriates with the appropriate technical and personal skills are involved, the 'friction' of cultural distance can be reduced; their presence enables an ongoing, everyday dialectic of mutual learning and compromises.

John Child and Livia Markóczy (1993) suggest several possible learning processes for local managers in joint ventures. These range from 'non-learning' to 'integrative learning'. The latter involves both cognitive and behavioural change, it is dependent on mutual trust and requires both sides to express and share their underlying understandings and behavioural norms. UK-Store's organisational structure and the management style of its expatriate staff appear to have facilitated just this kind of integrative learning. The evidence from UK-Store underlines the need for great care to be taken in the selection of expatriate personnel and for TNCs to ensure potential expatriates' cross-cultural suitability as well as their technical skills. A real test for the sustainability and efficacy of the firm's management approach, though, will come in the event of a business downturn, or even just a slower pace of expansion, when employees' expectations for individual advancement are less likely to be fulfilled.

Although StoreCo appears to have transferred successfully many of its parent-company HRM practices to China, such practices are refracted through host-country cultural and institutional lenses. The flat organisational hierarchy, for instance, means something rather different in the Chinese context. In transferring this parent-country approach StoreCo was, unwittingly, doing something quite radical in the host-country context. If we extrapolate from this, many other elements seen as 'transferred' might be subject to similar subtle processes of transformation. We might need to revisit studies that indicate the transfer of elements, go beyond managerial rhetoric and explore actual practices on the shopfloor and the ways they are interpreted and negotiated by actors.

This study has also indicated that HRM practices that are a source of competitive advantage in a firm's parent country might have their uniqueness enhanced in host countries. The transfer of a relatively flat hierarchy to a country accustomed to more rigid hierarchies appeared to leverage the competitive advantage of this management approach. Finally, the findings reinforce the view that specific HRM practices in multinationals' subsidiaries will be differentially shaped by the interplay of diverse forces (Rosenzweig and Nohria, 1994). This conclusion underlines the need to explore particular practices and to produce detailed, qualitative and contextualised case studies of workplaces, which pay attention to their insertion into local, national and global labour markets, economic and institutional structures, as well as global flows of capital and ideas. Diachronic studies will also be helpful to ascertain whether, as Philip Rosenzweig and Nitin Nohria (1994) suggest, as subsidiaries become more embedded in the local environment they increasingly take on the practices that prevail locally.

References

Bartlett, C. A., and S. Ghoshal (1998) *Managing across Borders: The Transnational Solution* (2nd edn.), London: Random House.

Beechler, S., and J. Z. Yang (1994) The transfer of Japanese-style management to American subsidiaries: contingencies, constraints, and competencies, *Journal of International Business Studies*, 25, 3, 467–91.

Child, J. (1994) *Management in China during the Age of Reform*, Cambridge: Cambridge University Press.

Child, J., D. Faulkner and R. Pitkethly (2000) Foreign direct investment in the UK 1985–1994: the impact on domestic management practice, *Journal of Management Studies*, 37, 1, 141–66.

Child, J., and L. Markóczy (1993) Host-country managerial behaviour and learning in Chinese and Hungarian joint ventures, *Journal of Management Studies*, 30, 4, 611–31.

Clark, T., C. Mabey and D. Skinner (1998) Experiencing HRM: the importance of the inside story, in C. Mabey, D. Skinner, and T. Clark (eds.) *Experiencing Human Resource Management*, London: Sage, 1–13.

Cooke, F. L. (2005) *HRM, Work and Employment in China*, London: Routledge.

DiMaggio, P. J., and W. W. Powell (1983) The iron cage revisited: institutional isomorphism and collective rationality in organizational fields, *American Sociological Review*, 48, 147–60.

Ding, D. Z., K. Goodall and M. Warner (2000) The end of the 'iron rice-bowl': whither Chinese human resource management?, *International Journal of Human Resource Management*, 11, 2, 217–36.

Easterby-Smith, M., D. Malina and Y. Lu (1995) How culture-sensitive is HRM? A comparative analysis of practice in Chinese and UK companies, *International Journal of Human Resource Management*, 6, 1, 31–59.

Edwards, P., A. Ferner and K. Sissons (1996) The conditions for international human resource management: two case studies, *International Journal of Human Resource Management*, 7, 1, 20–40.

Edwards, T., C. Rees and X. Coller (1999) Structure, politics and the diffusion of employment practices in multinationals, *European Journal of Industrial Relations*, 5, 3, 286–306.

Ernst and Young (2006) *Retail Revolution: A Look at Mergers and Acquisitions in China's Retail Industry*, Beijing: Ernst and Young China.

Ferner, A. (1997) Country of origin effects and HRM in multinational companies, *Human Resource Management Journal*, 7, 1, 19–37.

Ferner, A., and J. Quintanilla (1998) Multinationals, national business systems and HRM: the enduring influence of national identity or a process of 'Anglo-Saxonization', *International Journal of Human Resource Management*, 9, 4, 710–30.

Ferner, A., and M. Varul (2000) 'Vanguard' subsidiaries and the diffusion of new practices: a case study of German multinationals, *British Journal of Industrial Relations*, 38, 1, 115–40.

Francis, C.-B. (1996) Reproduction of *Danwei* institutional features in the context of China's market economy: the case of Haidian district's high-tech sector, *China Quarterly*, 147, 839–59.

Gamble, J. (2000) Localizing management in foreign-invested enterprises in China: practical, cultural, and strategic perspectives, *International Journal of Human Resource Management*, 11, 5, 883–903.

(2003) *Shanghai in Transition: Changing Perspectives and Social Contours of a Chinese Metropolis*, London: Routledge Curzon.

(2006a), Multinational retailers in China: proliferating 'McJobs' or developing skills?, *Journal of Management Studies*, 43, 7, 1463–90.

(2006b) Introducing Western-style HRM practices to China: shopfloor perceptions of employment in a multinational, *Journal of World Business*, 41, 4, 328–43.

(2007) The rhetoric of the consumer and customer control in China, *Work, Employment and Society*, 21, 1, 7–25.

Gill, R., and A. Wong (1998) The cross-cultural transfer of management practices: the case of Japanese human resource management practices in Singapore, *International Journal of Human Resource Management*, 9, 1, 116–35.

Goodall, K., and M. Warner (1998) HRM dilemmas in China: the case of foreign-invested enterprises in Shanghai, *Asia Pacific Business Review*, 4, 4, 1–21.

Hall, P. A., and D. Soskice (eds.) (2001) *Varieties of Capitalism: The Institutional Foundations of Comperative Advantage*, Oxford: Oxford University Press.

Harris, K., S. Baron and B. Davies (1999), 'What sort of soil do rhododendrons like?' Comparing customer and employee responses to requests for product-related information, *Journal of Services Marketing*, 13, 1, 21–37.

Lane, C. (1998) European companies between globalization and localization: a comparison of internationalization strategies of British and German MNEs, *Economy and Society*, 27, 4, 462–85.

Lockett, M. (1988) Culture and the problems of Chinese management, *Organization Studies*, 9, 4, 475–96.

Lu, Y., and I. Björkman (1997) HRM practices in China–Western joint ventures: MNC standardization versus localization, *International Journal of Human Resource Management*, 8, 5, 614–28.

Monks, K. (1996) Global or local? HRM in the multinational company: the Irish experience, *International Journal of Human Resource Management*, 7, 3, 721–35.

Mueller, F., and J. Purcell (1992) The Europeanisation of manufacturing and the decentralisation of bargaining: multinational management strategies in the European automobile industry, *International Journal of Human Resource Management*, 3, 1, 15–34.

Nohria, N., and S. Ghoshal (1994) Differentiated fit and shared values: alternatives for managing headquarters–subsidiary relations, *Strategic Management Journal*, 15, 491–502.

Purcell, W., S. Nicholas, D. Merrett and G. Whitwell (1999) The transfer of human resource and management practice by Japanese multinationals to Australia: do industry, size and experience matter?, *International Journal of Human Resource Management*, 10, 1, 72–88.

Rosenzweig, P. M., and N. Nohria (1994) Influences on human resource management practices in multinational corporations, *Journal of International Business Studies*, 25, 2, 229–51.

Sally, R. (1994) Multinational enterprises, political economy and institutional theory: domestic embeddedness in the context of internationalization, *Review of International Political Economy*, 1, 1, 161–92.

Smith, C., and P. Thompson (1998) Re-evaluating the labour process debate, *Economic and Industrial Democracy*, 19, 4, 551–77.

Taylor, S., S. Beechler and N. Napier (1996) Toward an integrative model of strategic international human resource management, *Academy of Management Review*, 21, 4, 959–85.

Townsend, A., D. Sadler and R. Hudson (1996) Geographical dimensions of UK retailing employment change, in N. Wrigley and M. Lowe (eds.) *Retailing, Consumption and Capital: Towards the new Retail Geography*, Harlow: Longman, 208–18.

Turnbull, P., and V. Wass (1998) Marxist management: sophisticated human relations in a high street retail store, *Industrial Relations Journal*, 29, 2, 98–111.

Warner, M. (1997) China's HRM in transition: towards relative convergence?, *Asia Pacific Business Review*, 3, 4, 19–33.

(1999) Human resources and management in China's 'hi-tech' revolution: a study of selected computer hardware, software and related firms in the PRC, *International Journal of Human Resource Management*, 10, 1, 1–20.

Whitley, R. (1992) *Business Systems in East Asia: Firms, Markets and Societies*, London: Sage.

Zhu, C. J. (2005) *Human Resource Management in China: Past, Current and Future HR Practices in the Industrial Sector*, London: Routledge Curzon.

7 Surviving through transplantation and cloning: the Swiss Migros hybrid, Migros-Türk

Gül Berna Özcan

Prelude

Labour Day celebrations were stormy at the headquarters of Migros in 1994.[1] The streets of Kadiköy, a middle-class mixed residential and office neighbourhood across the Bosporus from the prestige business district of Istanbul, were blocked with heavy traffic as demonstrators indulged in the routine clashes with police. Reporters on the scene became more enraged at the anarchistic turn of demonstrators, who uprooted flowers in the small parks they passed. The pillage of stores and other capitalist symbols was unusual, and many commentators suggested that this was a reaction to liberalisation and conspicuous consumption. Bad news for retailers such as Migros-Türk. They had just began to develop large-scale retailing and had to be sensitive to social tension, which, if combined with a downturn in the economic cycle, could have halted business growth altogether.

Despite his depressed mood and annoyance with the riot police, who had taken over the entire top floor and roof of his building in order to observe the demonstrators, the general manager, Bülent Özaydinli, was still excited about the future of his company. Despite his worries about social, economic and political disruptions, he was optimistic, and one of his remarks was prescient about Turkey's relations with Europe: 'With this retail transformation, Turkey is already in Europe even without EU membership.'

Eleven years later the new Migros-Türk headquarters was strategically located in a wealthy satellite town of Istanbul with abundant green areas and parks. The new general manager, Aziz Bulgu, was a veteran of the aggressive move into the Russian market that had helped to build the company's brand as 'Ramstore' in many of the countries comprising the Commonwealth of

Independent States (CIS).[2] Bulgu was more concerned about the intensified competition from foreign retailers than social unrest or political instability. Britain's Tesco had newly entered the Turkish market and, despite their earlier entry, Metro and Carrefour were just gaining confidence and beginning to expand their operations. Despite these global competitors, Migros-Türk was still the biggest and most widely spread retailer in the country, with a large stake in Russia and central Asia.

Introduction

In describing the development of the British department store Marks and Spencer, Gary Davies (1999) argues that the success of the company has been largely through organic growth and the managed evolution of a retail format that has changed slowly over the last 100 years. Such slow managed evolution, the author claims, can be explained by theories of the 'wheel of retailing' and the 'retail accordion'. In contrast, the case of Migros-Türk does not support these theories and the biological metaphors appropriate for it are not evolutionary. Even if we can trace cyclical patterns in other Turkish retail institutions, Migros's history is one of many temporal and spatial discontinuities from its origins in Switzerland to its domestication as part of the Koç conglomerate of Turkey. Studying the recent history of Migros can be better understood within the context of business transplants, technology and business transfers, which are inadequately understood and conceptualised in retail change theories. In this chapter I show that business change occurred through experiments of transplantation and cloning that ruptured the market with the introduction of alien retail institutions that had not evolved in the Turkish market. The move from Swiss Migros to Migros-Türk exemplifies a development from transplantation to an eventual successful hybrid existence through institutional and organisational changes in large-scale retailing.

In this chapter I show how the successful growth of Migros-Türk illustrates uneven organisational development interrupted by a fractured deployment of retail technologies. The case demonstrates the role of an agency in shaping organisational destiny in relation to the big waves of changes taking place in Turkish society and the economy. Despite the availability of mostly US and European retail technologies and management techniques, the uneven institutional diffusion of retail business models supports the view common among sceptics of global standardisation. Varying economic growth and the diversity of business practices indicate that homogenisation or global standardisation is not an inevitable result of the availability of technology. Instead, both the transfer process and the institutionalisation of technology and business models are highly unpredictable and discontinuous across sectors and economic spheres. This process is often affected deeply by the response of agents and institutions to changing environmental circumstances (i.e. market competition, regulation and social development). I demonstrate here that, due to these complexities, the organisational response is highly heterogeneous in the application of new business techniques and technology transfer.

Migros-Türk is analysed within this conceptual framework, showing how its success was engraved by its hybridisation, which eventually not only differed from its original Swiss company's business model but also set it apart from its domestic rivals. First, the Migros-Türk phenomenon is explored in terms of its business behaviour, organisational capacity and change agents. Second, the scene is set for the trajectory of the company within the societal and environmental changes in Turkey that have changed the business landscape dramatically from mostly state-controlled to a liberal market economy over the past three decades.

The search by the Istanbul municipal authorities for technical assistance in establishing a new food distribution agency resulted in the first internationally owned retail chain to enter the Turkish market. Thus, in 1954, the Swiss-owned cooperative Migros introduced its retail technology and know-how. First, mobile retailing began with trucks in order to provide an effective food service for Istanbul residents. Gradually, Migros introduced small stores for middle-class consumers. Stringent import substitution policies and the resultant scarcity of goods and services forced the Swiss co-operative to sell its business to one of the Turkish state-owned banks in 1974, a period of political turmoil in the country. This brought growth to a halt for the organisation, until it began to restructure itself some twenty years later. The change from a partly foreign-owned co-operative to Turkey's first national retailer accompanied deep changes in the market economy, society and retail technology. The survival of Migros-Türk is the result of its organisational capability as an institution, riding high on waves of retail change cycles in response to Europeanisation, deregulation and privatisation. As much as the institutional capabilities and opportunities created by environmental and technological changes, the role of key actors, such as the pioneering manager Bülent Özaydinli, its synergies with real estate developers and contractors, the strength of the Koç family conglomerate and the determination of a young and very ambitious group of middle managers behind the business have made Migros a far more successful retailer than its domestic rivals such as Gima and Tansaş.

This chapter is divided into five sections. The first section provides a general overview of retail change theories and offers a critical perspective on how a multiplicity of theories can be applied to business cases. It also highlights the peculiarities of this sort of single case study approach vis-à-vis aggregate sectoral studies. The second section introduces the early start of Migros within the context of cooperative establishments and their considerable importance in food distribution and retailing in the 1950s. An interim period of scarcity and turbulence is described in the third section, followed by an analysis of the cloning of Migros-Türk, based on European retailing, at a time of deregulation and liberalisation in the Turkish economy. The following section illustrates how the hybridisation of local know-how with retail technology characterised the successful internationalisation of the company. The conclusion argues that the company's success lies in its survival in a volatile environment. Its business change through the transplantation and cloning of foreign commercial technology has now produced a sustainable hybrid capable of developing its own retail technology and business structure.

Retail change and technology transfer

The essential elements of retail change theories focus on the dynamic interaction between retail forms (institutions) and their competition (markets). Businesses react to market forces to survive, while competition pushes retailers to devise an unending stream of new retail forms. In these approaches, institutions are very loosely defined, and range from individual firms or groups of firms to looser forms of organisation (chain stores, cooperatives, etc.) and national retail systems. For the most part, however, they refer to distinctive structures or techniques, such as a convenience stores, department stores, supermarkets, variety stores, shopping centres, discount stores, hypermarkets, etc.

Stephen Brown (1987) offers the most comprehensive account of retail change theories (see, for example, Roth and Klein, 1993, for ecological theories and Evans, Barnes and Schlacter, 1993, and Appel, 1972, for institutional evolution). First, environmental theory argues that changes in retailing are a function of developments in the socio-economic environment; such studies include cases and ecological and natural selection approaches.

Second, the cyclical theory suggests that change takes place in a rhythmic fashion and is characterised by the recurrence of earlier trends, such as the 'wheel of retailing' and retail life cycles. Third, conflict theory focuses on inter-institutional conflict, which occurs when new forms of retailing emerge, develop and disrupt traditional trade practices.

In studying Migros-Türk we make two important distinctions. First, theoretical generalisations on the evolution of retail forms offer limited scope for the research of an individual company. Second, we are studying a retailer in a developing economy in which mature Western retail forms have been transplanted and did not evolve in the dynamic context of markets and institutions. Thus, although the merits of environmentalist and ecological theoretical perspectives are apparent, their explanatory power is weak when it comes to the study of organisational survival as well as discontinuity. While most modern retail technologies and institutions enter emerging economies through foreign direct investment or technology transfer, there is little informed research on how domestic organisations use and reproduce these technologies.

Marketing scientists long ago suggested a direct relationship between economic development and retail institutions. The sophistication of retailing and distribution channels from production to consumption is regarded as a function of economic development. More levels of distribution and retail outlets are associated with higher economic development (Samiee, 1993; Hollander, 1986; Savitt, 1982). In many developing economies, the problem of scarcity and the mismatch between high urban demand and poor food supply and distribution have been commonly observed phenomena (Currie, 1968). On account of the low incomes, cultural differences in consumption habits and state-imposed price caps and other market distortions, many researchers questioned the merits of retail technology transfer to developing countries. Research in the 1980s concluded that Western retail techniques were not easily transferable or exportable (Yavaş, Kaynak and Borak, 1981; Goldman, 1982; Savitt, 1990). For example, Ronald Savitt (1990) has questioned whether economic development can be triggered by simply importing retail technology. Erdener Kaynak (1982, 1986) has emphasised the role of efficient marketing and distribution channels in food distribution and economic development. Ronan Paddison, Allan Findlay and John Dawson (1990) have linked the slow modernisation of retailing to peculiar supply and demand conditions in developing countries.

The success of technology transfer in this sector is highly dependent upon the customer profile and receptivity. Market penetration by supermarkets and hypermarkets is conditional on external factors such as customer mobility, household income and consumption habits. Similarly, supporting businesses in production, service and distribution are crucial for the success of large-scale retailing. Retailers in developing countries are often characterised by a large number of small, independent, family-run shops and wholesalers (Kaynak, 1982). Capital accumulation is modest and businesses lack knowledge of modern marketing techniques. Food distribution channels are described as long and household production widespread among the rural households and poor urban residents (Samiee, 1993). Paddison, Findlay and Dawson (1990) argue that the urban retailing system in developing countries appears to be chaotic by comparison with the spatial segregation and hierarchical ordering of developed economies. Periodic marketing, street selling, hawking and the informal sector not only constitute an important segment of the retail trade in these countries but also offer employment opportunities. Just as developing countries themselves display marked diversity and complexity, however, so does retailing in these countries. Their level of industrialisation, economic growth and size of population vary greatly, too. The emergence of mass markets across the world's big cities is changing retail landscapes, as well as consumption and shopping habits.

In the late 1980s some marketing scientist began to argue that urban people in developed and developing countries were converging on similar consumption patterns (Kaynak, 1986). Nonetheless, most Third World literature remained suspicious about the effects of the transfer of new retail outlets and technologies, focusing rightly on economic development and government control as indicating an underdeveloped retail and wholesale market in many developing economies. What has changed the retail sector of developing economies dramatically since the 1980s, however, has been global trade liberalisation and the internationalisation of large US and European retailers. Some have argued that government polices have been more influential in shaping the retail business in developing countries than market competition (Hollander and Boddewyn, 1974). Nevertheless, it remains the case that the diffusion of many Western products into domestic wholesale chains throughout the 1970s and 1980s altered distribution networks and tastes in developing countries long before supermarkets entered (Tokatlı and Eldener, 2002). The impact of media and internet technologies has also been substantial in opening up a new consumer age. Today many modern retail forms such as supermarkets and shopping malls are available in cities in the developing world, and these have profound effects on consumer behaviour, retail and distribution channels, and food production and marketing. The degree of market penetration by retail technology is still low, but for many middle-income developing countries supermarkets, hypermarkets and shopping malls are common features of the urban landscape.

Retail technology includes not just equipment and software but also the organisational moulding of these technologies through their use in design, store formats and marketing tools. It also involves knowledgeable participation on the part of shoppers. The use of computer technology in the retail industry began in the 1970s and 1980s for non-administrative tasks. The introduction of bar code readers and scanners provided major cost saving and efficiency gains to retailers (Walsh, 1993). Information technologies (IT) began to shape all aspects of retailing, from supply chain management to customer relationship management, in the 1980s. Electronic point of sale (EPOS)[3] and electronic data interchange (EDI) technologies are now widely used by retailers around the world (Lynch, 1990; Al-Sudairy and Tang, 2000). These technologies speed up the exchange of data and payment, and they enhance the spread of massive retail operations into different geographical locations. They also optimise delivery and logistics among suppliers, warehouses and retail outlets. Recent developments in information technologies have rationalised distribution channels, and extend the power of large-scale retailing vis-à-vis manufacturers and suppliers globally (Ducatel and Blomley, 1990). New IT tools, such as internet shopping, wireless scanning, new inventory management techniques, hand-held computers and automatic computer reordering, are being experimented with by global retailers.

These enabling technologies, although developed mostly in the United States, have been widely available to retailers worldwide. As Chandler (2005) has argued, however, importing a tool is not a transfer of technology in itself; rather, how that tool is used in an organisation and how it is subject to innovation mark an integrated learning base for an organisation. Indeed, as we illustrate in this case study, technology diffusion in modern retailing has been uneven and often shaped by institutional players and societal changes. The trajectory of Migros-Türk, Turkey's leading domestic and international retailer, can best be understood as part of the complex interplay between an engineered existence through the periodic upgrading of retail technology and broader institutional and environmental changes. In the following section we examine how Migros-Türk evolved as an organisation and how it responded to its changing environment.

The rise of cooperatives and the first transplantation of Migros

Migros-Türk originated in cooperative movements in Europe. Although consumer cooperatives never played a significant role in US retailing and distribution, they have played an important role in many western European countries. They were among the leaders in introducing self-service retailing to the European food traders, and by 1960 cooperatives accounted for one-tenth of all retail sales in Norway, Sweden, the United Kingdom, Switzerland, and Denmark (Jefferys and Knee, 1962). In the 1950s cooperative organisations expressed a sense of responsibility for the promotion of counterpart institutions in developing nations. Many of the advocates considered cooperatives an avenue for the social, as well as economic, advancement of people whose material resources were limited. Moreover, some proponents believed that cooperative activity closely resembled the ties of tribal or village life, and thus was particularly suitable to conditions in many poor countries (Hollander, 1970). As pointed out by Reed Moyer and Stanley Hollander (1968), developing country policy-makers who associated commercial trade with colonial powers or with unpopular ethnic minority groups felt a strong preference for cooperative enterprise.

Food distribution cooperatives were first introduced in Turkey in 1913, during the Balkan Wars, in order to cope with price increases and shortages. After the collapse of the Ottoman Empire the republican government aimed to fill market gaps in food processing and established state-run enterprises in meat, sugar and flour production. Although Turkey did not take part in the Second World War, its economy was severely affected. During the war the government introduced the National Protection Law, which aimed to control food prices and regulated the rationing of sugar, flour and bread. The state had an almost complete monopoly in modern foodstuffs processing and distribution, including staples such as fish, meat, milk, sugar, and tea. All the same, there were severe food shortages and distribution problems (Şamlı, 1964). Istanbul was a rapidly growing city and suffered the most. The newspapers at that time were reporting shortages of sugar and coffee every day, along with unpredictable price increases. Middle-class urbanites sought their food supplies from bazaars and small shops. The food-handling standards were poor, with no labelling, no proper packaging and no reliable measurements. Food was commonly wrapped in newspapers, and customers used their own shopping bags. In order to regulate food distribution and prevent black markets from growing, the first generation of supermarkets were initiated by municipalities, state companies and cooperatives in order to provide affordable and secure food delivery.

In the post-war period the municipality of Istanbul was determined to regulate foodstuffs retailing in the city and sent an expert, Ferruh Ilter, to the United States to learn about new retail practices. During this period Ilter learnt about Swiss Migros, and later he visited Switzerland. Upon his return he was appointed head of the economy division of the municipality, with responsibility for food pricing and distribution in the city. He quickly recognised the need for know-how in modern retailing in the city, and persuaded the mayor, the governor and the finance minister to support his idea of inviting the founder of Swiss Migros, Gottlieb Duttweiler, to bring that company's retail technology to Istanbul. He sent a formal invitation letter to Duttweiler in October 1953 (Oluç, 1956).

Gottlieb Duttweiler had begun food retailing in 1925, at the age of sixteen, and he emigrated to Brazil during World War I. Upon his return to Switzerland he acquired five old Ford trucks and began mobile retailing. His low prices quickly made him unpopular among established retailers. Although there were many difficulties, particularly during the early years, when Duttweiler was threatened with imprisonment because of his deviations from the price control laws, the organisation flourished throughout Switzerland. Migros expanded its business into food production, printing and even the film industry. By 1954 Migros had 289 retail stores (including ten supermarkets) and seventy trucks, nine butcher's shops and three clothing stores (Oluç, 1956).

The invitation to Istanbul and the municipality's commitments were serious. A group of experts from Swiss Migros accompanied the deputy manager, H. Hochstrasser, to Istanbul in January 1954. With the aim of providing 'cheap foodstuffs', the introduction of the Migros model was strongly supported by the municipality and the government. Following negotiations, the limited liability company Migros-Türk was established with the participation of nineteen shareholders, including Duttweiler and Hochstrasser, with TL500,000 total capital – equivalent to only a few thousand US dollars. As this was too small an amount to introduce the Migros way of retailing, the government supported the deal with a generous TL5 million credit scheme from the state-controlled Ziraat and Yapi Kredi Banks. Thus, the transplantation began. Swiss Migros sent the first general manager, Karl Ketterer, to Istanbul and eight Turkish civil servants went to Switzerland to be trained in accounting, packaging technologies, management and sales. Turkey had no automobile industry, so sixty trucks had to be imported from the United Kingdom. A warehouse was opened in Eminönü food market, where food was classified, weighed and packaged. A customised packaging machine was imported for this purpose. The arrival of the first twenty trucks, which paraded through the city, was greeted by excited crowds and accompanied by motorcycle policemen. The opening ceremony turned into a state celebration, with the participation of many Members of Parliament and ministers, along with the mayor and governor of Istanbul, on 30 September 1955. Trucks began operating on fixed neighbourhood routes and leaflets were delivered to residents about the time of truck delivery stops. This was a new concept of shopping time, and some contemporaries pointed out that observing clock time was not a common phenomenon for housewives; many households did not pay attention to, or even have, clocks at all!

At first, the trucks sold just twenty-nine categories of foodstuffs, totalling fifty items, and truck drivers used telephones to communicate their supply needs. The business was a great success, however. During the first few days the trucks were emptied by their fourth or fifth stop. In December 1957 the first store (with a total floor space of 114 sq. m.) was opened in Balıkpazarı, Istanbul; reports indicate that finding building material and store furniture was a real problem at the time. Migros-Türk's sales increased and the number of stores reached eight by 1959, despite rising inflation, high national debt and generally poor economic management by the ruling Democrat Party. Food shortages, high prices and the black market continued to be a problem for many in Istanbul. The company introduced roadside stands in the late 1950s, and by 1959 it had sixty trucks, eleven roadside stands and 327 employees. During this period the economy struggled, with a severe shortage of currency (inflation had risen to 90 per cent in 1958) and heavy foreign borrowing fuelled by clumsy populist politics, leading to a deep financial crisis. This, combined with the fears of traditionalist revivalism, triggered a military coup in 1960.

Despite the outward appearance of a successful transplantation, there were severe problems for the new company. First, Migros-Türk was encountering heavy financial losses. The government's price control of food products was the main concern of the Swiss partners and they deeply resented having to work in such an environment. Second, the company encountered considerable difficulty in securing spare parts and replacement units for trucks, because of import and foreign exchange controls. Truck maintenance costs tended to be high relative to sales volume. In addition, importing spare parts for trucks and other equipment took a long time and involved cumbersome bureaucratic procedures. A shipment of used trucks donated by the Swiss partners to replace badly deteriorated and obsolete units in the Turkish fleet was delayed for months over negotiations with the authorities about the appropriate customs duties. These difficulties all hindered the business. Third, the shortage of skilled people and a high turnover of sales assistants also became a problem as the business grew. Finally, the bad roads, harsh winters and hot summers made truck operations and food delivery difficult. Swiss Migros expressed its intention to leave and tried to negotiate a cooperative deal to sell shares to individuals, but neither the government nor the municipality had schemes in place that could implement this. Indeed, Swiss Migros began to think that it was expected to play a purely technical, advisory and marginal role. The venture reached the point of collapse by the end of the 1950s.

The government was determined to save Migros-Türk from collapse and bankruptcy, however. Negotiations continued and repeated assurances were given to the Swiss partners to persuade them to stay. Eventually they accepted a new deal. The company was recapitalised with TL9 million following the coup and Swiss Migros took a controlling share of 51 per cent in partnership with municipal and state organisations, including Istanbul municipality, the State Enterprise for Meat and Fishery Products and Ziraat Bank. With this new structure, Migros-Türk became a quasi-state-owned enterprise. According to plans in the late 1960s, the eventual aim was to turn Migros-Türk into a quasi-cooperative on the Swiss model (Hollander, 1970). This never happened, however. Retail stores began to operate in 1958 and they soon became more profitable than truck sales, accounting for over 60 per cent of total sales by 1967. The shift away from mobile retailing and small 'barrack-type' stands took Migros-Türk into more prosperous middle-class neighbourhoods. A buying office was set up in Mersin, in Turkey's southern agricultural heartland, and the company also began food processing in a minor way. Gradually direct purchases increased, from 18 per cent in 1961 to 59 per cent in 1967. Earnings increased in the late 1960s, closing the deficit gap.

Migros-Türk was initially opposed by small retailers and convenience stores, but most of these small retailers managed to retain their business, as supermarket penetration was slow with sales directed mainly to middle-class urbanites. In any event, the urban middle classes continued to patronise the periodic bazaars and other small retailers. This behaviour fits well with generalisations of customers in developing countries, described by Saeed Samiee (1993) as being characterised by: people buying smaller quantities, with frequent visits to small shops in their neighbourhood; customers requiring a large variety of products with minimal packaging; small retailers offering credit to their regular customers; and shopping functioning as an important form of social interaction. Ugur Yavaş, Erdener Kaynak and Eser Borak (1981) point out that shopkeepers would extend credit only to the customers whom they know; non-supermarket shoppers therefore see this as an important factor in their relations with the retailer.

By the end of the 1960s Swiss Migros was operating seventeen stores and thirty-five sales trucks. When Hollander studied Migros-Türk, he saw a positive picture:

Approximately thirteen or fourteen years of arduous efforts are really just beginning to bear fruit, and Migros-Türk is just beginning to be viable, a more self-reliant economic force. In the process it has become considerably more of a middle-class institution than was envisaged at the start of the venture. Its experience accords with the general rule that so-called Western or modern retailing techniques are most easily introduced in the middle- and upper income sectors of the developing economies. (1970: 87–8)

The Turkish urban middle classes were growing, but only slowly. Import substitution policies were bearing fruit in terms of industrialisation and the domestic production of foodstuffs. The first Turkish-made automobile, the Anadol, came out in 1967. The economy was heating up again, however, with inflation on the rise once more. Anti-American student demonstrations in 1968 were a landmark event in the intensifying political crisis, which eventually led to a military coup in March 1971. Migros-Türk's sales declined again during this period, in line with the deepening economic crisis.

The search for modern retailing and marketing in scarcity and turbulence

The 1970s were bloody and turbulent. Turkey might have been defending NATO's borders against the Soviet Union but the American dream never materialised. Despite heavy foreign borrowing industrialisation was slow, and the economy suffered periodic setbacks. Ideological divisions sharpened. Many intellectuals and students who supported leftist ideologies were against the exploitation of capitalist enterprises, while the ultra-nationalists and traditionalists were united in defiance of the subversive values of communism. From 1974 onwards there were street clashes between left- and right-wing youth groups across the country. Businesses did not escape the effects of the conflict, as industrial disputes and attacks exacerbated the crisis. Ever since the mid-1960s domestic production and investments had been dependent upon imports, for which there were limited financial resources. Coupled with the first and second oil shocks of the 1970s, inflation soared and remained high, and the economy went into a deep recession marked by severe shortages of goods, high unemployment and business closures. Turkey had to rely on workers' remittances from Europe for its foreign currency.

The scarcity of food and a rise in black market trade created shortages of basic foodstuffs in all major cities. State control brought inflexibility and further fuelled the black market. Retailers and wholesalers were accused of making unlawful profits. Swiss Migros was determined this time that it would pull out of the Turkish market. Rudolf Suter, a board member of Migros-Türk for the period of 1962–76, expressed the parent company's frustrations with the political and economic instability in the country, identifying the price controls imposed by the state as the most important difficulty Migros-Türk faced, and arguing that the business could not be maintained with this imposed price regime while inflation and costs were rising. Swiss Migros considered selling its shares to a cooperative, but there was no buyer. The government was worried about market disruptions and urged Swiss Migros not to harm consumers in such hard times. Suter approached several of Turkey's largest businessmen, among them Vehbi Koç, the founder of the Koç family conglomerate, which was then beginning to invest in food processing and had just opened TAT, a canned food factory. Koç had risen in business from trade and once owned a small convenience store himself. This background is believed to have played a role in his decision to buy Migros-Türk despite the turbulent economic and political environment.

A new beginning was engineered when Migros-Türk Limited was finally established, on 13 January 1975, the name being retained after an agreement had been reached with Swiss Migros. At that date the company was still only an Istanbul-based retailer, with sixteen stores, thirty-two trucks and 707 employees. Most of the equipment and merchandise was old and the facilities were in a dire condition. First the Koç family raised the capital from TL9 million to TL50 million. Then they brought in several young and successful managers, who ended up staying with the company for decades. The most influential of those were Oktay Irsıdar and Hulki Halisbah, who gave long service as board members and helped to establish business networks and a solid supply chain. The new Migros-Türk endured more than a decade of slow growth while it upgraded its facilities. Indeed, no significant technology upgrading took place until 1990, and its first store outside Istanbul, in Izmir, Turkey's third largest city, was opened only in 1988, thirteen years after Koç had acquired the major stake in the company. By this time Migros-Türk was no longer a pacesetter in modern retailing, and the Koç family preferred to see the company 'hibernate', maintaining only the existing routines.

In the light of the economic crisis of the 1970s, both the government and marketing experts argued that large supermarkets and cooperatives could resolve price increases and food shortages. The main debate concentrated on whether Turkey was ready for large modern stores (Oksay, 1979; Koparal, 1988). Scholars were also debating these issues in connection with developing countries (Goldman, 1981, 1982). The growing private sector was not interested in large-scale retailing, however. Consequently, the second generation of supermarkets were developed as consumer cooperatives and in conjunction with local governments in order to cope with price increases and to provide a regular supply of foodstuffs. Local governments played a particularly significant role in establishing supermarkets and special stores known as Tanzim Satış, which emerged with municipal management in the major cities. Local governments also intervened in food distribution channels and tried to crowd out middlemen in the distribution channel. Not many of these stores thrived, however. Tansaş, an enterprise of the municipality of Izmir, set up in 1973, did succeed adapting supermarket technology in the 1980s and further expanding its business during the 1990s. Gima also prospered, as did the Ordu Pazarlari, a supermarket chain, which was established for members of the Turkish armed forces.

The cloning of Migros-Türk with market liberalisation

The 1980 military coup stopped the bloodshed of the 1970s and initiated economic liberalisation, but it narrowed the scope for democracy. The first elected government did not take power till 1983, led by Turgut Özal, an admirer and friend of the United Kingdom's prime minister, Margaret Thatcher, and the United States president, Ronald Reagan. He quickly began deregulating the closed economy, following IMF and World Bank prescriptions. Starting from the mid-1980s government policies aimed to reduce the direct role of the state in the economy through deregulation, and the privatisation of state-owned food-processing enterprises came into effect in 1987. The minor share held by state banks in Migros-Türk was sold to the Koç family. Koç opened four new stores in Izmir in 1988 and began assessing the future of the business in light of the more competitive environment. Urban incomes were rising, along with car ownership, which increased twentyfold between 1970 and 1990 (see http://ekutup.dpt.gov.tr/ekonomi/gosterge/tr/1950-04/esg.htm). The same year the first modern shopping mall, Galleria, opened in Istanbul, with the French store Printemps as its anchor.

Metro, the German cash and carry store, entered the Turkish market in 1990, followed by France's Carrefour in 1991. The French Prusinic and Istanbul municipality opened Turkey's biggest supermarket, Belpa, in Merter, a working-class district of Istanbul, in 1991 (Aydin, 1992). These were followed by other European retailers (Özcan, 2001). The liberalisation policies aimed at changing the outlook for the Turkish economy, thereby influencing society as a whole. Copying Western-style retailing and shopping malls was seen as a visible symbol of this change. Thus, the government actively encouraged modernisation through incentives to large domestic and international retailers (Tokatlı and Özcan, 1998).

Although official moves to effect a policy change from import substitution to liberal economic development took place in the early 1980s, the real impact of the liberal trade regime began to make itself felt only in the 1990s. The customs union agreement with the European Union in 1995 marked the single most important development in reducing trade barriers and eliminating the state protection that had previously been extended to domestic businesses, with high tariffs and exemptions. The flow of foreign direct investment into Turkey was persistently small compared with that into eastern Europe, but remaining within the range of $1 to 2 billion until 2003 (see http://ekutup.dpt.gov.tr/ekonomi/gosterge/tr/1950-04/esg.htm), the large retailing sector proved to be the most attractive one for European investors. At a time when their home markets were becoming saturated and planning restrictions for new urban location were tightening, many large retailers were looking for international expansion. Successful applications of IT made large-scale retailing more efficient and profitable. Early comers were French and German investors, followed by Dutch, Belgian and American firms. The 1990s witnessed many activities and consolidation efforts. Despite their early entry, French retailers – with the exception of Carrefour – have not been successful in Turkey.

For the first time large conglomerates and banks took an interest in retailing, attracted by the advantages of daily cash generation and customer data. Bank-owning conglomerates, such as Fiba Holding and the Doğuş group, acquired Gima and Tansaş, respectively (Özcan, 2000). Credit buying allowed suppliers to be used as surrogate banks by retailers, with credit purchases consisting of a significant share of the stock. (This is a general phenomenon as large retailers gain a powerful position in the market vis-à-vis manufacturers and suppliers, (see Plender, Simons and Tricks, 2005.) More importantly, with this credit advantage, the daily cash generated in retailing was dumped into 'hot money' markets with high interest rates. With inflation running at around 60 to 80 per cent, short-term interest rates reached 100 per cent and higher. Anecdotal evidence reveals that many large retailers invested their cash in this money market. Land development and speculation generated further benefits to those, such as Carrefour, that were able to purchase large areas and develop new shopping space to rent or sell. These alternative capital-generating techniques became widespread among domestic retailers as well.

After more than a decade of hesitation the Koç family decided to enter large-scale retailing and update its retail technology. From 1990 onwards Migros-Türk began imitating European retailers in using state-of-the-art-technology. The technology and marketing aspects of supermarket and hypermarket retailing were carefully studied and American consultants were hired. The Koç family was ready to pour in resources in order to make this cloning work but, more importantly, they retained the valued 'old guards' while making room for new ideas and managers. This organisational transformation facilitated the use and absorption of new retail technologies.

The newly appointed chairman of Migros-Türk, Bülent Özaydinli, came up with a ten-year plan. The old guard managers were suspicious of the big expansion and, later, even became opposed to internationalisation efforts. Nevertheless, the new chairman and new managers were able to persuade the board members and the Koç directors. A group of young and well-educated university graduates was hired and many stayed on and grew in stature with the business. The top universities were the main source of new ideas and management techniques in the country, and these young managers were ready to absorb the new retail technology. The transforming retailing business fitted well with their expectations for modernisation in Turkey as well. The ideological confrontations of the 1960s and 1970s had been marginalised by the 1990s. Migros-Türk was able to recruit from the growing pool of young graduates in the fields of marketing, economics and IT studies. Özaydinli secured the success of the business by cultivating the loyalty and ability of middle managers and professionals. Their response was positive, and many devoted their work to the domestic and international success of the company. Throughout our interviews these managers stressed their pride in the speed of the expansion. As one said, 'We were growing so quickly, for a while opening one store per week, it became extremely exciting and challenging' (interview with Kerim Tatlıcı, manager, July 2005).

In 1991 the store format was updated on similar lines to those of Swiss Migros, although there were no formal business links. Around the same time the first Gulf War began and Turkey agreed to join the coalition forces led by the United States and the United Kingdom. The war ruined the economy of south-eastern Turkey, as trade and oil pipeline revenues were lost. Kurdish separatists' guerrilla training camps operated from northern Iraq and further destabilised the situation. The increased political insecurity also slowed down the aggressive pursuit of European retailers. Migros-Türk was accustomed to the bumpy nature of the Turkish economy and politics, however, and usually enjoyed good relations with political parties as an affiliate of Koç, then the biggest Turkish conglomerate. With this confidence and market understanding, it was able to make a major leap forward at a time when other large international retailers were busy consolidating their entry gains in Istanbul. The technology acquisition and in-house software development were successful; the new store format was working; and customers were enthusiastic. Secure in this knowledge, the company developed a goal of opening two stores per week in 1996.

The survival of a hybrid through technology absorption and internationalisation

Other momentous political events were taking place during this period as well. In 1989 the eastern bloc began to crumble, and in 1991 the Soviet Union was dismantled. This was both a big ideological shock and an unexpected economic opportunity for Turkey. The motto of the 1970s – 'Communists to Moscow!' – was quickly buried in the public psyche. Trade, tourism and business links grew rapidly between Russia and Turkey. Economic and cultural ties with the formerly little-known central Asian Turkic-speaking states also grew. Turkish construction companies, which were successful in the Middle East and north Africa, were among the first to enter the Russian market. They gained a good reputation and developed an understanding of and links with the political elite and bureaucracy there. Thousands of shuttle traders from CIS countries flocked to the northern Black Sea towns of Trabzon and Rize, and Istanbul's Laleli district became a major hub for shuttle traders from eastern Europe, Russia and central Asia in the 1990s (Yükseker, 2003). Turkish entrepreneurs began seeking business fortunes in central Asia and Russia, leading to the establishment of many Turkish-owned companies. Economic and political reforms linked to the European Union accession talks and political consolidation led to further positive developments. The rate of inflation finally came down to a single-digit figure in 2003, after twenty years when rates had averaged some 60 per cent. Business confidence increased, with exports, mainly industrial, and tourism revenues soaring from 2000 onwards.

The Turkish retail market continues to offer enormous room for the entry of large retailers: the top three retailers' market share is only 12 per cent, compared to 57 per cent in Germany and 64 per cent in France. Despite the fact that the growth of GDP had taken the per capita figure past the $5,000 level, however, intraregional and urban inequalities remained major problems, with a widening skill gap and poor public services in many cities and rural areas. Nonetheless, the affluence of the urban middle classes continued to increase. Credit sales soared as the number of bank credit cards jumped from 766,000 in 1991 to 14 million in 2001. The resistance of small retailers and their associations to the spread of big retail chains and shopping malls has recently led to the drafting of new laws on opening hours and planning restrictions, similar to the comparable attempts by small retailers in western Europe. There has been further consolation in the sector with the sale of Tansaş, Gima and Kipa, Migros-Türk's respons being the acquisition of 78.1 per cent of the shares of Tansaş[4]. This acquisition brought another 206 stores, in several regions of Turkey, and some 5,000 more employees to the company.

Opening up the domestic market to international competition made conglomerates such as Koç realise the need for technology and business upgrading. Many large and medium-sized family conglomerates that had grown behind the protective walls of the import substitution policies began seeking new opportunities through internationalisation. The Koç business group succeeded in building its home appliance brands, such as Beko, in the UK market. Özaydinli and his managers also recognised the potential of the CIS and Russian markets and needed to build friendly relations based on mutual interest, but Russia was unknown to them. The solution was found with a business synergy with the large construction company Enka, which had a good business record in Russia.[5] Thus, while large TNCs such as Tesco were securing their position in the eastern European market, Migros-Türk made the strategic decision to expand principally in Russia and central Asia.

In many ways this was a wise decision, as it was almost impossible for an emerging Turkish retailer to enter the European market. In Russia and central Asia, however, Migros-Türk's stores have become the symbol of modern retailing: in 2006 the company had three stores in Azerbaijan, ten shopping malls and forty-nine stores in Russia and two shopping malls and five stores in Kazakhstan; it also had stores in Bulgaria and one store and a hypermarket in Macedonia. The first test case of international expansion came in Baku, as Azerbaijan was culturally and physically closest to Turkey, and this was followed by investments in Russia and Kazakhstan, and, in the Balkans, Bulgaria and Macedonia, making Migros-Türk an international retailer in less than ten years. With the Ramstore brand, Migros entered the Russian market during the economic crisis in 1998. The managers' belief in the future of the Russian economy and its ability to bounce back made them friends in Kremlin. Ramstores were welcomed by Russian politicians and consumers at a time when Russia was not an attractive market for large Western retailers and there were still food shortages.

While aggressively pursuing international market opportunities, Migros-Türk has moved to occupy the whole extent of the retail accordion in the market with a range of small and large outlets, small discount stores for low-income families, cooperation with small shop keepers, internet shopping and a wholesaler business. With its range of retail formats the company captures the lower and upper ends of urban sprawl, competing directly with small convenience stores and wholesalers as well as large European retailers. Internationalisation has changed the financial structure of Migros-Türk as well: 51 per cent of shares are now owned by Koç and the rest is traded on the Istanbul Stock Exchange, 80 per cent of which is owned by foreign investors. Formerly the company was self-reliant and used mainly the financial resources of the holding group, but this also changed as it began using external funding, including an International Finance Corporation loan for $60 million to further its expansion in Moscow in 2002 (see www.ifc.org).

Over the last ten years or so the company has expanded its technological capabilities in retaining, restoring and using data. While European retailers were slow in bringing their state-of-the-art IT applications to the Turkish market, Migros-Türk became the pacesetter in the use of retail technologies such as bar codes, electronic labelling, virtual marketing, electronic self-service and business-to-business applications, although the financial crisis in 2001 did slow some of the technology applications. Standard NCR (the National Cash Register)[6] technologies were used, but almost all the company software represents in-house production adapted to the needs and priorities of the company. Along with business growth, information technologies were employed more aggressively and imaginatively to rationalise and standardise the business processes and transactions; an IT master plan was prepared in the late 1990s. Due to supply chain problems and production faults the company was encountering large losses every day, and this is still a common problem for retailers in Turkey. The business-to-business applications aimed to rationalise the supply chain, they succeeded in moving the supplier receipt and ordering process to internet speed.

All the stores are now electronically linked to each other, and also to more than 70 per cent of the 635 supplier companies, and this increases efficiency of shelf and stock control. The 2.5 million receipts that are, on average, processed each year are now dealt with electronically, offering enormous time and cost advantages. The introduction of IT has aided efficient delivery and stock control, and the improved distribution network for suppliers has enhanced organisational capabilities – and profits. By setting up a wholesale business and internet site, Migros-Türk is attempting to shape its business relations with suppliers, producers and customers. This combined with the penetration of IT-aided business practices in transactions, is changing the business culture and attitudes in retailing and wholesaling. Kangurum.com, initiated in 1998, provides internet shopping facilities, with 75,000 products from over sixty stores, and marked another first in Turkish retailing. The loyalty card scheme, Migros Club Card, began in 1998 and reached 4.5 million customers by 2005, and the targeted marketing has become more sophisticated and speedy.

The success of technology use was achieved through enhanced organisational capabilities. A new human resources and employment policy was put in place in 1990 with the appointment of young and dynamic managers to responsible positions. The number of female managers and employees also increased. This long-term dedication and ability to integrate young and ambitious professionals and managers seem to be the key to the success of the retail technology adaptation by Migros-Türk. With long-term mutual commitment by staff and firm, the organisational knowledge and capabilities generated in the lower and higher echelons of the management team has remained within the company. The company claims a continuing interest in the training and skills development of its workforce. A retail management institute was opened in 2000 at Koç University to give executive training and courses to managers and professionals about new retail technologies and trends. Members of staff were regularly sent abroad to make observations and attend conferences and trade fairs, further instilling loyalty. The speed of the business, its range of activities and the complexity of its market analysis techniques excite many of those involved.

Analysis and conclusions

The success of Migros-Türk cannot simply be explained by its first-mover advantages. Nor is it a story of continuous institutional evolution. Migros's growth trajectory saw it evolve into a hybrid form that became neither a Swiss business nor simply a mirror of a typical Turkish conglomerate. What this shows is that these hybrid organisations can emerge through business and technology transplantations, and if they can take advantage of internationalisation they can even be pacesetters in other markets for business development and technology transfer. Nevertheless, the case of Migros also shows that the process of hybridisation requires decades of organisational deployment, periodic hibernation and a determined and reliable source of capital if it is to succeed against a backdrop of market competition, state intervention and political and social volatility.

Migros-Türk had a rocky existence until the 1990s. Its organisational development stalled in the 1970s and the 1980s, when it was caught up by local chains, such as Gima and Tansaş. It was not Migros-Türk that took the first IT-monitored supermarket technology to Turkey. Turkey's first and biggest supermarket emerged from a partnership between the municipality of Istanbul and its French partner in 1991, but this enterprise failed within a few years. As in the 1950s and the 1970s, municipalities and government intervention changed the market circumstances and competitive pressures.

After more than a decade of passive survival, Migros began to import cutting-edge technology as part of its new vision in the 1990s. While retail technology has been available to other domestic firms and was also successfully disseminated through the regional chains, only a few players were able to generate their own organisational capability to grow and compete internationally. There are several reasons for this. First, the Koç Group was committed to its push for growth. Compared to large conglomerates such as the Doguş Group, which acquired retail chains but failed to manage and expand them, Koç was able to retain the business ware, expertise and organisational capability of Migros-Türk. It valued its old guard while bringing in new blood. Second, unlike other provincial rivals such as Beğendik and Yimpaş, it enjoyed a much bigger pool of managerial and financial assets and traded on its established reputation. Koç's name helped Migros-Türk to recruit top professionals and exploit synergies with businesses such as Enka, a major construction group, and other suppliers. Third, the vision of the general manager, Bülent Özaydinli, was supported by the managers of the Koç group throughout the 1990s. Finally, the technology adaptation was managed successfully by an able, young and highly motivated workforce, and achieved through an ability to build a new organisation while growing very rapidly.

The growth of Turkish Migros since 1990 has been remarkable. The company now operates in 853 stores (including seventy-three Ramstores abroad), reaches 218 million people in five countries and employs more than 15,000 people. A comparison of Migros-Türk with several global retailers puts its achievements in perspective, however. The total turnover of all large retailers in Turkey was estimated to be around €3 billion in 2005, whereas large European retailers active in Turkey, such as Carrefour and Metro, each had over €60 billion turnover from their global operations. In 2005 the annual sales of Migros-Türk were just €1.2 billion. Europe's big retailers have been growing aggressively and penetrating world markets over the past two decades through mergers and acquisitions, not by organic growth. In 2004 the leading European retailer, Carrefour, achieved more than €90 billion in sales in more than thirty countries, with most sales in its home market, France. The second largest, Metro, made €64.1 billion sales through its 2,400 stores in twenty-nine countries, with somewhat less reliance on its home market, Germany (see www.foodanddrinkeurope.com/news/).

Another comparison with Swiss Migros also reveals interesting results. After years of hesitation and the unsuccessful acquisition of a local chain in Austria, Swiss Migros chose to remain a mainly Swiss cooperative business. Internationally insignificant and fully entrenched in its home market, in 1991 the Swiss Migros assembly of delegates voted for international expansion, first into France. French people who worked in Switzerland and lived near the Swiss border were considered natural potential customers. A similar expansion strategy was applied to Germany. Interestingly, while Migros-Türk was discovering totally different markets, such as Russia, Swiss Migros was concerned with retaining its product range and principles in bordering countries[7]. International expansion has not been the main objective of the cooperative and it continued to consolidate its conservative home market. As a result of its successful operations in the small but wealthy Swiss market, unhindered by foreign competition, Swiss Migros has been able to develop stable market relations over the years. More than a half of Swiss households, some 1.9 million people, held Migros shares in 2004. By that year Swiss Migros was one of the country's top twenty enterprises, employing around 81,000 people (Ulrich, 2005). The turnover of Swiss Migros was €13 billion, with 1,292 stores in just three countries.

The trajectory and size of Swiss Migros clearly illustrates the modesty of Turkish Migros's achievements, and the main difference appears to be not in the organisational capabilities or strategic vision but in other respects. The first is the nature of and the difference between the home markets.

Migros-Türk has been operating in a low per capita income environment in a large country in which spending power has been at least five to six times lower than in Switzerland. Political and regional volatility generated further business uncertainty and hindered long-term business growth. Second, capital accumulation in the hands of domestic family conglomerates such as Koç, despite their close ties with the ruling political parties, has been slow in Turkey. This is partly due to the fact that, until the 1980s, many were operating in a closed economy with almost no potential for international expansion. This is why Turkish conglomerates were latecomers to internationalisation, had low levels of capital accumulation and limited local market growth. Finally, the modern management practices and skilled manpower needed to steer large operations emerged only after the 1980s.

Notes

This chapter is dedicated to the memory of a good colleague and friend, Colin Simmons, formerly Professor of Economics at Salford University. I am very grateful to Messrs Kerim Tatlıcı and Atilla Övündür of Migros-Türk and Ms Yasemin Kuytak for their help.

1. Although the registered name of the company is Migros-Türk, 'Migros' is also commonly used. In this chapter, unless stated as 'Swiss Migros', 'Migros' is used interchangeably for 'Migros-Türk'.
2. The Commonwealth of Independent States emerged after the dismantling of the Soviet Union. The CIS countries are Armenia, Azerbaijan, Belarus, Georgia, Kazakhstan, Kyrgyzstan, Moldova, the Russian Federation, Tajikistan, Turkmenistan, Ukraine and Uzbekistan.
3. EPOS is defined as the collection in real time at the point of sale, and the storing in a computer file, of sales and other related data by means of a number of electronic devices (Lynch, 1990). Electronic fund transfer (EFT) units attached to EPOS allow the automatic debiting of funds from customers' bank accounts for their purchase (Al-Sudairy and Tang, 2000).
4. Tansaş was established in 1973 by the Izmir municipality to provide affordable meat and coal to urban residents. In 1993 32.98 per cent of the shares were sold to the public. Subsequently the majority stake passed to the Doğuş Holding Group, and it merged with Macrocenter of Doğuş in 2002.
5. Ramstores are operated by Ramenka, incorporated in the Russian Federation in 1997. Migros, Enka and Entrade currently own 50 per cent, 38 per cent and 12 per cent of Ramenka, respectively (see www.ifc.org).
6. John H. Patterson founded the National Cash Register company, maker of the first mechanical cash registers, in 1884, and since the 1950s the company has evolved to become a leading technology provider for retailers (see www.ncr.com/en/history/history.htm).
7. The conservatism I refer to here is in a business strategy sense, and is not linked to Swiss Migros's principle of not selling alcohol, tobacco, war toys or pornographic material.

References

Al-Sudairy, M. A., and N. K. H. Tang (2000) Information technology in Saudi Arabia's super-market chains, *International Journal of Retailing and Distribution Management*, 28, 8, 341–56.

Appel, D. (1972) The supermarket: early development of an institutional innovation, *Journal of Retailing*, 48, 1, 39–53.

Aydın, K. (1992) *Retailing and Socio-economic Characteristics of Department Store Customers* [in Turkish], Istanbul: Gri Ajans.

Brown, S. (1987) Institutional change in retailing: a geographical interpretation, *Progress in Human Geography*, 11, 181–206.

Chandler, A. D. (2005) *Inventing the Electronic Century: The Epic Story of the Consumer Electronics and Computer Industries*, Harvard Studies in Business History, Cambridge, MA: Harvard University Press.

Currie, L. (1968) Marketing organization for underdeveloped countries, in R. Moyer and S. C. Hollander (eds.) *Markets and Marketing in Developing Economies*, Homewood, IL: R. D. Irwin, 117–29.

Davies, G. (1999) The evolution of Marks and Spencer, *Service Industries Journal*, 19, 3, 60–73.

Ducatel, K., and N. Blomley (1990) Rethinking retail capital, *International Journal of Urban and Regional Research*, 14, 2, 207–27.

Evans, K. R., J. Barnes and J. Schlacter (1993) A general systems approach to retail evolution: an existing institutional perspective, *International Review of Retail, Distribution, and Consumer Research*, 3, 1, 79–100.

Goldman, A. (1981) Transfer of retailing technology into the less developed countries: the supermarket case, *Journal of Retailing*, 57, 5–29.

  (1982) Adoption of supermarket shopping in a developing country, *European Journal of Marketing*, 16, 1, 17–26.

Hollander, S. C. (1970) *Multinational Retailing*, East Lansing, MI: Michigan State University Press.

  (1986) A rearview mirror might help us drive forward: a call for more historical studies in retailing, *Journal of Retailing*, 62, 1, 7–10.

Hollander, S. C., and J. J. Boddewyn (1974) Retailing and public policy: an international overview, *Journal of Retailing*, 50, 1, 55–66.

Jefferys, J. B., and D. Knee (1962) *Retailing in Europe: Present Structure and Future Trends*, London: Macmillan.

Kaynak, E. (1982) *Marketing in the Third World*, New York: Praeger.

  (1986) *Marketing and Economic Development*, New York: Praeger.

Koparal, C. (1988) *Zincirleme Mağazaların Organizasyon Yapıları ve Beymen Mağazalarindaki Inceleme* [A Study of the Organisational Structure of the Chain Stores and the Case of Beymen], Study no. 268, Anadolu: Anadolu University Publications.

Lynch, J. E. (1990) The impact of electronic point of sale technology (EPOS) on marketing strategy and retailer supplier relationships, *Journal of Marketing Management*, 6, 2, 157–68.

Moyer, R., and S. C. Hollander (eds.) (1968) *Markets and Marketing in Developing Economies*, Homewood, IL: R. D. Irwin.

Oksay, K. (1979) *Büyük Magazacilik ve Tüketim Kooperatifçiği* [Large Stores and Consumer Cooperatives], Study no. 41, Ankara: Turkish Cooperatives Agency.

Oluç, M. (1956) Migros-Türk, *Istanbul University Ikitisat Fakültesi Mecmuası*, 16, 1–4, 213–49.

Özcan, G. B. (2000) The transformation of Turkish retailing: survival strategies of small and medium-sized retailers, *Journal of Southern Europe and the Balkans*, 2, 1, 105–20.

(2001) Patterns of vertical and horizontal integration in Turkish retailing, *European Retail Digest*, 32, 35–41.

Paddison, R., A. M. Findlay and J. A. Dawson (1990) Retailing in less developed countries: an introduction, in A. M. Findlay, R. Paddison and J. A. Dawson (eds.) *Retailing Environments in Developing Countries*. London: Routledge, 3–51.

Plender, J., M. Simons and H. Tricks (2005) Cash benefit: how big supermarkets fund expansion by usuing suppliers as bankers, *Financial Times*, 7 December, 17.

Roth, V. J., and S. Klein (1993) A theory of retail change, *International Review of Retail, Distribution, and Consumer Research*, 3, 2, 167–83.

Samiee, S. (1993) Retailing and channel considerations in developing countries: a review and research propositions, *Journal of Business Research*, 27, 103–30.

Savitt, R. (1982) A historical approach to comparative retailing, *Management Decision*, 20, 4, 16–23.

(1990) Retail change and economic development, in A. M. Findlay, R. Paddison and J. A. Dawson (eds.) *Retailing Environments in Developing Countries*, London: Routledge, chap. 2.

Şamlı, C. (1964) Wholesaling in an economy of scarcity: Turkey, *Journal of Marketing*, 28, 55–8.

Tokatlı, N., and Y. Eldener (2002) Globalisation and the changing political economy of distribution channels in Turkey, *Environment and Planning A*, 34, 217–38.

Tokatlı, N., and G. B. Özcan, (1998) The state and the corporate private sector in the recent restructuring of Turkish retailing, *New Perspectives on Turkey*, 18, 79–113.

Ulrich, J. (2005) *Migros (Switzerland)*, Thunderbird School of Global Management, Geneva, available at www.thunderbird.edu/pdf/about_us/case_series/a12050002.pdf.

Walsh, J. P. (1993) *Supermarkets Transformed: Understanding Organisational and Technology Innovations*, New Brunswick, NJ: Rutgers University Press.

Yavaş, U., E. Kaynak and E. Borak (1981) Retailing institutions in developing countries: determinants of supermarket patronage in Istanbul, Turkey, *Journal of Business Research*, 9, 367–79.

Yükseker, H. D. (2003) *Laleli–Moskova Mekigi: Kayit Disi Ticaret ve Cinsiyet Iliskileri* [Laleli-Moskow Shuttle: Infomal External Trade and Gender Relations] Istanbul: Iletişim Yayinlari.

Part III

Society as Open and Closed

Preface: Society and comparative differences

Robert Fitzgerald

International comparisons quickly reveal the complexities of societies and systems, and push us towards the (albeit tricky) task of explaining the origins and consequences of their differences and similarities. The debate has too often been conducted according to the binary choice of national institutions or the forces of globalisation, and, equally frequently, with a limited interpretation of history (static certainly, ahistorical probably). One problem is the view that economies are fundamentally national in origin, but subject to the pressures of internationalisation in the last two decades. It would be taking revisionism too far to deny the ease of modern communications, or the secular rise in world trade and investment. There are lessons, however, from the first wave of 'globalisation' during the nineteenth century.

Rajeswary Ampalavanar Brown's contribution to this volume demonstrates the historical importance of international business. Her account of Arab business groups indicates their role in the long-term development of south-east Asia, and it undermines the notion that the worldwide economy is a product of Westernisation, or even colonialism. Andrew Popp similarly employs detailed historical case studies, and questions the idea that regional clusters emerge fundamentally protected from international influences. Industrial districts in England in the nineteenth century were an integral part of a mainly open world economy. Popp argues that comparisons have to be conducted at many levels of scale, and that industrial districts draw on their local, national and international capabilities to formulate specific competitive solutions. National institutions have influence, but each regional cluster will have its own characteristics. As a result, there is no single dominant archetype (as has been suggested elsewhere), and an historical pathway analysis based on adaptation and complexity is offered in place of clusters that succeed through their innate, cultural foundations. Popp applies the SSD model directly to review the related influences of the global, national and local. In addition to the general features of competitive markets, and their rising worldwide dimensions, we need to account for differences between industries, in their uses of technology, variations in operational scale, degrees of internationalisation or the extent of political and national institutional controls. By extension, even firms, their subsidiaries and single plants may have unique characteristics.

Axel Haunschild analyses the very particular features of the German theatrical industry, given the weight of historical legacy, the influence of national institutions, the lack of international competition and the relevance of cultural aims over economic ones. He usefully adapts the SSD model to highlight the distinctiveness of its employment structures, but suggests, too, that there may be lessons for sectors heavily influenced by national institutions (most obviously, the public sector) or dependent on high levels of creativity or individual skills (various professional services). Nonetheless, despite German theatre having a strong national and non-market focus, it has become subject to reform pressures inspired by alternative models from overseas. Haunschild's contribution illustrates the value of case study if we are to understand the formation and reformulation of industries, companies or organisations. So, in addition, does Alice Lam, whose choice of examples uncovers differences in knowledge creation and the application of science between multinationals operating in the same industry. She shows that strategies and structures are shaped by a complex mixture of home-country, host-country, transnational and product market influences. Multinationals are not simply imprints of the institutions found within their country of origin.

In chapter 8 Brown offers an historical analysis of Arab business groups that operated in south-east Asia from the early nineteenth century through to the middle of the twentieth, and reviews their role in trade, finance, real estate development, finance, manufacturing and shipping. She reveals a significant and early example of international enterprise, one that confronts associations of globalisation with recent events or 'Western' business models. The analysis begins by posing some fundamental questions. To what extent were Muslim groups from the nineteenth century onwards able to use diverse regional sites to amass and utilise commercial knowledge and skills? Why, by the late 1960s, were they dislodged from flourishing trading and financial positions in Singapore, Java, Hyderabad and Aden? Previous explanations have focused upon the clash between Islam and modernity, and criticise business structures based on a conservative, hierarchic, communal identity. Brown looks beyond socio-economic trends previously identified. She demonstrates how powerful Chinese, Japanese and Korean capitalists, assisted by state patronage, were critical to the restructuring of south-east Asian economies. In effect, the emergence of the 'newly industrialising economies' (NIEs) marginalised the Arab business groups.

In her analysis of the rise of Arab capitalism, Brown shows that the influence of culture on business and economic development is at best ambiguous. There were diverse interpretations of Islam, and, consequently, adequate accommodation between religious ideals and business pragmatism. Indeed, the act of interpreting or then reinterpreting religious ideals tended to legitimise vested political and commercial interests. South-east Asia and China composed a vibrant intra-Asian economy that survived even the 1930s depression and World War II. With the passing of the old colonial regimes, new independent nations in south-east Asia attempted to imitate the state-driven industrialisation of Japan. They favoured their own firms, and, for a number of reasons, most notably minorities from the Chinese diaspora. Just as British trading companies lost their role, partly as an expression of anti-imperialism and economic sovereignty, so too were the commercial and investment opportunities of the Arab groups disadvantaged. Furthermore, the Middle East shifted from an open economy with weak states to a closed economy with authoritarian rule between 1910 and 1973. This change undermined both migration and economic growth. Their homeland, the Hadramaut, sapped their capital, frittering remittances in religious wars, and avaricious states unhindered by strong governance rules or a counterbalancing bureaucracy left few productive investments in infrastructure, property and agriculture. The Arab business groups ultimately lost both their international base of operations in Asia and economic opportunities at home. The detailed historical record undermines any simple analysis that Chinese entrepreneurs adapted to the circumstances of the twentieth century thanks to their dynamic Confucian culture, whereas Arabs were hindered by conservatism and anti-business values.

Haunschild, in chapter 9, uses detailed research on the German theatrical employment system to analyse the influence of national institutions and the relevance of global 'best practice' ideas. He states that an history is essential to any understanding of local theatre practices in Germany and, therefore, to evaluating the impact of external forces. Long-term developments have shaped national rules and practices fundamentally, providing stable employment and ensemble groups in an industry tending by its nature towards project-based activities and transient work relations. The theatrical employment system is well established within the German historical political structure and its corporatist tradition of industrial relations and occupational labour markets. Acknowledging that the theatrical employment system is often characterised by flexible and temporary forms of labour, Haunschild uses ideas about the ability of national institutions to generate stable business practices, but he states, too, that these tend to neglect new challenges faced by actors and relevant institutions.

He considers the application of the SSD model directly, which weighs general characteristics associated with markets and competition alongside national context and standardising global forces. He adapts the SSD framework to accommodate the particular features of the theatrical industry, such as the inter-organisational character of careers and networks, as well as the coexistence of artistic, political and economic goals. He acknowledges that other countries have reduced public subsidy for the arts, and so, in Germany, the balance between the economic and cultural logics of creative production has to an extent been altered at the organisational level. Nonetheless, German theatres overall still face little economic pressure within their product markets or from international competition, thanks to a funding system that supports art for art's sake, and to the highly national character of theatrical art. Deviations from funded actor ensembles can be observed, as can attempts to abolish restrictions stemming from collective bargaining. Artists are most at risk from alternative models, and one possible trajectory is the emergence of a dynamic network capable of forming productions on a project basis, as is prevalent in most other countries and in other creative industries such as film and media. A market-based form of production could be regarded as a spreading form of capitalism in line with a dominant neoliberal discourse. Interestingly, this discourse refers to project-based knowledge work in general. The theatre provides a unique and idiosyncratic example that resists generalisation. In the case of German theatre, there exists a strong example of important and persistent national institutions that limit the global convergence of organisational practices. Even robust and powerful national institutions are increasingly challenged by globalising forces, however. Current debates about change can be understood only when the historical and societal roots of management practices and employment systems are taken into account. It is evident, moreover, that this conclusion is especially relevant whenever effectiveness and efficiency criteria are less clear, as in the case of the cultural industries, the professional service industries or the public sector.

In chapter 10 Popp explores the apparent contradiction between the global and the national dimensions of business. He questions a discourse based on competing claims for their pre-eminence as causes of contemporary economic and organisational change. Instead, he looks at the local dimension, or, more precisely, the industrial district. The key spatial dimension implicit in the industrial district concept provides a unique vantage point on debates about the future direction of modern capitalism. If the local can be shown to be of consequence to economic organisation, then where, one might ask, does that leave both the national and the global? Popp builds on a series of historically rooted case studies of English industrial districts. He uses these examples to present a reappraisal of conventional readings on the industrial district concept. Districts, empirically and conceptually, are neither examples of a unique, isolated hyperlocalism nor explicit and rooted rebukes to the supposed 'placelessness' of the global. In contrast to debates in recent decades over national clusters, Popp argues for a return to the thin, open model of the industrial district that admits the possibility of different organisational solutions, in different contexts, to the challenges of clustering under conditions of advancing globalisation.

Popp notes the existence, survival and even proliferation of industrial districts. His reinterpretation of literal sites – industrial districts themselves – enables us to see how the forces outlined within the SSD model intersect to produce complex and contingent outcomes beyond the simple choice of either national systems or global level forces. He criticises concepts that became dominant from the 1970s onwards, following the discovery and celebration of the 'Italianate' model. This approach concentrated on innate, cultural, unique or 'deterministic' characteristics that lead to fairly impervious systems. It followed that the British business system was incapable of generating 'true' industrial districts. At the same time, districts and clusters came increasingly to be promoted as an industrial policy panacea, both in mature economies facing deindustrialisation and in emerging economies seeking to develop capabilities. Were industrial districts simply particular to each locale, or were lessons to some degree generalisable? Popp presents detailed empirical and historical evidence on the evolution of key industrial districts in England.

The district emerges not as a third site, competing with the national and the global, but a site in which factors operating at a range of different spatial scales interact. It is from this interaction that a large element of the complexity found in the districts is derived. As a result, Popp sees industrial clusters as possessing characteristics that actually allow them to flourish in markets with globalising tendencies. Moreover, industrial districts vary greatly across space and time, even in a single nation such as the United Kingdom. They have strong generic features, but also substantial, institutionally mediated differences at the national and local levels. The formation of these variations is not strongly determined or culture-bound but contingent and contested. The advocacy of one type of district (largely Italian) demonstrates a dominance archetype, but ignores both the generic characteristics of districts and critical, embedded variations at the locale. A thin, open model of the industrial district admits the possibility of different organisational solutions to the common challenges of clustering.

Lam argues in chapter 11 that MNCs are knowledge-creating organisations that span diverse institutional contexts and possess the ability to transfer knowledge across national borders. In the past, the ways in which MNCs created value from knowledge was conceptualised as a linear diffusion from the home country to overseas units. More recent theoretical and empirical research recognises that knowledge creation occurs throughout internationally dispersed units. The MNC is conceived of as an international knowledge network that creates, integrates and applies knowledge in multiple locations. In science-based sectors in particular, innovation strategies since the early 1990s have been based on the development of 'international learning companies', which can utilise overseas laboratories as 'knowledge incubators' in order to maximise technological distinctiveness. A significant part of scientific knowledge and technological capabilities is tacit, and embedded in local innovation networks and scientific human resources. As a result, the sharing and transfer of knowledge across organisational and national borders are inherently difficult. Much of the existing analysis of MNCs' knowledge transfer problems focuses on the cognitive dimension and the role of intra-corporate mechanisms. Lam draws attention, instead, to the societal aspect of transferring and creating knowledge across major institutional and national boundaries.

Lam shows how patterns of knowledge production within and between firms are powerfully shaped by wider societal factors, especially nationally constituted organisational forms and labour markets. For example, large Japanese firms characterised by stable employment relationships and strong organisational identities have been able to develop strong capacities for internal tacit knowledge creation. By contrast, Anglo-American firms tend to rely more on external tacit knowledge based on flexible, open occupational labour markets and interorganisational flows of personnel. This implies that the kind of network relationships and societal support needed for the generation and transmission of tacit knowledge may differ significantly between national contexts. Lam's main aim is to explore how MNCs, characterised by contrasting home-based models of organisational learning, adopt varying strategies for solving the tacit knowledge problem. Her study explores how the home-based models of learning interact with the local host-country context to shape MNCs' abilities. The evidence presented generally supports the 'social embeddedness' thesis, namely that home-based institutions provide the basis for the development of an MNC's transnational social spaces, and so strategic behaviour and organisational forms will continue to diverge. The concept of 'transnational social space' so far neglects the external dimension of a firm's transnational social space, and puts too little emphasis on the dynamics of organisational learning. The host-country dimension cannot be so easily ignored. Furthermore, countries with their own institutional arrangements develop and reproduce quite different social and innovative capabilities in specific industries and sectors.

It is possible to portray the multinational as the epitome of footloose, cosmopolitan capitalism. MNCs may acquire particular characteristics from their transnationality, but, to varying degrees, they carry with them the influences of both home and host nations. Even this potent bearer of global, rootless uniformity has to be studied at the global/regional, the national and the regional/local levels, and the variations between industries and product markets are noteworthy. Modern-day US and Japanese corporations differ extensively from the historical Arab investment and trading groups of southeast Asia, the past and current industrial districts of England and Italy, and the very national (but not isolated) example of German theatre. Although complexity and circumstances deny the possibility of simple explanation or one dominant factor (such as national institutions, culture or globalisation), comparisons when applied at differing levels do present opportunities for insight. It is, perhaps, untidy, but it is not necessarily uncomfortable.

8 Capitalism and Islam: Arab business groups and capital flows in south-east Asia

Rajeswary Ampalavanar Brown

Introduction

This is an historical analysis of Arab capitalism in south-east Asia from the early nineteenth century to the present. It attempts to trace the critical phases of this capitalist evolution, determining its specific role in trade, finance, real estate development, manufacturing and shipping. It poses fundamental questions. How did the Arab[1] groups use diverse regional sites to amass information, disseminate and achieve improved regional economic performance over a long period, from 1830 to the 1960s? Why, therefore, were they dislodged by the late 1960s from these flourishing trading and financial positions in Singapore, Java, Hyderabad and Aden? Did religious identity and institutions create an inability to respond to the dramatic capitalist transformation sweeping south-east Asia after 1960? Were key turning points in capitalist development determined by the technological innovation and markets or by Islamic economics? Here Arab sub-economies, as reproduced in halawa (remittance) shops, Islamic partnerships, contracts, trust and religious morality, and charitable endowments (*waqf*), are analysed alongside a contiguous relationship with the economic interactions occurring between Muslim business and Chinese, Japanese and European capitalists and state capitalism, and their changing responses and strategies to economic change in the region.

Timur Kuran (1996, 2003b) sees the crisis in Arab capitalism as a product of Islamic economics and Islamic business structures aggravated by a conservative hierarchic communal identity. Bernard Lewis (2002) hints at dramatic changes in Islamic society and institutions, a development he argues is purely a product of internal pressures in Arab society and economics. E. L. Jones (1988: 97) raises the question of whether religion was 'exercising a certain brake on the economy. Conceivably even a lower average probability of independent growth than in say Christendom.' He goes on to argue, however, that, if the environment provides the appropriate conditions, religion can be circumvented. This is similar to Maxime Rodinson's (1973) thesis of the economic irrelevance of Islam, since interpretations of its message were diverse and Muslims could select what was relevant and appropriate and reject Islamic norms of economic behaviour that could distort development.

Finally, did Islam promote norms of economic behaviour that disadvantaged these groups? Islamic economics have emphasised interest-free banking (*riba*), wealth redistribution through taxation (*zakat*) and the creation of *waqf*. Other crucial economic precepts are the ethic of hard work, frugality and honesty. Are these 'serious impediments in the creation of capitalist structures?' Kuran (2004c: 137–47) argues, rightly, that Islamic economics has been exploited to legitimise and promote vested interests. This engenders a serious absence of individual freedom and stakeholding. What emerges, he suggests, is a conservative, communal hierarchic yoke inimical to progress. *Riba* and *zakat* are unrealistic in a free market economy facing serious competition from Western and Chinese capitalism and the Islamic *waqf* is inefficient, corrupt, exploited by the wealthy to secure their assets for posterity through charity, a form of custodianship and 'guilt relief'.

Kuran (1996: 438–42) also identifies the Islamic inheritance system as inhibiting both the transformation of Arab corporations into joint-stock firms and, more broadly, the economic modernisation of the Middle East. The insistence of Islamic economics on consensus weakens debate, and there is a serious divergence between public discourse and private belief. This creates a chain reaction in which an emphasis on Islamic purity negates outside influences and distorts truths in the interests of securing consensus. Potential hazards are ignored and policy failures are pervasive, which are then attributed to Western imperialism rather than to inherent flaws in the indigenous economic and political structures. This phobia with Western civilisation leads to Islamic texts being scrutinised for ideas that differentiate Islamic economics from Western economics. 'From Mawdudi onward, the moral discourse of Islamic economics has cultivated the view that behaviour standards of Islam are fundamentally at odds with those of the West.'[2]

I argue that the economic context within which Arab business operated in south-east Asia before 1960 was conducive to growth and influence; in contrast, the independent states after 1960 posed an attritional threat to this influence. The socio-economic trends identified by Lewis and Kuran were occurring at a time when powerful Chinese, Japanese and South Korean capitalists, assisted by state patronage, were critical to the restructuring of south-east Asian econo-mies; the emergence of the NIEs effectively marginalised the Islamic capitalists. This introduces another difficulty, however: why did they not adapt? After all, the Indian diaspora adapted with success (Markovitz, 2000).

There are, therefore, a number of ideas that are coherent but have to be tested through an empirical analysis. First, is the Arab failure to change partially explained by Islamic economics? Did their methods of capital accumulation, their financial institutions and conservative ideologies in political, social and religious institutions, create a reluctance to innovate and respond to change, thus thwarting any serious adaptation? Was religion, in Jones's (1988: 97) memorable phrase, in effect 'exercising a certain brake on the economy'?

It is striking that, while a few Arab capitalist families dominated lucrative niches in trade, shipping and real estate from the 1880s to the 1960s in parts of Penang, Singapore and Indonesia, there were no precise evolutionary trends in their development, as occurred among the Chinese in south-east Asia (Clarence-Smith, 1997, 1998, 2000, 2002a, 2002b; Ellen, 1996). The continuity and changes that occurred within Chinese capitalism were not reproduced within the Arab world. In the nineteenth and twentieth centuries the Chinese moved from revenue farming to banking to the creation of conglomerates, each phase introducing new merchant groups with their distinct functional ambitions. Their enterprise also needed the state and other significant networks, such as the Japanese and European networks (Brown, 1994, 2000). In contrast, the Arabs, though achieving truly impress-ive growth in three economic phases, 1750–1880, 1880–1940 and 1941–68, by 1970 had been seduced into government and academic life in south-east Asia and the Yemen. Those nurturing capitalist ambitions moved into Saudi Arabia and Kuwait. Roy Ellen (1996: 250–2) concludes that their small size, distorted further by their assimilation, and their lack of powerful trading networks signalled their economic stagnation. I take the argument one step further. While the Arabs successfully created multinational trading and manufacturing links, their weak economic institutions and relationships, their limited interaction with other trading diasporas and fluctuating, highly inconsistent relations with the state in south-east Asia and with their warring feudal sultanates in the Hadramaut sapped their entrepreneurial vigour. The Chinese flourished in a booming Asia-Pacific rim, but the Arabs faced an impoverished homeland, and could operate only within a rigid rentier econ-omy in parts of the Middle East, including Saudi Arabia (Field, 1984; Owen, 1993; Fawzy and Galal, 1999; Kuran, 2004b).

Karl Polanyi (1957) has argued that economic acts occur in socially con-structed frameworks, with interactions of capital, political power and social organisation determining capitalist evolution. Arab capitalists were more Kirznerian (Kirzner, 1973).[3] They readily identified opportunities for exploi-tation, yet were unable to create the structures, the relationships and the power to sustain their hold in these areas. Their success in economic diversi-fication is clear from the description below of the major Arab capitalists in Indonesia and Singapore. This diversification was achieved frequently, with limited assistance from the state or foreign joint venture partners. Their business strategy was complex and individualistic as well as communal, driven by niche selection in terms of viable economic initiatives.

This chapter pursues nine main lines of argument. First, it analyses the economic sectors in which Arab entrepreneurship dominated in south-east Asia, and asks why they were dislodged from these sectors by the late 1960s. Second, in securing answers to this puzzle, it tests Kuran's (2003b) hypothesis that the crisis in Arab capitalist development was a result of serious con-straints within Islam, in particular the Islamic laws on inheritance, wealth redistribution through *zakat* and the creation of *waqf*. Third, the chapter then considers the strengths and weaknesses in Arab business institutions and the legal framework of Arab commerce. Fourth, there is an analysis of the structure and organisation of Arab business and the legitimacy of various business partnerships and business contracts, with a resultant focus on their spatial concentration in certain ports and parts of the hinterland in south-east Asia and the Middle East. Did this spatial distribution create serious fragmentation, to the detriment of capitalist growth? What was the nature of 'trust' within this multinational Arab capitalist evolution? Fifth, I consider the impact of capital flows, particularly remittances from south-east Asia to the Hadramaut. The failure of the Arabs to move from moneylending activities to formal banking is contrasted with developments within the Chinese and Chettiar diasporas in the region.

Sixth, the chapter then turns to evaluate relations within the Arab diaspora and with other trading groups. How did they respond to differing business cycles, to competition and to demands for restructuring and innovation? Seventh, I appraise their relations with the state in south-east Asia and the Middle East. Eighth is a consideration of the highly factionalised and hier-archical character of the Arab commercial community, separated by class, religious and intellectual divisions. Kuran considers this hierarchic, conser-vative outlook as a by-product of Islamic economics, which fosters a serious lack of individual freedom. This so-called 'aloofness' of the Arab capitalist elite has to be tested against serious empirical evidence from south-east Asia. Finally, the chapter traces the indigenisation of Islamic economic ideology and concludes by asking whether Arab capitalist institutions in south-east Asia were shaped by religious ideology or by endogenous economic developments. Were Arab responses to capitalism in the region unique in their interpretation of religious ethics and ideology – were they flexible and yet gritty in their responses?

Economic dominance

By the 1960s Arab capitalist ambitions in south-east Asia had been blown away. Having survived – indeed, prospered – in the colonial period, not least against the challenges of the Chinese and Indian commercial diasporas, the Arab community went into serious decline at the hands of the independent governments of Indonesia and Singapore. Their homeland had sapped their capital through remittances, had introduced unstable religious forces and had provided few opportunities for productive investment.

It has to be emphasised and reiterated, however, that in contemporary Malaysia, Indonesia and Singapore there remain significant groups of successful Arab capitalists. The bin Talib family in Indonesia and Singapore, the Aidid family in Indonesia and the Buchori (Bukhari) Group in Malaysia have carved out powerful niches in the region's economic growth in the contemporary period. Moreover, there have also been distinct signs of Arab economic resurgence in the last two decades. These Arab families are wholly assimilated into local Muslim society, however, and hence are apprehensive over asserting their Middle Eastern background and origins, particularly in a region sensitive to race and identity in economic issues.

Next I focus on some general characteristics of Arab migration. A look at the influence of their spatial dispersion is central to an understanding of the nature of business organisation and networks. This also clarifies and forms part of the structural perspective on Arab capitalism in the south-east Asian economies since 1830.

The Arab migration to south-east Asia from the early nineteenth century onwards was principally from the Hadramaut. The majority were male *sayyids* (claiming descent from the Prophet Muhammad). The *shaykh* (religious teachers), the *qabail* (armed tribal groups) and the *masākīn* (poor) were increasingly present in the inter-war year (van den Berg, 1886: 74, 129). In the Netherlands East Indies (NEI) there were some 52,000 Arabs in 1885, rising to

71,335 in 1930 and to around 100,000 in 1956; in Singapore and Penang there were about 2,000 Arabs in 1885, rising to 2,591 in 1930 and to some 6,000 in 1956 (*Volkstelling*, 1935; Redkin, 1995). In NEI and Singapore throughout this period the Arabs constituted less than 1 per cent of the population; the pure Arab component of the total Muslim population in Singapore until 1947 was 5 to 6 per cent. By 1980 they accounted for 0.1 per cent of the total population in Singapore, while Muslims accounted for 16 per cent of this total population (Singapore Department of Statistics, 1981: 31). In Java the Arab component remained at less than 1 per cent into the 1960s. The impression is that the assimilation of these groups was intensive, accompanied by a decline in foreign-born Arabs throughout the region (Ellen, 1996; Singapore Department of Statistics, 1980; Lim, 1987: 21; *Asiaweek*, 1992; Tinbergen and Derksen, 1941).[4]

By the 1880s the Arabs in Singapore, Surabaya, Batavia and Pekalongan had carved out powerful niches in trade, shipping, and real estate. The al-Kâf (Alkaff) family, *sayyids* from the Hadramaut, rose from the mid-nineteenth century onwards. Three brothers, Abdullah, Muhammad and Shaykh, were prominent traders in spices, sugar, coffee and textiles, trading with the Middle East, India and Europe. Much of their profits found its way into properties, and hotels in Singapore. Between 1886 and 1907 Alkaff was the largest property group on the island (Alkaff transcript, n.d.: 1–4). They also subsidised road construction in the Hadramaut and invested in mosques, schools, textile mills and agriculture, moving from tax farming in the Shihr in 1919. They had a diversified economic empire in south-east Asia, which included major shipping interests.

The Arabs were also dominant in real estate. In 1885 25 per cent of Singapore's real estate was in Arab hands, the comparable levels in Surabaya and Batavia being 20 per cent and 15 per cent, respectively (van den Berg, 1886: 136). Of the seventeen largest estates in Batavia in 1886, ten belonged to the Arab minority. By 1931, among the seventy-five listed large estates in Batavia, only five revealed Arab ownership (Heuken, 1996: 70). The decline had begun in 1924, brought about by Dutch policies on land ownership and by rising competition from the Chinese.

In Singapore the Arabs formed a major landowning elite, in possession of 80 per cent of the largest estates by 1926 (Vlieland, 1931: 87). They also owned prestigious hotels, including Raffles Hotel and Hotel de l'Europe. Between 1826 and 1910 Shaykh Alkaff acquired high-value properties in Alkaff Quay, Collyer Quay, Beach Road, Tanjung Pagar and Orchard Road, and following his death in 1916 the net value of his estate exceeded

S$3 million (Alkaff transcript, n.d.: 14). He also owned vast properties in the Hadramaut and Java. Despite the setback of the recession in the 1930s, Arabs in Singapore possessed the highest proportion of urban property, with thirteen families owning assets valued at S$2.5 million (Ingrams, 1937: 150). By 1968, however, Arabs owned only 20 per cent of urban land in Singapore, the decline resulting from urban renewal programmes introduced by the state and the impoverishment of the Arab elite (Lim, 1987: 21). In Indonesia, in the 1960s, Arabs still held interests in commercial property, but here too they had been overtaken by the Chinese (Heuken, 1996) This enfeeblement of the Arab capitalists as a result of state action manifested itself throughout south-east Asia, India, the Sudan, Ethiopia and Yemen in the years following World War II.

Another sector that provided a crucial source of capital and profits was shipping. A significant share of the Arab shipping monopoly, which dated from 1819, was centred on Singapore. The only challenge to this arose from the Netherlands Indies Steam Navigation Company after 1869, when the NEI government secured for the company a share of the Javanese export trade to Europe. The British India Steam Navigation Company had from 1863 made inroads into shipping in the Far East. The inter-island shipping in south-east Asia and the pilgrim traffic to Jiddah remained with the Arabs, however; here the Chinese offered no competition. By 1888 the Dutch Koninklijke Paketvaart Maatschappij (KPM) was concentrating on the NEI while Holts carved out a share of the routes from Singapore and Melaka. The Germans concentrated on Bangkok and the Pacific Islands, but their defeat in World War I crushed their ambitions.

Sayyid Alsagoff owned the Singapore Steamship Company, which briefly possessed Chinese partners and an English captain (Alsagoff 1963: 9, 11–12);[5] the funds were derived from investments in Java. Another Arab, Salem Muhammad bin Talib, was one of the wealthiest Arabs, and he teamed up with the Japanese in north Sulawesi (Clarence-Smith, 2002b: 237–42). The Dutch curbed this activity, but Arabs still flourished in the lucrative coastal shipping trade. In the Indian Ocean, Hadramis faced the Moplah Muslims, and further west they encountered Omani competition; in the inter-war decades the Parsees were another major competitor. The Hadramis were acquiring a share of the contraband trade in arms smuggling and slave trade during this period, with the al-Attas family from Singapore prominent in this. The serious challenge at this time came from improved technology and the creation of European cartels through the Shipping Conference Agreement, which set price rates and specific routes for each shipping concern and specific cargoes and types of passengers. Thus, the Europeans' superior technology, organisation and capital enabled them to create global networks linking NEI to the Pacific, Australia and North America. The Arabs, with their divisive family enterprises, unstable capital base and poor technology, concentrated on sailing ships as they possessed only a limited number of steamships, and lost market share in the pilgrim trade.

The Chinese were adapting, by forging lucrative partnerships with Japanese and European shipping interests. It was the Japanese occupation that dealt the final blow, however. The Arabs were accused of having pro-European sympathies, and so Chinese shipping replaced some of the European shares in this period, despite the anti-Japanese attitudes of the majority of the Chinese. After 1966 a combination of technological changes, the introduction of containerisation and the forward and backward integration of shipping with warehousing, insurance, finance and telecommunications ended the chances of the remaining Arabs. The merger of P&O with Nedlloyd, the emergence of state-owned shipping companies and the aggressively low-cost shipping of the Japanese and south Koreans put paid to any lingering ambitions they might have had.

Their failure to respond and adapt is stark. It reveals a failure to restructure their corporations, devise new techniques of capital accumulation and absorb new technology – a failure deepened by the lack of long-term networks with other capitalists and with some of the newly independent states in the region. Throughout this period the Arabs were shifting funds from shipping into real estate, moneylending and manufacturing (Dick and Rimmer, 2003). Sadly, in all three sectors they were derailed by the aggressive new competition and unfavourable state policies in independent south-east Asia.

In shipping, one activity that proved highly lucrative was related to the Hajj. The Alsagoff and al-Hibshi families were major financial brokers. In 1881 the Alsagoff family was accused by the British of enslaving the poor through the Hajj (Roff, 1974: 38–9). Laws were subsequently introduced, in 1901 and 1906, to curb these excesses (*Straits Settlements Gazette*, 1901, 1906). As a result, the Hajj, which had originated as an individualistic endeavour in the pre-colonial period, was now organised and controlled by the governments in Indonesia and Malaya. The numbers of pilgrims from Java stood at around 5–6,000 between 1872 and 1926; for Singapore and Malaya there were dramatic increases between 1910 and 1924, but numbers fell in 1933, though they had recovered by 1936 (McDonnell, 1986: 626–40). The cost was around 500–600 Straits dollars for pilgrims from Singapore and 445 guilders for those from Indonesia (Eisenberger, 1926: 32; Tagliacozzo, 2003). Between 1954 and 1974 the number of pilgrims from Indonesia rose from 10,000 to 60,000 and the costs tripled. In Malaysia, the government established the Pilgrim Fund Tabung Haji in 1968, and by 2004 it had 4.5 million savers with total deposits of some 10 billion ringgit (Tabung Haji, 2004: 3).

These developments clearly marginalised the Arab position, both in the financing and in the shipping of the pilgrim traffic. The centrality of the Hajj for Arab trade and finance between south-east Asia and the Middle East is clear. Ashin Das Gupta (1982: 430) sees the Hajj as 'the principal draw for trade in the Indian Ocean'. This view is not shared by Michael Pearson (1994: 158), however, who sees the growth of Jiddah as an international trading port since the eighteenth century as separate from that of Mecca. Nevertheless, for south-east Asia the Hajj was critical in the internationalisation of Arab capital, intertwining devotion with regional business information, political patronage and the evolution of complex financial networks, as seen in the potted histories of Arab entrepreneurs. In the pre-colonial and colonial eras the Hajj resulted in the growth of charitable endowments, savings and capital accumulation that financed infrastructural projects in the Middle East, as well as stimulating intraregional trade and capital flows. In south-east Asia this role was usurped by the independent governments of the region.

This scenario of Arab economic dominance in the pre-colonial and early colonial periods followed by decline from the late colonial period was replicated in the textile industry. In the batik industry in Indonesia, the one-time dominance by the Arabs was declining by the 1950s. In Java in 1931 130 major batik enterprises were owned by the Arabs, 727 were in Chinese hands and Indonesians had 3,515. By 1942 Arabs held 22 per cent of all mechanised looms, 10 per cent of the weaving mills and 28 per cent of hand looms, while the Chinese held shares of 31 per cent, 16 per cent and 35 per cent, respectively. Arabs also owned many of the larger establishments (Sutter, 1959: 42–77). Between 1949 and 1957 President Sukarno introduced a form of nationalisation that absorbed the large textile mills of the Arabs and the Dutch (Makarim, 1987: 25–41). The import substitution industrialisation phase of the 1950s and 1960s introduced a system of auctions of licences and contracts that favoured the Chinese and a few *pribumi* (indigenous) capitalists with close connections with the state. The ascendance of the military and General Suharto after 1966 finally sealed the fate of the Arabs.

The rise in Indonesia of large, vertically integrated textile enterprises from the early 1970s, with clear state and foreign multinational support, led to the rapid demise of the Arabs. Political interference under President Suharto increased the concentration among textile producers. Texmaco (Indian-owned) and Argo Manunggal (Chinese-owned), with horizontal linkages of producers to suppliers, foreign-owned TNCs and the Indonesian state, achieved an increased market share and profitability, edging out smaller Arabs and *pribumi* firms (Brown, 2004a). Suharto's (1989) entrenched view was that Indonesian society possessed serious undercurrents of violence that were tribal, hierarchic, ill-disciplined and disorderly, lacking in a sense of duty. This nurtured in him an excessive belief in the commercial competence of the Chinese, whom he consequently emphasised in his economic planning (*Tempo*, 1980). The only competitor to survive without state aid was Indorama Synthetics, owned by the Lohia family, who concentrated on chemicals – they were able to expand their polymer division – and on downstream activities, chiefly fabric and resin production. This group possessed powerful Indian ethnic networks in Europe, the United States, Japan and Australia.

In Singapore the combined effects of the transition to a state dominated by the Chinese majority and the rather precise state economic planning sealed the fate of this Kirznerian entrepreneurial elite. So too in Malaysia, with its rising state capitalism, the Arabs – with some notable exceptions in Johor and Penang – either receded from the economic scene or coalesced into the indigenous bourgeoisie.

My argument is that the economic landscape from 1966 ensured the rise of a highly concentrated form of capitalism dominated by the Chinese, tapping into state rents and alliances with foreign capital and edging other minorities, including the Arabs, into subservient, unstable rent-seeking, and thereby pro-ducing flawed companies. The increasingly entrenched nature of this Chinese capitalism in south-east Asia and the decline of Arab entrepreneurship after 1960 is similar to the decline of Arab trading minorities in the Middle East a century earlier. There, Greek, Jewish and Armenian trading groups supplanted the Arabs by operating without the constraints of Islamic legal procedures and strictures on interest, the confusion over contracts and partnerships, and the general overload of Islam's 'moral economy' on Arab capitalism (Kuran, 2004a, 2004b). In the case of south-east Asia, Islam was peripheral to these dramatic developments. State capitalism and entrenched Chinese entrepreneurship squeezed out the Arabs, who increasingly turned to high political office instead, demonstrating that they were part of an assimilated indigenous elite.

Inheritance and Islamic charities

The description and analysis of this variegated pattern of Arab economic presence and circulation in south-east Asia needs to be analysed through an institutional perspective, focusing on the integral elements of Islamic inheritance, *zakat* (taxation) and *waqf* (charities) as shaping their capitalist responses. Was their mixed success and failure on the global scene explained by adherence to these Islamic tenets, or should we emphasise certain traits of capitalism occurring under colonial and post-colonial regimes, and unpredictable political developments both in the region and the Hadramaut?

Equally, a major share of the responsibility for this fractured development is often attributed to the Arab family Islamic inheritance laws and the wealth redistribution through *zakat* and *waqf*. This assessment is accurate: Islamic inheritance law did indeed add to this fragmentation and discord (Kuran, 2003b). The family estate was divided among the children (daughters as well as sons), spouses, parents, distant relatives; all were entitled to a share. This equal distribution of wealth, in conjunction with the pervasive polygamous relationships, produced uneconomic outcomes. Indeed, complicated lawsuits were common, resulting in the premature dissolution of firms and family estates. I would argue, however, that such tensions were also common to the Chinese and Hindu Indian commercial communities, even though they practised primogeniture. What is different here is the fact that the Arab diaspora had faced serious political turbulence in the Hadramaut since the nineteenth century, and the threat of expropriation of wealth by the state and warring factions remained (Freitag, 2003). It is this political instability that complicated the inheritance of some of these wealthy Arabs, such as Alkaff. The wills of Alkaff and Alsagoff in Singapore reveal that political affiliations and religious divisions exerted a more brutal impact on their estates than pure Islamic laws of inheritance (Lim, 1987; Alsagoff, 1963; Alkaff transcript, n.d.; Watts, 1947).

Furthermore, in practice, Islamic family law was enforced with greater flexibility than is generally perceived. Differences exist between the Shafis, the Hanafis and the Hanbalis, while within the Sunnis themselves interpretations differ greatly. The Bohra Muslims, like other Shia Muslims, have retained the Hindu law of inheritance, and were some of the wealthiest merchants in the Arabian peninsula and the Horn of Africa.

In order to avoid fragmentation and reduce tension within the family, the wealthy patriarch often established a charitable endowment (*waqf*), which controlled the estate. Trustees of the *waqf* could be the founding family, individuals of reputable status, mosque committees and village headmen. The *waqf* itself could be divided into private (*waqf zurri*) endowments for the family, though this was still dedicated for communal charities, and public (*waqf khairi*). The public *waqf* could be exploited for private gain (Kuran,

2001). A major issue in Arab capitalist development is this ethic of mutual social responsibility and how it neutralises the atomising effects of capitalism. This is enshrined in the *waqf*, whereby the wealthy endow property, build hospitals, schools and orphanages and even assume responsibility for the building of roads and infrastructure and the economic modernisation of the state. Does the *waqf* inhibit capital accumulation or is this harnessing of the 'moral economy' supportive of the capitalist order, founded on social solidarity, brotherhood and cooperation? Charles Tripp (2006: 58–66) mounts a brilliant defence both of the writings of Rafiq al-Azm on profits from property, which are endowed to the *waqf*, and of the Salafis, including al-Qasimi of Damascus, who urged a reconciliation of modern technology with Islamic law. Islamic responses thus sharpen adaptation to global capitalism (Tripp, 2006: 108). Equally, he sees *zakat* and the redistribution of wealth as creating greater self-sufficiency and growth (136). It would, therefore, be useful here to see how far these institutions aided or confused the Arabs' role in south-east Asian capitalism.

From 1830 many of these charitable trusts in Singapore, Java and the Hadramaut were a persistent source of litigation and tension (Communities of Singapore, 1996; Alkaff transcript, n.d.: 20; *Straits Times*, 1907; *Utusan Melayu*, 1908). The purpose and management of these trusts were shrouded in secrecy. First, they were often exploited by the wealthy classes to ensure that their property and assets passed from one generation to the next without loss to the state or to taxation. Second, while establishing a lineal descent group with exclusive rights to endowment revenues, the management was often autocratic and open to fraud. The building of mosques, schools and public kitchens, income from properties, and religious publications, all of which were connected to the trusts, were managed and transferred with no clear coherence of purpose. There was no clear legal jurisdiction and nor were the different operations defined. Another complication was the difficulty in separating the religious aspects of the endowment from the non-religious. The religious base provided an atmosphere of honesty and integrity but this was compromised by family greed and violence.

The ambitions of the family, in terms of desire for official titles, private financial gains or even political favours, often intruded on the trust's activities. Even the founder's directives were frequently discarded. The institution lacked transparency and flexibility, and often fraud or violent disputes forced the authorities to intervene and confiscate the assets. It could have been a focus of long-term capital accumulation, as was the case with the Chinese lineage. The lack of structures and legitimacy, however, introduced another source of volatility.

Endowments of land and real estate were in the main for charity and only a third was assigned to the heirs, yet, because of polygamy, there were increased family tensions, exacerbated by warring ethnic and religious factions. Confusion thus reigned in the *waqf*. By 1910 this institution was on the decline in south-east Asia. Two important *waqf* that had survived in Singapore since 1855 faced internal and external threats. The Alsagoff *waqf*, named the Sayyid Muhammad bin Ahmad Wakaff Fund and in existence from 1885, was dedicated to the maintenance of a mosque, burial sites and schools in Singapore and the Hadramaut, and to assisting pilgrims to Mecca (Lim, 1987: 78–80). The second, established in 1888, belonged to Alkaff, whose trusts in the Hadramaut were more powerful than those in Singapore; they financed schools, hospitals, religious centres and road building in Tarim and Seyu (Freitag, 2003). Nonetheless, many of the properties and assets associated with these two endowments were neglected, as a result of inadequate management, fraud, misappropriation and tension between the heirs (Lim, 1987: 78–80; Transcript of R. Jumabhoy, n.d.: 160–9; Harn, 1963).

In independent Singapore, the Alsagoff Group lost valuable properties because of the expiring of leases and the compulsory acquisition of properties by the government as part of its urban renewal programme; no fewer than thirty *waqf* were involved in this loss in the period 1965 to 1978 (Majlis Ugama Islam Singapura, 1973–80; see also Ter, 1985, and Muslim Trust Fund Association, 1984). In the Hadramaut Alkaff and Alsagoff lost their properties to the communist government of Yemen in 1967 (Lekon, 2003; for more recent developments, see Ariff, 1991).

An interesting comparison can be drawn here with the Chinese lineage and property endowments in China in the period 1830–1939. The common holding of property defined through lineage and territorial identity was a critical focus of Chinese financial and commercial networks stretched out across China, Hong Kong, Vietnam, Thailand, Malaya/Singapore and Indonesia. As properties were held in the name of the ancestors, there was a nesting of corporations within the lineage. Mutual compassion and material motivation and ambitions were coordinated through lineage and leadership. Detailed accounts were maintained and, within this collective, the lineage interacted with the state. Large properties not only provided income for the poor but also channelled funds for trade across this region. They held ancestral halls, temples and orphanages as well as remittance houses coordinating capital flows and institutions that were adapted for economic cooperation and interaction with the state and with Chinese and foreign commercial networks. Although fraud did exist, the organisational structures and accountability differed dramatically from the Islamic *waqf*, which the patriarch and, on his death, his family controlled even though they were frequently the main beneficiaries. This produced a short-term outlook, in contrast to the Chinese lineage. The Chinese lineage also averted the fragmentation of properties, since Confucian laws of inheritance meant that, while males inherited, to the exclusion of females, an equal share for all the sons was deemed to be prejudicial to the continuity of the legacy. The lineage therefore introduced hierarchic structures whereby vast properties could be organised at the level of the lineage, not the family. Lineage and village often coalesced in this property-holding arrangement, becoming part of an international economic network (Freedman, 1958; Cohen, 1976; Matsubara, 2004).

It is clear, therefore, that Chinese lineage properties were better administered than *waqf* properties in south-east Asia. There was confusion over legal rights with the latter, and this accounted for the neglect. In more recent years the *waqf* has aroused the suspicions of a number of governments, on the grounds that it could constitute a conduit for filtering through funds for acts of terrorism in Thailand, Indonesia and the Philippines, as subversive financial flows are difficult to separate from legitimate ones (Abuza, 2003). Another important relationship between Islamic economics and Arab economic development is the *zakat*, an obligatory tax aimed at wealth redistribution (Kuran, 2003a). *Zakat* funds, unlike *sadaqqat al-fitr* monies, which were voluntary contributions, were assigned to well-defined projects. Some of the funds were directed to investment in land and properties and the building of mosques, schools and orphanages.

In the nineteenth century the Dutch in Indonesia permitted fund-raising for these charitable institutions, and identified the local religious functionaries who were to be in charge of the collection, under the supervision of the *priyayi* (indigenous bureaucracy) (for more details, see the Snouck Hurgroaje letters in Gobee and Adriaanse, 1959, and Ibrahim, Siddique and Hussain, 1985). With the Japanese occupation, which started in 1942, the government asserted control over *zakat* collection. Islamic associations as well as the shariah courts were contracted to undertake these collections in Sumatra and Java. In independent Indonesia *zakat* collection was delegated to local government officials, and by 1986 civil servants were fully responsible, thus intensifying government control over the ulama (priests). This pattern was repeated by the other independent governments throughout south-east Asia. Two crucial aspects of *zakat* are relevant to our debate on Islam and economic development. These centre on capitalist initiatives under *zakat*, which provided credit for cottage industries, for religious schools and scholarships for the poor and for self-improvement projects. *Zakat* thus helped formalise the membership of associations and mosques, while distributing aid to the needy. This function was inherited by the social foundations established by the state under Suharto, but they were open to fraud and the expropriation of valuable funds by his cronies.

Thus, although communal cohesion was achieved, the potential for capitalist joint enterprises needing trust and transparency was aborted by the lack of structures and legitimacy. Wealthy groups accumulated and dissipated the funds on luxury lifestyles. *Sadaqqa* and *fitrah*, paid largely during Ramadan (the month of fasting), were soon linked to kinship and brotherhood groups, and this religious identity was divisive and volatile and harmful to joint economic ventures. They succeeded only in introducing layers of Islamic identity rather than cohesion and welfare within these partnerships.

Business structure

The foregoing analysis of Islamic institutions revealed how they could have underpinned and stabilised the emergence of a cohesive bourgeoisie but were hampered in this by the serious lack of clear organisation and legitimacy and an absence of separation of public and private interests. Only a critical analysis of Arab business structure and organisation would be able help clarify or confirm whether there was a process of unilinear decline in the economic position of Arabs in the region from the peak in the inter-war decades to a subsidiary role in independent south-east Asia. Alternatively, was their attempt to reconstruct their business operations independent of the state and Asian business diasporas after 1967 limited or hampered by the weakness of their business institutions, in particular that of family enterprise and Arab partnerships? While the Chinese trading diaspora compensated for its weakness in business organisation through a major alignment with the states in south-east Asia and their expanding networks, was the Arab minority already stretched to the limit in attempting to control a global network of such a magnitude that even peripheral defects in its business structure become fatal to its long-term growth and prosperity? Was this task of reorganising the business structure and networks difficult because of Islam or because of the structure and mode of operations, or was the ultimate fate of Arab merchants and their capacity for developing new specific skills and acquiring knowledge of changing global markets decided by deficient business organisation? The importance of business organisation to business

Table 8.1 Arab commercial firms with capital of over 10,000 guilders, 1885

Location	Number of firms	Percentage of total firms
Singapore	80	29.0
Surabaya	43	15.6
Palembang	37	13.4
Batavia	22	8.0
Pekalongan	18	6.5
Semarang	14	5.1
Sumemenep	12	4.3
Others	50	18.1
Total	276	100

Source: Clarence-Smith (1997: 305).

success cannot be regarded as merely conjectural in the light of the following analysis.

As we have seen, a contributory factor to this fractured capitalist development on the past of the Arabs was their weak commercial infrastructure, and this insight is confirmed by this study. They held a significant share of the corporate economy in Singapore and Java in 1885, as seen in table 8.1. This important position in the corporate structure of the region continued into the first part of the twentieth century. Serious weaknesses existed in both the commercial and organisational structures, however, and in the employment of viable commercial contracts. The Arab enterprise was dominated by the founding patriarch, and after his death the firm's future prospects were often ravaged by family rivalries, occasionally descending into violence. The murder in April 1907 of Sayyid Abd al-Qadir Alsagoff was a consequence of family feuds (Roff, 2002). This case, though extreme, reveals the insecurities prevailing within corporations. While Chinese family enterprises in south-east Asia were able to construct large-scale corporations through networks based on dialect and kinship ties, Arab corporations have remained confined to single families, with no examples of corporate constellations, corporate sets or corporate webs in the Arab system. The cause of such a serious absence is not cultural but the small size of the community and factionalism.

Although there is evidence of Arab joint-stock firms in the inter-war decades, the family firm continued to dominate. The authoritarian paternalism, combined with clannism (*al-asabiya*), within these corporations was a serious source of friction and a constraint on long-term growth and innovation. Moreover, the ambiguous, often vacillating relations with the states in Asia and in the Hadramaut introduced uncertainty. Awad bin Marta, a leading joint-stock firm in the inter-war years, prospered, but by the 1940s it was facing difficulties (Post, 1996), for which there are a number of explanations.

First, the spatial concentration of the Arab diaspora necessitated a structured and cohesive organisational framework and the employment of viable commercial techniques and instruments. There are scattered data available on different types of partnership contracts for the period 1876 to 1937, in the archives of Java Bank, Chartered Bank, Mercantile Bank and HongKong Bank. A *mudaraba*[6] contract with twenty participants covering trade in textiles and investments in land in Surabaya and Pekalongan explains that Alkaff in Surabaya, Aldjoeffrie in Semarang and Alatas of Pekalongan had financed trade missions since 1906 and had been in existence for twelve years. The partnership faced bankruptcy in 1934, facing litigation not only by creditors but also by family members. Java Bank held bad and doubtful debts of 1 million guilders in 1934 (Java Bank files of 25 January 1906, 30 October 1933 and 24 February 1937). The families' heirs were inconsistent in their attitude towards the continuation of the projects and sought foreclosure rather than reorganisation. The *mudaraba* contract needed a clear-cut demarcation between those merchants who stayed in Java or Singapore and the travelling merchants. Alkaff moved between Singapore and Tarim and Aden but the strong opposition to him in the Hadramaut meant that the duration of these partnerships was often limited. Second, the Java Bank records appear to contain many reports of tensions while the Hongkong Bank records reveal far less friction. The *mudaraba–musharaka*[7] relationships in Java appear less structured, more fluid, while the partnerships in Singapore were often embedded in investments in hotels, land and property. The third feature is that the partnerships overlapped in terms of product as well as market. The bank records reveal the dominance of a few large capitalists; bank officials also admitted to anxiety over such dominance, particularly as the loans were large and often shrouded in secrecy.

Trust

The spatial concentration of the Arab diaspora also affected business organisation. There were difficulties in monitoring economic activities, further aggravated by Islamic legal constraints. If the Arabs had possessed intermediaries in the ports and regions in which they traded, this would have reduced the operational difficulties. Sindhis in Shikapuri operated successfully from west Africa to Kobe because of kinship and religious networks. The Sindh and Gujarati networks also possessed clear apprenticeships in the firm, with varying tiers of employees ranging from kin, salaried managers to shop assistants and servants (Markovitz, 2000). This, together with the use of flexible partnerships and contracts, however limited in duration, enhanced their ability to adapt to different environments and changing circumstances. They developed a reputation for honesty and piety, and had access to information, and it was the agency structure that lay at the heart of their success; equally, it was this lack of agency ties that lay at the core of the Arab capitalists' difficulties. The Arabs had few stable patrons to absorb the risk, and, indeed, their connections to the Hadramaut feudal elite increased their risk. They faced the moral hazard issue because, with their spatial spread from Maluku to the Hadramaut, they were a highly mobile group, lacking clear corporate governance, transparency and accountability. As their trading sites were dispersed, when they left sons and nephews to coordinate activities over a vast range the risks and instability grew (van den Berg, 1886: 50, 124–7). It follows, therefore, that a connected issue here is trust.

The high profile of these few Arab capitalists produced a situation in which 'trust' led to investment without adequate safeguards and one's social and religious status was more important than economic efficiency. It was also inevitable that the small, pious investor would be exploited by the elite capitalist class. The 'moral economy', which gave rise to informal networks based on family and friends, was seriously unstable. Kuran's (2004c: 38–54) view is that the Islamic sub-economy as represented in Arab networks lacked individual freedom, was conservative and did not have the ability to present a coherent commercial communal cohesiveness. Religious piety often descended into public lies and private exploitation. My contention is that the Arabs lacked the intermediaries crucial in these dispersed sites; relying on anonymous partners raised the fundamental risks.

The foregoing analysis has revealed how the emergence of a cohesive bourgeoisie was hindered by the absence of clear business structures, legitimacy and an absence of separation of public and private interests. A financial history of the Arabs also reveals similar organisational impediments to long-term economic progress. Furthermore, their interactions with diverse regional trading networks from the nineteenth century were coordinated through different currencies – Asian and colonial currencies as well as the Maria Theresa dollar.

Remittances

Their operations between south-east Asia and the Middle East were coordinated partly through hawala (remittance) shops. These were money changers as well as agents transferring payments for primary commodities – slaves, horses, textile and minerals – over a huge area. They were, in effect, dealing with promissory notes and bills of exchange (*suftaja*), and also engaging in a form of financial derivatives because of the different prices of currencies and goods in Batavia, Singapore, Bombay and Aden. Although many of these transactions were defined by trust and much of the lending was through family and friends, risk was still very high – partly because of piracy. These deposits were derived from the remittances of the community to the homeland, as well as advance payments on crops and other purchases, and they were used by the proprietors of the hawala shops to speculate on land and property. Cases of default and mishandling were recorded. The informal nature of these operations has persisted into the contemporary period, with migrant workers from south-east Asia who are working in the Middle East still remitting money through hawala shops because of the advantageous exchange rates offered and the low commission charged. The records of the Chartered Bank in Singapore and the Java Bank in Batavia for the years 1908 to 1933 reveal their serious worries about the threat posed by the hawala shops to their foreign exchange business. Operations, though small in scale, were carried out extensively in Singapore, Indonesia, Malaya, Thailand, India and into the Arakan peninsula, sustained in part by the pilgrim traffic and remittances to the Hadramaut. This concentration within individuals translated into a lack of structures capable of transformation into formal banks. Despite working in diverse currencies and possessing superb market information, the individuals failed to exploit such knowledge and become bankers. The reasons for this failure are complex.

Arab moneylending too was necessarily limited in scale, being confined mainly to urban centres in Indonesia and Singapore. There were three types of moneylending activities: first, the straightforward lending of money, albeit often at exorbitant rates of interest, drawing the wrath of the Dutch bureaucrats; second, advances on crops; third, loans to the peasants, to the bureaucrats and the state in south-east Asia and the Hadramaut. The Alsagoff Group maintained substantial lending to the Sultan of Johor between the late nineteenth century and the first decade of the twentieth. The Alkaff Group also combined a portfolio of financial interests in south-east Asia and the Hadramaut, which included tax farming in Shihr and loans to the sultan in Tarim and to the Nizam of Hyderabad.

These moneylending activities were localised, however, and often lacking in clear specialisation. This lack of specialisation meant that their lending outlets were constantly changing, moving across vast areas, and again lacking in organisational structures. Thus, despite their knowledge and expertise in terms of markets, currencies, trade and shipping, they were unable to create a grid parallel to that of the Western, Chinese and Indian financiers. The small size of the Arab community, aggravated by the factions and tensions within families, worsened their prospects. Arab capital remained subordinate to Chinese, as they had monopolistic advantages in commodity production and trade, with valuable comprador links to Western capital. In areas such as the Tarim basin in the Hadramaut they faced sanctions on high interest charges, while in other areas they had the freedom to charge what interest rates they wanted.

This variety in financial institutions is also reflected in the remittance business. Some were transported by kinsmen and friends, some were sent via banks in Singapore, Bombay and Aden. Wealthy Arabs in south-east Asia sent 200,000 Indian rupees per month to the Hadramaut in the 1920s. By 1937 remittances of £630,000 were entering the Hadramaut through letters of credit (Ingrams, 1937: 142; Clarence-Smith, 2005). Since 1907 Alsagoff had coordinated remittance transfers through couriers, Western banks and Arab agents in Tegal, Singapore, Hyderabad and Aden. These transfers also involved multiple currencies: Javanese coins, the Singapore dollar, the Indian rupee, the Maria Theresa dollar, the Italian lira and Saudi Arabian coins. Large transactions were confined to the Maria Theresa dollar and the Indian rupee, as both were on the silver standard and facilitated exchange. By 1940 remittances were carried out largely in the rupee.

These remittances had some impact on the Hadramaut economy, in improving agriculture, transport and food and subsidising luxury imports. Nevertheless, there was continuing pressure on the Arabs to maintain their moneylending activities and invest in land and property. Concern over this preference for rentier capitalism was being voiced after World War II (Watts, 1947). This development contrasts with what happened in connection with Chinese remittances from south-east Asia to southern China, which resulted in increased trade and investment. The Chinese remittance houses were linked to the south-east Asian rice trade, and these financial groups formed banks through partnerships, based on dialect groups (Brown, 1994: 123–41).

In contrast, the Hadramaut remittances were absorbed by the warring factions in the homeland, and investment was limited.

The Arabs in south-east Asia had pursued a highly sophisticated and complex financial system, and yet they had not ventured into banking. Why? William Clarence-Smith (1997) advances the theory that the divisions within the Arab community over usury and increased religious concern over the issue put a brake on the plans of Hadramis envisaging setting up joint-stock banks on Chinese lines: 'Charging interest could be disguised in private arrangements between individuals . . .' There are difficulties in accepting this interpretation. Arab moneylending activities continued into the post-war period, with prominent families from Singapore financing the Chinese and the Malay elite in Malaya and Singapore. Later, in the 1960s, Hong Leong in Singapore and Malaysia was a recipient of Arab funds both local and foreign, which after 1980 led to coordinated joint venture arrangements with the Saudi elite in Hong Kong and New York (Brown, 2004b). Quek Leng Chan's partnership with Prince al Waleed of Saudi Arabia in hotel investments in the United States and Europe was a continuation of earlier ties with Arab money-lenders and financiers in Singapore.

I would argue that, unlike the Chinese and the Chettiars, the Arabs faced difficulties in pooling resources, and unlike the Chettiars had less access to Western banks for on-lending to agriculturalists and urban workers (Brown, 1994: 173–88). Second, the Chettiars specialised in finance, and had a regionally widespread network of moneylenders: one firm had branches from Chettinad to Burma, Malaya, Indonesia and Hong Kong. Third, the Chettiars had operations in wholesale as well as retail credit markets within a transregional context. Hence, despite their severe losses in south-east Asia in the Drepression of 1931, they were able to move back to south India, engaging in formal banking and participating in the heavy industrialisation drive, later in the 1930s. Fourth, in this multinational banking the use of diverse funds was assisted by the use of *hundi* (promissory notes) to transfer capital throughout Asia. In addition, the Chettiars maintained a system of guarantor (*adathi*) and clearing facilities. Their knowledge on variable interest rates, fostered by close links to grass roots borrowers and to Western financial institutions in the metropolis, provided a clear advantage. Chettiars exploited the porous nature of south-east Asia, which had no restraining boundaries, no controls on capital flows and an absence of serious competition from financial brokers, including the Arabs. Arabs were confronted with a serious lack of durable, long-term, interregional financial networks in Asia, the Middle East and north Africa.[8] This lack of strong organisational features on the part of financial institutions meant they were overtaken by the Chinese in south-east Asia and by the Indian, Jewish and Greek minorities in the Arabian peninsula (Kuran, 2004a).

Trading diasporas

The Arabs were a small minority who had to adapt to changing trade patterns as the south-east Asian moved from pre-colonial, to colonial to post-colonial regimes. The difficulties in this adaptation were not, as Kuran argues, a consequence of culture, control by religious conservatives and a society lacking public discourse on economic challenges (Kuran, 2004a, 2004b; Ozcan, 2004). Rather, the Arab decline here was driven by increased competition from other trading communities and from state capitalism. Rising Chinese, Japanese and European competition in Asia, and Indian competition in the Arabian peninsula, exacerbated by emerging state capitalism in south-east Asia and Yemen, blew their ambitions away, reducing them to exotic minorities languishing in their decaying 'palaces'. Some escaped to other parts of Asia and into Saudi Arabia and north Africa. The disparate spread of these Hadrami merchants discouraged the spread of durable business organisations and business partnerships. There was overlapping between headquarters in Singapore and the Hadramaut. The relations were of flexible duration and used varieties of finance. The partnerships thus differed according to the information and expenses required. The Alkaff family firm, formed in Surabaya in the early nineteenth century, moved to Singapore in mid-century, but the capacity for family firms in general to grow and strengthen was missing because of friction and tension. Trading profits remitted to the Hadramaut were frittered away in religious and political initiatives.

If they had adhered to an ascetic model of enterprise, like the Chettiars in south-east Asia, and the Gujaratis in Asia and Africa, the Arabs might have succeeded. It was the aggressive, ruthless competition that sealed their demise, however. The Arabs had powerful mercantile relations in the seventeenth and eighteenth centuries, when the mercantilist states of south-east Asia created monopolies in trade and in the collection of customs and port duties using Arab merchants as intermediaries. This continued into the nineteenth century with the emergence of the colonial powers, the Dutch and the British, and the rise of European and Chinese capitalists. The Hadrami migrants from the early nineteenth century onwards faced competition in revenue farming, which was dominated by the Chinese, who with the funds derived in this way were already creating multinational enterprises in the nineteenth century. These activities introduced invaluable control over labour and production, assisted by the rise of Chinese syndicate capitalists, loosely linked from Singapore to Malaya, Indonesia, Thailand, Hong Kong and China. The intra-Asia trade and industrialisation, driven by the Japanese since the nineteenth century, were also assisted by these Chinese networks (Brown, 1994). Faced with this, the Arabs, in true Kirznerian mode, grasped opportunities and grew at an impressive pace, but the lack of institutional structures defeated them in the long term. Ironically, the policies brought in by the independent states of south-east Asia disadvantaged many Arab capitalists, seducing their elite into government and academic life.

In their trade with India and the Middle East they had carved out lucrative niches. Alkaff had secured the revenue farm contract in the Shihr in 1919, owned real estate and agricultural land and was moneylender to the sultanate of Kathiri, as well as to the Qu'ayti sultan and local chiefs. He built the road between Tarim and the port of Shihr and he was also a defence contractor. In 1924, however, he lost his contract for Shihr customs collection, which was handed over to an Indian, Hajeebhoy Lalljee, for 80,000 Maria Theresa dollars. This contract was for six years, but Alkaff lost the bid because of his lower price estimate. Another Indian, Abdoolabhoy Lalljee, held the contract for Mukalla for 160,000 Maria Theresa dollars per year (Abdoolabhoy Lalljee to First Assistant Resident, 1922; Jumabhoy Lalljee to First Assistant Resident, 1927; Note on the revenue of Shihr and Mokalla, 1928).

This competition between the Bombay merchants and the Arabs was politically manipulated by the sultans and tribal chiefs. The Indian Muslims were bidding with high prices for these contracts, subsidising their losses through their trade profits. Alkaff, in contrast, was heavily committed on projects for political reform of the Hadramaut and the building of roads, schools and mosques, using both the customs revenues as well as trading profits for these philanthropic acts. The Indian merchants also had efficient business structures, with branches in Aden, Mukalla, Bombay, Calcutta and the Far East. These were business units with financial institutions managed by the extended family. Many of them were Bohra Muslims, a Gujarati group similar to the Ismailis, who believed in the coexistence of religion and the secular world. These Shia minorities used a combination of religion and modern economic institutions to strengthen their financial growth. Some of the Bohras retained Hindu laws of inheritance, and interest was charged on loans. Here we have a case of Gujarati cultural customs of ascetic piety shaping their Islam and determining their economic actions. They were a powerful group, both in India and abroad, revealing a work ethic, thrift and discipline combined with a belief in wealth creation and accumulation, through a partnership model that included the extended family and Bohra adherents (Markovitz, 2000; Lekon, 2003).

These Indian merchants also had a crucial advantage in their widespread use of the Indian rupee in the Arabian peninsula. Diverse Indian networks, such as the Khojas, Bohras, Ismailis, Gujarati Hindus and south Indian merchants in Aden, Bahrain, Dubai, Oman, and Kuwait, dominated this rupee bloc, which was replaced by new currencies from 1950. The rerouting of trade after 1950 to Europe, the United States and within the Middle East further conspired against these Arab groups from south-east Asia.

The decline of the Arab trading diaspora after 1960 is also related to the decline of Aden after the communist takeover of South Yemen in 1967. Aden as a leading port for the Arabian peninsula, Horn of Africa and Asia collapsed overnight. Earlier, Aden had preserved critical trade routes in produce, financial services, shipping, insurance and revenue farming activities through partnerships and joint-stock corporations, sustained by abundant inter-national capital flows. In the 1940 and 1950s famines, political conflicts and ideological warfare sapped these networks (Lekon, 2003: 24–6). Simultaneously, south-east Asia was increasingly integrated into a Pacific rim dominated first by Japan and later by South Korea and China as well.

It is this changing political dimension that needs to be kept in focus. The consolidation of commercial organisations and techniques through state patronage and privilege was essential for capitalist growth in south-east Asia. To make the transformation from niche traders to global players, the Arabs needed political patronage. The Arabs in Singapore held advisory positions in local and colonial government, but unlike the Chinese were marginalised in state economic initiatives, particularly after 1960. The immature and weak financial institutions that the Chinese had in the early twentieth century was compensated for by ties with local and European power brokers. In the nineteenth century the Arabs enjoyed some alliances with the state in lucrative revenue-forming monopolies in Johor, Java and the Hadramaut (Fernando and Bulbeck, 1992: 59; Trocki, 1979: 128, 175, 218–26). Alkaff held revenue farm contracts in the Shihr and surrounding areas in 1919, and attempted to build a power base in the Hadramaut through a close relationship with Resident Adviser W. H. Ingrams and, before him, the sultan. Both bestowed economic and religious responsibilities, but not privileges. Alkaff faced financial extortion and ruin at the hands of the sultan, and was saved only by British intervention. Alsagoff was a confidant of the Sultan of Johor, Abu Bakar, and gained land and economic privileges. The other state connection that was economically valuable to the Arabs was in Hyderabad, where they extracted revenues from tax farming, moneylending and in providing mercenaries from the late nineteenth century onwards (Khalidi, 1997; Field, 1984).

The bin Laden family, having enjoyed the patronage of the Saudi monarchy since the 1930s, were able to construct the largest building firm in Saudi Arabia, while the Mahfouz family acquired a controlling stake in the National Commercial Bank, the largest bank in the Middle East since the 1960s. The Baeshen, Bassamah and Binzagr Groups in the food industry carved out successful regional enclaves. The Barooms in construction, and the Bugshans in heavy equipment leasing, prospered during the oil boom of the 1970s. The majority of these businesses were linked to the house of Saud. The bin Laden Group secured the contracts for road building in Saudi Arabia and Kuwait from the 1970s to the 1990s. Their kinsmen in south-east Asia and Yemen were making a quick exit to high government posts and academic life; just a cursory glance at the Alatas clan in Indonesia, Singapore and Yemen reveals this. The clan produced a distinguished foreign minister in the Suharto government, a president of Yemen and a prominent intellectual, Syed Hussein Alatas (Kazuhiro, 2005). I am not denying the existence of pockets of Arab capitalists throughout contemporary south-east Asia, but they are not a powerful bourgeoisie, and are frequently lumped with, or assimilated into, indigenous capitalist groups.

The next issue that may explain some of the difficulties faced by Arab capitalists in restructuring and adapting to fresh competition in this region can be attributed to the stratified, hierarchical, social, religious and regional divisions and identities. Stratification among the Arabs increased with the rise of non-sayyid migration from the end of the nineteenth century, and increased the rivalry between the *sayyid*, who claimed descent from the Prophet Muhammad, and the *masākīn* (poor). This was also reflected in the reformist al-Irshad opposition to the conservative Alawi faction in the period 1914 to 1934, which frequently spilled over into inter-family and intergenerational rivalry. In the 1920s the younger Hadramis in Java sought the integration of these factions but they were frustrated by the dominance of certain capitalist elites and a lively press, which, together with developments in the Hadramaut, continued to nourish these tensions. It is ironic that, while the high-status religious elite (*sayyids*) was dominant in commerce, their religious piety acted to divide and constrain the economic well-being of the community as a whole. The quality and religious affiliation of entrepreneurs were emphasised, and often the economic attributes of a project were subordinated to status and filial piety. This engendered idiosyncratic economic behaviour.

Among the many factors commonly identified as contributing to the Arabs' weakness in capitalist growth is their high levels of consumption. The Arab diaspora, too spatially distributed, divided by volatile politics and factionalism and enduring high risk, indulged in luxury living. Alkaff and Alsagoff built palatial mansions and Japanese tea gardens, held lavish parties entertaining the colonial authorities and spent money seeking titles and honour from the governing regimes, both in south-east Asia and the Hadramaut. Alkaff was a motor racing enthusiast, and frittered away a fortune on fast cars. These internal flaws of a few members of Arab society were not serious enough in themselves, however, to deter rapid capital accumulation. The Hadrami success is even more remarkable considering that it was achieved with smaller demographic and economic resources than the Chinese.

The ecology of capitalism

At the outset it was established that it was environment and economic institutions rather than Islam that determined the success or failure of the Arab bourgeoisie in south-east Asia. It would therefore be pertinent here to trace how Islamic economic ideology in south-east Asia was indigenised and emancipated itself from any interpretations that constrained economic achievements in a ruthlessly competitive global economy. This literature underlines the problems of Islam and capitalist development, but this discourse had differing intrinsic endogenous factors for south-east Asia. The Islamic movements in the region emphasised the similarities between Islam and the West rather than the differences.

Sarekat Islam was formed in 1912 to assist Muslim traders to compete with the Chinese, in the batik industry, and it intersected with the Javanese reformist movement, the Muhammadiyah, in Yogyakarta (Nakamura, 1983). Islamic identity was seen as an expression of anti-Chinese, anti-colonial sentiments, and by the 1920s it had become a 'plea for Islamic unity from the periphery to the centre in turmoil' (Feillard, 2003: 16; see also Laffan, 2003). Sarekat Islam stressed socialism and was inspired by the Turkish revolution of Kemal Attaturk, revealing naïvety as to the latter's secularism. The Saudi occupation of Mecca in October 1924 and the rise of the Wahhabi movement introduced a brief interlude of Islamic orthodoxy. The economic boom of the 1920s, however, particularly in west Sumatra, created a leaning towards capitalism by the Kaum Muda, the powerful young reformist group in Indonesia. The rise of regional identities in Indonesia in the inter-war decades had a further influence on the pro-capitalist ideology sweeping Indonesia and Malaya. The factionalism between the Alawi (conservative) and al-Irshad (reformist) wings that characterised the period 1914 to 1934 led young Irshadis to emphasise wealth creation through a lively local press. The religious affiliation, piety and status of entrepreneurs and the economic attributes of their projects were stressed. Al-Irshad's hostile attitude to *sayyids*' dominance was clear. The Irshadis, dominated by wealthy non-*sayyids*, emphasised self-empowerment, hard work, honesty and responsibility, and built schools and established journals. The group revealed an obsessive concern with financial matters, in line with its belief that the economic backwardness of Muslims could be overcome through a technical education incorporating jurisprudence, science and mathematics besides theology and Arabic. This radical modernism was reinforced by a classless, anti-colonialist ideology. Dutch colonial attitudes and their patronage of the *sayyids* and the Chinese were seen as a threat to Muslim advancement.

This continued into the post-war decades, when Syed Hussein Alatas (1977) identified Dutch and British colonial images of the 'lazy native' as politically motivated. Alatas sought to emphasise the similarities between Islam and Protestantism: the virtues of hard work, a fear of God, honesty, integrity and frugality. The only difference was the Calvinist stress on pre-determinism and the link between wealth and personal salvation. The theological debate in independent Indonesia went further and affirmed Maxime Rodinson's thesis of the economic irrelevance of Islam, since interpretations were diverse and Muslims could select what was relevant and appropriate (Rodinson, 1973: 31). The 'insurmountable obstacles' were created by European imperialism, a view shared by the Islamic Marxist Dr Muhammad Hatta, who was vice-president of Indonesia in the 1950s. Islam posed no obstacle to capitalist development. 'If material circumstances are ripe for development, the beliefs and values of Muslims will not stand in the way' (Jones, 1988: 97). Indonesians and Malay Islamists, including Taufik Abdullah, also stressed the similarities between Puritan Islam and the Protestant work ethic and economic prosperity (Abdullah, 1979). Masfuk (2002: 30), an influential Indonesian intellectual, sees the Koran as encouraging wealth creation, and espouses an ideology akin to that of American self-improvement: Islam idolises the self-made man, and believes in rational management similar to that advocated by Peter Drucker, David McClelland (1961), Norman Vincent Peale, Dale Carnegie and Stephen Covey (1989).

The American self-development literature was compared to the economic goals and hard work enshrined in Islam. It is this continuous redefinition, the rational responses to the outside, that Jacob van Leur has described as the 'thin and flaky glaze' of South-east Asia's adoption of foreign influences (van Leur, 1983: 278–89). The innate flexibility, the 'third way' response in south-east Asia, is in stark contrast to the rigidities of China, India and the Middle East. The 'cultural protectionism' of Kuran is therefore missing in our analysis of capitalism and Islam in south-east Asia.

Dutch scholarship has also revealed divergent views. Lodewijk van den Berg, writing in 1886, saw Islam as a pernicious influence on growth (Van den Berg, 1886; see also Dostal, 1984: 50).[9] In the mid-twentieth century Clifford Geertz (1963) emphasised the bourgeois traits of the santri (religious education) in parts of Java. The consensus is that, while religion does shape economic and political processes, religion in turn is shaped by history and politics. The 'imagined umma' (Islamic community) has varied over time, space and region, as have its responses to politics, society, economics and capitalism.

Notes

I am grateful to Professor William Clarence-Smith and Professor William Roff for useful comments on this chapter. I am also indebted to Christian Lekon, Rahman Tang Abdullah, Samsol Bujang, Laura Newby and Gwenael Feillard for assistance on Muslim groups in Aden, south China, Malaysia and Indonesia. I am also grateful to Peggy Wintin, Abu Bakr and Nuha Vannet for further assistance with Arab definitions and technical phrases.

1. Arabs in south-east Asia were principally from the Hadramaut in the Arabian peninsula, which is present-day Yemen. The migration from the mid-eighteenth century to 1967 focused on Indonesia, Singapore and Malaysia. Today they are largely assimilated into the indigenous Muslim population of the region.

2. Sayyid Mawdudi was a Pakistani social thinker who envisaged Islam as a 'complete way of life', including ethical education, medicine, law, politics and economics: see Mawdudi (1947).

3. The difference between a Kirznerian type of entrepreneur and the occasional Schumpeterian entrepreneur is that the former is alert to opportunities but such exploitation of opportunities occurs in a state of disequilibrium. Such entrepreneurs possess confidence. Schumpeter's entrepreneur is highly innovative and thereby disturbs the world through innovation. Schumpeter (1942) believed that corporate growth and innovation would make the entrepreneur obsolete. Israel Kirzner, in contrast, believed that large corporations would attract entrepreneurs and afford them greater scope for their alertness, confidence and skills. This argument is similar to that of Lewis (1993: 347–57). Lewis also refutes Rodinson's thesis that decline is a consequence of political structures.

4. By the 1990s some 200,000 Arabs, principally of Hadrami descent, existed in Indonesia (Hamid, 1994: 143). There were several Arab millionaires in south-east Asia. In 1921 they had total investment of 24 million guilders in Indonesia, compared to that of 36 million for Japanese investors and 340 million for Chinese investments. In 1936 Arabs in Indonesia contributed an average annual income tax payment of 3,000 guilders, while the Chinese paid 2,000 guilders and Europeans 4,000 guilders (Cator, 1936: 64).

5. The Alsagoff Group also had diversified interests but was powerful in pilgrim shipping and in inter-island transport, acting briefly in the 1880s as an intermediary for Holts and Dutch Indies Railroad Company (NISM). By the 1930s the group was suffering a decline in receipts from shipping because of the emerging Dutch and British shipping cartels (see Buckley, 1965: 564).

6. *Mudaraba* is a contract between two partners, the financier and the manager. Profit is distributed between the two partners in accordance with the ratio upon which the two partners have agreed. Financial loss is borne only by the financier. The manager's share is restricted merely to the ultimate profits.

7. *Musharaka* is similar to *mudaraba*, but both partners participate in the provision of capital and management, and share in the profit and loss. Profits are distributed according to agreed ratios, while losses are distributed in proportion to one's share of the capital invested. *Murabaha* is a sale agreed at a specified profit. It is in essence an advance sale with the seller bearing the risk. This contract was used in transporting horses, slaves and minerals over a vast region, where risks were high, and when fraud, death or piracy could have destroyed the entire enterprise (Yousef, 2004: 65).

8. Fully Islamic banks emerged only in the 1970s in Malaysia, Pakistan, Iran and Sudan. An Islamic Bank in Dubai, established in 1975, achieved limited success. In Malaysia greater success was achieved through conventional banks having a limited Islamic banking division. Forms of finance undertaken by these Islamic banks included (1) equity finance, including a contract of profit-sharing (*uqud-ishtirak al-mudaraba*); (2) trustee profit-sharing (*al-musharaka*) and joint venture profit-sharing; and (3) debt financing from *al-bai/al-tijara/al-Dayun* (deferred contracts on exchange), *al-bai bithanan ajil* (deferred instalment sales), *bai al-murabaha* (deferred lump sum sales), *al-ijara* (leasing), *bai al-salaam* (sales), *bai alistisna* (sale on order) and *riba al-nasiah* (interest-based lending), although such interest-based debt financing is forbidden (*haraam*).

9. Walter Dostal argues that the *sayyids* hoarded capital, were rent capitalists, held labour in debt bondage and lavished consumption on palaces and mosques. They had short-term aims because of their migratory culture.

References

Books and articles

Abdullah, T. (1979) *Agama etos kerja dan, perkembangan ekonomi*, Jakarta: Jawa.

Abuza, Z. (2003) Funding terrorism in Southeast Asia: the financial network of Al Qaeda and Jemaah Islamiya, *Contemporary Southeast Asia*, 25, 2, 169–99.

Alatas, S. H. (1977) *The Myth of the Lazy Native: A Study of the Image of the Malays, Filipinos and Javanese from the Sixteenth to the Twentieth Century and its Function in the Ideology of Colonial Capitalism*, London: Frank Cass.

Alsagoff, S. M. (1963) *The Alsagoff Family in Malaysia, A.H. 1240 (1824) to A.H. 1382 (1962)*, Singapore: Mun Seong Press.

Ariff, M. (ed.) (1991) *The Islamic Voluntary Sector in Southeast Asia*, Singapore: Institute of Southeast Asian Studies.

Brown, R. A. (1994) *Capital and Entrepreneurship in South East Asia*, Basingstoke: Macmillan.
   (2000) *Chinese Big Business and the Wealth of Asian Nations*, Basingstoke: Palgrave Macmillan.
   (2004a) Conglomerates in contemporary Indonesia: concentration, crisis and restructuring, *South East Asia Research*, 21, 3, 401–5.
   (2004b) Capital structure puzzle: the Hong Leong Group in Malaysia, in S. -L. Wong (ed.) *Chinese and Indian Diasporas: Comparative Perspectives*, Hong Kong: Hong Kong University Press, 95–138.

Buckley, C. B. (1965) *An Anecdotal History of Singapore in Old Times*, Kuala Lumpur: University of Malaya Press.

Cator, W. J. (1936) *The Economic Position of the Chinese in the Netherlands Indies*, Chicago: University of Chicago Press.

Clarence-Smith, W. G. (1997) Hadhrami entrepreneurs in the Malay world, c. 1750 to c. 1940, in U. Freitag and W. G. Clarence-Smith (eds.) *Hadhrami Traders, Scholars and Statesmen in the Indian Ocean, 1750s to 1960s*, Leiden: Brill, 297–314.
   (1998) The economic role of the Arab community in Maluku, 1816 to 1940, *Indonesia and the Malay World*, 26, 74, 32–49.
   (2000) Arab entrepreneurs in the Malay world in the 1930s recession, in B. Boomgaard and I. Brown (eds.) *Weathering the Storm: The Economies of Southeast Asia in the 1930s Depression*, Leiden: KITLV and Singapore Institute of Southeast Asian Studies, 229–48.
   (2002a) Horse trading: the economic role of Arabs in the Lesser Sunda Islands, c. 1800–1950, in H. de Jonge and N. Kaptein (eds.) *Transcending Borders: Arabs, Politics, Trade and Islam in Southeast Asia, 1870–1990*, Leiden: KITLV, 143–62.
   (2002b) The rise and fall of Hadhrami Arab shipping in the Indian Ocean, c. 1750 – c. 1940, in D. Parkin and R. Barnes (eds.) *Ships and the Development of Maritime Technology in the Indian Ocean*, London: Routledge Curzon, 227–58.
   (2005) Entrepreneurial strategies of Hadhrami Arabs in southeast Asia, c. 1750s–1945, paper presented to the International Conference on Yemeni-Hadramis in Southeast Asia: Identity Maintenance or Assimilation?, Kuala Lumpur, 22–5 August.

Cohen, M. L. (1976) *House United, House Divided: The Chinese Family in Taiwan*, New York: Columbia University Press.

Covey, S. R. (1989) *The Seven Habits of Highly Effective People: Restoring the Character Ethic*, New York: Simon and Schuster.

Das Gupta, A. (1982) Indian merchants and the trade in the Indian Ocean, c. 1500–1700, in I. Habib and T. Raychavdhuri (eds.) *Cambridge Economic History of India*, vol. I, c. 1200–c. 1750, Cambridge: Cambridge University Press, 407–33.

Dick, H., and P. J. Rimmer (2003) *Cities, Transport and Communications: The Integration of Southeast Asia since 1850*, Basingstoke: Palgrave Macmillan.

Dostal, W. (1984) Squire and peasant in Tarim: a study of 'rent capitalism' in southern Arabia, in D. Walter (ed.) *On Social Evolution*, Vienna: Horn, 228–52.

Eisenberger, J. (1926) *Indie en de Bedevaart naar mekka*, Leiden: M. Dubbeldeman.

Ellen, R. F. (1996) Arab traders and land settlers in the Geser-Gorom archipelago, *Indonesia Circle*, 70, 237–52.

Fawzy, S., and A. Galal (eds.) (1999) *Partners for Development: New Roles for Government and Private Sector in the Middle East and North Africa*, Washington, DC: World Bank.

Feillard, G. (2003) Instilling the spirit of capitalism to the ummah: the making of an Islamic work ethic in Indonesia, paper presented to the Conference on Diasporas, Islam and Capitalism in Asia and Beyond, Asia Research Institute, National University of Singapore, 5 December.

Fernando, M. R., and D. Bulbeck (eds.) (1992) *Chinese Economic Activity in the Netherlands India: Selected Translations from the Dutch*, Singapore: Institute of Southeast Asian Studies.

Field, M. (1984) *The Merchants: The Big Business Families of Arabia*, New York: Overlook Press.

Freedman, M. (1958) *Lineage Organization in South Eastern China*, London: Athlone Press.

Freitag, U. (2003) *Indian Ocean Migrants and State Formation in Hadhramaut: Reforming the Homeland*, Leiden: Brill.

Geertz, C. (1963) *Peddlers and Princes: Social Development and Economic Change in Indonesian Towns*, Chicago: University of Chicago Press.

Gobee, E., and C. Adriaanse (eds.) (1959) *Ambtelijke adviezen van C. Snouck Hurgronje*, The Hague: Nijhoff.

Hamid, A. (1994) *Dutch Policy against Islam and Indonesians of Arab Descent in Indonesia*, Jakarta: LP3ES.

Harn, L. C. (1963) The Arab population of Singapore 1819–1959, BA thesis, Department of Sociology, National University of Singapore.

Heuken, A. (1996) Arab landowners in Batavia/Jakarta, *Indonesia Circle*, 68, 65–74.

Ibrahim, A., S. Siddique and Y. Hussain (1985) *Readings on Islam in Southeast Asia*, Institute of Southeast Asian Studies: Singapore.

Ingrams, W. H. (1937) *A Report on the Social, Economic and Political Condition of the Hadhramaut*, London: His Majesty's Stationery Office.

Jones, E. L. (1988) *Growth Recurring: Economic Change in World History*, London: Clarendon Press.

Kazuhiro, A. (2005) The history of Hadhrami migration to South East Asia: the case of the Al-Attas Family, in U. Akira, O. F. Bajunid and Y. Tomoko (eds.) *Proceedings of the JCAS Symposium Population Movement beyond the Middle East: Migration, Diaspora and Network*, Osaka: Japan Centre for Area Studies, National Museum of Ethnology, 165–83.

Khalidi, O. (1997) The Hadhrami role in the politics and society of colonial India, 1750s to 1950, in U. Freitag and W. G. Clarence-Smith (eds.) *Scholars and Statesmen in the Indian Ocean 1750s–1960s*, Leiden: Brill, 67–81.

Kirzner, I. M. (1973) *Competition and Entrepreneurship*, Chicago: University of Chicago Press.

Kuran, T. (1996) The discontents of Islamic economic morality, *American Economic Review*, 86, 438–42.

(2001) The Provision of public goods under Islamic law: origins, impact and limitations of the *waqf* system, *Law and Society Review*, 35, 841–97.

(2003a) Islamic redistribution through *zakat*: historical record and modern realities, in M. Bonner, M. Ener and A. Singer (eds.) *Poverty and Charity in Middle Eastern Contexts*, New York: State University of New York Press, 274–93.

(2003b) The Islamic commercial crisis: institutional roots of economic underdevelopment in the Middle East, *Journal of Economic History*, 63, 414–46.

(2004a) The economic ascent of the Middle East religious minorities: the role of Islamic legal pluralism, *Journal of Legal Studies*, 33, 2, 475–515.

(2004b) Why the Middle East is economically underdeveloped: historical mechanisms of institutional stagnation, *Journal of Economic Perspectives*, 18, 3, 71–90.

(2004c) *Islam and Mammon: The Economic Predicaments of Islamism*, Princeton, NJ: Princeton University Press.

Laffan, M. F. (2003) *Islamic Nationhood and Colonial Indonesia: The Umma below the Winds*, London: Routledge Curzon.

Lekon, C. (2003) Capitalist activities in Hadhramaut 1882–1967: rational, political or traditional, paper presented to the Conference on Diasporas, Islam and Capitalism in Asia and Beyond, Asia Research Institute, National University of Singapore, 5 December.

Lewis, B. (1993) *Islam in History: Ideas, People and Events in the Middle East*, Chicago: Open Court.

(2002) *What Went Wrong? The Clash between Islam and Modernity in the Middle East*, London: Perennial.

Lim, L. S. (1987) The Arabs of Singapore: a sociographic study of their place in the Muslim and Malay world of Singapore, BA thesis, Department of Sociology, National University of Singapore.

McClelland, D. C. (1961) *The Achieving Society*, Princeton, NJ: Van Nostrand

McDonnell, M. (1986) The conduct of the Hajj from Malaysia and its socio-economic impact on Malay society, Ph.D. thesis, Columbia University, NY.

Majlis Ugama Islam Singapura (1973–80) *Annual Report*, Singapore: Religious Council of Singapore.

Makarim, W. (1987) The political economy of the Indonesian textile industry under the New Order government, Ph.D. thesis, Ohio State University.

Markovitz, C. (2000) *The Global World of Indian Merchants 1750–1947: Traders of Sind from Bukhara to Panama*, Cambridge: Cambridge University Press.

Masfuk (2002) *Orang Jawa Miskin, Orang Jawa Kaya: Cara Menjadi Milyuner [The poor Javanese, the Rich Javanese: Both Seek to Become Millionaires]*, Jakarta: Republika.

Matsubara, K. (2004) Law of the ancestors: property holding practices and lineage social structures in nineteenth century south China, DPhil thesis, Oxford University.

Mawdudi, S. A.-A. (1947) *The Economic Problem of Man and its Islamic Solution*, Lahore: Islamic Publications.

Muslim Trust Fund Association (1984) *80th Anniversary Publication*, Singapore: Religious Council of Singapore.

Nakamura, M. (1983) *The Crescent Arises over the Banyan Tree: A Study of the Muhammadiyah Movement in a Central Javanese Town*, Jakarta: Gadjah Mada University Press.

Owen, R. (1993) *The Middle East in the World Economy 1800–1914*, London: Methuen.

Özcan, G. B. (2004) Trust and market exchange: the case of Islamic companies, unpublished paper.

Pearson, M. N. (1994) *Pious Passengers: The Hajj in Earlier Times*, New Delhi: Sterling.

Polanyi, K. (1957) *The Great Transformation: The Political and Economic Origins of Our Time*, Boston: Beacon Press.

Post, P. (1996) The formation of the pribumi business elite in Indonesia 1930s to 1940s, *Bijdragen tot de Taal-, Land-en Volkenkunde*, 152, 4, 87–110.

Redkin, O. I. (1995) Migration in Wadi Amd and Wadi Daw'an after World War II: economic and cultural effects, paper presented to the School of Oriental and African Studies conference on Hadramaut and the Hadrami Diaspora, Late Eighteenth Century to 1967, London, April.

Rodinson, M. (1973) *Islam and Capitalism* (trans. B. Pearce), New York: Pantheon.

Roff, W. R. (1974) *The Origins of Malay Nationalism*, Kuala Lumpur: Penerbit University Malaya.
    (2002) Murder as an aid to social history: the Arabs in Singapore in the early twentieth century, in H. de Jonge and N. Kaptein (eds.) *Transcending Borders: Arab Politics, Trade, and Islam in Southeast Asia*, Leiden: KITLV, 91–108.

Schumpeter, J. A. (1942) *Capitalism, Socialism and Democracy*, New York: Harper and Row.

Singapore Department of Statistics (1980) *Census of the Population of Singapore*, Singapore: Government Printers.
    (1981) *Census of the Population of Singapore 1980*, Singapore: Government Printers.

Straits Settlements Gazette (1901) Singapore: Government Printing Office.
    (1906) Singapore: Government Printing Office.

Suharto, R. (1989) *Pikiran, Ucapan dan Tindakan: Otobiografi Seperti Dipaparkan kepada G. Dwipayana dan Ramadhan K. H.* [*Thoughts and Action: The Autobiography of Suharto as Narrated to G. Dwipayana*]. Jakarta: D. H. Jakarta.

Sutter, J. O. (1959) Indonesianisasi: a historical survey of the role of politics in the institutions of a changing economy from the Second World War to the eve of the general elections, 1940–1955, Ph.D. thesis, Cornell University, NY.

Tabung Haji (2004) *Annual Report, Hasten Towards Prosperity*, Kuala Lumpur: Tabung Haji Publications.

Tagliacozzo, E. (2003) Financing devotion: the long duree economics of South East Asia's pilgrimage to Mecca, paper presented to the Asia Research Institute conference on Diasporas, Islam and Capitalism in Asia and Beyond, Singapore, 5 December.

Ter, K. L. (1985) *The Law of Charities: Cases and Materials, Singapore and Malaysia*, Singapore: Butterworths.

Tinbergen, J., and J. B. O. Derksen (1941) Nederlansch-Indie in cijfers, in W. H. van Helsdingen and H. Hoogenberk (eds.) *Daar werd wat groots verricht: Nederlandsch-Indie in de twintigste eeuw*, Amsterdam: Elsevier, 508–25.

Tripp, C. (2006) *Islam and the Moral Economy: The Challenge of Capitalism*, Cambridge: Cambridge University Press.

Trocki, C. A. (1979) *Prince of Pirates: The Temenggongs and the Development of Johor and Singapore 1784–1885*, Singapore: Singapore University Press.

Utusan Melayu (1908) 4 January 1908.

van den Berg, L. W. C. (1886) *Le Hadhramout et les Colonies Arabes dan L'Archipel Indien*, Batavia: Government Printing Office.

van Leur, J. C. (1983) *Indonesian Trade and Society: Essays in Asian Social and Economic History*, The Hague: W. van Hoeve.

Vlieland, C. A. (1931) *British Malaya: A Report on the 1931 Census and on Certain Problems of Vital Statistics*, London: Crown Agents for the Colonies.

Volkstelling 1930 (1935) Part VII, Batavia: Landsdrukkerij.

Yousef, T. M. (2004) The murabaha syndrome in Islamic finance: laws, institutions and politics, in C. M. Henry and R. Wilson (eds.) *The Politics of Islamic Finance*, Edinburgh: Edinburgh University Press, 63–80.

Manuscripts

Abdoolabhoy Lalljee to First Assistant Resident, Aden (4 September 1922), Oriental and India Office Collection, R/20/A/1407, British Library, London.

Alkaff transcript, National Archives of Singapore (n.d.) A000124, Singapore.

Communities of Singapore, Singapore: Oral History (1996), National Archives of Singapore, part 3, A000377, Singapore.

Jumabhoy Lalljee to First Assistant Resident, Aden (9 July 1927), Oriental and India Office Collection, R/20/A/1414, British Library, London.

Note on the revenue of Shihr and Mokalla (1928), Oriental and India Office Collection, R/20/A/3255, British Library, London.

Shaykh Alkaff's wills (6 February 1910), Oriental and India Office Collection, R/20/A3874, British Library, London.

Syed Mohsen Alsagoff transcript, National Archives of Singapore (15 January 1983), B000523, Singapore.

Transcript of R. Jumabhoy, National Archives of Singapore (n.d.), A00074, Singapore.

Watts, A. F, *Some notes on the rural economy of Wadi Hadhramaut* (1947), Oriental and India Office Collection, R/20/B/2033, British Library, London.

Newspapers

Asiaweek, 31 July 1992.

Straits Times, 13 November 1907.

Tempo, 26 July 1980.

Utusan Melayu, 4 January 1908.

Challenges to the German theatrical employment system: how long-established institutions respond to globalisation forces

Axel Haunschild

Introduction

This chapter draws on the example of the German theatrical employment system to analyse the tensions between national institutions and current external market and internationalisation forces. From an economic perspective, creative industries share certain features – such as the uncertainty of demand, the intrinsic motivation of workers/artists, the infinite variety of products, time pressures in project-based production and the omnipresence of ranking processes (Caves, 2000). Employment arrangements and work organisation in industries producing, for example, films, radio or television programmes, theatre and music are sometimes seen as a model for flexible work in a global and competitive economy. Comparing nations, however, reveals development paths that have led to different institutional environments for creative production such as theatre. Professional theatrical production is marked by project-based teams that bring together craft-oriented talents and professions (including actors, directors, costume designers, lighting designers and stage designers) to produce an output defined as a play or a performance. Despite the common characteristics of theatrical production, language boundaries and varying national roots and traditions have resulted in specific ways of organising theatrical work in different countries. These differences comprise, for example, ways of financing or funding theatrical work, ways in which actors and other theatre workers are educated and trained, and the terms and conditions of employment or work contracts.

The chapter concentrates on the German theatrical employment system. German theatre is characterised by (i) a large number of public repertoire theatres, (ii) a combination of stability and flexibility within the workforce, resulting from relatively stable teams working under temporary contracts, and (iii) collective bargaining, which sets some restrictions on employers' strategies. These features differ from most other existing national solutions. The chapter sketches the developments that have led to the current characteristics. More concretely, it shows how historical preconditions have shaped recent perceptions of efficiency and success, as well as the acceptability of working conditions and task assignments to both workers and employers. These national institutions and institutionalised rules provide stability and reduce uncertainty despite inter-firm mobility and transient work relations. This national model has increasingly come under threat, however. This is because (global) market forces put pressure on public subsidies. Additionally, solutions and developments in other countries, such as the withdrawal of state subsidies in the United Kingdom during the 1980s, or more project-based forms of theatre organisation in the Netherlands, offer alternative organisational and funding models, which are now being debated in Germany. This chapter shows how these pressures and internationalisation forces challenge the established system, how they are reformulated within current debates and how they lead to amendments and adaptations of the system. It refers to David Marsden's theory of employment systems to highlight the emergence and stability of existing institutional rules. This view, though, tends to neglect the challenges and dynamics that institutions and actors face. Therefore, the chapter also refers to the SSD framework developed by Smith and Meiksins (1995; see also Smith, 2005). This framework distinguishes between system, societal and dominance effects in order to explain variations in organisational practices and forms. Smith (2005: 603–4) sees, within a multinational company, a 'three-way tension of (a) generic features of capitalism and (b) particular forms of management and labor derived from the nationally embedded context ... and (c) standardizing forces derived from dominant or global actors as they represent best practices to the firm'. The SSD framework will have to be adapted to the features of the theatrical industry analysed in this chapter, however, such as the interorganisational character of careers and networks, as well as the coexistence of artistic, political and economic goals. The chapter supports the idea that an historical understanding of local practices and institutions is essential for developing analytical concepts and frameworks aimed at explaining current globalisation forces and their local consequences.

Background: cultural and creative industries

In the past two decades we have witnessed a remarkable increase in the literature on the economics of creative production, on the management and organisation of creative production within firms and within industries, and on the nature of creative production in general (Becker, 1982; Menger, 1999; Benhamou, 2000; Caves, 2000; Howkins, 2001; Throsby, 2001; Jeffcutt and Pratt, 2002; Davis and Scase, 2000). The term 'creative industries' (Caves, 2000) has been used to specify a growing and, according to many observers, fascinating and increasingly relevant sector of the economy. Three dominant perspectives can be identified, and they are used to advocate the uniqueness of creative industries and the legitimisation of creative industries research (see Eikhof and Haunschild, 2005, for a more detailed and critical account of these perspectives).

The first major characteristic within creative industries research is to focus on an industry's *output* or the *products*, respectively. Richard Caves (2000: 1), for example, defines creative industries as those industries 'supplying goods and services that we broadly associate with cultural, artistic, or simply entertainment value'. Following this line of thought, industries with outputs such as fine art, books, music, films, TV programmes and theatre performances are clearly regarded as creative industries, but entertainment industries such as the production of video games and special interest newspapers, as well as services in tourism and gastronomy (e.g. theme parks), can be included.

A second approach is to focus on the *content of labour*. Richard Florida (2002), for example, asserts that some occupations per se can be regarded as creative work, and so creative industries or creative classes can be identified by clustering employees or individuals of certain professions. To Florida (2002: 8), these constitute the creative class, who 'are paid to create and have considerably more autonomy and flexibility [...] to do so' than those 'primarily paid to execute according to plan'. Since the creation of 'new ideas, new technology and/or new creative content' is not limited to arts, music and entertainment, but is also a core phenomenon of science and engineering, architecture and education, this perspective further broadens the definition of creative industries.

The third perspective focuses on the *production structure*. Caves uses his product-focused definition of creative industries to look at 'why those activities [resulting in creative outputs] are organized the way they are' (2000: 1).

He identifies seven properties that characterise creative production (2–10), and concentrates on three main areas, namely product markets, production inputs and production processes (see Eikhof and Haunschild, 2005). Product markets in the creative industries are marked by the existence of *infinite varieties* of a product. Combined with the fact that product consumption is an individual experience and less easy to predict than in other industries (*nobody knows*), producers face higher uncertainties (and thus risks) in markets for creative products. Moreover, many creative products feature specific forms of durable rents (*ars longa*), requiring structures of property rights and contracting. Workers in the creative industries care about their products (*art for art's sake*) and creative work input is vertically differentiated (*A list/B list*). Although artists claim to produce art for art's sake, they have to be concerned about their market value in order to be included in the production of art at all. In many creative industries, production requires a high degree of flexibility both with respect to quantitative and qualitative inputs. It is carried out in changing teams of members with various capabilities and qualifications (*motley crews*). More directly than in most other industries, economic profitability is linked to the use of time according to an exact schedule (*time flies*). All inputs have to be available at the right time – their substitution is difficult, if not impossible, compared to non-creative production – and this factor requires specific forms of management.

Using these properties to distinguish creative industries from 'the rest of the economy where creativity plays a lesser (if seldom negligible) role' (Caves, 2000: 2), Caves enhances the product perspective. He does so by taking into account the structural embeddedness of creative production, as represented in market characteristics, property rights and features of production processes. The *production structure* perspective suggests that there are common and shared features of creative industries, in contrast to a focus on idiosyncratic (national or local) institutionalised patterns of production. In the following, one specific industry (theatre) in a specific national context (Germany) will be introduced.

Methodology: the empirical study

This chapter draws on qualitative empirical data and secondary data from a research project on German theatre conducted by the author and Doris Eikhof between 2000 and 2003. The overall aim of the project was to describe the German theatre industry as an employment system and to analyse various aspects of theatrical employment at individual, organisational and industry levels. Primary data collected include forty-five semi-structured, in-depth interviews (see King, 1994, and Miles and Huberman, 1994). The first set of ten interviews was carried out in a public theatre that is situated in a city with approximately 500,000 inhabitants. This theatre includes an opera house with orchestra and ballet, so employing about 900 people in total, of whom about one-third are artistic staff. The study focused on the theatre company. Interview partners included both members of the theatre's management group and actors. A second set of five interviews was conducted with representatives of intermediary organisations: the national employers' and employees' associations (Deutscher Bühnenverein, and Genossenschaft Deutscher Bühnen-Angehöriger), the state-run work agency for actors (Zentrale Bühnen-, Fernseh- und Filmvermittlung – ZBF) and a state-run theatre school. All relevant inter-firm institutions were analysed to explore their function within the employment system. The results of these interviews were used to validate some of the claims of the respondents in the first part of the study (see also Haunschild, 2003).

Based on these first fifteen interviews, a more detailed study of the individual aspects of employment was carried out. A third set of qualitative interviews (thirty in all) was conducted with theatre actors, theatre students, directors and a theatre manager in two public theatres situated in a city with approximately 2 million inhabitants. Additional information was collected by participant observation, which comprised attending premiere celebrations, gatherings after shows, rehearsals and other cultural events (e.g. readings), as well as informal discussions mainly with freelance artists. To validate the subjective information collected in the interviews, the material was contrasted with information from secondary data sources (Yin, 1994), such as statistical reports (e.g. by Deutscher Bühnenverein and Genossenschaft Deutscher Bühnen-Angehöriger), media coverage on German theatre industry and artists in newspapers and practitioner journals, and information given on theatre and intermediary organisation websites.

A brief history: the uniqueness of German theatre

The German theatre scene is unique. Historically grounded in the decentralised structure of princedoms and electorates, the large number of local court theatres with their own buildings and ensembles in existence at the end of the eighteenth century have bequeathed 151 state-supported theatres (Stadttheater, Staatstheater and Landestheater). These theatres receive around 80 per cent of their annual budgets from public subsidies (a total of €2 billion per year) and hold groups of about twelve to sometimes fifty actors and actresses (ensembles) employed on a temporary basis (Deutscher Bühnenverein, 2004). Until the second half of the twentieth century most German theatres of artistic relevance were organised as sub-departments of public administration, and often did not even have their own finance or personnel departments. All expenses were accounted for directly by the respective city or state administration. Today, 43 per cent of public theatres are still organised this way. Most of the theatres among the remaining 57 per cent are limited corporations with the respective city or state as the sole owner. Despite their theoretical independence as organisations, the public owners of these theatres still finance 80 to 95 per cent of their annual budget and automatically account for any overspend (Pitz and Köhn, 2001). German theatre managers are responsible to the local government for the theatres' overall artistic production, and have to legitimise the use of public funding. Once a manager is hired, however, the city or state government does not have any direct means of control until the manager's contract runs out. It may try to exercise political influence over a manager's artistic and economic decisions – by, for instance, threatening not to renegotiate the manager's contract – but even this threat has proved to have little effect on theatre managers convinced of their artistic vision (Eikhof and Haunschild, 2007).

In contrast to state-owned theatres in many other countries, and in contrast to commercial theatres, their German public counterparts are repertoire theatres. In other words, there is a repertoire of fifteen to twenty plays, and the performances of each play are spread over the theatre season, usually with no play being performed for more than one or two days running. Private and independent theatres exist as well, but, in terms of artistic quality and reputation, the public theatres account for what is recognised as 'the' German theatre industry.

Ensemble contracts in Germany are temporary contracts with a duration of one, two or, occasionally, three years. These ensembles or theatre companies usually remain stable for at least some years and are supplemented by so-called 'guests'. Theatre ensembles are therefore located firmly within the basic principles of organising work in the arts, as outlined by Howard Becker (1982: 81), who has noted permanent employment and organisational careers in conjunction with the freelance system. The considerable authority of theatre managers (and directors), which is derived from the right to artistic freedom, facilitates task assignments and hire-and-fire decisions according to individual tastes (i.e. for artistic reasons).

The 'Normalvertrag Bühne' (NV Bühne, formerly NV Solo), which arose from multi-employer collective bargaining, provides a mutually accepted framework for these contracts, and applies in addition to employed directors, stage designers and so on. Multi-employer bargaining sets an institutional framework and restricts the scope of German theatres to make use of flexible employment and the assignment of tasks to actors. The theatre management has the right to terminate contracts every autumn at the end of the theatre season (for so-called artistic reasons), but there are certain rules limiting the scope of employers, especially periods of notice giving actors half a year to present themselves to potential employers, the right to a personal explanatory conversation, and severance pay. There are written and unwritten rules regulating adequate minimum task assignment (they usually have the right to play two main roles in a season), and there are some restrictions on working hours, as well as a fixed minimum salary for beginners. There are no restrictions concerning the arrangement of particular tasks or the circumstances of job assignments.

The NV Bühne dates back to the end of the nineteenth century, having been negotiated in 1874 between the 'Cartellverein der Bühnenvorstände' for the employers (founded in 1846, and today called the Deutscher Bühnenverein) and the Bühnengenossenschaft (founded in 1871). The aims of the union from the beginning were the limitation of employers' authority, the improvement of social security for theatre artists and the support of professional off-the-job training for actors (Waidelich, 1991a). Support for off-the-job training by inter-firm institutions is a general characteristic of an employment system based on an occupational labour market, as is predominant in Germany (Marsden, 1999: 224, 264–5). Even if the influence of these institutions is not as strong in the theatre as in the German apprenticeship system, training is a concern for both employer and employee associations, as well as the state-run work agency for actors (the ZBF), which belongs to the national employment office and has local branches in five large German cities. These branches record the data of all actors graduating from drama school, and they operate as employment agencies. ZBF representatives provide cost-free help to both actors and theatres in the matching and recruitment process. The ZBF is contacted mostly when guest actors are needed who have qualities (the type of character, or certain physical characteristics) not available in the ensemble. It is also useful for small theatres, which are not attractive for young actors, and have problems in hiring qualified actors.

Although the NV Bühne is a central feature of the German theatrical system, it covers fewer than one-third of the work arrangements for the

9–10,000 professional actors in Germany (Deutscher Bühnenverein, 2004; Haunschild, 2004a). Actors not engaged on the basis of the NV Bühne work (a) as 'guests' engaged for a certain play, (b) for a part of the season, (c) in private, commercial or 'free' theatres and (d) not as theatre actors but in film, TV and radio productions, or, alternatively, (e) they are unemployed.

The terms of employment and the institutional framework sketched above have been the reference point and ideal of a theatre actor's work arrangements in Germany for more than 200 years (see Waidelich, 1991a). East German theatres before the German reunification differed considerably from this model, however. The theatre world in the former German Democratic Republic (GDR) involved a strong collective culture and protection of workers: homogeneous training, lifetime employment and stable forms of artistic cooperation (de Verdalle, 2003). Consequently, theatres in eastern Germany have had to undergo significant changes in the last fifteen years. The differences between East and West German theatre reveal that there is no 'natural' or inevitable institutional structure of theatre work. Rather, the same historical roots can lead to very different (idiosyncratic) systems of work, employment and production. Nevertheless, the German solutions, in the former GDR as well as in recent Germany, both mirror the corporatist German employment and industrial relations system, marked as it is by co-determination and regulation (Bamber, Lansbury and Wailes, 2004; Crouch, 2003; Hassel, 1999; Lane, 1992; Marsden, 1999, 2000; Muller, 1999; Weitbrecht, 2003). All the same, the (widely studied) role of the guilds and unions in the US film industry (Christopherson and Storper, 1989; Paul and Kleingartner, 1994) shows that the role of inter-firm institutions in German theatre cannot be explained by its national context alone. The inter-firm institutions described can be interpreted as institutions that have coevolved with other labour market institutions and employment rules in theatre. In the following section, the current (though increasingly challenged) theatrical employment system is explained in more detail.

Stability: the theatrical employment system

The brief historical overview has shown how the existing characteristics of the German theatrical system are based on strong traditions. In this section, the institutional framework is described more concretely by referring to Marsden's (1999) theory of employment systems and by regarding organisational practices as being embedded in an *interorganisational employment system*, which comprises rules of job design and task assignment, the labour market, inter-firm institutions and the education system. The theory of employment systems combines an embeddedness or institutionalist perspective (e.g. Hollingsworth and Boyer, 1997; Powell and DiMaggio, 1991; Whitley, 1999) with economic and functionalist explanations of institutional arrangements (e.g. Williamson, 1975).

This employment system for German theatre artists is marked by inter-organisational projects, high labour mobility and contingent work arrangements, but it is also characterised by the above-mentioned ensemble structure providing (temporary) stability for the workforce. The creative industries in general offer instructive examples of how institutional frameworks can reduce uncertainty and provide some stability within such a flexible labour market (see also the above-outlined 'seven properties' that characterise creative production according to Caves, 2000). Several studies of artistic labour markets and other industries marked by high labour mobility emphasise the importance of transorganisational networks and occupational or industrial communities (Arthur and Rousseau, 1996; Blair, 2001; Faulkner and Anderson, 1987; Jones and Walsh, 1997; Sydow and Staber, 2002; Tolbert, 1996). These collective structures enable individuals to build up reputation, to signal skills and market value (Jones, 2002) and to develop norms of good performance at an interorganisational level. They provide employers with otherwise non-accessible information on (potential) workers. Other institutional structures enforcing stability in a project-focused industry comprise royalty-type incomes, market intermediaries and education (Marsden, 2004), as well as certain belief systems and lifestyles supporting mobility and transient work relations.

Artistic job starters in the German theatrical system usually graduate from state or private drama schools. Since state schools accept only a small number of applicants, being one of their graduates can be seen as a first proof of artistic talent. Having passed the recruitment decision as a second gateway, following initial training, actors must continuously gain new job experience, achieve recognition and build a network of ties to colleagues, directors and theatre managers. Accordingly, the German theatrical employment system is stabilised by intra- and interorganisational networks and an occupational community including 'professional' theatre artists and excluding non-artists (Haunschild, 2003). Employees' and employers' associations negotiate industry-wide formal rules of the game (see above) and labour market intermediaries (agent, state work agency) help to match job requirements with the artists' characteristics and skills (see Haunschild, 2004a, for a more detailed account of these labour market institutions). Finally, an artistic or bohemian lifestyle functions as a 'social glue', holding the community together and creating a fit between individual preferences and work requirements (Eikhof and Haunschild, 2006). This outlined institutional framework helps individuals (artists) and organisations (theatres) reduce the uncertainties of artistic and economic success.

Threats: globalisation, economisation and market pressures

According to Marsden (2000: 322), employment systems are 'institutional frameworks that enable firms and workers to organize their collaboration while protecting both parties from certain kinds of opportunistic behaviour'. This conceptual perspective has been used above to characterise (traditional and stable) institutional structures in German theatre. This macro perspective tends to neglect the pressures, tensions, and conflicts that individuals face in an employment system marked by considerable flexibility and mobility requirements, however. Furthermore, the employment system perspective tends to neglect the dynamics of the whole institutionalised employment system or industry. This latter aspect is relevant in the context of this chapter.

Undoubtedly, there are external pressures that force artists, arts managers, collective bargaining partners and the politicians responsible for arts and culture to defend and adapt the existing theatrical employment system. The sources and directions of these pressures or forces are difficult to identify, though. In this section I try to single out some of these challenges to and their consequences for the German theatrical system by using the SSD framework (Smith and Meiksins, 1995; Smith, 2005). This framework suggests that national (or regional) practices or behavioural patterns interfere with dominance effects based on economic power, and with universalistic systemic features of capitalism.

One basic difficulty of applying the SSD framework to theatres results from the fact that (i) cultural industries are based on artistic as well as economic logics of practice (Bourdieu, 1993, 1999; Eikhof and Haunschild, 2007) and (ii) there is no international, let alone global, market and competition for theatrical 'products'. Therefore, the SSD framework is useful for identifying some tensions between national institutions and external forces. The example of theatre also reveals difficulties in clearly distinguishing and isolating societal, system and dominance effects.

My analysis in the following focuses mainly on economic challenges and their consequences for the employment system, as characterised above. I do not discuss details of new forms of management and financial accounting in theatres, which have increasingly been discussed in theory and practice (see, for example, Hoegl, 1995, Kommunale Gemeinschaftsstelle für Verwaltungsvereinfachung, 1989, and Waidelich, 1991b). There is, furthermore, a debate on the artistic quality of German theatre in comparison to theatre productions in less (or non-) subsidised, more project-based systems of production, such as in the Netherlands, the United Kingdom or the United States. An analysis of this artistic debate would be beyond the scope of this chapter.

The biggest threat to the existing system, specifically the repertoire system with standing ensembles, is budget restrictions. There is clear evidence that almost all the 151 public theatres have had to deal with considerable budget cuts (Dermutz, 2004; Königstorfer, 2005; Kümmel, 2005; Laudenbach, 2003; Seeger, 2003; Spahn, 2002b). In some cases this has led to threats to their existence (for example, in Freiburg, Bremen, Würzburg and Lübeck, and in many East German theatres) and even theatre closures (the Schillertheater in Berlin). In most other cases budget restrictions have led to attempts to increase economic efficiency and to changes in human resource policies (see more details below). Even when budgets are stable, theatres still face considerable economic pressure, because most members of the workforce are administrative and technical workers who are employed on the basis of collective agreements in the public sector. This also holds for members of the orchestra and choir. These workers benefit from collective agreements on pay rises and working time reductions. The resulting higher expenditures for this group of workers imply the need to achieve savings in the areas of artistic contracts and budgets for costumes, stage design, music and so on. In extreme cases, maintaining the theatre building and paying administrative and technical staff as well as the orchestra may require cutbacks in actors, dancers and opera singers. This situation has been critically discussed in theatres as well as in the media (Berger, 2002; Laudenbach, 2003; Seeger, 2003; Wüllenweber, 2006), and different solutions are being debated (see next section).

What are the forces that place the German theatrical system under threat? In contrast to (multinational) enterprises, German theatres are not exposed to a global market. Theatre provides an example of an isolated field at the national level. In the case of Germany, the decentralised structure of princedoms and electorates has led to a large number of local court theatres with their own buildings and ensembles, resulting in today's unique state-supported theatre scene. German theatres compete economically with other theatres near to them and with other alternative entertainments, in the sense that they have to fill their auditoria (at least to a certain or politically given degree). They also compete with other theatres for artistic reputation. The quality of artistic output is hardly measurable, however (Bourdieu, 1993, 1999; Krebs and Pommerehne, 1995; Throsby, 2001), and only loosely coupled with economic efficiency. Observable budget cuts have a direct impact on theatre management, but they do not result directly from market forces, in the form of reduced sales or market shares.

The economic pressure on German theatres is related to tight public budgets at national and regional (Bundesländer, councils) level, and to a general discourse influenced by 'neoliberal' ideas that emphasise the advantages of free market coordination. We can, therefore, identify different levels of influence. Public budgets depend on tax income, which is lower when companies' profits decrease or consumers' salaries are less. It is not the aim of this chapter to examine the reasons for the crisis of public finance in Germany. What can be said is that competition of a more globalised nature enhances the pressure on public budgets. It is difficult to typify this as either a system or a dominance effect, however. The overall tendency of introducing market mechanisms to formerly hierarchically and bureaucratically organised spheres can currently be regarded as a dominant logic, which becomes more influential in a variety of societal spheres and discussed from different (often critical) perspectives (Beck, 1992; Boltanski and Chiapello, 2005; Bourdieu, 1997; Chomsky, 1998; Coleman, 1990; Drori, 2006; Forrester, 1996; Giddens, 1990; Haunschild, 2004b; Sennett, 1998). This 'neoliberal' discourse is rooted in an idealisation of free market economies and criticism of recent economic problems in coordinated market economies such as those of France and Germany (Crouch, 2003; Ebbinghaus, 1999). It therefore bundles dominant ideas about a 'successful' capitalist system. As an ideological and normative model, it is taken up and propagated by dominant actors (politicians, in our case) to enforce (allegedly) best practice. Dominance here is clearly of a symbolic (Smith, 2005: 616) and abstract nature, and closely linked to system effects.

The consequences of these threats are, nevertheless, real. On the other hand, the more an industry is isolated, and the more competitive success is based on the interpretative and non-economic (in this case artistic and cultural processes, and politics), the less economic systems and dominance effects can explain the current dynamics of organisational practices. In the following section, some specific nationally or societally influenced responses to threats to the German theatrical employment system are examined.

Responses: debates, strategies and local practices

Current budget cuts reveal how much the German theatrical system depends on public subsidies; to what extent its work and production structures are institutionalised and form a well-established employment system; and how fragile this system nonetheless is with respect to external political changes. This fragility follows from the vital role of the ensemble. As outlined above, it is often the case that reduced budgets can be met only if expenditures for artistic inputs are reduced. Therefore, growing economic pressures on the German system of public subsidy limit the ability of theatres to maintain an ensemble structure, while challenging the existing and established institutional framework.

Indeed, there is a tendency to substitute 'guest actors' on a project basis for ensemble members. The existing (limited) security for ensemble members may erode in the future, and the employment system characterised by ensembles could move towards project-based production, as has happened in the US film industry since the 1950s (Christopherson and Storper, 1989) or the British and German television industries since the 1980s and 1990s (Dex *et al.*, 2000; Windeler and Sydow, 2001). Such a change of the employment rules would have far-reaching consequences for artists as employers and employees or workers (see also Eikhof and Haunschild, 2006, 2007) and would either involve a reallocation of labour market risks or require new collective structures. Furthermore, HRM practices would have to respond to changes in the predictability and quality of labour supply, and new patterns of skill development, recognition and transmission would have to evolve (Marsden, 1999: 25–7; see also de Verdalle, 2003, for details of a transformation of the ensemble structure at Staatsschauspiel Dresden after German reunification). It is because of this crucial and highly institutionalised role of the ensemble that there is a widely accepted consensus that it is a valuable asset of German theatre (see, for examples, the statements of fourteen theatre directors in the October 1997 issue of the journal *theater heute*). Most individual and collective actors involved in theatrical production seek to preserve and maintain the existing model.

There are, however, different and often contradictory strategies to achieve the survival of the ensemble. Whereas the union concerned (the Genossenschaft

Deutscher Bühnen-Angehöriger) postulates the inclusion of artists in the collective bargaining scheme for the public sector and the codification of (sufficient) governmental support for culture in the German constitution, the employers' association (the Deutscher Bühnenverein) supports the abolition of the existing protection for administrative and technical workers in order to gain more financial leeway for artistic inputs. Another demand on employers is to relocate the collective bargaining process more to the theatre level, which has already happened in some cases, particularly in eastern Germany, where financial pressures are more threatening. A role model for such a strategy is the theatre in Weimar (the Deutsches Nationaltheater), which was supposed to merge with the theatre in Erfurt. The 'Weimarer Modell' is based on the idea that all workers in effect surrender their rights resulting from collective agreements and that a new legal form of organisation provides much more financial independence and flexibility (Märki, 2002; Raue and Hegemann, 2003). Since this model interferes with German traditions of industrial relations, as well as existing forms of cooperation and consent, it is seen as critical by the union and by many theatre managers (Grundmann, 2002; Spahn, 2002a). The theatre actors themselves, because of their restricted individual bargaining power, have very little ability to influence current developments. Since few theatre artists are interested in 'humdrum' collective representation and even fewer are members of the Genossenschaft Deutscher Bühnen-Angehöriger (or of the very small association the Interessenverband Deutscher Schauspieler), there is no actual collective voice that is powerful. This is surprising to some extent, as recent changes to employment policies have further weakened their position in the labour market, since a large pool of qualified workers, which is a typical phenomenon of the creative industries (Caves, 2000; Menger, 1999), is ready to replace ensemble members.

In the three theatres studied, their strategies for coping with the current challenges differed. Whereas one theatre sought to maintain the existing ensemble structure, producing a mix of common folk entertainment and avant-garde plays, another theatre in the same city pursued a strategy of more project-based productions with freelance actors. Interviews with actors working for this latter theatre showed that the working conditions provided were perceived as precarious and, in some cases, demotivating. The third theatre studied is more difficult to manage, since it includes an opera house with orchestra and ballet. No clear strategy of cost management could be identified in this case. Nevertheless, the theatre manager and his team did admit that there was capacity for savings, though they also stated that there was a dilemma: if they talked about potential savings in public, they would incur further budget cuts.

Another, even more wide-ranging issue is the impact of economic logic versus artistic logic. Eikhof and Haunschild (2007) show that, when the artistic logic of practice is utilised economically, economic logic tends to crowd out artistic logic. They analyse in the main the market behaviour of artists, principally their self-marketing and the subordination of the private and personal aspects of life to their job (see also Eikhof and Haunschild, 2004). Moreover, the economic pressures and market forces discussed in this chapter, as well as their (indirect) consequences for individual artists and organisations, can have a critical impact on artistic motivation and self-perception. Since changes in the institutional framework take a long time to negotiate and are difficult to realise, these tensions have to be dealt with on an individual basis. Whereas successful theatre managers and actors can afford to play the role of mavericks, resigning (or threatening to resign) from their job when the business world (that is, budget restrictions or expected box-office sales) becomes too dominant, many theatre artists face the prospect of having to abandon their artistic profession.

Conclusions: traditions, forces and ambiguities

The German theatrical employment system is a well-established industry with a long tradition rooted in Germany's historical political structure, as well as in a national German employment system that is marked by a corporatist tradition of industrial relations and occupational labour markets. At the same time, however, the theatrical employment system is characterised by flexible forms of labour, which is untypical for Germany. The ensemble, a group of theatre actors employed on a temporary basis, provides flexibility and, at the same time, a stable work environment for a certain period of time. The institutional framework of this theatrical employment system has evolved during the last 200, or even 300, years. This chapter has referred to Marsden's theory of employment systems to emphasise the stability-providing function of this framework.

Any focus on this stability suppresses the current dynamics and challenges. Some of these dynamics and challenges, which result from economic pressures and a discourse stressing the importance of market forces, have been examined in this chapter with reference to the SSD framework. Recently, cuts in public budgets have led to cuts in theatre budgets and stimulated discussions about efficacy and efficiency amongst theatre managers. Using public funding to achieve cultural goals in a cost-efficient way has gained significantly in importance as a managerial goal in the last decade or so. As a result, the economic logic of creative production has become more explicit at the organisational level (Eikhof and Haunschild, 2007). Whereas the societal effects can clearly be traced back to the national employment system and the idiosyncratic German theatrical employment system, an identification of system and dominance effects has been more problematic. This is because German theatres still face little economic pressure from product markets and international competition, due to the overall public funding system and the national character of theatrical art. Nonetheless, budget restrictions put the prevailing ensemble system under threat and reveal the fragility of the system.

Responses to these threats have not yet been able to find ways of changing the institutionalised traditional system, which is marked by a high degree of inertia. Deviations from the focus on ensemble actors can be observed, however, as can attempts to abolish restrictions stemming from collective bargaining, particularly in the case of administrative and technical staff. One paradoxical effect is that artists, who already represent the most precarious group of workers with flexible work arrangements, are coming under even more pressure, and they are most at risk from alternative models. One possible trajectory is the emergence of a project-based dynamic network form of production, as is prevalent in most other countries and in such other creative industries as film and media. A market-based form of production could be regarded as a spreading form of capitalism in line with a dominant neoliberal discourse (Boltanski and Chiapello, 2005; see also Fenwick, 2002, Opitz, 2004, Storey, Salaman and Platman 2005, and Sennett, 1998). Interestingly, this discourse refers to the creative industries as a role model for project-based knowledge work in general (see, for example, Florida, 2002).

On the one hand, theatre provides a unique and idiosyncratic example that hardly seems capable of generalisation. On the other hand, the case of German theatre provides a strong example for the importance and persistence of national institutions that limit the global convergence of organisational practices. It is an example that reveals how even robust and powerful national institutions are increasingly being challenged by globalising forces. Additionally, the example of theatre sheds some light on the very individual consequences of such dynamics. This chapter has argued that the current debates on and the changes that follow from external (or global) forces can be understood only when the historical and societal roots of management practices and employment systems are taken into account. It is evident, moreover, that this conclusion is especially relevant whenever effectiveness and efficiency criteria are less clear, as in the case of the cultural industries, the professional service industries or the public sector.

References

Arthur, M. B., and D. M. Rousseau (eds.) (1996) *The Boundaryless Career: A New Employment Principle for a New Organizational Era*, New York: Oxford University Press.

Bamber, G., R. Lansbury and N. Wailes (eds.) (2004) *International and Comparative Employment Relations* (4th edn.), London: Sage.

Beck, U. (1992) *Risk Society: Towards a New Modernity*, London: Sage.

Becker, H. S. (1982) *Art Worlds*, Berkeley, CA: University of California Press.

Benhamou, F. (2000) The opposition between two models of labour market adjustment: the case of audiovisual and performing arts activities in France and Great Britain over a ten-year period, *Journal of Cultural Economics*, 24, 301–19.

Berger, J. (2002) Geisterhaus, *Süddeutsche Zeitung*, 29 November, 13.

Blair, H. (2001) You're only as good as your last job: the labour process and labour market in the British film industry, *Work, Employment and Society*, 15, 1, 149–69.

Boltanski, L., and E. Chiapello (2005) *The New Spirit of Capitalism*, London: Verso.

Bourdieu, P. (1993) *The Field of Cultural Production: Essays on Art and Literature*, New York: Columbia University Press.

(1997) Le précarité est aujourd'hui partout, in P. Bourdieu *Contre-feux*, Paris: Liber-Raisons d'agir, 95–101.

(1999) *Die Regeln der Kunst: Genese und Struktur des literarischen Feldes*, Frankfurt: Suhrkamp.

Caves, R. E. (2000) *Creative Industries: Contracts between Art and Commerce*, Cambridge, MA: Harvard University Press.

Chomsky, N. (1998) *Profit over People: Neoliberalism and Global Order*, New York: Seven Stories Press.

Christopherson, S., and M. Storper (1989) The effects of flexible specialization on industrial politics and the labor market: the motion picture industry, *Industrial and Labor Relations Review*, 42, 331–47.

Coleman, J. S. (1990) *Foundations of Social Theory*, Cambridge, MA: Belknap Press.

Crouch C. (2003) The state: economic management and incomes policy, in P. Edwards (ed.) *Industrial Relations: Theory and Evidence in Britain* (2nd edn.), Oxford: Basil Blackwell, 10–23.

Davis, H., and R. Scase (2000) *Managing Creativity: The Dynamics of Work and Organization*, Buckingham: Open University Press.

de Verdalle, L. (2003) La transition théâtrale dans l'ex-RDA: vers la recherche de nouvelles formes de régulation organisationelle, *Sociologie du Travail*, 45, 385–405.

Dermutz, K. (2004) Landschaft mit Kriegern *Die Zeit*, 8 January, 40.

Deutscher Bühnenverein (ed.) (2004) *Theaterstatistik 2002/2003*, vol. xxxviii, Cologne: Deutscher Bühnenverein.

Dex, S., J. Willis, R. Paterson and E. Sheppard (2000) Freelance workers and contract uncertainty: the effects of contractual changes in the television industry, *Work, Employment and Society*, 14, 2, 283–305.

Drori, G. S. (ed.) (2006) *Globalization and Organization: World Society and Organizational Change*, Oxford: Oxford University Press.

Ebbinghaus, B. (1999) Does a European social model exist and can it survive?, in G. Huemer, M. Mesch and F. Traxler (eds.) *The Role of Employer Associations and Labour Unions in the EMU*, Aldershot: Ashgate, 1–26.

Eikhof, D. R., and A. Haunschild (2004) Arbeitskraftunternehmer in der Kulturindustrie: ein Forschungsbericht über die Arbeitswelt Theater, in H. J. Pongratz and G. G. Voss (eds.) *Typisch Arbeitskraftunternehmer? Befunde der empirischen Arbeitsforschung*, Berlin: Sigma, 93–113.

 (2005) What makes an industry creative? A comparison of team sports and transorganizational cultural production, paper presented at the European Group for Organizational Studies Colloquium, Berlin, 30 June–2 July.

 (2006) Lifestyle meets market: bohemian entrepreneurs in creative industries, *Creativity and Innovation Management*, 15, 234–41.

 (2007) For art's sake! Artistic and economic logics in creative production, *Journal of Organizational Behavior*, 28, 528–38.

Faulkner, R. R., and A. B. Anderson (1987) Short-term projects and emergent careers: evidence from Hollywood, *American Journal of Sociology*, 92, 879–909.

Fenwick, T. (2002) Transgressive desires: new enterprising selves in the new capitalism, *Work, Employment and Society*, 16, 4, 703–23.

Florida, R. (2002) *The Rise of the Creative Class: And How It's Transforming Work, Leisure, Community and Everyday Life*, New York: Basic Books.

Forrester, V. (1996) *L'horreur économique*, Paris: Librairie Arthème Fayard.

Giddens, A. (1990) *The Consequences of Modernity*, Cambridge: Polity Press.

Grundmann, U. (2002) Ein Modell und viele Fragen, *Die Deutsche Bühne*, 5/2002, 46–7.

Hassel, A. (1999) The erosion of the German system of industrial relations, *British Journal of Industrial Relations*, 37, 483–505.

Haunschild, A. (2003) Managing employment relationships in flexible labour markets: the case of German repertory theatres, *Human Relations*, 56, 899–929.

 (2004a) Employment rules in German theatres: an application and evaluation of the theory of employment systems, *British Journal of Industrial Relations*, 42, 685–703.

 (2004b) Contingent work: the problem of disembeddedness and economic reembeddedness, *Management Revue*, 15, 74–88.

Hoegl, C. (1995) *Ökonomie der Oper: Grundlagen für das Musiktheater-Management*, Bonn: ARCult Media.

Hollingsworth, J. R., and R. Boyer (eds.) (1997) *Contemporary Capitalism: The Embeddedness of Institutions*, Cambridge: Cambridge University Press.

Howkins, G. (2001) *The Creative Economy: How People Make Money from Ideas*, London: Penguin Books.

Jeffcutt, P., and A. Pratt (2002) Managing creativity in the cultural industries, *Creativity and Innovation Management*, 11, 225–33.

Jones, C. (2002) Signalling expertise: how signals shape careers in creative industries, in M. Peiperl, M. Arthur and N. Anand (eds.) *Career Creativity. Explorations in the Remaking of Work*, Oxford: Oxford University Press, 209–28.

Jones, C., and K. Walsh (1997) Boundaryless careers in the US film industry: understanding labor market dynamics of network organizations, *Industrielle Beziehungen*, 4, 58–73.

King, N. (1994) The qualitative research interview, in C. Cassell and G. Symon (eds.) *Qualitative Methods in Organizational Research: A Practical Guide*, London: Sage, 14–36.

Kommunale Gemeinschaftsstelle für Verwaltungsvereinfachung (1989) *Führung und Stewerung des Theaters*, Cologne: Kommunale Gemeinschaftsstelle für Verwaltungsvereinfachung.

Königstorfer, T. (2005) Schwierige Balance zwischen Kunst und Kommerz, *Rotary Magazin Deutschland und Österreich*, 4/2005, 19–23.

Krebs, S., and W. W. Pommerehne (1995) Politico-economic interactions of German public performing arts institutions, *Journal of Cultural Economics*, 19, 17–32.

Kümmel, P. (2005) Die Erpressung hat funktioniert, *Die Zeit*, 3 November, 50.

Lane, C. (1992) European business systems: Britain and Germany compared, in R. Whitley (ed.) *European Business Systems*, London: Sage, 64–97.

Laudenbach, P. (2003) Wir können auch anders, *brandeins*, 10.

Märki, S. (2002) Das Weimarer Modell (interview by M. Helbing), *Theater der Zeit*, April, 4–5.

Marsden, D. (1999) *A Theory of Employment Systems: Micro-foundations of Societal Diversity*, Oxford: Oxford University Press.

   (2000) A theory of job regulation, the employment relationship, and the organisation of labour institutions, *Industrielle Beziehungen*, 7, 320–47.

   (2004) The 'network economy' and models of the employment contract, *British Journal of Industrial Relations*, 42, 659–84.

Menger, P.-M. (1999) Artistic labor markets and careers, *Annual Review of Sociology*, 25, 541–74.

Miles, M. B., and A. M. Huberman (1994) *Qualitative Data Analysis* (2nd edn.), London: Sage.

Muller, M. (1999) Human resource management under institutional constraints: the case of Germany, *British Journal of Management*, 10, S31–S44.

Opitz, S. (2004) *Gouvernementalität im Postfordismus: Macht, Wissen und Techniken des Selbst im Feld unternehmerischer Rationalität*, Hamburg: Argument-Verlag.

Paul, A., and A. Kleingartner (1994) Flexible production and the transformation of industrial relations in the motion picture and television industry, *Industrial and Labor Relations Review*, 47, 663–78.

Pitz, C., and M. Köhn (2001) Öffentliche Trägerschaft – aber wie?, *Die Deutsche Bühne*, 7, 26–9.

Powell, W., and P. DiMaggio (eds.) (1991) *The New Institutionalism in Organisational Analysis*, Chicago: University of Chicago Press.

Raue, P., and J. Hegemann (2003) Spielplan ohne ver.di, *Die Zeit*, 27 February, 41.

Seeger, A. (2003) Wenn der letzte Vorhang fällt, *Hamburger Abendblatt*, 21 January 2003.

Sennett, R. (1998) *Corrosion of Character: The Personal Consequences of Work in the New Capitalism*, New York: Norton.

Smith, C. (2005) Beyond convergence and divergence: explaining variations in organizational practices and forms, in S. Ackroyd, R. Batt, P. Thompson and P. S. Tolbert (eds.) *The Oxford Handbook of Work and Organization*, Oxford: Oxford University Press, 602–25.

Smith, C., and P. Meiksins (1995) System, society and dominance effects in cross-national organizational analysis, *Work, Employment and Society*, 9, 2, 241–67.

Spahn, C. (2002a) Apparat frisst Kunst, *Die Zeit*, 2 May, 39.

   (2002b) Spielen ohne Spielraum, *Die Zeit*, 5 December, 41.

Storey, J., G. Salaman and K. Platman (2005) Living with enterprise in an enterprise economy: freelance and contract workers in the media, *Human Relations*, 58, 1033–54.

Sydow, J., and U. Staber (2002) The institutional embeddedness of project networks: the case of content production in German television, *Regional Studies*, 36, 215–27.

Throsby, D. (2001) *Economics and Culture*, Cambridge: Cambridge University Press.

Tolbert, P. S. (1996) Occupations, organizations, and boundaryless careers, in M. B. Arthur and D. M. Rousseau (eds.) *The Boundaryless Career: A New Employment Principle for a New Organizational Era*, New York: Oxford University Press, 331–49.

Waidelich, J.-D. (1991a) Theatermanagement/Theaterorganisation, part 1, *Problemaufriß und Geschichte des Theatermanagements bis zur Gegenwart*, Hagen: Fernuniversität.

(1991b) Theatermanagement/Theaterorganisation, part 2, *Strukturen und Rezepturen der gegenwärtigen Theaterarbeit*, Hagen: Fernuniversität.

Weitbrecht, H. (2003) Human resource management and co-determination, in W. Mueller-Jentsch and H. Weitbrecht (eds.) *The Changing Contours of German Industrial Relations*, Munich: Hampp.

Whitley, R. (1999) *Divergent Capitalisms: The Social Structuring and Change of Business Systems*, Oxford: Oxford University Press.

Williamson, O. E. (1975) *Markets and Hierarchies*, New York: Free Press.

Windeler, A., and J. Sydow (2001) Project networks and changing industry practices: collaborative content production in the German television industry, *Organization Studies*, 22, 1036–60.

Wüllenweber, W. (2006) Absurdes Theater, *Stern*, 28/2006, 115–24.

Yin, R. K. (1994) *Case Study Research* (2nd edn.), London: Sage.

10 Between the global and the national: the industrial district concept in historical and comparative context

Andrew Popp

Introduction

This chapter seeks to explore the apparent contradiction between the global and the national, and the competing claims for the pre-eminence of each of these as analytical units through which to understand contemporary economic and organisational change, by focusing instead on one aspect of the local: the industrial district. The important spatial dimension to the industrial district concept, necessary to its very definition, provides us with a unique vantage point on this debate. If the local can be shown to matter to economic organisation, then where does that leave both the national and the global? By focusing on the importance of the regional we can see that neither the national nor the global can be considered complete analytical scales. The existence, survival, even proliferation, of districts and clusters would appear to throw down a challenge to these two competing narratives: that of the persistence of national systems as against that of globalising convergence. This challenge is real, and allows us to argue that a reinterpretation of the industrial district, both as a concrete phenomenon and as a theoretical construct, enables us to see more clearly how at one crucial (literal) site – the district itself – those forces contained within the SSD model intersect to produce complex and contingent outcomes that deny explanation in terms of either national systems or global-level forces.

With regard to the district itself, my aim is to attempt to escape the essentialist and internalist understandings of districts that became dominant from the 1970s onwards as a result of the discovery and celebration of the 'Italianate model' (Paniccia, 2002). This model became increasingly closed rather than open, and increasingly thick rather than thin, in its prescriptions – a process that led, for example, to implicit claims that the British business system, for one, was incapable of generating 'true' industrial districts (Zeitlin, 1995). Thus, a certain uniqueness, largely defying explanation, was claimed for the few canonical examples allowed. At the same time, districts and clusters came increasingly to be promoted as an industrial policy panacea, both in mature economies facing deindustrialisation and in emerging economies seeking to develop stronger capabilities. Were districts really the particular outcome of a certain few business systems (e.g. Italy, Germany) or were their lessons generalisable at the global level, and do our answers to these questions relate to the national versus the global?

Thus, as well as seeking to rethink the district, I also aim to use it as a lens in order to focus better on the complexity of ongoing economic and organisational shifts, whether within or between firms, or between firms and wider institutional settings, or at subnational, national or supranational levels.

The chapter is structured as follows. It begins with sections exploring, respectively, definitions of districts, and how districts have been studied and to what effect. Detailed empirical evidence is then presented on the evolution of certain key industrial districts in England before going on to consider how they relate to the meta-narratives of globalisation versus business systems and how the industrial district might be understood in the light of the SSD model. An important element of these empirical cases will be the use of an historical methodology. The chapter concludes by considering the roles to be played by path dependency, contingency and complexity in the evolution of both specific industrial districts and the industrial district concept in general.

The industrial district concept

There is no settled definition of the industrial district. Some key characteristics can, however, be outlined. First, and most importantly, industrial districts are spatial concentrations of populations of firms linked by shared and interdependent processes, products, and product and labour markets and by various forms of exchange, transactional or otherwise – from dependence on each other for inputs to the next stage of the value chain to the sharing of many different types of information. It is also normally assumed that firms will be relatively numerous – perhaps in the hundreds, even – and will also typically be small and medium-sized enterprises (SMEs). These assumptions are often left rather underdeveloped and untested, however. How many is many? Why should firms typically be small? Are size disparities between firms always low and, if not, why not and with what effect? Many of these prescriptions have been subject to little empirical testing or validation. Even the size of spatial areas that might legitimately be thought of as constituting a district remains problematical. Indeed, Mark Casson (1999: 6) has accused much of the district literature of 'casual empiricism'. It is also typically assumed that the district will be articulated on the vertical axis (that is, that it will be vertically disintegrated), mitigating competition on the horizontal. Further, structural change and growth is held to occur through processes of cross-fertilisation and, in particular, spin-offs from existing firms. These processes lead to an ever finer articulation of the industrial structure of the district as new firms emerge to exploit niches that incumbent firms are either unwilling or unable to occupy.

Second, despite the underspecified and under-researched nature of some of these structural 'markers', they are not inconsequential, for in the decentralisation of resources and structures in industrial districts lies their potential to generate the external economies of scale and scope that lie at the heart of their economic rationale. Importantly, these external economies – first identified by Alfred Marshall (1919) in the late nineteenth century – should be considered as dynamic, operating over and above the regular economies of agglomeration that obtain in most sizeable urban settings, derived from thick markets for a range of inputs. It is these dynamic external economies of scale and scope, created not simply through flexible subcontracting networks but through knowledge spillovers, that make both the industrial district itself and its constituent firms resilient and competitive. Also associated with the existence of external economies are patterns of deepening specialisation (at the level of the firm) and strengthening capabilities. It should be added, though, that there have been few empirical demonstrations of the existence of external economies; instead, their presence is normally inferred (Broadberry and Marrison, 2002). Many districts, their firms serving speciality markets for high-quality and high-value-added goods, or for the technically innovative, whether for final consumers or other industrial users, augment their competitive advantage through the privileging of skill and the pursuit of strategies of flexibility. Flexibility is also, typically, a product of the district as a whole, emerging from the myriad potential interconnections thrown up by the close proximity of multiple specialised firms

Thus, third, the combination of structural characteristics outlined above not only generates dynamic external economies of scale and scope but also promotes a particular climate for entrepreneurship and innovation that is encouraging to both. Indeed, the structural properties and a climate that facilitates entrepreneurship and innovation are self-reinforcing, as new actors enter the district in order to pursue fresh avenues thrown up by innovatory insights yielded by the existing productive capabilities.

Nonetheless, as Charles Sabel and Jonathan Zeitlin (1997: 20) have noted, in districts the 'central problem of industrial organization ... is the coordination of decentralization'. As this suggests, it is possible that in one of the industrial district's greatest strengths, its decentralisation, we also find one of its greatest potential weaknesses. Therefore, fourth, it is further assumed that these structural characteristics, powerfully reinforced by the embeddedness and socialisation of actors within a distinctive local milieu, will somewhat naturally produce a governance system that seamlessly aligns interests within the district, leading to effective and efficient coordination of resources – 'a local institutional capability to respond collectively' (Amin and Thrift, 1992: 580). In other words, the decentralised resources of the district, distributed widely amongst many different firms, institutions and individual actors, are bound together into a coherent system through a district-wide governance system. This is important; clustering produces systemic effects such that districts may be said to be more than the sum of their parts (Swann, 2005). How this binding together is achieved and then maintained remains problematical, however. In the Italian literature and in those studies inspired by it, these characteristic governance arrangements are the result of a deep social embedding of actors within a context unique to the specific district, and they produce a unique blend of both cooperation and competition. As Udo Staber (1996: 248) states very clearly, 'The embeddedness of firms in a distinctive local social fabric is a key feature of the industrial district model'. This embedding, it is claimed, has real effects on business practices and economic structures and performance in districts, producing an 'ethos that reconciled and gave immediate human content to the claims of competition and ambition on the one hand and community and co-operation on the other' (Sabel and Zeitlin, 1985: 152). This is, perhaps, the most controversial element of the industrial district concept, however – with some voices becoming increasingly sceptical about the efficacy, existence or even necessity of deep social embedding (Popp, 2001, 2005; Wilson and Popp, 2003; Gaggio, 2006).

Finally, the spatial dimension needs to be emphasised, particularly the importance of proximity to all the above effects. A spatial element is central, rather than incidental, to the industrial district concept – hence its ability to throw a revealing light on the tension between the national and the global. The industrial district concept considers the functioning of the economy at an extremely localised micro level; the characteristics of the specific district are considered to be highly locationally specific. This is because proximity, wherever found, is thought to generate particular advantages, from easy and effective knowledge spillovers generated through the face-to-face transmission of hard to codify tacit knowledge to transaction-cost-lowering trust founded in the deep personal knowledge of co-actors. Above and beyond these generic products of proximity, however, lies an emphasis on the importance of *place*; in other words, individual real districts are deeply rooted in space and time. As Marshall (1919: 284–7) observed in his original remarks on the industrial district, each provided a particular 'industrial atmosphere', and, crucially, these unique industrial atmospheres 'cannot be quickly acquired ... [but] yield *gratis* to the manufacturers ... great advantages that are not easily to be had elsewhere: and an industrial atmosphere cannot be moved'. Or, as Andrea Colli has expressed it more recently, 'Networks of producers develop *primarily* thanks to the fact of being in the same place' (1998: 79; emphasis added). Again, however, a note of caution needs to be sounded, for detailed empirical studies of a range of districts, particularly those outside Italy, increasingly suggest that reality rarely supports Bennett Harrison's (1992: 478) simple linear model, which runs from 'proximity to experience to trust to collaboration to enhanced regional economic growth'.

The intention in this section has been, first, to introduce the industrial district concept and, second, to begin to suggest some of the ways in which that concept or model is now being contested. It is this second theme that is now picked up in the following section.

'Representing' the industrial district: the industrial district as a model

First, I must emphasise that I see industrial districts as real, concrete phenomena, occurring in many different places and at many different times. As such, they are worthy of serious study. It is also the case, however, that the industrial district, as a concept, has developed considerable rhetorical, even symbolic, power. In many ways, claimants for the industrial district have tried to have it both ways – proclaiming both the inimitability, the specificity, of the individual district whilst proselytising on the model's behalf on the basis of the construction of a (highly restrictive) 'ideal typical'. Thus, in its ideal-typical form, the industrial district has become a worthy companion to the purer models of national systems and economic globalisation. Opening up the industrial district, seeing what is essential, what is context-specific, why they vary and how they change may help us similarly open up for inspection the false analytical dichotomies presented in the national versus global debate. I would agree with the editors of this book that, at the level of the district, as well as at that of its constituent firms, diversity and complexity have been underestimated (see chapter 1).

Work on industrial districts has gathered pace from the mid-1970s onwards, to form what is now almost a tidal wave. Districts have been 'discovered' nearly everywhere, from their original home in Italy to Mexico and Taiwan, and all points in between. This voluminous literature, which is impossible now to survey fully in a short piece, has ranged from – as already suggested – rank empiricism to a thrust towards the construction of a strongly normative 'ideal-typical' that has also become increasingly narrowly defined. So strong has been the emphasis in some of these perspectives on a few certain supposedly key qualities, such as a harmonious and cohesive 'community market' (Dei Ottati, 2003), that we have reached the distinctly strange position in which it can be argued that, despite providing the whole foundation of the industrial district concept, Marshall 'did not observe industrial districts' due to the presence in his examples of 'relationships . . . organized by contracts' (Piore, 1992: 436–7). As Zeitlin (1995: 102) observes, it is the 'height of perversity to argue that whilst Alfred Marshall invented the [industrial district] concept in turn-of-the-century Britain, its true empirical referent would only appear in Italy half a century later'. The industrial district model is an object lesson in the consequences of drawing our models of the economy and its organisations in ever tighter and more exclusive terms. Thus, I echo Zeitlin (102) in seeking a 'necessary move . . . away from a "thick", "closed" model of the industrial district based on a stylized account of the Italian experience towards a "thin", "open" model capable of accom-modating a variety of empirically observable forms'. Vitally, such a thin, open model would 'not assume that industrial districts are necessarily flexible, consensual or otherwise successful' (102). Moreover, such a reformulation should also seek to escape the determinism inherent in the strong embed-dedness perspective on districts, in which actors are relatively passive 'enac-tors' of the sociocultural forces and structures inscribed on them in the process of embedding (Gaggio, 2006).

How, though, is such a reformulation to be achieved? First, I do not believe that a significant way forward lies in the construction of taxonomies of alternative forms of industrial district (Markusen, 1996). Instead, it is perhaps more useful to enquire into how these theoretical mutations arose, and then, through theoretically informed empirical work, not simply to adumbrate a series of 'varieties' of industrial district but instead to ask how variation arises. The next section addresses these questions through a survey of empirical historical work on a series of English industrial districts

English industrial districts

Zeitlin (1995) may once have asked 'Why are there no industrial districts in England?', but I would contend that there have been (and still are) many industrial districts there. The study of these sites from an explicit industrial district perspective is a relatively recent phenomenon, however (Hudson, 1989). To a considerable degree, much of this recent, largely historical work on English industrial districts may be thought of as a reaction to the Italianate model that rose to pre-eminence in the 1980s. Work on English industrial districts has tended to stress not just the vibrancy and strengths of these clusters but also their potential weaknesses and, perhaps most importantly, the extent to which, in the way in which they were constituted internally, particularly in terms of district-level governance, they displayed much higher levels of contestation and much less harmony than had been claimed for the Italian exemplars. In particular, the concept of 'social embeddedness,' at least in its strongest and most deterministic forms, appears highly problematical in the context of English districts (Popp, 2000; Carnevali, 2003a). As we have already seen, one reaction has been to suggest that the English districts were, because of these very characteristics, simply not districts at all. I think a much more satisfying approach is to ask from where the differences stem.

First, with much of the English work having been conducted by historians, a typically longer time frame was adopted. This brought into much sharper focus the questions of the sustainability and vulnerability of industrial districts as the question of crisis and decline was necessarily confronted. Commentators had already begun to note the often extremely optimistic tone of some of the writing on Italy. Ian Taplin and Jonathan Winterton (1995: 618), for example, accused Michael Piore and Charles Sabel (1984), Sabel and Zeitlin (1985) and others of 'euphoria' and of writing little more than 'fables' that made for 'enchanting reading', and the work on English districts has fed into this growing vein of more cautious or even sceptical analysis. A further effect of the fact that historians conducted this work has been that the long time frames involved have highlighted the importance of both temporal and spatial context. The variations found between different districts in the same country and in single districts across time suggest strongly that the contrasts between English and Italian districts outlined above are not simply the outcome of country-level effects, as might be claimed from a national systems perspective, but must instead be the result of more complex forces

As a result, an attempt has been made to explore the dynamics of clustering in England in a more systematic fashion, whilst at the same time controlling for country-level effects. The result was a series of case studies contained in a volume edited by John Wilson and Andrew Popp (2003). Districts/sectors covered by the studies included Lancashire cotton textiles, Yorkshire wool textiles, chemicals on Merseyside, the metallurgical/engineering complex around Darlington, the Coventry engineering complex, Sheffield steel and cutlery, the Birmingham jewellery quarter (BJQ), glove manufacturing in Worcester and defence industries in Lancashire. The findings were reinforced by those from earlier studies of the North Staffordshire Potteries (Popp, 2000, 2001, 2003a).

First, it is important to stress the status of these different agglomerations as industrial districts – at least, according to relatively thin and open definitions. All exhibited many of the core characteristics outlined above: spatial concentration, a myriad of (often small) interdependent partial-process firms, strongly entrepreneurial and innovative climates, structural dynamics driven by spin-offs and cross-fertilisations, innovative solutions to the problems of district-wide governance and, in many cases, distinctive local milieu. They also varied in important ways, however. Some, such as the BJQ, contained very many (hundreds) of small firms showing little significant size disparity, whereas the Potteries contained just as many firms but also showed vast variations in firm size, while in yet others, such as Widnes chemicals, a smaller number of firms clustered around a few lead firms. Districts also showed varying degrees of sectoral focus, from the multiple overlapping engineering trades centred on Coventry to the mono-industrial focus of Worcester, the Potteries and the BJQ, and differing spatial dimensions, from the very small area covered by the BJQ to the much larger Lancashire cotton industrial region.

Most importantly, though, they experienced very differing fortunes across time. The Lancashire cotton textile industry enjoyed prolonged emergence, triumph and maturity but equally prolonged decline. Widnes emerged as both a town and an industrial district centred almost exclusively on chemicals, but was also relatively rapidly absorbed into the corporate structures of first the United Alkali Company (UAC), from 1890, and then Imperial Chemical Industries (ICI), from 1926, shifting in the process from autonomous industrial district to just one element in a branch plant economy controlled from metropolitan headquarters. The Potteries still cling to their specialisation but are currently under considerable duress as manufacturing moves progressively overseas, and might soon break apart, whilst the BJQ remains a vibrant and relatively unchanged micro-district (Carnevali, 2003b). The challenges of growth, maturity and then decline provoked varying governance responses in different districts. Lancashire remained for a long time the epitome of the 'automatic' coordination most favoured by Marshall, but lapsed into inward-looking cliques of interlocking director-ships as difficulties mounted early in the twentieth century (Toms and Filatotchev, 2003). In contrast, the similarly structured wool textile industry in West Yorkshire was much more successful in forging successful trade associations, an experience repeated in the BJQ, where at one time opportunism threatened to engulf the trade, but not in the north Staffordshire Potteries. In Widnes, exogenous technological threats led to merger and the first steps away from districtisation. Networks were found everywhere but had very different foundations, from pragmatism and common interests to kinship and co-religion.

In confronting this mosaic of similarities and differences, Wilson and Popp posed three sets of core, interrelated questions. As historians, their focus was naturally on plotting and understanding patterns of change. Thus, first, they asked what the drivers of change were in industrial districts. Second, they set out to explore how context influenced how the pressure for change was interpreted and acted upon. Third, they sought a closer understanding of the mechanisms within the district that mediated and accommodated these pressures for change.

With regard to the first of these, the drivers, the point to highlight immediately, as Marshall did, is the imperatives of shifts in markets and technologies. As Peter Swann, Martha Prevezer and David Stout (1998: 2) have noted, district dynamics are likely to be closely related to technological issues. This much is obvious. Instead, what needs to be asked is how technological and market change acts on districts. First, neither is a purely exogenous force – as the influence of either national systems or global convergence might be thought of. Rather, the actors in the districts studied, whether firms, entrepreneurs or associations, always attempted to shape and reshape the factors of production available to them. Similarly, they were not inert in the face of the market. Often serving speciality consumer markets, producers in English industrial districts certainly had to do their best to meet the demands of the marketplace, but they were also convinced – often rightly – that the market could be persuaded to buy the new designs and desires created by often highly inventive and skilled workers and owners. Technologies, markets and producers therefore existed in a symbiotic balance that evolved in a path-dependent fashion as capabilities developed – not in isolation but through the process of interaction with the surrounding world.

Thus, a progressive, entrepreneurially driven elaboration of technological bases and capabilities, developing in step with constantly widening and changing national and international markets, was a major force driving the evolution of all English districts. For some this was a path to a dead end, however, and for others one to constant renewal. Important here was the ability of districts either to act as innovation systems themselves, as in Coventry, for example (Lloyd-Jones and Lewis, 2003), or to effectively absorb innovations made elsewhere, as in Worcester (Coopey, 2003). In contrast, the Widnes chemical industry, committed to the 'Leblanc process' for the manufacture of alkali, found itself trapped during a period of rapid and very radical, exogenous technological change in the final quarter of the nineteenth century.

For some, such events can be construed as examples of technological 'lock-in'. Only very rarely does technology follow an unbending trajectory to which firms and districts are helplessly bound, however. The key to survival lies in the ability to foster diversity and to build afresh on the complementarities in existing products, technologies and practices; failure to do so is an institutional rather than a technological one. An exemplar of success in English industrial history is Coventry, which progressively elaborated on the capabilities involved in precision trades such as the making of textile machines and watches to move, in turn, into manufacturing bicycles, motorbikes, motorcars and machine tools. For R. Lloyd-Jones and M. J. Lewis (2003), it was a pattern of spin-offs from lead 'seed corn' firms, facilitated by key local entrepreneurs such as James Starley and Alfred Herbert, that made this strategy of technological and product profusion possible. When no such 'social habit' has been implanted, however, then profusion can be difficult. In the Manchester industrial district, as John Wilson and John Singleton (2003) show, incumbent firms signally failed to build the basis for a diverse product and technological platform, despite the example offered by the US manufacturing firms that began to populate nearby Trafford Park industrial estate from the late nineteenth century onwards.

At the same time, I cannot ignore the dynamic impact of markets and competition. As Marshall (1919: 287) observed, the 'opening out of new sources of supply or new markets for sale may quickly overbear the strengths which old districts have inherited from past conditions'. For the advocates of flexible specialisation as a response to the increased levels of turmoil that seemed to characterise world markets from the mid-1970s onwards, and that seemed to undermine the economic rationale of mass production wedded to mass consumption that had driven the rise of the 'Chandlerian' corporation, market change favours the capabilities of the district. Nonetheless, whilst this might be true in the context of the business cycle, allowing the speciality producers in districts to make rapid and ongoing but small shifts, it is not so clear that this is always true in the context of more radical secular market change. Worcester, as a centre of industry, was destroyed by the fall from grace of the glove as an essential item of clothing (Coopey, 2003). Moreover, when secular change is combined with a constant reconfiguration and expansion of markets, as occurs under internationalisation, itself driven by changes in the technologies of transport and communication, then this ensures that 'this world competition, however free it may become, can lead to no finality, no settled appointment of industrial activity to the several parts of the world' (Hobson, 1906: 159). Again, handling the most radical shifts in markets and competition seems to depend on fostering the same kind of diversity in institutions and capabilities that also facilitates technological dynamism.

There was also clear evidence of strong structural dynamics operating alongside those derived from markets and technologies, however. Crucially, these structural dynamics appear to be largely systemic and contingent rather than strategic. Key to understanding these structural dynamics, which, as we shall see, feed into a district life cycle, is careful attention to changing barriers to entry and exit from the district. In particular, in contrast to much of the district literature, which tends to be highly enthusiastic about the multiplication of small firms that can occur, the studies found that these structural dynamics are by no means always positive in their effects. Over the life of a district, resources accumulate and thicken, leading to continually falling barriers to entry. At the same time, unrestrained entry can be encouraged by a local sociocultural valorisation of entrepreneurship. The outcome can be severe structural congestion and heightened localised competition of destructive proportions. Alternatively, when barriers to exit are simultaneously low, the often redundant resources thus released can be recycled in new, ever larger waves of start-ups, creating a similar condition of structural overcrowding. Thus, mature districts may exhibit high levels of internal competition and a breakdown in competitive norms (Popp, 2005). Reintroducing technology as an issue, the coincidence with similar moments of maturity in the product life cycle can act particularly powerfully to frustrate change.

I would argue that structural lock-in, observable only through the long-itudinal study of populations of firms in districts, is best revealed and analysed through historical methods.

Furthermore, understanding these structural dynamics also requires a perspective on agency. It is agency, especially individual decisions by actors to enter a district, that creates the conditions for a structural lock-in that over time acts to constrain incumbents and other entrants. Therefore, at the root of the systemic nature of industrial districts there lie many, many individual acts of choice and agency (Popp, 2005).

Of course, the impact of these various drivers also depends on the wider context in which they are experienced, over which regional systems and individual actors tend to have less influence. It is not possible to examine any district in isolation from wider systems – including the national and the international. In particular, the findings suggest, it is important to establish the extent to which local networks are able to connect to, intersect with, learn from and influence other systems operating at a range of geographical scales. These systems might relate to technology, commerce, politics, law or, more broadly, society and culture.

In this area a particularly high degree of importance can be attached to contingency. Given the wide time span covered by Wilson and Popp's studies, from the mid-eighteenth century to the late twentieth, I am able to suggest that, due to a range of environmental factors, the date of a district's formation is important to its subsequent development. This is to point out the need not simply for longitudinal studies but for an awareness of historical time. These environmental factors include physical and socio-economic infrastructure, from systems of transport and communication to education systems, through political and legislative regimes – as expressed, for example, in company law – to the development, already noted, of markets of supply and demand. The effects of changes in environmental conditions over histor-ical time show themselves in several different ways. First, we can observe a shortening and speeding up of the district life cycle. Thus, in many English districts, the country being the world's first industrialiser, the take-off, critical mass and maturity phases of the life cycle were extremely prolonged and the decline phase relatively so. Examples include the Lancashire cotton industry and the north Staffordshire Potteries. In contrast, the Widnes chemical industry moved through the entire cycle from nascent district to absorption into a branch plant economy in the period 1848 to 1926.

The study of older and earlier districts highlights the additional impor-tance of relative regional underdevelopment, which tends to promote reliance, for both governance issues and access to resources, on highly localised, close-knit and informal networks, often drawing on existing ties such as are offered by kinship and co-religion (Caunce, 2003; Cookson, 2003). This conclusion highlights how contingency varies in the magnitude of its impact across the life cycle of the district. It therefore makes very little historical sense to talk of district 'design'. Instead, structures and practices emerge in an iterative way, through, if one likes, an inductive, trial and error experimentation (Popp and Wilson, 2007).

The importance of secular market change as a dynamic driver of district development has already been noted. In contrast, I would portray the shorter-term business cycle more as an element of contingent context. Thus, both Sue Bowden and David Higgins (2003) and Richard Coopey (2003) highlight how apparently core district attributes, such as high-trust networks, could actually change very rapidly under the effect of short-term shifts in the business cycle – and were thus highly dependent, for their meaning or even existence, on specific environmental conditions. These arguments are echoed in Dario Gaggio's (2006) recent long-run study of two Italian jewellery districts.

Even having specified key drivers and having explored some of the ways in which context can shape reactions, however, we are still left with the questions of why districts develop in different ways. Why one choice over another? Why one time or place and not at another? What forces are at work when change is either hastened or blocked? Central here are questions of governance and resources. In order for a district to adapt and evolve, existing resources have to be reordered and perhaps even new resources not yet present in the district recruited and mobilised. Lock-in represents an inability to pursue and achieve such reorderings and recruitments, and perhaps even a failure to recognise that such reorderings may be necessary. The central problem is that, given what I have already said about the structures of districts, these responses must occur under conditions of decentralisation. The district literature typically places a very heavy emphasis on the importance of networks, variously defined, in meeting these challenges. Networks, for example, are held to be one of the key mechanisms through which resources are shared across firms. Network analysis needs to go beyond this static formulation, however, in order to take account of how the reordering of resources outlined above may be handled.

These studies all attest to the importance of networks. I also share Nohria's (1992: 12) note of scepticism, however, when he notes that 'the network organization has been reified as the new-ideal type of organization'. Networks, in and of themselves, are not fail-safe solutions to the challenges of achieving order in decentralised and sometimes contested districts.

Nonetheless, several key points can be made. First, the presence of networks is a reflection of the systemic qualities of districts. Furthermore, just like capabilities and technologies, they too evolve in iterative, path-dependent ways. I also contend that networks must necessarily be seen as interpenetrating two other governance forms with which they are often explicitly contrasted, namely markets and hierarchies. In reality, and in analytical terms, the three cannot be separated neatly. Firms and districts simultaneously employ a mix of markets, hierarchies and networks in the pursuit of their goals. The balance of this mix might go some way to explaining differing outcomes in situations demanding change.

Second, I argue for close attention to how actors actively construct networks and their positions within them, in contrast to the strong embeddedness perspective, which tends to see network membership and position as determined by the possession of certain sociocultural attributes. Networks are not then simply structuring institutions that variously constrain or enable different actors at different times; instead, they are also important vehicles for agency and power. This is not to say that agency is not compromised or that actors are not embedded to some extent. Clearly, systems of norms, values and social structure do impact on behaviours. This is to argue against the reification of networks as an ideal-typical organisational form, however, as warned against by Nohria (1992), and it is to argue that they are not objective phenomena that exist independently of those actors that constitute them; understanding them calls for what the editors of this volume have called 'situated analysis', or what an historian might term 'historical method'.

Having made these key observations about the nature of networks as governance mechanisms in industrial districts, I wish to address three specific aspects more directly: their relationship to other structures and institutions – in other words, their embeddedness; their efficacy; and their spatiality. First, whilst many of these cases did contain evidence of a role for wider social structures in the creation and maintenance of networks in districts, little evidence was found for what sociologist Mark Granovetter (1992: 28) has called 'strong social embeddedness'. Such scepticism about some of the stronger claims made for the effects of social embeddedness would chime with the scepticism displayed elsewhere in this volume with regard to, for example, the pervasiveness of national system effects. Simple interpretations of the effects of social embeddedness demand that we have simple but

ultimately unsustainable understandings of the roles and identities that
people adopt and of the meaning they give to their economic and organisational lives.

This argument can be made more concrete through reference to several
cases drawn from the histories of English industrial districts. First, the case of
Widnes shows the extent to which a strong social embeddedness position on
district governance depends on static constructions. The town of Widnes
simply did not exist when John Hutchinson established the first chemical
works there in 1848. There was no local sociocultural fabric in which
the industry could be embedded. Certainly, a local society and culture did
emerge – but the stress here should fall on the word 'emerge'. Sociocultural
frameworks are always emergent, in the act of formation, rather than finished
and constant. If sociocultural frameworks are not constant, however, then
neither are they uncontested, even in the most cohesive-seeming of industrial
districts.

The North Staffordshire Potteries should be a perfect site, if any is to be
found, for studying the effects of strong social embeddedness. This industry,
by the late nineteenth century, had already been established in the region for
at least 200 years. The district showed considerable apparent homogeneity, its
population being very largely indigenous to the immediate locale and showing strong adherence to several sociocultural norms, such as nonconformism
in religion. Despite these conditions, however, the vital economic issue of
entrepreneurship – particularly the question as to which classes in society
could legitimately aspire to the condition of entrepreneurship – came to be
extremely contested in this period. Different individuals in the same societal
setting placed very different constructions on the meaning of entrepreneurship, and did so by drawing on equally contested understandings of local
identity (Popp, 2003b). Moreover, these were not sterile, theoretical discussions, but instead impacted directly on individual and aggregate behaviours,
making the governance of the district as a whole extremely difficult at the
very moment it was facing very severe external threats – from those very
forces I have already discussed: a changing international political economy
and a changing competitive environment (Popp, 2005). Similarly, in the
Birmingham jewellery quarter, any embeddedness that was present in the
multitudinous small-firm population – a 'canonical' industrial district – was
signally incapable of combating that which the 'Italianate' model claims it
should be able to: opportunism and malfeasance. Instead, the district in the
late nineteenth century was plagued by an endemic dishonesty. Adherence to
standards and norms of behaviour had instead to be consciously engineered

through the formation of the Birmingham Jewellery Association (BJA), which acted quite literally as a policeman for the industry (Carnevali, 2003a, 2003b).

It is also significant that, in Birmingham, effective trade governance – when achieved – owed much to a few lead actors, for Wilson and Popp's studies repeatedly highlight an important role for leadership in regional business networks, as predicted in the models of economist Casson (1999, 2003). In Worcester, Birmingham, Coventry, Widnes, Sheffield and others, network formation and operation were driven forward by small groups of key figures. Networking is, as Casson (1999, 2003) argues, a highly entrepreneurial function. It is not particular network structures (or even the presence of networks, as much evidence of 'bad' networking was also found) that act as powerful determinants of regional economic performance but, rather, the quality of the entrepreneurship for which networks serve as a vehicle. These arguments again contrast with much of the district literature, and at the same time lead to the question of the effectiveness of networks as governance mechanisms in industrial districts.

Here there is considerable ambiguity. Lloyd-Jones and Lewis (2003) argue that, in Coventry, networks functioned well at the local level to forge and govern a vibrant and successful district but were much less successful at the national level, and failed to engender the kinds of political capital that might have been extremely useful to the town. Networks might also be said to have been successful in Widnes – but largely in the sense of managing decline relatively smoothly (Popp, 2003a, 2006). Other studies – Wilson and Singleton (2003) on Manchester, Steve Toms and Igor Filatotchev (2003) on Lancashire cotton textiles and Bowden and Higgins (2003) on wool versus cotton textiles– offer very strong critiques of the sometimes negative, sclerotic effects that networks could have on host districts. In particular, all these studies, as well as Gill Cookson (2003) on Darlington, emphasise the tendency for networks to become more inward-looking and less responsive to external stimuli over time – tendencies that impeded accountability and blocked the kind of reordering of resources stressed above as vital to the regeneration and longevity of districts. It can, therefore, safely be concluded that networks were not always able to meet the evolving governance challenges faced by a district over its life cycle.

The differing extent to which districts were able to meet new challenges had implications for and was also influenced by the depth, strength and nature of the linkages forged with wider systems (an interaction of differing spatial spheres that belies simplistic national versus global dichotomies). Thus, many of our cases provided support for the importance of extra-local, especially metropolitan, links posited in Casson's (1999, 2003) theoretical work on regional business networks. This was clearly true in Darlington, Lancashire, Coventry, Sheffield and Worcester. Further, it was also found that there were broad changes in what might be referred to as 'district spatiality over time', not least because the historical evolution of English districts unfolded alongside a concurrent evolution in national and international regimes and markets. These effects were reflected in the evolution of individual districts. In the earliest stages of district formation, therefore, particularly those furthest back in historical time, network linkages were densest at a highly localised level. Intuitively, however, any deepening specialisation and division of labour at the local level must be accompanied by a widening of other linkages. In this sense, at least, the 'global' and the 'local' are far from mutually exclusive. What might be termed 'centripetal' and 'centrifugal' forces thus remain in tension within the district throughout its history.

In summation then, these cases, subjected to rigorous historical method, demonstrate how industrial districts, as organisational environments, are subject to complex sets of dynamic drivers operating equally from within and from without, which are in turn refracted through the contingent influence of both varying contexts and the highly varied, always emergent, governance mechanisms that they generate. I have also emphasised throughout the way in which all these factors and effects, given their path-dependent nature, can be comprehended properly only through genuine historical awareness. This sensitivity to historical time, I have further argued, must be matched by attention to the differing impacts of systems operating at various spatial scales – from the micro-local to the international. The outcome is an understanding that, somewhat in contrast to the dominant Italian literature, sees industrial districts as complex, sometimes contested places in which there is not necessarily a correlation between the fact of spatial clustering and a single organisational response. Instead, the economic logic behind clustering and districts can find many different organisational expressions. This brings us to reflections on how this work on districts might relate to and inform the wider themes developed in this volume.

Conclusion: districts, meta-narratives and the SSD model

First, as suggested at the outset of this chapter, the industrial district poses a challenge to the contrasted narratives of national systems versus globalisation.

This is not because, as it might at first seem, it proposes a third, conflicting narrative – that of the pre-eminence of local systems – but because it is so clearly a site at which factors operating at a range of different spatial scales interact. It is from this interaction that a large element of the complexity found in the districts explored above is derived.

To an extent, this argument depends on a reappraisal of the standard statement of the industrial district model, which, with its essentialist and inward-looking perspectives, has not sufficiently confronted the conflicting analyses based on national systems versus global convergence. In its spatial boundedness and strong social embeddedness, and therefore its implied 'return to place' (Amin and Thrift, 1992: 572), the classical industrial district model is an argument both for a hyper-distinctive localism and for reified societal effects that are so strong as to be overwhelmingly deterministic. In Ann Markusen's words, it is thought that it is the spatial specificity and distinctiveness of districts that enables them to 'adapt and flourish *despite* globalizing tendencies' (1996: 294; emphasis added). They are 'sticky places' in 'slippery space', their very *placeness* confronting the *placenessness* of globalisation. At the same time, they are pressed into the service of national stereotypes – the 'Italianate' propensity to form districts as against the English inability to.

I would argue that Wilson and Popp's historically rooted analyses have shown these claims to be fallacies, however. Industrial districts vary greatly across space and time, even in a single nation such as the United Kingdom. They are not fixed and unchanging, either in their internal constitution or in their relationship to the wider world. This is true of individual districts over time, let alone across different districts. Moreover, their defining spatial concentration could not exist apart from a concurrently expanded interaction with the wider world, if only simply for orders for their goods.

By shifting the focus backwards and forwards throughout the chapter, between Italy and England, and between the late nineteenth and late twentieth centuries, we have seen not only the incompleteness of the national versus global analyses but also the various components of the SSD model at work. Thus, the industrial district clearly has strong generic features, but it can be seen to also be subject to different political economies, from the laissez-faire climate of late nineteenth-century England to the Communist- or Christian-Democrat-dominated districts of the so-called 'Third Italy', leading to substantial, institutionally mediated differences between different sites. These differences also reflect societal effects, but societal effects that are contingent and contested, even at the micro level, rather than strongly determined, as in the social embeddedness perspective characteristic of many district studies.

Furthermore, in the shift of understanding of what does and does not constitute a district, which has accompanied the shift in the study of districts from the model's origins in England to its new home in Italy, we see dominance effects. The 'Italianate' model became for a while in the late twentieth century a dominant archetype; a recipe to be transmitted around the world, rooted in national circumstances but generalised for a wider stage. I have sought here to begin to challenge that dominant archetype, by subjecting it to intense empirical, historical study. The result, I hope, will contribute to a return to a thin, open model of the industrial district that admits the possibility of different organisational solutions, in different contexts, to the common challenges of clustering.

References

Amin, A., and N. Thrift (1992) Neo-Marshallian nodes in global networks, *International Journal of Urban and Regional Research*, 16, 571–87.

Bowden, S., and D. Higgins (2003) 'Much ado about nothing?' Regional business networks and the performance of the cotton and woollen textile industries, c.1919–c.1939, in J. F. Wilson and A. Popp (eds.) *Industrial Clusters and Regional Business Networks in England, 1750–1970*, Aldershot: Ashgate, 90–111.

Broadberry, S., and A. Marrison (2002) External economies of scale in the Lancashire cotton industry, 1900–1950, *Economic History Review*, 55, 51–77.

Carnevali, F. (2003a) 'Malefactors and honourable men': the making of commercial honesty in nineteenth-century industrial Birmingham, in J. F. Wilson and A. Popp (eds.) *Industrial Clusters and Regional Business Networks in England, 1750–1970*, Aldershot: Ashgate, 192–207.

(2003b) Golden opportunities: jewelry making in Birmingham between mass production and specialty, *Enterprise and Society*, 4, 272–98.

Casson, M. C. (1999) *Analysing Regional Business Networks: An Economic Perspective*, discussion paper, Department of Economics, University of Reading.

(2003), An economic approach to regional business networks, in J. F. Wilson and A. Popp (eds.) *Industrial Clusters and Regional Business Networks in England, 1750–1970*, Aldershot: Ashgate, 19–43.

Caunce, S. (2003) Banks, communities and manufacturing in West Yorkshire textiles, c.1800–1830, in J. F. Wilson, and A. Popp (eds.) *Industrial Clusters and Regional Business Networks in England, 1750–1970*, Aldershot: Ashgate, 112–29.

Colli, A. (1998) Networking the market: evidence and conjectures from the history of the Italian industrial districts, in W. Felderkirchen and T. Gourvish (eds.) *European Yearbook of Business History*, vol. I, Aldershot: Ashgate, 75–92.

Cookson, G. (2003) Quaker networks and the industrial development of Darlington, 1780–1870, in J. F. Wilson and A. Popp (eds.) *Industrial Clusters and Regional Business Networks in England, 1750–1970*, Aldershot: Ashgate, 155–73.

Coopey, R. (2003) The British glove industry, 1750–1970: the advantages and vulnerability of a regional industry, in J. F. Wilson and A. Popp (eds.) *Industrial Clusters and Regional Business Networks in England, 1750–1970*, Aldershot: Ashgate, 174–91.

Dei Ottati, G. (2003) The governance of transactions in the industrial district: the 'Community market', in G. Becattini, M. Bellandi, G. Dei Ottati and F. Sforzi (eds.) *From Industrial Districts to Local Development*, Cheltenham: Edward Elgar, 73–94.

Gaggio, D. (2006) Pyramids of trust: social embeddedness and political culture in two Italian gold jewelry districts, *Enterprise and Society*, 7, 19–58.

Granovetter, M. (1992) Problems of explanation in economic sociology, in N. Nohria and R. Eccles (eds.) *Networks and Organization: Structure, Form and Action*, Cambridge, MA: Harvard University Press, 25–56.

Harrison, B. (1992) Industrial districts: old wine in new bottles?, *Regional Studies*, 26, 469–83.

Hobson, J. (1906) *The Evolution of Modern Capitalism: A Study of Machine Production*, London: Walter Scott.

Hudson, P. (1989) *Regions and Industries: Perspectives on the Industrial Revolution*, Cambridge: Cambridge University Press.

Lloyd-Jones, R., and M. J. Lewis (2003) Business networks, social habits and the evolution of a regional industrial cluster, in J. F. Wilson and A. Popp (eds.) *Industrial Clusters and Regional Business Networks in England, 1750–1970*, Aldershot: Ashgate, 229–50.

Markusen, A. (1996) Sticky places in slippery space: a typology of industrial districts, *Economic Geography*, 72, 293–313.

Marshall, A. (1919) *Industry and Trade: A Study of Industrial Technique and Business Organisation and their Influences on the Condition of Various Classes and Nations*, Basingstoke: Macmillan.

Nohria, N. (1992) Introduction: Is a network perspective a useful way of studying organizations?, in N. Nohria and R. Eccles (eds.) *Networks and Organizations: Structure, Form and Action*, Cambridge, MA: Harvard University Press, 1–22.

Paniccia, I. (2002) *Industrial Districts: Evolution and Competitiveness in Italian Firms*, Cheltenham: Edward Elgar.

Piore, M. (1992) Fragments of a cognitive theory of technological change and organization structure, in N. Nohria and R. Eccles (eds.) *Networks and Organizations: Structure, Form and Action*, Cambridge, MA: Harvard University Press, 430–44.

Piore, M. J. and C. F. Sabel (1984) *The Second Industrial Divide: Possibilities for Prosperity*, New York: Basic Books.

Popp, A. (2000) Trust in an industrial district: the Potteries, c.1850–1900, *Journal of Industrial History*, 3, 29–53.

   (2001) *Business Structure, Business Culture and the Industrial District: The Potteries, c.1850–1914*, Aldershot: Ashgate.

   (2003a), Networks and industrial restructuring: the Widnes district and the formation of the United Alkali Company, 1890, in J. F. Wilson and A. Popp (eds.) *Industrial Clusters and Regional Business Networks in England, 1750–1970*, Aldershot: Ashgate, 208–28.

   (2003b) 'The true potter': identity and entrepreneurship in the North Staffordshire Potteries in the late nineteenth century, *Journal of Historical Geography*, 29, 317–35.

   (2005) 'An indissoluble mutual destiny': the North Staffordshire Potteries and the limits of regional trade associationalism, *Organization Studies*, 26, 1831–50.

(2006) Governance at points of corporate transition: networks and the formation of the United Alkali Company, 1890–1895, *Enterprise and Society*, 7, 315–52.

Popp, A., and J. F. Wilson (2007) Life-cycles, agency and contingency: English industrial districts in historical perspective, *Environment and Planning A*.

Sabel, C. F., and J. Zeitlin (1985) Historical alternatives to mass production: politics, markets and technology in nineteenth-century industrialization, *Past and Present*, 108, 133–76.

(eds.) (1997) *World of Possibilities: Flexibility and Mass Production in Western Industrialization*, Cambridge: Cambridge University Press.

Staber, U. (1996) The social embeddedness of industrial district networks, in U. Staber, N. Schaeffer and B. Sharma (eds.) *Regional Business Networks: Prospects for Prosperity*, Berlin: de Gruyter, 148–74.

Swann, G. M. P. (2005) Clustering: where does it all end, paper presented at the British Academy of Management Annual Conference, Oxford, 13–15 September.

Swann, G. M. P, M. Prevezer and D. Stout (eds.) (1998), *The Dynamics of Industrial Clusteriing: International Comparisons in Computing and Biotechnology*, Oxford: Oxford University Press.

Taplin, I. M., and J. Winterton (1995) New clothes from old techniques: restructuring and flexibility in the US and UK clothing industries, *Industrial and Corporate Change*, 4, 615–38.

Toms, S., and I. Filatotchev (2003) Networks, corporate governance and the decline of the Lancashire textile industry, in J. F. Wilson and A. Popp (eds.) *Industrial Clusters and Regional Business Networks in England, 1750–1970*, Aldershot: Ashgate, 68–89.

Wilson, J. F., and A. Popp (eds.) (2003) *Industrial Districts and Regional Business Networks in England, 1750–1970*, Aldershot: Ashgate.

Wilson, J. F., and J. Singleton (2003) The Manchester industrial district, 1750–1939: clustering, networking and performance, in J. F. Wilson and A. Popp (eds.) *Industrial Clusters and Regional Business Networks in England, 1750–1970*, Aldershot: Ashgate, 44–67.

Zeitlin, J. (1995) Why are there no industrial districts in England?, in A. Bagnasco and C. F. Sabel (eds.) *Small and Medium Size Enterprises*, London: Pinter, 93–114.

11 Transnational learning and knowledge transfer: a comparative analysis of Japanese and US MNCs' overseas R&D laboratories

Alice Lam

Introduction

Multinational corporations are unique knowledge-creating organisations, because of their structural position spanning diverse institutional contexts and their ability to transfer knowledge across national borders (Kogut and Zander, 1993, 1995; Gupta and Govindarajan, 2000). Recent research has emphasised the learning and knowledge-creating aspects of foreign direct investment, and the growing importance of networks of foreign subsidiaries as new sources of competitive advantage (Frost and Zhou, 2000; Birkinshaw, 1997; Frost, Birkinshaw and Ensign, 2002). In the past, the ways in which the MNC created value from knowledge was conceptualised as a linear process of knowledge diffusion from the home country to the overseas unit. More recent theoretical and empirical research on MNCs recognises increasingly that knowledge creation occurs not only at the home base but in all the firm's far-flung dispersed units (Nohria and Ghoshal, 1997; Frost, 2001). The MNC is increasingly recognised as an international knowledge network that creates, integrates and applies knowledge in multiple locations (Almedia, Song and Grant, 2002; Subramaniam and Venkatraman, 2001). Especially in the science-based high-technology sectors, one notable recent trend has been the extension of firms' research and development activities and competence portfolios on a global scale to augment their knowledge base and to gain access to unique human resources (Howells, 1990; Florida, 1997; Kuemmerle, 1997). It has been noted that one of the main changes in the innovation strategies of MNCs since the early 1990s has been the move towards 'international learning companies', and the utilisation of overseas laboratories as 'knowledge incubators' to generate new scientific knowledge that can underpin their technological distinctiveness (Meyer-Krahmer and Reger, 1999; Pearce and Papanastassiou, 1999; Lehrer and Asakawa, 2002, 2003).

MNCs pursue global knowledge sourcing in search of emerging new scientific knowledge and technological capabilities, a large part of which is tacit and embedded in local innovation networks and scientific human resources. The sharing and transfer of knowledge across organisational and national borders is inherently difficult; the problem is even greater in the case of tacit knowledge, which is difficult to articulate and communicate across wide geographical and social spaces because of its experiential and socially embedded nature. Much of the existing analysis of MNCs' knowledge transfer problems focuses on the cognitive dimension and the role of intracorporate mechanisms in dealing with it (Teece, 1977, 1981; Martin and Salomon, 2003a, 2003b; Gupta and Govindarajan, 2000). In this chapter I draw attention also to the societal aspect of the problem that MNCs have to face when they attempt to transfer and create knowledge across major institutional/societal boundaries.

There are two dimensions of the tacit knowledge problem in MNCs. The first arises from the experiential nature of tacit knowledge – that is, the classic Michael Polanyi (1958, 1966) problem as depicted in his observation that 'we know more than we can tell'. Here, Polanyi draws our attention to the deeply personal and experiential nature of tacit knowledge that defies easy articulation and communication. Tacit knowledge, in this sense, is a form of 'knowing' and is inseparable from action because it is constituted through action (Orlikowski, 2002). It is learnt by direct interaction and transmitted through shared experience and the development of common understanding in particular contexts. The experiential nature of tacit knowledge may create significant barriers to organisational learning and knowledge creation within the MNC because of the difficulty in engendering interactive learning and maintaining mutual knowledge (Cramton, 2001; Sole and Edmonson, 2002) within its geographically dispersed and socially diverse knowledge structures (Foss and Pedersen, 2003; Becker, 2001). MNCs face a distributed organisational learning problem in general but the problem becomes especially complex when the creation and transfer of new (tacit) knowledge is at stake, as in the case of the global dispersion of R&D and innovation activities.

The second problem originates from the socially embedded nature of tacit knowledge, and the barriers that MNCs may encounter when they seek to create and transfer it across major societal boundaries. There is a large comparative literature demonstrating how the building of firm-level skills and knowledge accumulation is heavily influenced by wider socio-economic forces and the institutional framework at the national and regional levels (Whitley, 1999; Lam, 1997, 2000; Lam and Lundvall, 2000). Max Boisot (1995) argues that there is a relationship between the codifiability of knowledge, societal culture and institutions. Lam (2000, 2002) demonstrates how patterns of knowledge production within and between firms are powerfully shaped by wider societal factors, especially nationally constituted organisational forms and labour markets. For example, large Japanese firms characterised by stable employment relationships and strong organisational identities have been able to develop strong capacities for internal organisational tacit knowledge creation. By contrast, Anglo-American firms tend to rely more on external tacit knowledge generation based on flexible, open occupational labour markets and interorganisational flows of person-embodied tacit knowledge. This implies that the kind of network relationships and societal support needed for the generation and transmission of tacit knowledge may differ significantly between different national contexts. Thus, knowledge is tacit also in the sense that common rules and taken-for-granted assumptions shared between actors are important for its successful transfer. When MNCs seek to tap into locally embedded tacit knowledge and capabilities they have to develop close external network relationships with a variety of local actors and manage the interaction between R&D communities in the home country and in the host region. The ease of local learning and knowledge transfer may depend on the dynamics of interaction between the MNCs and host-regional context, and the extent to which the R&D communities of MNCs are able to develop social and relational proximity with their local counterparts.

While these two dimensions of the knowledge transfer problem are conceptually distinct, in practice they are closely related. One might argue that the societal aspect of the problem represents an accentuation of the cognitive problem in a cross-national context within which the cognitive barriers to knowledge transfer have their origins in the wider institutional environment. These institutional forces are not always obvious to firms, and become apparent only when they attempt to engage in learning that spans institutionally defined contextual divides (Gertler, 2003: 94; Lam, 1997).

The main aim of this chapter is to explore how MNCs, characterised by contrasting home-based models of organisational forms and learning, adopt different strategies for solving the tacit knowledge problem. I examine the problem under the US 'professional-oriented' and the Japanese 'organisational-oriented' models of learning and innovation (Lam, 2000, 2002). While the former relies on an external learning strategy and open recruitment of scientists and engineers in a professional-oriented labour market for knowledge renewal, the latter builds its innovative capabilities on a well-established internal labour market with a strong emphasis on internal knowledge creation. My study seeks to understand how MNCs, rooted in these two divergent national models of learning and innovation, draw on their distinctive home-based organisations and competencies to develop their transnational learning strategies. I also explore how home-based models of learning interact with the local host-country context to shape MNCs' abilities to harness local tacit knowledge. The empirical research is based on four in-depth case studies carried out in the R&D laboratories of US and Japanese MNCs operating in the United Kingdom.

Background: overseas R&D as a knowledge incubator

The global dispersion of R&D has been driven increasingly by firms' needs to acquire new knowledge and capabilities, and to gain access to unique human resources (Cantwell, 1995; Dunning and Wymbs, 1999; Howells, 1990; Florida, 1997; Kuemmerle, 1999a, 1999b). Since the mid-1980s the overseas R&D units of many MNCs have no longer confined themselves to transferring parent-company technology to host countries but have been developing major innovations for the global market by leveraging the unique knowledge resources of some host-country environments. Alexander Gerybadze and Guido Reger (1999) argue that the proliferation of national innovation systems and knowledge centres at various locations throughout the world has strengthened the incentives for MNCs to go for global knowledge sourcing. When deciding to establish or expand R&D abroad, firms are increasingly motivated by the wish to gain access to sophisticated resources that cannot be found anywhere else. These changes are clearly demonstrated in Robert Pearce and Marina Papanastassiou's (1999) survey of the evolution of overseas R&D laboratories in the United Kingdom. The authors distinguish three different roles for laboratories: support, locally integrated and internationally interdependent categories. The study shows that the internationally interdependent type, the main aim of which is to generate new scientific knowledge, has emerged as the most prevalent type of laboratory in MNCs' units in the United Kingdom.

A key element in the global learning strategies of MNCs has been the growth of transnational collaborative relationships with academic institutions. This trend is particularly prominent in the science-based industries, in which the traditional barriers between scientific and technological disciplines are breaking down, and there is an increased interchange between basic and applied research. Forging close links with academic institutions helps both to speed up innovation and to broaden the boundary of knowledge exploration. Large MNCs also seek to establish strong links with local higher education institutions so as to gain early access to the best students and academic researchers. In the dynamic technological fields, competitive advantage increasingly depends on tacit competence and unique configurations of knowledge resources. The recruitment of scientific personnel is one of the main ways for MNCs to tap effectively into new clusters of knowledge located abroad.

Although US firms have been able to draw upon a strong academic science base at home to support their radical innovation strategies, they are subject to intense competitive pressures to broaden the scope of innovative search. Since the early 1990s many leading US MNCs have sought to create a global scientific space through their worldwide R&D networks and academic links (Gerybadze and Reger, 1999). In contrast, Japanese companies are relative latecomers in setting up R&D facilities abroad. Since the late 1980s, however, many Japanese firms in the electronics and pharmaceutical sectors have become increasingly concerned with the need to develop more creative research organisations with greater capabilities in basic research and radical innovation (Methé, 1995; Roehl, Mitchell and Slattery, 1995; Methé and Penner-Hahn, 1999). The relative weakness of the academic science base at home and the historical institutional separation between universities and industry (Coleman, 1999; Nakayama and Low, 1997; Hane, 1999) have prompted Japanese firms to go abroad to search for productive university ties and set up basic research facilities. MNCs increasingly internationalise their university collaborations in general, but Japanese firms appear to have internationalised their university collaborations to a greater extent (Granstrand, 1999).

Mark Lehrer and Kazuhiro Asakawa (2002, 2003) use the term 'offshore knowledge incubators' to describe R&D units established in a foreign environment with the strategic objective of building close ties with local universities and research organisations in order to capture and cultivate new scientific and technical knowledge to support their parent MNCs' global innovation strategies. This type of overseas unit poses special managerial and organisational challenges for the MNC, because of the tacitness and localised nature of the knowledge involved and the open-ended knowledge creation process that they undertake within globally dispersed organisational contexts. The mandate of these overseas knowledge incubators is to search for new (breakthrough) scientific knowledge that, potentially, has high economic and commercial value for the MNC. New knowledge tends to be developed in tacit form and to be highly personal, initially known by one person or a small team of scientists making a discovery, and it is difficult to transfer to others (Zucker, Darby and Armstrong, 2002). The complexity of scientific and technical knowledge also means that it tends to remain tacit for a long time. Capturing such knowledge requires MNCs to foster interaction between scientists, both among their employees and with outsiders. A major challenge for the MNC, then, is the creation of a transnational learning space, linking its internal organisational networks with external, locally embedded networks for capturing and transferring knowledge across organisational and institutional boundaries.

The social embeddedness of MNCs and transnational social learning space

The existing literature identifies two different strategies for creating a common social space to coordinate geographically dispersed learning activities within MNCs. The 'learning region' strategy, popular among economic geographers and innovation scholars (Maskell and Malmberg, 1999; Howells, 2002; Lawson and Lorenz, 1999), argues that spatial proximity and the creation of strong external knowledge networks closely embedding the firm in the local innovation systems may be a potential solution. The core assumption is that the local context or geographical space provides the crucial social environment, in which actors develop relational proximity, common codes of communication and shared norms that guide social interaction and facilitate the flow of tacit knowledge. In contrast, the second strategy is based on 'communities of practice' (COP) and the idea that the creation of organisational space and strong relational proximity could facilitate the flow of knowledge across geographical and institutional boundaries (Amin and Cohendet, 2000; Brown and Duguid, 1996, 2000a). It emphasises the importance of developing a distinctive organisational space and shared work practices and identity as key factors promoting the generation and transmission of tacit knowledge.

The relative dominance of these two different strategies may vary between firms of different national origins, as suggested by the institutional approach, which stresses the influence of home-based institutions on the structure and behaviour of MNCs (Whitley, 1999, 2001; Morgan, 2001; Pauly and Reich, 1997; Doremus *et al.*, 1998). In a similar vein, the literature on national innovation systems stresses the impact of distinctive national institutions on firms' innovation patterns and technological trajectories (Lundvall, 1992; Nelson, 1993; Hollingsworth, 2000; Pavitt and Patel, 1999). Drawing on this earlier work, I argue in this chapter that the transnational learning activities of MNCs and their strategies for harnessing local knowledge will bear the strong imprint of home-country societal effects. This does not imply the replication of home-based organisational forms and learning patterns in the global arena, however, but refers to the ways in which MNCs draw upon their existing organisational competencies and expertise to develop their transnational learning spaces.

Whilst recognising that home-country institutions provide the main basis from which MNCs develop their globalisation strategies, I consider also host-country institutions as part of the social context within which the activities of MNCs are embedded. This is because the act of globalisation itself can be considered to be part of a firm's strategy to develop new competences and organisational routines, taking the local subsidiaries as potential sources of new ideas (Birkinshaw, 1997; Child, Faulkner and Pitkethley, 2000). This is especially relevant in the globalisation of R&D, which represents an important strategy of organisational and technological learning (Frost, 2001; Hollingsworth, 2000). Learning is, essentially, a social and interactive process, rooted in spatial and relational proximity (Gertler, Wolfe and Garkut, 2000; Lundvall, 1992; Saxenian, 1994). MNCs are attracted to places rich in knowledge sources and technological capabilities, in order to exploit the innovative richness arising from the social dynamics of local learning. A subsidiary's ability to gain access to local knowledge sources is likely to be dependent upon its embeddedness in the host-country context and the social relations of technological innovation (Frost, 2001; Blanc and Sierra, 1999; Zanfei, 2000). Proximity between home-based institutions and the host context may facilitate the local embeddedness of MNCs and their ability to harness local tacit knowledge.

Accordingly, I suggest that US MNCs will tend to adopt the 'learning region' approach, taking advantage of their strong organisational capacity for external learning and knowledge creation through open professional networks spanning organisational and institutional boundaries (Saxenian, 1996; Cohen and Fields, 1999). The liberal market institutional environment within which US firms are embedded allows them considerable flexibility to extend their organisational and human resource systems across institutional and geographical boundaries. Further, given that both the US and UK employment systems are organised around liberal market institutions and share a similar higher education and research base, this institutional proximity may also reinforce the local embeddedness of US MNCs. In contrast, Japanese MNCs are more likely to adopt the organisational 'communities of practice' approach, relying on their unique organisational capacity for internal tacit knowledge creation through the development of shared identities and problem-solving routines within organisational networks (Nonaka and Takeuchi, 1995; Dyer and Nobeoka, 2000). The strong emphasis of Japanese firms on internal tacit knowledge creation and their tightly integrated organisational and business systems, however, may limit their ability to exploit locally embedded knowledge. One would also expect Japanese R&D laboratories in the United Kingdom to face greater institutional barriers to local learning because of the greater divergence between the local institutions and Japanese MNCs' domestic institutions.

The empirical study explores the ways in which US and Japanese MNCs develop their transnational social spaces for learning, and how the two different strategies for transnational learning unfold in practice. While both sets of MNCs have to deal with the cognitive aspect of the tacit knowledge transfer problem, the varying degree of institutional proximity between the home and local context would imply an asymmetry in the societal aspect of the problem. The comparison between the US and Japanese MNCs in the UK context brings out the importance of the varying degrees of institutional proximity: the cross-societal knowledge transfer problem. The study also seeks to illustrate the dynamic interplay of the various 'embeddedness effects' on the MNCs' transnational learning activities and the tensions arising from different cross-cutting forces within the transnational social spaces.

Research methods and the sample

The research is based on four case studies of two US MNCs, one in the information and communications technology (ICT) sector (US-ICT) and the other in pharmaceutical (US-Pharma), and two Japanese MNCs, also from the same two sectors (J-ICT and J-Pharma). They are all large transnational firms operating in the science-based industries. The two ICT firms are comparable in terms of their size, the scale of their R&D investment and the duration of their R&D operations in the United Kingdom. US-ICT's Bristol laboratory was established in 1985, J-ICT's Cambridge laboratory

(JCL) in 1989. The two companies in the pharmaceutical sector, however, cannot be claimed to be directly comparable, because of the substantial differences in their size and R&D investment. Moreover, US-Pharma's R&D site in the United Kingdom was established in 1955, whereas J-Pharma's London laboratory (JLL) was initiated in 1990. The 'bias' of the sample is inevitable, in view of the contrasting national patterns of sectoral development in pharmaceuticals between the two countries.

The case studies focus on the MNCs' R&D laboratories in the United Kingdom. All four units chosen for the study are research labs with the objectives of exploring new technologies or researching new scientific fields. They can be described as 'knowledge incubators'. The two US laboratories are part of US MNCs' globally distributed network of R&D centres, whereas the Japanese ones are campus-based laboratories, reflecting the distinctive pattern of Japanese overseas R&D investments. The data were collected by semi-structured interviews with senior managerial and technical staff in R&D, human resource and academic liaison groups, as well as those directly engaged in external collaborative activities. The semi-structured questionnaires covered three main areas: (i) international R&D organisation and global knowledge-sourcing strategies; (ii) patterns of interaction with local universities and research institutes; and (iii) the role of human resource strategies in global coordination and local knowledge sourcing. A small number of interviews were also conducted with the MNCs' local academic partners in order to gain a deeper understanding of the knowledge transfer process.

In the case of the Japanese firms, interviews were also carried out with senior management at the headquarters in Japan. This was necessary for collecting essential company information not readily available in the United Kingdom. The contacts with the headquarters were also important for gaining access to the laboratories in the United Kingdom. The Japanese interview sample was much smaller, owing to the difficulties in gaining access to key staff in Japan and the small scale of the local laboratories. Access to J-Pharma in Japan was relatively restricted and only four interviews were carried out. Nonetheless, this was compensated for by the fact that the two interviewees at the headquarters in Japan had previously worked in the overseas laboratories in the United States and United Kingdom, and were able to provide rich information on the role of these laboratories. The interviews in Japan were conducted in Japanese and, in the United Kingdom, in English. The interviews with the two US MNCs were conducted between 1999 and 2000, those with the Japanese MNCs during 2001. The interview sample is shown in table 11.1. All the interviews were recorded and transcribed.

Table 11.1 The interview sample

Company	US-ICT	US-Pharma	J-ICT	J-Pharma
Number of company interviews (with technical and managerial staff in R&D and HR functions)	11	16	7	4
Number of interviews with local academic partners	2	3	1	1

These data were supplemented by company documents, press releases and other relevant published materials.

A comparative analysis of the case studies

Table 11.2 gives a profile of the international R&D organisation of the four companies studied. The case studies reveal some significant contrasts between the US and Japanese MNCs' in their global R&D structures and coordinative mechanisms, and the ways in which they seek to tap into local knowledge. These differences generally support the hypothesis that the US MNCs have a tendency to adopt the 'learning region' strategy whereas the Japanese opt for the organisational 'communities of practice' strategy.

International R&D organisation and distributed organisational learning: integrated networks versus the hub model

MNCs adopt a variety of global R&D structures and management styles in coordinating globally dispersed R&D units (Chiesa, 1999; Gassman and von Zedwitz, 1999; Reger, 1999). The two US MNCs examined here have sought to build an integrated form of network R&D organisation on a global basis since the early 1990s. An important policy focus of the R&D organisational restructuring in recent years has been to enhance the global coordination and integration of the geographically distributed research laboratories into the global knowledge networks. The global R&D structure can be characterised as that of an 'integrated network', whereby the central R&D evolves into a competency centre among interdependent R&D units that are closely connected by flexible and diverse coordination mechanisms. In both the US case study companies, the development of global research programmes and projects has played an increasingly important role in coordinating dispersed innovation. An important objective of the US MNCs' global knowledge

Table 11.2 A profile of the international R&D organisation of the four companies

Company	US-ICT	US-Pharma	J-ICT	J-Pharma
Industrial sector	Computing and communication	Pharmaceutical	Electronics, computing and communication	Pharmaceutical
Mode of international R&D organisation	Integrated network	Integrated network	Hub model	Hub model
R&D headquarters	United States and United Kingdom (distributed lab)	United States	Japan	Japan
Global R&D structure and coordinating mechanisms	R&D is distributed between corporate laboratories and R&D groups at divisional level; central R&D is globally distributed, employing 800 people in six sites around the world. Research organised into four programmes (aligned with four businesses) that can be located anywhere in the world. Global project teams as coordinating mechanisms	Global R&D division employs approximately 12,000 employees, with six discovery sites; central research organised as a globally distributed network. Project management as a key managerial tool for the coordination of global R&D; research teams and project managers, located at different sites, increasingly work in coordination with each other	Seven corporate research labs in Japan, employing a total of 2,700 research staff, with the central research lab being the largest, employing 930 research staff. Global (tripolar) research networks include four R&D centres in the United States and five sites in Europe; the US facilities employ a total of sixty people and, in Europe, around thirty. The European sites are coordinated by a parent organisation, the Corporate Technology Group, based in the United Kingdom. Japanese expatriate (research) manager from central R&D as key coordinating and liaison person	Central research in Japan functions as the nucleus of drug development activities and employs around 400 research staff. Overseas R&D facilities were commenced through the establishment of a research lab in Boston in 1989 (sixty staff), and the initiation of the London lab in 1990 (forty staff); these together form the company's tripolar research network, with the central lab in Japan acting as the focal link. Japanese expatriate managers/researchers as key coordinators

	Bristol laboratories (UK), the company's second largest research lab and among the premier corporate research labs in Europe, employing around 200 people	Central research (UK), the company's European headquarters for the discovery and development of new drugs and the largest research facility outside the United States, with 1,500 employees (640 R&D staff) at the site	Cambridge laboratory (UK), a campus-based lab aiming at creating new concepts of advanced electronic/opto-electronic devices, employs ten research staff and collaborates with twenty-five university researchers	London laboratory (UK), a campus-based lab with its initial focus on basic research in cell and molecular biology, has recently shifted towards more applied research working in close integration with central R&D in Japan; employs forty research staff, including some scientists seconded from Japan
Role of local labs (units investigated)				
Links with local universities/research	Strategic partnerships with local universities as part of global university relationships programme Hybrid research organisation	Postdoctoral collaboration; grant and fellowship training programmes; and strategic research collaboration Strategic recruitment specialists to develop strategic relationships with universities	'Institutionalised' university partnership and 'embedded laboratory' approach; focused and limited in scope	'Institutionalised' university partnership; focused and limited in scope
Recruitment and local labour market links	Important; tapping into wider European labour market	Important; increasingly moving towards 'Europeanisation' for PhD and postdoctoral recruitment	Not important	Not important

sourcing strategies has been to broaden their global scientific space and external knowledge networks. The local laboratories enjoy a clearly defined and coordinated autonomy within the MNC groups in terms of their R&D and business strategies, and relationships with local education and research systems. Both companies manifest a strategic aim to build a systematic and all-encompassing approach to the way they interact with local universities and research organisations. Gaining access to and the recruitment of scientific personnel appears to be a key strategic objective of their academic links. Moreover, the companies are also increasingly seeking to enlarge their space for the search of scientific expertise by tapping into the wider European labour markets. The local regional context provides an important social context within which the US MNCs construct their learning spaces, and seek to integrate the local knowledge sources within their global R&D networks.

The two Japanese cases examined here are both university-based laboratories, and their approach to tapping into the foreign scientific academic knowledge base can be considered as typical of Japanese firms (Turner, Ray and Hayward, 1997). They were established about ten years ago and the companies have made a large investment in them. They represent the European nodes in the companies' tripolar global research network. The R&D organisation of the Japanese MNCs approximates the 'hub model': the central research laboratories at home maintain tight control over decentralised activities by means of long-term R&D programmes as well as by resource allocation and close monitoring through personnel allocation. Both laboratories are managed by Japanese research scientists dispatched from central R&D at home. The pharmaceutical company's initial attempt to appoint a foreign research director and grant its London laboratory autonomy had proved to be 'unsuccessful' from the viewpoint of the parent company. This subsequently led the company to dispatch a Japanese research manager to reintegrate the overseas unit within its domestic research facilities (see below). The Japanese MNCs have sought to create tight 'organisational spaces' across geographical boundaries to support their transnational learning activities.

The cases studies also show that the two sets of companies use different mechanisms for integrating distributed organisational learning. The US MNCs adopt a project-team-level coordination strategy focused on the development of integrative management practices that encourage individuals from different parts of the organisation to interact and communicate with each other once the knowledge creation task (project) has been identified. Within the US MNCs, the development of global research programmes provides a common cognitive space for integrating and guiding R&D activities among the dispersed scientific and technical communities. The US MNCs increasingly rely on multi-site projects for coodinating their globally dispersed R&D activities. For example, US-ICT's corporate R&D is organised into four research programmes, corresponding to the four core business areas. These programmes cut across different laboratories, which can be located anywhere in the world. Labs are organised into departments, which are subdivided into projects. The project groups constitute the basic structure of work organisation in the laboratories. The company places an increased emphasis on the development of global project teams and systematic human resource strategies to support global coordination and knowledge transfer.

In the case of US-Pharma, the central project management function has assumed an increasingly important role in coordinating globally distributed R&D. The company has recently developed the Common Planning and Scheduling System (COMPASS), which is universally adopted by the research labs worldwide. The intention, according to the project manager interviewed, is to have a set of common definitions and codes to enable the company to 'roll up' all the projects into a portfolio view. In both companies, projects provide focal points for developing common knowledge and shared practices within their global knowledge networks. Projects assume an identity within the global organisation, allowing the members to relate to it and provide a shared context for knowledge sharing. They also generate organisational standards and procedures that help to reduce the cognitive and social distance between project participants (Mendez, 2003). In this regard, the project or task provides what Catherine Cramton (2001) refers to as the 'common ground' for generating the 'mutual knowledge' that aids knowledge transfer in dispersed collaboration. Projects also allow the companies a great deal of organisational and spatial flexibility to extend their reach to different knowledge pools and resources, internally as well as externally. Their temporary nature and the limited scope of 'common knowledge' built around specific tasks/teams, however, mean that the flow of tacit knowledge may be confined within these boundaries.

The Japanese MNCs, by contrast, rely on an organisational-level integrative strategy, aiming at maintaining a cohesive internal tacit knowledge production system. In fact, a core strategy of the Japanese case study companies has been to limit the 'dispersedness' of their global knowledge structures so as to ease transnational learning. This is achieved by limiting the size of their overseas laboratories and the scope of their links with local institutions, and reducing the uncertainty in their knowledge search by focusing on specific technological fields closely related to their home-based core competencies. Both the Japanese laboratories looked at in the study are located on a campus and focused on specific technological fields. The two companies use a combination of formal control structures and informal socialisation and person-oriented mechanisms to integrate their geographically dispersed learning activities. The overseas laboratories are under the formal control of Corporate R&D Planning Group at home, and the managers and key technical staff responsible are Japanese. For example, J-ICT's European R&D sites are coordinated by a parent organisation, the Corporate Technology Group, based in the United Kingdom. The management team of the group is exclusively Japanese, comprising a general manager and four local laboratory managers. Indeed, a distinctive approach adopted by the Japanese MNCs is the reliance on expatriate managers (scientists) as key liaison individuals in bridging the relationships between the home and local laboratories. These expatriate managers play a critical role in transferring home-based organisational routines and work practices to the local laboratories, and fostering strong interpersonal connections between the home and local R&D communities.

The manager of J-ICT's Cambridge laboratory is a Japanese researcher from the central R&D function who acts as the key liaison person between J-ICT and the local laboratory. He visits Japan twice a year to report on progress and decide the future objectives of the Cambridge lab. J-ICT also makes intensive use of progress reviews and frequent written reports for monitoring the progress and research direction of JCL. Likewise, the director of J-Pharma's London lab is an experienced Japanese researcher dispatched from central R&D who considers his task to be to 'integrate and bridge' basic and applied research, and to 'educate' the local researchers on drug development. One can argue that the Japanese MNCs have sought to extend their firm-centred communities of practice across geographical boundaries in order to promote common standards, routines and values (i.e. a corporate culture) that supports the integration of dispersed R&D into corporate business strategies.

While the US MNCs seek to develop project-related 'common knowledge' as a cognitive base to promote tacit knowledge transfer, the Japanese MNCs appear to rely on 'shared identity' to promote trust and attachment to the organisation in order to ease the transfer of tacit knowledge. Indeed, Ikujiro Nonaka and Hirotaka Takeuchi's (1995) model of organisational knowledge creation stresses the importance of socialisation and organisational emotional engagement in facilitating the sharing and transfer of tacit knowledge. This organisational integrative strategy is costly, however, and depends on the existence of a relatively stable organisational membership base. This inevitably means that it cannot easily be extended across wide spatial and social boundaries.

Network construction and local learning: 'strategic university partnerships' versus the 'embedded laboratory' approach

The case studies also show a significant contrast between the US and Japanese MNCs in their patterns of local learning and abilities to embed themselves in the local innovation networks. Here, a key problem facing the MNCs concerns the potential barriers to cross-societal learning arising from the socially embedded nature of tacit knowledge. Developing close network ties and personal links with local scientists is important for capturing locally embedded tacit knowledge. The evidence suggests that the US MNCs have been able to develop extensive network ties with the local scientific communities through strategic university partnerships and the recruitment of scientific personnel to encourage the flow of person-embodied tacit knowledge across organisational boundaries. The Japanese MNCs, on the other hand, appear to be more limited in the scope of their local network construction, and they have not developed the US type of broad-based university links and human resource strategies. Instead, their local laboratories are rather small and set up as university research centres engaging in relatively focused research collaboration with the university scientists. The recruitment of local scientific personnel does not appear to be a key motive behind the collaboration. This approach reflects a conscious strategy adopted by the Japanese companies to create their own distinctive organisational spaces and social network support within a foreign institutional context that differs significantly from the domestic one.

US MNCs: strategic university partnerships and regional scientific networks

The two US MNCs looked at in this study have sought to develop deep institutional links with key local universities and use wide external networks of scientists/collaborators to facilitate interorganisational flows of knowledge. The main mechanisms for local knowledge sourcing comprise three components: (i) developing 'strategic partnerships' with key universities for human resource flows and recruitment; (ii) using hybrid research organisations and collaborative projects to facilitate joint work and the transfer of knowledge; and (iii) using 'star scientists' as focal links in local innovation networks.

A key aspect of the US MNCs' strategies for tapping into the local labour markets and scientific communities has been the development of close ties with local universities and research organisations. The main objective of the companies is to focus attention and concentrate resources on a small number of key institutions from which they are most likely to acquire their people and knowledge. The term 'strategic partnership' is often used to denote an intention to forge long-term, multidimensional ties and trusting relationships with preferred institutions. The relationships are usually sustained by a range of linking mechanisms, including research collaboration, industrial inputs to curriculum development, student placements and exchanges of scientific staff.

Since the mid-1990s US-ICT has been making a conscious policy effort to develop more systematic and stronger links with universities. A new position responsible for academic links was created in 1995 at the Bristol laboratories. The mandate of this new role is the development of a 'Strategic University Relations Programme' on a global scale together with their US counterparts. The strongest focus is placed on long-term relationship-building rather than on the acquisition of specific expertise or technologies. The intention behind such partnerships, according to a senior manager responsible for university links in US-ICT, is to have 'early access to the best ideas and trusted access to the best people'. By becoming a trusted partner in the academic community, US-ICT would be in a better position to catch the students early while retaining the opportunity to influence the education and training of future employees. Likewise, US-Pharma has sought to develop a more focused and targeted approach in the ways it relates to higher education institutions. The director of Human Resources in Central Discovery described recruitment as a very 'tough' area. Forging closer academic links has become so important that the company has recently created 'strategic recruitment specialists' in chemistry and biology, staffed by scientists with PhD qualifications, to liaise and develop strategic relationships with their preferred institutions.

A major challenge facing MNCs' global knowledge sourcing concerns the development of organisational mechanisms for cultivating and capturing commercially valuable new scientific knowledge at the local level. As already noted, new scientific breakthrough knowledge tends to be tacit and highly personal, usually known only by a single person or a small team of discovering scientists, and is difficult to transfer to others. According to Lynne Zucker, Michael Darby and Jeff Armstrong (2002), the most effective means for the sharing and transfer of such knowledge requires bench-level collaboration between firm and discovering academic scientists, enabling one to see how the science is done. Discovering scientists are typically willing to transfer knowledge primarily in the context of their ongoing laboratory work. The participation of firm scientists in bench-level teamwork with discovering university scientists also facilitates the formation of a shared cognitive framework that makes the new knowledge understandable and usable for the firm.

Hybrid research organisations and collaborative projects are the main mechanisms used by the US MNCs to engage local academic scientists in joint work. US-ICT, for example, set up a hybrid research institute in mathematics in the mid-1990s as part of the company's initiative to widen its research base and explore new avenues of knowledge. The hybrid research centre sits at the interface between US-ICT's Bristol laboratories and its partner university in the region. It provides a forum for collaborative research and personnel exchanges. The core research staff comprise a mixed blend of US-ICT researchers, academic scientists jointly appointed by the company and university, and postdoctoral and PhD students working on projects jointly supervised by the academic and company scientists. These people represent a kind of 'joint human capital' shared between the company and the university. The professional networks and problem-solving experiences spanning the two sectors constitute important mechanisms for the joint production and sharing of new knowledge.

At the core of the US MNCs' strategies for developing close ties to the local scientific communities is the desire to gain access to a small number of 'star scientists' who can act as focal links in the local innovation networks. The term 'star scientist' is used to refer to the top, renowned academic scientists, who have accumulated unique sets of scientific expertise and social networks that underpin their superior knowledge production capabilities (Zucker, Darby and Armstrong, 2002a; Bozeman and Mangematin, 2004). 'Star scientists' are vital sources of knowledge and academic interfaces for firms on account not only of the value of their deep scientific expertise but, more critically, their connections to the wider scientific networks and their 'brokering' role in knowledge transfer. As noted by Fiona Murray (2004), a firm's close ties to an individual scientist may result in that scientist contributing both human and social capital to the networks of collaboration. The social capital of the focal scientists includes their local laboratory networks of researchers and doctoral students as well as the more widely dispersed academic peers in their specialist fields.

The two US companies looked at in this study have developed their local university partnerships through the personal contacts and deep engagement of such 'star' academic scientists in the collaborative relationships. US-Pharma, for instance, has recently engaged in a five-year, large-scale consortium research project with a university in Scotland. The engine behind the creation of the project was a 'star' bio-scientist who had developed strong personal links with the company through consultancy activities and advisory board membership. Over the years this professor had become a vital source of intellectual capital for US-Pharma, through joint research and his key role in creating and transferring early discovery results (tacit or non-codified knowledge) via direct personal contacts with the company scientists. More critically, he has also acted as a magnet for attracting postdocs and other top scientists to his laboratory, providing a source of reliable researchers for collaborative projects and a potential source of recruits for the companies.

Likewise, US-ICT's strategic partnership with a university in the west of England also revolved around a key scientist who had been an industrial researcher in computer science for fifteen years before joining academia. His relationship with US-ICT dated back to his years in industry, when he had built a strong reputation in both the business and academic communities. His arrival at the university gave a strong impetus to the partnership, through the funding of research projects and the drawing up of a broad framework agreement to facilitate personnel-based exchanges, including student placements, visiting staff arrangements and the participation of firm scientists in curriculum development and project supervision. Thus, not only does this professor represent a centre of expertise for US-ICT, he is also the main conduit through which the company gains early access to students and influences their training. He is also the focal point for the firm to establish a 'local window' of scientific contacts 'to generate links with other kinds of research groups around the world', to put it in the words of the professor.

It is apparent from the above analysis that the professional networks of scientists provide a common cognitive and social basis for the US MNCs to create permeable organisational boundaries and build close ties with the local scientific communities. The construction of extensive external networks ties through gaining proximity to key scientists and universities constitutes a main channel for the US MNCs to tap into local knowledge sources and capture emerging tacit knowledge.

Japanese MNCs: 'embedded laboratories'

Japanese companies' motives for developing overseas academic links are very different from those of their US counterparts. They appear to use globalisation as a strategy to compensate for the weakness of home-based institutions in basic science, and to 'disrupt' their established, firm-centred learning patterns (Nakayama and Low, 1997; Methé, 1995; Westney, 1993). Both the laboratories studied are located on a campus and engaged in rather focused research activities through institutionalised collaboration with the partner universities.

Locating their laboratories on campus serves two important purposes. The first is to gain immediate access to qualified scientific personnel. Japanese companies are relative latecomers to the global R&D scene, and their laboratories are 'unknown' entities to many European scientists. They are only too aware of the potential difficulties in competing with other well-established European and US laboratories for talented scientists in a tight labour market. Thus, setting up university-based laboratories helps to project them as sponsors of world-class research and attract qualified local scientists (Lehrer and Asakawa, 2002). The second purpose is to use the laboratories as focal points for constructing organisational spaces to facilitate on-site (*genba*) learning and the transfer of tacit knowledge. Both the laboratories are relatively small, enabling the companies to extend their 'communities of practice' approach across geographical boundaries through deep interactions with the various parties involved. The empirical evidence suggests that J-ICT's COP approach has met with greater success than that of J-Pharma. The latter's attempt to (re)integrate its London laboratory with the R&D system at home, after an initial 'hands-off' period, appeared to have caused intense organisational strain and alienated the local scientists.

'Embedded laboratory' as organisational space for transnational learning: J-ICT's Cambridge laboratory

J-ICT refers to its Cambridge laboratory as an 'embedded' laboratory. This involves the research group of JCL being physically located within the same building as the microelectronics research centre (MRC) of the university, the frequent sharing of research staff and information, and intimate cooperation in research. J-ICT considers the main advantage of an embedded laboratory to be the opportunity to interact face to face with the local researchers and develop a sense of shared understanding, so as to influence the purpose and targets of research identified within MRC. The Japanese manager interviewed stresses the importance of 'working together' and being 'in the same place' for relationship building with the university scientists:

So, as you see here, through the one door, J-ICT's area and the university's area are just next door. And, in the daytime, you can't distinguish which person is a university person . . . So we have a very deep collaboration – close collaboration, really. So far, I think everything came quite smoothly. The very important factor is that we are working so closely every day . . . So we have been discussing the research and administration every day . . . (Japanese laboratory manager, JCL)

Indeed, one of the main roles of JCL is to integrate the fundamental research conducted at the university with the strategic objectives of the company. The subject areas and research direction of JCL are regularly discussed at an annual advisory committee meeting at Cambridge, involving people from J-ICT and the collaborating academics. As highlighted by the laboratory manager of JCL, the collaboration is not simply a case of 'asking university people, please do this sort of research and we want to receive some results'. Rather, as researchers from JCL and MRC work together, it strives to achieve a common understanding and to direct research towards the same goal, though this is not effortless. The following comments made by the Japanese manager and a Cambridge researcher are illustrative.

The biggest difficulty is . . . we employ basically the researchers with physics background. So they have a strong motivation to achieve some research goals. But, as an industry, we have certain direction and targets. So to discuss the target and also to reach an agreement, by concerning research from Japan, that is somehow one of the most difficult parts. And also the approach and the way of thinking for the research here is very different from those in Japan . . . So it's very useful that we have the opportunity to discuss such a target from the beginning with university staff and also students so they understand fully what's going on. I think that's the most important benefit [of adopting the embedded laboratory approach]. (Japanese laboratory manager, JCL)

. . . [The collaborative relationship] needed very careful day-to-day management, very strong communication on both sides . . . So, on both sides, it takes a lot of work, a lot of day-to-day communication, both locally and between the local managers, and also between our manager here and the hierarchy in Japan. Between Prof X and the hierarchy with the lab at the university, and also at other levels within those hierarchies as well . . . (Cambridge researcher, JCL)

At the time of the study there were three ongoing collaborative projects, one of which had reached a stage of product development in collaboration with the central research laboratory in Japan. The project started ten years ago at the initiation of JCL, with research on single electron devices lasting for seven years, representing a cumulative learning period necessary to gain the expertise that formed the foundation of this invention. JCL regards its role in interfacing the 'scientific' with the 'development' world as critical for the successful innovation. This interface involves the sharing and transfer of tacit knowledge between Cambridge and central research in Japan, through developing common understanding and bridging the different cognitive frameworks between the Cambridge scientists and the development engineers in Japan. Japanese managers are, effectively, mediators between the two different knowledge communities: the corporate centre in Japan, rooted in one community, and the foreign researchers, rooted in another. A Cambridge researcher described JCL as 'a buffer between the corporate side and the university side'. The Japanese manager pointed out that having the Japanese staff on-site at JCL was vital for the interface and knowledge transfer:

That's our role. That's the reason why we need the Japanese staff here, myself and two more Japanese ... And also the interface between the scientific world and the development world is very, very difficult to fill so we are working very hard ... For scientific purposes, to show the scientific results clearly, there is a certain way to prepare the sample and prepare the end results. But to use that for the actual products there are a lot more data necessary to show, to convince the people working in the factory. So it takes more than the initial scientific work to get some engineering data. That's done jointly with people on the central research laboratory. We don't have enough expertise here, but by collaborating with the people in central research we try to get some necessary data. (Japanese manager, JCL)

The evidence thus far suggests that the JCL–Cambridge collaboration has been a success, both in terms of tangible outputs and its apparent strategic importance for J-ICT. Both the J-ICT management and researchers at Cambridge describe the partnership as 'stable and successful'. A number of factors might have contributed to this. First, JCL has been able to embed itself within the university both physically and socially. It has established strong personal and social network ties, albeit on a limited scale, within the university, and engaged in reciprocal knowledge sharing. A senior Cambridge researcher interviewed emphasises the importance of the 'two-way process' and how JCL 'brings in a lot of extra scientific expertise and knowledge to the university group'. Second, J-ICT has made large investments in its domestic R&D and established a strong scientific culture at its central laboratory at home. This facilitates scientific communication with the overseas researchers and the appropriation of scientific breakthroughs. Finally, and perhaps more critically, J-ICT has been able to extend its corporate COP approach to its overseas laboratory, through an emphasis on management processes that lead to the formation of common understanding and shared identity among its local laboratory staff. Concern was placed not only on gaining access to scientific expertise but also on instilling a sense of shared identity through intense communication and subtle socialisation, so that the key local researchers get to know the company and its established routines. A local Cambridge researcher talks about the importance of 'careful daily management' of relationships in 'little things', such as wearing a suit, when he visits the Japanese headquarters in Maidenhead, 'because there everybody wears suits and if I turned up dressed up like this I wouldn't be taken seriously'. He also boasts of the strong links that his team has developed 'with everybody at every level and also up to board level within the central research lab [in Japan]'. It appears that the intensive personal interaction and frequent two-way visits of researchers have facilitated the development of 'relationship-specific heuristics' (Uzzi, 1997) that helps to ease the cognitive and societal barriers to tacit knowledge transfer.

It is worthy of note, however, that JCL is relatively small. Its collaborative objectives and research focus have remained highly specific, and tightly connected with the product innovation strategy at home. This indicates that the innovative capabilities may be limited or circumscribed, in that if it were more extensive it would be able to conduct a more varied spectrum of research and broaden its scope of knowledge search.

'Embedded laboratory' and problems in local embedding: J-Pharma's London laboratory

J-Pharma's London laboratory was initially conceived in order to focus on basic, curiosity-driven research that might provide new drug candidates, which would then be developed at the Tsukuba research laboratories in Japan. Initially the lab was given sufficient independence to carry out this mandate. The appointment of a US scientist with strong connections with local academics represented a conscious attempt on the part of J-Pharma to signal its commitment to basic research and the local embedding of the laboratory. During the first five years, despite the formal, centralised management structure, JLL was able to establish close links with the university, and engaged in various exchange activities. This was made possible through the effort of the US scientist director and a small group of university academics initially involved in setting up the laboratory, as noted by one of the professors:

[S]o with J-Pharma in the first five years, remember, the structure was identical. The Japanese had absolute control, J-Pharma had absolute control of what went on there [at JLL], but because of the director and the people he hired, and so on, it was terrific. There was a lot of flow back and forth, we collaborated with them, we published with them, as did other people in the university. Students were flown here. I mean, it was like part of the university, it was tremendous. (London professor, JLL)

After a few years without producing what were felt to be significant drug candidates, however, it was reintegrated within the research activities of the Tsukuba lab. JLL currently collaborates on projects with the Tsukuba laboratory, whereby project team members concurrently conduct research on the same project. Tight control is maintained through project management and intensive two-way communication between the two labs via the internet and visits by researchers. The role of JLL appears to have shifted from being that of an 'innovator' in the global R&D network to a 'contributor' within the product development system at home.

The reason given for this dramatic change of research orientation and management, according to the interviews with J-Pharma, was the fact that, despite three or four years of investment, no new drug candidates had been discovered. It was stated in the interviews that the president of J-Pharma, an MBA graduate, became impatient for some return on the investment made. This expectation and the subsequent change of direction seem remarkable, however, given that J-Pharma's president had stated that the aim of JLL was 'to produce good medicines for the central nervous system. It will take at least five to six years – and in many cases more than 10 years – to reach that stage' (*Financial Times*, 1990). It can be argued that the change in research orientation partly reflects the 'failure' of J-Pharma to gain an understanding of the research process conducted at JLL and hence to evaluate its research progress appropriately. The tangible output of drug candidates used to evaluate the achievements of JLL may not be a sufficient measure of the success of the collaboration. The academic at the University of London responsible for the initial setting up of JLL repeatedly pointed out in the interview that 'there were some very serious misunderstandings' about the nature of doing basic research and the role expected of JLL.

[T]he real problem was this misunderstanding about direction from the beginning. Their claim was they had always had the same thing in mind, they wanted to see drugs on line in three to five years, and that was not on the table in the early years ... We on the advisory board were under the impression that what J-Pharma wanted was to have a first-rate research institute focused on XX disease. Basically, doing basic research for drugs that would emerge from principles fifteen, twenty years – this was long-term research ... (London professor, JLL)

It would appear that the 'misunderstanding' was caused partly by the different expectations and taken-for-granted assumptions concerning basic science on the part of industry and university. The problem can be accentuated when it involves a Japanese company and a Western academic partner because of the added difficulties arising from 'cross-societal' differences in attitudes towards science and dominant modes of knowledge production. Japanese society traditionally accords greater respect to engineers than to scientists in laboratories and universities (Chikudate, 1999; Coleman, 1999). The dominant technical logic of Japanese pharmaceutical companies has traditionally been weighted towards the development of products based on existing scientific knowledge, as opposed to the basic research needed to create new scientific knowledge (Methé, 1995; Kneller, 2003). Thus, Japanese companies may find it difficult to understand and appreciate the basic assumptions of exploratory science upheld by Western scientists. Nobuyuki Chikudate (1999) notes that the cognitive and social distance between the 'managerialism' of Japanese pharmaceutical companies and Western 'scientism' often leads to communication breakdown in cross-border partnerships.

The dramatic shift in the research direction of JLL also reflects the strength of the dominant technical logic and power of control of existing organisational routines. Japanese pharmaceutical companies have traditionally built their success on using a cohesive internal product development system to achieve world-class product output levels despite their small size compared with major global rivals (Roehl, Mitchell and Slattery, 1995). The system is geared towards internal knowledge creation and transfer. The presence of a non-Japanese laboratory director at JLL posed a challenge to the cohesive product development system: it created difficulties in communication and internal knowledge transfer from the viewpoint of the central laboratory. It was considered by head office that the foreign research director sought 'too much independence' and could not be held accountable for the direction of research: 'Foreign director has his own thoughts and own opinions ... Our president thought the lab director should be Japanese' (interview with Japanese director at JLL). Indeed, the change of research director at JLL, from an American academic scientist to a Japanese researcher with many years of drug development experience at home (but no previous overseas experience), can be considered as an attempt to reintegrate the local laboratory, and to harness and exploit its research results. Following the appointment of the Japanese research director, JLL became more integrated within J-Pharma.

The dramatic change in research direction and the departure of the US director resulted in very high staff turnover, with a half of the research staff leaving, and the subsequent alienation of numerous academics and the cessation of substantial links with the university. There is now little formal collaboration between JLL and the university. Informal contacts and personnel exchanges also appear to be minimal. One of the key academics initially active in the links claims that JLL is now 'a non-entity to the university'. He describes the change in research direction as 'a shock, an enormous disappointment', and reckons that 'none of the really good basic research at the university will ever find its way through the doors of J-Pharma'. This is because the community of academic scientists on the campus no longer felt that they were connected. This raises questions about its long-term ability to build academic links and tap into the local knowledge networks. J-Pharma itself has also expressed doubts about the value on return for the investment in JLL and its long-term viability.

The collaboration between J-Pharma and the University of London has not been considered a success by either of the parties concerned. J-Pharma has not been able to sustain its initial effort in organisational learning, and has failed to establish close ties with the local academic community. The experience of JLL demonstrates the tension involved in the adaptation and integration of this dispersed centre of learning within J-Pharma's global knowledge network (Asakawa, 2001). This manifests an inherent management problem in global R&D amplified in a cross-societal context, in that J-Pharma lacks the necessary organisational competence in managing its European laboratory and understanding the process of basic discovery research. Although J-Pharma is one of the most research-intensive Japanese pharmaceutical companies, its R&D investment remains very small. The company's traditional weakness in basic research and its strong reliance on a cohesive product development system means that it may not have developed the necessary organisational capacity for developing effective links with external networked actors and for harnessing the tacit knowledge of research conducted abroad. Indeed, recent evidence suggests that Japanese pharmaceutical companies continue to pursue an 'autarkic' innovation strategy, relying predominately on in-house R&D for drug discovery and the long-term employment of master-level graduates in cohesive teams (Kneller, 2003) – despite the increased exposure of the industry to international competition since the late 1990s and signs of a breakdown of long-term employment in other sectors. Japanese pharmaceutical companies' strong emphasis on in-house R&D stands in stark contrast to the network strategy pursued by their US and European counterparts. The 'misunderstandings' between J-Pharma and its partner university highlighted in the case study are symptomatic of the communication and social distance between them.

Discussion

The case studies show that the US MNCs have sought to use the local regional context as the main social space in which network ties are constructed with local scientists to facilitate interorganisational flows of tacit knowledge. They have been able to exploit their strong capacity for external learning through open professional network ties among scientists spanning industry and academia, and to extend the spatial reach of their global scientific space. Particularly notable are the ways in which the US MNCs use network ties with 'star scientists' for tapping into local scientific networks and broadening the scope of knowledge search. In contrast, the Japanese MNCs have relied on the creation of tight organisational spaces across geographical boundaries to support site-specific learning and intra-organisational tacit knowledge transfer. Learning within such communities of practice tends to focus on clearly defined agenda and is closely linked to the companies' core competencies. Key local scientists are used as 'bridging persons' for channelling the flow of knowledge between the local laboratory and the parent company. This approach builds on Japanese companies' traditional strength in promoting an internal tacit knowledge production system through organisational bonds and shared identities. It also reflects a conscious adaptive strategy for reducing the learning uncertainties in a foreign institutional context that differs significantly from the domestic one. Lehrer and Asakawa (2003: 774) note that US and Japanese firms operating R&D laboratories in Europe face *asymmetric* conditions on the basis of their home-based systems. Their study shows that Japanese laboratories in Europe have encountered greater difficulties in managing the relationship with the external R&D occupational communities.

The divergent patterns of transnational learning observed in the two sets of companies illustrate the contrasting logics of two distinctive national models of learning manifest in the global context. The US 'professional-oriented' model of organisation and knowledge building enables companies to have considerable flexibility to extend their human resources and learning systems across institutional and geographical boundaries. US firms have traditionally relied on open recruitment and the interorganisational mobility of scientific personnel as a main mechanism for acquiring person-embodied tacit knowledge to support their radical innovation strategies (Finegold, 1999; Hage and Hollingsworth, 2000; Whitley, 2000). Moreover, historically they have established strong institutional links with academia, leading to a greater degree of human resource mobility between the two sectors and the formation of research networks within a global scientific space (Mowery and Rosenberg, 1993; Hane, 1999; Zucker, Darby and Torero, 2002; Mahroum, 2000). The professional-oriented career structures and open employment systems facilitate the development of a decentralised global R&D structure through project management, and allow overseas units a greater degree of autonomy in local recruitment. It could be argued that US firms in general enjoy a 'comparative institutional advantage' in developing transnational learning spaces to broaden the scope of knowledge exploration. This advantage is reinforced when they locate their R&D units in an environment where labour market institutions and systems of higher education are congruent with those at home. Institutional proximity between the home- and host-country contexts appears to have eased horizontal network construction and led to a higher degree of local embeddedness on the part of the US MNCs.

The Japanese MNCs, on the other hand, appear to be more limited in the scope of their local network construction, and they have not developed the US type of broad-based university links and human resource strategies. Japanese MNCs, in general, tend to be tightly integrated and seek to maintain a high degree of internal organisational proximity and coherence (Westney, 1999). They develop their internationalisation strategies by building on and extending their existing technological expertise to overseas markets. This is achieved by maintaining a close integration between the technological competencies based at home and those developed overseas. The Japanese approach to product innovation is characterised by a tight integration between R&D and manufacturing operations and the frequent rotation of people across functional boundaries (Kenney and Florida, 1993; Lam, 1996). This particular feature of the Japanese innovation system inhibits the decentralisation of R&D to foreign subsidiaries. Moreover, Japanese firms have historically built their innovative capabilities on a well-established, firm-based internal labour market with a strong emphasis on internal tacit knowledge creation (Nonaka and Takeuchi, 1995; Lam, 1997). The high degree of intra-organisational mobility of R&D personnel is accompanied by a relative absence of horizontal mobility (Dirks et al., 2000).

The firm-based human resource system in R&D is further reinforced by the institutional separation between industry and academia, and the tendency among Japanese firms to 'grow' their own PhDs rather than recruiting those trained at universities (Nakayama and Low, 1997; Westney, 1993; Coleman, 1999). Japanese firms have limited experience in conducting basic research and developing external network ties with the academic scientific community. Their strong emphasis on internal tacit knowledge creation has inhibited their ability to exploit locally embedded tacit knowledge in foreign contexts. Moreover, when they set up R&D units in the United Kingdom they are operating in a host institutional environment very different from their domestic one, and have to deal with the tension of cross-societal differences in knowledge creation. The Japanese 'organisational-oriented' model of work organisation cannot be enmeshed easily with the UK 'occupation-oriented' R&D communities without the use of bridging mechanisms. It would have been much more difficult for the Japanese MNCs to build the sort of horizontal networks connecting the company and external R&D communities as observed in the case of the US MNCs. Instead, the Japanese MNCs have sought to use firm-centred communities of practice as mediating mechanisms to support transnational learning. The extension of such communities of practice across geographical and institutional boundaries, blending action at a distance and local practices, provides a social space within which the companies seek to develop relational proximity with local collaborators to support the joint production of knowledge. One can argue that the Japanese companies are substituting the local context with organisational context as the main social space for local learning. The spatial reach of organisational communities of practice is inherently limited, however, because 'you can only work closely with so many people . . .' (Brown and Duguid, 2000b: 143); hence the limited embeddedness of the Japanese MNCs in the local innovation systems.

Within these distinctive national patterns observed in the two sets of MNCs, one can also observe sectoral differences in the case of Japan: the COP strategy appears to have met with greater success in the case of J-ICT than in that of J-Pharma. One possible explanation for this is the relative competitive strength of the two sectors within the Japanese national innovation system, which has influenced their capacity for external learning. There are substantial differences between the ICT and pharmaceutical industries in terms of their domestic R&D capabilities and global competitiveness (Kitschelt, 1991; Odagiri and Goto, 1996). The Japanese ICT and electronics industry has been able to maintain a large domestic R&D capability and sustain its global competitiveness over the last three decades. The J-ICT scientists have basic research experience and appear to be able to engage in 'knowledge trading' with local scientists, which opens up the potential for 'mutual assimilation' in their collaborative ventures. Conversely, the Japanese pharmaceutical industry is younger, and its firms are much smaller in size and have less well-developed domestic R&D capacity. Historically, there has been significant underinvestment in R&D in the pharmaceutical sector. It is apparent from the case study that J-Pharma had difficulties in understanding the basic assumptions of discovery research, which subsequently caused a communication breakdown between JLL and its university partners. Robert Kneller (2003: 1823) notes that there is a tendency for Japanese pharmaceutical companies to seek mainly codified results from foreign partners rather than to engage in ongoing exchange involving tacit as well as codified knowledge. Since a firm's absorptive capacity is a function of its level of prior related knowledge, and those with a greater capacity for internal R&D are also able to contribute more as well as learn extensively from it (Cohen and Levinthal, 1990), it could be argued that J-ICT's relative domestic strength in R&D has enabled it to have the absorptive capacity to appropriate the scientific discoveries made in its overseas units, and also to engage in more effective external learning. By contrast, J-Pharma does not benefit from a strong scientific base, and accordingly is less endowed with the necessary organisational competence to engage in external learning and benefit from the knowledge gained from its overseas research facilities.

The differences in the international competitive strengths of the two companies have also had an impact on their relative ability to exert control over the collaborative relationships and to gain acceptance as 'insiders' in the local R&D communities in order to develop relational proximity. Smith (2005) uses the term 'dominance effects' to describe the uneven nature of economic power in the global economy and the tendency for the economically powerful actor to take the lead in developing organisation and management practices considered to be efficient. One could observe such 'dominance effects' at play in the case of J-ICT. The company is a global leader in a sector in which Japan has gained international competitive strength, and the associated model of organisation and management has been perceived as global 'best practice'. This implies that J-ICT may be perceived as a 'collaborator of choice' by its academic partner, and has been able to gain trust and exert influence over the collaborative relationship. By contrast, Japanese pharmaceutical companies are less well-known players in the global R&D communities and are operating in a sector in which European and US companies command greater international reputation (Thomas, 2001). Thus, it is not surprising that J-Pharma encountered greater difficulties in exerting control over its UK university partner, and that its subsequent attempt to do so has resulted in the alienation of the local scientists. Such sectoral differences in market strength and dominance appear to be less evident in the case of the US firms.

Conclusions

In this chapter the experiences of four MNCs, headquartered in two countries, the United States and Japan, have been contrasted in order to examine the influence of home-based models of organisation and learning on their global R&D and transnational knowledge creation activities. The analysis has focused on how the MNCs adopt different strategies for solving the tacit knowledge transfer problem, and the ways in which home-based models of learning interact with the local host-country context to shape the nature and boundary of the MNCs' transnational learning spaces and their ability to harness local tacit knowledge.

The evidence presented generally supports the 'social embeddedness' thesis of the institutional perspective, namely that home-based institutions provide the basis for the development of MNCs' transnational social spaces, and thus their strategic behaviour and organisational forms will carry on diverging. It shows that home-country societal effects continue to exert a powerful influence on MNCs' mode of operation even in global R&D activities that represent an important strategy of organisational learning. This is clearly illustrated by the US firms' reliance on 'geographical space' as the main site for learning and knowledge creation, as contrasted with the Japanese firms' use of 'organisational space'. These differences are manifestations of the contrasting logics of the US 'professional-oriented' and the Japanese 'organizational-oriented' models of learning in the global arena.

Three further related points are worthy of attention. The first concerns the concept of 'transnational social space'. Morgan's (2001) and Whitley's (1999, 2001) original analysis of this concept focuses narrowly on the internal governance structures and application of firms' existing competencies. It neglects the external dimension of firms' transnational social space and puts too little emphasis on the dynamics of organisational learning within MNCs. My analysis has incorporated the external, local networks of firms. It suggests that external networks and the local embeddedness of the subsidiary R&D units are critical to organisational learning and innovation within MNCs. The innovative behaviour of MNCs cannot be fully understood without taking into account how national institutions shape their transnational learning spaces, encompassing the internal as well as external networks.

The second point concerns the need to revise the notion of 'social embeddedness' to accommodate a role for the host-country context in the explanatory framework. Learning is essentially a social and interactive process rooted in relational proximity, and therefore the ability of an MNC to harness local knowledge is also influenced by the dynamics of interaction between home-based and local institutions. When the institutional frameworks between the home and host regional contexts are similar, as in the case of the United States and United Kingdom, firms may succeed in achieving a high degree of local embeddedness. Contrarily, firms' local embeddedness may be limited and their learning activities circumscribed when operating across major boundaries between distinct national systems, as in the case of Japanese firms in the United Kingdom. An important implication is that the notion of institutional proximity should be taken into account in exploring the subtle interplay between home- and host-country societal effects on the global practices of MNCs.

A final point to note is that the emphasis on national institutional logic underlying the learning and innovative behaviour of MNCs does not imply national uniformity and the absence of sectoral variation. Countries with different institutional arrangements develop and reproduce varied systems of economic organisation, with different social and innovative capabilities, in particular industries and sectors (Sorge, 1991; Biggart and Orru, 1997). The globalisation of innovation may indeed reinforce, and not dismantle, nationally distinctive patterns of innovation (Cantwell, 1995). In this chapter I have illustrated with case studies the social dynamics underpinning this process. Future research should examine in greater detail whether the differences in the global R&D organisation and learning activities of MNCs support their differing innovation trajectories.

Note

Financial support for my research was provided by the European Commission's Directorate General for Science, Research and Development under the Targeted Socio-Economic Research Programme.

References

Almedia, P., J. Song and R. M. Grant (2002) Are firms superior to alliances and markets? An empirical test of cross-border knowledge building, *Organization Science*, 13, 2, 147–61.

Amin, A., and P. Cohendet (2000) Organisational learning and governance through embedded practices, *Journal of Management and Governance*, 4, 93–116.

Asakawa, K. (2001) Organizational tension in international R&D management: the case of Japanese firms, *Research Policy*, 30, 735–57.

Becker, M. C. (2001) Managing dispersed knowledge: organizational problems, managerial strategies, and their effectiveness, *Journal of Management Studies*, 38, 7, 1037–51.

Biggart, N. W., and M. Orru (1997) Societal strategic advantage: institutional structure and path dependence in the automotive and electronics industries of east Asia, in A. Bugra and B. Usdiken (eds.) *State, Market and Organizational Form*, Berlin: Walter de Gruyter, 201–39.

Birkinshaw, J. (1997) Entrepreneurship in multinational corporations: the characteristics of subsidiary initiatives, *Strategic Management Journal*, 18, 3, 207–29.

Blanc, H., and C. Sierra (1999) The internationalisation of R&D by multinationals: a trade-off between external and internal proximity, *Cambridge Journal of Economics*, 23, 187–206.

Boisot, M. H. (1995) *Information Space: A Framework for Learning in Organizations, Institutions and Culture*, London: Routledge.

Bozeman, B., and V. Mangematin (2004) Editor's introduction: Building and deploying scientific and technical human capital, *Research Policy*, 33, 565–8.

Brown, J. S., and P. Duguid (1996) Organizational learning and communities of practice: toward a unified view of working, learning and innovation, in M. Cohen and L. Sproull (eds.) *Organizational Learning*, London: Sage, 58–82.

  (2000a) Mysteries of the region: knowledge dynamics in Silicon Valley, in C. M. Lee, W. F. Miller, M. G. Hancock and H. S. Rowen (eds.) *The Silicon Valley Edge: A Habitat for Innovation and Entrepreneurship*, Stanford, CA: Stanford University Press, 16–39.

  (2000b) *The Social Life of Information*, Boston: Harvard Business School Press.

Cantwell, J. A. (1995) The globalisation of technology: what remains of the product cycle model?, *Cambridge Journal of Economics*, 19, 155–74.

Chiesa, V. (1999) 'Technology development control styles in multinational corporations: a case study', *Journal of Engineering and Technology Management*, 16: 191–206.

Chikudate, N. (1999) Generating reflexivity from partnership formation: a phenomenological reasoning on the partnership between a Japanese pharmaceutical corporation and Western laboratories, *Journal of Applied Behavioral Science*, 35, 3, 287–305.

Child, J., D. Faulkner and R. Pitkethley (2000). Foreign direct investment in the UK 1985–1994: the impact of domestic management practice, *Journal of Management Studies*, 37, 141–66.

Cohen, S. S., and G. Fields (1999) Social capital and capital gains in Silicon Valley, *California Management Review*, 41, 2, 108–30.

Cohen, W. M., and D. A. Levinthal (1990) Absorptive capacity: a new perspective of learning and innovation, *Administrative Science Quarterly*, 35, 128–52.

Coleman, S. (1999) *Japanese Science: From the Inside*, London: Routledge.

Cramton, C. D. (2001) The mutual knowledge problem and its consequences for dispersed collaboration, *Organization Science*, 12, 3, 346–71.

Dirks, D., M. Hammert, J. Legewie, H. Meyer-Ohle and F. Waldenberger (2000) The Japanese employment system in transition, *International Business Review*, 9, 525–53.

Doremus, P. N., W. W. Keller, L. W. Pauley and S. Reich (1998) *The Myth of the Global Corporation*, Princeton, NJ: Princeton University Press.

Dunning, J. H., and C. Wymbs (1999) The geographical sourcing of technology-based assets by multinational enterprises, in D. Archibugi, J. Howells and J. Michie (eds.)

Innovation Policy in a Global Economy, Cambridge: Cambridge University Press, 184–224.

Dyer, J. H., and K. Nobeoka (2000) Creating and managing a high-performance knowledge-sharing network: the Toyota case, *Strategic Management Journal*, 21, 345–67.

Financial Times (1990) Japanese put pounds 50 m into university research, *Financial Times*, 12 September.

Finegold, D. (1999) Creating self-sustaining high-skill ecosystems, *Oxford Review of Economic Policy*, 15, 1, 60–81.

Florida, R. (1997) The globalization of R&D: results of a survey of foreign-affiliated R&D laboratories in the USA, *Research Policy*, 26, 85–103.

Foss, N., and T. Pedersen (2003) *The MNC as a Knowledge Structure: The Role of Knowledge Sources and Organisational Instruments in MNC Knowledge Management*, Working Paper no. 03–09, Danish Research Unit for Industrial Dynamics, Aalborg University.

Frost, T. S. (2001) The geographic sources of foreign subsidiaries' innovations, *Strategic Management Journal*, 22, 101–23.

Frost, T. S., J. M. Birkinshaw and P. S. Ensign (2002) Centres of excellence in multinational corporations, *Strategic Management Journal*, 23, 997–1018.

Frost, T. S., and C. Zhou (2000) The geography of foreign R&D within a host country, *International Studies of Management and Organization*, 30, 2, 10–43.

Gassman, O., and M. von Zedwitz (1999) New concepts and trends in international R&D organization, *Research Policy*, 28, 231–50.

Gertler, M. S. (2003) Tacit knowledge and the economic geography of context, or the undefinable tacitness of being (there), *Journal of Economic Geography*, 3, 75–99.

Gertler, M. S., D. A. Wolfe and D. Garkut (2000) No place like home? The embeddedness of innovation in a regional economy, *Review of International Political Economy*, 7, 4, 688–718.

Gerybadze, A., and G. Reger (1999) Globalization of R&D: recent changes in the management of innovation in transnational corporations, *Research Policy*, 28, 251–74.

Granstrand, O. (1999) Internationalization of corporate R&D: a study of Japanese and Swedish corporations, *Research Policy*, 28, 275–302.

Gupta, A. K., and V. Govindarajan (2000) Knowledge flows within multinational corporations, *Strategic Management Journal*, 21, 473–96.

Hage, J., and J. R. Hollingsworth (2000) A strategy for the analysis of idea innovation networks and institutions, *Organization Studies*, 21, 5, 971–1004.

Hane, G. (1999) Comparing university–industry linkages in the United States and Japan, in L. M. Branscomb, F. Kodama and R. Florida (eds.) *University–Industry Linkages in Japan and the United States*, Cambridge, MA: MIT Press, 20–61.

Hollingsworth, J. R. (2000) Doing institutional analysis: implications for the study of innovations, *Review of International Political Economy*, 7, 4, 595–644.

Howells, J. (1990) The internationalization of R&D and the development of global research networks, *Regional Studies*, 24, 6, 495–512.

(2002) Tacit knowledge, innovation and economic geography, *Urban Studies*, 39, 5/6, 871–84.

Kenney, M., and R. Florida (1993). *Beyond Mass Production: The Japanese System and Its Transfer to the US*, Oxford: Oxford University Press.

Kitschelt, H. (1991) Industrial governance structures, innovation strategies, and the case of Japan: sectoral or cross-national comparative analysis, *International Organization*, 45, 4, 454–93.

Kneller, R. (2003) Autarkic drug discovery in Japanese pharmaceutical companies: insights into national differences in industrial innovation, *Research Policy*, 32, 1805–27.

Kogut, B., and U. Zander (1993) Knowledge of the firm and the evolutionary theory of the multinational corporation, *Journal of International Business Studies*, 24, 4, 625–46.

(1995) Knowledge, market failure and the multinational enterprise: a reply, *Journal of International Business Studies*, 26, 2, 417–26.

Kuemmerle, W. (1997) Building effective R&D capabilities abroad, *Harvard Business Review*, 75, 2, 61–70.

(1999a) Foreign direct investment in industrial research in the pharmaceutical and electronics industries: results from a survey of multinational firms, *Research Policy*, 28, 179–93.

(1999b) The drivers of foreign direct investment into research and development: an empirical investigation, *Journal of International Business Studies*, 30, 1, 1–25.

Lam, A. (1996) Engineers, management and work organization: a comparative analysis of engineers' work roles in British and Japanese electronics firms, *Journal of Management Studies*, 33, 2, 183–212.

(1997) Embedded firms, embedded knowledge: problems of collaboration and knowledge transfer in global cooperative ventures, *Organization Studies*, 18, 6, 973–96.

(2000) Tacit knowledge, organizational learning and societal institutions: an integrated framework, *Organizational Studies*, 21, 3, 487–513.

(2002) Alternative societal models of learning and innovation in the knowledge economy, *International Social Science Journal*, 171, 67–82.

Lam, A., and B.-A. Lundvall (2000) Innovation policy and knowledge management in the learning economy: the interplay between firm strategies and national systems of competence building and innovation, paper presented at the OECD High Level Forum on Knowledge Management, Ottawa, 21–2 September.

Lawson, C., and E. Lorenz (1999) Collective learning, tacit knowledge and regional innovative capacity, *Regional Studies*, 33, 305–25.

Lehrer, M., and K. Asakawa (2002) Offshore knowledge incubation: the 'third path' for embedding R&D labs in foreign systems of innovation, *Journal of World Business*, 37, 297–306.

(2003) Managing intersecting R&D social communities: a comparative study of European 'knowledge incubators' in Japanese and American firms, *Organization Studies*, 24, 5, 771–92.

Lundvall, B.-A. (1992) *National Systems of Innovation: Towards a Theory of Innovation and Interactive Learning*, London: Pinter.

Mahroum, S. (2000) Scientists and global spaces, *Technology in Society*, 22, 513–23.

Martin, X., and R. Salomon (2003a) Knowledge transfer capacity and its implications for the theory of the multinational corporation, *Journal of International Business Studies*, 34, 4, 356–74.

(2003b) Tacitness, learning and international expansion: a study of foreign direct investment in a knowledge-intensive industry, *Organization Science*, 14, 3, 207–311.

Maskell, P., and A. Malmberg (1999), Localised learning and industrial competitiveness, *Cambridge Journal of Economics*, 23, 167–86.

Mendez, A. (2003) The coordination of globalized R&D activities through project teams organization: an exploratory empirical study, *Journal of World Business*, 38, 96–109.

Methé, D. T. (1995) Basic research in Japanese electronic companies: an attempt at establishing new organizational routines, in J. K. Liker, J. E. Ettlie and J. C. Campbell (eds.) *Engineered in Japan: Japanese Technology Management Practices*, New York: Oxford University Press, 17–39.

Methé, D. T., and J. D. Penner-Hahn (1999) Globalization of pharmaceutical research and development in Japanese companies: organizational learning and the parent–subsidiary relationship, in S. L. Beechler and A. Bird (eds.) *Japanese Multinationals Abroad: Individual and Organizational Learning*, New York: Oxford University Press, 191–210.

Meyer-Krahmer, F., and G. Reger (1999) New perspectives on the innovation strategies of multinational enterprises: lessons for technology policy in Europe, *Research Policy*, 28, 751–76.

Morgan, G. (2001) The multinational firm, in G. Morgan, P. H. Kristensen and R. Whitley (eds.) *The Multinational Firm: Organizing across Institutional and National Divides*, Oxford: Oxford University Press, 1–24.

Mowery, D. C., and N. Rosenberg (1993) The US national innovation system, in R. R. Nelson (ed.). *National Innovation Systems: A Comparative Analysis*, Oxford: Oxford University Press, 29–75.

Murray, F. (2004) The role of academic inventors in entrepreneurial firms: sharing the laboratory life, *Research Policy*, 33, 643–59.

Nakayama, S., and M. F. Low (1997). The research function of universities in Japan, *Higher Education*, 34, 245–58.

Nelson, R. R. (1993). *National Innovation Systems: A Comparative Analysis*, Oxford: Oxford University Press.

Nohria, N., and S. Ghoshal (1997) *The Differentiated Network: Organizing Multinational Corporations for Value Creation*, San Francisco: Jossey-Bass.

Nonaka, I., and H. Takeuchi (1995) *The Knowledge-creating Company*, Oxford: Oxford University Press.

Odagiri, H., and A. Goto (1996) *Technology and Industrial Development in Japan*, Oxford: Clarendon Press.

Orlikowski, W. J. (2002) Knowing in practice: enacting a collective capability in distributed organization, *Organization Science*, 13, 3, 249–73.

Pauly, L. W., and S. Reich (1997) National structures and multinational corporate behaviour: enduring differences in the age of globalization, *International Organization*, 51, 1, 1–30.

Pavitt, P., and P. Patel (1999) Global corporations and national systems of innovation, in D. Archibugi, J. Howells and J. Michie (eds.) *Innovation Policy in a Global Economy*, Cambridge: Cambridge University Press, 94–119.

Pearce, R., and M. Papanastassiou (1999) Overseas R&D and the strategic evolution of MNCs: evidence from laboratories in the UK, *Research Policy*, 28, 23–41.

Polanyi, M. (1958) *Personal Knowledge: Towards a Post-Critical Philosophy*, London: Routledge and Kegan Paul.

(1966) *The Tacit Dimension*, New York: Doubleday.

Reger, G. (1999) How R&D is coordinated in Japanese and European multinationals, *R&D Management*, 29, 1, 71–85.

Roehl, T., W. Mitchell and R. J. Slattery (1995) The growth of R&D investment and organizational changes by Japanese pharmaceutical firms, 1975–1993, in J. K. Liker, J. E. Ettie and J. C. Campbell (eds.) *Engineered in Japan: Japanese Technology Management Practices*, New York: Oxford University Press, 40–69.

Saxenian, A. (1994) *Regional Advantage: Competition and Cooperation in Silicon Valley and Route 128*, Cambridge, MA: Harvard University Press.

  (1996) Beyond boundaries: open labour markets and learning in the Silicon Valley, in M. B. Arthur and D. M. Rousseau (eds.) *The Boundaryless Career: A New Employment Principle for a New Organizational Era*, New York: Oxford University Press, 23–39.

Smith, C. (2005) Beyond convergence and divergence: explaining variations in organizational practices and forms, in S. Ackroyd, R. Batt, P. Thompson and P. S. Tolbert (eds.) *The Oxford Handbook of Work and Organization*, Oxford: Oxford University Press, 602–25.

Sole, D., and A. Edmondson (2002) Situated knowledge and learning in dispersed teams, *British Journal of Management*, 13, S17–S34.

Sorge, A. (1991) Strategic fit and the societal effect: interpreting cross-national comparisons of technology, organization and human resources, *Organization Studies*, 12, 2, 161–90.

Subramaniam, M., and N. Venkatraman (2001) Determinants of transnational new product development capability: testing the influence of transferring and deploying tacit overseas knowledge, *Strategic Management Journal*, 22, 359–78.

Teece, D. J. (1977) Technology transfer by multinational corporations: the resource cost of transferring technological know-how, *Economic Journal*, 87, 242–61.

  (1981) The market for know-how and the efficient international transfer of technology, *Annals of the American Academy of Political and Social Science*, 458, 81–96.

Thomas, L. G. (2001) *The Japanese Pharmaceutical Industry*, Cheltenham: Edward Elgar.

Turner, L., D. Ray and T. Hayward (1997) *The British Research of Japanese Companies*, London: Japan/Anglo-Japanese Economic Institute.

Uzzi, B. (1997) Social structure and competition in interfirm networks: the paradox of embeddedness, *Administrative Science Quarterly*, 42, 35–67.

Westney, D. E. (1993) Country patterns in R&D organization: the United States and Japan, in B. Kogut (ed.) *Country Competitiveness and the Organizing of Work*, New York: Oxford University Press, 36–53.

  (1999) Changing perspectives on the organization of Japanese multinational companies, in S. L. Beechler and A. Bird (eds.) *Japanese Multinationals Abroad: Individual and Organizational Learning*, New York: Oxford University Press, 11–29.

Whitley, R. (1999) *Divergent Capitalisms: The Social Structuring and Change of Business Systems*, Oxford: Oxford University Press.

  (2000) The institutional structuring of innovation strategies: business systems, firm types and patterns of technical change in different market economies, *Organization Studies*, 21, 5, 855–86.

  (2001) How and why are international firms different? The consequences of cross-border managerial coordination for firm characteristics and behaviour, in G. Morgan, P. H. Kristensen and R. Whitley (eds.) *The Multinational Firm: Organizing across Institutional and National Divides*, Oxford: Oxford University Press, 27–68.

Zanfei, A. (2000) Transnational firms and the changing organization of innovation activities, *Cambridge Journal of Economics*, 24, 515–42.

Zucker, L. G., M. R. Darby and J. S. Armstrong (2002) Commercializing knowledge: university science, knowledge capture, and firm performance in biotechnology, *Management Science*, 48, 1, 138–53.

Zucker, L. G., M. R. Darby and M. Torero (2002) Labor mobility from academe to commerce, *Journal of Labor Economics*, 20, 3, 629–60.

Part IV

The Search for Global Standards

Preface: Dominance, best practice and globalisation

Chris Smith

The chapters in this section examine the ideas of dominance and best practice, the tendency for prescriptions for ways of working or organising business to emerge as pre-eminent standards that all organisations should follow because they offer the universal benefit of superior performance. The idea of 'dominance' is employed within the SSD framework to check two tendencies within the bipolar thinking around convergence and divergence between countries.

First, within the divergence camp is the idea that societies face each other with equivalence: equally efficient and effective ways of organising. If this were the case, progress and change would be difficult to explain. By introducing the idea of 'dominance' such equality is rejected; instead, societies face each other with both difference and relative strengths, and some societies evolve techniques or practices that are (for a period) celebrated as 'modern', 'superior' or 'best practice'. These are paraded by consultants and academics as new paradigms or concepts for organising work and management, whether scientific management, just-in-time production or the flexible firm. The problem with a simple equivalence position – the United Kingdom and France have different ways of doing business – is that it ignores a ranking process evident at the system level: capitalist competition naturally places companies (and countries) against each other, and so the system part of the SSD model introduces inequality.

Furthermore, from a variety of capitalism or societal effects approach, one cannot explain diversity as producing diffusion of ideas from one society to another and an appetite for new ideas about management or working. If all is 'functionally equivalent' competition between equally effective and efficient societies, change can, logically, be only internal or endogenous. Clearly, however, ideas developed in one country or company are held up as 'models' for other countries to emulate, and are actively diffused by companies and agents across societies. In this sense societies do not simply face each other as isolated, integral actors. One cannot explain diffusion from variety, therefore one needs to introduce some mechanism for saying – symbolically as much as materially – how capitalist societies face each other as non-equals, and some evolve what are deemed 'modern', 'best' or 'leading' ways of doing things that others seek to emulate, and agents (such as academics and consultants) promote and diffuse as ideas/practices the genesis of which lies in one society but the distribution of which is more widespread.

Second, dominance is important because novel developments remain unsettled, with lead societies or companies changing over time, so the idea of dominance challenges the standardisation and sameness assumptions within the idea of convergence or globalisation, which view the world of work as becoming permanently standardised and uniform. The rotational element is partially tied to the economic performance of different capitalist economies, but is also based on experimentation with ways of working and managing that come from the separation of capital (system effects) and countries (societal effects). Dominance effects are different from the unevenness at the system level. There is also a tendency, however, for the three effects to get mixed up, for a country to be seen as a dominant case; and the reverse, for country effects to be transmuted into system effects – part of what it is to be capitalist at any one time. In this sense, Taylorism and Fordism have been used to characterise a new 'phase of capitalist development' and not simply the ideas or practices of particular individuals or firms from one particular society. Dominance is temporary and it has a lot of myth or symbolic capital attached to it, because agents active in knowledge competition (academics, consultants, etc.) are always looking for new ideas/techniques/paradigms to sell to business/society, and hype or rhetorical claims form part of this marketing of ideas. Academics construct and deconstruct all the time. One needs to be able to get theoretically from dominance to system and to society – and treat them as connected.

The chapters in this section explore different types of best or dominant practices and their interaction with society- and system-level considerations. Alan Pilkington, in chapter 12, offers a 'historical' account of the appeal of 'Japanisation' in the 1980s and early 1990s, and why the message of a single method of manufacturing was a particular one (the Toyota story) and not common to other Japanese firms, and certainly not appropriate as a universal panacea for non-Japanese players.

The concept of dominance within the SSD model explains the appeal of all things Japanese during the 1980s and the decontextualisation of Japanese practices/history through social scientists and management gurus seeking to champion a new story and one message to sell to the world. Japanese practices moved from being societally bounded to having global reach as orders for Japanese products grew (trade), but, more importantly, Japanese TNCs moved out of Japan to set up production operations internationally. This shift from societal message to dominant message reflects the cyclical upswing in the Japanese economy relative to the United States and Europe, which produced a search for an explanation of success that was learnable or movable, and not simply connected to Japanese territory. The invention of the concept of 'lean production' as a global panacea occurred through a process of abstraction and conceptualisation, but it reached a willing audience only because of Japanese economic success (a temporary 'dominance'), and the sense in which not to adopt 'lean' would be irrational. Firms that adopt such best practices are promised a substantial improvement in performance, but, as the case studies in the chapter show, this was largely illusionary in the case of UK companies in the car industry.

Commentators have noted the lack of correlation between imitation and competitive advantage, but the reasons for this failure have not been so adequately explored. Pilkington uses evidence from the United Kingdom's automobile industry to illustrate the impact of 'Japanisation' and attempts to copy 'best practice'. The chapter argues that business strategy, rather being influenced by 'best practice' or common fads, ought to fit within the firm's strategic capabilities, particular histories and product markets. In other words, manufacturing strategy should follow a contingency road more than a best-practice one. Drawing on the author's field studies in the UK automobile industry, this chapter suggests that managers should not try dogmatically to impose such supposed 'best practices' but, instead, should concentrate on the development of their specific strategic competencies and the alignment of manufacturing with corporate strategy.

The extensive debate on Japanisation in the West has followed a pathway of learning or diffusion from a new, apparently superior model or recipe to other countries – the practice carried through the TNC as a boundary-spanning agency. Chapter 13, by Michael Gold, is not about the diffusion of one dominant model; neither is it about knowledge transfer through a boundary-spanning agency such as the TNC. It is, rather, about learning through multiple sources, from low-level state functionaries to multi-country contexts. Gold analyses the diffusion of active labour market policies (ALMP) across the member states of the European Union as a result of peer review processes designed to promote the transfer of 'good practice'. Dominance, power and a single standard are absent – hence the case presents a rather diffuse and complex set of outcomes and processes, because there does not exist a single template (best practice or dominant model), neither is there a powerful agency of diffusion, such as a TNC.

Analytically, the chapter argues for logic of 'fit', or appropriateness, with ideas that sit comfortably within another cultural or institutional context more likely to be admired if not straightforwardly adopted. Therefore, Gold writes against the idea of 'best practice' (the notion that a good idea/practice will automatically be diffused). He suggests instead that what gets taken up is politically expedient – accepting an idea if it brings EU funding, for example – as well as using what is popular/fashionable – the idea that some practices appear dominant because they are trendy or 'flavour of the month', a lot of borrowing being superficial and based on trend or isomorphism. Finally, Gold looks at what is culturally/institutionally appropriate – the fit argument. He deconstructs the concept of 'transfer' into its elements – such as policy goals, content, instruments and so on – and then demonstrates the kinds of constraints that operate at different levels. For example, labour market goals (such as employment rate targets) are comparatively easy to transfer. The content and instruments of policies that perform well in one country may, however, encounter a variety of constraints if transfer is attempted (including administrative, institutional, legal and cultural constraints, amongst many others). The chapter concludes that 'organisational learning' is a fruitful framework for analysing the processes involved in peer review, though politicians and national administrations are generally concerned more with the public relations effects of 'good' or 'bad' recommendations from the European Commission than with genuine longer-term opportunities for learning.

Chapter 14, by Chris Hackley and Amy Rungpaka Tiwsakul, explores the role of advertising agencies as vehicles for sustaining global 'brands', the presence of which is a key element of the notion of globalisation. Advertising agencies act as important nodes in the system of organisational communication that sustain brands as internationally recognised entities. Promoting the global is carried out through some quite specific organisational forms, however, and the worldwide influence of brand advertising and marketing communication is realised by means of the culturally specific management practices of international advertising agencies. This chapter draws on empirical studies of the work processes of advertising management in the United Kingdom, United States and Thailand to explore the intracultural specificity that underlies and sustains the notion of the cross-cultural brand.

Advertising management is a far from a unified field. As long as corporations have sought to impose models of bureaucratic efficiency on their ad agencies, the agencies have found ways to circumvent and undermine these controls to realize their 'creative' ideal. Agency life is typically fraught with conflict between client and account team, creative and account management, creative and research: and between account teams and their agencies. Such tensions are resolved in varied ways in different agencies, both within and between cultures, and hence a common nonconformist tendency seen in ad agencies may nevertheless be translated in different ways in different contexts. The global role of advertising agencies since the turn of the last century has been to legitimise corporatism and clear an ideological path for a lifestyle of consumption (Marchand, 1985, 1998). They have drawn on art, aesthetics and poetic forms of expression to create inspiring visions of consumption, all the while simultaneously satisfying the clients' mechanistic criteria of business accountability. Ad agencies are often thought to be the very antithesis of sober, rational business practice, while marketing is thought of as the organisational function that unites consumer need and organisational innovation. It can be argued, however, that the chief way in which marketing gives consumers 'what we want' is in a symbolic sense, our imagined 'need' realised in the promotional communication that valorises manufactured objects by drawing on a parasitic relation with non-consumer culture (McCracken, 1986). This global pattern is filtered through particular agencies within their local cultural context, which is the topic of interest in this chapter.

Arguably, then, advertising agencies' internal management practices are central to the sustenance of global consumer culture. One message emerging from recent studies is that Theodore Levitt's (1983) notion of the 'globalized' market, to be realised, has to rest on ad agencies' understanding of the cultural specificity of consumption and communicative practice. The authors observe a tendency for dominant players (US and UK advertising agencies' formats) to get imposed on other countries – Thai advertising has been heavily influenced by the US model, with US agencies establishing their working methods (hierarchical, client-driven) in their Thai subsidiaries, for example. Nevertheless, Hackley and Tiwsakul conclude, on the basis of fieldwork in the different advertising agencies, that local cultures do get reflected through ad agencies, and so Thai advertising does reflect Thai culture. Hence 'the dominance of the Western management values of global communications conglomerates on Thai agency branches was, it seems, contested by and mediated through the national cultural mores and practices that Thai consumers and professionals bring to the production, and the consumption, of advertising'.

Axel Haunschild, Dirk Matten and Lutz Preuss, writing in chapter 15, explore for the first time the relationship between organised labour and corporate social responsibility within Europe as CSR increasingly becomes embraced by industry on the Continent. Being largely a concept embedded in Anglo-American capitalism, however, with its emphasis on voluntary action rather than regulation, the transfer of CSR to the European setting has resulted in some tensions. A range of activities that may fall under CSR in the United States, such as the corporate provision of health care or education, have mostly in Europe been part of the social institutional framework (Matten and Moon, 2005). Additionally, the corporate discretion of CSR is at odds with the more regulated frameworks in many European nations, which grant employees and trade unions a well-defined and codified scope to influence corporate decision-making (Bamber, Lansbury and Wailes, 2004; Dobbin and Boychuk, 1999; Marsden, 1999). The impact of CSR on organised labour in Europe is, accordingly, one of the most interesting examples of the impact an ascendant archetype from a dominant society can have on elements of the national business systems of other countries.

The chapter teases out the tensions between system effects, societal effects and dominance effects as applied through three case studies. Generic (system-wide) trends in capitalism – the increased internationalisation of capital; the growing power of TNCs and the reduced power of nation states; increased problems of institutional fragmentation between subsidiaries of TNCs – put policies that aim to link together the social conditions of workers internationally on the agenda. Second, these policies, such as CSR, originate in a particular type of capitalist society and are received in divergent types of capitalist society. In other words, both home- and host-country 'societal effects' are important for the diffusion and reception of CSR. Third, globally speaking, one version of CSR is hegemonic or dominant, and this is associated with the world's dominant economic power that, relative to other economic forces (in Asia or Europe), is currently 'top dog'. This has symbolic and real effects, and one of the drivers of CSR in its current version is explained by this association between one version of CSR (American) with the hegemonic role this power has in the world – hence the 'dominance effect'.

The authors note that, across the Continent, a number of distinct union positions on CSR can be identified. Such differences can be explained by two factors: on the one hand, by the relative strength of the union, which in turn is significantly influenced by the national industrial relations framework; on the other hand, a union position on CSR is shaped by the degree to which the respective industry or national economy is exposed to the pressures of global markets. Hence, unions that are in a relatively weak position in rather open national economies – such as GMB in the United Kingdom – see CSR predominantly as a threat, as transferring yet more power and discretion to managers. By contrast, unions that enjoy a relatively strong position in traditionally corporatist countries – such as LO in Denmark – claim for themselves to be drivers of CSR. An altogether different situation exists in eastern Europe, where unions lack the legitimacy and influence to shape the emerging CSR agenda.

CSR is clearly a novel challenge for unions in Europe. Has the rise of this notion, which is becoming internationally dominant, meant that we see a convergence of union positions across Europe, however? One indicator for such potential convergence is the general union insistence that the voluntary nature of CSR must not mean a replacement of legally codified employee rights. The full answer, however, is more complex, as union positions on and responses to CSR differ not only between national industrial relations frameworks but also within countries, depending on the strength of the individual unions. In any event, the conclusion is justified that unions in Europe are adapting themselves to the changing circumstances, and also aim to adapt the US concept of CSR to their requirements. In other words, the repackaging of a national practice – CSR – of a dominant nation – the United States – into apparently neutral requirements to be adopted in other national settings (Smith, 2005) does not proceed without resistance to and adaptation of the dominant practice.

In chapter 16, the final chapter, Fiona Moore explores the tensions between 'national' and 'international' identities within MNCs. Taking the case of two German MNCs, one a bank and one an automobile manufacturer, and using Erving Goffman's approach to strategic self-presentation, Moore uses ethnographic research to examine how each attempts to be seen less as localised 'German' companies and more as globalised 'international' companies. The result not only has implications for the dominance effect and best practice debates but also calls into question the concept of 'culture management', and whether it is in fact possible for companies to remake their own image and/or internal culture according to their needs. The 'drivers' of internationalism and 'diluters' of national identity within corporations are the product market, the nature of the clients/customers and ownership. The contrast between the bank and the manufacturing company highlights different contingencies, and these in turn influence whether company or territory (national or international) informed the discourse on identity in the groups of managers interviewed and observed. For the bank, client and markets are more in Germany, and this tie reinforces Germanness; for the car firm, the product focus and global market for these means that Germany is only another market amongst others. In this way Moore shows that, at times, nationality is a stereotype, at others the basis of policy initiatives, at others a source of personnel, at others a source of particular expertise and at others the origins and substantive base of the organisation. Nationality is therefore partially negotiated, partially determined. The bank chose to identify itself as German with an international focus, and the automobile manufacturer to identify itself more as an international company with German roots. These different forms of identification relate to the company's history, strategy and product, and the nature of relations between branch and head office, as well as events that have had an impact on the company (mergers, restructuring programmes and so forth).

References

Bamber, G., R. Lansbury and N. Wailes (eds.) (2004) *International and Comparative Employment Relations* (4th edn.), London: Sage.

Dobbin, F., and T. Boychuk (1999) National employment systems and job autonomy: why job autonomy is high in the Nordic countries and low in the United States, Canada, and Australia, *Organization Studies*, 20, 257–91.

Levitt, T. (1983) The globalization of markets, *Harvard Business Review*, 61, 3, 92–107.

McCracken, G. (1986) Culture and consumption: a theoretical account of the structure and movement of the cultural meaning of consumer goods, *Journal of Consumer Research*, 13, 1, 71–84.

Marchand, R. (1985) *Advertising and the American Dream: Making Way for Modernity 1920–1940*, Los Angeles: University of California Press.

(1998) *Creating the Corporate Soul: The Rise of Public Relations and Corporate Imagery in American Big Business*, Los Angeles: University of California Press.

Marsden, D. (1999) *A Theory of Employment Systems: Micro-foundations of Societal Diversity*, Oxford: Oxford University Press.

Matten, D., and J. Moon (2005) A conceptual framework for understanding CSR, in A. Habisch, J. Jonker, M. Wegner and R. Schmidpeter (eds.) *Corporate Social Responsibility across Europe*, Berlin: Springer, 339–60.

Smith, C. (2005) Beyond convergence and divergence: explaining variations in organizational practices and forms, in S. Ackroyd, R. Batt, P. Thompson and P. S. Tolbert (eds.) *The Oxford Handbook of Work and Organization*, Oxford: Oxford University Press, 602–25.

12 The unravelling of manufacturing best-practice strategies

Alan Pilkington

Introduction

Despite the emergence of the manufacturing strategy concept over thirty years ago (Skinner, 1969), there is still a recurrent trend in manufacturing management towards the adoption of best practices (Pilkington, 1998, 1999). The 'Japanisation' of production systems, in particular, was seen as a key means of generating industrial success in the 1980s and 1990s. Japanese practices and the resulting 'lean' mantra were moved from being societally bounded to having global reach, as Japanese products spread and Japanese TNCs moved out of Japan to set up production operations internationally. This shift mirrored the cyclical upswing in the Japanese economy relative to America and Europe, and produced a search for an explanation of success that was learnable and/or movable and not simply connected to Japanese territory.

This chapter explores the validity of a single lean system through the identification of the different operating methods found in Japanese car manufacturers during the period, and so challenges the notion and value of the best-practice approach. Data from US and UK industry show a lack of advancement from adopting Japanisation and so following the best-practice route. The transition of practices from Japan can be viewed as a transfer of structurally bounded strategies into a dominant system, and, in essence, the invention of 'lean' is a process of abstraction and conceptualisation that is able to reach a willing audience largely because of Japanese economic success. The economic dominance of Japan at the time heightened the appeal and generated a sense in which not to adopt 'lean' would be irrational. Evidence from the early adopters contradicts the often blanket assertions concerning leanness that are still often repeated today, however (Schlie and Yip, 2000; Womack and Jones, 1996; Nicholas and Soni, 2006; Åhlström, 1998; Liker,

2003). In reflection this analysis suggests that managers should concentrate on strategic competences and aligning manufacturing with corporate strategy, which does not always mean a lean approach.

Strategy and manufacturing divergence

The development of different production systems is one area of management studies that, traditionally, has followed practice more closely than others, with a succession of popular approaches being reported and analysed in detail. Unfortunately, manufacturing management has repeatedly chosen to follow the latest approach as a panacea (Wheelwright and Bowen, 1996) without considering its place in the firm's business strategy (Pilkington, 1998, 1999). There has been a lack of integration of manufacturing management with the growing complexity and acceptance by practitioners of business-level strategy concepts such as generic strategies (Porter, 1980) and core competencies (Prahalad and Hamel, 1990). Strategic approaches to manufacturing management have been missing in the models of just-in-time production (Schonberger, 1982), lean production (Womack, Jones and Roos, 1990), flexible manufacturing (Goldhar and Jelinek, 1983; Meredith, 1987) and total quality management (Hall, 1987). This is despite the number of researchers claiming the need to integrate manufacturing as a strategic weapon into corporate strategy (Skinner, 1969; Hill, 1985; Buffa, 1984; Cohen and Zysman, 1987; Hayes and Wheelwright, 1984). The manufacturing management approaches have been proclaimed as best practice, or advanced management techniques (AMTs), and assumed by manufacturing managers to generate competitive advantage (Skinner, 1996) irrespective of the corporate strategy of the firm into which they have been introduced. Some conceptual models have been made to explore the linkages between and among manufacturing strategy, business strategy and performance (Kotha and Orne, 1989; Nemetz and Fry, 1988; Parthasarty and Sethi, 1992; Ward, Bickford and Leong, 1996), but they are stylised and general without addressing the specific processes at work in the development of AMTs and the reasons for manufacturing management techniques to develop out of kilter with corporate strategy. In large part, this separation of manufacturing from the general business-level models is believed to have been as a result of the attractiveness of best-practice routes in which a particular operating method (normally Japanese and car manufacturing in origin) appears to provide competitive advantage to one firm and so is appropriated by many others.

This chapter explores the way that manufacturing managers and research-ers have remained embedded in a best-practice mode despite its rejection by the general strategy literature as lacking creativity and leverage. It is based on original research by the author reported in greater depth elsewhere (Pilkington, 1998, 1999). The development of manufacturing is analysed by deconstructing the dominant theme of the 1990s – Japanese lean production. A central theme is the tension between the suggested best-practice strategy and the practices of the firms taken as exemplars. In essence, I show that Japanese car manufacturers, the source of many of the techniques, do not follow the strategy of best practice themselves. Given this problem, it is important to assess how successful the Japanese manufacturing approach has been in transforming manufacturing industry in the United Kingdom and United States.

Japan and best practices

In manufacturing management the 1980s were dominated by researchers analysing the AMTs of newly competitive Japanese firms in an attempt to identify the key to their success. As table 12.1 shows, the dramatic rise of the Japanese car industry from small beginnings to overtake the much larger United States as the world's leading manufacturer of cars was worthy of investigation. The examination of the new leaders led to the isolation of particular Japanese operating methods, however, and the marketing to man-agers of individual approaches such as JIT and TQM. The 1990s saw challenges

Table 12.1 International car production, 1950–90

	Japan	United States	United Kingdom	France	Italy
1950	1,594	6,665,863	522,515	257,292	101,310
1955	20,268	7,920,186	897,560	561,465	230,978
1960	165,094	6,674,796	1,352,728	1,175,301	595,907
1965	969,176	9,305,561	1,722,045	1,423,365	1,103,932
1970	3,178,708	6,550,203	1,640,966	2,458,038	1,719,715
1975	4,568,120	6,717,177	1,267,695	2,546,154	1,348,544
1980	7,038,108	6,375,506	923,744	2,938,581	1,445,221
1985	7,646,816	8,184,821	1,047,973	2,632,366	1,389,156
1990	9,947,972	6,077,449	1,295,611	3,294,815	1,874,672

Source: Society of Motor Manufacturers and Traders (1993: 54).

to the approach of promoting a single trait of Japanese firms as the key to manufacturing supremacy, as it was argued that the examples of faltering firms trying to adopt Japanese practices had failed because the individual techniques were not independent and required the support of the others for successful implementation. For example, it is now rare to find discussion of JIT in isolation from TQM (Goyal and Deshmukh, 1992; Smith *et al.*, 1994), and the development and inclusion of Japanese HRM practices in the simultaneous engineering model of product development (Voss and Winch, 1996).

This reconstruction of the Japanese manufacturing elements has gone even further, and they are now often considered under one banner with a range of titles, though they are most widely known as *lean production* (Krafcik, 1988). The power of the argument, that the Japanese had a better way of manufacturing and that everyone should copy it or their firms would fail, was too strong for managers to resist. Where did these best-practice models come from, however, and why was the direct and causative link to corporate strategy lost? This rush to follow 'one best way' was occurring at the time when corporate strategy was discounting such strategy as plan approaches (Mintzberg and Miller, 1988), and even the notion of contingency or generic approaches, were being challenged by developments of competency and capability (Kay, 1993). How did lean production get such a tight hold on the collective manufacturing view, and why was the strategy element ignored? To consider this it is necessary to dissect the background and development of the dominant lean production concept.

Examining lean production

The study by the International Motor Vehicle Programme (IMVP) of the world automobile industry was instrumental in promoting the idea of leanness, largely through the book *The Machine that Changed the World* (Womack, Jones and Roos, 1990). This text, and several others from the project group (Clark and Fujimoto, 1991; Lamming, 1993), exposed to the world the idea that Japanese car manufacturers had developed a new form of production, or a generic package of operating methods, that was as a whole more efficient than existing ideas of mass production. Lean production became the model for 1990s manufacturing, and many managers extended their existing Japan-inspired JIT and TQM programmes accordingly. Similarly, many manufacturing researchers accepted the lean model almost completely and extended it, now under the term 'mass customisation'

(Kotha, 1995), through studies in many different countries (Kaplinsky, 1995), but largely without revisiting the basis of the original model (Delbridge and Oliver, 1991). Moreover, this process continues to this day (Holweg and Pil, 2004; Oxtoby, McGuiness and Morgan, 2002; Schlie and Yip, 2000; Nicholas and Soni, 2006; Liker, 2003).

The IMVP's description of lean production shows that their account of the system is based largely on the operations of Toyota, previously recorded by Taiichi Ohno (1978), Yasuhiro Monden (1983), Shigeo Shingo (1989) and Michael Cusumano (1985), but, as a result of the style of the text, it is portrayed as a generic system adopted by all Japanese firms. The focus on Japan as a manufacturing miracle was not misplaced, but, as table 12.2 shows, the IMVP claim that the Japanese were twice as effective as American manufacturers was perhaps not entirely accurate (Williams *et al.*, 1992). All motor manufacturers increased their output gradually in the late 1980s, with Japan remaining the country to beat, but there was no radical realignment as a result of the widespread adoption of Japanisation. The discrepancies between the leading car manufacturing nations largely remain the same as in the 1980s.

The Japanese car industry was an area worthy of investigation, and the IMVP exposed Toyota's production system as significantly different from those of other players in the global market, but, with the exception of Honda, the analysis of the remaining Japanese manufacturers showed levels of performance only comparable to international firms in the industry, and they were hard hit by the subsequent recessions in the Japanese economy. The decline in Honda and Toyota's profits, the losses posted by Nissan and the takeover of Mazda by Ford led to questions being raised concerning the nature of Japanese firms' success (see table 12.3). External factors, such as

Table 12.2 Comparison of value added per motor vehicle employee (dollars), 1986–90

	1986	1987	1988	1989	1990
Canada	57,350	58,649	71,943	76,311	74,105
Japan	67,075	84,538	103,548	105,433	107,874
South Korea	18,757	23,607	28,069	34,063	44,539
Spain	24,571	42,146	49,443	48,341	53,891
Sweden	42,776	52,413	63,433	62,723	63,229
United Kingdom	32,263	39,984	46,720	50,547	53,340
United States	77,787	80,403	89,034	94,912	89,219

Source: Darnay (1996: 617–18).

Table 12.3 Net income (loss) for Japanese car manufacturers (million yen), 1990–6

	Toyota	Honda	Nissan	Mazda
1990	441,302	81,648	116,013	23,438
1991	431,450	76,273	48,831	26,652
1992	237,841	64,877	101,295	9,314
1993	176,465	37,157	(55,998)	1,280
1994	125,807	23,699	(86,915)	n/a
1995	131,953	61,525	(166,054)	n/a
1996	256,977	70,801	(88,418)	n/a

Note: 1994 saw Toytota reduce the dividend it paid to shareholders.
Source: Company reports and accounts, various years.

quiescent home markets and currency fluctuations, have eliminated any advantage that even the best lean firms might have derived from their operating systems.

Examining the operating systems of the individual Japanese car manufacturers reveals how Toyota and Honda differed from their competitors and were able to weather the economic storm more successfully. If manufacturing managers are to learn more than just how to copy systems from others with little consideration of how they evolved or what their weaknesses are, they need to understand the strategies that led Toyota and Honda to the systems they chose.

Japanese car-making strategies

One element of the IMVP study that led to the promotion of the idea that all Japanese firms have similar operating systems was the aggregation of data, apparently to protect individual firm's confidences, into a country-based analysis. When the individual systems of the Japanese firms are analysed in more detail and in isolation from each other, it becomes clear that they are not similar at all. Table 12.4 reveals how different operating strategies realise themselves in comparative measures of the operating structures of the Japanese car manufacturers. The figure of labour's share of value added is telling, as it represents how the firms have removed labour costs from the manufacturing process. Labour costs typically account for about 70 per cent of the value added in car manufacturing, and so any reduction in labour content makes a significant increase in the productivity of the system.

Table 12.4 Manufacturing effectiveness of Japanese car manufacturers, 1990

	Ratio of stocks to plant and equipment	Value added/ stocks	Labour's share of added value (%)
Honda	49.8	7.0	50.9
Toyota	13.5	14.1	42.2
Nissan	28.7	5.7	68.5
Mazda	13.9	8.1	64.9

Source: Williams *et al.* (1994: 18, 33, 52).

Toyota's system is highly efficient at using labour, allowing the firm great flexibility in investment and market strategies. Honda is also ahead in reducing the labour content of its vehicles, largely through investment in technology, whilst the other Japanese firms perform at around the same levels as the rest of the industry.

Another advantage for Toyota over its domestic competitors is as a result of the levels of stocks in its manufacturing system, but the figures here could mislead, as examination of Honda's relatively weak position on value added to stocks shows that Honda has work in progress (WIP) levels as low as Toyota's but average levels of stocks comparable with the others. This suggests that Honda and Toyota both have very effective and efficient manufacturing systems that are able to move material through the plant at a high rate, using lower labour levels (and thus costs) than other manufacturers, in Japan as well as elsewhere. It is important not to dwell too long on these statistics, as perhaps researchers have in the past, but to examine how the operating systems of these firms function and how they evolved.

The attention to labour reduction in Toyota was first publicised by Cusumano (1985), who described it as a waste reduction philosophy and compared it to the approach at Nissan. He explained the differences by considering the relative historical performances and trajectories of each firm. Toyota's focus on waste has been used in making a range of products, including sewing machines and prefabricated buildings, but it evolved slowly from a system first used to free capital from WIP at a time of crisis (Ohno, 1978). Unfinished goods were mounting up as poor deliveries caused shortages of key parts in the assembly operation. By reducing the level of stocks in the production process, and assembling each product in a batch of one, Toyota was able to identify the shortages and prevent the assembly of vehicles that could not be completed. This was the start of the JIT system, which moved on to removing labour from the production system as it evolved. The development of JIT is covered in great detail by Shingo (1989) and, in particular, Ohno (1978), one of the engineers who developed the original concepts.

The heart of making the Toyota system work is the *kanban* – a system that links one production operation to the next, matching the production of parts closely to the demand established in the final assembly area. In essence, the Toyota system takes orders from customers (but only those that fit a pre-determined plan) and then responds rapidly by assembling the car to the specification demanded. The level of vertical disintegration and a focus on removing labour costs from vehicle manufacture means that Toyota's suppliers also have to respond to the changes in customer demands. The use of a highly tiered supply network that relies on many small family firms, beyond the main suppliers, helps Toyota insulate itself from labour costs. The costs associated with flexibility are much lower for the third- and fourth-tier suppliers than for Toyota itself. As a result, Toyota produces cars cheaply and carries very low levels of stocks, which move rapidly out to the customer. Nissan is perhaps the only other firm to follow the general lean model, but its attempt at introducing Toyota's JIT at a time of financial instability was not a total success and it was not able to match the low levels of labour needed to produce at Toyota (Vasilash, 1991), and as a result it has been hit very hard by the downturn in the Japanese economy.

Similarly, Honda aspires to manufacturing efficiency and waste reduction targets, but the driving force behind its operations strategy is to support the quality of engineering design. Honda's founder, Soichiro Honda, was primarily an engineer, and he firmly believed that customer satisfaction was derived from the engineering excellence of his products. These were originally motorcycles, but eventually he moved to capture a slice of the more lucrative car market, despite opposition from the post-war Ministry of International Trade and Industry (MITI), which sought to protect the existing players in the market from competition (Sakia, 1984). Honda's production systems, used for both motorcycles and cars, seek to minimise variations in the manufacturing process in an attempt to ensure that the vehicle meets the design specifications. The manufacturing strategy is to produce vehicles in large batches, not the batch-of-one/JIT approach favoured by Toyota. Repetition is seen as the key to producing vehicles that conform to the engineering specifications. With such a strategy comes a focus on product specification simplification, and stable production schedules that evolve slowly over a long period of time. This is quite unlike the rapid response of the Toyota system, but shares some JIT techniques (notably the *kanban* system) to ensure the smooth running of the final assembly operation, and close links to component manufacturing areas and suppliers. As a result, the Honda lines often resemble those of Toyota, but with more raw material stocks and a planning system that is fixed up to six months in advance of manufacture. Honda has a relatively weak standing in its home market, but has gained valuable sales overseas as a result of its ability to design and manufacture engines able to meet increasingly stringent emissions regulations, particularly in the United States.

It was purchases of Honda engines and access to the company's manufacturing facilities and their associated operating systems that the United Kingdom's Rover Group had recourse to during the 1980s. Rover, which has been studied from many angles as an example of the demise of the British car industry (Robson, 1984; Whipp and Clark, 1986; Dunnett, 1980; Williams, Williams and Haslam, 1987; Church, 1994; Wood, 1988; Holweg and Oliver, 2005), proves an interesting case of the failure of the Japanisation theme. Despite a decade of working closely with one of the world leaders in its industry, all Rover achieved was something of a stay of execution through the 1980s and early 1990s, and was finally sold to BMW by its cash-starved parent, British Aerospace (BAe), in 1994. In Honda, Rover had access to what was believed to be one of the key exponents of lean manufacturing, and should have been able to build a future modelled on Japanese techniques. This transformation should have been easier for Rover than for other organisations that did not have such a link to help learn Japanese manufacturing principles.

Why Rover was unable to achieve a continued revival of its fortunes at the modest levels of the late 1980s can be explained only by considering the capabilities and context of the firm, which become clear when examples of change within the firm are examined (Pilkington, 1996a). The pressures arising from its downward financial performance, the spiralling decline of engineering resources and a reliance on the highly competitive UK market during a period of economic recession were the key reasons for Rover's lengthy demise (Pilkington, 1996b). Apart from being restricted by its own capabilities, as a result of failing financial health due to mounting debts in the 1970s, Rover had another barrier to learning lean production from Honda: its lack of fully considering the strategy implications of its chosen manufacturing route. Rover's sales strategy was the careful targeting of niche sections of the British car market with distinctive and high-appeal vehicles, but Honda's manufacturing systems had not been developed to be responsive in the way the Toyota-based lean model of Japanese car manufacturing had. Honda does exhibit the HRM policies common to most Japanese firms, and these were transferred, after a fashion, into Rover (Muller, 1991; Towers, 1992). The efficiency and conformity of Honda's own systems were sacrificed, however, to meet the needs of the ailing UK manufacturer in its struggles to capture market share in a highly competitive market suffering the effects of recession. The structural factors that had forced Rover to turn to Honda in the first place eventually caught up with it. The extended downturn in the UK market further squeezed the funding for new models to a limit that its parent could not support, and the firm was sold (Holweg and Oliver, 2005).

The production systems at Mazda are perhaps closer to those of Toyota than Honda, but not because of any similarities in the firm or strategy. Mazda's goal has been to take advantage of products that appeal to niches in the market, as a result of its small size, relative to its competitors in the Japanese market, and a greater reliance on export markets following a period of near-collapse in the 1970s. The standard approach to production line design, as adopted at most car manufacturers, is for a facility to be dedicated to making one model. If the complexity of the process is increased to accommodate more than one model then the risks involved, and the complexity of managing such a facility, lead to reduced efficiency. During the 1980s Mazda developed production lines that could build fifteen models using the same facilities, believing that the reduced efficiency would be overcome by a reduction in break-even volume. The approach was based on the Toyota batch-of-one/JIT system, but expanded with the addition of labour-intensive operations to provide batch-of-one manufacture for any of the fifteen different models. The reduction in the company's break-even volume for each new model was to give Mazda access to the niche markets and enable higher prices to be set for more desirable products (Pilkington, 1995). The strategy was only an engineering and manufacturing success, however, as the economic and market situation dampened its commercial performance. Mazda now concentrates more on efficiency in its assembly systems, in keeping with the development of common models with Ford, its new owner.

The differences in operating and manufacturing strategies between the Japanese firms become more marked when their transplant factories are examined. For example, the UK operations of Toyota are as different from those used in Japan as are those of its other foreign operations and the General Motors (GM) collaboration NUMMI (New United Motor Manufacturing Inc.). The IMVP study itself indicated that the productivity of the NUMMI plant did not match its Japanese comparator Takaoka, because of the structure of the supply network. Similarly, the Nissan plants in the United States and United Kingdom look unlike their lean parent plants in Japan and more like the simple final assembly plants that any overseas firm would establish in a new market. Again, this reflects the development of capabilities and strategy: a parent company with a new assembly operation to feed a growing market develops a new supply base and slowly expands as the plant becomes established.

In the most influential article echoing and advancing the manufacturing strategy concept in the post-lean era, Robert Hayes and Gary Pisano (1994) argue that manufacturing's most valuable weapon is not arrived at by copying the techniques of others but through flexibility in order to react to changes in the environment and so achieve long-term strategic goals. It was this process that first led to the emergence of the Japanese car manufacturers as global players, as each one evolved different practices to achieve its own strategies, determined by its own particular situation. When this idea is applied to the lean model and the individual strategies of the Japanese car manufacturers are examined, it becomes clear that they did *not* follow a single strategy but, rather, each had its own approach, not all of which achieved the same levels of success.

In summary, the Japanese car manufacturers have very different operating systems from each other. Those that have been more resilient to the recent downturn in the Japanese economy have systems that are tailored specifically to support the business-level strategy of the firm. Toyota occupies a dominant position in the market and sells in large volumes – hence a strategy based on cost and production efficiency is the one that the production systems support. Honda has its historically derived engineering focus as the main reason for its rigid brand of leanness, whilst Mazda's low-volume, export-led niche market products led it to a now discredited mixed-model-based production strategy. Nissan used to be the dominant player in the market but lost its position to Toyota, and needed to develop alternative strategies to compete, but has deviated from the IMVP pattern as it compromised in its efforts as a result of integrating the approach into pre-existing practices. The Japanese themselves have not followed the best-practice approach but, instead, the capability- and contingency-based concepts of aligning production systems to corporate strategy (Holweg and Pil, 2004). We cannot guess as to what the situation would be now had the alignment of operating systems been with the business-level strategies of the 1980s and had manufacturing managers pursued the alignment of the best-practice route with their corporate goals, but we can analyse the relative success of the Japanisation theme.

Japanisation: a successful strategy?

One would expect to see a significant convergence of Western firms on the operating models of the Japanese car manufacturers as they adopted, wholesale, the best practices of the IMVP. Evidence comparing international manufacturing, despite being clouded by economic instability during the early 1990s, suggests that the Japanisation theme has led to a degree of restructuring. Table 12.5 compares the evolution of US and UK manufacturing industry and the automotive sectors during the 'Japanisation' era. The data use census information on the pattern and distribution of stocks to identify any changes as a result of Japanisation. The WIP data show how the levels of in-process stock in the manufacturing operations have altered, with a pattern emerging of a steady reduction of WIP in automobile manufacturing operations, but with little overall change to the total manufacturing activities of both countries. This is despite the additional pressures from a global

Table 12.5 US and UK manufacturing structures, 1973–92

| | Value added to WIP (1973 as base level) | | | | Finished goods stocks as percentage of all stocks | | | |
| | All manufacturing sectors | | Automobile manufacturing | | All manufacturing sectors | | Automobile manufacturing | |
	United States	United Kingdom	United States	United Kingdom	United States	United Kingdom	United States	United Kingdom
1973	1.0	1.0	1.0	1.0	30.5	22.2	8.4	27.8
1975	0.9	1.0	0.7	0.9	31.3	25.9	8.5	31.3
1977	1.0	0.9	0.9	0.9	31.5	27.5	9.3	34.6
1979	0.9	0.9	1.0	1.0	30.1	27.3	10.0	39.3
1981	0.9	0.8	1.1	1.0	31.5	28.3	11.1	47.2
1983	0.9	0.9	1.1	1.3	32.8	28.9	12.9	54.3
1985	0.9	1.0	1.4	1.6	32.5	29.7	13.2	58.0
1987	1.0	1.1	1.7	1.6	31.7	30.4	17.1	57.1
1989	0.9	1.2	2.4	2.2	31.6	32.0	19.5	62.9
1991	1.0	1.3	2.2	1.9	32.9	33.0	16.2	60.6
1992	1.1	1.3	2.2	2.2	34.3	32.6	15.7	59.6

Note: Index figures are used to overcome differences in the way that value added is calculated in the United States and United Kingdom. Similarly, it should be stressed that the make-up of the automobile sectors in each census is slightly different, and that US SIC code 3711 and UK Class 35 have been used to compile the table. *Source:* Calculated from data in the *US Survey of Manufactures*, and *UK Census of Production*, various years.

recession. The success of Japanisation in the car industry is to be expected, given the emphasis on stock reduction techniques resulting from the instability of the markets during the period examined and the arrival of transplant operations that push the mix of firms more towards the assembly of vehicles from parts produced elsewhere. The fortunes of the car manufacturing firms failed to show the great reversal that had been hoped for, however, and they are still bumping along, just managing to break even.

Table 12.5 also shows the level of finished goods to all stocks, an indicator of whether the manufacturing stocks have been entirely removed or merely pushed to another part of the chain. These data illustrate the penalty of the advances in WIP reduction, most evidently in the UK car industry, in which there has been a marked growth in the level of finished products as the stock is squeezed from one part of the supply chain, downstream into the sales network. The UK figures themselves show that in 1973 the combined values of raw materials and WIP was more than twice that of finished goods (£623 million to £240 million), but by 1990 the situation was reversed (£1,353 million to £2,526 million). The lean model has much to say concerning the management of suppliers and the adoption of JIT, but many of the messages concerning finished products, order management and customer delivery appear to have been diluted along the way as manufacturing managers picked the best practices whilst their sales departments persevered with existing systems. In the UK car industry traditional build-to-order systems have been severely tested by the move to lean production. The market was the scene of increasingly competitive practices, which have forced a move towards sales from stock policies as a means of making aggressive strategies and discounting effective. This has not been so marked in the case of the US car industry, for which the market has traditionally been one in which most vehicles are sold from stocks that have always been carefully managed.

The recommendation of a pursuit of Japanisation has had the positive result of reduced stock levels as firms were persuaded to introduce JIT and supplier management programmes, and the car industry should congratulate itself. Nonetheless, the overall result has been a shifting of liabilities from manufacturing and supply onto the sales networks. The firms that have been most successful in reducing manufacturing stocks have experienced the largest increase in finished product stocks. Firms have pursued the Japanisation theme without fully appreciating the strategy of those who developed it and, as a consequence, have gained little advantage for their efforts. The adoption of best practice may appeal to a company as a way of catching up with competitors, but normally by the time the approach has been implemented the competitors have moved on and the company remains in the same relative situation that it was in beforehand. In some cases the best-practice strategy can even make a firm's situation worse, as it finds itself selecting practices that do not suit its operating environment and limit its future choices. This was the situation at Rover, where the Honda systems failed to deliver the level of performance expected, and even prevented the firm from pursuing its sales-led recovery strategy.

Conclusions: align manufacturing and corporate strategy

The failure of Japanisation has shown that a best-practice approach is unlikely ever to provide transformations in organisational performance, as has been reflected in the general strategy literature for some time with its development of contingency and competency models. Closer examination of the parallel manufacturing strategy literature, however, also supports the need for integrating manufacturing and business-level strategy (Skinner, 1969). Either deliberately, or by chance, the Japanese car manufacturers from which the majority of the best practice was acquired followed an integrated strategy model aligning manufacturing with corporate strategy, and built capability in the existing systems, rather than disposing of their systems and acquiring new solutions as they came into fashion. This building of capabilities is a time-consuming and delicate process, as can be seen by the less than perfect attempts of Nissan and Mazda, for which the alignment was not total or the business-level strategy was inappropriate. This alignment of manufacturing with the rest of the corporate strategy has been ignored in many firms pursuing best practices, with, for example, the manufacturing manager being rewarded for reducing costs even when the rest of the organisation has been trying to compete on product differentiation.

As has been seen, the notion of lean production as a well-defined approach universally adopted throughout the Japanese car industry is inaccurate. There may be some factors that all Japanese firms have as a result of their national situation, such as HRM policies and the tiered supply network, but these factors have been used to establish production systems that have radically different aims and procedures. The variations in business strategy, and therefore manufacturing philosophies, of the Japanese car manufacturers reflect the impact of differing market forces on the companies – in particular, the volume of sales, past experience and the differing capabilities of the organisations. As the business-level strategy literature has been stressing for some time, competitive success comes from a strategy that challenges the norms and aligns all the business units into a common purpose. Merely trying to catch up, as the Japanisation and best-practice strategies still recommend to this day, is insufficient in the long term, despite its attractiveness and apparent ease of implementation.

The question remains as to whether chief executives in the future will be wary of the claims of manufacturing managers when they declare that the adoption of best-practice production systems can reduce costs and generate competitive advantage whatever the focus of the firm's corporate strategy. In most cases the appeal of copying a system found in a successful firm, coupled with the need to produce results quickly, will prevent the integration by practitioners of more sensitive strategy models. We need to escape best practice and resurrect the notion of manufacturing as being capable of generating competitive advantage, but only when it is aligned with the corporate strategy and not pulling against it.

References

Åhlström, P. (1998) Sequences in the implementation of lean production, *European Management Journal*, 16, 3, 327–34.

Buffa, E. (1984) *Meeting the Competitive Challenge*, Homewood, IL: Dow-Jones Irwin.

Church, R. (1994) *The Rise and Decline of the British Motor Industry*, Cambridge: Cambridge University Press.

Clark, K., and T. Fujimoto (1991) *Product Development Performance*, Boston: Harvard Business School Press.

Cohen, S. C., and J. Zysman (1987) Why manufacturing matters: the myth of the post industrial economy, *California Management Review*, 29, 9–26.

Cusumano, M. A. (1985) *The Japanese Automobile Industry: Technology and Management at Nissan and Toyota*, Cambridge, MA: Harvard University Press.

Darnay, A. (ed.) (1996) *Ward's Manufacturing Worldwide: Industry Analyses Statistics*, New York: Thompson Gale.

Delbridge, R., and N. Oliver (1991) Narrowing the gap? Stock turns in the Japanese and Western car industries, *International Journal of Production Research*, 29, 10, 2083–95.

Dunnett, P. (1980) *The Decline of the British Motor Industry: The Effects of Government Policy, 1945–1979*, London: Croom Helm.

Goldhar, J., and M. Jelinek (1983) Plan for economies of scope, *Harvard Business Review*, 61, 6, 141–8.

Goyal, S., and S. Deshmukh (1992) A critique of the literature on just-in-time manufacturing, *International Journal of Operations and Production Technology*, 12, 1, 18–28.

Hall, R. (1987) *Attaining Manufacturing Excellence*, Homewood, IL: Dow-Jones Irwin.

Hayes, R., and G. Pisano (1994) Beyond world-class: the new manufacturing strategy, *Harvard Business Review*, 72, 1, 77–86.

Hayes, R., and S. Wheelwright (1984) *Restoring Our Competitive Edge: Competing through Manufacturing*, New York: Wiley.

Hill, T. (1985) *Manufacturing Strategy: The Strategic Management of the Manufacturing Function*, Basingstoke: Macmillan.

Holweg, M., and N. Oliver (2005) *Who Killed MG Rover?*, working paper, Centre for Competitiveness and Innovation, Judge Business School, Cambridge University, available at www-innovation.jims.cam.ac.uk (last accessed 5 June 2006).

Holweg, M., and F. Pil (2004) *The Second Century: Reconnecting Customer and Value Chain through Build to Order*, Cambridge, MA: MIT Press.

Kaplinsky, R. (1995) *Easternisation: The Spread of Japanese Management Techniques to Developing Countries*, Ilford: Frank Cass.

Kay, J. (1993) *Foundations of Corporate Success*, Oxford: Oxford University Press.

Kotha, S. (1995) Mass customisation: implementing the emerging paradigm for competitive advantage, *Strategic Management Journal*, 16, 21–43.

Kotha, S., and D. Orne (1989) Generic manufacturing strategies: a conceptual synthesis, *Strategic Management Journal*, 10, 3, 211–31.

Krafcik, J. (1988) The triumph of lean production, *Sloan Management Review*, 30, 1, 41–52.

Lamming, R. (1993) *Beyond Partnership: Strategies for Lean Supply*, London: Prentice-Hall.

Liker, J. (2003) *The Toyota Way: 14 Management Principles from the World's Greatest Manufacturer*, New York: McGraw-Hill.

Meredith, J. (1987) The strategic advantages of the factory of the future, *California Management Review*, 29, 27–41.

Mintzberg, H., and D. Miller (1988) The case for configuration, in J. Quinn, H. Mintzberg and R. James (eds.) *The Strategy Process: Concepts, Contexts, Cases*, Englewood Cliffs, NJ: Prentice-Hall, 518–24.

Monden, Y. (1983) *Toyota Production System: Practical Approach to Production Management*, Norcross, GA: Industrial Engineering and Management Press.

Muller, F. (1991) A new engine of change in employee relationships, *Personnel Management*, 23, 7, 15–24.

Nemetz, P. L., and L. W. Fry (1988) Flexible manufacturing organisations: implications for strategy formulation and organisation design, *Academy of Management Review*, 13, 4, 627–38.

Nicholas, J., and A. Soni (2006) *The Portal to Lean Production: Principles and Practices for Doing More with Less*, Boca Raton, FL: Auerbach.

Ohno, T. (1978) *Toyota Production System: Beyond Large-scale Production*, Cambridge, MA: Productivity Press.

Oxtoby, B., A. McGuiness and R. Morgan (2002) Developing organisational change capability, *European Management Journal*, 20, 3, 310–20.

Parthasarty, R., and S. Sethi (1992) The impact of flexible automation on business strategy and organisational structure, *Academy of Management Review*, 17, 1, 86–111.

Pilkington, A. (1995) Japanese production strategies and competitive success: Mazda's quiet revolution?, *Journal of Far Eastern Business*, 1, 4, 15–35.

(1996a) *Transforming Rover: Renewal against the Odds, 1981–1994*, Bristol: Bristol Academic Press.

(1996b) Learning from joint venture: the Rover–Honda relationship, *Business History*, 38, 1, 90–114.

(1998) Manufacturing strategy regained: evidence for the demise of best-practice, *California Management Review*, 41, 1, 31–42.

(1999) International joint ventures: dependency in manufacturing and design, *International Journal of Operations and Production Management*, 19, 5/6, 460–73.

Porter, M. E. (1980) *Competitive Strategy: Techniques for Analyzing Industries and Competitors*, New York: Free Press.

Prahalad, C., and G. Hamel (1990) The core competence of the corporation, *Harvard Business Review*, 68, 3, 79–91.

Robson, G. (1984) *The Rover Story: A Century of Success*, Cambridge: Stevens.

Sakia, T. (1984) *Honda Motor: The Men, the Management, the Machines*, Tokyo: Kodansha International.

Schlie, E., and G. Yip (2000) Regional follows global: strategy mixes in the world automotive industry, *European Management Journal*, 18, 4, 343–54.

Schonberger, R. (1982) *Japanese Manufacturing Techniques: Nine Hidden Lessons in Simplicity*, London: Collier Macmillan.

Shingo, S. (1989) *A Study of the Toyota Production System from an Industrial Engineering Viewpoint*, Cambridge, MA: Productivity Press.

Skinner, W. (1969) Manufacturing: missing link in corporate strategy, *Harvard Business Review*, 47, 3, 139–46.

(1996) Three yards and a cloud of dust: industrial management at century end, *Production and Operations Management*, 5, 1, 15–24.

Smith, S., D. Tranfield, M. Foster and S. Whittle (1994) Strategies for managing the TQ agenda, *International Journal of Operations and Production Technology*, 14, 1, 75–88.

Society of Motor Manufacturers and Traders (1993) *Motor Industry of Great Britain 1993: World Automotive Statistics*, London: Society of Motor Manufactures and Traders.

Towers, J. (1992) A new deal, *Manufacturing Engineer*, 71, 4, 45–7.

Vasilash, G. (1991) Discovering Japan, *Production*, 36, 1, 39–50.

Voss, C., and G. Winch (1996) Including engineering in operations strategy, *Production and Operations Management*, 5, 1, 78–91.

Ward, P., D. Bickford and G. Leong (1996) Configurations of manufacturing strategy, business strategy, environment and structure, *Journal of Management*, 22, 4, 597–626.

Wheelwright, S., and H. Bowen (1996) The challenge of manufacturing advantage, *Production and Operations Management*, 5, 1, 59–77.

Whipp, R., and P. Clark (1986) *Innovation and the Auto Industry: Product, Process and Work Organization*, London: Pinter.

Williams, K., C. Haslam, S. Johal and J. Williams (1994) *Cars: Analysis, History, Cases*, Oxford: Berghahn Books.

Williams, K., C. Haslam, J. Williams, A. Cutler, A. Adcroft and S. Johal (1992) Against lean production, *Economy and Society*, 21, 3, 321–53.

Williams, K., J. Williams and C. Haslam (1987) *The Breakdown of Austin Rover: A Case-study in the Failure of Business Strategy and Industrial Policy*, Leamington Spa: Berg.

Womack, J. P., and D. T. Jones (1996) *Lean Thinking*, New York: Simon and Schuster.

Womack, J. P., D. T. Jones and D. Roos (1990) *The Machine that Changed the World: The Triumph of Lean Production*, London: Macmillan.

Wood, J. (1988) *Wheels of Misfortune: The Rise and Fall of the British Motor Industry*, London: Sidgwick and Jackson.

13 Policy transfer and institutional constraints: the diffusion of active labour market policies across Europe

Michael Gold

Introduction

Attempts by the European Union to create the social dimension have undergone major revisions over the last twenty years or so. From reliance on directives and regulations it has shifted, since the late 1980s, towards a focus on negotiation, social dialogue and other 'soft' forms of regulation. At the same time, policy priorities have also shifted, from workers' rights and issues in industrial relations towards employment creation and active labour market policies. The context for these changes included a growing build-up of rigidities on the supply side across the European Union since the 1970s, the increasing share of public expenditure in gross national product (GNP), the rise in real labour costs and worsening unemployment, amongst other factors, all of which were seen as unsustainable in the long term (OECD, 1988).

The European Commission's White Paper on growth, competitiveness and employment, adopted at the Brussels summit in December 1993, focused on training, flexibility in the labour market and work reorganisation amongst other means of reducing the level of unemployment across the European Union (European Commission, 1993). The Essen summit in December 1994 also focused on combating unemployment as the main plank in social policy. It advocated measures to promote training, increase the job intensity of growth, reduce non-wage labour costs, move from passive to active labour market policies and target groups particularly hard hit by unemployment (European Commission, 1994: 8–9).

These shifts in emphasis at EU level were eventually consolidated in the Treaty of Amsterdam (1997), which introduced the European Employment Strategy (EES). The EES – amongst other elements – requires member states to submit national action plans (NAPs) for employment every year to the Commission, in an attempt to foster greater transparency in labour market policy across the European Union. For the first five years each NAP covered four standard 'pillars': employability, entrepreneurialism, adaptability and equal opportunities. The pillars were further subdivided into a number of guidelines, which varied year by year: in the 2002 NAPs there were eighteen guidelines in total (*Official Journal of the European Communities*, 2002). The system of 'pillars' and 'guidelines' was subsequently reorganised into a more simplified framework of ten guidelines, known as the 'ten commandments', which remain the same over a three-year, rather than a one-year, cycle. They were preceded by three 'overarching and interrelated objectives', namely full employment, the quality and productivity of work, and social cohesion and inclusion (Watt, 2004: 125). In 2005 the strategy was again revisited by the European Commission and Council. There are now only eight guidelines, defined for the period 2005–8, with employment policies more integrated into macroeconomic and micro-economic policies (*Official Journal of the European Union*, 2005). The foundation of the system – based on common guidelines, indicators and joint evaluation – remains the same as before, however.

Between 1998/99 and 2002/3, the period covered in this chapter, each member state drew up its NAP in line with the earliest formula noted above, and submitted it to the Commission for evaluation. Each NAP was first of all dispatched to two other member states, so that they could lead the discussion at a two-day meeting held in Brussels, where the Commission, as well as an ad hoc group of the Employment Committee and the member states, could ask questions (a procedure known as the 'Cambridge process'). The Commission would subsequently organise a series of 'bilateral' meetings with each individual member state, attended by the national government and, generally, the social partners concerned as well, at which the main points of the NAP were discussed and clarified. From 2000 the Commission would also then issue recommendations to each member state for further action. These recommendations varied in number, but it was expected that the concerns raised would be addressed in the following year's NAP. The Commission subsequently drew up its annual Joint Employment Report, containing a résumé and assessment of each member state's policy direction. Recommendations and the Joint Employment Report were duly adopted by the Council, and formed the basis for any amendments to the guidelines in the coming year – and so the process turned full circle.

The NAPs therefore reflect national priorities in active labour market policies, but their submission is a treaty obligation and they must be presented under a standard format – until 2003 as 'pillars' and 'guidelines', now as broader guidelines – adopted by the Council, formerly on a one-year, now on a three-year, cycle. Peer review and evaluation remain very much an integral part of the cycle.

This procedure thereby combines 'soft' with 'hard' law elements, and decentralisation with coordination, and is known technically as the 'open method of coordination' or OMC (Hodson and Maher, 2001). The OMC developed out of moves towards European Monetary Union (EMU) and, in particular, the Stability and Growth Pact of 1996, which required member states in the Eurozone to submit convergence programmes in line with the Commission's broad economic policy guidelines setting out macroeconomic priorities. These guidelines were enforced principally through the financial markets, public opinion and peer review, though financial sanctions were also envisaged in extreme cases (Dyson, 2000). Since then, however, the OMC has been extended to cover a variety of other policy areas regarded as 'sensitive', such as information society, social inclusion, pensions and employment. Whilst 'hard' law often underpins these areas – the stability and growth pact and the NAPs being examples – coordination is complemented by a range of 'soft' measures 'involving the exchange of best practices, the use of benchmarking, national and regional-level target-setting, periodic reporting, and multilateral surveillance' (de la Porte, 2002: 38). The OMC thus combines 'carrot' with 'stick', and is well suited to areas of integration either outside the scope of the treaties or else characterised by institutional divergences and national jealousies. In such areas, peer pressure has increasingly been seen as the most effective tool to promote compliance with EU policy objectives (Jacobsson, 2004; Zeitlin, Pochet and Magnusson, 2005).

'Beacon' programmes

Indeed, as part of this framework, article 129 of the treaty itself encourages initiatives 'aimed at developing exchanges of information and best practices, providing comparative analysis and advice as well as promoting innovative approaches and evaluating experiences ...' (Euroconfidentiel, 1999). These initiatives, the focus of this chapter, have now been formalised as a further process of peer review amongst the member states of the European Union alongside the Cambridge process referred to above. The Commission requests all member states both to host their own 'beacon' ALMP programmes and to make their own visits to those hosted by other member states ('beacon' is the author's, not the Commission's, term). The first peer review round (1999–2001) contained twenty-six such beacon programmes presented by thirteen of the then fifteen member states, with each one attracting between two and nine member state visitors (a total of 122 separate visits). These programmes included social responsibility programmes for enterprises in Denmark, access routes to employment for young people in France, reducing the gender digital divide in Germany and lifelong learning in the United Kingdom, amongst many others. The second round (2003/4) included sixteen programmes, from a follow-up to the national programme for ageing workers in Finland to the personalised action programme for a new start in France. The selection of specific programmes by member states for this kind of window display is voluntary, but the four pillars under which they do so – as part of the NAPs process – is compulsory. Amongst the twenty-six programmes organised in the first round, ten focused on the employability pillar, six on entrepreneurialism, seven on adaptability and two on equal opportunities (one – the French 'new services, new jobs' programme – featured twice, under entrepreneurialism and equal opportunities, respectively).

The peer review visits examined in this chapter provide a rich source of information that can be used to examine the 'soft' processes of regulation on which the OMC depends. Each peer review visit is written up as a report that follows a broadly comparable structure. The report outlines the labour market programme under review, explains its design, implementation and funding, and examines the role of the government and social partners in it. The report then analyses the results of the programme, the number of beneficiaries, and the obstacles, challenges and problems that face it. It also identifies issues of special interest to the peer countries. In the final section it discusses the potential for transfer to other countries. Each visiting peer country will have sent along two reviewers – a government official, generally from the ministry of labour, and an independent expert. Each one is invited to comment on aspects of transferability to his/her own country and the constraints that might arise. These comments provide an unparalleled insight into the parameters of labour market policy transfer, as assessed by the experts.

So, for example, in November 2000 the UK Department of Education and Employment and the Treasury hosted a peer review meeting entitled Tax and Benefit Reform in the UK: Making Work Pay. The meeting, attended by six peer review countries, focused on the Working Families Tax Credit as part of a package of tax and benefit reforms introduced by the Labour government since 1997. Following presentations and discussion of the reforms, each member state present commented on the transferability of the experience and on its learning value. Austria, for example, expressed concern that tax credits based on the household could act as a disincentive for female employment, which it wished to raise. In Ireland, the problem was that many people have been taken out of the bottom end of the tax system, so tax relief would not benefit them. In the Netherlands, by contrast, a similar approach to that of the United Kingdom was being adopted, but concerns there centred on the high cost of the reforms and their sustainability in the event of recession. The other peer review countries – Belgium, Finland and Italy – offered further observations about transferability. Constraints in these cases included divergent policy objectives (Austria), the operation of the tax system (Ireland) and the costs involved (Netherlands). In this example, the Dutch appeared to derive greatest advantage from the visit as they focused on the design details of the policy that interested them most. Nevertheless, the hosts – the United Kingdom – also noted the trend towards a greater degree of evidence-based policy formulation: 'In this context it is very useful to gather information from other countries.'

This chapter focuses, then, on how peer review and peer pressure promote policy transfer and cross-jurisdictional learning amongst member states in relation to these beacon programmes. The link between peer review and policy transfer is particularly significant. The peer review reports analysed here explicitly refer to transferability and policy transfer in an attempt to foster the diffusion of best practice. The diffusion of best practice is itself a critical element in the open method of coordination, as 'soft' law increasingly usurps the role once played by 'hard' law in establishing an employment-centred EU social dimension. Constraints on diffusion may well hinder the achievement of the European Union's labour market policies.

The chapter covers the first round of beacon programmes (1999–2001). It is based on analysis of the published peer review reports available on the internet (http://peerreview.almp.org/en; see also ÖSB Consulting, 2001) and on interviews carried out in the first six months of 2003 with a sample of the government officers and independent experts responsible for making the visits and reporting back with findings. It thereby sheds light on the effectiveness of the OMC in diffusing best practice, changing behaviour and creating greater convergence in labour market policy in the longer run.

Policy transfer and cross-jurisdictional learning

In a review of the literature, David Dolowitz and David Marsh (1996: 344) define policy transfer as 'a process in which knowledge about policies, administrative arrangements, institutions etc. in one time and/or place is used in the development of policies, administrative arrangements and institutions in another time and/or place'. They maintain that policy transfer has always existed, but that the process has accelerated since World War II with the rapid growth of communications. Those who defend and those who criticise the policy transfer approach both acknowledge that interest in these processes has burgeoned recently (Evans and Davies, 1999, and James and Lodge, 2003, respectively). Indeed, the Economic and Social Research Council (ESRC) financed the Future of Governance Programme, which embraced around thirty projects (including one on which this chapter is based) designed to illuminate the process of policy transfer and cross-jurisdictional learning across a wide range of areas, including health, housing, constitutional law and tax compliance, amongst many others (see www.futuregovernance.ac.uk).

There are a number of attractions to the policy transfer approach when studying the diffusion of ALMP across the European Union. The first is that the peer review process explicitly attempts to promote the transferability of ALMP, and so provides an ideal setting for the application of concepts and methods of analysis drawn from the policy transfer literature. The second attraction of this approach is that it is, arguably, empirically testable. By defining the scope of the policy under review – as is done in the next section – it should be possible to track the degree to which it can be 'exported' to another jurisdiction and the success with which this is carried out. Third, the distinction made between 'voluntary' and 'coercive' transfer along a spectrum of obligation (Dolowitz and Marsh, 2000) fits the development of the OMC within the European Union rather well; that is, as noted above, the annual submission of NAPs to the Commission by member states is a treaty obligation, and the Lisbon and Stockholm summits set explicit labour market targets for member states to meet, relating principally to employment rates amongst men and women (Goetschy, 2003). Member states remain free to select their own ways of hitting these targets according to their own domestic circumstances and institutional frameworks, however. The diffusion of best practice through the peer review process therefore becomes critically important for the success of the OMC, which becomes the forum that encourages member states to display their best practice from which others may draw lessons. Such lesson drawing may involve copying, adapting, hybridising, synthesising or inspiring (Rose, 1993: 30).

The idea of 'best practice' here does not therefore imply homogenisation or standardisation, as in the debate on best-practice production concepts, such as quality circles or just-in-time. Rather, issues arise about the selection of practices and the processes of active interpretation required to assess whether they would or would not suit local conditions. As we see below, there is nothing inevitable about these processes, as the assessment by the peer reviewers may uncover a whole battery of constraints – administrative, financial, institutional and so on – that they believe could impede successful transfer of the practice in question.

Finally, the policy transfer process helps to illuminate the degree to which convergence – of labour market objectives, ideologies, institutions, policies and instruments, amongst other elements – is taking place amongst member states. There is an extensive literature on 'convergence' processes, and analysis of policy transfer – along with the factors that encourage it – helps to explain the parameters within which convergence is, or is not, taking place (Smith, 2005; see also chapter 2). A focus on the precise nature of the object of transfer provides a comparative framework within which to contrast *areas* of convergence, the *pace* at which they are taking place and the *constraints* that impede their development. Economic liberalisation and the national deregulation of labour markets underpin pressures towards convergence, but these may be accelerated or decelerated by policy-makers given the significance of politics as 'in part an independent factor' in these processes (Hyman, 2006: 243). In this context, policy-makers are involved in choosing to adopt or adapt a range of solutions to problems as identified and defined in the NAP guidelines. The assessment of government advisers and independent experts of the transferability of ALMP between member states provides a significant perspective on the constraints of convergence. The *means* through which policy may converge may include emulation, elite networking, harmonisation and certain penetrative processes (Bennett, 1991).

The kinds of diffusion analysed in this chapter present some striking contrasts with those found elsewhere in the literature. Elsewhere, the model generally assumes a dominant or strong 'object' of transfer, which is then tracked as it is exported to other countries. For example, American production methods, such as Taylorism, and use of the multidivisional company structure (the 'M-form'), may be diffused through TNCs or by their imitators in host countries (Kogut and Parkinson, 1993), or by management consultants (Littler, 1982). Government agencies, such as the US Technical Assistance and Productivity Program, have been involved in other instances of the diffusion of learning processes (McGlade, 2000). The extensive debate on 'Japanisation' has followed a similar course, with studies of the ways in which new, apparently superior production methods have been exported to other countries by means of multinational companies or other transnational agencies (Womack, Jones and Roos, 1990; Oliver and Wilkinson, 1992; Abo, 1994; Elger and Smith, 2005).

The kinds of learning analysed in this chapter do not fall into this pattern. The peer review visits discussed here do not focus on the diffusion of one dominant model, nor do they involve knowledge transfer through the mediation of transnational agencies. Rather, they explore the processes of learning from multiple sources through low-level government officials and consultants based on multi-country comparisons. Notions of dominance, power and a single 'best practice' are notably absent, which helps to explain the nature of the complex and variable sets of processes and outcomes involved.

Reasons for visits

All the EU member states, apart from Greece and Luxembourg, hosted at least one labour market programme in the first peer review round, and the same number again offered further programmes, or sometimes follow-ups, under the second round. The interviews at the ministries of labour in ten of the member states in relation to the first round reveal a variety of reasons for hosting a programme. The member state may simply be proud of its success, it may be seeking ideas for further improvement or it may want to make its own point. Ireland, for example, in offering its programme Building Sustainable Competitive Advantage in October 2001 hoped to draw attention to the significance of the demand side of labour market policy, which it saw as underestimated in relation to supply-side issues. (This programme promotes sustainable domestic business in the manufacturing and internationally traded services sectors.) A further motive is to 'play the game' with the Commission and avoid criticism for not taking part. Greece failed to offer a programme because the NAP process had itself been insufficiently well organised internally, and the officials responsible had been too junior to drive events forward – a failure that was being rectified through reforms within the ministries involved. Not all programmes were equally popular, however. Spain drew only two peer review countries with its agreement on employment stability whilst the United Kingdom drew nine with its programme on lifelong learning.

Similar motivational variety underpins the choice of a member state to visit a particular programme. Those interviewed in the ministries of labour were often vague or unclear about the criteria for selection, not least because decisions were often decentralised to other departments, or even to other ministries (such as education, in the case of lifelong learning). In addition, there was little continuity of government representatives at programmes, either because of staff turnover or because specialists were despatched rather than generalists and the contingents varied. Reasons for attending included the desire to analyse approaches to a similar problem or to learn about a particular aspect of policy (such as evaluation), or a member state wishing to vaunt its own policies in the peer review arena. In a couple of cases, two non-EU countries attended (Bulgaria and Norway). Ireland attended four of the twenty-four programmes in the first round, whilst Greece and Luxembourg – which had hosted none at all – each attended eleven.

Few patterns of interaction emerge, except that Ireland and the United Kingdom each visited all the others' programmes. Both countries obviously share a common language and certain historical ties, but these patterns did not materialise elsewhere. For example, French- and German-speaking countries did not necessarily visit each other, nor did members of contiguous communities, such as Benelux and the Nordic countries. The single most important criterion for selection was simply technical: did the programme in question offer a potential peer review country any possible ideas or solutions to problems that it too shared? This suggests that the peer review programme as a whole does indeed provide a genuine framework for pooling approaches to ALMP. The peer review countries are self-selected, instrumental and keen to learn – surely a fertile ground for policy transfer.

What might be transferred

The next question to consider centres on the 'objects' of potential transfer – that is, what a peer review country might believe to be appropriate to transfer. Each peer review report summarises the observations made by each visiting country on what might, at least technically, be transferable. This issue has also been addressed in the academic literature. Indeed, Dolowitz and Marsh (2000) list a set of possible objects of transfer: policy goals, content, instruments and/or programmes, institutions, ideologies, ideas/attitudes and negative lessons (that is, what to avoid doing).

The research carried out by Bernard Casey and me largely bears out the validity of these categories, with the emphasis very much on policy *goals*, such as improving the transfer of young people from education to work or increasing the activity rates of older workers. We need to be aware, however, that these 'objects' often become difficult to disentangle and identify in practice – generally because they are so deeply embedded in institutional frameworks – and that the categories themselves need to be refined.

For example, the *principles* on which policy is based, such as targeting, individual counselling, partnership or mainstreaming, are also frequently a focus of attention. Most of the member states that visited the national programme for ageing workers in Finland, for instance, commented favourably on how it mainstreamed the social integration of older people through education, health and labour market policies. Italy appreciated the partnership approach adopted by France in its access routes to employment for young people, which it felt was important as it embarked on decentralising its own ALMP. In many cases, countries commented favourably on how programmes adopted individualised counselling for vulnerable groups, such as the young or long-term unemployed. An example can be found in the comments of the Dutch peer reviewers on the Finnish national programme for ageing workers.

Furthermore, in many cases member states consider that only certain *aspects* of a programme merit transfer. This leads at times to a rather 'pick and mix' perspective on policy-making. Peer reviewers sometimes focused on very narrow features of a programme for transfer, such as the use of IT in handling applications to register businesses or self-certification as a means for fulfilling certain administrative requirements – points made by Luxembourg when reviewing the Italian programme for reducing administrative burdens on enterprises. The United Kingdom, in its comments on Portuguese programmes for the integration of long-term youth and adult unemployed (the Inserjovem and Reage Programmes), similarly highlighted their detailed procedures as possible areas for learning (procedural manuals, insertion teams, individual dossiers and the follow-up). Such aspects of policy are so decontextualised that they are often little more than 'good ideas'. More broadly, Sweden felt it could learn from the way in which the United Kingdom's New Deal led specifically to accredited qualifications for young unemployed people, and all peer review countries expressed interest in the Swedish programme on women entrepreneurs. They agreed that it was possible to examine the general setting of the programme and the ideas behind it 'rather than trying to transfer the measure itself'. They focused on the role of women advisers in the programme, the development of an electronic network to support it, its long-term nature and its built-in system of evaluation.

There is little interest in the transfer of *institutions* – indeed, the Dutch explicitly discounted the centralised approach to lifelong learning in the

United Kingdom as they have relied on adapting their own, decentralised infrastructure: 'Foreign systems cannot be imported,' they argued. Nevertheless, there is greater interest expressed in *policy 'models'*. Sweden, for example, admired the Italian model of the one-stop shop for entrepreneurs setting up new businesses as it provided a 'clear picture' for the reduction of administrative burdens on enterprises.

It was unusual for countries either to reject or accept a *programme* under review in its entirety. Nonetheless, all five peer review countries rejected the French model for legislation on the reorganisation and reduction of working time, mainly because, they maintained, such matters should be left to negotiations and because of the alleged damage caused to competitiveness. By contrast, three of the four peer review countries believed that the German programme for reducing the gender digital divide was at least 'highly relevant' (Spain) or else wholly transferable (Austria and Finland). Denmark, however, did not support single-sex training courses – on which the German programme depended – and claimed that, in any event, more women in Denmark used the internet than men.

Arguably, the member states already share – or at least have been encouraged to develop – a similar supply-side *ideology* as an approach to labour market problems through the European Employment Strategy. As we have seen, the EES involves the exchange of best practice, benchmarking and the use of peer pressure to tackle member states that are insufficiently active in meeting the targets set (Biagi, 2000). The diffusion of this ideology through the emergence of so-called 'epistemic communities' of peer reviewers, based in ministries of labour and independent research establishments, sustains the peer review process itself and makes it meaningful to the participants.

Indeed, the analysis in this section reveals the extent to which patterns of shared assumptions and understandings of ALMP across the European Union have become established. One of the most significant functions of the peer review process is the opportunity it provides for structured reflection and discussion. When examining the Portuguese Inserjovem and Reage Programmes for long-term youth and adult unemployed, the Dutch participants were led to ponder on their own schemes for preventive action, which were less voluntary: 'An issue that arises is whether compulsion will enhance the feeling of joint responsibility that will motivate job seekers to take their own initiatives as well.' Similarly, the Austrian programme on Territorial Employment Pacts (TEPs) engendered a lively debate on the optimal scale of intervention that should be envisaged, the role of private sector participation and cooperation with other local-level initiatives, amongst other issues. Many further examples could be given illustrating how participants used the peer review process as a kind of policy forum to air ideas, test opinions and gain critical feedback on existing or proposed policies. The learning experience for those involved is quite intense – though, as we see later on, this experience appears rarely to get passed on.

Constraints on transfer

Nevertheless, there are clearly many instances when member states do not wish to transfer any part of the active labour market programmes they visit. This may be because labour market conditions are different. For example, high levels of unemployment in Greece would make the Danish system of compulsory employability enhancement unworkable, as the jobs are simply not there to go to, or the low level of self-employment in Finland rendered inappropriate the Italian one-stop shops for business set-ups. The programme presented might not be relevant: France, Sweden and the United Kingdom all claimed that they had no problems with sources of venture capital, so that that aspect of the Irish programme on sustainable competitive advantage had little interest for them. Countries might also be confident in their existing policies, or simply reject the policy orientation in the programme they visited.

France, for example, stated that it did not encourage fixed-term contracts as they were still seen as precarious forms of employment, and therefore it renounced the very premise of the Dutch Flexibility and Security Act (1999), one aim of which was to promote this and other forms of flexible employment. The United Kingdom explained that, in response to German and Italian programmes for bridging benefits for self-employment, it favoured easing the young unemployed into dependent employment, and that these programmes therefore did not fit its domestic policy framework.

In some cases, peer reviewers admitted that the problem might centre on a lack of political commitment. The United Kingdom agreed that the Finnish programme for national workplace development offered ideas on how to fill a policy gap – relating, for instance, to networking between companies – but added that 'transferability depends on the degree of political will that exists'. In other cases, there was scepticism about the longer-term viability of a programme if economic conditions were to change. All peer reviewers criticised the Belgian 'Rosetta Plan' – designed to launch young people into employment – on this ground. Under the plan, private companies are legally required to fill a 3 per cent quota with young employees, and public services a quota of 1.5 per cent. The reviewers noted that the plan 'works well during a period of growth, but is likely to be more difficult for firms to apply in the event of recession or stagnation'. Peer reviewers made similar observations about the national programme for ageing workers in Finland, saying that 'the programme had hopped on to a moving train'. It was still too early, they claimed, to identify the results deriving from the programme and those deriving from the upturn in the economy. Indeed, on other occasions, countries simply preferred to await fuller evaluation before deciding on the merits of a programme, which was Austria's position on UK lifelong learning.

This chapter focuses below on constraints on transferability, however – that is, the difficulties that member states argued that they would face in attempting to adopt the aspects of programmes that they did consider to be at least partly appropriate for transfer. Analysis of these constraints reveals insights into the parameters of the policy transfer process.

Administrative and financial constraints

Administrative bottlenecks were sometimes considered a problem. Both Finland and Italy commented that a unified policy on lifelong learning in the United Kingdom was possible because the same ministry covered employment, education and training. In Italy, several ministries are responsible for different aspects of the educational system, and 'there is little or no coordination between and integration of all institutions involved in the supply of education and training', which would cause difficulties in pursuing a similar policy. Greece raised the issue of staff workloads as a problem when considering the German immediate-action programme for the training, qualification and employment of young people ('JUMP'). The Greek peer reviewers appreciated the breadth and flexibility of the programme but added that the burden it would place on their staff in the public employment service, and the costs involved, would cause problems in implementation.

Spain has no tradition of generous ALMP, and most expenditure so far goes on passive payments. Therefore, transfer of the German JUMP scheme would face 'administrative, coordination and cultural obstacles and is therefore hardly conceivable at the moment'. Indeed, Spain has no history of in-house training or apprenticeships, and there is a lack of coordination between the three actors involved in supplying vocational training: the education authorities, the public employment service and the trade unions.

The cost of programmes was a further factor mentioned as a constraint on a number of occasions. Individualised counselling for vulnerable groups is expensive, and – as Sweden pointed out with respect to the Danish youth unemployment programme and the United Kingdom's New Deal – it would have to be assessed on the merits of the case. All peer reviewers expressed concern at the financial obstacles involved in the Portuguese programme for training in micro- and small enterprises, not least because it was financed largely by the European Social Fund.

'Reform overload' also appeared occasionally as a disincentive to adopt new policies. Greece referred on several occasions to reforms to its public employment service, and the resulting high levels of workload on staff. The Netherlands also referred to reforms in its public employment service and social security system that, it claimed, would hinder the adoption of otherwise attractive aspects of the Danish employability enhancement programme.

Institutional constraints

Peer reviewers also referred to a battery of institutional constraints – in the form of their country's legal, industrial relations, political, social security or tax systems – that might require overhaul to establish the policy in question. There is a well-known literature on 'institutionalism' and 'national business systems' in which much of the following analysis may be contextualised (see, for example, Lane, 1989, Hollingsworth and Boyer, 1997, and Whitley, 1999).

In some cases, peer reviewers observed that their country lacked the relevant supporting infrastructure. The French programme for access routes to employment for young people in danger of exclusion ('TRACE') relies for its delivery on 'missions locales', a network of information and resource centres for young people. Both Denmark and Finland noted how TRACE was embedded in this particular element of French institutional life and that it would be unrealistic to set up similar centres.

Diverging legal frameworks were frequently cited as barriers to transfer. France, for example, in commenting on the Danish programme on the social responsibility of enterprises, pointed out that in France policies on disabled workers, collective redundancies and working time are legally based, in contrast with Denmark, where the approach is voluntary. Meanwhile, Luxembourg pointed out that flexible labour legislation in Denmark meant a relatively high level of labour turnover, and hence a continual supply of vacancies for those who had undertaken activation measures under the country's employability enhancement programme. Luxembourg has stricter legislation on hiring and firing, however, and so there would be less chance of finding work, rendering the scheme less effective – and it rejected the possibility of changing the law.

Closely linked to legal frameworks are systems of industrial relations. All peer reviewers noted that working time was a matter for negotiation in their countries, not legislation, as in France, which meant that the French model of working time reorganisation and reduction was largely invalid for their countries. Indeed, patterns of social partnership feature prominently as significant variables between industrial relations systems. Denmark, France and Italy noted that the UK system of lifelong learning would not fit into their own domestic patterns of social partnership. Portugal commented, in relation to the Dutch Flexibility and Security Act, that 'a new form of dialogue between the social partners' would be necessary before it could consider transfer.

A further institutional factor centres on taxation and social security systems. Luxembourg's approach to the disabled is based on a social assistance model. It therefore believed that attempts to introduce the approach enshrined in the Austrian programme Arbeitsassistenz (support for the integration of disabled people into the labour market) would 'create considerable tension'. Institutional problems would also hamper the Dutch in relation to the same Austrian programme: while the public sector still carries responsibility for the case management of the disabled, rehabilitation and reintegration have been privatised. The benefits structure also informed comments on other programmes. Spain pointed out that both the Danish youth unemployment programme and the UK New Deal combine activation measures with reductions in unemployment benefit if an individual will not participate. In Spain, however, the young unemployed are covered by neither social assistance nor unemployment insurance, eligibility for which requires six and twelve months' work experience, respectively. As a result, the 'stick' implicit in these programmes would have no effect. Portugal made a similar point in relation to the Danish employability enhancement programme – namely that compulsory activation would not work as unemployment benefits are so low – whilst the Netherlands maintained that it would be impossible to cut unemployment benefits and reduce welfare benefits to those refusing to work as welfare benefits are close to the minimum wage and there is 'a sort of poverty trap'.

Political structures also play a part in impeding the diffusion of good practice. The Italian one-stop shop approach to establishing businesses appealed to the German peer reviewers as there are a multiplicity of agencies involved in Germany. The German federal government lacks jurisdiction over the state governments (Länder) to require them to adopt such an approach, however, though there might be other ways to spread their example. By contrast, Spain would find it difficult to establish competence centres – a key element in the German programme on reducing the digital divide – because it is decentralising labour market functions to the regional level. It added that it would welcome information on how Germany coordinated these centres. Belgium, too, noted that its 'main obstacle to transferability' with regard to the Finnish national programme for ageing workers was the regionalised structure of the state and 'its ensuing dispersion of competences concerning economic, employment and social issues'.

Cultural and attitudinal constraints

Finally, countries sometimes referred to cultural or attitudinal constraints that would require much work to overcome. Belgium, for example, was very interested in the Danish programme of corporate social responsibility as there had been much discussion of the insertion of social clauses into calls for tender, on similar lines to the Danish model. At the same time, however, 'the need for wholesale cultural change' was emphasised. This is because both employers and unions would need to accept the concept of CSR on account of its improvement to work organisation and company performance, not on account simply of the economic subsidies it might attract. Austria too observed that attitudes amongst the social partners and local authorities would have to change before this Danish programme could succeed domestically.

Belgium, Greece, Portugal and Spain all observed that existing domestic attitudes to women at work would undermine any attempt to adopt the Swedish programme on women entrepreneurs. Greece pointed out that these cultural differences – set against a contrasting labour market situation for women – 'might need attention first before thinking about implementing the Swedish programme'.

Successful transfer?

Overall, there emerge very few substantiated examples of successful transfer in these peer review reports, though the use of Territorial Employment Pacts – a highly adaptable policy instrument – appears to provide an unusual exception. The Austrian presentation of its TEPs revealed that a number of countries have already introduced them: four in Austria, two in Luxembourg, three in Portugal and twenty-six in Finland. Indeed, Finland had gone ahead 'on the basis of positive experiences in Ireland'. It also became clear that Germany had introduced similar pacts as well, but under different names. As a result of the discussions, the Commission representatives present 'were pleased to note that while the individual TEPs were still struggling with structural and policy issues, the basic idea appeared to be on the right track'.

Policy transfer and convergence

In the light of these findings, this chapter finally addresses the question of whether the analysis of the peer review process throws any light on the extent to which a convergence of ALMP may be taking place across the European Union, and hence a convergence of labour market regulation more generally.

The development of the social dialogue at EU level since the 1980s, its consolidation into the Maastricht Treaty and the subsequent adoption of a number of directives – notably those covering parental leave, part-time work and fixed-term contracts – based on agreements between the social partners at EU level have had a major impact on the social dimension. The widespread creation of European works councils, the progress of sectoral-level social dialogue and the launch of EMU have similarly helped to enhance the role of the social partners to various degrees and at various levels. Some commentators have accordingly argued that these developments – underpinned by the EES – imply significant moves towards EU-level labour market regulation (Jensen, Madsen and Due, 1999; Léonard, 2001).

This chapter acknowledges these pressures and the progress of EU-level regulatory mechanisms but maintains that their influence on domestic regulatory frameworks remains limited. This is because the scope for policy transfer and lesson learning in the area of ALMP itself remains limited. Even though the EES has established labour market targets, the evidence reveals that member states will rely on their own home-grown means – administrative, institutional and legal – to meet them. Indeed, this is not surprising in view of the Commission's inability to create a social dimension based on 'hard' law during the 1980s and 1990s and its subsequent fallback on to the use of 'soft' law and the OMC (Goetschy, 1999). Member states have resisted the harmonisation of labour market regulation – the creation of a genuine 'level playing field' – in favour of non-binding instruments such as the Social

Charter and the OMC, both of which leave domestic regulatory mechanisms largely intact.

This analysis demonstrates how restricted the impact of the OMC is likely to remain, however, at least insofar as its peer review process is concerned. Member states may face a variety of labour market challenges – such as low participation rates amongst ethnic minorities, women and older workers – and were even required to attain certain targets to improve them by 2005 (Stockholm summit) and 2010 (Lisbon summit), yet peer reviewers frequently expressed little more than polite interest in how other member states were striving to hit these targets. Sometimes they suggested that a host programme was successful only because of an economic upturn, or they might question its sustainability or use the visit as a platform to explain their own policies.

Indeed, even in those cases when peer reviewers enthusiastically endorsed policies for possible transfer, the question arises: what happens next? Our interviews with a sample of government and independent peer reviewers across ten EU member states revealed a state of inertia. The reports might have been written up and posted on the internet, but their circulation within and between government departments and other ministries remained very poor. The website was not advertised, and not one departmental seminar or briefing paper for wider circulation could be detected amongst our cases. Reports were not sent to the social partners, and comparatively senior government officials in relevant policy areas had frequently not even heard of the peer review process. One reason for this lack of diffusion was the relatively junior status of many of the government officials sent as peer reviewers and the lack of continuity of their experience, largely because ministries sent 'experts' on one-off visits rather than 'generalists' for a series of visits. A further reason, however, is that ministries had simply not come to grips with the potential of the peer review exercise: there was no *institutionalised* diffusion through seminars, conferences, chapters or other attempts to feed systematically through to other ministries, social partners or interested agencies.

The impact of peer review is possibly greater on the host programme organisers than on the visitors, however: in a survey of host-country officials, 38 per cent reported 'adaptations or developments' of the policy presented during peer review (ÖSB Consulting, 2001: 3). Some respondents pointed out that it was not possible to identify influences or that it was still too early to assess the potential impact of peer review. Overall, though, the impression is that host officials benefited from the attention paid to them by their colleagues from other countries and from the discussion, rather than from any attempts to engage in policy transfer, of which very few examples were reported (ÖSB Consulting, 2001: 19).

This bears out our own finding, that peer review is more likely to develop as a *learning process* amongst labour market technicians or experts from the member states, which results in a degree of 'tweaking' of existing policies. In other words, it establishes a forum in which ideas, suggestions and observations may be exchanged and thrashed out to test their validity and appropriateness in varying complex domestic frameworks. As Richard Rose (1993: ix) puts it: 'Understanding under what circumstances and to what extent programs effective elsewhere will work here is an essential element in lesson drawing.' What this implies is that peer review programmes will be generally assessed for their 'logic of appropriateness' (Knill, 1998). Put another way, policy transfer will be considered only within the framework of complex institutional networks covering administration, finance, industrial relations, legal matters, social security and taxation – and, furthermore, generally only within the narrow parameters agreeable to the key policy-makers, such as operating procedures and methods of implementation. Indeed, we can expect that 'no more than small or incremental steps – no more than muddling – is ordinarily possible' (Lindblom, 1979: 517). This is at least Euro-level muddling, however, rather than merely its counterpart at national level.

Conclusions

The peer review process has led to a greater awareness of the range of ALMP instruments that exist across the European Union. It has helped to consolidate the learning of the 'epistemic community' of participating experts, but the extent to which it leads to 'promoting innovative approaches' through policy transfer remains problematic. There are several reasons for this. Diffusion may depend on political expedience, such as the availability of EU funding, or on fashion and the desire to be seen following the latest trends. The 'community of experts' responsible for diffusion is itself fragmented and changing, and – so far – unable to integrate itself into the mainstream policy drivers of the relevant government ministries. Above all, practices are most likely to be admired, if not adopted (as there are so few examples of adoption), if they are seen to sit comfortably within the domestic institutional, legal or cultural context. Indeed, the recognition of best practice *as* 'best practice' largely depends on this context.

The constraints on transfer therefore remain formidable: the perceived institutional embeddedness of ALMP is a striking feature of the analysis of this chapter. In particular, there is no evidence that peer review is leading to any broader convergence in ALMP. Whilst overall employment objectives are indeed laid down at EU level in the form of targets under the EES, labour market conditions and institutional frameworks across the member states remain so diverse that – without genuine regulation and harmonisation at EU level – the impact of the OMC is likely to remain strictly limited.

Note

This chapter is based on research financed under the ESRC's Future of Governance Programme (1999–2003). The project 'National Action Plans: Policy Transfer and Social Learning in the EU' was coordinated by Bernard Casey. The author presented the findings contained in this chapter to the annual conference of the British Universities Industrial Relations Association in July 2003. Some of the material has subsequently appeared in Casey and Gold (2005).

References

Abo, T. (ed.) (1994) *Hybrid Factory: The Japanese Production System in the United States*, Oxford: Oxford University Press.

Bennett, C. J. (1991) Review article: What is policy convergence and what causes it?, *British Journal of Political Science*, 21, 215–33.

Biagi, M. (2000) The impact of the European Employment Strategy on the role of labour law and industrial relations, *International Journal of Comparative Labour Law and Industrial Relations*, 16, 2, 155–73.

Casey, B., and M. Gold (2005) Peer review of labour market programmes in the European Union: what can countries really learn from one another?, *Journal of European Public Policy*, 12, 1, 23–43.

de la Porte, C. (2002) Is the open method of coordination appropriate for organizing activities at European level in sensitive policy areas?, *European Law Journal*, 8, 1, 38–58.

Dolowitz, D., and D. Marsh (1996) Who learns what from whom: a review of the policy transfer literature, *Political Studies*, 44, 343–57.

(2000) Learning from abroad: the role of policy transfer in contemporary policy-making, *Governance*, 13, 1, 5–24.

Dyson, K. (2000) EMU as Europeanization: convergence, diversity and contingency, *Journal of Common Market Studies*, 38, 4, 645–66.

Elger, T., and C. Smith (2005) *Assembling Work: Remaking Factory Regimes in Japanese Multinationals in Britain*, Oxford: Oxford University Press.

Euroconfidentiel (1999) *The Rome, Maastricht and Amsterdam Treaties: Comparative Texts*, Brussels: Euroconfidentiel.

European Commission (1993) *Growth, Competitiveness, Employment: The Challenges and Ways Forward into the 21st Century*, White Paper, COM (93)700 Final, Brussels: Commission of the European Communities.

 (1994) Essen European Council: Conclusions of the Presidency, in *Bulletin of the European Union*, December, Brussels: Commission of the European Communities, 7–27.

Evans, M., and J. Davies (1999) Understanding policy transfer: a multi-level, multi-disciplinary perspective, *Public Administration*, 77, 2, 361–85.

Goetschy, J. (1999) The European Employment Strategy: genesis and development, *European Journal of Industrial Relations*, 5, 2, 117–37.

 (2003) EU social policy and developments in worker involvement, in M. Gold (ed.) *New Frontiers of Democratic Participation at Work*, Aldershot: Ashgate, 29–50.

Hodson, D., and I. Maher (2001) The open method as a new mode of governance: the case of soft economic policy coordination, *Journal of Common Market Studies*, 39, 4, 719–46.

Hollingsworth, J. R., and R. Boyer (eds.) (1997) *Contemporary Capitalism: The Embeddedness of Institutions*, Cambridge: Cambridge University Press.

Hyman, R. (2006) Structuring the transnational space: can Europe resist multinational capital?, in A. Ferner, J. Quintanilla and C. Sánchez-Runde (eds.) *Multinationals, Institutions and the Construction of Transnational Practices*, Basingstoke: Palgrave Macmillan, 239–55.

Jacobsson, K. (2004) Soft regulation and the subtle transformation of states: the case of EU employment policy, *Journal of European Social Policy*, 14, 4, 355–70.

James, O., and M. Lodge (2003) The limitations of 'policy transfer' and 'lesson drawing' for public policy research, *Political Studies Review*, 1, 2, 179–93.

Jensen, C. S., J. S. Madsen and J. Due (1999) Phases and dynamics in the development of EU industrial relations regulation, *Industrial Relations Journal*, 30, 2, 118–34.

Knill, C. (1998) European policies: the impact of national administrative traditions, *Journal of Public Policy*, 18, 1, 1–28.

Kogut, B., and D. Parkinson (1993) The diffusion of American organizing principles to Europe, in B. Kogut (ed.) *Country Competitiveness: Technology and the Organizing of Work*, Oxford: Oxford University Press, 179–202.

Lane, C. (1989) *Management and Labour in Europe: The Industrial Enterprise in Germany, Britain and France*, Aldershot: Edward Elgar.

Léonard, E. (2001) Industrial relations and the regulation of employment in Europe, *European Journal of Industrial Relations*, 7, 1, 27–47.

Lindblom, C. E. (1979) Still muddling, not yet through, *Public Administration Review*, 39, 6, 517–26.

Littler, C. R. (1982) *Development of the Labour Process in Capitalist Societies: A Comparative Study of the Transformation of Work Organization in Britain, Japan and the USA*, Aldershot: Gower.

McGlade, J. (2000) Americanization: ideology or process? The case of the US Technical Assistance Program, in J. Zeitlin and G. Herrigel (eds.) *Americanization and Its Limits: Reworking US Technology and Management in Post-war Europe and Japan*, New York: Oxford University Press, 53–75.

OECD (1988) *Why Economic Policies Change Course: Eleven Case Studies*, Paris: Organisation for Economic Co-operation and Development

Official Journal of the European Communities (2002) Council decision of 18 February 2002 on guidelines for member states' employment policies for the year 2002, *Official Journal of the European Communities*, L/60, 1 March, 60–9.

Official Journal of the European Union (2005) Council decision of 12 July 2005 on guidelines for the employment policies of the member states, *Official Journal of the European Union*, L/205, 6 August, 21–7.

Oliver, N., and B. Wilkinson (1992) *The Japanization of British Industry: New Developments in the 1990s*, Oxford: Blackwell.

ÖSB Consulting (2001) *Evaluation of Peer Review Programme on Active Labour Market Policy 2000–2001*, Vienna: ÖSB Consulting, available at http://peerreview.almp.org/pdf/evaluation-report-10-01.pdf.

Rose, R. (1993) *Lesson Drawing in Public Policy*, Chatham, NJ: Chatham House.

Smith, C. (2005) Beyond convergence and divergence: explaining variations in organizational practices and forms, in S. Ackroyd, R. Batt, P. Thompson and P. S. Tolbert (eds.) *The Oxford Handbook of Work and Organization*, Oxford: Oxford University Press, 602–25.

Watt, A. (2004) Reform of the European Employment Strategy after five years: a change of course or merely of presentation?, *European Journal of Industrial Relations*, 10, 2, 117–37.

Whitley, R. (1999) *Divergent Capitalisms: The Social Structuring and Change of Business Systems*, Oxford: Oxford University Press.

Womack, J. P., D. T. Jones and D. Roos (1990) *The Machine that Changed the World: The Triumph of Lean Production*, London: Macmillan.

Zeitlin, J., P. Pochet and L. Magnusson (eds.) (2005) *The Open Method of Coordination in Action: The European Employment and Social Inclusion Strategies*, Brussels: Peter Lang.

Comparative management practices in international advertising agencies in the United Kingdom, Thailand and the United States

Chris Hackley and Amy Rungpaka Tiwsakul

Introduction

According to some cultural theorists, advertising is deeply implicated in the phenomenon of globalisation, yet the management of advertising agencies has attracted much less attention from researchers than advertising itself. Analyses of the cultural economy of advertising have tended to neglect the constitutive management practices of agencies, preferring instead to see advertising as an institution driven by exogenous cultural and economic forces. In this chapter we review a range of research into advertising to substantiate this position before outlining some of the literature that deals with the main roles, functions and processes of advertising production. We then draw on several empirical studies, including some previously unpublished data, to try to pull together strands of advertising management practices in three countries: the United Kingdom, Thailand and the United States.

Advertising and promotional strategies and styles differ very much around the world, in response to national and regional marketing communications environments. Language, economic history and consumer culture, the communications and broadcasting infrastructure and legal and regulatory environments, among other things, create contrasting priorities for ad agencies and clients. This applies even when they are selling the same products in different countries. The management of advertising within agencies around the world, however, does not differ so strikingly, and employees in international agency groups can be quite mobile internationally. Nevertheless, agencies tend to have a very local feel. In the course of the interviews that inform this chapter we came across account planners from Birmingham, England, working in New York in top Madison Avenue agencies, a Thai creative director who had previously worked in American-based agencies, a Welsh account director working for a Japanese-owned Bangkok-based agency, and an American psychology graduate working as head of planning in a London agency. The majority of agency employees we encountered were nationals, though. This might be expected, since mass commercial communication demands a highly nuanced grasp of local idioms and social practices. There might be another reason for the national bias, however. Advertising tends, in each country, to be a relatively small, elite creative industry, and the networks that operate within it are not easy to penetrate.

Ad agency origins and organisation

Most of the large agencies are part of global communication conglomerates and they boast a cross-national perspective, but there are also small, local organisations. Ad agencies began around the late eighteenth century/early nineteenth century in the United Kingdom and United States, as brokers selling advertising space. Often the agency acted for only one or a few print publications. In many cases the head of the agency had a proprietorial interest in the media vehicle in which advertising space was being sold (McFall, 2004). The early agencies often had no division of labour, with one individual winning clients, conducting research, designing strategy, writing copy and deciding on media. As time went on, however, and agencies began to employ specialist artists, writers and client services staff, the traditional agency began to take form. Only around the beginning of the twentieth century did a division of labour begin to emerge within agencies, as the industry sought to professionalise and win greater respectability.

The demands of advertising production dictate the organisation of roles and management mechanisms in agencies to a large extent, so, on a superficial level at least, ad agency management seems to conform to roughly the same template the world over. The traditional 'full-service' agency undertakes any communications-related activity a client demands. This might include a full strategic review of the brand based on consumer and marketing research, leading to a multi-channel creative campaign. It can include other strategic consulting services: one account planner at a northern English branch of a major American agency was designing customer satisfaction survey instruments for a theme park in addition to her research work supporting the development of a promotional campaign. Clients have often taken advantage of ad agencies' strategic perspective and skills for consulting services. In other cases agencies might fulfill any part of a client's marketing communications or branding activity, such as the consumer research, the strategic planning or the creative production.

The traditional agency structure, though, is under threat. Full-service agencies are no longer the default option for major brand clients, as media and direct mail agencies, and small, specialist creative boutiques, are increasingly making inroads into the big advertising accounts. One of the reasons for this is that media audiences are fragmenting so quickly into harder to reach subcultural groupings, and new communications channels and vehicles are developing so rapidly, that even the top agencies frequently have to outsource parts of campaigns to specialists with up-to-date knowledge and relevant skills. Agencies increasingly rely on young staff for their understanding of new media. Nonetheless, even if an agency doesn't necessarily do all the work itself, it still has to *manage* consumer and market research, communications strategy and creative work, and media channel mix. It also has to manage clients. As a result, generic management processes and functions can be identified in all but the most idiosyncratic agencies.

In outline, agency management processes can be summarised thus. Work is organised in account teams. On big accounts, more than one account team might be working on parts of the same account. The account team consists of account executive, account planner or researcher, creative team, and a number of ancillary roles such as art production and 'traffic' or administration management. The account handler (also called client services manager) liaises with the client and reports to the account director. The account 'planner' or researcher generates the consumer insight that will provide the hook of consumer reality on which to hang the advertising fantasy, and reports to the director of planning. The creative team devises an ad in response to the creative brief, and reports to the director of creativity. The account team collectively reports to the agency head, and is responsible to the client.

Agency brands and their management styles

Within this generic management process, however, there are significant differences in emphasis. These differences may seem minor in terms of management process, but to industry professionals they are crucial and far-reaching. In all the countries we have studied, agencies like to regard themselves as distinct from other agencies in the same country (or the same city) in some aspect of their management style. The style of management in an agency is one of the defining features of the agency 'brand'. For example, some agencies are considered straight-laced and hierarchical, focusing on business values and placing great emphasis on smooth client relations. Some long-standing East Coast US agencies have this reputation. Others are regarded as more creatively risky agencies, in which aesthetic values (as opposed to instrumental commercial values) are prized and risks are taken in an anarchically informal working culture. Still others prize their 'account planning' approach, which keeps the consumer in the advertising development loop and (according to the agencies) ensures that the communications strategy is based on empirical insight as well as creative flair. Several British agencies, and a few West Coast US ones, particularly cleave to the 'account planning philosophy' of advertising development.

Some agencies have a planned approach to recruitment that gives them a distinctive climate: one London agency is famous for hiring the top Oxbridge graduates in maths, history and classics. Its understated climate contrasts with the louder, brasher, more macho working-class ethos in some other London agencies. Some agencies are owned by a global group but dominated by local people and a local working approach, as one Bangkok agency was when we visited it. It prides itself on its informal style and closeness to the creative, brand-conscious and humour-loving mentality of the Thai consumer. This agency has since been bought out by the parent company, and the Thai employees have now set up their own independent agency. Other agencies are heavily influenced by the culture and management controls of their international owners. American and Japanese firms in particular have established the now advanced Thai advertising industry, generally by imposing their own management models onto the local context. The result is an attractive blend of high advertising production values with a characteristically Thai humour and aesthetic.

An exploration of comparative management practices in cross-national ad agencies therefore needs to tease out quite elusive management issues that are, nonetheless, significant in their implications for the workers producing the advertising as well as for the consumers consuming it. As we will see below, however, ethnographically inspired descriptions of management practices within agencies have been surprisingly few in number.

Critical cultural accounts of advertising

The relative neglect of the material practices of advertising production

The advertising industry is highly developed and its output attracts a great deal of attention but, oddly, ad agencies remain enigmatic organisations, and what happens in them is not at all well documented. The practice-based marketing literature is very culpable in this respect. Standard marketing texts treat advertising as a subdiscipline of marketing management but they do not deal in ethnographic or other situational accounts of management practice, focusing instead on abstract, normative frameworks (e.g. Kotler, 1980; discussions in Ardley, 2005, and Hackley, 1998, 2003a). This results in a highly generalised, and idealised, account of the ways in which marketing management professionals play out their organisational roles (Brown, 1995). It might appear from such an account that the process is as simplistic as doing some market research, designing a product, then getting an agency to make you a nice ad. Even the more specialised marketing communications texts display the same tendency to avoid situational specifics in favour of abstract models, with only cursory treatment of the internal dynamics and conflicts of marketing or advertising management (Buttle, 1995). Managerial 'marketing communications' texts (e.g. Shimp, 1997, and Pickton and Broderick, 2002) normally offer few (if any) citations to ethnographic or other deeply descriptive work in ad agencies to support the explications of creativity, strategy formulation, advertising production and the integration of research into advertising.

These activities can be classed under what agencies call the 'advertising development process'. This is a general label for the management of account teams in agencies, and it contains many activities. It is the conduct of these activities, and the organisational climate within which they are undertaken, that gives advertising its distinctiveness as unique creative industry. Agencies vary greatly, however, in the way they manage and undertake the advertising development process. As we have noted, the managerial marketing literature tends to underplay this variation in favour of a generic account. The human detail of management practice in ad agencies is neglected not only by the marketing literature, however; the critical cultural literature also neglects it, though for a different reason. Whereas the managerial marketing literature draws an ideologically tinged picture of a relatively unified and cohesive domain of marketing practice, the critical literature uses a generic account of ad agency management to support accounts of advertising's cultural influence.

Critical cultural studies of advertising neglect to give detailed attention to the managerial, technical and economic imperatives that drive advertising practice, tending instead to focus on the analysis of advertising texts (e.g. Williamson, 1978, Barthes, 2000 [1957], and Goldman, 1992). For critical researchers, marketing in general is a key component of the ideological process whereby cultural meanings are inscribed into commodities (Holt, 2002, citing Baudrillard, 1998). Marketing's cultural authority is said to be facilitated, mobilised and articulated by advertising. For Douglas Holt (2002), the application of scientific management principles to advertising from the 1920s fostered the idea that consumers could be controlled by advertising in the interests of the corporations. This momentum accelerated in advertising as post-war psychologists of behaviourism and group influence were co-opted into the advertising game, most famously in the case of behavioural psychologist J. B. Watson (1930), who applied his theories of learning devised while a research academic to his later career as an advertising man. The sense of advertising as a device of mass control managed by a detached class of expert behavioural scientists has been powerful in popular notions of the topic (e.g. Packard, 1959), as well as in both practitioner-based and critical cultural accounts of advertising.

Mark Tadajewski (2006) suggests that McCarthyism and the Cold War influenced the financial, institutional and political drivers behind marketing scholarship, resulting in an accentuated emphasis on 'scientific' research in marketing informed by the quantitative behavioural sciences. As a result, ethnographic studies that tried to reveal and explicate the complex and negotiated management practices that actually obtain in agencies were rather ruled out of bounds in mainstream management business schools, and are more likely to be found among the work of cultural and communication studies scholars. Work such as this tends to be marginalised within mainstream business schools because of their emphasis on a more prescriptive managerial agenda.

Critically inclined marketing and consumer research academics have characterised advertising as a major feature of postmodern consumer culture, especially for its role in producing brands as cultural resources for the production of social identity (Elliott and Wattanasuwan, 1998; Firat and Venkatesh, 1995; Brown, 1994). The position here is that, while there is nothing new about goods having symbolic as well as utilitarian value, advertising is presented as a hybrid realm that binds culture and commerce into commodity signs on a scale and within a communications infrastructure that is historically unprecedented. Although such accounts are seductive, Liz McFall (2004) suggests that their neglect of the material practices and, in particular, the historical context of advertising practices is a serious flaw. She suggests that these accounts implicitly assume that advertising in the modern era is more pervasive and more persuasive than in any other era. Studies of historical archives of advertising show that this is not necessarily the case, if the technologies of advertising media are understood in their historical context. There was never an era in which advertising was quaintly informative; ever since it has been recorded it has made use of integrated media, attention-getting spectacle, emotional appeals and visual rhetoric. Another flaw that McFall reads into the epochal advertising literature is this. Advertising is characterised as a hybrid institution that breaches the cultural and economic domains. It takes meanings extant in non-advertising culture and re-forms them as commodity signs in juxtaposition with marketed brands. This characterisation might rest on an implicit duality between culture and economy, but McFall points out that these two domains are mutually constitutive. She argues that it was never true that culture and economy could be demarcated clearly into two domains, one purely economic, the other purely cultural.

On the other hand, it can hardly be denied that new media technologies and the lateral integration of media interests have created a historically new environment for advertising that, in turn, may well have some subtle effects on the way consumers read and engage with it. For example, studies have shown how advertising is consumed for its own sake as a cultural resource for social positioning in ways quite unconnected with consumption of the actual advertised products (Ritson and Elliott, 1999; Tiwsakul and Hackley, 2007). Furthermore, the interactive involvement of consumers with brands through branded websites, blogs and chatrooms is possible only because of contemporary technologies and techniques of brand marketing communication. If, following Michel Foucault (1984, cited in McFall, 2004), labels such as 'modernist' are regarded not as periodisations but as an attitude or a spirit, then we can understand why many consumer researchers have been keen to characterise contemporary consumption phenomena (especially in connection with advertising) and their social implications as postmodern, the better to distinguish them from anthropologically based studies of the symbolic nature of ownership and the display of goods (e.g. Belk, 1988). Be this as it may, our concern here is that accounts of advertising and its purported role in creating and sustaining a postmodern consumer culture have emphasised the interpretation of advertising and consumption phenomena while neglecting to offer an account of how, why – and, indeed, if – agencies accomplish these phenomena.

We can, therefore, see why ethnographic or other situational accounts of work in ad agencies might undermine the agenda of both managerial and critical accounts of advertising's role. The managerial accounts privilege an advertising agency that operates as a sub-field of marketing management, supplying the promotional 'P' of the four Ps of the 'marketing mix'. Critical cultural accounts see ad agencies as the symbolic factory creating marketing commodity signs by juxtaposing cultural signs with commercial ones. Notwithstanding this, it is not the purpose of this chapter to explore fully the omissions of either category of advertising literature. The point here is to set the context for this chapter by indicating something of the current state of published research on ad agencies. The next step in the chapter is to outline some of the main themes in research on the cultural role and influence of advertising, so as to set current agency practices within a sense of the role and purposes of advertising.

What do ad agencies do?

One view of ad agencies is that they are, simply, a layer of marketing management concerned with raising awareness of brands. Many typical marketing texts and much research in the field rests on the assumption that advertisements persuade individual consumers to change brands or trial new products. Specialist advertising texts tend to allow that its strategic role can be more complex and subtle than this (Hackley, 2005). In the critical literature advertising's key role as a conveyor of ideology is emphasised. The historical role of advertising in legitimising corporate activity and establishing the preconditions for a consumer culture has received detailed historical attention from Roland Marchand (1998), who describes how ad agencies enabled the big American corporates to overcome popular resistance to their growing power at the start of the twentieth century. When critical questions about their influence over American life were asked at presidential level, the ad agencies responded with an onslaught of promotional imagery and rhetoric conferring small-town human values on the faceless corporations. This may have helped establish a baseline of acquiescence for the ad agencies' subsequent role in the production of a culture of promotion (Marchand, 1985; Wernick, 1991).

Many critical cultural studies of advertising have placed ad agencies at the centre of Max Horkheimer and Theodor Adorno's (1944) 'culture industry'. In this role they are thought to be deeply implicated in the production of a seamless, mediated world that links production and consumption under the guise of entertainment. Regardless of the biases of the Frankfurt School, the culture industry thesis seems on the face of it to have found its apotheosis in the way major ad agencies have become a hub connecting movies, TV studios, newspaper groups and brand marketing organisations, all seeking mutually

advantageous ways to cross-promote their various brands in entertainment/
communication contexts (Hackley, 2003a; Tiwsakul, Hackley and Szmigin,
2005; Hackley and Tiwsakul, 2006). The resulting 'intertextuality' (O'Donohoe,
1997) of the consumer experience of advertising seems to be at least one aspect
of the field in which precise historical parallels are difficult to see.

Building on the mutual interests of advertising and commerce and their
joint power to influence news and entertainment, it has been argued that
advertising is the 'super-ideology' of our time (Elliott and Ritson, 1997). This
ideological force is made possible by the panoptic research surveillance of ad
agencies as they use many quasi-anthropological techniques to scrutinise
consumers' inner motivations and unconscious behaviour (Hackley, 2002).
Nonetheless, while many critical research perspectives place advertising and
ad agencies implicitly or explicitly at the hub of this ideological process as
prime movers in the transfer of meaning from culture to consumption
(McCracken, 1986), they differ on the extent to which agencies are an active
presence or a passive instrument of the structural relation between production and consumption. For example, Judith Williamson (1978) offers a
detailed textual analysis of advertisements to highlight their apparent role
in linking and conflating culture and economy, but has nothing to say about
the internal agency mechanisms, techniques and processes that make this
possible. In fact, many critical accounts of advertising (such as Leiss *et al.*,
2005, and Wernick, 1991) implicitly place ad agencies in the role of 'cultural
intermediary' (Bourdieu, 1984), acting to transform non-advertising meanings into commodity signs. One problem with such accounts is that most
leave this transformational process explained only sketchily; the internal
workings of the ad agency are, it seems, of great significance, but they remain
enigmatic.

This is a significant omission. McFall (2004) argues that critical studies of
advertising present particular challenges because of the relative lack of empirical grounding for key implicit assumptions. For example, semiotic analyses of
advertising texts (Barthes, 1973 [1957], 1977 [1964]) tend to assume that there
is a duality between culture and economy. Advertisements, explicated through
the expertise of the semiotician, are supposed to take meanings from authentic
culture and juxtapose them imaginatively with images of commodities, creating commodity signs. There is no examination of the precise way ad agencies
do this; they are assumed to be the fulcrum around which this transformation
from authenticity to artifice turns. If a dialectical relation is supposed in which
economic and cultural meaning are bound up with each other, then the
ideological transformation from authentic meaning to myth becomes less

easy to describe. For McFall (2004), semiotic analyses suffer from other under-specified assumptions. In addition to the assumed duality of commercial and non-commercial culture, there is an assumed historical evolution of advertising from an epoch of functional, rational consumption to one of symbolic, emotional consumption. As we note above, supporting this epochal distinction is an assumption that the techniques of advertising have become progressively more persuasive and more pervasive. Where once advertising was factual and information-based, it is now symbolic and lifestyle-based – or so the story goes. Seductive though such assumptions may be, as McFall notes, there is little historical evidence to substantiate such an historical distinction. 'Thus contemporary forms of advertising practice are seen as emblematic of an underlying structural change, producing a new hybrid form of cultural/economic practice. Advertising is thereby described as a culture industry (Lash and Urry, 1994) staffed by practitioners blending symbolic expertise with economic aims in a "third wave" creative revolution (Mort, 1996; Nixon, 1997)' (McFall, 2004, p. 98).

Critical ethnographic studies of ad agencies

Critical accounts of advertising, and also practice-based accounts, then, often assume that the production of advertising is known and understood while it is consumption that requires examination. There are some ethnographic accounts of life in ad agencies, most from a critical theoretical perspective (e.g. Alvesson, 1998, Miller, 1997, and Moeran, 1996), that are helpful in providing some insight into the material practices of advertising, though generally these have not been assimilated into text-based analyses of advertisements. Hackley (2002) has examined the research practices of ad agencies to explore their 'panoptic' role in the production of consumer culture, arguing that they carry out a largely unacknowledged but extensive and penetrating surveillance of consumers and consumption through their marketing and consumer research practices, and that their skills in this surveillance are key to the function they perform as a conduit between consumers and marketing institutions. As Hackley (2003a, 2003b) has also noted, the suggestion that ad agencies are part of a system of cultural transformation is not unproblematic, partly because exactly how agencies operate is obscured by the degree of internal tension, conflict and contradiction found. More effective expositions of ad agency dynamics might create a more compelling empirical basis for analyses of advertising's cultural and economic role.

Ad agencies, then, are elusive and enigmatic organisations to study. They can often seem folksy, disorganised and parochial places. Most are relatively small businesses in a small industry, even though many are, as we have seen, legally linked as arms of giant communications corporations. Many people attracted to work in them for the opportunity to exercise their creative skills draw on aesthetics and the liberal arts for their cultural reference points, while many others have a hard-nosed business mentality. If they didn't have to act as an arm of brand marketing, with all the supposed accountability and formality of process that implies, ad agencies could be understood as arts or cultural organisations. They occupy this uniquely contradictory site as cultural intermediaries, however, one foot in popular culture, one foot in the arts, and an arm in business. How, then, can we discuss the management practices of ad agencies in a global context?

What sort of management occurs in an ad agency?

In anthropology and organisation studies, organisations have often been conceived in terms of three dimensions: the formal, the informal and the environmental (Wright, 1994). Ad agencies have bureaucratic systems and procedures of management and accountability, and they have highly developed informal systems that often seem to override the formal systems. They also intersect with the environment through two points at either end of a continuum. At one end they intersect with brand marketing clients, and they do so by speaking the language of business. At the other end they have an ethnographer's inside-out understanding of the cultural practices of consumption and communication, earned through their formal and informal systems of consumer research (Hackley, 2002). Finally, they have another point of contact in the middle of this continuum. This is the world of aesthetic and liberal arts, which supply the preferred cultural references points of many ad agency professionals and form the raw symbolic material of advertisements (Hackley and Kover, 2007).

Linguistically, then, ad agencies master three competing vernaculars: those of business, art and popular culture. Their position is further complicated because these three incompatible vernaculars are often located in different nation states (leaving aside problematic conceptualisations of 'national' culture; McSweeney, 2002). If the agency is a subsidiary of a national conglomerate then the governing management culture is that of the global head office, and it has to be superimposed onto the local agency culture. To take one example, major American-based ad agencies tend to be organised along more formal, hierarchical lines than British ones, and they often have a different view of what accountability means in advertising. Consequently, culture clashes can be common. Another source of competing vernaculars is the international account that requires, say, one agency to market a brand in a different country. For example, a British account director in an American-owned London agency might be accountable to American group executives, a French client and British colleagues for a campaign designed for the South African consumer market. This can result in a drift towards a mid-Atlantic advertising vernacular unless the local agencies are allowed (or take) the creative initiative.

Another difficulty raised by studying the management processes of ad agencies is that they have seldom been regarded as exemplars of excellence in management practice. The history of advertising management might be regarded as a persistent attempt to manage the unmanageable. As long as corporations have sought to impose models of bureaucratic efficiency on their ad agencies, the agencies have found ways to circumvent and undermine these controls so as to impose their own creative vision. Ad agency creatives are convinced that clients do not understand marketing communication. They have to be helped, or made, to understand. Not surprisingly, then, agency life is typically fraught with conflict between client and account team, creative and account management, creative and research: and between account teams and their agencies (Kover and Goldberg, 1995; Hackley, 2003b, 2003d). 'Management' seems a slightly grandiose term for the organisation of such a fractious bunch.

Ad agencies are often thought to be the very antithesis of sober, rational business practice while marketing is thought of as the organisational function that unites consumer need and organisational innovation. It can be argued, however, that the main sense in which marketing gives consumers 'what we want' is in a symbolic sense, our imagined 'need' realised in the promotional communication that valorises manufactured objects by drawing on a parasitic relation with non-consumer culture (Cook, 2001; McCracken, 1986). Management in ad agencies is, in some ways, separated from the discourses and practices of management in manufacturing or commercial services. As a hybrid form of organisation, in the sense of being neither completely bureaucratic nor informal but both, ad agencies have generally eluded the management fashions and trends that have proved so influential in other industries. Within the advertising industry, debates about best practice tend to focus on what might be called operational techniques and processes rather than management styles.

As a result, ad agencies do not seem to conform easily to a model of organisation: they are polymorphs. They are bureaucratic, with stated systems, procedures and internal paper trails of accountability. Agencies claim to possess specialised technologies for understanding the workings of the consumer's 'black box' and for creating communications that will resonate with meaning for the chosen kind of consumer. These systems are highly flexible and implemented pragmatically, however, and often seem to dissolve altogether when agencies are studied first-hand. Advertising is a collective endeavour characterised by negotiation between the various functional roles (Richards, Macrury and Botterill, 2000). Hackley (2000) looks at ways in which ad agency professionals construct their own sense of professional identity by internalising the instrumental discourse of the agency. Hackley (2003d) explores the contrasting implicit model of the consumer that each member of the account team deploys in his/her interactions with colleagues. McFall (2004: 73, citing Fish, 1980) suggests that the articulation of a campaign in an ad agency is 'bound up with the production and "reaffirmation" of organisational roles and occupational "habiti"' and this entails being 'caught up in the reproduction of particular organisational identities'. In this broad sense, ad agencies could be seen as places where the order is negotiated (as in Strauss *et al.*, 1963, and Wright, 1994) to a considerable extent through both formal and informal social systems.

Ad agencies are hybrid organisations, operating at the intersection of creative, cultural industries and bureaucratised commercial business. They have creative people, and there is a strong belief within the industry that creative geniuses have to be given a lot of management rope if they are to produce the best work. Other creative staff see themselves as cultural ethnographers, translating the meanings and practices of non-marketing culture into symbols for sale. Agencies have their researchers, their strategists and also their business managers, the account executives, who are expected to speak the same language as clients and who ensure that the bottom line is always served. Agencies, then, flip between accountable, formally controlled and bureaucratised business processes and informal, uncontrolled and creative processes, depending on the circumstances with a given account.

So, when looking at ad agencies in different countries, they can be easier to characterise by their similarities than by their differences. They are, as we have noted, all doing pretty much the same thing, but within a different social and political history, economy and culture, which gives their work a distinct context. Points of difference in management practices can, therefore, be as hard to establish as points of convergence, because of the great variability within the field.

Advertising agencies' internal management practices, then, are arguably central to the maintenance of a globalised sense of consumer culture. One message emerging from recent studies is that Levitt's (1983) notion of the 'globalized' market must, to be realised, rest on ad agencies' understanding of the cultural specificity of consumption and communicative practice in different regions. Through this understanding agencies are able to translate bounded brand identities into globally recognised commodity signs, thereby giving purchase to the notion of a global consumer culture. As we shall see in the next section, though, the cultural understanding of agencies is itself a bounded thing, set within particular historical and cultural conditions.

Comparative ad agency management cultures

Thai ad agencies

Like many Asian countries, Thailand has sharply contrasting areas of urban development and rural poverty. Thailand is one of the leading Asian economies in advertising expenditure (Punyapiroje, Morrison and Hoy, 2002) and has a sophisticated advertising culture in terms of advanced production techniques and creative strategy. The Thai advertising industry has been heavily influenced by an influx of foreign agencies, such as the American JWT (the agency formerly known as J. Walter Thompson); Saatchi and Saatchi, from the United Kingdom; the world's largest communications conglomerate, Dentsu from Japan; and the French-owned Publicis agency group. Nevertheless, much Thai advertising has a Thai 'feel', reflecting the Thai consumer's preference for humorous, visual, creatively imaginative and soft-sell advertising (Sherer, 1995). Many Thai ads emphasise aesthetic beauty and loving relationships, though this occurs in a context of a dominance of Western brands. Thai culture (and Asian culture in general) might be particularly open to Western consumption practices because of the prestige and inferred social status attached to ownership of Western brands (Suphap, 1993; Tirakhunkovit, 1980). This phenomenon has reached such an extent that indigenous Thai industry has a problem marketing home-grown products when they are not regarded as desirable as Western brands by Thai consumers.

Thai ad agencies employ a range of nationalities, including many Thais. Their operating approaches are broadly similar to Western agencies, with one apparent exception: consumer research. Whereas Western consumers are often willing to open up to strangers in focus groups or other research scenarios with their personal insights about consumption, Asian consumers are generally not. The notion of speaking candidly to a stranger about personal matters, such as one's economic decision-making, is a problematic one in many Asian cultures. Even if they do participate in research, south-east Asian consumers may be reluctant to show a lack of respect by offering opinions that appear to contradict those of others. Consequently, research is not much use, and agencies instead have to rely on their insider knowledge of Thai consumption practices. One agency, Publicis of Bangkok, which was until recently owned and run by Thais, has a novel solution to this that they call 'streetsmarts'. This involves all members of an account team taking part in the consumption activity in question: for example, in a campaign brief for a coffee milk substitute very popular in Thailand, all the account team members would go for trips to public coffee houses to watch the rituals of consumption first-hand (Hackley, 2005). This may seem unremarkable, and in Western agencies it is common for quasi-ethnographic observation to be used in the pursuit of insights into the social practices of consumption in particular consumer contexts. What is unusual is the participation of all members of the account team. In Western agencies such a team-oriented approach might threaten the role demarcations and authority of the different account team members. The role of consumer research in Western ad agencies is hotly contested (Kover, 1996) because it is a potential source of power within the account team (Hackley, 2003c). The account team member who 'owns' insights into consumers wields authority with clients and colleagues. In Western agencies it is often convenient for the consumer insights to be owned by one individual (usually the account planner or researcher) so that line management accountability can be maintained. This causes a great deal of conflict in Western agencies, but, nevertheless, the practice of allocating the research 'voice' to one individual within the account team is still adhered to.

In Thailand, as elsewhere, local agencies owned by overseas conglomerates have difficulty maintaining the integrity of their way of doing things under pressure to conform to the management systems of the owner. This Thai-run agency, which used to operate under a French agency brand, has since been taken over operationally by the brand owners while the Thais have left to set up their own agency. It appears that the more communal Thai style of organising advertising development was not understood or appreciated by the Western owner. Another Bangkok agency, owned by a Japanese conglomerate, seems to have a much more formal, Western-style management culture. It holds major accounts (including Thai government accounts) but is known as a creatively conservative agency. The account teams do include Thai people, but they seemed (to us) to be subordinate to the Western account team head. This is global advertising development practice with a Thai input, as opposed to a distinctively Thai, creativity- and consumer-led advertising development process. The campaigns that were described and shown to us had a standardised, corporate feel, though of course it was a very large agency and we could not be sure that these campaigns were typical of the agency's style.

In a British-owned Bangkok agency a Thai creative director (who had been employed before in American agencies) told us of a similarly top-down style of managing advertising development, though with a clear Thai flavour as regards creative practices and standards. It is probably fair to say that the predominant model of Thai ad agency management is American, characterised by a hierarchical agency structure interpolated with Thai creative values. This model seems to work reasonably well in comparison with, say, Malaysia, where the intrusion of Western advertising styles is seen by many to produce culturally clumsy and insensitive results ('patronising' was the view of one Malaysian advertising professional we interviewed). The success and prestige of Thai advertising may be attributed to the willingness of Western agencies and brands to adapt, at least to some degree, to the national sensibility. It may also be the case that Thai consumers are friendlier towards, or more tolerant of, Western styles of communication than their counterparts in some other south-east Asian countries.

Advertising agencies in the United States

US advertising is known for the predominance of the 'rational' appeal. Direct appeals to the consumer's sense of value tend to be more common than in the United Kingdom, Europe and many Asian countries. This hard-sell tone is, in part, driven by the 'scientific management' emphasis that is seen in American marketing. There is much effort put into the measurement and prediction of consumer behaviour. American ad agencies are (so we were told by senior practitioners in New York agencies) dominated by a 'copy testing' mentality. The advertising copy and creative execution is tested at every stage of development with data from consumer surveys and experiments. A negative copy test result can result in a lost account, or a lost job; that is, if a group of consumers in an experiment record negative attitudes towards a given ad, it's back to square one for the creative team. Several New York agency personnel expressed wry admiration for the creative standards of British advertising. They regretted that copy testing was so much bigger in the American than in the British advertising industry.

US agencies, especially the conservative, big East Coast agencies, are known as hierarchical, client-driven organisations. Advertising folklore has it that the client is king, and clients tend to be against advertising that does not appear to be making a hard sell. So the character and tone of American advertising is influenced by the client-driven need for obvious accountability. Creatively risky advertising is more difficult for the client to justify to the board, so it tends not to get made. On the other hand, copy testing yields quantitative results that are powerful rhetorical devices for the persuasion or reassurance of clients and other non-creative stakeholders. American agencies do employ anthropologists for their skills in ethnographic consumer research, but one of these told us that he used his anthropological skills to generate the insights that drove his work, and his statistical skills to impress and reassure clients. This suggests that a scientistic ideology may be so ingrained in American advertising that agencies have to deploy a double standard just to keep accounts.

It is, of course, true that many American agencies have the highest of creative standards, while many also do not conform to the laced-up, client-driven management model. Several West Coast agencies, for example, are well known for their strengths in research and creativity. Comments from interviewees typically reinforced the formal, hierarchical stereotype of US agency management, however. In American agencies the account executive is often the only account team member permitted to speak to the client. The researcher and creative team are kept in the background, while the account executive leads the team and takes the major decisions about the interpretation and use of consumer research and the creative executions that should be presented to the client. One US national working as an account planner in a New York agency summed this scenario up by saying that the client's marketing director, and the agency account executive, had 'quantitative MBAs from Wharton' that, he suggested, led to a cultural divide within the agency between the 'suits' on the one side and the creatives and account planners on the other. In fact, while this account planner was aligning himself with the aesthetic values of the creative team in opposition to the instrumental business mentality of the client and account executive, most agencies suffer from conflict between the creatives and the account planners as well.

American advertising is rich and varied, as are agency management styles, but there are predominant themes clearly evident from our range of interviews, and from previous research. These themes can be summed up in terms of control and accountability. Control over creative content is exercised through the technologies of 'copy testing', and the aim of this control is to hold creative workers, and the agency, to account. This generates some cynicism and bitterness from advertising creatives, and perpetuates the control of senior agency management, ostensibly in the interest of the client. While creatives feel that they know what 'works', the agency management has the power to decide what is good or poor work. The results of 'scientific' management measures and techniques are the resource that agency management draw upon to justify their judgements on particular creative executions. The 'hard sell' tone characterising much US advertising results from this close control of creativity. That is not to say that American advertising is not visually creative, as creative and production standards can be high, but creative executions tend to be tied closely to sales conversation narratives that are very clear about the values and benefits of the product. Advertising narratives that are more opaque are considered risky.

It has to be acknowledged that US advertising culture seems to fit its consumers. American advertising professionals candidly dismissed it as 'shit' in several interviews, but the ethnic diversity of consumers in New York and California means that subtlety and sophistication in advertising are likely to be missed by much of the non-native English-speaking audience. The value-driven advertising might reflect the needs of the mass advertising audience. On the other hand, the imposition of copy testing might in itself limit creativity in American advertising because it imposes a hierarchical corporate control over the creative development process. In turn, this drive to control and bureaucratise advertising creativity might be linked to broader narratives of 'scientific' management ideology and control (Zeitlin and Herrigel, 2000; Kogut, 1993.)

Advertising agencies in the United Kingdom

UK advertising has a prestigious global reputation for its sophistication and creative values. This comes from an agency culture in which the creative authority can be held by the agency. What this means is that clients are regarded as strategic partners who are experts in their brand but who are not experts in communication. Therefore, the agency has the moral authority to argue a given point of view with clients, rather than simply conforming to client values and expectations in the interests of retaining the account. This perhaps somewhat idealised picture has support from American agency interviewees, who spoke admiringly of the license that British agency professionals have to contradict clients' views. They also spoke of their admiration for the creative culture of British advertising, a culture that facilitated creative executions in which 'you don't have to tell the consumer everything'. This comment refers to the softer-sell, narrative-driven character of much British advertising, which is regarded (by some) as creatively superior to the more direct, hard-sell ads typical in the United States. The sales-driven style of American advertising is partly a reflection of the influence that clients wield over creative development. They feel that they need to justify the spending on the ad with a very direct sales pitch. The most creatively striking campaigns often arise from the climate of mutual trust between client and agency, however, which gives the agency much greater creative latitude. Put simply, the client trusts the creative vision of the agency, hands the agency a large cheque and lets it get on with it. This trust seems to characterise the most eminent creative campaigns from British agencies. Campaigns for Guinness, Sony and Honda come to mind.

The creative culture of advertising in the United Kingdom seems more benign that that in the United States. We did not hear any mention of the 'copy testing' that American advertising creative professionals bemoan ('copy testing is the bane of our life') from any British-based advertising professional. There was, though, much more discussion of 'creative research' than there was from American-based employees. Creative research entails understanding the consumer milieu through qualitative methods (often ethnography-derived). The aim is to generate insights into the social practices of consumption in specified contexts, so that these insights can be incorporated into the creative execution to create a sense of reality and resonance that consumers will connect with. This general approach of integrating qualitative insights into creative development is labelled a 'planning philosophy' of advertising development, and is much lauded by several British agencies. The 'planning philosophy' is by no means universally accepted; the industry can't even agree on what the term means. Some of its basic tenets, however, such as the use of qualitative research to gain insight into target consumers, a team approach to creative development and a willingness to create advertising that is not entirely explicit to consumers, seem fairly widely agreed upon.

British agencies have a reputation for being somewhat more collegial and less hierarchical than American ones. In practice, however, they are no less riven by conflict between creative, account planning and account executive. Within British advertising culture, though, more effort seemed to be made by interviewees to play the conflict down, though there were enough references to tantrums and 'cup throwing' for it to be clear that conflict (usually between creatives and everyone else) is common. American creatives seemed more direct or candid about the state of relations between themselves and other account team professionals. The management style in British agencies seemed rather understated, or perhaps more coded than American management style. The impression given by agencies was of informality, but also professionalism. Some British agencies are known for a ribald, macho culture, with punchbags hanging in the open-plan office, beer fridges, basketballs and guitars lying around the office. Others are very understated, quiet but intense places. Most seem to share an air of informality, and some have luxurious fittings, adding to the sense of being elite places for elite people.

This informality, and the emphasis on creativity, for which British ad agencies are known, should not be taken as a lack of accountability. To be sure, there are maverick creative agencies that keep clients at arm's length and resist accountability. In general, moreover, British management style is known for its individuality, innovativeness and lack of close adherence to procedure, compared to management styles more typical in, say, Japan (Storey, Edwards and Sisson, 1997; Elger and Smith, 2005). In most cases, though, effort is made to justify and account for the effects of advertising. The account planner and account director are often jointly charged with the task of writing up case studies that show how a campaign effectively solved a client marketing problem. In some, they draw on statistical techniques such as multivariate analysis to try to isolate the advertising cause and the sales effect. In others, more qualitative reasoning is used. These case studies are often entered for prestigious industry awards for creativity or for advertising effectiveness. The importance of awards in the advertising industry, all over the world, should not be underestimated. In a relatively small, business-to-business context, awards are a badge of achievement. They are crucially important for the careers of creative professionals as well as bringing prestige to the agency brand.

Conclusions: cross-cultural studies of advertising management and the SSD model

In this chapter we have discussed the ways in which advertising and its management are theorised in various different literatures because of the mutual interdependence between these strains of research. The way one conceives of advertising is influenced by the view one holds of the professionals who create it. The character and consequences of what advertising professionals produce changes if these professionals are viewed as a social elite of 'cultural intermediaries', as managerial functionaries or merely as cogs in the capitalist wheel. As we have seen, many theorisations of advertising and its management do not include detailed accounts of the organisational dynamics that obtain within international advertising agencies. In the latter part of this chapter we have drawn together and summarised the findings from a number of studies based on 'ethnographic interviews' to try to look beneath the stereotypes and reveal something of the complexities of work in these enigmatic yet apparently influential organisational forms.

Smith and Meiksins (1995) suggest that variations in cross-cultural organisational forms cannot be fully explained by any simple account of global or local management practices but are subject to the influence of system, society and dominance effects. Seen in these terms, advertising agency management, for all the superficial similarity of its generic processes and working methods, appears to be characterised by system effects that are 'institutionally mediated' and uneven in their influence around the world. The emphases on, respectively, client accountability, creativity and consumer research varies greatly within agencies, depending on the extent to which they adhere to a particular advertising management tradition. There is a degree of system incommensurability in the sense that some systems, such as the British 'planning philosophy' of advertising development, do not fit so well into the agency culture of the United States or Thailand.

This comment leads us into a consideration of the dominance effect. We have noted that, for example, Thai advertising has been heavily influenced by the American model, with American agencies establishing their working methods (hierarchical, client-driven) in their Thai subsidiaries. We also noted, however, that Thai advertising reflects Thai culture. In fact, many Thai ads are more British than American in style, given the love of humour evident in the advertising of both Thailand and the United Kingdom. This, we suggest, is because the dominant organisational systems have had to adapt to local cultural practices. All the international ad agency groups we visited in Thailand employ Thais, and Thais have a distinctive way of working. In the case of one agency we visited, the cultural tensions between Thai working practices and the needs of head office for more Western management systems had become critical. There was a parting of the ways.

That agency had been entirely populated by Thai workers, however. Others succeeded in a mutual accommodation, bolting Thai creative sensibility and local knowledge onto more Western management practices, usually by employing a multinational workforce. The dominance of the Western management values of global communications conglomerates on Thai agency branches was, it seems, contested by and mediated through the national cultural mores and practices that Thai consumers and professionals bring to the production, and the consumption, of advertising.

References

Alvesson, M. (1998) Gender relations and identity at work: a case study of masculinities and femininities in an advertising agency, *Human Relations*, 51, 8, 969–1005.

Ardley, B. (2005) Marketing managers and their life world: explorations in strategic planning using the phenomenological interview, *The Marketing Review*, 5, 2, 111–27.

Barthes, R. (1973 [1957]) Myth today, in R. Barthes *Mythologies* (trans. A. Lavers), London: Paladin, 109–59.

(1977 [1964]) The rhetoric of the image, in R. Barthes *Image-Music-Text* (trans. S. Meath), London: Fontana, 32–51.

(2000 [1957]). *Mythologies* (trans. A. Lavers), London: Vintage.

Baudrillard, J. (1998) *The Consumer Society: Myths and Structures*, Newbury Park, CA: Sage.

Belk, R. (1988) Possessions and the extended self, *Journal of Consumer Research*, 15, 2, 139–68.

Bourdieu, P. (1984) *Distinction: A Critique of the Judgement of Taste*, London: Routledge.

Brown, S. (1994) Marketing as multiplex: screening postmodernism, *European Journal of Marketing*, 28, 8/9, 27–51.

(1995) *Postmodern Marketing*, London: Routledge.

Buttle, F. (1995) Marketing communications theory: what do the texts teach our students?, *International Journal of Advertising*, 14, 297–313.

Cook, G. (2001) *The Discourse of Advertising*, London: Routledge.

Elger, T., and C. Smith (2005) *Assembling Work: Remaking Factory Regimes in Japanese Multinationals in Britain*, Oxford: Oxford University Press.

Elliott, R., and M. Ritson (1997) Post-structuralism and the dialectics of advertising: discourse, ideology, resistance, in S. Brown and D. Turley (eds.) *Consumer Research: Postcards from the Edge*, London: Routledge, 190–248.

Elliott, R., and K. Wattanasuwan (1998) Brands as symbolic resources for the construction of identity, *International Journal of Advertising*, 17, 2, 131–44.

Firat, A. F., and A. Venkatesh (1995) Liberatory postmodernism and the re-enchantment of consumption, *Journal of Consumer Research*, 22, 3, 239–67.

Fish, S. (1980) *Is There a Text in This Class?*, Cambridge, MA: Harvard University Press.

Foucault, M. (1984) What is enlightenment?, in P. Rabinov (ed.) *The Foucault Reader*, London: Penguin Books, 32–50.

Goldman, R. (1992) *Reading Ads Socially*, London: Routledge.

Hackley, C. (1998) Management learning and normative marketing theory: learning from the life-world, *Management Learning*, 29, 1, 91–105.

(2000) Silent running: tacit, discursive and psychological aspects of management in a top UK advertising agency, *British Journal of Management*, 11, 3, 239–54.

(2002) The panoptic role of advertising agencies in the production of consumer culture, *Consumption, Markets and Culture*, 5, 3, 211–29.

(2003a) 'We are all customers now': rhetorical strategy and ideological control in marketing management texts, *Journal of Management Studies*, 40, 5, 1325–52.

(2003b) IMC and Hollywood: what brand managers need to know, *Admap*, 38, 10, 44–7.

(2003c) Account planning: current agency perspectives on an advertising enigma, *Journal of Advertising Research*, 43, 2, 235–45.

(2003d) How divergent beliefs cause account team conflict, *International Journal of Advertising*, 22, 3, 313–32.

(2005) *Advertising and Promotion: Communicating Brands*, London: Sage.

Hackley, C., and A. J. Kover (2007) The trouble with creatives: negotiating creative identity in advertising agencies, *International Journal of Advertising*, 26, 1, 63–78.

Hackley, C., and A. R. Tiwsakul (2006) Entertainment marketing and experiential consumption, *Journal of Marketing Communications*, 12, 1, 63–75.

Holt, D. (2002) Why do brands cause trouble? A dialectical theory of consumer culture and branding, *Journal of Consumer Research*, 29, 1, 70–90.

Horkheimer, M., and T. W. Adorno (1944) *The Dialectic of Enlightenment*, New York: Continuum.

Kogut, B. (ed) (1993) *Country Competitiveness: Technology and the Organizing of Work*, Oxford: Oxford University Press.

Kotler, P. (1980) *Marketing Management; Analysis, Planning, Implementation and Control* (4th edn), Englewood Cliffs, NJ: Prentice-Hall.

Kover, A. J. (1996) Why copywriters don't like advertising research – and what kind of research might they accept?, *Journal of Advertising Research*, 36, 2, 8–12.

Kover, A. J., and S. M. Goldberg (1995) The games copywriters play: conflict, quasi-control, a new proposal, *Journal of Advertising Research*, 35, 4, 52–68.

Lash, S., and J. Urry (1994) *Economies of Signs and Space*, London: Sage.

Leiss, W., S. Kline, S. Jhally and J. Botterill (2005) *Social Communication in Advertising: Consumption in the Mediated Marketplace* (3rd edn.), London: Routledge.

Levitt, T. (1983) The globalization of markets, *Harvard Business Review*, 61, 3, 92–107.

McCracken, G. (1986) Culture and consumption: a theoretical account of the structure and movement of the cultural meaning of consumer goods, *Journal of Consumer Research*, 13, 1, 71–84.

McFall, L. (2004) *Advertising: A Cultural Economy*, London: Sage.

McSweeney, B. (2002) Hofstede's model of national cultural differences and their consequences: a triumph of faith – a failure of analysis, *Human Relations*, 55, 1, 89–117.

Marchand, R. (1985) *Advertising and the American Dream: Making Way for Modernity 1920–1940*, Los Angeles: University of California Press.

(1998) *Creating the Corporate Soul: The Rise of Public Relations and Corporate Imagery in American Big Business*, Los Angeles: University of California Press.

Miller, D. (1997) *Capitalism: An Ethnographic Approach*, London: Berg.

Moeran, B. (1996) *A Japanese Advertising Agency: An Anthropology of Media and Markets*, London: Curzon.

Mort, F. (1996) *Cultures of Consumption: Masculinities and Social Space in Late Twentieth-century Britain*, London: Routledge.

Nixon, S. (1997) Circulating culture, in P. du Gay (ed.) *Production of Culture/Cultures of Production*, London: Sage, 177–234.

O'Donohoe, S. (1997) Raiding the postmodern pantry: advertising intertextuality and the young adult audience, *European Journal of Marketing*, 31, 3/4, 234–54.

Packard, V. (1959) *The Hidden Persuaders*, New York: Mckay.

Pickton, D., and A. Broderick (2002) *Integrated Marketing Communications*, London: Pearson Education.

Punyapiroje, C., M. Morrison and M. Hoy (2002), A nation under the influence: the creative strategy process for advertising in Thailand, *Journal of Current Issues and Research in Advertising*, 24, 2, 51–65.

Richards, B., I. Macrury and J. Botterill (2000) *The Dynamics of Advertising*, London: Routledge.

Ritson, M., and R. Elliott (1999) The social uses of advertising: an ethnographic study of adolescent advertising audiences, *Journal of Consumer Research*, 26, 3, 260–77.

Sherer, P. M. (1995) Selling the sizzle: Thai advertising crackles with creativity as industry continues to grow, *Asian Wall Street Journal Weekly*, 1, 6–7.

Shimp, T. A. (1997) *Advertising, Promotion and Supplemental Aspects of Integrated Marketing Communications* (4th edn.), Orlando, FL: Dryden Press.

Smith, C., and P. Meiksins (1995) System, society and dominance effects in cross-national organisational analysis, *Work, Employment and Society*, 9, 2, 241–67.

Storey, J., P. Edwards and K. Sisson (1997) *Managers in the Making: Careers, Development and Control in Corporate Britain and Japan*, London: Sage.

Strauss, A., L. Schatzman, D. Ehrlich, R. Bucher and M. Sabshin (1963) The hospital and its negotiated order, in E. Friedson (ed.) *The Hospital in Modern Society*, New York: Macmillan, 147–69.

Suphap, S. (1993) *Thai Culture and Society: Values, Family, Religion and Tradition* (8th edn., in Thai), Bangkok: Thai Watanapanich.

Tadajewski, M. (2006) The ordering of marketing theory: the influence of McCarthyism and the Cold War, *Marketing Theory*, 6, 2, 163–99.

Tirakhunkovit, V. (1980) Why Thais do not like Thai products? (in Thai), *Monthly Business Journal*, Bangkok: Thailand Thurakij, 22–9.

Tiwsakul, A. R., and C. Hackley (2007) Young Thai and UK consumers' experiences of television product placement: engagement, resistance and objectification, in M. Craig-Lees, G. Gregory and T. Davis (eds.) *Asia-Pacific Advances in Consumer Research*, vol. VII, Sydney: Association for Consumer Research, 372–7.

Tiwsakul, A. R., C. Hackley and I. Szmigin (2005) Explicit, non-integrated product placement in British television programmes, *International Journal of Advertising*, 24, 1, 95–111.

Watson, J. B. (1930) *Behaviorism* (rev. edn.), Chicago: University of Chicago Press.

Wernick, A. (1991) *Promotional Culture: Advertising, Ideology and Symbolic Expression*, London: Sage.

Williamson, J. (1978) *Decoding Advertising: Ideology and Meaning in Advertisements*, London: Marion Boyars.

Wright, S. (ed.) (1994) *The Anthropology of Organizations*. London: Routledge.

Zeitlin, J., and G. Herrigel (eds.) (2000) *Americanization and Its Limits: Reworking American Technology and Management in Post-war Europe and Japan*, Oxford: Oxford University Press.

15 Corporate social responsibility in Europe: what role for organised labour?

Axel Haunschild, Dirk Matten and Lutz Preuss

Introduction

Corporate social responsibility has increasingly become embraced by indus-try in Europe. Being largely a concept embedded in Anglo-American capita-lism, however, with its emphasis on voluntary action rather than regulation, the transfer of CSR to the European setting has resulted in some tensions. A range of activities that may fall under CSR in the United States, such as the corporate provision of health care or education, have in Europe been under-taken largely on a tax-financed basis (Matten and Moon, 2008). Additionally, the corporate discretion of CSR is at odds with the more regulated frame-works in many European nations, which grant employees and trade unions a well-defined scope to influence corporate decision-making (Dobbin and Boychuk, 1999; Marsden, 1999; Bamber, Lansbury and Wailes, 2004). The impact of CSR on organised labour in Europe is therefore one of the most interesting examples of the impact an ascendant archetype from a dominant society can have on elements of the national business systems of other countries.

Interestingly, this topic is not widely discussed currently, and there seems to be a reluctance in both the industrial relations community to engage actively with CSR (Royle, 2005) and the CSR/business ethics literature to examine the role of trade unions (Preuss, Haunschild and Matten, 2006). Furthermore, there is considerable suspicion among trade unions of CSR, and it is only recently that major players have started engaging with the topic (e.g. Deutscher Gewerkschaftsbund, 2005). The sparse literature on the topic suggests a rather conflict-ridden relationship between CSR and organised labour, with writers judging CSR a threat to trade unions and works councils (Capron and Quairel, 2004; Sobczak, 2004). Our chapter aims to provide greater insight into this field of research by looking at some recent cases of European companies engaging in CSR. Our interest is in elucidating the role of works councils and/or trade unions in these processes.

The chapter opens with a conceptual overview embedding our topic in more long-standing debates in management studies on national differences in organisational practices. We also briefly outline current aspects of the CSR debate and assess their links with industrial relations issues and organised labour more generally. We then move on to present recent research conducted collaboratively between three teams of researchers from France, Belgium and the United Kingdom. The three case studies all deal with the involvement of works councils and/or trade union representatives in the implementation process of CSR elements in three European companies. They are based on original research by the three teams, which was carried out using qualitative interviews and document analysis. After presenting the cases in some detail, we discuss key findings from this exploratory research. Finally, we offer some conclusions for the ongoing research agenda in the field of CSR and industrial relations.

A theoretical lens for understanding organised labour in Europe

Following Paul Edwards and Tony Elger (1999), capitalism constitutes a generic form of economic activity that is shaped by property rights, the accumulation of capital through competition and incessant innovation in both products and production processes. Nonetheless, distinctive national characteristics can be made out, as this generic form is shaped by the inter-action with institutional actors – such as firms, organised labour and the state – in a concrete cultural setting. These national versions of capitalism have grown historically, but they are not fixed for ever. Rather, firms operating in these are in turn subject to isomorphic pressures (DiMaggio and Powell, 1983) to adopt what counts globally as 'best practice', whether it is the Fordist organisation of production, quality circles or CSR. Hence, Smith (2005: 603) sees, within a TNC, a 'three-way tension of (a) generic features of capitalism and (b) particular forms of management and labor derived from the nation-ally embedded context ... and (c) standardizing forces derived from domi-nant or global actors as they represent best practices to the firm'. Applied to our topic, we can thus say that the generic features of capitalism have led to different industrial relations systems across Europe, which in turn are chal-lenged by CSR as an emerging new paradigm.

Capitalism as a political economy and technological system of production is shaped by a number of features that set it apart from other forms of human economic activity. At the centre of the system is the coordinating role of the market. While there is a degree of stability in some markets, producers generally do not know in advance what quantity of goods and services they are able to sell at what price (Smith, 1811 [1776]). Legally enshrined property rights, including property rights in the productive resources, divide society into waged labourers and employers. Work is undertaken for private gain rather than collective good or community status; it is, again, the market that determines the price and quantity of labour. Although labour cannot just be seen as a commodity, there is nonetheless an inherent conflict in capitalism between waged employees and the owners of capital. Waged labour is directed by managers, who are themselves employed as agents of the owners. Since the exact nature of the labour effort can rarely be specified in advance, there is also an inherent conflict between worker and management. Competition leads, furthermore, to a technological dynamism, with a myriad of firms competing to bring new products to the market. This dynamism often leads to a decrease in price for many products as process innovation allows these to be manufactured more cheaply, or it can lead to an increase in the choice in consumer goods (Schumpeter, 1992 [1942]). Technological dynamism also requires workers and managers to keep updating their skills or risk exclusion from the labour market however. Such a description of capitalism is, of course, an ideal type one, as in most societies markets coexist with forms of non-market allocation, private ownership with degrees of public ownership or wage labour with self-employment and unpaid work (Hyman, 2004).

When applied to a specific setting, these generic features of capitalism become subject to an adaptation process. Historical circumstances and cultural values mould capitalist institutions in distinctly national ways and produce a variety of organisational forms and practices. In many cases the adaptation process has been of such a magnitude that scholars have coined the notion of national business systems (Whitley, 1992, 1999) or national forms of capitalism (Albert, 1993). Such differences exist in the relative importance of the stock market and institutional investors in company financing (Hyman, 2004). There are differences in work organisation, whether managerial control is achieved through strict discipline or via the encouragement of responsibility. National differences are also evident in the degree to which employers perceive themselves as being responsible for providing training. To a large extent such national differences are imposed or reinforced by the state, as in national legislation that prohibits or limits monopolies to larger or smaller degrees. Equally, governments differ in the distribution of funding for education, welfare and health, which in turn shapes the position of an individual within the labour market (Hyman, 2004).

In contrast to the more liberal market economy of the United Kingdom, most other European countries have a more coordinated market economy, where a dense network of institutions subjects the decisions of the individual economic actors to limitations of a collective and at times normative kind (Hyman, 2004). These coordinated market economies share a number of distinct features (Ebbinghaus, 1999). Employment is seen not just as a contractual matter but also as a social relationship, and therefore these countries show a broad acceptance of the need for collective regulation of employment to protect the weaker party. As a consequence, individual contracts are often subject to overriding collective ones, which largely determine remuneration and working conditions. Employee input or grievances can be addressed through a formal system of workplace representation, which is often enshrined in law. Moreover, organised labour and industry associations often have a legally enshrined role in the administration of welfare state functions.

Despite such similarities, Europe is better understood as a group of social models. André Saphir (2005) distinguishes four models – Nordic, Anglo-Saxon, Continental and Mediterranean – and analyses their performance in terms of both efficiency (whether they provide sufficient incentives to work) and equity (whether they keep the risk of poverty for the population relatively low). Nordic countries achieve both high employment and low poverty. Continental countries, such as Germany and France, achieve a low poverty risk, but are hampered in the efficiency of their social model by their stricter employment protection. Mediterranean countries, such as Italy and Spain, rank low on poverty avoidance, as do Anglo-Saxon countries, (the United Kingdom and Ireland), but in the latter employment rates are higher due to their lower degree of employment protection. Saphir argues that Anglo-Saxon and Continental countries demonstrate a trade-off between efficiency and equity; whereas the United Kingdom has an efficient but inequitable social model, the German one is more equitable but far less efficient. The high Scandinavian score on both scales, while partly a result of these countries having smaller national economies, is also explained by the greater investment in education, and hence human capital, that these countries undertake.

Such national differences can lead to an uneven process of economic development, which can be observed at various levels. At a national level certain countries become economically more powerful than others, and societies are then no longer equal in their prospects of further economic development. Differences arising from the national remoulding of generic capitalist features are also visible at the level of technology. Both can – individually or in combination – create an international dominance effect, although this is usually of limited duration. The best-studied example of such temporary dominance is probably the success of the Japanese model during the 1970s and 1980s. The rise of the Japanese economy was ascribed to its historically grown pattern of strong links between manufacturers, suppliers and banks within the *keiretsu* structure, as well as the promise of lifelong employment for workers in the core firms of these groupings. These were accompanied by technological innovations, such as the concept of total quality management. As the attempts at adopting these features to non-Japanese contexts show, however, the diffusion process led to the societal origins being neutralised and the focus being directed to technical aspects. In other words, any dominance is also, at least in part, of a symbolic nature (Smith, 2005).

Having reviewed the shared and divergent patterns of capitalism within Europe, we will now examine the impact these have on the reception of CSR in European companies. We enquire what differences there are regarding the degree to which management in diverse European settings involves employee representatives in setting CSR priorities or what, conversely, the role of global pressures in the adoption of CSR practices is. Last but not least, our chapter aims to investigate whether European conceptualisations of CSR differ from US ones, and what implications such differences can have for unions and works councils in European companies.

The rise and spread of CSR in Europe

The 1990s saw a return to dominance of US capitalism, and with it the emergence of another symbolic notion: that of corporate social responsibility. Proponents of CSR argue that companies need to address an entire spectrum of obligations to society, including – but not limited to – economic and legal ones. CSR has thus been defined as 'actions that appear to further some social good, beyond the interests of the firm and that which is required by law' (McWilliams and Siegel, 2001: 117). Similarly, the Green Paper by the European Commission (2001) defines CSR by its voluntary nature. Other authors have argued that CSR need not be an altruistic activity but that it can be applied in a strategic sense, and hence a business case for CSR can be made (Porter and Kramer, 2002; Vogel, 2005; Husted and de Jesus Salazar, 2006). Such definitions do not, however, address the question of what corporate obligations the concept should entail. One attempt at classifying the CSR requirements of companies is Archie Carroll's (1979, 1991) pyramid, which bases CSR on economic responsibilities, upon which legally required and morally expected responsibilities can be met and which culminates in discretionary philanthropic responsibilities.

The range of specific activities that are demanded of companies in the name of CSR is, again, vast. They are expected to integrate social preferences into product development or manufacturing processes. Within the firm, issues relating to employee rights and non-discrimination are raised. Companies are approached for donations by educational establishments, sports clubs or symphony orchestras. They are encouraged to contribute to community development projects, such as the redevelopment of derelict urban areas (Husted, 2003). There is no agreement yet in the CSR literature as to what the content of CSR should be. Perhaps the best-known initiative internationally to identify a list of possible problem areas that should fall under CSR is the UN Global Compact (Kell, 2003). Launched in 2000, it consists of ten universal principles in the areas of human rights, labour relations, the environment and anti-corruption that companies across the world can subscribe to. The labour principles require business to uphold the freedom of association and guarantee an effective recognition of the right to collective bargaining; to eliminate all forms of forced and compulsory labour; to abolish child labour; and to eliminate discrimination in respect of employment and occupation.

CSR is by no means a new idea (Carroll, 1999). After Howard Bowen's (1953) landmark book, an early voice in the academic debate was that of Levitt, who warned in 1958 that 'business's job is not government', and vice versa (47) – an argument that was taken up in Milton Friedman's well-known article in the *New York Times Magazine* in 1970. Since the 1950s CSR seems to have gone through waves of interest, yet over the last decade interest by both corporate critics and managers has been steadily increasing again. This is a result of three related developments (Vogel, 2005; Habisch and Jonker, 2005). First, political changes have led to a relative erosion of the power of national governments in industrialised countries. This is especially evident in their decreasing ability to control large TNCs, but it is also apparent in the persistence of social welfare problems, such as large-scale unemployment. Second, civil society in industrialised countries has undergone important changes in recent decades. There is now a growing awareness of environmental problems and persisting social inequality. This awareness is coupled with new opportunities for addressing political and social concerns parallel to traditional party politics. Third, in the economic sphere we see an increasing mobility of corporations and a growing importance of financial markets for economic success. Magnified by media pressure and advances in IT, these three sources of pressure have raised expectations that business – given its growing economic role in society – should play a more prominent social role too.

In Europe, the academic debate on CSR is relatively young, but it is increasingly gaining momentum (Garriga and Melé, 2004). A particular focus has been on the practices of CSR in management education (Mahoney, 1990; Matten and Moon, 2004), the use of CSR tools (Langlois and Schlegelmilch, 1990; Kolk, 2005) and philanthropic donations for educational, social or environmental causes (Brammer and Pavelin, 2005). As this literature shows, these areas of CSR and their implementation in European companies have become widespread only quite recently. The rise and spread of CSR as an American idea can, incidentally, be observed in all parts of the globe, for instance in Africa, Australasia, South America and south, east and south-east Asia (Moon and Sochacki, 1996, 1998; Birch and Moon, 2004; Fukukawa and Moon, 2004; Chapple and Moon, 2005; Puppim de Oliveira, 2006; Visser, Middleton and McIntosh, 2005; Welford, 2005). There is thus evidence that generic – i.e. system-wide – trends in capitalism, such as an increased internationalisation of capital, the growing power of TNCs and the reduced power of nation states, as well as increased problems of institutional fragmentation between subsidiaries of TNCs, put policies on the corporate agenda that aim to link together the social conditions of workers internationally.

Given such a global expansion of CSR, the concept can be described, in the sense of Smith (2005) above, as a standardising force that is propagated by dominant actors and that is taken as representing best practice. At the same time, CSR is still part of a reshaping of generic capitalist features by national institutions, and it carries a strong national imprint. It is a corporate response to criticism regarding the role of business in society that has been moulded by American society, with its emphasis on voluntary action over regulation; hence the transfer to other parts of the globe, such as Europe, where capitalism has been shaped in a somewhat different fashion, is bound to lead to some tensions. A range of activities that may fall under CSR in the United States, such as the corporate provision of health care, education or sponsorship of the arts, have in Europe largely been financed through higher rates of taxation. Expenditure on health care or education is seen as the duty of government, and so European companies have been less inclined to engage in philanthropic activities than American ones (Palazzo, 2002). Likewise, issues relating to good corporate governance and employee and managerial remuneration have in the United States often been settled by corporate policy, whereas most European countries either are characterised by extensive legislation covering such areas (Matten and Moon, 2008) or resolve these issues in what is often referred to as a 'corporatist approach', assigning social responsibilities to business by way of close and consensual ties between business associations, government and representatives of civil society, most notably employees (Molina and Rhodes, 2002).

Furthermore, the corporate discretion of CSR is at odds with the more regulated frameworks in many European nations, which grant employees and trade unions a well-defined and codified scope to influence corporate decision-making and which hence take care of many elements of the firm-level CSR policies in US corporations (Dobbin and Boychuk, 1999; Marsden, 1999; Bamber, Lansbury and Wailes, 2004). Given the cultural differences that underlie the notion, one can expect differences as to who counts as a legitimate stakeholder and who should consequently be consulted in the process of drawing up and implementing a CSR policy. With regard to organised labour, the question therefore arises of the extent to which unions and works councils in European companies should be involved in CSR activities. Equally, industry associations in Europe often take part in the design and review of the institutional framework governing business. At European Union level, such tripartite consultation has become institutionalised as social dialogue (Marginson, 2005).

The impact of CSR on organised labour in Europe is, therefore, one of the most interesting contemporary examples of the impact that an ascendant archetype from a dominant society can have on elements of the national business systems of other countries. It once again highlights the mutual influences between national business systems and the dominant mode of doing business. Just as the dominant mode influences and changes national business systems beyond its home system, it itself gets adapted and reinterpreted. Moreover, the topic of unions and CSR illustrates the challenges of international CSR research. This concerns particularly the question of whether an international operationalisation of CSR is possible in the first place, since each TNC has its own home-country-based organisational heritage and hence a predisposition towards a specific interpretation of CSR, which inevitably comes into contact and possibly conflict with those of the multiple host countries (Arthaud-Day, 2005).

The case studies

Methodology

We have applied a multiple case study approach (Yin, 2003) in order to compare union reactions to and involvement in CSR in different national and sector contexts. While it could be argued that this research method is limited in terms of the generalisation of its results, in particular across sectors (Hammersley and Gomm, 2000), a case study approach in comparative international business issues is particularly recommended in situations when a rather recent phenomenon is still insufficiently understood (Ghauri, 2004). The case material introduced in this section is based on empirical studies in three European coordinated market economies: France (Brabet, 2006), Belgium (Van Liederkerke and Louche, 2006) and Germany (Haunschild, Matten and Preuss, 2006). All the case studies were part of an EU-funded project initiated and coordinated by Eurocadres, the Council of European Professional and Managerial Staff, based in Brussels. Since the three cases cover only a small selection of European countries as well as three different industries (the textile industry, the agri-food sector and car manufacturing), this empirical approach has an explorative character, and is meant to be a first step towards an exploration of the role of unions or works council in CSR projects of European firms. All three case studies are based on semi-structured interviews as well as an analysis of secondary data. Case study 1 is not anonymised but case studies 2 and 3 have been, as in the original publications of the cases.

In the following section we first outline and then compare the cases. This comparison focuses on those CSR aspects that were relevant in the case firms, the involved actors and their strategies as well as an overall evaluation of the role of unions or works councils in each case. Whereas the original case data are more detailed in some respects, we have selected those aspects of the cases that shed light on the general relationship between CSR activities and union or works council involvement.

Case study 1: Van de Velde

The case company is a Belgian family company specialising in designing, manufacturing and trading luxury lingerie and underwear. Most production has been relocated to Hungary, Tunisia and China, and at the time of writing the company was in a healthy social and financial situation. Taking up a trade

union request concerning labour standards and working conditions in foreign branches, Van de Velde decided in 2003 to employ an independent audit
office to examine the compliance of all production sites with the global social
accountability standard SA8000, developed and overseen by Social
Accountability International (SAI). SA8000 is an example of a code of conduct that can be considered as a typical and extremely popular CSR tool
(Bondy, Matten, and Moon, 2006). Codes mainly help companies to commit
themselves voluntarily to certain ethical standards in countries in which the
institutional framework is weak and the risk of human rights and labour
standard violations is high. Of the many approaches to self-regulation,
SA8000 is one of the strictest and most rigid standards, in particular with
regard to child labour.

Van de Velde's board of management sought to limit the union's influence
in the project but at the same time agreed to keep the certification process
open and transparent. The union, in return, promised to keep all problems
emerging from the auditing process internal. The certification process started
in Belgium and was then extended to the foreign branches. In Belgium, the
certification process led to a formalisation of HRM procedures and practices,
while major European suppliers were asked to commit themselves to SA8000
norms and standards too. Audits of the overseas branches revealed different
problems. In Hungary the implementation of SA8000 was more difficult
than expected, but it was achieved independently by the site in 2005. In
Tunisia it was difficult to find an appropriate auditor, and the more hierarchical authority structures have restricted the required collaboration and
dialogue. In addition, the rapid growth of the site limits the attention that
management currently devotes to SA8000. The most difficult case is China,
however. The branch there is more independent from Van de Velde, and it
refuses SA8000 certification since it already has a Worldwide Responsible
Apparel Production (WRAP) certificate, which is less demanding than
SA8000. Furthermore, the state policy of compulsory pregnancy tests for
female employees contradicts SA8000 values, and, at the same time, changing
this practice is beyond the decision-making power of Van de Velde.

Although the trade union has not been deeply involved in the certification
process, it can be seen as the triggering factor, and it regards the Van de Velde
project as a pilot project for union involvement in CSR. Despite the initial
fears of union members that SA8000 might make relocation of work to
foreign sites even easier, the union fairly quickly acted as a sort of in-house
non-governmental organisation (NGO), creating within the company 'an
international solidarity feeling that was previously not present' (Van

Liederkerke and Louche, 2006: 14). It also helped to mobilise people within the union around the CSR issue. Moreover, it initiated the establishment of contacts with union representatives in all the countries that Van de Velde has plants in (or NGO representatives, in the Chinese case). Management assessed the whole project positively regarding the formalisation of internal procedures, as well as reputation and image, but also stated that shareholders' and stakeholders' (and also competitors') interest in the project (and in CSR in general) had been rather limited. This, together with the high costs, has led Van de Velde's board of management to the conclusion that a continuation of audits to maintain the certificate might not be worthwhile. According to both parties, management and the union, however, the SA8000 project has strengthened an already good relationship and has created mutual trust.

Case study 2: Groupe Agro Alimentaire (AA Group)

This French case company employs about 90,000 people and is acting globally in the agri-food sector (dairy products, drinks, biscuits and cereal products). Its business strategy is based on organic growth and a combination of independent business units with common policies, programmes and tools. The company has a long tradition of dealing with social responsibility issues. More than three decades ago a two-pronged social and economic project, launched by the former managing director and the human resource director, turned the company into a 'social showcase'. Current activities, such as environmental and social responsibility reports or the AA Way guide (explained below), still refer to this project. AA signed up the UN Global Compact as well as agreements with international trade union organisations, and set up a European works council before this became enshrined in EU law.

The AA Way was designed by AA managers in 2000 as a reaction to the increasing globalisation of the company. The main aim of the AA Way was to 'enable the AA culture to be conveyed whilst clarifying standards and to be enriched by sharing best practice ... It was used to bring together information that was vital for reporting in the framework of the NRA law and the Global Compact, but also information that was vital for controlling the Business Units and managing environmental and social risks' (Brabet, 2006: 24). Reporting topics include workers, consumers, suppliers, the environment, civil society and shareholders. The chapter on workers specifically refers to respecting human rights at work; guaranteeing equality; focusing attention on people; investing in people; promoting the unionisation of employees; seeking better performance through values; establishing conditions for dialogue with workers and their representatives; and respecting ethical regulations.

According to the international food sector trade union UIF (a 2005 statement, quoted in Brabet, 2006: 21), AA respects trade union rights and negotiates with unions at every level. There is a long tradition of international meetings and shared policies between management and unions, covering, for example, the provision of adequate information to trade unions and other workers' representatives, gender equality, and a policy for providing training. In 2004 UIF and AA agreed on twenty social indicators in order to evaluate the extent to which agreements have been put into practice. Unions or other stakeholder representatives were not involved in the design of the AA Way, however. In addition, the implementation of the AA Way across the whole company and its business units has been monitored by a management steering committee. Although self-assessment in the business units includes worker participation, unions are not involved.

Case study 3: STARCAR

The case company is one of the major global car manufacturers, with production facilities in twenty countries and some 384,000 employees. Headquartered in Germany, the company is the country's second biggest car manufacturer and the fifth globally. Internationalisation of the company was pushed forward by a merger with a US company some years ago. The company describes itself as comparatively decentralised, with its headquarters playing a coordinating role. STARCAR is deeply embedded in the traditions and characteristics of the German industrial relations system. The corporate works council (Gesamtbetriebsrat) is the most important committee in this respect, representing about 160,000 employees in Germany. At the global level, employees are represented by the world employment committee (WEC), formally accepted by the company as the bargaining partner for global agreements in 2002. Both employer's and employees' representatives describe their relationship as constructive, characterised by an open discussion culture, mutual trust and reliability as well as a willingness to share information.

In 2000 STARCAR's chief executive officer (CEO) signed the UN Global Compact, which includes a commitment to meet standards in the areas of human rights, labour standards, environment and anti-corruption. Since then CSR has become a topic of considerable debate in STARCAR. In 2002, the WEC and STARCAR signed the company's 'corporate social responsibility principles'. These principles have the status of a plant bargaining agreement (Betriebsvereinbarung) or international framework agreement in the terms of the International Metalworkers' Federation. They concentrate on social rather than environmental issues, including human rights (forced labour, child labour, equal opportunities, equal pay for equal value), working conditions (the protection of health, compensation, working hours, training, suppliers) and relations between employer and employee representatives.

CSR was initially promoted by the top managers, who signed the UN Global Compact without previous debate or consultation with either the works council or the human relations (HR) department. At the same time, the works council approached the HR department in order to negotiate mutual and binding global CSR agreements. This initiative was influenced by similar negotiations at Germany's no. 1 car manufacturer as well as requests from IG Metall (the chief metalworkers' union in Germany) and the International Metalworkers' Federation. Whereas the HR department at first refused to negotiate a legally binding CSR commitment, the initiative taken by top management persuaded it to start negotiations on CSR principles. The main strategic aim of the workers' representatives can be seen in going beyond one-sided company initiatives ('soft law') to achieve a legally binding commitment ('hard law'). The existing agreement is seen as a framework that now has to be developed further in order to specify its more general terms. In addition, procedures to enforce CSR agreements are to be developed.

Overall, STARCAR's works council is in a strong position in CSR-related topics. It has been able to use CSR, as well as its institutional strength based on the German industrial relations system, as leverage in subsidiaries, which are not subject to German law. Through the mechanism of a contractual framework and its legal status, CSR within the global group no longer has the character of a voluntary initiative on the part of the employer. The works council may not be the driver of all group-wide CSR activities but it definitely is a major CSR player, internationally promoting the codification and enforcement of STARCAR's CSR activities.

Comparative discussion of case research

The three cases are different with respect to industry, company size and national industrial relations system, but they also share some common characteristics. All the cases show that CSR-related topics have been taken up as a reaction to an internationalisation of business. The initial drive for adopting CSR ideas in the first place came from external developments and stakeholder expectations. The role of the unions was different in the three cases, however. Whereas in the case of Van de Velde the union requested and promoted an audit of the company's social responsibility, in the cases of AA Group and STARCAR management initiated CSR activities without union demands and even without union consultation.

The cases also show that most aspects covered by the notion of CSR are not new for managers or unions in coordinated market economies. While there is now a broad range of concepts and terms used to describe new and increasingly expected corporate responsibilities (such as corporate social responsibility, sustainability, business ethics, compliance management and corporate governance), a shared language still has to be developed. Furthermore, all cases demonstrate the increasing demand on unions and works councils to internationalise their activities. This requires the development of knowledge of these foreign branches in addition to mobilising home-country workers around the problems in these branches. There is also a growing need to be aware of different national industrial relations systems, and rules of global worker representation and co-determination within TNC settings have to be developed and put into practice. An increase in intra-firm competition, which is likely to happen in most companies in the near future, would make worker representation far more difficult at the international level and is likely to cause conflicts between national unions and works councils. What has also been revealed by the cases is that traditional union issues are increasingly taken up by other actors such as NGOs, which often use a wider notion of social responsibility, including not only social but also environmental issues, and often a general critique of capitalism as well.

In the case companies unions have not seen CSR as a threat (see Preuss, Haunschild and Matten, 2006, for contrasting examples). The consequences of the CSR activities for the internal bargaining power of workers' representatives differ in the three cases, however. At Van de Velde, as well as at STARCAR, employer's CSR initiatives were not perceived as attempts to undermine or weaken the trust-based relationship between company and workers' representatives; rather, CSR has been used to maintain and strengthen the relationship. At AA Group, CSR did not have a negative impact on unions' position either; involvement in CSR-related activities remained unclear nonetheless, and not satisfactory from the unions' perspective (Brabet, 2006). The comparison of the three cases is summarised in table 15.1, which also provides some further company details.

Table 15.1 Trade unions and CSR: three TNC case studies

	Case study 1: Van de Velde	Case study 2: Groupe Agro Alimentaire (AA Group)	Case study 3: STARCAR
Country	Belgium, large part of production in Hungary, Tunisia and China	France, TNC	Headquarters in Germany, merger with large US company
Industry	Garment/textile industry	Agri-food sector (dairy products, drinks, biscuits, cereals)	Automobile industry
Company details	Family company, 3,000 employees	TNC, 90,000 employees, independent business units	TNC, 380,000 employees; worldwide production sites and sales organisation
CSR project	External SA8000 accreditation for working conditions in foreign branches	Internal 'AA Way' as strategic concept linking reporting and measurement of economic and social issues	Company initiatives (external UN Global Compact) and framework agreement between employer and works council (CSR principles)
External forces and drivers	Criticism and boycotts in textile and clothing sector; relocation of production sites	Problems of integration in a globalised company	Internationalisation; CSR activities of major competitor; union and works council demands
Role and strategy of management	Board of management reacts to trade union demand with launch of SA8000 project; attempts to limit trade union influence in the project but keeps the process open and transparent	Long tradition in social responsibility management; recognition of and respect for workers representatives and unions as partners, but attempts to limit trade union influence in the AA Way project	Company initiatives fostered by top management as well as collective bargaining with national and international works councils; close cooperation with workers' representatives
Role and strategy of unions or works council	Trade union request as starting point for SA8000 accreditation; establishment of contacts with unions or NGOs in countries of foreign subsidiaries	Disappointment about lack of influence in AA Way project	CSR as catalyst for internationalisation and continued role of involvement in strategic decision-making; strives for mutual and binding agreements ('hard law')
Other relevant actors	SA8000 project accompanied by consultants; difficulties in finding capable auditors in Tunisia; problems implementing project at all sites, particularly at more independent Chinese branch; NGO replaces union contact in China	No evidence in case study	Increasing but so far informal engagement with NGOs
Summary	Management and unions see the SA8000 accreditation project as success; due to high costs and lack of stakeholder interest, however, the continuation of the project is in doubt	Despite a long tradition of reflective CSR management and a good relationship between company and worker representation, unions play a minor role in current initiatives that link social responsibility and business activities	STARCAR's works council is in a strong position in CSR-related topics; it uses CSR as leverage in subsidiaries that are not subject to German law; due to a contractual framework, CSR is no longer only a voluntary initiative of the employer

Discussion

Here we consider the case material with reference to the theoretical framework outlined at the beginning of this chapter, Smith's (2005) model of understanding variations in organisational practices and forms. The discussion focuses on the system, society and dominance effects that shape the roles unions and works council (can) play in current CSR projects. The three case studies highlight a number of important issues: first, in terms of understanding the spread of CSR as a new management idea; second, regarding our understanding of how these new management ideas become 'translated' and contextualised in different national and societal contexts; and, third, about the nature of the globalisation process and the forces of dominance currently shaping global capitalism.

Turning to the first aspect, the system effect, leading to some global universalisation of management practices, refers – among other things – to 'global technology or techniques and ways of working that are diffused as common standards' (Smith, 2005: 612). Interestingly, in all three of our cases we found that CSR entered the respective companies through global standards and systems of self-regulation. In the French and German cases, the key initiating element was the company joining the UN Global Compact, which led to the diffusion and implementation of CSR policies and practices within the respective organisations. In the Belgian company, CSR got on the agenda through the implementation of the global workplace standard SA 8000. In spite of variety in the industry, size and national background of the companies, we can identify CSR as a manifestation of a 'managerial discourse [. . .] creating common methodologies regardless of the sector or country in which the firm is operating' (Smith, 2005: 613). In a similar vein, the concern with CSR in these companies was not raised through their domestic operations. Rather, as the case of Van de Velde probably makes most clear, the adoption of CSR was triggered by the fact that the company is operating globally and faces stakeholder expectations of responsible behaviour in areas in which no mandatory legal framework forces it to do so.

As Dirk Matten and Jeremy Moon (2008) argue, this global spread of CSR can be understood from the perspective of new institutionalism. Following the analysis of the spread of the international quality standard ISO 9000 by Isin Guler, Mauro Guillén and John Muir MacPherson (2002), they suggest three isomorphic pressures as being instrumental to this phenomenon. The Belgian case exemplifies what we could see as isomorphic pressures: following the scandals around sweatshops, most notably those involving Gap and Nike in the late 1990s, the garment industry faced considerable pressure from NGOs, consumers and other stakeholders to maintain minimum standards in their overseas operations. By contrast, the German case revealed strong traits of mimetic processes, as the move into CSR was very much perceived to be the result of top management following a trend among TNCs to sign the UN Global Compact. Finally, the French case highlights normative pressures, as CSR in AA was chiefly considered to be a state-of-the-art strategic concept for integrating certain areas of its global operations.

Our cases also shed an interesting light on the second aspect of Smith's model, societal effects and the role of national divergence in management practices. To begin with, our research has highlighted the fact that CSR is not a European idea, and that for all three companies the engagement with these issues was a rather recent phenomenon that had not hitherto been practised. Moreover, all the companies engaged in CSR for reasons other than many of the classic issues in the original, US-style practice of CSR, such as corporate philanthropy (Brammer and Pavelin, 2005), education (Timpane and Miller McNeil, 1991; Dowie, 2001) or health care (Hacker, 1997). For all the companies in our cases CSR got on the agenda because of issues arising beyond their home country, most notably in connection with the global supply chain (Van de Velde), subsidiaries in less developed countries (STARCAR) or the global governance of social responsibility within the global organisation (AA Group). Accordingly, CSR becomes contextualised within a specifically European agenda, without the baggage evident in its American genesis.

Our research also highlights the fairly different approaches to employee stakeholders on either side of the Atlantic. The role and rights of employees have been a long-standing item on US-style CSR agendas. This is neatly captured in a comment by the president of Studebaker Motor Company nearly a century ago (quoted in Heald, 1970: 36):

The first duty of an employer is to labor . . . It is the duty of capital and management to compensate liberally, paying at least the current wage and probably a little more, and to give workers decent and healthful surroundings and treat them with utmost consideration.

CSR sees the employer as the pivotal agent and conceptualizes his/her responsibility in terms of the *duties* he/she has to fulfil. On the opposite side, Europe has a long and vibrant tradition of conceptualising these responsibilities in terms of the *rights* of employees, which are embedded in and enforced through a dense network of mandatory regulation, often referred to as the 'European social model' (Hyman, 2001a, 2001b, 2005). As Royle (2005) has shown, it is exactly at this point that US companies – otherwise known as leaders in the CSR field – struggle to embrace the different nature of industrial relations in Europe. Our research highlights these tensions in an interesting way. First, many of our respondents expressed concern regarding the voluntary nature of these initiatives, and the French case in particular shows that trade union representatives perceived the initiatives – though in themselves laudable – as a potential threat to their position. At STARCAR the works council was very eager not just to implement CSR policies but to integrate them into the usual regulatory framework of an agreement that transforms the voluntary commitments of employers into a mandatory and codified right of employees.

Second, the industrial relations framework in many European countries makes it a necessity for companies to involve their works council through the co-determination process, which turns works councils or trade union representatives into a 'natural partner' for CSR issues. This is certainly the case at STARCAR and Van de Velde, although the evidence of AA Group suggests that this is not necessarily the typical practice, and further research is required to ascertain the detailed determinants of union involvement in CSR. Finally, the examples of STARCAR and, most notably, Van de Velde provide evidence of a relatively active role for organised labour in CSR. As they are traditionally involved in many CSR-related issues, unions can assume, as it were, the role of an in-house NGO in pushing and implementing the CSR agenda throughout the global operations of a European company. In the two latter cases worker's representatives served as contact points for engaging with other civil society actors, and thus provided a pre-existing infrastructure for companies to engage with stakeholders – a phenomenon largely unmentioned in the predominantly US-authored stakeholder literature.

With regard to the third aspect, the dominance effects in Smith's model, one might argue that the spread of CSR is part of a broader Americanisation of global business practices. For some years now many commentators have been commenting on the export of the 'American model' of management practices to Europe (e.g. Djelic, 1998, and Mayer and Whittington, 2002). More recently, authors such as David Held (2004) have argued that, following the end of the Cold War and especially following the rise of global terrorism after September 2001, we have witnessed what he refers to as the 'Washington Consensus', which aims to shape economic and political processes according to the preferences of the only remaining superpower. Assisted by actors such as the World Bank, the IMF, the WTO and others, the world economy has been characterized by a shift towards further economic liberalisation, privatisation and deregulation, placing TNCs in a pivotal global economic role. Hand in hand with these trends, corporations have increasingly taken up CSR in order to forestall or circumvent imperative regulation by national governments. Many commentators therefore see CSR as part and parcel of such a global shift (e.g. Bakan, 2004) and one of the key initiatives in the CSR area, the UN Global Compact, as a blatant example of even the United Nations being co-opted into this approach, which makes commitment to labour, human rights or environmental standards just an area of voluntary corporate discretion rather than of stringent national or supranational regulation (Monbiot, 2000; Bendell, 2004). Interestingly, in two of our three cases the initiative to engage in CSR was indeed triggered by the UN Global Compact, and in the Belgian case it was the adoption of one of the most-discussed global standards of corporate voluntary self-regulation (SA 8000) that led the company to engage in CSR. In this sense, then, CSR can in fact be interpreted as a reflection of the current dominance of the American model of capitalism, in particular the focus on shareholder value maximisation and the economic liberty of corporations.

From a trade union perspective this approach appears rather problematic, as codified worker's rights do not necessarily feature high on this agenda, if they are addressed at all. Indeed, trade union representatives heavily criticised the UN Global Compact as having been drawn up to the exclusion of the trade union movement, with these actors only recently starting to be integrated (Baker, 2004). As the French case shows, in becoming 'socially responsible' the company can in fact largely ignore its workers' official representatives. At the global level in particular we see that corporations, mostly by adopting codes of conduct, are in fact privatising the governance of workers' rights, and use CSR as a substitute for traditional industrial relations frameworks (Arthurs, 2005). While this can still be considered an improvement in developing countries with poor governance and low enforcement of workers' rights (see Blowfield and Frynas, 2005, for an overview), it becomes problematic in Europe, where employees have traditionally been protected by a fairly solid regulatory regime. Many commentators, though, have argued that current trends towards the regulation of industrial relations across the European Union tend to erode and weaken this position (Hyman, 2001b). Conspicuously, with its latest initiative in the area of CSR the European Commission has departed from the long-standing tradition of multi-stakeholder consultation (including organised labour) and has launched its new 2006 'European Alliance for CSR', which focuses solely on corporations and excludes other stakeholders' representatives such as NGOs and trade unions

(Gardner, 2006). Against this backdrop, the spread of CSR might indeed become a threat to the influence of trade unions and works councils, in which case it might actually be the French case, rather than the German and the Belgian ones, that is pointing to the way ahead.

Conclusions: towards a European research agenda on CSR

The exploratory research discussed in this chapter, though limited and hardly capable of being generalised, highlights some important issues for further research. First, we would argue that the 'export' of what is basically a US concept to Europe exposes the nature of CSR as an 'essentially contested concept' that is 'appraisive' (or considered as valued), 'internally complex' and having relatively open rules of application (Moon, Crane and Matten, 2005: 433–4). European corporations focus on different aspects of CSR from their North American counterparts, and they face a different institutional setting for their attempts to provide a new meaning for their role of 'responsible' societal actors. Ultimately, the recent European interest in CSR points to a necessity to define and contextualise CSR in different national and regional contexts.

Second, our research has shown that – though largely ignored in the contemporary CSR literature – trade unions and their representatives play an active role in CSR, in some cases even a genuinely pivotal one. The relative differences in responses, strategies and practices, however, suggest that there is still a large field of investigation in order to establish what the antecedents, contingencies and success factors of an involvement of trade unions in the CSR agenda might be. Finally, our research raises questions regarding the nature of the relation between organised labour and CSR. Two of our cases have suggested a relatively benevolent and harmonious integration of CSR, while the French case in particular might raise concerns about the impact of CSR on the role of trade unions. The jury is still out, therefore, on whether the currently rather apprehensive tone in much of the literature on CSR from a trade union perspective only partly captures the situation in an adequate fashion.

References

Albert, M. (1993) *Capitalism vs. Capitalism: How America's Obsession with Individual Achievement and Short-term Profit Has Led It to the Brink of Collapse*, New York: Four Walls Eight Windows.

Arthaud-Day, M. L. (2005) Transnational corporate social responsibility: a tri-dimensional approach to international CSR research, *Business Ethics Quarterly*, 15, 1, 1–22.

Arthurs, H. W. (2005) Private ordering of worker's rights in the global economy: corporate codes of conduct as a regime of labour market regulation, in W. Cragg (ed.) *Ethics Codes, Corporations and the Challenge of Globalization*, Cheltenham: Edward Elgar, 194–211.

Bakan, J. (2004) *The Corporation: The Pathological Pursuit of Profit and Power*, New York: Free Press.

Baker, J. (2004) Labour and the Global Compact: the early days, in M. McIntosh, S. Waddock and G. Kell (eds.) *Learning to Talk: Corporate Citizenship and the Development of the UN Global Compact*, Sheffield: Greenleaf, 168–82.

Bamber, G., R. Lansbury and N. Wailes (eds.) (2004) *International and Comparative Employment Relations* (4th edn.), London: Sage.

Beaujolin, F. (2004) *European trade unions and corporate social responsibility: Final report to the European Trade Union Confederation*, Brussels: ETUC.

Bendell, J. (2004) Flags of inconvenience? The Global Compact and the future of the United Nations, in M. McIntosh, S. Waddock and G. Kell (eds.) *Learning to Talk: Corporate Citizenship and the Development of the UN Global Compact*, Sheffield: Greenleaf, 146–67.

Birch, D., and J. Moon (2004) Corporate social responsibility in Asia, *Journal of Corporate Citizenship*, 13, Special Issue, 18–149.

Blowfield, M., and J. G. Frynas (2005) Setting new agendas: critical perspectives on corporate social responsibility in the developing world, *International Affairs*, 81, 3, 499–513.

Bondy, K., D. Matten and J. Moon (2006) Codes of conduct as a tool for sustainable governance in multinational corporations, in S. Benn and D. Dunphy (eds.) *Corporate Governance and Sustainability: Challenges for Theory and Practice*, London: Routledge, 165–86.

Bowen, H. R. (1953) *Social Responsibilities of the Businessman*, New York: Harper and Row.

Brabet, J. (2006) From the two-pronged social and economic project to the AA Way: CSR at loggerheads with globalisation and increasing profitability, in *A Curriculum for Responsible European Management (REM)*, Brussels: Eurocadres, 19–27, available at www.eurocadres. org/en/areas_of_action/responsible_european_management/publications_and_material/ publications/a_curriculum_for_responsible_european_management.

Brammer, S., and S. Pavelin (2005) Corporate community contributions in the United Kingdom and the United States, *Journal of Business Ethics*, 56, 15–26.

Capron, M., and F. Quairel (2004) *Mythes et réalités de l'entreprise responsable*, Paris: La Découverte.

Carroll, A. B. (1979) A three-dimensional conceptual model of corporate performance, *Academy of Management Review*, 4, 4, 497–505.

(1991) The pyramid of corporate social responsibility: toward the moral management of organizational stakeholders, *Business Horizons*, 34, 4, 39–48.

(1999) Corporate social responsibility: evolution of a definitional construct, *Business and Society*, 38, 268–95.

Chapple, W., and J. Moon (2005) Corporate social responsibility in Asia: a seven country study of CSR website reporting, *Business and Society*, 44, 4, 415–41.

Deutscher Gewerkschaftsbund (2005) *Corporate Social Responsibility (CSR): Neue Handlungsfelder für Arbeitnehmervertretungen*, Düsseldorf: Deutscher Gewerkschaftsbund.

DiMaggio, P. J., and W. W. Powell (1983) The iron cage revisited: institutional isomorphism and collective rationality in organizational fields, *American Sociological Review*, 48, 147–60.

Djelic, M.-L. (1998) *Exporting the American Model: The Postwar Transformation of European Businesses*, Oxford: Oxford University Press.

Dobbin, F., and T. Boychuk (1999) National employment systems and job autonomy: why job autonomy is high in the Nordic countries and low in the United States, Canada, and Australia, *Organization Studies*, 20, 257–91.

Dowie, M. (2001) *American Foundations: An Investigative History*, Cambridge, MA: MIT Press.

Ebbinghaus, B. (1999) Does a European social model exist and can it survive?, in G. Huemer, M. Mesch and F. Traxler (eds.) *The Role of Employer Associations and Labour Unions in the EMU*, Aldershot: Ashgate, 1–26.

Edwards, P., and T. Elger (1999) *National States and the Regulation of Labour in the Global Economy*, London: Mansell.

European Commission (2001) *Promoting a European Framework for Corporate Social Responsibility*, Green Paper, Brussels: Commission of the European Communities, available at http://europa.eu.int/comm/employment_social/soc-dial/csr/greenpaper_en.pdf.

Friedman, M. (1970) The social responsibility of business is to increase its profits, *New York Times Magazine*, 13 September, 32–3.

Fukukawa, K., and J. Moon (2004) A Japanese model of corporate social responsibility? A study of website reporting, *Journal of Corporate Citizenship*, 16, 45–59.

Gardner, S. (2006) Pushing business-driven corporate citizenship, *Ethical Corporation*, April, 8–9.

Garriga, E., and D. Melé (2004) Corporate social responsibility theories: mapping the territory, *Journal of Business Ethics*, 53, 1/2, 51–71.

Ghauri, P. N. (2004) Designing and conducting case studies in international business research, in R. Marschan-Piekkari and C. Welch (eds.) *Handbook of Qualitative Research Methods for International Business*, Cheltenham: Edward Elgar, 109–24.

Guler, I., M. Guillén and J. M. MacPherson (2002) Global competition, institutions and the diffusion of organizational practices: the international spread of the ISO 9000 quality certificates, *Administrative Science Quarterly*, 47, 207–32.

Habisch, A., and J. Jonker (2005) Introduction, in A. Habisch, J. Jonker, M. Wegner and R. Schmidpeter (eds.) *Corporate Social Responsibility across Europe*, Berlin: Springer, 1–9.

Hacker, J. S. (1997) *The Road to Nowhere: The Genesis of President Clinton's Plan for Health Security*, Princeton, NJ: Princeton University Press.

Hammersley, M., and R. Gomm (2000) Introduction, in R. Gomm, M. Hammersley and P. Foster (eds.) *Case Study Method*, London: Sage, 1–16.

Haunschild, A., D. Matten and L. Preuss (2006) CSR and the internationalisation of employment relations: the case of a German car manufacturer, in *A Curriculum for Responsible European Management (REM)*, Brussels: Eurocadres, 29–35, available at www.eurocadres.org/en/areas_of_action/responsible_european_management/publications_and_material/publications/a_curriculum_for_responsible_european_management.

Heald, M. (1970) *The Social Responsibilities of Business: Company and Community, 1900–1960*, Cleveland, OH: Press of Case Western Reserve University.

Held, D. (2004) *Global Covenant: The Social Democratic Alternative to the Washington Consensus*, Cambridge: Polity Press.

Husted, B. W. (2003) Corporate governance choices for corporate social responsibility, *Long Range Planning*, 36, 481–98.

Husted, B. W., J. de Jesus Salazar (2006) Taking Friedman seriously: maximizing profits and social performance, *Journal of Management Studies*, 43, 1, 75–91.

Hyman, R. (2001a) *Understanding European Trade Unionism: Between Market, Class and Society*, London: Sage.

   (2001b) The Europeanization – or the erosion – of industrial relations?, *Industrial Relations Journal*, 32, 4, 280–94.

   (2004) Varieties of capitalism, national industrial relations systems and transnational challenges, in A.-W. Harzing and J. van Ruysseveldt (eds.) *International Human Resource Management: An Integrated Approach* (2nd edn.), London: Sage, 411–32.

   (2005) Trade unions and the politics of the European social model, *Economic and Industrial Democracy*, 26, 1, 9–40.

Kell, G. (2003) The global compact: origins, operations, progress, challenges, *Journal of Corporate Citizenship*, 11, 35–49.

Kolk, A. (2005) Environmental reporting by multinationals from the Triad: convergence or divergence? *Management International Review*, 45, Special Issue 1, 145–66.

Langlois, C., and B. Schlegelmilch (1990) Do corporate codes of ethics reflect national character? Evidence from Europe and the United States, *Journal of International Business Studies*, 21, 4, 519–39.

Levitt, T. (1958) The dangers of social responsibility, *Harvard Business Review*, 36, 5, 41–50.

McWilliams, A., and D. S. Siegel (2001) Corporate social responsibility: a theory of the firm perspective, *Academy of Management Review*, 26, 117–27

Mahoney, J. (1990) *Teaching business ethics in the UK, Europe, and the USA: A Comparative Study*, London: Athlone Press.

Marginson, P. (2005) Industrial relations at European sector level: the weak link?, *Economic and Industrial Democracy*, 26, 4, 511–40.

Marsden, D. (1999) *A Theory of Employment Systems: Micro-foundations of Societal Diversity*, Oxford: Oxford University Press.

Matten, D., and J. Moon (2004) Corporate social responsibility education in Europe, *Journal of Business Ethics*, 54, 4, 323–37.

   (2008) 'Implicit' and 'explicit' CSR: a conceptual framework for a comparative understanding of corporate social responsibility, *Academy of Management Review*, 33, 2 (in press).

Mayer, M., and R. Whittington (2002) The evolving European corporation: strategy, structure and social science, in M. Geppert, D. Matten & K. Williams (eds.) *Challenges for European Management in a Global Context*, Basingstoke: Palgrave, 19–41.

Molina, O., and M. Rhodes (2002) Corporatism: the past, present and future of a concept, *Annual Review of Political Science*, 5, 305–31.

Monbiot, G. (2000) Getting into bed with business: the UN is no longer just a joke, *Guardian*, 31 August, 18.

Moon, J., A. Crane and D. Matten (2005) Can corporations be citizens? Corporate citizenship as a metaphor for business participation in society, *Business Ethics Quarterly*, 15, 3, 427–51.

Moon, J., and R. Sochacki (1996) The social responsibility of business in job and enterprise creation: motives, means and implications, *Australian Quarterly*, 68, 1, 21–30.

—— (1998) New governance in Australian schools: a place for business social responsibility?, *Australian Journal of Public Administration*, 55, 1, 55–67.

Palazzo, G. (2002) US-American and German business ethics: an intercultural comparison, *Journal of Business Ethics*, 41, 195–216.

Porter, M. E., and M. R. Kramer (2002) The competitive advantage of corporate philanthropy, *Harvard Business Review*, 80, 12, 56–68.

Preuss, L., A. Haunschild and D. Matten (2006) Trade unions and CSR: a European research agenda, *Journal of Public Affairs*, 6, 3/4, 256–68.

Puppim de Oliveira, J. A. (2006) Corporate citizenship in Latin America: new challenges for business, *Journal of Corporate Citizenship*, 21, Special Issue, 17–20.

Royle, T. (2005) Realism or idealism? Corporate social responsibility and the employee stakeholder in the global fast-food industry, *Business Ethics: A European Review*, 14, 1, 42–55.

Saphir, A. (2005) *Globalisation and the Reform of the European Social Models*, Brussels: Bruegel.

Schumpeter, J. A. (1992 [1942]) *Capitalism, Socialism and Democracy*, London: Routledge.

Smith, A. (1811 [1776]) *An Inquiry into the Nature and Causes of the Wealth of Nations*, London: Cadell and Davies.

Smith, C. (2005) Beyond convergence and divergence: explaining variations in organizational practices and forms, in S. Ackroyd, R. Batt, P. Thompson and P. S. Tolbert (eds.) *The Oxford Handbook of Work and Organization*, Oxford: Oxford University Press.

Sobczak, A. (2004) La responsabilité sociale de l'entreprise: menace ou opportunité pour le droit du travai?, *Relations Industrielles*, 59, 1, 3–28.

Timpane, P., and L. Miller McNeil (1991) *Business Impact on Education and Child Development*, New York: Committee for Economic Development.

Van Liederkerke, L., and C. Louche (2006) Van de Velde case: the challenges of implementing SA8000, in *A curriculum for responsible European management (REM)*, Brussels: Eurocadres, 7–16, available at www.eurocadres.org/en/areas_of_action/responsible_european_management/publications_and_material/publications/a_curriculum_for_responsible_european_management.

Visser, W., C. Middleton and M. McIntosh (2005) Corporate citizenship in Africa, *Journal of Corporate Citizenship*, 18, Special Issue, 17–124.

Vogel, D. (2005) Is there a market for virtue: the business case for corporate social responsibility, *California Management Review*, 47, 4, 19–45.

Welford, R. J. (2005) Corporate social responsibility in Europe, North America and Asia: 2004 survey results, *Journal of Corporate Citizenship*, 17, 33–52.

Whitley, R. (ed.) (1992) *European Business Systems: Firms and Markets in Their National Contexts*, London: Sage.

—— (1999) *Divergent Capitalisms: The Social Structuring and Change of Business Systems*, Oxford: Oxford University Press.

Yin, R. K. (2003) *Case Study Research: Design and Methods*, Thousand Oaks, CA: Sage.

16 Can 'German' become 'international'? Reactions to globalisation in two German MNCs

Fiona Moore

Introduction

While a number of companies have adopted the philosophy that, once they reach a certain degree of globalisation, they can, and should, divorce themselves from their national origins and become 'international' instead, sociological and anthropological research on social identity questions whether any company should – or, indeed, can – become completely 'global' in this fashion. Through applying a system, society and dominance approach to case studies of the British operations of two German multinationals, one a bank ('ZwoBank') and one a car company ('AutoWorks'), I examine how they took different approaches to the process of being seen as 'international', study the impact of this process upon the management culture of the organisation and conclude with a look at more general implications for cross-cultural management and international human resource management.

'Made in Germany' or 'Made by Siemens': the problem outlined

The dominance effect, hyperglobalisers and convergence

Although it may seem counter-intuitive in light of the evidence to the contrary, the 'hyperglobaliser' and 'convergence' philosophies continue to exist, and to contribute to the idea that companies can become truly international. In this section I challenge this idea using SSD theory.

David Held, Anthony McGrew, David Goldblatt and Jonathan Perraton (1999) identify hyperglobalisers as follows: that they assume that the processes of globalisation are bringing about a new era in which nation states are decreasing in importance and old divisions are being eroded in favour of a new, more egalitarian economic system (3–5; see also Ohmae, 1990). Furthermore, they argue, people are becoming more globally aware and inclined to think in global, rather than local, terms; ultimately, both people and companies will cease to regard national identity as anything more than a quaint trait. The hyperglobalist stance thus holds that the processes of globalisation are bringing about a new era that will differ categorically from any that has come before.

This ties in with the theories of best practice and convergence. Exponents of convergence argue that, gradually, companies are coming to adopt the same practices worldwide, and that these practices will be the 'best' ones: the ones said to be the most effective and efficient practices for all companies (Sako, 1994). Although numerous challenges to this idea exist (e.g. Royle, 2000), it remains a popular one among businesspeople, and consequently one that influences corporate policy at all levels (Liesch, Steen and Kastelle, 2006). Most of the people interviewed in connection with this chapter implicitly assumed that globalisation meant an inevitable detachment from the national, and the convergence of practices. The idea that companies can become 'international' is thus inspired by a hyperglobalist perspective, as well as by the theories of best practice and convergence.

These views are challenged by system, society and dominance effect theory, however. According to Smith and Meiksins (1995), the practices of certain economies within the global market come to dominate in terms of modes of production, becoming seen as 'best practice'. This is then mitigated by the cultures from which the company originates and in which it operates (see also Kristensen and Zeitlin, 2004), and the economic system – in this case, capitalism – that informs it. Therefore, the culture of an organisation is less a matter of a hyperglobalising tendency towards pure 'best practice', divorced from national influences, and more a kind of *bricolage*, in which the corporation's culture evolves along particular lines according to its history and circumstances. I now consider how this applies to the case of German companies.

Being German: 'Germanness' in the international business context

Before we go further, it is worth briefly exploring the concept of 'Germanness' within this context. The concept is difficult to pin down, and too complex to be dealt with in much detail here, but I do consider some of the more common ways that it was used with my informants. More general, abstract aspects of Germanness – the concept of *Heimat*, for instance, and the German education system – will not be discussed in detail (interested readers are referred to Moore, 2005: chap. 3, for a more extensive treatment).

The way in which my interviewees conceived of Germanness can be broken down into three related categories: people, products and companies. In the case of people, the concept of 'Germanness' did not refer simply to German origin, or to having German ancestry (see Applegate, 1990), but also to a repertoire of character traits: non-Germans in the company would often refer to themselves (or colleagues) as 'acting German' or 'turning German' if they believed that they displayed one or more of those traits. These included either actual efficiency or an (unfulfilled) desire for efficiency and order (the German concept *Ordnung* has associations not only with order but with cleanliness, purity and general 'rightness'; see Moore, 2005: 45–6), conservatism and long-term orientation and, in some cases, a focus on Germany (sometimes styled as a kind of parochialism).

In the case of products, those described as 'German' (leaving aside tourist goods and popular ethnic foodstuffs) tended to be high-quality, traditionally manufactured goods, such as cars, household appliances, tools and scientific equipment. While IT products such as Siemens' mobile phones and computers were also coming to be described as 'German', this was a relatively recent development; as late as 1998 pundits were fearing that Germany would remain outside the IT revolution (Economist, 1998; see also Abel and Itterman, 2003: 110–11), and it was also, for the most part, confined to the products of a single company (i.e. Siemens). Luxury or body care products, such as Wella shampoo, and medicines, such as Bayer pharmaceuticals, were not often cited by interviewees as 'German' products, even if the company was known to be German or German-owned. 'German' products were thus confined to a fairly narrow range and usually associated with manufacturing.

Finally, in the case of companies and corporate cultures, 'Germanness' tended to be associated with a long-term focus, a concentration on the German economic market and the local labour market, corporate social responsibility and the association with certain products described in the paragraph above. This long-term focus was most remarked upon in the banking sector, which in the United Kingdom tends to be very short-termist (though it was not unknown in other sectors: AutoWorks' decision to take over the 'Lewis Motors' plant, discussed below, was held up by the company and its supporters as an example of how they were willing to invest time and money in restoring a failing local company). CSR activities tended to focus on the local area: AutoWorks, as noted below, maintained a strong connection to community organisations, and ZwoBank London had displays of art by London artists on its walls, in an echo of the German art and photographs on the walls of the Frankfurt head office. More negatively, however, Germanness in a company could be associated with a reluctance to embrace new ideas, German chauvinism or a refusal to change even when change was necessitated. Finally, specific companies could also be specifically associated with Germanness: Siemens has been mentioned above and will be discussed in greater detail below, but the list also included BMW, Volkswagen, Audi, Braun and Bosch.

While this discussion is by no means exhaustive, it does cast some light on which symbols, images and attitudes were considered indicative of 'Germanness' by my interviewees in and around both companies. I now consider how these symbols play out in the specific case of the 'Made in Germany' trademark.

Made by whom? German companies, national and global identity

For over 100 years the 'Made in Germany' trademark has apparently been a source of national pride for Germans. The rise of globalisation, however, coupled with negative associations that can arise with regard to German national identity have meant that some German MNCs are attempting to adjust their corporate culture so that their products are instead seen as 'Made by [company name]', rejecting a national identity in place of one based on the sale of international products, in line with the hyperglobalising trend discussed above. In this section I consider this phenomenon and what impact it has on the development of identity through the deployment of symbols in German MNCs.

Initially imposed upon German goods by UK manufacturers concerned about competition from cheaper and better foreign products in the late nineteenth century, the 'Made in Germany' mark consequently became a source of pride for Germans in symbolising that their manufacturing systems had actually outstripped those of the British. This focusing of national pride on companies and manufactured goods intensified following World War II, when, as Peter Lawrence (1980: 13) notes, fear of the consequences of focusing nationalistic feelings on German military and cultural achievements meant that Germans turned instead to German companies and their successes in the international sphere as a source of national pride. This can be summed up in a *Der Spiegel* cover (reproduced in Hughes, 1994) depicting a globe made up of German MNCs with the subtitle *Weltfirma Deutschland* (roughly, 'Germany the Global Corporation'), and also in a monograph by David Head (1992), tellingly entitled *'Made in Germany': The Corporate Identity of a Nation*, examining this phenomenon in detail. Head also discusses how the 'Germanness' of a product – its perceived connection to Germany and German stereotypical traits – is used to sell German products; Audi and Volkswagen both advertise their cars internationally using German slogans, and many other German manufacturing companies (e.g. Braun) emphasise the idea that Germans are good at engineering. The mark 'Made in Germany' and the image of certain products as German has therefore been a mark of pride for Germans historically, giving them a strong connection to national culture.

More recently, however, there have been moves away from this, with a 1995 Wolff Olins identity research survey considering the then recent move by German-based electronics company Siemens to replace its trademark 'Made in Germany' with one reading 'Made by Siemens' in an attempt to seem 'more global' and/or 'less German' by identifying the company with a well-known and internationally used range of products rather than with its national origin. This trend has continued subsequently, as can be seen in news reports concerning the attempts of the German state, in advance of the 2006 football World Cup, to 'rebrand' itself as a globally engaged, multicultural nation and do away with internationally held images of German folk culture (lederhosen, sausages, folk dancing, etc.) on the grounds that these were actively damaging to the international perception of Germany (see BBCi, 2006b, and a Channel 4 News story entitled 'Double Deutsch' broadcast on 4 January 2006; see also the numerous websites set up by the German government to promote this transnational and multicultural image to tourists and World Cup attendees, such as Germany, Land of Ideas – www.land-of-ideas.org – or Germany 2006 – http://wm2006.deutschland.de/EN/Navigation/Home/home.html). A number of German businesspeople, in interviews conducted between 1999 and 2003, argued that they saw nothing wrong with the practice of identifying a product with its company rather than its company's national origin, pointing out that if the product was not actually made in Germany (as many, in the age of globalisation, are not) there was no real reason why the company should be seen as German, and that it was more accurate for it to adopt a self-designation indicating its status as a multinational group (Moore, 2005: 276–7). One might equally compare it to Apple's recent decision to brand the popular iPod music players with the designation 'Designed in California, Made in China' (BBCi, 2006c). There thus seem to have been moves on the part of well-known German multinationals, and on the part of the German government, to encourage people to think less in terms of 'German', and more in terms of 'international', identity when dealing with German companies, with possible implications for the ongoing debate over whether national cultures show increasing degrees of convergence or divergence under globalisation (Mueller, 1994).

There are also a number of reasons why German companies might choose to emphasise an international rather than a German image. Germany is still associated in some circles, particularly in the British business context, with Nazism; Germans in the City of London, in interviews and conversation, deliberately defined themselves in opposition to the community of German refugees from Nazi persecution (and their descendants), who were also present in London in noticeable numbers; the Nazi period went virtually unmentioned in all the corporate promotional material that I collected during and after my fieldwork – including, interestingly, that of corporations that had been shut down during the Nazi period (e.g. Deutsche Genossenschaftsbank) and could not therefore be said to have political skeletons in their closets. The main exceptions were cases in which the company had established a reparations programme following disclosures of having benefited financially from the Nazi regime (*Financial Times*, 1999), and in those cases the company could be seen as making a virtue of necessity rather than employing its nationality to create a positive image. My research also found that negative images of Germans as Nazis tended to crop up in informal joking among non-German employees of certain German corporations, as a form of employee resistance (see Moore, 2005: chap. 6). By choosing to be seen as 'international', German companies thus avoid the whole issue of having to confront the war.

Despite this, however, there has been a lessening of the stigma associated with the Nazi regime in recent years: films such as *Downfall* (2004) and *The Bunker* (2001) have successfully explored the controversies of World War II from the German point of view while at the same time remaining free of any tinge of pro-Nazi sympathies, indicating that it is now increasingly possible for Germans to identify as such, even while referencing the World War II context, without necessarily evoking the negative imagery associated with the Nazi regime. While Germans initially seemed reluctant to express nationalist sentiment during the 2006 World Cup, the team's early success saw more displays of national pride amongst German fans (BBCi, 2006d). Germans may therefore avoid the controversy of World War II, and the negative associations of German nationalism, by choosing to avoid identifying as 'German'; this stigma seems to be increasingly becoming less and less relevant in terms of social identification, however.

Another reason to identify oneself or one's company as 'international' rather than 'German' is the fact that identifying with a particular nationality, while positive in some contexts, also appears to have negative connotations within the international business community, in the United Kingdom if nowhere else. Although most Germans whom I encountered in the United Kingdom were interested to hear that German businesses had a long history of success in the British context (one staff member even exclaiming ruefully: 'I wish somebody would tell the English about that!'), none of them showed any particular interest in spreading the information or in taking pride in the connection. As Sklair (2001) argues, however, this lack of connection with history fits well with the construction of the German businesspeople as a transnational capitalist class: an orientation towards business leaves little room for interest in history or roots other than as a personal quirk, and the focus on modernity, simultaneity and the present is in keeping with the fast-paced, postmodern ethic of a developing transnational elite. Nonetheless, a sense of national identity can prove an advantage in marketing products internationally, as witness recent adverts for Citroen cars screened in the United Kingdom that emphasise the association of French nationality with refinement, culture and taste, and the German examples cited above. German companies thus wish to be seen as 'international' because of the positive associations this image carries in international business circles; to avoid national associations entirely, however, could prove problematic for many German companies.

For a variety of reasons, then, German managers and businesses are increasingly presenting themselves in terms that can allow them to shift their self-presentation to vary between being seen as 'German' and 'international'. This chapter is an exploration of how this process of self-presentation takes place at two different companies, in different sectors, and the variations that took place within this process, following the comparative-historical approach employed by Peer Hull Kristensen and Jonathan Zeitlin (2004).

Identity and corporations: Erving Goffman and changes to corporate identity

For insight into the factors affecting the adoption of an 'international' rather than a 'German' identity/culture, we turn to Goffman's research into strategic self-presentation. Many of his works focus on exploring the ways in which strategic competition between actors (individual and/or group) takes place through identity and self-presentation, most famously in *The Presentation of Self in Everyday Life* (1956). Actors, Goffman (1961: 143) says, may define themselves predominantly according to a connection with one group, but within that there is a constant interplay of allegiances to many groups and institutions, with different ones prioritised in different situations according to which the actor feels best suits his/her aims, which have an impact on the relationships and social dynamics in which the actor is involved. Self-presentation, therefore, can be a key part of the strategies of social actors in their interactions with one another, and is an often overlooked influence on group strategy and action (Burns, 1992: 232). In the case of German companies, then, the expression of national identity forms part of a process of strategic self-presentation necessary for operation in the transnational business world.

My earlier research, following Goffman, has argued that MNCs and their managers use symbols of national identity as multivalent symbols through which they can present themselves in a shifting, complex fashion that trans-forms according to the way in which they wish to be seen at any given moment (see Moore, 2003, 2004, 2005). Furthermore, the process of identity does not take place in a vacuum but is a process of negotiation between different groups, which attempt not only to define themselves but to apply definitions to others, and to resist others' definitions.

This hypothesis is particularly relevant to the issue of whether or not companies, in this case German ones, *can* internationalise, as it argues that companies and managers can shift their self-presentation according to whether it is more advantageous for them to be seen as 'German' or 'inter-national', and thus be either convergent or divergent as it suits them. For instance, during my fieldwork I put to the representatives of two German business networking organisations in the United Kingdom, in two separate interviews, the question of whether a new trademark made the company more 'global' and/or less 'German' (Wolff Olins, 1995). One representative was dismissive of this notion, saying that people still 'see' Siemens as German. The representative of the second organisation placed the question in historical context, however, talking about how thirty years ago there had been a strong 'buy British' movement, but that today British people are more comfortable with the idea of buying German products, thanks largely to automobile adverts such as Audi's that emphasise the connection between German origin and engineering quality, and that, consequently, there is less strategic need now to de-emphasise the company's Germanness. The fact that the name 'Siemens' also connotes Germanness as well as the image of a transnational manufacturing concern suggests that the company can thus symbolically 'be' German when it is advantageous and that, when it is not, it can present itself as a 'rootless' transnational corporation, without altering the symbols used (see Head, 1992: 23, and Watson, 1995: 164). Through the discourse of 'German' versus 'international' identity, German companies can shift their self-presentation according to their situations and strategies, exhibiting both convergent and divergent traits.

Hyperglobalists to the contrary notwithstanding, then, the argument from anthropological and sociological studies of identity and self-presentation suggests that a company cannot 'lose' its associations with a particular national identity at will, supporting the SSD position. While identity can be strategically deployed, and certain aspects of identity emphasised, the way in which a group or corporation comes across is a factor of its history, tendencies, social make-up and relationships with other groups (see Cohen, 1985); changes in the way a company is seen are therefore a process of negotiation rather than of self-willed transformation.

Based on the above theories, therefore, I would hypothesise that German companies' attempts to become 'less German and more global' will not be totally successful but will result in a kind of hybrid identity, the make-up of which will be dependent on the history and make-up of the company, its branches and so forth, suggesting that what we have is not a case of corporations converging on a kind of abstracted 'best practice', or 'global culture' overwhelming 'national culture', but interactions between different influences at different levels according to circumstances.

Methodology

The methodologies employed in preparing this chapter are qualitative and, for the most part, ethnographic, based on participant observation fieldwork within two German companies, one, 'ZwoBank', a bank, the other, 'AutoWorks', a car manufacturer. In this section I briefly describe the two companies, their positions as MNCs in their particular sectors, and the methodologies used to obtain the relevant information about them.

Case study 1: ZwoBank

ZwoBank AG is a Frankfurt-based universal bank that, although one of the largest banks in Germany, with an above-average number of foreign branches, is still fairly limited in its international operations – a not atypical state of affairs in German finance (see Ebster-Grosz and Pugh, 1996). It has maintained a presence in London since the early 1970s, with a full branch being opened in the early 1980s. The longest-serving employee (a senior manager) had been with ZwoBank London for fifteen years at the time of this study, the shortest-serving (a trainee) three months. The branch had about 160 employees at the time of the study, including trainee, temporary and service employees. Of these, about one-third were German, Swiss or Austrian, one-tenth were non-German foreign employees and the rest originated from the United Kingdom. ZwoBank London is thus more or less typical of the London branches of German banks.

ZwoBank Zentrale (head office), by contrast, is a massive organisation housed in a complex of several modern buildings close to the centre of Frankfurt. It employs approximately 2,000 staff in total, with all staff members pertaining to particular departments generally being housed in the same area of the complex, but in separate, enclosed offices containing two or three people rather than the big open-plan offices of London branch. There were fewer non-German staff members in head office than there were non-English staff members in London; more people in head office were fluent in at least one foreign language (usually English) than in London branch, however. Although I could not obtain educational statistics on head office, I spoke with a number of people there who held postgraduate degrees, including doctorates, which was almost unheard of in London. Head office is thus much larger, less diverse and more focused on formal qualifications than London branch.

Fieldwork at ZwoBank was carried out between January and June 2000, with follow-up work done between July 2000 and January 2001, as part of an eighteen-month study of German bank branches and head offices (for confidentiality reasons, all names and some details of the bank and its staff members have been changed). Further follow-up visits were conducted to London branch in the autumn of 2003. During 2000 I conducted participant observation for six months, which involved coming into the bank every working day and having access to a desk in a shared office, the canteen and other basic staff resources. I also made three trips of ten days each to Frankfurt to visit ZwoBank's head office in April, September and October 2000. Formal interviews were conducted on a periodic basis over the course of the participant observation period, and the six months following it, with sixteen individuals at the London branch. Of these, six were expatriate Germans, five were Germans living permanently in the United Kingdom, two were English who had lived in Germany and three were English with no German connections outside the bank. In addition, formal interviews were conducted at ZwoBank's head office with six managers in the human resources department and one in a front office division, with follow-up work via telephone and e-mail. Each participant was interviewed between one and four times, with interviews lasting approximately an hour apiece. Bilingual interviewees were given the option of being interviewed in English or German; although most at the London branch chose English, and most at the head office chose German, no interview was conducted exclusively in a single language. During the 2003 follow-up visits four employees were reinterviewed using the same techniques. The interviews were also complemented by informal interviews with these and about twenty other members of the London office's staff, usually conducted over lunch or after work; the people who received informal, but not formal, interviews included five Germans living permanently in the United Kingdom, six non-Germans who had lived in Germany and nine non-German employees with no connection to Germany.

Case Study 2: AutoWorks

AutoWorks UK has a quite different history from that of ZwoBank in terms of its international activities. The plant at which my study was conducted started out as a small domestic British car manufacturer, here called Lewis Motors, in the early 1910s (Newbigging, Shatford and Williams, 1998: 12), remaining more or less under the same ownership until the late 1960s. During this time it rapidly became part of the culture of the local town, developing its own sports teams, bands, amateur dramatic societies and social club; at least some of the people working at the factory at the time of fieldwork confessed to being second- or even third-generation factory workers (see also Bardsley and Laing, 1999: 86, 95–104). In the mid-1990s, after thirty years of financial difficulties and changing ownership, the company was sold to a German MNC, known here as AutoWorks (Scarbrough and Terry, 1996: 5), which had itself started out as a domestically focused manufacturing company, but had begun to branch out after World War II, coming to global prominence in the 1970s and 1980s as a manufacturer of luxury and sports vehicles. Rather than starting as a German company and branching out as ZwoBank did, then, AutoWorks UK has a history of local association and international acquisition.

Today, the AutoWorks organisation emphasises strongly its global reach, the quality of its products and its flexibility. Two-thirds of the shop-floor workforce are employed through a temporary labour agency, with the explicit proviso that this is the section of the workforce most likely to be reduced during lean economic times. The factory operated on a shift system of two sets of four-day weekday shifts of ten hours each, the day shift running from Monday through to Thursday, with Friday as a day off for all line staff, and the evening one running from Monday through to Friday, with a rotating day off. There was also a three-day weekend shift of twelve hours each; the night shift on Fridays would start and finish two hours later than on other days of the week. Managers, however, maintained a more traditional nine-to-five, Monday-to-Friday routine in theory, although in practice many took advantage of work/life balance programmes to extend or change their working routines.

The fieldwork upon which this chapter is based took place intermittently between 2003 and 2005, with follow-up work ongoing at the time of writing. In 2003 I spent three months on the line in the final assembly area (colloquially referred to as 'assembly') of the plant, working as a temporary employee of the firm with their full knowledge and permission. Two tours were also taken of the full plant as an outsider. Subsequently, I have spent about twelve months, intermittently, working with a group of managers from the human resources department on two projects, one involving the development of a management education programme and one aimed at assessing how the workforce feel about the plant's management style; I also paid an exploratory visit to a comparable plant of the same company in Germany. Formal interviews were conduced with seventeen staff members in total. Most were in white-collar managerial and/or coordination functions, although some were shop-floor managers; four were German international managers. Most of the interviewees were associated with the final assembly area, but there were also some from the paint shop or body in white (the area where the unpainted car is assembled) sections as well. In some cases, follow-up interviews were conducted, normally over the telephone. Informal, unrecorded discussions were held with workers on the line during fieldwork, as well as with the HR managers with whom I worked on the two projects mentioned above. Any statistics cited in this chapter have been obtained from the firm, with permission.

The two companies dealt with here are thus both German, and both multinational, but have different histories of internationalisation and corporate structures, and the studied branches have different histories of establishment and different connections to the surrounding British culture. In the sections that follow I will explore how both companies went about trying to change their cultures to become 'more international', and how they succeeded and failed in different areas.

International but German: ZwoBank

In this section I consider the specific case of ZwoBank and how it attempted to internationalise, first through a matrix integration programme and later through a merger with another European financial company in the same sector, all the while encouraging clients to make the transition from seeing it as a 'German' company to seeing it as 'international'. The ultimate result was not a full transition to a global or even international orientation but to a form of self-identification as global with German roots, in which discourses of nationality versus globalisation became the focus for tensions and anxieties among managers.

Moves towards the international: the matrix integration and the merger

As implied in the description above, ZwoBank's historical focus has been on the German market, at the expense of others. London branch's primary function is to administer its foreign investments (as opposed to supporting German clients in the United Kingdom; see Moore, 2005), and it supported few non-German clients or enterprises. Employees also frequently referred to the branch's close-knit social structure and the strong presence of German and German-speaking employees within the bank as indications of 'Germanness'. Most employees therefore, at the time of the study, saw the bank as German and their particular branch as a kind of 'outpost' of the main bank rather than as part of an international group.

From its establishment until July 1999, London branch had operated more or less autonomously from the rest of the bank. It retained a traditional 'pyramid structure', in which the heads of individual departments reported to the general manager, who was the only staff member in regular contact with superiors in Frankfurt. Shortly before my fieldwork began, however, the company had embarked on a matrix integration programme, with the explicit intention of developing a more centralised structure in which the branches served as extensions of a Frankfurt-based head office. Under the matrix integration system, individual department heads were required to report directly to individual department heads in Frankfurt, making the bank's structure less a matter of individual national branches reporting to a German centre, as of globe-spanning departments radiating out from Frankfurt, in a shift from a multinational to a more transnational business strategy (see Bartlett and Ghoshal, 1992: 15–20). Consequently, many

London branch staff members who had previously had little to do with the Frankfurt office now found themselves reporting to a German 'global head', and there was an increased presence of visitors, expatriate employees and others associated with head office at the branch. In addition, many employees had to learn particular business practices that were commonly used at head office but that were less often employed in London. Unsurprisingly, a number of issues arose from the integration in London branch, mostly relating to employees having difficulty learning the new business practices, or to the failure of many employees to use the new reporting system, either through ignorance or in protest against its perceived lack of efficiency. The situation at the time of the study was thus one in which head office was attempting to introduce a new system to London branch, and correspondingly both exerting control over the branch and experiencing resistance from its overseas employees.

These changes were rationalised by both head office and branch employees in terms of their being necessary for the 'internationalisation' of the branch. Although the process could be seen as making the overseas branches more 'German', as the main result of the changes brought about by the matrix integration was that many employees were brought into closer daily contact with Zwobank Zentrale, and there was an increased presence of visitors and expatriates from Frankfurt at the London branch, instead people at both the branch and the head office spoke in terms of developing a 'global' institution through the new centralised structure, arguing that, as the structure involved closer contact between far-flung branches through the medium of the head office, this was a response to globalisation rather than an assertion of German dominance. At head office, those involved with the restructuring expressed the hope that the initiative would bring the foreign branches more into line with the domestic group, some saying that they felt that the increased contact would allow head office to learn from the branches, and vice versa. While London employees expressed their anxieties, which frequently manifested themselves through ethnic tensions with German international managers at the branch, due to the fact that German managers tended to be assumed (often wrongly) to be more sympathetic to the interests of head office than to London branch, they also all agreed that in the past the bank had been 'too German-focused', in that most of the bank's activities had concentrated on Germany and/or clients of German origin, and welcomed those aspects of the matrix integration that might allow them greater say in the decisions of the group. Although the bank's activities could be seen as either 'German' or 'globalising', employees at all levels focused on presenting them as the latter option.

Throughout the process, ZwoBank also emphasised its greater internationalism to its clients. Publicity material from this period emphasised the bank's international and/or European connections, with its historical roots in Germany being played down, and ZwoBank London's HR managers repeatedly talked about the need for the employees to see themselves more as a thrusting international company and less as a socialist, state-focused institution with a focus on supporting smaller enterprises, all of the latter being traits commonly associated with German finance (see Lawrence, 1980, and Watson, 1995). Internally and externally, then, the matrix integration was presented to me, colleagues and clients as a move away from 'Germanness' and towards 'internationalism'.

Following the matrix integration, however, ZwoBank attempted a merger with another bank in the same sector and of a comparable size, but of a different national origin, with a view to setting up a kind of European bank in that particular sector, and possibly taking in mergers and joint ventures with banks in other countries in the future. This openly internationalising move was generally spoken of as a positive development among managers I interviewed; they also expressed fears, however, that the company they were merging with was 'too different' from themselves – an opinion with nationalistic overtones, given that the main difference between the companies was their national origin, and also suggesting that there was a degree of tension within the company around shedding its 'Germanness' to become truly 'European'. Whereas the idea of becoming ostensibly international but, tacitly, remaining German-focused had appealed to staff during the conduct of the matrix integration, the concept of becoming part of a larger and decidedly Europeanised, if not globalised, banking group was regarded as a disturbing move that would damage ZwoBank's corporate identity. The discourse of 'Germanness' versus 'internationalism' thus became a focal point for tensions within the bank surrounding the merger, suggesting that the bank did not wish to go so far as to shed all connection with Germany in its self-presentation.

Culture, Germanness and internationalism

Culturally, even during and after the matrix integration, the bank's employees identified in ways that expressed an international or global connection but also always referred back to the bank's national origin, whether openly or tacitly. London branch's culture was said by employees of all nationalities to be 'a mix of English and German', and language mixing was also a symbol of collective identity among all groups. Many of the Germans who had been in the United Kingdom for some time, and non-Germans with a German connection, made their mixed status a point of pride. One department had an entire collective identity constructed around the fact that its members were the ones with greatest contact with Germany, but were located in the United Kingdom; virtually the whole team was bilingual. The valuation of mixed status thus provided a means of bridging different groups: it allowed employees to construct a conceptual social space in which German and English systems could combine in constantly changing ways to form new wholes, emphasising international connections without losing the symbolic connection with Germany.

Tensions within the bank also focused strongly on the dichotomy between the bank's 'German' and 'international' identities. London branch employees tend to regard themselves as relatively independent of head office, and frequently resent what they see as its intervention in a market that they feel they know better than head office does; a common complaint among staff (particularly UK-born) is that head office is 'too German for the London market'. UK-born employees have a range of jokes and perfor-mances expressing unspoken concerns about what they see as the domina-tion of the bank by the Germans; conflict frequently occurred over perceived differences between German and UK business systems, as in the case of one English employee who admitted to me that he frequently did not wait for head office approval when making a deal with a non-German business, as head office's approval procedures took what was perceived as an unreasonably long time in the short-termist City of London market (see also Ebster-Grosz and Pugh, 1996). The centralised structure of the group was also a sore point: while both London and head office view the organisa-tion as 'global', head office employees feel that this should take the form of a variety of branches around the world answering to a single central office, whereas London prefers a more decentralised approach focusing on a variety of local markets. In ZwoBank, then, both positive and negative aspects of the bank's identity included a combination of international focus and German roots.

Management development initiatives in London also focused less on encouraging staff to consider themselves as global and more in terms of developing positive Anglo-German relationships. For instance, a deliberate managerial initiative was set up with the aim of getting more British staff into the branch's top management, but none aimed at developing an international top management cadre within head office (in contrast to similar initiatives then in place at, for instance, Deutsche Bank and Vodafone). There was also an 'exchange programme' for junior managers, whereby they could spend three months at head office (and head office staff could visit London on a similar basis), and German trainees frequently went out to the branches; again, however, this was focused on head office employees going out to the branches and vice versa. Furthermore, the bank hired intercultural trainers to try and break down the barriers between the groups, as well as engaging consultants in cultural issues (including me). Language teachers were also hired, as learning German was regarded as the best way to understand German culture. A variety of initiatives therefore existed to try and encourage staff and management development in such a way as to develop an integrated Anglo-German organisation rather than an 'international' one.

The result: international, but German

The results of ZwoBank's activities with regard to changing its corporate culture to be less 'German' and more 'international' thus had the result that, while 'internationalism' remained a positive 'buzzword' around the bank, it continued to see itself, and be seen, as German-focused. The emphasis during the matrix integration programme, as before, was less about incorporating diverse national practices into a single global corporation and more in terms of internationalising German practices and ideals, in the same way that some critics of globalisation assert that what people think of as 'global culture' is simply the permeation of American culture worldwide (Tomlinson, 1991). Even if the company presented itself as an international entity, the German roots of the organisation were always there, if only tacitly.

This is also reflected in ZwoBank's ostensibly globalising activities. Although the company was supposedly developing itself into a global organisation through the matrix integration programme, in fact it was becoming more focused on the German head office as a driving factor in decisions and activities, causing employees to engage in a two-pronged self-presentation strategy: in public supporting the idea of the bank as an international entity, but privately considering it as being as 'German-focused' as it had been in the past. The integration itself was less a true matrix integration and more a centralised structure focused on Frankfurt. On ZwoBank's part, too, the whole move was, tacitly, client-driven rather than emerging from its own international expansion. When officials were asked why they were doing this, one explanation that usually cropped up sooner or later was that they provided financing for German corporate clients, many of which were trying to become 'international' rather than 'German' companies – suggesting that, if the clients had retained the 'German' focus, they would not have been so keen to gain an 'international' image. The idea of actually becoming part of an international group caused considerable anxiety, even though the company would not have undergone a loss of power or status due to the merger, and, indeed, stood to gain a greater international presence. Essentially, then, ZwoBank presented itself in such a way as to appear to be internationalising while nonetheless remaining more comfortable with a German focus.

The German focus also reflected the company's strategy and market niche. Whereas companies such as the above-mentioned Siemens have actual physical products that can be used in most places around the world, a German multinational bank is inherently going to have to deal with certain products, practices and/or clients that are specific to Germany, either through, as ZwoBank does, providing international products for German domestic clients or, as others do, providing banking services for German companies overseas or German investment opportunities for non-German investors. In such a situation, it can be an asset to emphasise the company's Germanness to some extent, in order to attract the sort of clients that would be interested in patronising this particular firm.

ZwoBank's approach was, therefore, essentially 'Made in Germany' rather than 'Made by Siemens': while the international connotations of the bank's German origins and centralised structure were emphasised, the bank made no real attempt to globalise itself, encourage employees to think of themselves in global terms or do anything other than to treat the world as an extension of Germany rather than the company as an international entity. This appears to be due largely to the bank's history, corporate culture and business strategy. I now consider how similar processes played out at the second case study under consideration, the car manufacturer AutoWorks.

German but international: AutoWorks

In contrast to ZwoBank, AutoWorks appeared to have little trouble in seeing itself, and being seen, as an international company; its German origins remained in its self-presentation, however, albeit in different ways from those seen at ZwoBank. The focus here is how discourses of Germanness versus internationalism played out in the car manufacturing sector.

Structure and international management

In contrast to ZwoBank, AutoWorks did not operate on a centralised plan but retained a fairly hands-off policy towards the branches. Although the British plant had a large number of Germans in its top management, the product in question was not emphatically treated as a 'German' car, and the car was being marketed under a separate brand name (although the parent company made no secret of its ownership of the plant and the product, the AutoWorks brand name was clearly visible on the plant itself and all publicity material, and most of the publicity and reviews regarding the factory's products emphasised the name of the parent company; despite this, the factory was frequently referred to locally by the name of its former owners, such as 'the old Lewis plant', or the product's name). From the outset, AutoWorks' managers' stated policy towards its acquisition had been that they would let the acquired company handle its own affairs and they would just provide local support; although they subsequently became more involved in the company's management, they retained the stated policy that the branches should essentially make their own decisions. AutoWorks thus acquired a degree of internationalisation in its self-image through decentralising and allowing local authority.

Another area in which AutoWorks engaged in an international agenda was with regard to connections between branches, and branch and head office. There appeared, for instance, to be a stratum of international managers who, like Nick Forster's (2000) 'true international managers', moved around the group every three years or so, and who were of diverse national origin (although my impression was that Germans nonetheless formed the greater number of them). Significantly, this policy also seemed to be the case within their German domestic operations, suggesting that nationality was not considered relevant in terms of how different branches were treated. As mentioned above, there were also exchange programmes at both worker and management levels whereby employees could spend time at another plant in the group, which took place throughout the whole MNC rather than being focused on connections between head office and its periphery; a number of workers (as well as managers) spoke of having taken part in exchanges or excursions aimed at teaching processes and other forms of knowledge transfer to Germany, other parts of continental Europe, southern Africa or America (as my accent is quite strongly Canadian, I discovered that some colleagues had initially assumed that I was an exchange worker from one of the company's American plants). At one point, passing through a managers' lounge, I saw a prominent advert seeking a host family for a German trainee coming to England on a three-month exchange, and also I heard of an incident in which a group of workers were brought in from the company's Portuguese plant to fill a temporary shortfall of skilled labour, and then sent back once local replacements had been found. The company thus engaged in practices that treated the company as a whole like an international group rather than a German centre with an international periphery.

International products: culture in AutoWorks

In AutoWorks, the main source of identification was focused not so much on national identity as on the cars that the plant produces, further encouraging workers and managers to identify less with the company's German origins and more with its internationally used products. When asked what they liked about working for the company, the managers generally said 'pride in the product' or 'pride in the company name', driving the company's cars and emphasising the AutoWorks association with luxury and technical excellence. Although workers did not tend to identify with the product (mainly citing the fact that, working close to it day in and day out, they found it less interesting than the managers, who were more distanced from its manufacture), they instead cited 'good pay' and 'good mates [i.e. friendships]' as their reasons for enjoying working at AutoWorks; significantly, the workforce was quite strongly international, with a single team of ten workers containing one Australian, one Canadian, two Caribbean, one black South African, one Czech and two Pakistani as well as two British staff members. The temporary labour agency that staffed the final assembly line emphasised the international nature of the staff in its orientation sessions. As such, then, when defining the company, both workers and managers employed international symbols rather than ones focused on its Germanness.

In keeping with the company's focus on dispersed branches as a means of developing an international image, it should also be mentioned that the workers tended to see the plant largely in local terms. The company's management traded on the long-standing history of the plant within the region, exploiting the local ties by, for instance, sponsoring local events and encouraging employees' charity and volunteer activities in the name of the plant. Consequently, periodic images of Germanness in the factory context – the fact that certain jobs within the factory had German or Germanic titles, that boxes of automobile parts were labelled in German and that many of the managers were German – simply became part of the background of a local enterprise, and the Germanness of the parent company of little import in daily interaction. Within the British context, also, German images can symbolise international connections as much as a particular nationality: when a BMW car was chosen for the then new James Bond Pierce Brosnan to drive in *GoldenEye*, rather than the traditional Aston Martin, this was held up by journalists as an example of how Bond was no longer simply British but an international globetrotter of British origin (Oakes, 1997). Ironically, then, the local connections of the plant encouraged workers to consider the company as 'international' rather than 'German'.

At the management level, however, Germanness became more of an issue, and the international self-presentation of the company was tempered with images of Anglo-German relations. There was an uneasy relationship between British and German managers similar to that in ZwoBank, stemming largely from the nature of the company's takeover and the usual tensions that exist between branches and head offices; as in ZwoBank, however, this centred around differences between British and German management practice in terms of work/life balance, attitude to the company, sense of humour and so forth. This also contributed to the company's self-perception as 'international', however, as one of the common complaints about the German managers related to the fact that many of them were part of the above-mentioned 'international stratum', who consequently spent relatively little time at that particular branch compared to the local managers before moving on to their next assignment, as illustrated in the following interview excerpt involving two line managers, an HR manager and me (all the managers concerned are British):

Manager no. 1: I've never had a problem with a German manager; I'll be honest with you.
Manager no. 2: But some of them are very 'rule-focused' rather than 'understanding'.

German managers were thus perceived within the company partly in terms of their nationality but also partly in terms of their being 'international' operatives, with it being difficult to separate the international and German components of their identities within the British context.

Managers also spoke of the company not only as Anglo-German but as involving international connections with a variety of different advantages. During the discussion within group interviews of the incident mentioned above in which Portuguese workers were brought in to fill a temporary shortfall in skilled labour, some line managers commented a couple of times on Portuguese 'expertise' in electronics, creating an image of a company drawing on diverse skills associated with particular nationalities: British with car design, German with engineering, Portuguese with electronics, and so on and so forth around the globe.

The result: German, but international

In contrast to ZwoBank, the situation as AutoWorks was closer to the 'Made by Siemens' paradigm than the 'Made in Germany' paradigm, in that it was capable of maintaining an identity with a strong international component, even if a German connection was inextricable from it, and most members emphasised a multinational corporate identity over one based on the company's German origins. While the company's origins were acknowledged tacitly in the use of German and German-inspired practices in publicity and internal activities, in the presence of German managers and in some aspects of its corporate culture, most employees in practice described their employer as a 'car manufacturer' rather than specifically a 'German company'. AutoWorks thus appears to have successfully developed an international corporate culture.

Despite this, however, while AutoWorks may have been seen as international, it nonetheless had a German connection that was inextricable from its international image. Among the German international managers, there was a strong sense that the German branches were the 'real' locus of the company's culture; in interviews, they spoke about how all the members of the German branches, including the workers, have a strong enthusiasm for both product and corporation, forming part of their identity, contrasting it with workers in overseas branches, who they saw as having more of a 'nine-to-five' attitude, enjoying the job but lacking true devotion to the brand. While this attitude was tacitly challenged by the British managers, it is fair to say that they also acknowledged the German branches as the driving force behind most company policy. As noted before, Germans dominated the international cohort of managers, meaning that there was, as at ZwoBank, something of a link between 'German' and 'international' in the company's culture. Although Germany was not the centre of AutoWorks' identity and international activities here as it was for ZwoBank, the German components of the company did dominate the group in subtle ways.

The positive value placed on internationalism was also not always unproblematic. Much of the tension between managers, as mentioned above, focused on Anglo-German relations, and the temporary importation of the Portuguese workers, while it was acknowledged as necessary, was also a

source of complaint for line managers, who felt that the imported workers'
English-language skills were lacking. Some managers were also disconcerted
by the rapid turnover of international managers, expressing the feeling that
they never really got to know the branch well enough in the short time that
they were there, and then there was a new person to deal with. Within
AutoWorks, then, the company's international image was also the source of
tension and resistance among managers and workers, who would have preferred a more locally focused identity.

AutoWorks, therefore, did succeed in developing a company that was
viewed by both employees and clients as 'international' rather than
'German', through focusing staff identity on the company's products and
through operating a decentralised network of interconnected branches. The
company could not totally escape an association with its national roots,
however, and, indeed, in the opinion of some managers, it would not have
been desirable to do so at all. I now conclude with a comparison of the
experiences of the two German companies.

Analysis: 'Made in Germany' or 'Made by Siemens'?

In the end, then, both ZwoBank and AutoWorks were able to develop their
corporate self-presentations in ways that emphasised their 'international'
nature while at the same time including 'German' aspects. Not only did both
companies do this in different ways, however, but the results were different
for both companies, in apparent contradiction to the hyperglobalist/strong
convergence perspectives. In this section, I briefly consider and summarise
the similarities and differences between the two companies' experiences, and
how each position emerged as a result of different historical and environmental factors.

ZwoBank: still local?

In the case of ZwoBank, the company was unable for the most part to lose its
'German' image, and was seen as being a German company with overseas
connections: attempts to develop the company into a group that both
perceived itself and acted as multinational, including strong input from
groups of other nationalities, were unsuccessful, and managers seemed to
regard attempts at developing an 'international' image that did not include a
strong 'German' component as problematic. While many global companies

do trade off a strong association of their product with a particular nationality (e.g. Coca-Cola or IKEA), as noted above, ZwoBank remained largely German-focused in its orientation, rather than focusing more on the global, as its general management intended.

One of the strongest factors preventing it from doing so was the way in which the discourse of identity was presented. Throughout, employees at ZwoBank spoke in terms of a German identity being *opposed* to an international identity, as if, in order for them to become a global company, they had to efface their Germanness and lose their local identity. As seen in the example of AutoWorks, though, an international identity does not have to mean losing the German components of that identity, and, indeed, some companies have traded on the associations of Germanness with quality and excellence in engineering. Furthermore, unlike AutoWorks, ZwoBank's 'internationalisation' programme consisted of expanding out German practices, rather than of spreading a variety of practices and skills from diverse branches throughout the group (see Bartlett and Ghoshal, 1992). Consequently, the company first set up a cultural paradigm that Germanness was incompatible with an identity as international, and yet insisted on prioritising German methods, meaning that the company essentially has to continue to see itself, and be seen, as German. By taking a particular line on the relationship of Germanness to internationalism, ZwoBank employees ensure that it is continually prioritised.

Although ZwoBank was not without international connections and operations, it remained firmly German in its identification – a state of affairs that was not quite what managers claimed they wanted, but that seemed to be more or less what the company felt more comfortable operating with, and that was most compatible with its culture and symbolic self-presentation, due to its particular circumstances. Whether this can be considered a 'failure to internationalise' is less certain, however.

AutoWorks: a global company?

In the case of AutoWorks, we see a company that appears to have been better able to present itself, and be seen, as an international rather than a German company, even though Germanness remained a more or less tacit presence within its identity. Rather than developing an identity genuinely focused on global symbols and practices, however, AutoWorks was seen as 'global' mostly because of its cultivation of a variety of local connections. In this section I explore the nature of this apparent paradox, and why it is not such a contradiction as it first appears.

In the first place, the UK branch's local associations, ironically, enabled people to see the company as a whole as global: rather than simply being a German company that had set up a plant or office in the neighbourhood (as, arguably, would be the case with ZwoBank), it was regarded as a local firm that had developed international connections. The company's hands-off policy was visible throughout the group: a visit to a German branch indicated that, while the two plants were visibly part of the same group, displaying the same logos and engaging in the same practices, there were differences in ethos, behaviour (e.g. the wearing of company uniforms, or ways of decorating the common leisure areas) and so forth. Although AutoWorks was able to be seen as international, it did so through cultivating local connections.

National discourses, rather than globalising ones, were also reflected in the way in which the British managers were willing to associate themselves with the global company's name. Whereas the German automotive industry has been relatively successful in the international sphere, the British car industry has experienced a variety of setbacks, culminating in the recent collapse of the Rover group (Scarbrough and Terry, 1996; Holweg and Oliver, 2005). Consequently, the executives were happy to associate themselves with an international car company, because it allowed them to associate themselves with a successful car industry rather than a failing one; to associate themselves deliberately with a German company would be to court a long-standing Anglo-German national rivalry, however (Hughes, 1994). Consequently, British executives embraced the discourses of internationalism relating to the company because they allowed them to trade on the historic success of the German car industry without seeming to abandon local patriotism. Local and national rivalries thus played into the developing internationalisation of the company.

Finally, the focus on the product was also used to encourage employees and outsiders to view the company as international. This again highlights another difference between the companies under consideration: whereas banking involves fairly nationally specific products because of financial regulations, cars and so forth are largely the same the world over. It has to be said, however, that manufacturing companies do have a tacit association with Germanness: asked to name a German company, interviewees in all sectors tended to name manufacturing companies, such as Volkswagen or Audi, ahead of financial or service corporations. Again, we see the use of national associations to develop an international image.

AutoWorks, therefore, appears on the surface to have engaged in a product and/or brand-name-associated globalisation of its identity as described in the above-mentioned Wolff Olins report. Ironically, though, it was able to do so only through exploiting national associations and symbols, including German ones.

Why stay national? The benefits of German identity for both companies

It should further be noted that, in both cases, the companies in question actively benefited from possessing a connection to Germany in terms of strategic self-presentation. AutoWorks, for instance, was not unaware that some of its sales were due to the German reputation for solid engineering and quality automotive construction; German bankers also said that the German reputation for reliability and long-term performance could be a positive asset when presenting themselves to non-German clients and rivals. Even the more negative associations of German identity that were brought up by the managers at ZwoBank – slowness, conservatism, parochialism – allowed them to define themselves by the particular problems they faced during their working day, and develop collective solidarity amongst themselves and with the employees of other German bank branches in London. German MNCs can thus benefit from asserting their national identity in particular circumstances.

Moreover, neither British nor German managers in either company were totally against the retention of the German connection, at least to some degree. All the German expatriate managers spoke of having been made welcome; many of the British employees at ZwoBank memorised short German phrases for use in conversation. At both companies, I would frequently hear employees explaining some quirk of policy or practice with the phrase 'It's a German thing'. At the same time, ZwoBank had possessed international connections even before its integration campaign began, through its overseas branches, meaning that, even at a time when the company was identifying itself particularly strongly as being German, the international component of its identity was still present. In practice, then, both companies incorporated both components in their identities, and emphasised both at different times.

The ZwoBank and AutoWorks examples thus bear out the indications of my earlier research that companies do not define themselves as 'German' or 'international' to the exclusion of all else but incorporate different images of Germanness and international awareness in their self-presentation, which are deployed differently and at different times, depending on the strategies of the company and its employees. I now consider in more detail the challenge that these two cases pose to hyperglobalist notions of best practice and globalising culture.

Culture and globalisation: how self-presentation connects the national and the international

The key factor regarding the differences between the companies' self-presentation therefore appears to be their culture, as developed through their history, associations and strategies. Both Ivo Strecker (1988) and Dan Sperber (1974) argue that cultures are built up through symbols, which change their meaning as the groups associated with them change and develop. As an example, consider the computer company Apple (cited in Deal and Kennedy, 1988: 21, 26, 197–8), the employees of which went from defining themselves as a market leader in the field of information technology to defining themselves as a quirky and creative alternative group, through using the same image of a rainbow-coloured apple, which goes from representing knowledge acquisition through its association with the garden of Eden to, more recently, representing a funky, environmentally aware, green ethos (fruit = natural, holistic); the association with the Beatles' company, Apple Corps (over which Apple has fought a number of lawsuits), also brings in an association with pop culture and the rebellious, experimental nature of the 1960s (BBCi, 2006a). In the cases that we have seen, German and international identities are differently expressed within the companies depending on their histories, sectors and strategies.

The fact that both the German firms studied here were either global or globalising companies is also significant. In his 1999 monograph *Globalization and Culture*, John Tomlinson (1999) argues that the key for companies, groups and individuals to operate on a global level is not for them to become fully detached from the local but to be able to operate simultaneously in the global and the local spheres. As noted elsewhere, companies frequently do this through the use of symbols (Moore, 2004). The differences between ZwoBank and AutoWorks with regard to their treatment of Germanness and internationalism reflected different strategies with regard to globalisation, the one pursuing a centralised, expansionist strategy with the other pursuing a dispersed, differentiated strategy, resulting in different patterns of identity (see Bartlett and Ghoshal, 1992). In the cases under discussion, then, we see the use of symbols by companies engaged in different strategies of globalisation as a way of being both global and local, being seen as 'international' but retaining local roots. Rather than converging on a general 'global business' culture and system of practices, then, both companies are informed by their culture, their intentions, the economic system they work within, the societies they are associated with and the hierarchies of world politics.

Both companies are therefore pursuing different strategies of globalisation in keeping with the cultures of the different institutions, with ZwoBank, German-focused from its outset and still maintaining Germany as the focus of its business, developing a discourse of internationalism through spreading German practices, policies and images abroad, and AutoWorks, focused on acquisition rather than expansion and with an internationally recognised product, globalising through emphasising the culture of the branches within the group. The differences between the groups' self-presentation as German and international thus reflect, and are products of, their strategies within the global business world; the continued associations of companies with national culture is thus not a 'failure to internationalise' but a natural aspect of working in the global sphere.

The results of this study also serve as an implicit critique of the tendency of management works to oversimplify definitions and descriptions of national culture and its impact on organisations (see also chapter 3). Both companies were of the same national origin, and yet their different histories, sectors and strategies meant that they had quite different results in pursuing what might superficially seem to be the same objective, supporting the SSD perspective that culture in companies is the result of a variety of influences, not simply the national and the global. At the same time, the results question the way in which Morgan (2005) characterises German companies as inherently 'more transnational' than, for instance, Japanese ones; while this may be the case for some German companies, it is by no means true for all, and one might likewise question whether all Japanese companies can be categorised according to the same degree of transnationalism. The two case studies discussed here thus indicate that a more complex approach to national culture is needed in the studies of international business and human resource management.

Further directions for research are suggested by this necessarily limited comparison. I am currently undertaking further studies with regard to Goffmanian self-presentation in corporate settings; while I have here been able to compare companies in two sectors, it might be worth considering other sectors as well as examining the way in which corporate self-presentation changes over time. More complex views of culture are also needed, as is the development and refinement of the use of qualitative methodologies in business studies (Marschan-Piekkari and Welch, 2004), and, consequently, the revision of classic works on culture in business in light of this. More research is also needed into the complicated role that culture plays with regard to change in organisations. The history and development of the relationship between national versus international/product-focused corporate identities might also be worth looking into; comparisons with companies of other national origins, for instance Japanese or South Korean MNCs, might also provide fruitful comparisons. Wider studies into nationality and self-presentation are thus being undertaken, and more need to be done, to develop the thesis of this chapter.

Conclusions

In sum, therefore, both ZwoBank and AutoWorks can be said to have 'German' and 'international' aspects to their identities, their products being seen both as 'Made in Germany' and 'Made by [company name]'. Nevertheless, the different approaches that each company takes, and the different identities that result, depend on the company's culture, history, business strategy, sector and so forth. Furthermore, this would appear to be less the result of a failure on the part of the companies to divorce themselves from their national roots and more a natural product of the processes of globalisation and the role of the local in furthering these (Tomlinson, 1999). As in Goffman's theories of self-presentation, then, both companies use symbols to present themselves in diverse ways, which shift according to their situation and which aspects of their identity they feel are most useful with regard to their particular strategy, with a view to emphasising the international aspects and/or the local aspects as needed, rather than switching from the one to the other.

In the case of the ZwoBank and AutoWorks studies, then, it seems that both companies used the same symbols both to indicate their international and their German connections. The companies did this in different ways, however, according to their different corporate cultures, with the result being different degrees of success in different areas, suggesting that globalisation, in business, is less a question of 'becoming global' and more one of negotiation between different factors, associations and cultural and systemic influences upon the company in question, in a vindication of ethnographic and sociological views of culture and identity.

References

Abel, J., and P. Itterman (2003) Exploring the boundaries of co-determination, in W. Müller-Jentsch and H. Weitbrecht (eds.) *The Changing Contours of German Industrial Relations*, Munich: Rainer Hampp, 103–18.

Applegate, C. (1990) *A Nation of Provincials: The German Idea of Heimat*, Berkeley, CA: University of California Press.

Bardsley, G., and S. Laing (1999) *Making Cars at Cowley: From Morris to Rover*, Stroud: British Motor Industry Heritage Trust.

Bartlett, C. A., and S. Ghoshal (1992) *Managing across Borders: The Transnational Solution*, London: Century Business.

BBCi (2006a) Apple giants do battle in court, BBCi, 29 March, available at http://news.bbc.co.uk/1/hi/entertainment/4854408.stm.

(2006b) Will Germany's World Cup push pay off?, BBCi, 7 June, available at http://news.bbc.co.uk/1/hi/business/5019830.stm.

(2006c) iPod 'slave' claims investigated, BBCi, 14 June, available at http://news.bbc.co.uk/1/hi/business/5079590.stm.

(2006d) World Cup 2006 report card, BBCi, 11 July, available at http://news.bbc.co.uk/1/hi/world/europe/5167600.stm.

Burns, T. (1992) *Erving Goffman*, London: Routledge.

Cohen, A. P. (1985) *The Symbolic Construction of Community*, London: Tavistock.

Deal, T. E., and A. A. Kennedy (1988) *Corporate Cultures: The Rites and Rituals of Corporate Life*, London: Penguin Books.

Ebster-Grosz, D., and D. Pugh (1996) *Anglo-German Business Collaboration: Pitfalls and Potentials*, London: Macmillan.

Economist (1998) Salesman Schroeder, *Economist*, 29 August, 16.

Financial Times (1999) Compensation for Nazi era labour to rise, 7 October, 4.

Forster, N. (2000) The myth of the 'international manager', *International Journal of Human Resource Management*, 11, 1, 126–42.

Goffman, E. (1956) *The Presentation of Self in Everyday Life*, Edinburgh: University of Edinburgh Press.

(1961) *Encounters: Two Studies in the Sociology of Interaction*, Indianapolis: Bobbs-Merrill.

Head, D. (1992) *'Made in Germany': The Corporate Identity of a Nation*, London: Hodder and Stoughton.

Held, D., McGrew, A. D. Goldblatt and J. Perraton (1999) *Global Transformations: Politics, Economics and Culture*, Cambridge: Polity Press

Holweg, M., and N. Oliver (2005) *Who Killed MG Rover?*, working paper, Centre for Competitiveness and Innovation, Judge Business School, Cambridge University, available at www-innovation.jims.cam.ac.uk.

Hughes, T. (1994) *The Image Makers: National Stereotypes and the Media*, London: Goethe Institute.

Kristensen, P. H., and D. Zeitlin (2004) *Local Players in Global Games: The Strategic Constitution of a Multinational Corporation*, Oxford: Oxford University Press.

Lawrence, P. (1980) *Managers and Management in West Germany*, London: Croom Helm.

Liesch, P., J. Steen and T. Kastelle (2006) Globalization and connectedness: a network approach to international business, in M. A. Von Glinow and T. Kiyak (eds.) *Proceedings of the 48th Annual Meeting of the Academy of International Business*, East Lansing, MI: Academy of International Business, 212.

Marschan-Piekkari, R., and C. Welch (2004) Qualitative research methods in international business: the state of the art, in R. Marschan-Piekkari and C. Welch (eds.) *Handbook of Qualitative Research Methods for International Business*, Cheltenham: Edward Elgar, 5–24.

Moore, F. (2003) Internal diversity and culture's consequences: branch/head office relations in a German MNC, *Management International Review*, 43, 2, 95–111.

—— (2004) Symbols of organization: informal ways of negotiating the global and the local in MNCs, *Global Networks*, 4, 2, 181–98.

—— (2005) *Transnational Business Cultures: Life and Work in a Multinational Corporation*, Aldershot: Ashgate.

Morgan, G. (2005) Understanding multinational corporations, in S. Ackroyd, R. Batt, P. Thompson and P. S. Tolbert (eds.) *The Oxford Handbook of Work and Organization*, Oxford: Oxford University Press, 554–76.

Mueller, F. (1994) Societal effect, organizational effect and globalization, *Organization Studies*, 15, 3, 407–28.

Newbigging, C., S. Shatford and T. Williams (1998) *The Changing Faces of Cowley Works*, Witney: Robert Boyd.

Oakes, P. (1997) Licensed to sell, *Guardian*, 17 December.

Ohmae, K. (1990) *The Borderless World: Power and Strategy in the Interlinked Economy*, London: HarperCollins.

Royle, T. (2000) *Working for McDonald's in Europe*, London: Routledge.

Sako, M. (1994) Training, productivity, and quality control in Japanese multinational companies, in M. Aoki and R. Dore (eds.) *The Japanese Firm: Sources of Competitive Strength*, London: Routledge, 84–116.

Scarbrough, H., and M. Terry (1996). *Industrial Relations and the Reorganization of Production in the UK Motor Vehicle Industry: A Study of the Rover Group*, Warwick Paper in Industrial Relations no. 58, University of Warwick.

Sklair, L. (2001) *The Transnational Capitalist Class*, Oxford: Basil Blackwell.

Smith, C., and P. Meiksins (1995) System, society and dominance effects in cross-national organizational analysis, *Work, Employment and Society*, 9, 2, 241–67.

Sperber, D. (1974) *Rethinking Symbolism*, Cambridge: Cambridge University Press.

Strecker, I. (1988) *The Social Practice of Symbolization: An Anthropological Analysis*, London: Athlone Press.

Tomlinson, J. (1991) *Cultural Imperialism: A Critical Introduction*, London: Johns Hopkins University Press.

—— (1999) *Globalization and Culture*, Cambridge: Polity Press.

Watson, A. (1995) *The Germans: Who Are They Now?* London: Methuen.

Wolff Olins (1995) *Made in Germany: A Business Survey of the Relevance of the National Badge and Its Image Associations*, London: Wolff Olins.

Index